COMMERCIAL PROPERTY

COMMERCIAL PROPERTY

Editor

Anne Rodell MA (Cantab), Solicitor

Contributors

Simon Halliwell, Clare Harris, Leona Mason, Stephanie McGuiness,
Lucy Morton, Anne Rodell, Robert Tam, Helen Watson
and Matthew White

Published by

College of Law Publishing,
Braboeuf Manor, Portsmouth Road, St Catherines, Guildford GU3 1HA

British Library Cataloguing-in-Publication Data
A catalogue record for this book is available from the British Library.

ISBN 978 1 910019 81 8

Typeset by Style Photosetting Ltd, Mayfield, East Sussex
Printed in Great Britain by Polestar Wheatons, Exeter

Preface

The aim of this book is to provide law students with a comprehensive introduction to the areas of property law particularly relevant to commercial property.

Part I of the book deals with areas relevant to property acquisition and development. These include structures for joint ownership, arrangements for funding, contractual arrangements with the seller, the need for planning permission, environmental considerations, contractual arrangements with members of the construction team and taxation. Part II takes the reader through the grant of a commercial lease, the assignment of that lease and its termination. Part III deals with the law relating to property and insolvency.

Although we hope that this book will provide a useful guide to trainee solicitors and others involved in commercial property work, it is primarily intended to complement the Stage 2 Advanced Property Law and Practice elective on the Legal Practice Course. This elective is only undertaken once the Stage 1 Property Law and Practice course has been completed. Apart from the matters specifically mentioned in Part I of this book, the conveyancing process for the transfer and leasing of commercial property is as described in the Legal Practice Guide entitled *Property Law and Practice* accompanying the Stage 1 course, so the conveyancing process is not dealt with in this book.

The University of Law would like to thank the Practical Law Company for authorising the use of the following documents in this book:

- Practice note on Overage Payments <http://uk.practicallaw.com/4-200-2514> (Chapter 3)

- Lease of floor(s) of an office block with guarantee and prescribed clauses <http://uk.practicallaw.com/9-218-6006> (Appendix 4)

- Diagrams on procurement <http://uk.practicallaw.com/9-329-1308> and linked documents (Chapter 9)

The current team of authors would like to acknowledge the valuable contributions made by Paul Butt, Neil Duckworth, Susannah Herbert, Sue Highmore and Vanessa Ralph to earlier editions of this book. The current team of authors bears responsibility for any failings in this edition.

The law is as stated as at 1 September 2014.

Anne Rodell

The University of Law
Guildford

About the Contributors

Simon Halliwell is a leading non-contentious construction law specialist who has worked on some of the largest construction projects both in the UK and internationally, acting for major developers, investment banks, blue-chip commercial organisations and governmental institutions. He founded *www.constructionlawexpert.com* as a niche construction law practice in November 2012 after over a decade of working at major global law firms in the City of London. After graduating with a law degree from Trinity Hall, Cambridge University, he joined 'magic circle' law firm, Linklaters LLP, and qualified into the non-contentious construction law department in 2003. Following moves to leading US law firm King & Spalding International LLP and Herbert Smith Freehills LLP, Simon set up *www.constructionlawexpert.com* and joined the long-established family firm of John J Halliwell & Co Solicitors as a partner in November 2012.

Clare Harris is a Senior Lecturer at the University of Law. She qualified as a solicitor in 1994, working as a commercial property lawyer for Edge Ellison (now Squire Sanders) and NatWest Bank. In 2001 she moved to the University of Law where she currently teaches property law and advanced property law. Clare is co-author of *Property Law in Practice*.

Leona Mason is a Senior Lecturer at the University of Law. She qualified as a solicitor in 1982 and was a partner in Underwood Solicitors LLP until 2004, specialising in property finance and secured lending. At the University, she teaches at the Moorgate Centre and has designed courses in Property Law & Practice and Finance & Capital Markets.

Stephanie McGuiness has been a senior lecturer at the University of Law since 2006, having trained and practised at Herbert Smith. She teaches at the Moorgate Centre on both the LPC (Property Law and Practice) and GDL (Contract) programmes.

Lucy Morton is the Professional Support Lawyer in the Planning team at leading international law firm, Herbert Smith Freehills LLP. Lucy qualified as a solicitor at the firm in 2008 and advises prestigious clients on the legal aspects of large-scale development and infrastructure projects. She also contributes to legal updates and publications in the fields of commercial property and planning law.

Anne Rodell is an Associate Professor at the University of Law. She qualified as a solicitor in 1989 and was an assistant solicitor in the Real Estate Department of Linklaters LLP until 1998. At the University, she currently designs courses in Land Law, Property Law & Practice and Advanced Property.

Robert Tam is a lawyer, lecturer and international development consultant. Robert trained with Clifford Chance in 2001. He then specialised in environment law in Sydney and London, with Ashurst and Travers Smith. He also taught the GDL, LPC and LLM at the University of Law for five years. Robert is now the Director of Eight Times Up: a global development and professional education consultancy, with predominantly law firm and international charity clients. He also continues to work as a project expert with the Centre for International Legal Cooperation (mostly in Uganda), and provide executive support to Pure Leapfrog: a pro bono carbon reduction charity.

Helen Watson is an Associate Professor at the University of Law. She qualified as a solicitor in 1994 and worked at Davies Wallis Foyster (now DWF). Helen currently teaches Business Structures, Taxation and Insolvency and is co-author of *Business Law and Practice*.

Matthew White is a partner at Herbert Smith Freehills LLP and is recognised as one of the United Kingdom's top planning solicitors. He works on large-scale commercial planning matters, with a focus on nationally significant energy and infrastructure projects and complex mixed-use masterplan developments. Matthew has expertise in all elements of contentious and non-contentious planning, including environmental impact assessment, compulsory purchase, planning inquiries and judicial review. He has advised on many high-profile and politically sensitive projects in recent years.

Contents

PREFACE   v

ABOUT THE CONTRIBUTORS   vi

TABLE OF CASES   xiii

TABLE OF STATUTES   xix

TABLE OF SECONDARY LEGISLATION   xxiii

LIST OF ABBREVIATIONS   xxvii

Part I	SITE ACQUISITIONS	1

Chapter 1	THE COMMERCIAL CONTEXT *Anne Rodell*	3
	1.1 What is commercial property?	3
	1.2 Who buys commercial property?	4
	1.3 Buying commercial property jointly	5
	1.4 Methods of structuring a property joint venture	6
	Review activity	8

Chapter 2	OBTAINING PROPERTY FINANCE *Leona Mason*	9
	2.1 Methods of finance	9
	2.2 Debt finance	10
	Review activity	14

Chapter 3	MATTERS OF CONTRACT *Anne Rodell*	17
	3.1 The contract of sale	17
	3.2 Different types of contract	18
	3.3 Overage	23
	Review activity	26

Chapter 4	PLANNING CONTROL *Matthew White & Lucy Morton*	27
	4.1 The planning system	27
	4.2 When is planning permission needed?	31
	4.3 Planning permission	40
	4.4 Application to the local planning authority	46
	4.5 Appeals against adverse planning determinations	51
	Review activity	55

Chapter 5	PLANNING OBLIGATIONS AND COMMUNITY INFRASTRUCTURE LEVY	
	Matthew White & Lucy Morton	57
	5.1 Introduction	57
	5.2 Planning obligations	58
	5.3 Government policy	59
	5.4 Unilateral undertakings	60
	5.5 Modification and discharge of planning obligations	60
	5.6 Community Infrastructure Levy	61
	5.7 CIL and planning obligations	66
	5.8 Practical points	67
	Review activity	68

Chapter 6	ENFORCEMENT OF PLANNING CONTROL *Matthew White & Lucy Morton*	69
	6.1 Introduction	69
	6.2 Definitions and time limits	69
	6.3 Certificates of lawful use or development (ss 191–192)	70

6.4	Right of entry for enforcement purposes (ss 196A–196C)	72
6.5	Planning contravention notice (ss 171C–171D)	72
6.6	Breach of condition notice (s 187A)	73
6.7	Enforcement notice (ss 172–182)	74
6.8	Stop notice and temporary stop notice (ss 183–187 and ss 171E–171G)	78
6.9	Injunctions (s 187B)	80
6.10	Appeals against enforcement notices (ss 174–177)	80
	Review activity	82

Chapter 7   ENVIRONMENTAL ISSUES   *Robert Tam*   83

7.1	Introduction to environmental law	83
7.2	Environmental risk management	85
7.3	Contaminated land	87
7.4	Nuisance	95
7.5	Environmental Damage Regulations	98
7.6	Environmental permitting and regulation	99
7.7	Climate change law and energy performance	102
7.8	Regulatory Enforcement and Sanctions Act 2008	106
7.9	Asbestos	106
7.10	Japanese knotweed	108
7.11	Flood risks	108
7.12	Sentencing guidelines: environmental offences	108
7.13	Environment Tribunal	109
	Review activity	109

Chapter 8   SEARCHES AND ENQUIRIES   *Anne Rodell*   111

8.1	Local search and enquiries	111
8.2	Planning matters	111
8.3	Drainage	112
8.4	Highways	112
8.5	Contaminated land	112
8.6	Commons registration	112
8.7	Enquiries of the seller	112
8.8	Flood searches	112
8.9	Survey and inspection	113
8.10	Investigation of title	113
	Review activity	114

Chapter 9   CONSTRUCTION PROJECTS   *Simon Halliwell*   115

9.1	Introduction	115
9.2	Who will be involved? The design and construction team	115
9.3	Different forms of procurement	118
9.4	Duties owed to third parties	125
9.5	Protecting third parties	128
9.6	Dispute resolution	132
	Review activity	133

Chapter 10   AN OUTLINE OF TAXATION OF COMMERCIAL PROPERTIES   *Anne Rodell*   135

10.1	Value added tax	135
10.2	Stamp duty land tax on leases	141
	Review activity	141

Part II   COMMERCIAL LEASES   143

Chapter 11   LANDLORD AND TENANT LAW   *Stephanie McGuiness*   145

11.1	Introduction	145
11.2	Lease/licence distinction	145
11.3	Security of tenure	146
11.4	Liability of the parties on the covenants in the lease	146
	Review activity	147

Chapter 12	AGREEMENTS FOR LEASE *Stephanie McGuiness*	149
	12.1 Introduction	149
	12.2 A typical agreement	149
	Review activity	153

Chapter 13	LEASE CONTENTS *Stephanie McGuiness*	155
	13.1 Introduction	155
	13.2 The 2007 Code for Leasing Business Premises in England and Wales	155
	13.3 Drafting leases	156
	13.4 Prescribed clauses leases	157
	13.5 The structure of the lease	158
	Review activity	162

Chapter 14	THE PARTIES TO THE LEASE AND THEIR LIABILITIES *Clare Haris*	163
	14.1 Introduction	163
	14.2 The landlord	163
	14.3 The tenant	165
	14.4 The guarantor	168
	Review activity	173

Chapter 15	THE PARCELS CLAUSE *Anne Rodell*	175
	15.1 Purpose	175
	15.2 Airspace and underground	175
	15.3 Fixtures	175
	15.4 Rights to be granted and reserved	176
	Review activity	177

Chapter 16	TERM *Anne Rodell*	179
	16.1 Introduction	179
	16.2 Break clauses	180
	16.3 Options to renew	181
	16.4 Impact of SDLT	181
	Review activity	182

Chapter 17	RENT *Anne Rodell*	183
	17.1 Introduction	183
	17.2 Amount	184
	17.3 Time for payment	184
	17.4 Other payments reserved as rent	184
	17.5 Suspension of rent	184
	17.6 Interest	184
	17.7 VAT	185
	Review activity	185

Chapter 18	THE RENT REVIEW CLAUSE *Clare Haris*	187
	18.1 The need for review	187
	18.2 Types of rent review clause	187
	18.3 The dates for review	189
	18.4 Working out the open market rent	190
	18.5 The assumptions	191
	18.6 The disregards	197
	18.7 The mechanism for determining the rent	199
	18.8 The late review	200
	18.9 Recording the review	200
	Review activity	201

Chapter 19	REPAIR *Stephanie McGuiness*	203
	19.1 Introduction	203
	19.2 Tenant's covenant to repair	204

19.3	Definition of the subject matter of the covenant	204
19.4	Extent of liability	204
19.5	Tenant's concerns and amendments	208
19.6	Enforcement of covenant by landlord	209
19.7	Covenant to yield up in repair	209
19.8	Decorating	209
19.9	Landlord's covenant to repair	210
	Review activity	210

Chapter 20	ALIENATION	*Clare Haris*	211
	20.1	Dealings with the premises	211
	20.2	Restrictions on alienation	213
	20.3	Seeking consent from the landlord	217
	20.4	Notice of assignment or sub-letting	220
	20.5	Virtual assignments	221
		Review activity	221

Chapter 21	USER	*Clare Haris*	223
	21.1	The need for a user covenant	223
	21.2	The permitted use	224
	21.3	The extent of the landlord's control	226
	21.4	Ancillary clauses	227
	21.5	Impact of competition legislation on user covenants	228
		Review activity	229

Chapter 22	ALTERATIONS	*Stephanie McGuiness*	231
	22.1	Introduction	231
	22.2	Lease controls	232
	22.3	Restrictions outside the lease	235
	22.4	Compensation for improvements	236
	22.5	The 2007 Code for Leasing Business Premises	236
		Review activity	236

Chapter 23	THE LANDLORD'S COVENANT FOR QUIET ENJOYMENT	*Anne Rodell*	237
	23.1	Nature of the covenant	237
	23.2	Negotiating the covenant	237
	23.3	Acts constituting a breach	238
		Review activity	238

Chapter 24	INSURANCE	*Clare Haris*	241
	24.1	Introduction	241
	24.2	The obligation to insure	242
	24.3	The obligation to pay for the insurance	244
	24.4	Compliance with the terms of the insurance	245
	24.5	The obligation to reinstate	245
	24.6	Rent suspension	247
	24.7	Termination	248
	24.8	Damage by uninsured risks	249
	24.9	Additional provisions	250
	24.10	Insurance by the tenant	250
		Review activity	250

Chapter 25	FORFEITURE	*Stephanie McGuiness*	251
	25.1	Introduction	251
	25.2	Express reservation of the right	251
	25.3	Waiver of the right to forfeit	252
	25.4	Strict procedural rules and relief against forfeiture	252
	25.5	Additional rules in special cases	255
	25.6	Position of sub-tenants and mortgagees on forfeiture	257

| | 25.7 | The 2007 Code for Leasing Business Premises | 257 |
| | | Review activity | 257 |

Chapter 26	LEASE OF PART *Clare Haris*		259
	26.1	Introduction	259
	26.2	Defining the demised premises	259
	26.3	Rights granted and reserved	259
	26.4	Repairs	260
	26.5	Service charges	261
	26.6	Sinking and reserve funds	266
	26.7	Insurance	266
	26.8	RICS Code of Practice for Service Charges	266
		Review activity	267

Chapter 27	SELLING THE LEASE *Clare Haris*		269
	27.1	Applications for consent to assign	269
	27.2	The landlord's licence	271
	27.3	Authorised guarantee agreements	272
		Review activity	272

Chapter 28	SUB-LEASES *Clare Haris*		273
	28.1	The nature of a sub-lease	273
	28.2	Reasons for sub-letting	273
	28.3	Consent to the sub-letting	274
	28.4	Liability to the head-landlord	275
	28.5	Drafting the sub-lease	275
		Review activity	278

Chapter 29	REMEDIES FOR BREACH OF COVENANT *Anne Rodell*		279
	29.1	Landlord's remedies	279
	29.2	Tenant's remedies	284

Chapter 30	METHODS OF TERMINATION *Stephanie McGuiness*		287
	30.1	Introduction	287
	30.2	Expiry	287
	30.3	Notice to quit	287
	30.4	Operation of break clause	288
	30.5	Surrender	288
	30.6	Merger	289
		Review activity	289

Chapter 31	THE LANDLORD AND TENANT ACT 1954, PART II *Anne Rodell*		291
	31.1	Introductory matters	291
	31.2	Termination under the Act	296
	31.3	The application to court	300
	31.4	Interim rents	301
	31.5	Grounds of opposition	303
	31.6	Compensation for failure to obtain a new tenancy	307
	31.7	The renewal lease	308
	31.8	The order for the new lease	310
	31.9	Procedural flowchart – s 25 notice	311
		Review activity	311

| **Part III** | **PROPERTY AND INSOLVENCY** | | **313** |

Chapter 32	INSOLVENCY AND ITS EFFECT ON COMMERCIAL PROPERTY *Helen Watson*		315
	32.1	Why insolvency matters	315
	32.2	Measures to reduce the perceived risk of insolvency	315
	32.3	Always establish the type of insolvency regime	316
	32.4	Identify the type of contract	318

32.5   Different types of insolvency regime   318
32.6   Setting aside transactions which have already been completed   323
32.7   The effect of a tenant becoming insolvent   325
32.8   Requiring the insolvency official to pay rent   332
32.9   Requiring the insolvency official to observe the lease covenants   333
32.10   Disclaimer and its effects   334

Appendices

Appendix 1   Review Activity Answers 339
Appendix 2   Prescribed forms of notice under the Landlord and Tenant Act 1954   357
Appendix 3   The Code for Leasing Business Premises in England and Wales 2007   371
Appendix 4   Lease of floor(s) of an office block with guarantee and prescribed clauses   383
Appendix 5   Specimen Authorised Guarantee Agreement   423
Appendix 6   Extracts from the Landlord and Tenant Act 1954, Part II   429

INDEX   447

Table of Cases

A

ABC Coupler and Engineering Co Ltd (No 3) [1970] 1 All ER 650   335
Actionstrength Ltd v International Glass Engineering [2003] 2 AC 541   171
Active Estates Ltd v Parness [2002] EWHC 893   336
Addiscombe Garden Estates v Crabbe [1958] 1 QB 513   292
Akasuc Enterprise Ltd v Farmar & Shirreff [2003] EWHC 1275 (Ch)   25
Akici v LR Butlin Ltd [2006] 1 WLR 201   254
Albany Holdings Ltd v Crown Estate Commissioners [2003] EWHC 1480   254
Allen v Corporation of the City of London [1981] JPL 685   42
Allied Dunbar Assurance plc v Homebase Ltd [2002] EWCA Civ 666, [2002] 27 EG 144, [2002] 2 EGLR 23   219, 276
Allied Dunbar Pension Services Ltd v Baker [2001] All ER (D) 46   275
Allnatt London Properties Ltd v Newton [1984] 1 All ER 423   289
Anglia Building Society v Secretary of State for the Environment and Another [1984] JPL 175   42
Anstruther-Gough-Calthorpe v McOscar and Another [1924] 1 KB 716   207
Artworld Financial Corporation v Safaryan [2009] 23 EG 94   289
Arundel Corporation v The Financial Training Co Ltd [2000] 3 All ER 456   289, 297
Ashburn Anstalt v Arnold [1989] Ch 1   145
Ashworth Frazer Ltd v Gloucester City Council [2002] 05 EG 133   219
Atlantic Computer Systems plc, Re [1990] EWCA Civ 20   332
Attorney-General v PYA Quarries Ltd [1957] 2 QB 169   97
Aubergine Enterprises Ltd v Lakewood International Ltd [2002] EWCA Civ 177   271
Avocet Industrial Estates LLP v Merol and Another [2011] EWHC 3422 (Ch)   180
Avonridge Property Co Ltd v Mashru [2005] UKHL 70   164

B

B&Q plc v Liverpool and Lancashire Properties Ltd [2000] EGCS 101   260
Bacchiocci v Academic Agency Ltd [1998] 1 WLR 1313   297
Bairstow Eves (Securities) Ltd v Ripley [1992] 2 EGLR 47   180, 349
Barclays Bank plc v Daejan Investments (Grove Hall) Ltd [1995] 18 EG 117   227
Barclays Wealth Trustees (Jersey) Ltd v Erimus Housing Ltd [2014] EWCA Civ 303   293
Barnes v City of London Real Property Co [1918] 2 Ch 18   263
Barr and Others v Biffa Waste Services Ltd [2012] EWHC Civ 312   96
Barrett v Morgan [2000] 2 AC 264   288
Barth v Pritchard [1990] 1 EGLR 109   305
Bates v Donaldson [1896] 2 QB 241   219
Bayliss v Secretary of State for Communities and Local Government [2013] EWHC 1612 (Admin)   30
Belcourt Estates Ltd v Adesina [2005] EWCA Civ 208   289
Betty's Cafes Ltd v Phillips Furnishing Stores Ltd [1959] AC 20   304
BHP Great Britain Petroleum Ltd v Chesterfield Properties Ltd [2001] EWCA Civ 1797, [2002] 2 WLR 672   164, 165
Bickerton's Aerodromes v Young (1958) 108 LJ 217   254
Billson v Residential Apartments Ltd [1992] 1 AC 494   255
Blockbuster Entertainment Ltd v Barnsdale Properties Ltd [2003] EWHC 2912   270
Bolton (HL) Engineering Co Ltd v Graham & Sons Ltd [1957] 1 QB 159   307
Booth v Thomas [1926] Ch 397   238
Broadgate Square plc v Lehman Brothers Ltd [1995] 1 EGLR 97, [1995] 01 EG 111   157, 195
Brown & Root Technology v Sun Alliance [1997] 18 EG 123   180
Burdle and Another v Secretary of State for the Environment and Another [1972] 3 All ER 240   32
Burt v British Transport Commission (1955) 166 EG 4   283

C

C&A Pension Trustees Ltd v British Vita Investments Ltd [1984] 2 EGLR 75, (1984) 272 EG 63   224
Cambridge Water Company v Eastern Counties Leather plc [1994] 2 AC 264   96
Campbell v Daejan Properties Ltd [2012] EWCA Civ 1503   261
Caparo Industries plc v Dickman [1990] 2 AC 605   128
Central Estates (Belgravia) Ltd v Woolgar (No 2) [1972] 1 WLR 1048   252
Central Estates Ltd v Secretary of State for the Environment [1997] 1 EGLR 239   199

Chartered Trust plc v Davies [1997] 49 EG 135   286
Cheryl Investments Ltd v Saldhana [1978] 1 WLR 1329   292
Cheverell Estates Ltd v Harris [1998] 02 EG 127   279
Church Commissioners for England v Secretary of State for the Environment (1996) 7 P & CR 73   32
Circular Facilities (London) Ltd v Sevenoaks District Council [2005] EWHC 865 (Admin)   87, 92
City of London Corporation v Fell [1993] 49 EG 113   166
Civil Service Co-operative Society v McGrigor's Trustee [1923] 2 Ch 347   254
Claire's Accessories v Kensington High Street [2001] PLSCS 112   181
Clarence House Ltd v National Westminster Bank plc [2009] EWHC 77 (Ch); [2009] EWCA Civ 1311   221
Claridge [2011] EWHC 2047 (Ch)   324
Clear Channel UK Ltd v Manchester City Council [2005] EWCA Civ 1304   146
Colman v Secretary of State for Communities and Local Government and RWE Npower [2013] EWHC 1138 (Admin) 30
Commercial Union Life Assurance Co v Label Ink Ltd [2001] L & TR 29   207
Cook v Shoesmith [1951] 1 KB 752   214
Cooper's Lease, Re (1968) 19 P & CR 541   219
Co-operative Insurance Society Ltd v Argyll Stores (Holdings) Ltd [1997] 23 EG 137   284
Coppin v Bruce-Smith [1998] EGCS 45   305
Corby Group Litigation v Corby District Council [2009] EWHC 1944   96
Coventry v Lawrence [2014] All ER (D) 245 (Feb)   96
Credit Suisse v Beegas Nominees Ltd [1994] 11 EG 151   207, 208
Creska Ltd v Hammersmith and Fulham London Borough Council (No 2) (1999) 78 P & CR D46   282
Cricket Ltd v Shaftesbury plc [1999] 3 All ER 283   293
Crown Estate Commissioners v Town Investments Ltd [1992] 08 EG 111   310
Croydon London Borough Council v Gladden [1994] JPL 723, CA   80
Cunliffe v Goodman [1950] 2 KB 237   304

D

D&F Estates Ltd v Church Commissioners for England [1989] AC 177   127
Daiches v Bluelake Investments Ltd [1985] 2 EGLR 67   285
Davies v Yadegar [1990] 1 EGLR 71   348
Dennis v Ministry of Defence [2003] Env LR 34   95
Department of the Environment v Allied Freehold Property Trust Ltd [1992] 45 EG 156   302
Doleman v Shaw [2009] EWCA Civ 283   336
Dolgellau Golf Club v Hett [1998] 2 EGLR 75, CA   306
Dong Bang Minerva (UK) Ltd v Davina Ltd [1996] 31 EG 87   271
Donoghue v Stevenson [1932] AC 562   127
Donovan v Secretary of State for the Environment [1988] JPL 118   74

E

English Exporters (London) Ltd v Eldonwall Ltd [1973] Ch 415   302
Envirocor Waste Holdings v Secretary of State for the Environment [1995] EGCS 60, QB   42
Esselte AB v Pearl Assurance plc [1997] 1 WLR 891   296, 297
Essexcrest Ltd v Evenlex Ltd [1988] 1 EGLR 69   295
Esso Petroleum Co Ltd v Fumegrange Ltd [1994] 46 EG 199   145
Esso Petroleum v Southport Corporation [1956] AC 218   98
Expert Clothing Service & Sales Ltd v Hillgate House Ltd [1986] Ch 340   254

F

Family Management v Grey (1979) 253 EG 369   196
Farr v Ginnings (1928) 44 TLR 249   219
Fawke v Viscount Chelsea [1980] QB 441   310
First Property Growth Partnership v Royal & Sun Alliance Services Ltd [2002] EWHC 305 (Ch), [2002] 22 EG 140 199
Fitzroy House Epworth Street (No 1) v The Financial Times Ltd [2006] EWCA Civ 329   180
Flairline Properties Ltd v Hassan [1997] 1 EGLR 138   292
Footwear Corporation Ltd v Amplight Properties Ltd [1999] 1 WLR 551   219, 220
Forbuoys plc v Newport Borough Council [1994] 24 EG 156   310
Fowles v Heathrow Airport Ltd [2008] EWCA Civ 1270   303
Friends Life Ltd v Siemens Hearing Instruments Ltd [2014] EWCA Civ 382   181, 288
Friends Provident Life Office v British Railways Board [1995] 1 All ER 336   165, 170
FW Woolworth v Charlwood Alliance Properties [1987] 1 EGLR 53   219

G

G & K Ladenbau (UK) Ltd v Crawley and de Reya [1978] 1 All ER 682   112

Gateshead Metropolitan Borough Council v Secretary of State for the Environment [1995] JPL 432, CA   42
Gemini Press Ltd v Cheryl Lindsay Parsons [2012] EWHC 1608 (QB)   180
Glass v Kencakes Ltd [1966] 1 QB 611   254, 352
Go West Ltd v Spigarolo [2003] EWCA Civ 17, [2003] 07 EG 136   270
Goldacre (Offices) Ltd v Nortel Networks (UK) Ltd (in administration) [2009] EWHC 3389 (Ch)   333
Goldmile Properties Ltd v Lechouritis [2003] EWCA Civ 49, [2003] 15 EG 143   238
Good Harvest LLP v Centaur Services Limited [2010] EWHC 330 (Ch)   169, 171, 173, 216
Graysim Holdings Ltd v P&O Property Holdings Ltd [1995] 3 WLR 854   292
Great Portland Estates plc v Westminster City Council [1985] AC 661, HL   42
Gurton v Parrot [1991] 1 EGLR 98   292

H

Hadley v Baxendale (1854) 9 Exch 341   126, 283
Hambleton District Council v Bird [1995] 3 PLR 8   80
Hancock & Willis v GMS Syndicate Ltd (1982) 265 EG 473   292
Harborough District Council v Wheatcroft & Son Ltd [1996] JPL B128   80
Harmer v Jumbil (Nigeria) Tin Areas Ltd [1921] 1 Ch 200   286
Havant International Holdings Ltd v Lionsgate (H) Investments Ltd [1999] EGCS 144   181
Havenridge Ltd v Boston Dyers Ltd [1994] 49 EG 111   245
Hazel v Akhtar [2002] EWCA Civ 1883, [2002] 07 EG 124   303
Hedley Byrne & Co Ltd v Heller & Partners Ltd [1964] AC 465   127
Herbert Duncan Ltd v Cluttons [1992] 1 EGLR 101   166, 183
Heronslea (Mill Hill) Ltd v Kwik-Fit Properties Ltd [2009] EWHC 295   351
Hills (Patents) Ltd v University College Hospital Board of Governors [1956] 1 QB 90   292
Hindcastle v Barbara Attenborough Associates [1997] AC 70   336
Historic Hotels Ltd v Cadogan Estates [1995] 1 EGLR 117   198
Hockley Engineering Ltd v V & P Midlands Ltd [1993] 1 EGLR 76   257
Holland and Another v Hodgson and Another (1872) LR 7 CP 328   176
Holme v Brunskill (1877) 3 QBD 495   170
Hopley v Tarvin Parish Council (1910) 54 JP 209   254
Horne & Meredith Properties v Cox, Billingsley [2014] EWCA Civ 423   303
Horsey Estate Limited v Steiger [1899] 2 QB 79   212
Hotgroup plc v Royal Bank of Scotland plc [2010] EWHC 1193   181
Hunt & Others v Optima (Cambridge) Ltd & Others [2014] EWCA Civ 714   128
Hunter v Canary Wharf Ltd [1997] 2 WLR 684   96
Hyman v Rose [1912] AC 623   255

I

International Drilling Fluids Ltd v Louisville Investments (Uxbridge) Ltd [1986] Ch 513, [1986] 1 All ER 321   218, 233

J

Janmohamed v Hassam (1976) 241 EG 609   19
Javad v Aqil [1991] 1 WLR 1007   293
Jolley v Carmel [2000] 43 EG 185   21
Junction Estates Ltd v Cope (1974) 27 P & CR 482   170
Junior Books v Veitchi [1983] 1 AC 520   127

K

K/S Victoria Street v House of Fraser (Stores Management) Limited [2011] EWCA Civ 904   169, 173
Kalford Ltd v Peterborough City Council [2001] EGCS 42   233
Kalra v Secretary of State for the Environment [1996] JPL 850, CA   34
Khatun v United Kingdom, European Commission of Human Rights, 1 July 1998   96
Kissel v Secretary of State for the Environment and Another [1994] JPL 819   42

L

Lambert v FW Woolworth & Co Ltd (No 2) [1938] 2 All ER 664   233
Lambert v Keymood Ltd [1997] 43 EG 131   243
Landmaster Properties Ltd v Thackeray Property Services [2003] 35 EG 83   282
Law Land Co Ltd v Consumers Association Ltd (1980) 255 EG 617   225
Lazari GP Ltd v Jervis [2012] EWHC 1466   322
Lee-Parker v Izzet [1971] 1 WLR 1688   285
Lee-Parker and Another v Izzet and Others (No 2) [1972] 2 All ER 800   19

Leeward Securities v Lilyheath (1983) 17 HLR 35   255
Leisure Norwich (II) Ltd v Luminar Lava Ignite Ltd & Others [2012] EWHC 951 (Ch)   333
Lemmerbell Ltd v Britannia LAS Direct Ltd [1998] 3 EGLR 67   181
Leschallas v Woolf [1908] 1 Ch 641   176
Linden Garden Trust Ltd v Lenesta Sludge Disposals Ltd; St Martins Property Corporation Ltd v
    Sir Robert McAlpine & Sons Ltd [1993] 3 WLR 408   130
Lister v Lane & Nesham [1893] 2 QB 212   206
Lock v Pearce [1893] 2 Ch 271   254
London Baggage Co (Charing Cross) Ltd v Railtrack plc [2000] EGCS 57   293
London Hilton Jewellers Ltd v Hilton International Hotels Ltd [1990] 1 EGLR 112   306
London Residuary Body v Lambeth Borough Council [1990] 2 All ER 309, HL   42
Lurcott v Wakeley & Wheeler [1911] 1 KB 905   206

M

M&P Enterprises (London) Ltd v Norfolk Square Hotels Ltd [1994] 1 EGLR 129   298
Malvern Hills DC v Secretary of State for the Environment [1982] JPL 439   45
Mannai Investment Co Ltd v Eagle Star Life Assurance Co Ltd [1997] AC 749   181, 288, 348
Mark Rowlands Ltd v Berni Inns Ltd [1986] 1 QB 211   242
Marks and Spencer plc v BNP Paribas Securities Services Trust Company (Jersey) Ltd [2014] EWCA Civ 603   180
Martin Retail Group Ltd v Crawley Borough Council (CC (Central London), 24 December 2013)   229
McCaw v City of Westminster Magistrates' Court (D) and Middlesex SARL [2008] EWHC 1504   97
McDougall v Easington DC (1989) 58 P & CR 201, CA   206
Meadfield Properties Ltd v Secretary of State for the Environment [1995] 03 EG 128   179, 348
Mellor v Watkins (1874) LR 9 QBD 400   289
Metropolitan Properties Co (Regis) Ltd v Bartholomew [1995] 14 EG 143   170
Ministerial Decision [1977] JPL 116   33
Mira v Aylmer Square Investments Ltd [1990] 1 EGLR 45   238
Morcom v Campbell-Johnson [1955] 3 All ER 264   206
Morgan Sindall v Sawston Farms (Cambs) Ltd [1999] 1 EGLR 90   266
Moss Bros Group plc v CSC Properties Ltd [1999] EGCS 47   219
Moule v Garrett and Others (1872) LR 7 Exch 101   166
Mount Eden Land Ltd v Folia Ltd [2003] EWHC 1815   270
Mourant & Co Trustees Ltd v Sixty UK Ltd (in administration) [2010] EWHC 1890   318
Mullaney v Maybourne Grange (Croydon) Ltd [1986] 1 EGLR 70   263
Mumford Hotels Ltd v Wheler and Another [1964] Ch 117   246
Murphy v Brentwood District Council [1990] 2 All ER 908   127

N

National Car Parks Ltd v The Paternoster Consortium Ltd [1990] 15 EG 53   309
National Car Parks Ltd v Trinity Development Co (Banbury) Ltd [2001] EWCA Civ 1686, [2001] 28 EG 144   145
National Carriers Ltd v Panalpina (Northern) Ltd [1981] AC 675   184, 248
National Grid Co plc v M25 Group Ltd [1999] 08 EG 169   266
National Westminster Bank plc v Arthur Young McClelland Moores & Co [1985] 1 WLR 1123   194
Newbury District Council v Secretary of State for the Environment; Newbury District Council v International
    Synthetic Rubber Co [1981] AC 578   43
Newham London Borough Council v Thomas-Van Staden [2008] EWCA Civ 1414   294
Next plc v National Farmers Union Mutual Insurance Co Ltd [1997] EGCS 181   271, 353
Nicholas v Kinsey [1994] 16 EG 145   294
Northways Flats Management Co v Wimpey Pension Trustees [1992] 31 EG 65   262
Norwich Union Life Insurance Society v Low Profile Fashions Ltd (1992) 21 EG 104   270
Norwich Union Life Insurance Society v Shopmoor Ltd [1999] 1 WLR 531   219
Nynehead Developments Ltd v RH Fibreboard Containers Ltd and Others [1999] 9 EG 174   286

O

O'May v City of London Real Property Co Ltd [1983] AC 726   310
Oceanic Village Ltd v Shirayama Shokusan Co Ltd [2001] All ER (D) 62 (Feb)   286
Orlando Investments v Grosvenor Estate Belgravia [1989] 2 EGLR 74   219
Osibanjo v Seahive Investments Ltd [2008] EWCA Civ 1282   252
Owen v Gadd [1956] 2 QB 99   238

P

P&A Swift Investments v Combined English Stores Group plc [1983] 3 WLR 313   164
Palisade Investments Ltd v Secretary of State for the Environment [1995] 69 P & CR 638, CA   35

Patel, Patel v K & J Restaurants Ltd, MP Catering Ltd [2010] ECWA Civ 1211	254, 352
Payne v Haine (1847) 153 ER 1304	205
Pearson v Alyo [1990] 1 EGLR 114	298
Peel Land & Property (Ports No 3) Ltd v TS Sheerness Steel Ltd [2013] EWHC 1658 (Ch)	176
Peel Land & Property (Ports No 3) Ltd v TS Sheerness Steel Ltd [2014] EWCA Civ 100	176
Perry v Stanborough (Developments) Ltd [1978] JPL 36	75
Petra Investments Ltd v Jeffrey Rogers plc [2000] 3 EGLR 120	286
Pick v Chief Land Registrar [2011] EWHC 206	321
Pillar Denton Ltd and Others v Jervis and Others [2014] EWCA Civ 180 (24 February 2014)	333
Platt v London Underground [2001] 20 EG 227	286
Plinth Property Investments Ltd v Mott, Hay & Anderson [1979] 1 EGLR 17	224
Pointon York Group plc v Poulton [2006] EWCA Civ 1001	292
Ponderosa International Development v Pengap Securities [1986] 1 EGLR 66	219
Port v Griffith [1938] 1 All ER 295	286
Post Office Counters Ltd v Harlow District Council [1991] 2 EGLR 121	225
Post Office v Aquarius Properties Ltd [1987] 1 All ER 1055	204, 205
Price v West London Investment Building Society [1964] 2 All ER 318	300
Proudfoot v Hart (1890) 25 QBD 42	205, 207
Prudential Assurance Co Ltd v Exel UK Ltd [2009] EWHC 1350 (Ch)	348
Prudential Assurance Co Ltd v Grand Metropolitan Estate Ltd [1993] 32 EG 74	198
Prudential Assurance Co Ltd v London Residuary Body [1992] 2 AC 386	179
Prudential Assurance Company Ltd & Others v PRG Powerhouse Ltd & Others [2007] EWHC 1002	318

Q

Qdime Ltd v various leaseholders at Bath Building (Swindon) [2014] UKUT 0261 (LC)	243
QFS Scaffolding Limited v Sable and Another [2010] EWCA Civ 682	289
Quick v Taff-Ely Borough Council [1986] QB 809	204

R

R (on the application of Crest Nicholson Residential Ltd) v SSEFRA & Others [2010] EWHC 561 (Admin)	93
R (on the application of Fidler) v Secretary of State for Communities and Local Government [2011] EWCA Civ 1159	70
R (on the application of Harris) v Haringey LBC [2010] EWCA Civ 703	42
R (on the application of National Grid Gas plc) v Environment Agency [2007] UKHL 30	93
R (on the application of Redland Minerals Ltd) v SSEFRA & Others [2010] EWHC 913 (Admin)	91, 93
R (SAVE Britain's Heritage) v Secretary of State for Communities and Local Government [2011] EWCA Civ 334	32
R v Del Basso and Another [2010] EWCA Crim 1119	77
R v Greenwich London Borough Council, ex p Patel [1985] JPL 851, CA	76
R v Hillingdon London Borough Council, ex p Royco Homes Ltd [1974] 1 QB 720	43
R v Kuxhaus [1988] 2 WLR 1005, [1988] 2 All ER 705, CA	81
R v West Oxfordshire District Council, ex p CH Pearce Homes [1986] JPL 523	50
Railtrack plc v Gojra [1998] 08 EG 158	300
Rainbow Estates Ltd v Tokenhold Ltd [1999] Ch 64	283
Ravenseft Properties Ltd v Davstone (Holdings) Ltd [1980] QB 12	205, 206
Ravensgate Estates Ltd v Horizon Housing Group Ltd [2007] All ER (D) 294	281
Receiver for Metropolitan Police District v Palacegate Properties Ltd [2001] 2 Ch 131	295
Romulus Trading Co Ltd v Comet Properties Ltd [1996] 2 EGLR 70	286
Romulus Trading Co Ltd v Henry Smith's Charity Trustees [1990] 2 EGLR 75	305
Royal Bank of Scotland plc v Jennings and Others [1997] 19 EG 152	157
Rugby School (Governors) v Tannahill [1935] 1 KB 87	254
Rushmer v Polsue and Alfieri Ltd [1906] 1 Ch 234	95
Rylands v Fletcher [1868] UKHL 1	97

S

Sabella Ltd v Montgomery [1998] 09 EG 153	297
Sage v Secretary of State for the Environment, Transport and the Regions [2003] 1 WLR 983	70
Savva v Hussein (1997) 73 P & CR 150	254
Scala House & District Property Co Ltd v Forbes [1974] QB 575	254
Scholl Manufacturing Ltd v Clifton (Slim-Line) Ltd [1967] Ch 41	298
Scottish & Newcastle plc v Raguz [2007] EWCA Civ 150	279
Sea & Land Power & Energy v Secretary of State for Communities and Local Government [2012] EWHC 1419 (Admin)	30
Segal Securities Ltd v Thoseby [1963] 1 QB 887	252
Shanley v Ward (1913) 29 TLR 714	219
Sight and Sound Education Ltd v Books etc Ltd [1999] 43 EG 61	297

Skilleter v Charles [1992] 13 EG 113   262
Smiley v Townshend [1950] 2 KB 311   281
Smith v Draper [1990] 2 EGLR 69   297
South Northamptonshire Council & Ward v Secretary of State for Communities and Local Government
    [2013] EWHC 11 (Admin)   30
Southport Old Links Ltd v Naylor [1985] 1 EGLR 66   298
Southwark London Borough Council v Mills and Others; Baxter v Camden London Borough Council
    [1999] 3 WLR 939   238
Sovmots v Secretary of State for the Environment; Brompton Securities Ltd v Secretary of State for the
    Environment [1977] 1 QB 411   42
Starmark Enterprises Ltd v CPL Distribution Ltd [2001] 32 EG 89 (CS)   199
Sterling Land Office Developments Ltd v Lloyds Bank plc (1984) 271 EG 894   225
Stevens v Bromley London Borough Council [1972] 2 WLR 605, CA   76
Stile Hall Properties Ltd v Gooch [1979] 3 All ER 848   299
Straudley Investments Ltd v Barpress Ltd [1987] 1 EGLR 69   348
Street v Mountford [1985] AC 809, [1985] 2 All ER 289   145, 212
Stringer v Minister for Housing and Local Government [1971] 1 All ER 65   41
Sunberry Properties Limited v Innovate Logistics Ltd (in administration) [2008] EWCA Civ 1261   333
Surrey County Council v Single Horse Properties Ltd [2002] EWCA Civ 367, [2002] 1 WLR 2106   296

T

Tesco Stores Limited v Dundee CC [2012] UKSC 13   41
Thames Heliport plc v Tower Hamlets LBC [1997] 2 PLR 72   32
Thatcher v CH Pearce & Sons (Contractors) Ltd [1968] 1 WLR 748   253
Tidswell v Secretary of State for the Environment [1977] JPL 104   74
Tindall Cobham 1 Ltd & Others v Adda Hotels (an unlimited company) & Others [2014] EWCA Civ 1215   216
Topland Portfolio No 1 Ltd v Smiths New Trading Ltd [2014] EWCA Civ 18   170
Transco v Stockport MBC [2003] UKHL 61   97
Transworld Land Co Ltd v J Sainsbury plc [1990] 2 EGLR 255   283
Tyco Fire & Integrated Solutions (UK) Ltd v Rolls Royce Motor Cars Ltd [2008] EWCA Civ 286   242

U

Ultraworth Ltd v General Accident Fire and Life Assurance Corporation [2000] 2 EGLR 115   281
United Dominion Trust Ltd v Shellpoint Trustees [1993] EGCS 57   257
United Scientific Holdings v Burnley Borough Council [1978] AC 904, [1972] 2 All ER 62   181, 199

V

Van Dal Footwear v Ryman Ltd [2009] EWCA Civ 1478   281

W

Wallington v Secretary of State for the Environment [1991] JPL 942, CA   33
Wallis Fashion Group Ltd v General Accident Life Assurance Ltd [2000] EGCS 45   310
Webber (CA) Transport Ltd v Railtrack plc [2004] 1 WLR 320   300
Welsh v Greenwich London Borough Council [2000] PLSCS 149   208
Welwyn Hatfield Council v the Secretary of State [2011] 4 All ER 851   70
Wembley National Stadium Limited v Wembley (London) Limited [2007] EWHC 756 (Ch)   164
Western Fish Products Limited v Penwith DC and Another (1979) 38 P & CR 7   47
Whiteminster Estates v Hodges Menswear (1974) 232 EG 715   219
Willis v Derwentside District Council [2013] All ER (D) 70 (Apr)   96
Willison v Cheverell Estates Ltd [1996] 26 EG 133   302
Winfrey and Chatterton's Agreement, Re [1921] 2 Ch 7   219
Wood v Secretary of State for the Environment [1973] 1 WLR 707, HL   33

Y

Youssefi v Mussellwhite [2014] EWCA Civ 885   303

Z

Zarvos v Pradhan [2003] 2 P & CR 9, [2003] EWCA Civ 208   305, 306

Table of Statutes

Agricultural Holdings Act 1986 293
Arbitration Act 1996 133, 199

Climate Change Act 2008 103
Common Law Procedure Act 1852
  s 210 253
Companies Act 2006 7
  s 172 105, 344
  s 859A 13
  s 1139 300
Competition Act 1998 228, 229
  s 2 228, 229
  s 9 228
Contracts (Rights of Third Parties) Act 1999 126, 275, 354
Control of Pollution (Amendment) Act 1989
  s 1 109
County Courts Act 1984
  s 139(1) 253
Criminal Law Act 1977
  s 6 251

Defective Premises Act 1972 209
Disability Discrimination Act 1995
  s 49 42

Energy Act 2011 106
Enterprise and Regulatory Reform Act 2013 28, 32, 35, 45
Environment Act 1995 88
Environmental Protection Act 1990 88, 108
  s 33 100, 108
  s 34 97, 100, 108
  s 37 107
  Part IIA (s 78A–78YC) 87, 88, 89, 92, 93, 94, 95, 98, 99,
    100
  s 78A(2) 88
  s 78A(4) 88
  s 78A(9) 89
  s 78B 88
  s 78C 90
  s 78E 90
  s 78F(2) 90
  s 78F(4) 90
  s 78M 93
  s 78M(5) 94
  s 78P(2) 92
  s 78U 95
  s 79 97
  s 80 97, 109
  s 82 97
  s 157 87, 94
  Sch 2 98
  Sch 3 100
  Sch 9 100
Equality Act 2010 42, 213, 220, 235

Growth and Infrastructure Act 2013 28, 46
  s 1 42

Growth and Infrastructure Act 2013 – *continued*
  s 6 48
  Sch 1 42

Health and Safety at Work, etc Act 1974
  s 33(1)(c) 107
Highways Act 1980 66, 67
  s 278 66
Housing Grants, Construction and Regeneration Act 1996
  Part II 133
Human Rights Act 1998 96
  Sch 1 251

Insolvency Act 1986 172, 315, 318, 319, 321, 322
  ss 1–7 318
  s 28 319
  s 44 320
  s 112 323
  s 126 331
  s 130 331
  s 145 171
  s 178 330, 331
  s 178(3) 334
  s 178(3)(a) 323
  s 178(4) 336
  s 178(5) 335
  s 238 324
  s 239 324
  s 241 325
  s 252 318, 319
  s 253 318
  s 254 318, 319
  ss 255–263 318
  s 284(1) 321
  s 285(1) 321, 327
  s 285(3) 321, 327
  s 285(4) 321
  s 316 327
  s 316(1) 335
  s 339 324
  s 340 324
  s 342 325
  Sch B1, para 43 322
Insolvency Act 2006
  s 178 334
  s 315 334

Land Charges Act 1972 301
Land Compensation Act 1973
  Part 3 362, 365
Land Registration Act 2002 157
  s 86 321
  Sch 3 301
  Sch 12 166, 167, 168
Landlord and Tenant Act 1927 209, 231, 236, 282, 300
  Part I (ss 1–17) 236
  s 18 281, 285

Landlord and Tenant Act 1927 – *continued*
  s 19(1)(a) 214, 215, 216, 218, 269, 274
  s 19(1A) 215, 217, 218, 220, 269, 272
  s 19(1C) 215
  s 19(2) 233, 234
  s 19(3) 227
  s 23(1) 300
  s 25 292
Landlord and Tenant Act 1954 146, 158, 162, 173, 181, 185,
  189, 190, 213, 217, 229, 272, 274, 276, 291, 295, 296,
  353, 354
  Part II (ss 23–46) 141, 146, 162, 179, 180, 181, 183, 212,
    219, 249, 275, 278, 287, 288, 289, 291–311, 322, 354,
    429–45
  s 23 292, 293
  s 23(1) 291
  s 23(1A)–(1B) 292
  s 23(3) 294
  s 24 166, 170, 183, 291, 296, 298, 358, 360, 363, 366
  s 24(2) 181
  s 24(2A) 358, 360
  s 24(2B) 360
  s 24(3) 293
  s 24A 159, 166, 183, 190, 296, 302, 358, 363
  ss 24B–24D 358, 363
  s 25 297, 298, 299, 300, 301, 302, 303, 305, 306, 307, 311,
    355, 357–62, 366, 368
  s 25(8) 358
  s 26 297, 298, 299, 300, 301, 302, 303, 305, 306, 307, 355,
    362–5, 366, 368
  s 26(6) 366, 368
  s 27 296, 297, 366
  s 27(1) 297, 354
  s 27(1A) 296, 297
  s 27(2) 297
  s 28 366
  s 29A 302, 358, 360, 365
  s 29A(2) 301
  s 29A(3) 365
  s 29B 301, 358, 360, 365
  s 30 298, 301, 303, 308
  s 30(1) 303, 359, 360, 362, 363, 364
  s 30(1)(a)–(c) 360, 364
  s 30(1)(d) 361, 364
  s 30(1)(e) 361, 362, 364, 365
  s 30(1)(f)–(g) 181, 361, 362, 364, 365
  s 30(1A)–(1B) 361
  s 30(2)–(3) 306
  s 31A 305, 309, 361
  s 34 190, 358, 363
  s 34(3) 310
  s 35 358, 363
  s 37 162, 362, 364, 365
  s 38 289
  s 38(1) 294
  s 38(2) 308
  s 38(4) 294
  s 40 294, 355, 366
  s 40(1) 365–7
  s 40(2) 367
  s 40(3) 368–70
  s 40(4) 370
  s 40(5) 367, 369, 370

Landlord and Tenant Act 1954 – *continued*
  s 40(8) 367, 369
  s 40B 367, 369
  s 41 292, 306
  s 41A 292
  s 42 306
  s 44 293, 358, 362, 365, 367, 370
  s 46 292
  s 46(2) 292, 361
  Part III (ss 47–50) 236
  s 67 358, 362, 365, 367, 370
Landlord and Tenant Act 1988 218, 220, 227, 269, 270, 271
  s 1 269, 274
  s 1(3)(b) 220
Landlord and Tenant (Covenants) Act 1995 146, 147, 163,
  164, 165, 167, 168, 172, 214, 215, 216, 269, 270, 271,
  272, 275, 279, 284, 286, 310, 320, 334, 348
  s 6 164
  s 8 164
  s 17 165, 166, 169, 279, 349
  s 18 165, 170
  s 24(2) 169
  s 25 169, 171
  s 28(1) 153
Law of Property Act 1925 160, 316
  s 44 275
  s 52 288
  s 61 160
  s 77 166, 167, 168
  s 101 319
  s 139 289
  s 141 165
  s 141(1) 164
  s 142 165
  s 142(1) 164
  s 144 218, 220
  s 146 159, 184, 253, 254, 255, 256, 257, 278, 282, 331,
    349
  s 146(2) 255
  s 146(4) 257
  s 147 256
  s 150 289
  s 196 22, 161
  s 196(3)–(4) 161
  s 205(1) 145
Leasehold Property (Repairs) Act 1938 209, 255, 256, 282
  s 1(5) 256
Limitation Act 1980 126, 280
Local Democracy, Economic Development and
  Construction Act 2009 133
Local Government Act 1972 47
  s 250(5) 55
Local Government Act 2003
  s 93 47
Localism Act 2011 28, 30, 40, 70
  s 109 30

Mental Health Act 1983
  s 99 172
Misrepresentation Act 1967
  s 3 161

Partnership Act 1890 7

Planning Act 2008 28, 46, 57, 62
Planning and Compensation Act 1991 28
Planning and Compulsory Purchase Act 2004 28, 45
    s 38(6) 29, 30, 31
    s 43 49
Planning (Hazardous Substances) Act 1990 101
Proceeds of Crime Act 2002 77

Race Relations Act 1976
    s 71 42
Recorded Delivery Service Act 1962 161
Regulatory Enforcement and Sanctions Act 2008 84, 94, 106
Rent Act 1977 367
Rent (Agriculture) Act 1976 367

Senior Courts Act 1981
    s 37 285
Sexual Discrimination Act 1975
    s 76A(1) 42
Supply of Goods and Services Act 1982 264
    s 4 116
    s 13 116

Town and Country Planning Act 1947 27
Town and Country Planning Act 1990 28, 31, 46, 62, 69, 70
    s 38(6) 341
    s 55 235
    s 55(1) 31
    s 55(1A) 31
    s 55(2) 33
    s 55(2)(a) 31
    s 55(2)(d)–(f) 33
    s 55(2)(g) 31
    s 55(3) 33
    s 55(5) 33
    s 56 45, 341
    s 56(4) 63
    s 57(1) 31
    s 57(2) 35, 38, 44
    s 57(3)–(6) 35
    ss 59–61 35
    s 61W 47
    ss 62–65 47
    s 65(8) 49
    ss 66–68 47
    s 69 47, 49, 71
    s 70(1) 41, 42, 43
    s 70B 49
    s 72(1) 42
    s 73 44, 48, 50, 51, 62, 68, 341
    s 73A 51, 68, 77
    s 75(1) 44
    s 78 51
    s 96A 51
    s 97 45
    s 106 57, 59, 60, 66, 67
    s 106(1) 58, 60
    s 106(2) 58
    s 106(3) 59, 60
    s 106(4) 58, 59, 60
    s 106(5)–(6) 59
    s 106(12) 59

Town and Country Planning Act 1990 – *continued*
    s 106A 60, 61
    s 106B 61
    s 106BA 60, 61
    s 106BC 61
    Part VII (ss 171–196) 69
    s 171A 69, 75
    s 171A(1) 75
    s 171B 70, 75
    s 171B(4)(b) 70, 75
    s 171BA 70, 75
    s 171C 72, 79
    s 171C(1) 73
    s 171C(5) 73
    s 171D 72
    s 171D(2)–(6) 73
    ss 171E–171G 78
    s 172 74, 75, 80
    s 172(1) 74
    s 173 74, 75
    s 173(1) 75
    s 173(2) 75, 78
    s 173(3)–(9) 75
    s 173(11)–(12) 77
    s 174 74, 75, 76, 77, 80
    s 174(1) 81
    s 174(2) 80
    s 174(2)(a) 79, 80
    s 174(3) 81
    s 174(3)(b) 81
    s 174(4) 81
    s 174(6) 81
    s 175 74, 75, 80
    s 175(5) 80
    s 176 74, 75, 80
    s 176(1) 80
    s 176(2) 77
    s 177 74, 75, 80
    s 177(1C) 80
    s 178 74
    s 178(1) 78
    s 179 74
    s 179(1)–(5) 77
    s 179(7)–(9) 77
    ss 180–182 74
    s 183 78
    s 183(1)–(3) 78
    s 183(6)–(7) 79
    s 184 78
    s 184(1)–(3) 78
    s 184(7) 79
    s 185 78
    s 186 78
    s 187 78
    s 187A 73
    s 187B 78, 80
    s 188 77, 78
    s 191 70
    s 191(1) 70
    s 191(4) 71
    s 192 71
    s 193(4) 71
    s 193(6) 71

Town and Country Planning Act 1990 – *continued*
    ss 196A–196C 72
    s 284 55
    s 285 76
    s 285(1) 76
    s 288 55, 71
    s 289 81, 82
    s 320 81
    s 320(2) 55
    s 322 55, 81
    s 336 52
    s 336(1) 31, 76
    Sch 1, para 1 28
Tribunals, Courts and Enforcement Act 2007
    Part 3 (ss 62–90) 280
    s 77 280
    s 81 281, 325–32
    Sch 12 280

Unfair Contracts Terms Act 1977 161
    s 8 161

Value Added Tax Act 1994
    s 49 140
    s 89 139

Water Act 2014
    Part 4 (ss 64–84) 108
Water Industry Act 1991
    s 111 109
Water Resources Act 1991
    s 24 100
    s 25 100
    s 104 89
    s 118 100
Wildlife and Countryside Act 1981 108

International legislation
European Convention on Human Rights 74, 251
    Art 8 96
UN Framework Convention on Climate Change
    Kyoto Protocol 1997 102

Table of Secondary Legislation

Building Regulations 2010 (SI 2010/2214) 104, 150, 235

Community Infrastructure Levy (Amendment) Regulations 2011 (SI 2011/987) 57, 63, 65
Community Infrastructure Levy (Amendment) Regulations 2012 (SI 2012/98) 57, 62, 63, 65
Community Infrastructure Levy (Amendment) Regulations 2013 (SI 2013/382) 57, 62, 63, 65
Community Infrastructure Levy (Amendment) Regulations 2014 (SI 2014/395) 57, 66
Community Infrastructure Levy Regulations 2010 (SI 2010/948) 57, 58, 61, 62, 63, 64, 65, 66, 67
    reg 6(2) 62
    reg 122 58, 60
Construction (Design and Management) Regulations 1994 (SI 1994/3140) 117
Construction (Design and Management) Regulations 2007 (SI 2007/320) 117
Contaminated Land (England) Regulations 2006 (SI 2006/1380) 94
Control of Asbestos at Work Regulations 2012 (SI 2012/632) 107
    reg 4 107, 108
    reg 4(1) 107
Control of Major Accidents Hazards Regulations 1999 (SI 1999/743) 344
Control of Substances Hazardous to Health Regulations 2002 (SI 2002/2677) 100, 101
Controlled Waste (England and Wales) Regulations 2012 (SI 2012/811) 108
CRC Energy Efficiency Scheme Order 2013 (SI 2013/1119) 103

Energy Performance of Buildings (Certificates and Inspections) (England and Wales) Regulations 2012 (SI 2012/3118) 104
    regs 5–7 104
    reg 9 104
    reg 10 105
    Part 4 (regs 17–21) 105
Environmental Damage (Prevention and Remediation) Regulations 2009 (SI 2009/153) 84, 98, 344
    reg 13 98
    reg 14 98
Environmental Permitting (England and Wales) Regulations 2010 (SI 2010/675) 99, 101
    Part A(1)–(2) 100
    Part B 100
    reg 7 99
    reg 12 99, 100, 101, 108
    reg 12(1) 99, 100
    reg 22 101
    reg 36 101
    reg 37 101
    reg 38 100, 101, 102, 108
    reg 38(1) 100

Environmental Permitting (England and Wales) Regulations 2010 – continued
    reg 41 102
    reg 57 102
    reg 60 101
    Sch 7A 99
    Sch 8 99
    Sch 9 99
    Sch 9A 99
    Schs 10–12 99
    Sch 13A 99
    Sch 14 99
    Sch 15A 99
    Sch 16 99
    Sch 17A 99
    Schs 18–19 99
    Sch 21 99, 100
    Sch 22 99, 100
        para 9 101
    Sch 23 99

Greenhouse Gas Emissions Trading Scheme Regulations 2012 (SI 2012/3038) 103

Insolvency Rules 1986 (SI 1986/1925) 315
    r 6.13 317

Land Registration (Amendment) (No 2) Rules 2005 (SI 2005/1982) 157
Land Registration Rules 2005 (SI 2005/1766) 157
    Sch 1A 157
Landlord and Tenant Act 1954 Part II (Notices) (England and Wales) Regulations 2004 (SI 2004/1005) 297, 298
    Sch 2 357–9

Producer Responsibility Obligations (Packaging Waste) Regulations 2007 (SI 2007/871) 101

Regulatory Reform (Business Tenancies) (England and Wales) Order 2003 (SI 2003/3096) 358, 360, 363, 367, 369
Regulatory Reform (Fire Safety) Order 2005 (SI 2005/1541) 344

Scheme for Construction Contracts (England and Wales) Regulations 1998 (Amendment) (England) Regulations 2011 (SI 2011/2333) 133
Scheme for Construction Contracts (England and Wales) Regulations 1998 (SI 1998/649) 133

Town and Country Planning (Appeals) (Written Representations Procedure) Regulations 2009 (SI 2009/452) 53
Town and Country Planning (Determination by Inspectors) (Inquiries Procedure) Rules (England) 2000 (SI 2000/1625) 54

Town and Country Planning (Development Management
    Procedure) (England) (Amendment) Order 2013
    (SI 2013/1238) 48, 50
Town and Country Planning (Development Management
    Procedure) (England) Order 2010 (SI 2010/2184) 27, 28,
    40
    art 1 40
    art 1(2) 41
    art 4 40, 41, 56
    art 11 49
    art 11(8) 49
    art 12 49
    art 13 49
    art 29 49
    art 31 50
    art 32 52
    art 33 51, 52, 53
    art 35 71
    art 36 50
Town and Country Planning (Enforcement Notices and
    Appeals) (England) Regulations 2002 (SI 2002/2682)
    regs 4–5 75
    reg 6 81
Town and Country Planning (Enforcement Notices and
    Appeals) (Wales) Regulations 2003 (SI 2003/394) 75
Town and Country Planning (Environmental Impact
    Assessment) Regulations 2011 (SI 2011/1824) 48, 49
Town and Country Planning (General Permitted
    Development) (Amendment) (England) Order 2013
    (SI 2013/1101) 35
Town and Country Planning (General Permitted
    Development) (Amendment) (England) (No 2) Order
    2013 (SI 2013/1868) 35–6
Town and Country Planning (General Permitted
    Development) (Amendment) (England) (No 3) Order
    2013 (SI 2013/2147) 36
Town and Country Planning (General Permitted
    Development) (Amendment) (England) (No 4) Order
    2013 (SI 2013/2435) 36
Town and Country Planning (General Permitted
    Development) Order 1995 (SI 1995/418) 27, 28, 32, 35–9,
    39, 55, 56, 62, 65, 70, 341, 342, 350
    art 1(5) 36, 38, 39
    art 3(5) 39
    art 3(10) 39
    art 4 39, 341
    Sch 2 35, 39
        Part 1 36
        Part 2 37
        Part 3 37
        Part 4 37–8
        Part 6 38
        Part 31 38
        Part 41 38
        Part 42 39
Town and Country Planning (Hearings and Inquiries
    Procedure) (Amendment) (England) Rules 2009
    (SI 2009/455) 54, 55
Town and Country Planning (Hearings Procedure)
    (England) Rules 2000 (SI 2000/1626) 55
Town and Country Planning (Inquiries Procedure) (England)
    Rules 2000 (SI 2000/1624) 54

Town and Country Planning (Use Classes) Order 1987
    (SI 1987/764) 27, 28, 33, 34, 35, 37, 193, 225, 230
    art 3(6) 34
    Sch 37
Transfrontier Shipment of Waste Regulations 2007
    (SI 2007/1711) 109

Value Added Tax (Land) Order 1995 (SI 1995/282) 140

Waste Electrical and Electronic Equipment Regulations
    2013 (SI 2013/3113) 100

EU secondary legislation
Directive 2003/87/EC Emissions Trading Scheme 102, 103
Directive 2004/35/EC Environmental Liability 98
Directive 2010/31/EU Energy Performance of Buildings 104
    Arts 8–9 104

Circulars 33, 42
DCLG Circular 11/95 44
    Appendix A 44
DCLG Circular 5/2005 58

Codes of Practice and Arbitration Rules
Code for Leasing Business Premises in England and Wales
    2007 155–6, 201, 217, 224, 236, 241, 243, 245, 247, 257,
    267, 272, 276, 350, 351, 371–81, 383
    para 4 189
    para 5 217
    para 6 267
    para 7 208
    para 8 224, 236
    para 9 241, 250
    para 10 257
Institution of Civil Engineers Arbitration Rules 133
International Chamber of Commerce (ICC) Arbitration
    Rules 133
London Court of International Arbitration Rules 133
DCLG Model Planning Conditions for Contaminated Land
    94
RICS Code of Practice on Service Charges in Commercial
    Property 2006 266
    s 2 267

Directions
Town and Country Planning (Demolition–Descriptions of
    Buildings) Direction 1995 31–2

Guidance
Contaminated Land Statutory Guidance 2012 90, 93, 94
    s 3 88
    s 4 88
    s 4.1 88
    s 4.3 89
    s 4.19 89
    s 4.33 89
    s 7 91
    s 7(c) 90
    s 7(d) 91
    s 7(e) 90
    s 7(f) 92
    s 7.3.2(b) 90

Contaminated Land Statutory Guidance 2012 – *continued*
    s 7.32 90
    s 7.66 92
    s 7.68–7.72 92
    s 7.79 90
    s 7.80–7.86 92
National Policy Practice Guidance 27, 28, 33, 44, 51, 54, 55, 59, 71, 74, 75

National Planning Policy Framework 29, 30, 42, 53, 59, 74, 94, 2728
    para 2 29
    para 14 29

National Planning Policy Framework – *continued*
    para 51 33
    para 195 41
    para 203 43, 59
    paras 204–5 59
    para 206 44
    para 207 74
    para 215 30

Planning Policy Statements 42
PPS 10 94
PPS 23 94, 344
Tan 21 (Wales) 94

List of Abbreviations

The following abbreviations are used throughout this book.

ADR	alternative dispute resolution
AGA	Authorised Guarantee Agreement
AMP	Asbestos Management Plan
BCN	breach of condition notice
CA 1998	Competition Act 1998
CGT	capital gains tax
CIL	Community Infrastructure Levy
CLEUD	certificate of lawful use or development
COSHH 2002	Control of Substances Hazardous to Health Regulations 2002
CRC Energy Efficiency Scheme	Carbon Reduction Commitment Energy Efficiency Scheme
CVA	company voluntary arrangement
DCLG	Department for Communities and Local Government
DAS	designs and access statement
DEC	Display Energy Certificate
Defra	Department for Environment, Food and Rural Affairs
DMPO	Town and Country Planning (Development Management Procedure) Order 2010
EA	Environment Agency
EA 1995	Environment Act 1995
EIA	environmental impact assessment
EPA 1990	Environmental Protection Act 1990
EPB Regulations 2012	Energy Performance of Buildings (England and Wales) Regulations 2012
EPC	Energy Performance Certificate
EPR 2010	Environmental Permitting (England and Wales) Regulations 2010
ERRA 2013	Enterprise and Regulatory Reform Act 2013
ES	environmental statement
EU ETS	European Union Emission Trading System
GAIA 2013	Growth and Infrastructure Act 2013
GHG	greenhouse gas
GIA	gross internal area
GPDO	Town and Country Planning (General Permitted Development) Order 1995
HMRC	HM Revenue & Customs
HSE	Health and Safety Executive
IA	Insolvency Act 1986
IVA	individual voluntary arrangement
LA 2011	Localism Act 2011

LDF	local development framework
LPA	local planning authority
LPA 1925	Law of Property Act 1925
LP(R)A 1938	Leasehold Property (Repairs) Act 1938
LRA 2002	Land Registration Act 2002
LTA 1927	Landlord and Tenant Act 1927
LTA 1954	Landlord and Tenant Act 1954
LTA 1988	Landlord and Tenant Act 1988
LT(C)A 1995	Landlord and Tenant (Covenants) Act 1995
NPPF	National Planning Policy Framework
NPV	net present value
OMR	open market rent
PA 2008	Planning Act 2008
PCA 1991	Planning and Compensation Act 1991
PCN	planning contravention notice
PCPA 2004	Planning and Compulsory Purchase Act 2004
PEA 1977	Protection from Eviction Act 1977
PINS	Planning Inspectorate
PPGs	planning policy guidance notes
PPS	Planning Policy Statement
RESA 2008	Regulatory Enforcement and Sanctions Act 2008
RICS	Royal Institution of Chartered Surveyors
SCPC	Standard Commercial Property Condition
SDLT	stamp duty land tax
SDO	special development order
SOS	Secretary of State for Communities and Local Government
SPV	special purpose vehicle
SPZ	simplified planning zone
SSSI	site of special scientific interest
TCEA 2007	Tribunals, Courts and Enforcement Act 2007
TCPA 1990	Town and Country Planning Act 1990
UCO	Town and Country Planning (Use Classes) Order 1987
VATA 1994	Value Added Tax Act 1994

SITE ACQUISITIONS

CHAPTER 1

THE COMMERCIAL CONTEXT

1.1	What is commercial property?	3
1.2	Who buys commercial property?	4
1.3	Buying commercial property jointly	5
1.4	Methods of structuring a property joint venture	6
	Review activity	8

1.1 WHAT IS COMMERCIAL PROPERTY?

Commercial property is property which is not designed or used for residential purposes, or for purposes associated with the primary industries such as agriculture and mining. The three main types of commercial property are offices (single office buildings and business parks), retail (individual shops, shopping centres, retail warehouses and supermarkets) and industrial (factories, warehouses and distribution centres). Together these represent about 86% of the commercial property market. The remaining 14% comprises properties used for leisure (pubs, restaurants and hotels), sport, education, the provision of utilities and healthcare (hospitals and nursing homes).

The value of UK commercial property at the end of 2013 was £683 billion, about 45% of the value of government bonds and 30% of the UK's stock market. Within that figure of £683 billion, retail accounted for £305 billion (45%), offices £195 billion (29%), industrial £126 billion (18%) and other commercial properties £58 billion (8%). Commercial property activities employed over 900,000 people and the sector contributed about £54 billion (3.8%) to the UK's GDP. (The figures quoted are taken from the *Property Data Report 2014*, produced by nine members of the Property Industry Alliance.) Although the residential property sector is seven times larger (by value) than the commercial property sector, the vast majority of residential properties are owned by private householders, so there is not as much scope for residential property investment as there is for commercial property investment.

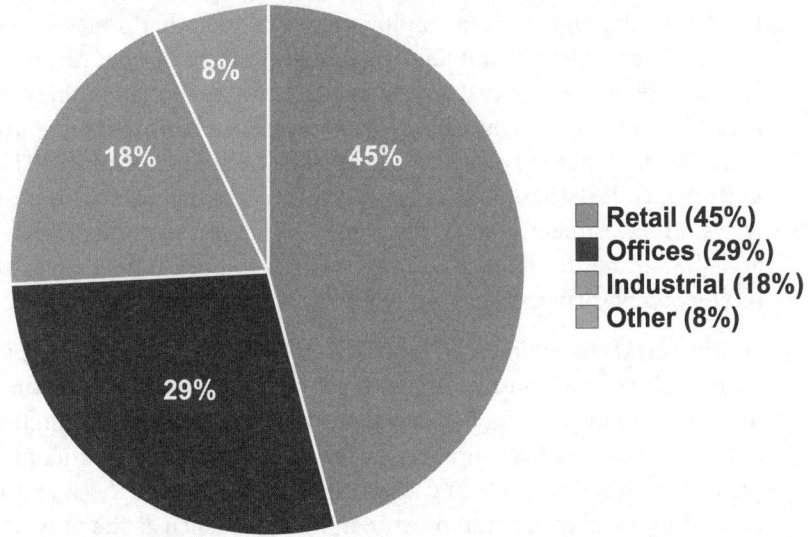

Figure 1.1   Value of UK commercial property at the end of 2013

This book will concentrate on two of the main types of commercial property, offices and retail, although most of what is covered in it will also be relevant to the other types of commercial property.

1.2   WHO BUYS COMMERCIAL PROPERTY?

1.2.1   Occupiers

About one-third of all commercial property is bought by owner-occupiers, who need land and buildings from which to conduct their business. Some of these occupiers want to buy a freehold or long leasehold interest in the property because they need certainty and complete freedom to deal with the property as the business dictates, but it does means that a lot of capital is tied up in the building. Other occupiers prefer to take a so-called 'rack rent lease', where the occupation cost is paid, usually quarterly, over the period of the lease by way of rent, rather than all at the beginning. In recent years, particularly among the large food retailers, there has been a move away from freehold ownership through 'sale and leaseback', where the freehold interest in the property is sold to an investor (thus releasing capital for use in the operating part of the business) and the occupier takes a rack rent lease instead.

1.2.2   Investors

The other two-thirds of all commercial property is bought by investors, who buy property to let out to others so that they can make an income from the rent and a profit from any increase in the capital value of the property. Although the capital value of commercial property suffered a considerable fall in 2007 and 2008, it remains popular with certain types of investor because the average lease offers an income stream of about five years. So the income return (or 'yield') from commercial property is reasonable (10.6% in 2013, less than that of buoyant UK equities but far better than gilts). Commercial property was the best performing asset class in 2010, and over the 42 years prior to 2013, commercial property produced annualised returns of almost 10.7%, somewhere between gilts and equities (see paragraph 12 of the *Property Data Report 2014*). Commercial property has tended not to track the performance of gilts and equities particularly closely, so including some commercial property in your investment portfolio is a way of diversifying and spreading risk. Moreover, by good management of tenants and/or refurbishment of a tired building, a property investor may be able to enhance the value of the asset, even in times of economic downturn.

There are two ways to invest in commercial property, directly or indirectly. Direct property investment involves buying a property in your own name or in the name of a group company, letting it out, taking responsibility for managing it and selling it on when you no longer require it. Although you can employ surveyors and other professionals to assist you, this still uses up a considerable amount of time and effort. It also means that you have to find a considerable amount of cash, or a loan, or a combination of both, to fund the initial purchase. An alternative way is to buy shares or units in a company that invests in a range of commercial and residential property, such as a real estate investment trust (REIT) or an offshore property unit trust (PUT). These indirect property investment vehicles offer opportunities for smaller levels of investment, some taxation advantages, less management responsibility and, arguably, greater flexibility as it may be easier to trade units than to sell a property. However, indirect property investment is beyond the scope of this book.

So who invests in commercial property? According to figures in the *Property Data Report 2014*, overseas investors held the largest block of directly-owned investment property (24%); UK insurance companies and pension funds held 19%; UK REITs and listed property companies held 14%; and UK private property companies held 14%. Traditional estates and charities and private investors held 4% and 3% respectively. Most of the remainder (22%) was held by investors providing indirect investment to others, such as the property unit trusts and pooled funds. Some of these units are bought by private individuals, but many are bought by the investors who also buy property directly. For example, in 2013 the UK insurance companies and pension funds invested £75 billion (2.7% of their total investments) in directly owned UK property, £42 billion (1.5%) in collective investment schemes and £39 billion (1.4%) in property company and REIT shares.

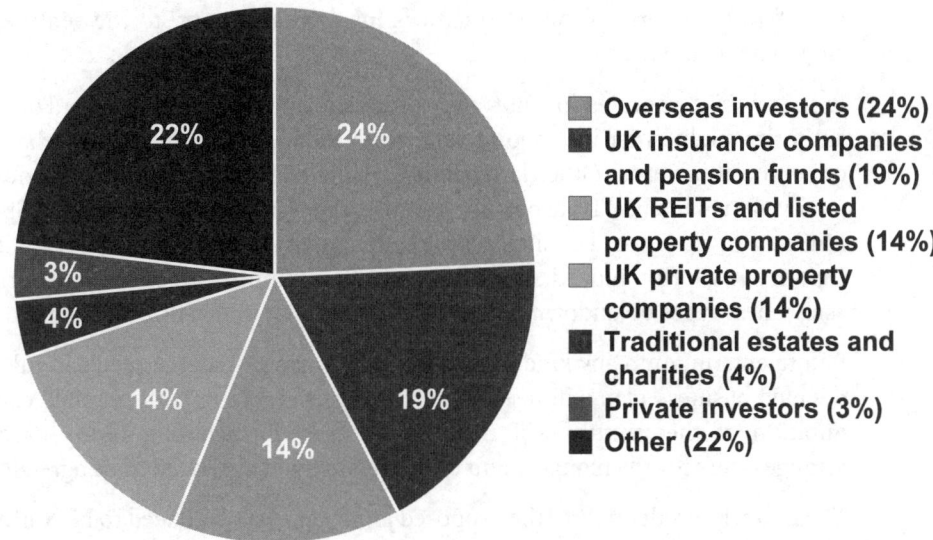

Figure 1.2   Investors in UK commercial property

1.2.3   Developers

Another way to make a profit from commercial property is to buy a property which is not being used to its full potential, construct some new buildings on the site, let at least some of the new buildings to quality tenants so that there is good income flow, and then sell the completed development to an occupier or an investor at a price greater than you have spent on the purchase and development of the property. Commercial property development stalled after the credit crunch of 2007 because of the difficulties developers experienced in obtaining loans to fund what is still seen as a risky activity, but in times of economic growth, when there is a shortage in the supply of new buildings, commercial property development returns.

Of course, the aims of occupation, investment and development are not mutually exclusive. For example, some larger investors develop property themselves, or participate in joint ventures with developers so as to spread the risks (see **1.3**). Some potential occupiers, particularly those looking for prestige headquarters buildings, may prefer to develop their own building or work alongside a developer in order to achieve a high degree of customisation.

1.3   BUYING COMMERCIAL PROPERTY JOINTLY

Both property investment and property development involve substantial financial risks. For example, between the summer of 2007 and the autumn of 2008, commercial property lost, on average, about 40% of its value. Property development is particularly risky because the economic conditions can worsen considerably in the months, sometimes years, between the purchase of the site and completion of the development. So, although it is sometimes the case that a developer will purchase a site and develop the site itself, this normally occurs only in the case of small-scale developments. In larger developments it is usual to find that the development will be a joint venture between two or more parties.

Joint ventures enable the cost and potential risks, and profits (if any), of a development scheme to be shared. So a developer might find it easier to obtain funding, and those wishing to invest funds (eg banks, pension funds, etc) can share in the profits of a development rather than just obtaining a fixed return. They may also have more control over the nature of the development.

Joint ventures also enable landowners and those without particular skills in a particular aspect of property development to undertake them competently. So, for example, the cleaning up of a seriously contaminated site would need the involvement of specialists. This service could always be purchased, ie a contractor is employed to clean up the site, but if the landowner/developer does not understand the issues involved it can be very difficult to manage outside contractors properly. If the contractor is involved as a party to the venture, such problems should be avoided.

Property joint ventures are not always carried out purely for profit. For example, a local authority might enter into a joint venture as a way of bringing about urban regeneration or other social benefits. Other landowning public bodies which have historically entered into joint ventures include Transport for London, the National Health Service, Sport England, the Ministry of Defence, housing associations, registered social landlords and the Olympic Delivery Authority. Indeed, the Home and Communities Agency was specifically set up to assist these types of landowner to get their surplus or under-utilised land redeveloped.

Before entering into any kind of joint venture, various matters need careful consideration. A detailed business plan will need to be put together, along with possible exit strategies. The duration of the venture will need to be agreed, including terms of dissolution. The arrangements for the management of the venture will also need to be agreed.

The financial credentials of the proposed joint venturers will need to be confirmed. The profit share (or share of the loss) and financial contributions of each party will have to be agreed, along with each party's involvement in the development works themselves. The form which the joint venture will take will also need to be established.

1.4   METHODS OF STRUCTURING A PROPERTY JOINT VENTURE

A joint venture set up for development purposes might involve, for example, the landowner, the developer, the funder and the ultimate occupier of the completed development. There are various ways in which such a joint venture can be structured. No one scheme is always appropriate, and the advantages and disadvantages of each option should be considered carefully. Often taxation will be of prime consideration, and specialist advice should be obtained with regard to the tax implications of the chosen scheme.

1.4.1   Contractual joint venture

This, in essence, involves the parties entering into a contract which sets out the terms of their agreement. These will include each party's financial commitment and duties in relation to the development, so the arrangement is very flexible and responsive to the parties' individual needs. If one of the parties already owns the property, there is no need to transfer the ownership of the site at the start of the joint venture as there is no setting up of a separate legal entity, so a charge to stamp duty land tax (SDLT) is avoided. The joint venture contract arrangement is 'tax transparent', so each party will be responsible for payment of income tax on its profits and capital gains tax (CGT) on its capital gains, and will get the direct benefit of any tax deductions and reliefs. Moreover, as the parties are in a mere contract together, it is less likely that one party would be liable for the actions of another (subject to the terms of the agreement). On the other hand, as there is no separate legal entity, there will be unlimited liability in relation to any losses. Thus the failure of the joint venture could result in threats to the continued existence of the contracting parties.

1.4.2   Joint venture partnership

In a joint venture partnership, the joint venture partners will enter into a partnership agreement to purchase the property. This agreement will again regulate the way in which risk and profits are shared and the roles and responsibilities of each partner. A joint venture partnership, like the joint venture contract, is very flexible and can be tailored to suit the needs of the partners. However, unlike a joint venture contract, a partnership is a legally recognised structure, governed by a statutory code in the Partnership Act 1890, so there is a default position when unexpected events occur.

The property will be held in the name of the partnership, so if the property is being acquired from a third party, a charge to SDLT will arise when the property is transferred from the third party to the joint venture partners. Alternatively, one of the joint venture parties might already own the property, in which case a charge to SDLT will arise when the property is transferred to the joint venture partnership (something that can be avoided by using a contractual joint venture instead). In either case, as the legal interest in property can only be held by up to four people, if there are more than four partners the legal interest will be held in the names of some of those partners, with the beneficial interest vesting in all of the partners, in specified shares.

As far as tax is concerned, a joint venture partnership is tax transparent, so each partner is taxed on its own share of the profits and capital gains separately, and each is able to choose how best to use its tax deductions and reliefs. As a partnership, there is no requirement to file an annual return, and the accounts will remain private.

The main disadvantage is that in the traditional unlimited liability partnership, each partner will be wholly liable for the debts and obligations of the partnership, so the partners have to know and trust each other to a very high degree. Moreover, each partner will have the authority to bind the partnership and its co-partners when dealing with third parties. However, parties can now choose to use a limited liability partnership (LLP). An LLP is a hybrid between a partnership under the Partnership Act 1890 and a limited company under the Companies Act 2006. An LLP shares many of the features of a traditional partnership (including tax transparency), but it also offers reduced personal responsibility for business debts. The LLP is a corporate body with a separate identity from the members, and the LLP itself is responsible for any debts that it incurs, rather than the individual members.

Joint venture partnerships have been commonly used to acquire property and are preferable to a simple contractual relationship where a long-term, complex project is contemplated.

1.4.3 Special purpose vehicle companies

This is a limited company set up for a particular purpose, eg to develop a particular site. The special purpose vehicle company (SPV) may be a subsidiary of just one company, but it can also be a jointly-owned subsidiary of several companies. The companies that set up the SPV are shareholders in it and have all of the usual rights of a shareholder. Different companies can invest different amounts in the property that the SPV purchases and receive differing profit shares. Although certain matters can be customised in a shareholders agreement, in default the arrangements will be governed by company law, which is a tried and tested framework with which the parties are likely to be familiar.

A key advantage of using an SPV is that the SPV will have limited liability. This means that the risk of a particular business venture can be isolated from the other businesses of the companies involved. If the property investment turns out to be a very bad one and the SPV becomes insolvent, the other interests of the shareholding companies are protected.

Another reason for choosing an SPV is that on completion of the development, it is possible to transfer ownership of the property by selling the shares in the SPV company, rather than by transferring the property itself. The benefit of this comes from the way stamp duty is charged. Stamp duty land tax is paid at the rate of 4% of the purchase price for all property costing more than £500,000. However, if you sell shares in a company, stamp duty is paid at the rate of 0.5% on the consideration. There are, however, special anti-avoidance SDLT rules which need to be considered in this context. As always, specialist taxation advice will be needed. Note also that although it is the buyer, rather than the seller, who pays the SDLT and who therefore benefits from the saving, as the buyer will be making an SDLT saving it may be prepared to pay a higher purchase price for the SPV than for the property, so the seller benefits too.

On the other hand, as a limited company governed by the Companies Acts, annual returns must be filed, which will result in administrative expense and a lack of privacy as to the company's structure and finances (LLPs also have to file annual accounts). When the joint venture is formed, the property will be held in the name of the SPV, so a charge to SDLT will arise when the property is transferred from the landowner to the SPV. There are also taxation issues other than SDLT to consider. The SPV itself will be assessed to corporation tax on the rental income and on capital gains from the property held as an investment, and the shareholder companies will pay corporation tax on the dividends issued by the SPV. This is sometimes referred to as 'double taxation'. For this reason, an SPV is perhaps more suited to a development which is to be disposed of within a short period of its completion rather than held as a long-term investment.

REVIEW ACTIVITY

1.   What are the three main types of commercial property?
2.   When choosing a commercial property from which to conduct its business, why might a business organisation prefer to rent a property than buy a freehold property?
3.   How do investors hope to make a profit from commercial property?
4.   How do developers hope to make a profit from commercial property?
5.   Why might an investor enter into a joint venture with others to develop a commercial property?
6.   Why might a contractual joint venture or a joint venture partnership be more tax-efficient for the parties than an SPV?
7.   In terms of reducing financial risk to the joint venture parties, which joint venture structures are most advantageous?
8.   Which joint venture structure is most efficient in terms of SDLT?

Answers to this Review activity may be found in Appendix 1.

CHAPTER 2

OBTAINING PROPERTY FINANCE

2.1	Methods of finance	9
2.2	Debt finance	10
	Review activity	14

2.1 METHODS OF FINANCE

One of the first considerations of any buyer of commercial property, whether the buyer is a developer, an institutional investor or simply a company looking to acquire premises from which to operate, is how to fund the acquisition. Even the largest commercial organisation is unlikely to have sufficient funds to buy the property without recourse to outside funding; and even if it does have the funds readily available, it may not make financial sense to use them. There may be tax advantages to borrowing the necessary funds, as discussed at **2.1.4**. There are a number of ways in which a company may finance an acquisition and/or development. These are considered below.

2.1.1 Share capital

Where the buyer is a company, it may consider issuing further shares to raise additional capital to invest in property. This method of raising funds may not be popular with the current shareholders of the company. Depending on the method used, a new issue of shares may result in reduced dividends as a current shareholder's percentage shareholding may be diluted, which will also affect voting power and capital rights. Further, if the company is a publicly listed company there will be additional regulations to consider before any such fund-raising may be considered. Details of these regulations are dealt with in *Public Companies and Equity Finance*.

2.1.2 Forward funding and equity funding

Institutional investors such as pension and life insurance funds have substantial sums of money at their disposal for investment. These investors will usually invest in property in addition to shares and bonds, in order to maintain a balanced investment portfolio. This investment may take the form of a simple purchase of an established commercial property (an office block or shopping centre) which has been let. The investor will receive the rental income stream from the tenants, and it will also hope that, over time, the capital value of the property will increase.

As an alternative to purchasing a property which has already been let, such investors may also take an active part in the development of suitable property. Examples of ways of doing this are discussed below.

2.1.2.1 Forward funding

In this instance, the institutional investor finances the development from the outset, acquiring the land and paying all the construction costs, including architects' fees, etc. The developer is paid a fee for its work and, once the development has been completed and let (to tenants with an agreed covenant strength), is paid a profit share. The developer may be prepared to accept a lower profit because there is less risk to the developer than if it had developed the property using its own funds. The investor will hope to have paid less for the completed and let property than if it had waited to buy the property until after the developer had built and let it.

2.1.2.2   Equity funding

In the case of equity funding, an investor and a developer will form a joint venture company to acquire the development site and undertake the development. The investor takes preference shares in order to be assured of a priority return on its investment. This way, the investor is participating in the profits and losses of the development.

2.1.3   Sale and leaseback

It is possible for the owner-occupier of a freehold property to raise funds against the value of its property and remain in occupation by entering into a sale and leaseback arrangement. The freehold interest in the property is sold; immediately following completion of the sale, the buyer leases it back to the seller/former owner, usually at a market rent. In this way the former owner can raise capital for whatever purpose it requires, eg working capital to acquire further premises for investment or development, etc. The buyer will see a return on its capital investment in the form of the rent paid by the former owner.

2.1.4   Debt finance

One of the most common ways of raising finance is to borrow, usually from a bank or building society. The attraction of borrowing for UK tax resident corporate borrowers is that they may be entitled to tax relief on any loan interest paid. Further, even if the buyer has sufficient cash to purchase the property without recourse to borrowing, the return it will get by investing the cash may be higher than the rate of interest it will pay on a loan. The remainder of this chapter will concentrate on debt finance, as this is probably the method you will encounter most often in practice.

2.2   DEBT FINANCE

2.2.1   Term sheet

A term sheet is a document which sets out the principal terms on which the lender is prepared to lend. It is produced following initial negotiations between the lender and the borrower, and is not usually intended to be legally binding as it is based on the limited information the lender has about the borrower and the property at this early stage. The term sheet will often be attached to a commitment letter or mandate letter which contains any terms which are intended to be legally binding at that stage, including provisions relating to payment of the lender's fees and expenses. Alternatively, it may be produced as a stand-alone document which clearly states that the parties do not intend the document to bind them legally, save in respect of the payment of fees.

Typically a term sheet will include brief details of the following:

(a)   the borrower;

(b)   the lender;

(c)   the amount of the loan and the period during which the borrower can request release of the loan monies;

(d)   any provisions relating to the release of the loan in stage payments, called tranches, which may be the case where the loan is to finance a development project;

(e)   the purpose of the loan;

(f)   the interest rate;

(g)   the date for repayment of the loan and the repayment schedule;

(h)   any provisions relating to repayment of the whole or part of the loan prior to the date for repayment (called prepayment);

(i)   the security required for the loan;

(j)   the conditions precedent which must be satisfied by the borrower prior to the loan being made;

(k)   the representations and warranties which the borrower must make as to both its status and the property, many of which will be deemed repeated throughout the period of the loan;

(l)   the undertakings and financial covenants to be given by the borrower with which the borrower must comply throughout the period of the loan;

(m)   the events which will constitute events of default under the loan agreement;

(n)   the costs to be paid by the borrower.

2.2.2   Due diligence

Prior to issuing the term sheet the lender will have undertaken a certain amount of due diligence in respect of the borrower to assess the risk that the borrower will be unable to meet the payments due under the loan. Once the terms of the loan have been accepted by the borrower, by signing and returning either the commitment letter, or the term sheet itself if it has been produced as a stand-alone document, the next phase of the due diligence process can commence. The lender will undertake a more detailed analysis of the borrower, its constitution and powers if it is a corporate borrower, and of the property to be purchased. At this stage the lender will also instruct its solicitors to prepare a first draft of the loan agreement, sometimes referred to as the facility agreement or credit agreement.

2.2.3   Loan agreement

The term sheet and any commitment letter are the starting point for negotiation of the loan agreement. It is not uncommon for the term sheet to use generic language such as 'The Loan Agreement will contain the usual conditions precedent applicable to this type of facility'. The loan agreement will incorporate the provisions outlined in the term sheet, but the brief outline of conditions precedent, representations and warranties, undertakings and financial covenants will become detailed provisions. The precise nature and number of these clauses will depend upon the nature of the borrower and its business, and the extent of any issues identified during the continuing due diligence process.

The borrower needs to consider the provisions in the loan agreement carefully, as it needs to be satisfied that it can comply with the provisions in order to obtain the loan and, further, that any repeating representations and warranties and any undertakings and financial covenants are not drafted in such a way that they restrict the borrower's ability to run its business.

Part of the due diligence process to be undertaken at this stage will be the investigation of title to the property. This will often result either in changes to the terms outlined in the term sheet, or in additional terms.

For example, a satisfactory valuation of the property will generally be a condition precedent which must be satisfied prior to the release of the funds. The lender will have proposed a loan-to-value ratio when negotiating the terms of the loan. If the property is valued at less than anticipated, this can affect the proposed loan. Generally, the property is the principal security for the lender. The lender will need to be satisfied that a sale of the property by the lender as mortgagee, in the event of a default by the borrower, will achieve sufficient funds to repay the loan, any accrued interest, and the legal costs and charges incurred by the lender in recovering the loan. The loan-to-value ratio is intended to ensure that there is a margin by which the value of the property exceeds the loan. The margin should be sufficient to cover accrued interest, etc, and to alleviate the possibility of the lender suffering a shortfall in recovering the loan either due to a decline in property values generally, or due to the property simply being sold for less than anticipated. In order to meet the loan-to-value ratio a lower valuation will result in a reduction in the amount the lender is willing to lend.

In addition to being concerned with the valuation of the property, the lender will also wish to be satisfied that the property has good and marketable title. As mentioned above, on a default by the borrower the lender will wish to sell the property as mortgagee to repay the loan, interest, costs and charges. If there are any defects in the title this could cause a delay in the sale, thereby causing further interest to accrue, or enable a buyer to renegotiate the price. This increases the risk of the lender suffering a shortfall. For example, if investigation of title reveals a subsisting breach of covenant, the lender may require restrictive covenant indemnity insurance to be put in place prior to the release of funds. This would be added as a further condition precedent.

The loan agreement will also include the detail of provisions such as events of default. If a borrower breaches a term of the loan agreement, the lender will want the ability to terminate the loan and demand repayment of all outstanding principal and interest (known as 'acceleration'). The most common events of default are as follows:

(a)   failure to pay any capital, interest, fees or expenses;

(b)   breach of any representation or warranty, undertaking or covenant in the loan agreement or the security documents;

(c)   the insolvency of the borrower;

(d)   the borrower becoming involved in any litigation or similar proceedings;

(e)   it becomes unlawful for the borrower to continue to perform its obligations under the loan agreement;

(f)   a material adverse change in the borrower's position or circumstances;

(g)   cross-default if the borrower defaults under another contract, ie another loan agreement in favour of this or any other lender.

Each of the above may be an indication that the borrower is, or may soon be, in some financial difficulty and unable to comply with its obligations under the loan agreement. Once an event of default has occurred, depending on the seriousness of the breach, the lender may decide to accelerate the loan. Alternatively, if the breach is minor or technical in nature, the lender may permit the loan to continue but may take this opportunity to renegotiate the terms of the loan, for example increasing the interest rate to compensate the lender for any increased risk the lender perceives in continuing.

2.2.4 Security

2.2.4.1 Need for security

The loan agreement will provide that prior to the release of any funds, the security specified in the loan agreement must be in place. A loan agreement relating to the acquisition or re-financing of commercial property will generally require the following:

(a)   A charge by way of legal mortgage. The lender has the same protection, powers and remedies as if it had a 3,000-year lease (or for a leasehold property a term of one day less than the lease). Any fixtures affixed to the property may be included in this security automatically.

(b)   A fixed charge over any plant and machinery which is not affixed to the property.

(c)   An assignment of any rental income generated by the property.

(d)   A floating charge over all the assets and undertaking of any corporate borrower as a catch-all to cover anything not specifically charged by the security above and incorporating a negative pledge. The importance of a negative pledge is discussed at **2.2.4.2**.

Clearly, the borrower will not be in a position to complete the security prior to acquisition of the property, and cannot complete the acquisition of the property without the release of funds. In a commercial property transaction it is likely that the lender and borrower will be separately represented. The solicitors acting for the lender will expect to have the security executed, but undated, and in their possession prior to the release of funds. The security will then be completed immediately following completion of the acquisition.

2.2.4.2 Perfection of security

It is essential that any steps required to perfect the security are taken to ensure that the security is valid against third parties and to achieve priority over other security interests.

If the borrower is a company registered in England and Wales, the first step is to register the security at Companies House. Since 6 April 2013, all charges created by a UK company are registrable at Companies House (unless they fall into one of the exceptions) (Companies Act 2006, s 859A). 'Charges' includes a charge by way of legal mortgage over land. Registration of a charge is made using Form MR01, which must be sent to the Registrar of Companies, together with a certified copy of the charge and the relevant fee, within 21 days beginning with the day after the date of creation of the charge.

If the security is not registered at Companies House it will be void against any administrator, liquidator and creditors of the borrower, and the debt it secures becomes immediately repayable.

Priority between floating charges is governed by their date of creation if properly registered. However, a charge by way of legal mortgage and a fixed charge will rank in priority to a floating charge. It is for this reason that most lenders will stipulate that a floating charge in the lender's favour must contain a negative pledge on the part of the borrower not to grant any further security. If the borrower then acts in breach of the negative pledge, this will be an event of default enabling the lender to accelerate the loan. Although a negative pledge acts as a constraint on the borrower in terms of granting further security, the negative pledge does not amount to a security interest and so is not binding on the subsequent lender. Any new mortgage or charge would be effective security as between the borrower and the subsequent lender. Any such security will have priority over the floating charge, unless the subsequent lender has notice of the negative pledge at the time it takes its security. In this case, priority is reversed and the subsequent lender's new security, although valid, will rank behind the floating charge. In addition, it is arguable that the subsequent lender may be subject to an action for the tort of interfering with contractual relations and should hold any new security on trust for the original lender. Since 6 April 2013, details of any negative pledge must be given on Form MR01, and therefore a subsequent lender who searches the register will have actual notice of the negative pledge and be bound by it. It is not yet clear what the position will be in respect of constructive notice for those who have not searched the register.

Once registration of the security at Companies House has been completed, any charge by way of legal mortgage must be registered at Land Registry. If the transaction involves an acquisition of land, registered or unregistered, the application for registration of the borrower's title either as a dealing with registered land or as a first registration will also include an application to register the charge. If the transaction involves a re-finance of existing borrowing secured on a registered property, an application will be made to register the discharge of any existing security and registration of the charge. If the transaction involves the re-finance of unregistered land, completion of the charge will trigger first registration of the land.

Where the transaction involves registered land, the application for registration of the dealing must be made on the appropriate application form, accompanied by the correct documentation and fee, and must be received by Land Registry within the priority period afforded by the land registry search made prior to completion of the transaction.

Where the application is for first registration of title, this must be made within two months of the transaction which induces first registration.

Priority of charges relating to registered land is generally governed by the date of registration. First registered in time will rank ahead of charges subsequently registered, irrespective of the date of creation. The order of priority can be altered by the lenders entering into a contractual arrangement called a deed of priority and applying to have this noted on the register.

It is common for the lender to require registration of a restriction on the title at Land Registry providing that no disposition of the property will be registered without a written consent signed by the lender. This restriction prevents the borrower creating a further charge in favour of a subsequent lender without the consent of the original lender. The original lender will have first-ranking security and, on a sale by a mortgagee in possession, the sale proceeds will first be applied in discharging the original loan. Nevertheless, the lender may prefer that the borrower does not create a subsequent charge. The reason for this is that on completion of a subsequent charge, the lender will lose a degree of control in respect of the property. A subsequent lender may seek to exercise its power of sale on a default by the borrower under the subsequent loan (or on a cross-default), whereas the original lender may not wish to take this step but to give the borrower time. Further, once notice of a subsequent charge has been given, the original lender can make further advances with first-ranking security only if the steps detailed at **2.2.4.3** have been taken.

2.2.4.3   Further advances

Where the loan relates to the acquisition or re-finance of an existing commercial property or a development site, the loan agreement will generally provide for the loan to be released by the lender in one sum, on request, once all conditions precedent have been satisfied.

Where the loan relates to a development project, however, the loan agreement may provide for the loan to be released in tranches, as the development progresses. The loan agreement will usually specify that an architect's certificate, certifying that the development has reached a certain stage, must be produced to the lender prior to the release of the next tranche required to finance the next stage of the development.

The charge by way of legal mortgage will secure the whole loan. However, it is necessary to protect the first-ranking security of the further tranches which will be classed as further advances.

If the property is registered, an application can be made to Land Registry to note the lender's obligation to make further advances, ie release the further tranches. Alternatively, the parties may agree that the original charge secures a maximum amount, and an application can be made to Land Registry to note this on the register. Registration of the obligation or the agreement preserves the priority of the original charge. It puts any subsequent lender on notice that there may be further advances to be released pursuant to the original charge, and those further monies will, on default by the borrower, be repaid to the original lender, together with the original loan, prior to any monies due to the subsequent lender.

If the property is unregistered, any further advance by the original lender will rank ahead of any monies secured by a subsequent charge if the original lender has no notice of the subsequent charge at the time of the further advance or the original charge imposes an obligation to make further advances, in which case the further advances have priority, whether or not the original lender has notice of the subsequent charge.

REVIEW ACTIVITY

Scenario

Ross Developments (Spice Quay) Limited ('Ross') has negotiated the purchase of a former warehouse building (Unit 3) in Spice Quay, an area adjacent to Canary Wharf, for a sum of

£10,000,000. Unit 3 was constructed in 1925, and was used for the storage of spices and fruits until 2005. It has been empty since that date. Ross intends to convert the warehouse into offices, adding a large glass and steel extension in the process, and is in discussion with an institutional investor which has expressed an interest in buying the property once it has been fully developed and let.

Ross is financing the acquisition and development with a loan from Western Bank plc ('Western') and has received a commitment letter and term sheet confirming a proposed loan of £7,000,000 towards the acquisition of Unit 3 and a further £7,000,000 towards the development costs, to be released in tranches of no less than £1,000,000 against architect's certificates certifying completion of certain stages of the development. The term sheet contains only brief details of the agreed terms.

Western has instructed your firm to act on its behalf in connection with the preparation and perfection of its security. Ross is separately represented.

You have received a copy of the valuation report in respect of Unit 3. The surveyor has noted:

(a)   The rear wall of the building is bowing, and there are some diagonal cracks running between the windows on the first and second floors. It is not clear whether these cracks relate to settlement which took place many years ago, or whether any movement is recent.

The solicitors acting for Ross have investigated title to the property and have reported the following issues to you:

(b)   The sellers are currently in dispute with the owners of an adjoining property (Unit 4) regarding a right of way over Unit 3 to access Unit 4 (which is also in the course of development). The right of way runs over the proposed site of the extension to Unit 3.

(c)   Three years ago Unit 3 and the surrounding area suffered severe flooding.

Question

Western and Ross are negotiating the provisions of the loan agreement. Western is keen to proceed with the loan, but does not want to release the loan if there are any risks in doing so. Explain the risks to Western and, in the light of the issues arising from the valuation and investigation of title, suggest provisions to be included in the loan agreement which will give Western the protection it needs.

Answers to this Review activity may be found in Appendix 1.

CHAPTER 3

MATTERS OF CONTRACT

3.1	The contract of sale	17
3.2	Different types of contract	18
3.3	Overage	23
	Review activity	26

3.1 THE CONTRACT OF SALE

As in residential conveyancing, it is the seller's solicitor who will draft the contract of sale for the purchase of a commercial property for submission to the buyer's solicitor for approval. The seller's solicitor will probably use a form of contract incorporating the Standard Commercial Property Conditions (SCPCs) and will draft the contract adopting the same drafting principles applicable in residential conveyancing. Further, on the sale of a green field site, where the seller's main interest is in the receipt of money and the buyer's in obtaining vacant possession, he will include clauses similar to those used in residential conveyancing. It is only where matters are complicated (eg by the need to obtain planning permission before completion) that drafting techniques will differ from residential conveyancing.

The following points are particularly relevant to the sale of a commercial property:

(a) The seller is likely to insist upon the payment of a full 10% deposit on exchange of contracts and is unlikely to agree to accept a reduced deposit. The buyer, being in business, should be able to pay the usual contractual deposit, but he is likely to insist that the deposit is to be held by the seller's solicitor as stakeholder, and he may insist that the interest on the deposit (which may itself amount to a sizeable sum) is to be paid to the buyer at completion. However, some larger organisations will be able to agree a reduced deposit, or even to dispense with the payment of a deposit altogether, on the basis that the size and reputation of the organisation is a sufficient guarantee that completion will take place.

(b) It will be very important to the commercial buyer of a development site to ensure that the contract provides for vacant possession of the whole of the site at completion so that the buyer's development plans are not frustrated. In most cases there is an implied term for vacant possession, but for the avoidance of doubt an express term should be included.

(c) Value added tax (VAT) must be dealt with clearly in the agreement. The danger for the buyer is that if the contract is silent as to VAT, and after exchange of contracts the seller (being a person registered for VAT) elects to charge VAT on the purchase price, the buyer will have to add VAT to the purchase price. The buyer may want to ensure that the contract contains an express warranty by the seller that he has not, before exchange, elected to charge VAT on the purchase price, and that he will not do so thereafter, or that the purchase price is paid inclusive of VAT. In any case, the buyer will want to make enquiries of the seller to ascertain his intentions regarding VAT on the purchase price. VAT on property is dealt with more fully at **10.1**.

(d) The seller, having entered into a bargain with a chosen buyer, will usually want to deal with the chosen buyer alone and will, therefore, want to ensure there is a clause in the contract which prevents the buyer from assigning the benefit of the contract to a third party. Further, the seller will often attempt to prevent the buyer from entering into a sub-sale of the property, by stipulating that the seller cannot be required by the buyer to execute a transfer of the property to anyone other than the buyer. (This last clause does not prevent a sub-sale but makes it less attractive to the buyers, since SDLT will be payable both on the transfer to the buyer and on the buyer's transfer to the sub-buyer.)

(e)   Frequently, the seller will deal with the possibility of the buyer becoming bankrupt, or going into liquidation or becoming subject to other insolvency proceedings before completion of the sale, by giving himself the right to rescind the contract upon any such event. This frees the seller to arrange a sale to another buyer without the delay of having to await completion and the expiry of a notice to complete.

(f)   If the buyer has agreed to pay all or part of the seller's legal and other expenses in connection with the sale, the contract should so provide.

(g)   Express provision should be made, where appropriate, for the grant and reservation of easements and the imposition of covenants. If the seller is retaining some adjoining or neighbouring land, he will be anxious to retain some control over the future development of the property.

(h)   Where the property already has the benefit of planning permission obtained by the seller, the benefit of that permission will automatically pass to the buyer, since planning permission enures for the benefit of the land concerned (unless it states otherwise). The buyer will no doubt want to develop in accordance with the plans and specifications upon which the application for permission was based, but copyright in those plans and specifications will be retained by the architect who drew them up in the first place. The buyer should therefore ensure that the contract provides for the seller to assign to him, or procure the grant to him, of a valid licence to use the plans and specifications.

(i)   If the land is sold without the benefit of planning permission, the seller may wish to make provision for the payment of 'overage' should planning permission for development be granted in the future. Where land is sold without planning permission for development, the price would have been fixed on the basis of its current use, eg agricultural. If planning permission for development is granted, its value will increase considerably. The seller may wish to share in that increase, and so the contract may provide for the buyer to make an additional payment (the overage payment) should planning permission be granted (see **3.3.3**).

3.2   DIFFERENT TYPES OF CONTRACT

Sometimes the sale will be by simple private treaty; sometimes it will be by way of auction or tender; and sometimes the nature of the transaction may justify a departure altogether from the straightforward kind of sale and purchase contract. There are many types of commercial contracts which can be entered into by a seller and buyer of a commercial site, catering for widely different circumstances, and the agreement between the seller and buyer will need to reflect the bargain they have struck. This section of this chapter considers the four most common alternative forms of agreement: conditional agreements, call options, put options and pre-emption agreements.

3.2.1   Conditional agreements

There will be occasions when one of the parties to the contract will be either unable, or unwilling immediately to enter into an unconditional agreement for the sale or purchase of the property, and so arrangements may be made to effect a conditional exchange of contracts. The seller is usually reluctant to agree to a conditional exchange, since what the seller ordinarily seeks is the security of knowing that his buyer is firmly committed to paying over money on a specified date for completion.

A conditional contract rarely serves a useful purpose for the seller. It is normally the buyer who suggests a conditional exchange of contracts, in a situation where the buyer is anxious to avoid losing the property to another buyer but is not yet in a position to commit himself irrevocably to the purchase.

3.2.1.1   Types of conditional agreements

A conditional agreement may be useful in the following situations:

(a)   where planning permission for development of the site has not yet been obtained;

(b)   where the results of the buyer's local search and enquiries of the local authority have not yet been received;

(c)   where vacant possession of the site is not yet available owing to the existence of a tenancy agreement in respect of all or part of the site, which the buyer requires to be terminated;

(d)   where the property is leasehold, and the consent of the landlord is required but has not yet been obtained for the proposed assignment to the buyer (see also SCPC 10.3), or for alterations to the property, or for a change in the use of the property proposed by the buyer.

Great care must be taken to distinguish between a contract which contains a condition precedent to the formation of the contract itself (in which case no contract exists unless and until the condition is performed), and a contract which contains a condition precedent to the performance of certain specified obligations (in which case a binding contract is immediately created, but if the condition is not fulfilled the specified obligations, typically the obligations to complete the sale and purchase, never come into effect). In drafting the contract, the seller's solicitor should make it expressly clear which type of agreement is intended. If the former type of contract is used then, despite the fact that the parties have entered into a written agreement, effectively they will still be in the same position as if negotiations were continuing since, until the condition has been satisfied, no binding contract exists and either party is free to back out. The condition must be fulfilled before any part of the contract comes into effect. If the latter type of contract is used (and in order to obtain a degree of certainty and commitment, both of the parties are likely to favour this type), a binding contract immediately comes into effect so that neither party can back out without the other's consent while the condition still remains to be performed, and the parties must comply with any obligations they have taken on to work toward fulfilment of the condition. If the condition is not ultimately fulfilled, the contract terminates, unless the party for whose sole benefit the condition was inserted waives the benefit of the condition and elects to proceed.

3.2.1.2   The condition

Certainty is required with conditional agreements. If the court cannot judge with certainty whether the conditionality of the contract has been removed, the court will reluctantly declare the entire contract void. Hence, in *Lee-Parker and Another v Izzet and Others (No 2)* [1972] 2 All ER 800, a contract which was stated to be conditional upon the buyer obtaining a satisfactory mortgage was held to be void since the concept of a satisfactory mortgage was too vague and indefinite. By way of contrast, in *Janmohamed v Hassam* (1976) 241 EG 609, a contract which was conditional upon the receipt of a mortgage offer satisfactory to the buyer was held to be valid, since the court was prepared to imply an obligation upon the buyer to act reasonably in deciding whether the mortgage offer was satisfactory to him.

In drafting the conditional clause, the seller's solicitor should clearly set out what is required to be done, by whom, and by when, in order for the contract to become unconditional. Consider the following situations by way of example:

(a)   If the buyer has not yet received the results of his local search and replies to enquiries of the local authority, the contract can be made conditional upon the buyer receiving what he considers to be satisfactory results and replies, by a stipulated date. The contract should contain an obligation upon the buyer to submit the correct forms to the local authority and to pay the fees (in case he has not already done so). Upon receipt of the search certificate and replies, the buyer should be obliged to notify the seller of receipt, indicating one of three things:

(i)   that the buyer considers the results and replies to be satisfactory, in which case the contract proceeds to completion; or

(ii) that the buyer considers them to be unsatisfactory, in which case the contract becomes unenforceable, and the contract should provide for the return of the deposit to the buyer and of the evidence of title to the seller; or

(iii) that the buyer is prepared to waive the benefit of the condition.

Such a contract is heavily weighted in favour of the buyer, since it is up to him to determine whether or not the condition has been satisfied. A more neutral and objectively based conditional clause could make the contract conditional upon the receipt by the buyer of a set of results and replies to the local search and enquiries which disclose no adverse matters of a kind which would materially affect the value or beneficial use or occupation of the property by the buyer. This type of clause may not be favoured by the buyer since it leaves scope for argument.

(b)   If the buyer is not prepared to complete without the benefit of planning permission for the type of development he proposes to carry out on the property, the contract could be made conditional upon the receipt of an 'acceptable' planning permission by a stipulated date. Again, the buyer should be obliged by the contract to submit a valid planning application without delay, to serve the correct statutory notices, and to pay the fees for the application. Consideration ought to be given as to whether provision should be made so that, upon refusal of permission (which ordinarily would render the contract unenforceable), the buyer may be allowed or, perhaps, obliged to pursue an appeal.

Particular consideration must be given to the definition of an 'acceptable' planning permission. It ought to be one which is granted pursuant to an application, precise details of which are set out in the contract and which is subject only to the usual planning conditions imposed by statute (eg conditions imposing time limits for the commencement of development), or which relate simply to the materials to be used or the provision of works of landscaping, or which are conditions which the buyer should reasonably accept. If this clause appears to be too objectively based for a developer's liking, he can be given control over the conditionality of the contract (in the same way as above) by having a clause which allows him to accept or reject the suitability of the permission, or to waive the benefit of the clause.

3.2.1.3   Time for performance

The condition must be satisfied either by a stipulated date, or, if none is stated, by the contractual completion date or, if neither, within a reasonable time. It is good practice to stipulate in the contract a long-stop date by which the condition must be satisfied. The contract can then provide that if the condition is fulfilled by that date, completion is to take place within 14 or 21 days of the contract becoming unconditional. The contract should be drafted to oblige one party to notify the other that the contract has become unconditional (eg if the buyer receives the outstanding local search then, unless the seller is notified, the seller will not know that the contract has become unconditional and that a completion date has been triggered).

If fulfilment of the condition depends upon action by one of the parties (eg the submission of a local search, or the making of an application for planning permission by the buyer), that party should not be able to rely upon his own inaction to argue that the contract has become unenforceable due to the non-fulfilment of the condition. To avoid this situation arising, the contract should place a contractual obligation upon the party of whom action is required to act diligently/with all reasonable speed and best/reasonable endeavours, and to pay the costs of the action required (eg search fees, planning application fees). However, in *Jolley v Carmel* [2000] 43 EG 185, the Court of Appeal was prepared to adopt a construction of a conditional contract that was commercially realistic and practical, and to imply terms into it to that end. In particular, terms were implied that the buyer would use reasonable efforts to obtain planning permission within a reasonable time. What was reasonable would depend upon the circumstances that actually existed and would not be judged by an objective test. It was also implied that the seller would do nothing to hinder the grant of the planning permission. It was held that the buyer would not be in breach of the implied term to obtain planning permission so long as any delay in obtaining the permission was attributable to causes beyond the buyer's control and so long as the buyer had not acted negligently or unreasonably.

3.2.2 Option agreements

3.2.2.1 Call options

The usual form of option agreement entered into with a landowner (referred to as a 'call' option) gives the buyer, as grantee of the option, the right within a specified time to serve notice upon the landowner requiring it to transfer the property either at an agreed price, or at the market value of the property at the time the option notice is served. Whilst a conditional agreement is useful to a buyer who is trying to commit a landowner to a sale of land at a time when the buyer is not able unconditionally to commit himself, call options have many more varying uses for the buyer, and are particularly useful for a developer buyer attempting to piece together a development site. Under a conditional contract, unless the contract is drafted in a manner which favours the buyer, the buyer is usually obliged to complete the purchase at the contract price once the condition has been fulfilled, even though in the meantime market conditions have caused him to rethink the development. With a call option, the buyer can exercise the option if he wants to, or he can let it lapse if market conditions are no longer in his favour. While this is clearly not ideal for the seller, call options are usually granted for a non-returnable option fee. So the buyer is purchasing the right to require the seller to sell, and is compensating the seller for the uncertainty as to whether the sale will actually proceed and the inconvenience of not being able to dispose of the property elsewhere in the meantime.

Once the call option has been entered into, the buyer acquires an immediate equitable interest in the land which the buyer must protect by registration of a Class C(iv) land charge, in the case of unregistered land, or by a notice, in the case of registered land.

3.2.2.2 Put options

A 'put' option is a contract that enables a landowner to require the potential buyer to buy the property, subject to the terms of the contract as to price, time limits, etc. There is no obligation on the seller to sell. Again, the option is often granted in return for a non-returnable fee, but in the case of a put option, it will be the seller who pays the buyer to take the risk that he may be required to purchase the property. Put options, while offering maximum flexibility to landowners, confer little benefit on developers so are much less common than call options.

Put options do not create an interest in land and so cannot be protected by registration at Land Registry.

3.2.2.3 Uses of options

An option agreement may be useful in the following situations:

(a)   Where planning permission for development proposed by the developer has not yet been applied for, the developer may consider securing a call option over the land before investing resources into making an application for permission. Once the application succeeds, the call option can be exercised by the developer. This is very similar to a conditional agreement, but with a call option, the developer may be able to delay the exercise of the option until he is prepared to part with his money and commence development, whereas under a conditional agreement, as soon as the condition has been satisfied, the developer will have to complete.

(b)   Moreover, with a call option the developer can decide not to exercise the option at all if economic conditions are no longer right for the development.

(c)   Where the land proposed as the site for development is sub-divided amongst landowners and there is no guarantee that all of them will sell, the developer can assemble the development site gradually, by acquiring call options over each parcel of land. Once the entire site is under call option, the developer can then apply for planning permission (it would not make financial sense to do so beforehand), and then once permission has been obtained, he could exercise each call option.

(d)   Where a developer developing a site feels that there is some prospect of being able to expand the development at some future date, he may attempt to acquire a call option over adjacent land which can be exercised when the prospect becomes a reality.

A speculator may attempt to acquire call options over land where there is little immediate prospect of obtaining planning permission (eg because the land forms part of the green belt, or is land not allocated for any particular purpose in the local planning authority development plan). The speculator may either adopt a wait-and-see approach in the hope that planning policy in the area changes, or (as is more likely to be the case) may invest time and resources in seeking to influence planning policy to get the land released for development purposes when the next draft development plan is being prepared. In this way, developers build up considerable land banks to be drawn upon when conditions are right.

3.2.2.4   Terms of an option

An option will grant the one party the right to call for the property, or require the purchase of the property, by serving a written notice on the other within a specified period. Regardless of whether it is a put option or a call option, time limits are construed by the courts to be of the essence of the agreement. The option agreement should set out the correct method of serving the option notice, or alternatively incorporate the provisions of s 196 of the Law of Property Act 1925 (LPA 1925) into the agreement. In specifying a time for the service of the notice, care should be taken to ensure that the grantor has sufficient powers vested in him to grant an option capable of being exercised within the time period proposed.

The option will usually be granted in consideration of an option fee, which can be nominal but is more likely to be a considerable sum, depending upon the development potential of the land. When the option is exercised, the agreement will usually require the land to be transferred to the buyer for a further consideration (a credit or discount sometimes being given for the option fee already paid) which may be fixed by the agreement at the outset, or may be determined at the time of the exercise of the option either by reference to the market value of the land at that time or by reference to the development value of the land as ascertained by a valuation formula set out in the agreement. It should be noted that both the option agreement and the subsequent transfer of the land are subject to SDLT. Further, because of the VAT implications of the transaction, the buyer should ensure that the agreement clearly states that any option fee he has to pay and the purchase price is inclusive of VAT. There may also be capital gains tax (CGT) implications for the landowner, since an option is treated as an asset for CGT purposes, separate from the land itself, which is disposed of in consideration of the option fee.

Provision should be made in the agreement for the deduction of title and the raising of requisitions on title after the option notice is served, and for the other usual conveyancing steps which need to be taken before completion. It is usual for the option agreement to incorporate a set of conditions of sale (eg, the SCPCs current at the time of the option agreement). In many cases, the developer will want title to be deduced before the option agreement is entered into (requisitions on title then being barred), and it will then require the seller to enter into a condition in the agreement not to incumber the land any further without the developer's consent.

3.2.3 Pre-emption agreements

A right of pre-emption, sometimes known as a right of 'first refusal', obliges a seller who wishes to sell its property within an agreed pre-emption period to offer it first to the developer. The pre-emption agreement will provide that if the landowner decides to sell the property, it must first serve a notice offering it to the developer. If the developer wishes to buy the property on the terms set out in the landowner's notice, it must serve an acceptance notice, whereupon a binding contract for sale will come into existence. If the developer does not serve an acceptance notice within the agreed timescale then the landowner is free to sell the property to a third party. The key point to note is that unlike a call option (see **3.2.2.1**), a right of pre-emption does not oblige the seller to sell the property to the developer, or indeed to sell it at all.

3.3 OVERAGE

The University of Law would like to thank the Practical Law Company for authorising the adaptation in this publication of the following section on 'Overage Payments' – see <http://uk. practicallaw.com/4-200-2514>. For further information about the Practical Law Company, visit <http://uk.practicallaw.com/> or call 020 7202 1200. © Legal & Commercial Publishing Limited 2014.

Many contracts for the sale of development land will include provisions with for the possible payment by the buyer of 'overage'. Overage provisions are generally used where a seller wishes to share in any potential development value in a property that might be realised after completion of a sale. So, a seller is likely to require an overage payment from the buyer where there is a reasonable belief that value will be added when the land is redeveloped, or when permission for change of use is granted in the future, or when a proposed development produces more profit than expected due to a rise in sale prices or an increase in the number of units authorised by the planning consent. An overage obligation requires the buyer to make a further payment to the seller, representing a share of the increased market value of the property after the occurrence of an agreed event. The seller can therefore maximise its return from the sale by realising the current market value of the property immediately, without losing out on future increases in value by having sold the property before the full development potential is actually realised.

It is sometimes said that the existence of overage should not affect the initial sale price, but this is not always true. The insistence on overage provisions in a deal may well affect the initial purchase price that the buyer is willing to pay for the land. It will certainly involve more legal work, and the greater costs and potential delays associated with it. It will thus always be a question of judgement of the commercial issues involved as to whether the provision is justified.

3.3.1 'Overage' or 'clawback'?

The terms 'overage' and 'clawback' are often used interchangeably, and there is no generally accepted definition of either term.

The term 'clawback' is generally used in the public sector where land is sold at a discount which the seller is entitled to recover on particular events occurring in the future. For example, if a buyer acquires property at a discount and resells within a stated period (eg a local authority house under the 'right to buy' legislation), the discount might be 'clawed back'. Also, additional payments that become due on the grant of planning permission may be described as 'clawback' in the public sector, rather than 'overage', presumably on the basis that the extra value in some way really belonged to the public purse all along and it is being 'clawed back' to where it belongs.

The public sector also sometimes draws a distinction between payments representing part of the increase in value of a property due to an event such as the grant of planning permission (which it calls clawback), and payments representing a share in the sale proceeds following completion of the development (which is referred to as overage).

However, in the private sector, both of these types of payment are normally described as overage.

3.3.2   'Positive' or 'negative' overage

Overage provisions are sometimes described as being either positive or negative in character.

'Positive overage' methods involve the seller extracting an express promise from the buyer to make a further payment if a particular specified event (such as redevelopment) should occur in the future. The way in which the payment will be calculated and the trigger event for payment must be carefully defined in advance.

'Negative overage' methods, however, occur when the seller imposes a restrictive covenant, or another mechanism such as retaining a ransom strip, that *prevents* a particular development or change of use from taking place. In such a case there is no need for a specific promise to pay overage, as the seller has control over the situation. The development cannot take place without the seller's consent, and the seller can then require payment of an additional sum in return for the release of the covenant or the sale of the ransom strip.

3.3.3   Drafting considerations

As overage provisions usually reflect complex arrangements, the parties and their solicitors must take particular care to ensure that the documentation reflects precisely what has been agreed. This is obvious, but the problem with overage is that this can be very difficult to achieve. It is not enough just to have an agreement in place which provides for the payment of overage; it is also necessary for the seller's solicitor to ensure that the payment will actually be made – to secure the payment of the amount due. So, as well as setting out how the overage payment is to be calculated and when it is to be payable, both parties' solicitors need to consider carefully all the various combinations of events which might happen over the period of the overage being potentially payable. This can be problematic given the difficulty in predicting future events and the state of the property market over what may be many years. Obviously, issues such as the possible liquidation or insolvency of the buyer must be considered. What if the liquidator then exercises his right to disclaim onerous contracts? How might all these events impact on the payment of the overage? And the more complex the provisions, the greater the risk that mistakes, oversights and omissions will occur.

3.3.3.1   The trigger event

The first thing that will need to be agreed between the parties – and clearly stated in the contract – is precisely when the overage payment will become payable. This 'trigger' event for payment could be, for example:

(a)   the grant of planning permission for specified development or change of use;

(b)   the implementation of such planning permission;

(c)   the practical completion of a development;

(d)   the disposal of the property with the benefit of planning permission;

(e)   the disposal of the completed development;

(f)   the disposal of individual units (eg houses) at more than a stated price;

(g)   the amount of profit on the completion of a development exceeding a stated amount.

Ideally, a seller would like the payment to be triggered when the increase in value actually occurs, eg on the grant of planning permission. Equally, a buyer would prefer to have to make the payment only when it has actually realised that increase in value, eg on the sale of the completed development. And often the buyer will wish to impose a time limit on the period during which it is at risk of having to pay overage – five years, 10 years or whatever.

3.3.3.2   The amount of the overage payment

Of equal importance to both seller and buyer is the amount of the payment to be made. This could be, for example:

(a)   a percentage of the increase in value of the land;

(b)   a percentage of the profit made on the development;

(c)   a percentage of the profit made on the development if it exceeds a specified amount;

(d)   a percentage of the sale price of units if that exceeds a specified amount.

The amount of negotiation that might be necessary before agreement is reached on precise figures in relation to any of these can well be imagined.

3.3.3.3   Securing the overage payment

It is the seller's solicitor's responsibility to ensure that adequate security is given to the seller to protect the future payment and ensure that it will be made if the appropriate trigger event occurs. Without adequate security, overage provisions may be virtually worthless. In *Akasuc Enterprise Ltd v Farmar & Shirreff* [2003] EWHC 1275 (Ch), the defendant firm failed to incorporate appropriate provisions in an agreement to protect an overage payment. As a result, the claimant lost an opportunity to obtain a further £250,000. The court considered that it was the firm's responsibility to ensure that the documentation contained an appropriate mechanism to secure the overage payment and that it had been negligent.

There are various ways in which overage obligations can be drafted and secured, and the most appropriate method should be chosen to suit the particular circumstances. The methods differ according to whether a negative or positive overage provision has been agreed. Normally, the seller will need recourse in some form or other against either the land itself or the buyer's successors in title. For example:

(a)   a positive covenant by the buyer to make a further payment to the seller on the occurrence of a specified event, perhaps supported by a guarantee or bond from a third party, combined with a buyer's covenant to ensure that any successor in title will enter into a similar commitment to the seller;

(b)   a legal charge over the property following completion, enabling the seller to sell the land and recover the overage from the sale proceeds if the overage payment is not made as agreed;

(c)   a seller's lien over the property for unpaid purchase price, enabling the seller to apply to court for an order of sale if the overage payment is not made as agreed;

(d)   a freehold right of re-entry, whereby the property reverts to the seller if the overage payment is not made as agreed;

(e)   a restrictive covenant against building on the land or using it for specified purposes, which will be released by the seller only when the overage payment is made;

(f)   the seller retains ownership of a piece of land (a 'ransom strip') so that the buyer cannot develop the land until the overage payment is made and the seller sells the ransom strip to the buyer or grants a right of way over it.

These methods are not exhaustive and each has its own advantages and disadvantages which are outside the scope of this book. Further information on overage agreements may be obtained from the Practical Law Company at <http://uk.practicallaw.com/4-200-2514>.

REVIEW ACTIVITY

1.   ABC Developments Ltd ('ABC') is interested in buying a plot of former agricultural land in Dorset which already has the benefit of planning permission for the conversion of three existing barns to light industrial units. However, given the current economic climate, ABC is unlikely to be able to obtain funding for the conversion on acceptable financial terms in the next couple of years. While ABC has been deliberating, the seller has become impatient and is threatening to sell the land to a rival developer.

      What type(s) of contract with the seller would you recommend to ABC in this situation?

2.   You act for Mulcaster Borough Council ('MBC') which is looking to dispose of some land that is surplus to requirements since the privatisation of the refuse collection service. Its preferred option is to sell the land to a local housing association which would build much needed social housing, but the housing association is constantly prevaricating whilst it waits to see if its funding will be renewed. In the meantime, a national house building chain has expressed an interest in buying the site for private residential development. MBC would like to give the housing association more time to make a decision, but cannot allow the situation to drag on indefinitely.

      What type(s) of contract with the housing association would you recommend to MBC in this situation?

Answers to this Review activity may be found in Appendix 1.

CHAPTER 4

PLANNING CONTROL

4.1	The planning system	27
4.2	When is planning permission needed?	31
4.3	Planning permission	40
4.4	Application to the local planning authority	46
4.5	Appeals against adverse planning determinations	51
	Review activity	55

4.1 THE PLANNING SYSTEM

The town and country planning system is designed to ensure that land is used in a planned and appropriate manner. It was first introduced by the Town and Country Planning Act 1947. Prior to that, such controls had been sought by local bye-laws and by private arrangements such as the use of restrictive covenants. The system is a creature of statute and as such is governed by detailed regulations, but policy at both the central and local government level also plays an important part. Accordingly, planning is governed by public rather than private law.

The planning system is currently in a state of flux. The Government is focusing on planning as a means to bring forward economic growth, as well as giving the 'power to plan' back to local communities. The result has meant significant changes to the planning system in the last three years or so, including the introduction of a raft of measures intended to remove uncertainty from, and to speed up, the planning process.

This chapter will begin with an overview of the structure of the town and country planning system. It will then consider the key trigger of the system, namely that for certain kinds of development, planning permission is required before that development can take place. Next it will look at planning permission in its own right, including what types of planning permission can be obtained, what factors influence whether planning permission will be obtained (and on what terms) and the effect of planning permission once obtained. The chapter will conclude by looking at how that permission, if needed, can be obtained either directly from the local planning authority (LPA) or on appeal.

For the sake of brevity, the following abbreviations have been used:

DCLG   Department for Communities and Local Government

DMPO   Town and Country Planning (Development Management Procedure) (England) Order 2010

GPDO   Town and Country Planning (General Permitted Development) Order 1995

NPPF   National Planning Policy Framework

NPPG   National Planning Practice Guidance

UCO   Town and Country Planning (Use Classes) Order 1987

Note that the DCLG website (a section within the Government's website, <www.gov.uk>) and the Planning Portal (<www.planningportal.gov.uk>) are useful resources where many of the policy and other documents mentioned below can be found.

The NPPF and NPPG were added to a new online resource in March 2014 (<http://planningguidance.planning portal.gov.uk>).

4.1.1   Legislation

The principal Act is the Town and Country Planning Act 1990 (TCPA 1990). This has been substantially amended by the Planning and Compensation Act 1991 (PCA 1991), the Planning and Compulsory Purchase Act 2004 (PCPA 2004), the Planning Act 2008 (PA 2008), the Localism Act 2011 (LA 2011), the Growth and Infrastructure Act 2013 (GAIA 2013) and the Enterprise and Regulatory Reform Act 2013 (ERRA 2013). All references in this and the following two chapters to 'the Act' are to the 1990 Act as amended, unless the contrary is stated. The Act sets out the main framework of the planning system. The majority of the detail (including procedural rules and regulations, prescribed forms and many more substantive matters) is provided by a vast body of delegated legislation.

4.1.2   Central and local government

4.1.2.1   The Department for Communities and Local Government

The DCLG is the central government department with responsibility for town and country planning. It has three broad classes of function under the Act, namely legislative, administrative and quasi-judicial.

As regards legislative powers, the Act contains many powers for the Secretary of State for Communities and Local Government (SOS) to make orders, rules and regulations, usually by statutory instrument. Examples include the UCO 1987, the DMPO 2010 and the GPDO 1995, all of which will be considered below.

The SOS's administrative powers include the dissemination of policy guidance that, until recently, came through a variety of documents such as circulars, planning policy guidance and planning policy statements. With effect from 27 March 2012, the Government replaced many of these separate documents with a single National Planning Policy Framework (NPPF), which will be considered further below. The Government also published simplified planning guidance to replace the 6,000 or so pages of previous existing planning guidance. The National Planning Practice Guidance (NPPG) was launched online on 6 March 2014 (see website link above).

The SOS also has powers to 'call in' a wide variety of matters for his own consideration (such as development plan documents and applications for planning permission). In a recent expansion to his jurisdiction, the GAIA 2013 now also permits applicants for prescribed types of major development to make planning applications and certain other applications directly to the SOS with a view to development being brought forward more quickly. In cases where the relevant LPA has been designated by him as not performing its function of determining applications adequately, the SOS will therefore take on the LPA's role.

Lastly, as regards quasi-judicial powers, the SOS is the person to whom an appeal is made in the first instance against most decisions of a planning authority. In particular, appeals lie to him in respect of a refusal of, or conditions imposed on, a planning permission or the service of an enforcement notice by an LPA.

4.1.2.2   Local government

Subject to any express provision to the contrary, all references in the Act to an LPA should be construed as a reference to both the relevant county planning authority and district planning authority. The county council is the county planning authority and the district council is the district planning authority. The county planning authority normally has exclusive jurisdiction over mineral planning, and development control and enforcement which relate to 'county matters'. 'County matters' are defined in Sch 1, para 1 to the Act, as being concerned with minerals and operational development falling partly within and partly outside a national park. The district planning authority has exclusive jurisdiction over development control and enforcement which does not concern a county matter, and hazardous substances. Responsibility for the preparation of the development plan is considered below (see **4.1.3**).

Where unitary councils have been established (ie there is just the one tier of local government), those councils will normally be the LPAs for all purposes.

Note that, since devolution, the Welsh Assembly has had responsibility for the overall planning system in Wales. Some differences will therefore arise when dealing with properties in Wales. In London, some town and country planning functions are undertaken by the Mayor.

4.1.3 'The development plan'

4.1.3.1 The importance of the development plan

The development plan sits at the heart of the town and country planning system. When applying for planning permission (and in other instances, such as the service of an enforcement notice – see **6.7**), it is the development plan that is the main document for determining the outcome of the decision. The development plan aims to ensure that land is used in a planned and appropriate fashion by setting out policies to govern development control in a given area. By s 38(6) of the PCPA 2004:

> If regard is to be had to the development plan for the purpose of any determination to be made under the planning Acts the determination must be made in accordance with the plan unless material considerations indicate otherwise.

Policy guidance on the importance of the development plan can be found at para 2 of the NPPF, where DCLG advises that:

> This National Planning Policy Framework does not change the statutory status of the development plan as the starting point for decision making. Proposed development that accords with an up-to-date Local Plan should be approved, and proposed development that conflicts should be refused unless other material considerations indicate otherwise. It is highly desirable that local planning authorities should have an up-to-date plan in place.

Developers therefore will need to look very carefully at the development plan as a starting point to see if it contains any policy on the development proposed; if it does so and the proposal is not in accordance with the plan, any planning application is unlikely to succeed in most cases.

The development plan is not the sole factor, however (despite its pre-eminent position): any local finance considerations, so far as material to the application, and any other material considerations must also be taken into account including, crucially now, the NPPF. Material considerations will be considered further at **4.3.2** below.

Although the NPPF does not form part of the development plan, it nevertheless has a significant role in planning decisions.

At the heart of the NPPF is a presumption in favour of sustainable development, which is intended to foster growth in a challenging economic climate. Paragraph 14 of the NPPF states that the presumption should be 'seen as a golden thread running through plan-making and decision-taking'. For plan-making, it means that LPAs should positively seek opportunities to meet the development needs of their area and that local plans should meet those needs, with sufficient flexibility to adapt to rapid change, unless the adverse impacts of doing so would significantly and demonstrably outweigh the benefits when assessed against the policies in the NPPF taken as a whole, or if specific policies (eg, those protecting designated areas) in the NPPF indicate that development should be restricted. For decision-taking, it means, unless material considerations indicate otherwise, approving development proposals that accord with the development plan without delay and, where the development plan is absent, silent or relevant policies are out-of-date, granting permission unless the adverse impacts of doing so or specific policies indicate development should be restricted (as described above).

The NPPF was published on 27 March 2012 and came into effect on the same day. Its content does not affect the statutory requirement in s 38(6) for LPAs to determine planning applications in accordance with the development plan unless material considerations indicate otherwise. However, the NPPF does provide guidance on the weight to be given to its policies in the decision-taking process from that date. Paragraph 215 requires that

> due weight should be given to relevant policies in existing plans according to their degree of consistency with [the NPPF] (the closer the policies in the plan to the policies in the Framework, the greater the weight that may be given).

Note that the roles of and weight to be given to s 38(6) and policies in the development plan, particularly in the light of the adoption of the NPPF, have been the subject of a number of recent cases which have confirmed that applications are to be determined in accordance with the local development plan unless material considerations indicate otherwise, and that the NPPF can be a material consideration that is capable of outweighing the policies in the local development plan. However, it is not to be read as part of the development plan. (See *Sea & Land Power & Energy v Secretary of State for Communities and Local Government* [2012] EWHC 1419 (Admin), *South Northamptonshire Council & Ward v Secretary of State for Communities and Local Government* [2013] EWHC 11 (Admin), *Colman v Secretary of State for Communities and Local Government and RWE Npower* [2013] EWHC 1138 (Admin) and *Bayliss v Secretary of State for Communities and Local Government* [2013] EWHC 1612 (Admin).)

4.1.3.2   Meaning of 'development plan'

Historically, the development plan was made up of two documents: the 'structure plan' (normally prepared by the county planning authority, which detailed the broad, strategic development policy for the regional area); and the 'local plan' (prepared by the district planning authority, which contained more detailed policies for the specific area of that district). In the case of unitary authorities, the development plan was a single document, the unified development plan, which covered both issues in one document.

The structure plan and local plan system was, until recently, gradually being replaced by a system of regional strategies (prepared by Regional Development Agencies) and local development frameworks (LDFs) (prepared by the the LPAs). The LDF is a portfolio of documents, including a core strategy and proposals map (essentially the replacement of the old 'local plan') but also documents covering ongoing monitoring of the implementation of the core strategy and other matters. There are detailed transitional provisions, but in essence, pending adoption of the LDF, former local plans were allowed to continue in operation and are referred to as 'saved' plans. All regional strategies have now been revoked by the SOS pursuant to the power in s 109 of the LA 2011.

In short, the 'development plan' means the policies in any development plan document that has been adopted within an LDF and any 'saved' local plan policies, and any neighbourhood development plans (see below) that have been adopted. Enquiry should be made on a case-by-case basis to determine the current position.

Note that, since devolution, the Welsh Assembly has had responsibility for the overall planning system in Wales. Some differences will therefore arise when dealing with properties in Wales. In the case of London, the Mayor's London Plan forms part of the local plan and therefore provides the planning framework for London Boroughs alongside each individual LPA's own LDF.

Neighbourhood development plans

The LA 2011 introduced new rights and powers for local communities to establish general planning policies for the development and use of land in a neighbourhood. These policies are called 'neighbourhood development plans', which must focus on enabling, not restricting, development.

The creation of neighbourhood development plans can be led by town and parish councils or 'neighbourhood forums', which are community groups designated to take forward neighbourhood planning in areas without parishes. Town and parish councils and neighbourhood forums are required to apply to the LPA to be designated a 'qualifying body' to produce a neighbourhood development plan. A neighbourhood development plan must also be approved, and adopted as soon as reasonably practicable by an LPA, if more than half those voting have voted in favour of adopting the plan at a referendum held for that purpose. Neighbourhood development plans must have regard to national policy, be in general conformity with an LPA's development plan policies and be compatible with EU obligations and human rights requirements. Once adopted, a neighbourhood development plan will become part of the development plan for the purposes of s 38(6) of the PCPA 2004.

The first neighbourhood plan was adopted by Eden District Council on 11 April 2013; and a plan for Thame was adopted by South Oxfordshire District Council on 18 July 2013. There have been numerous neighbourhood plans adopted since, and these are an important planning consideration with statutory weight and as part of the wider development plan. Those areas with a neighbourhood plan in place receive a greater portion of CIL funding (see **Chapter 5**).

4.2 WHEN IS PLANNING PERMISSION NEEDED?

The basic rule is to be found in s 57(1) of the Act, which states that planning permission is required for the carrying out of any 'development' of land. The term development is defined in s 55(1) as

> the carrying out of building, engineering, mining or other operations in, on, over or under land, or the making of any material change in the use of any buildings or other land.

The term 'development' thus has two mutually exclusive parts to it, namely the carrying out of operations and the making of a material change of use.

It is possible to apply to the LPA for certification that any current or proposed use or operation is lawful. This is considered at **6.3**.

4.2.1 Operations

4.2.1.1 Operational development

Operational development is defined in ss 55(1A) and 336(1) of the Act. 'Building operations' include rebuilding, structural alterations of or additions to buildings, and other operations normally undertaken by a person carrying on business as a builder. 'Engineering operations' include the formation or laying out of means of access to highways. 'Mining operations' and 'other operations' are not defined in the Act. The demolition of buildings will be considered separately at **4.2.1.2**.

Works for the maintenance, improvement or other alteration of a building which affect only the interior of the building, or which do not materially affect its external appearance, and which do not provide additional space underground do not constitute development (s 55(2)(a)). However, increasing retail floor space by internal works (eg the construction of a mezzanine floor) will require planning permission in England if the increase is more than 200m^2.

4.2.1.2 Demolition

Demolition falls within the definition of operational development (s 55(1A)) but, under s 55(2)(g), the SOS has the power to identify works of demolition to which this will not apply. A new Direction was made by the SOS, in force since 4 March 2014 – the Town and Country Planning (Demolition – Descriptions of Buildings) Direction 2014. The 2014 Direction set out the types of demolition that would not count as development and therefore would not require planning permission. These types of demolition are now limited to: (a) any building the cubic content of which, measured externally, does not exceed 50 cubic metres; and (b) the whole or any part of any gate, fence, wall or other means of enclosure (where not in a conservation area).

This 2014 Direction clarified the position on demolition following a case in the Court of Appeal, R (SAVE Britain's Heritage) v Secretary of State for Communities and Local Government [2011] EWCA Civ 334 which had decided that certain provisions in the previous demolition Direction (dated 1995) were unlawful. The 2014 Direction also revoked the 1995 Direction.

Before the SAVE Britain's Heritage case in 2011, the 1995 Direction had set out a broader list of categories of demolition which were exempt from the requirement for planning permission, including listed buildings, buildings in a conservation area, scheduled monuments and buildings other than dwelling houses or buildings adjoining dwelling houses. The effect of the SAVE Britain's Heritage case, as confirmed by the 2014 Direction, was to restrict the categories of demolition which are permitted without express planning permission.

In practice, however, where the demolition does not form part of wider environmental impact assessment (EIA) development (see **4.4.2.1**), such permission is usually granted by the GPDO 1995, subject to conditions such as the need to secure prior approval from the LPA for the proposed method of demolition in certain circumstances.

Note that also, as regards demolition of listed buildings and scheduled monuments, whatever the requirement for planning permission, consents under the legislation dealing with the historic environment will be needed, eg listed buildings consent, unless this requirement is removed by provisions in the ERRA 2013.

For demolition in a conservation area, the ERRA 2013 removed the requirement for conservation area consent for demolition in a conservation area and replaced this with a requirement for approval of such demolition to be covered under a planning permission, to reduce duplication of consents. This provision came into force on 1 October 2013 and demolition in a conservation area without the required approval is a criminal offence. Enforcement arrangements (see **Chapter 6**) have also been changed to reflect this streamlined approach to development planning.

4.2.2   Material change of use

In order to constitute development, a change of use must be material. The Act does not define what is meant by 'material'.

Case law makes it clear that the question as to whether a change of use is material is one of fact and degree in each case. It follows, therefore, that the courts will not normally interfere with a planning decision on the question of the materiality of a particular change of use unless the decision is totally unreasonable on the facts, or the deciding body has misdirected itself as to the relevant law. Note, however, the following general points decided by case law:

(a)   It is necessary to look at the change in the use of the relevant 'planning unit'. In many cases this will be the whole of the land concerned, ie the land in the same ownership and occupation. Occasionally, particularly with larger sites, a single occupation may comprise two or more physically distinct and separate areas which are occupied for substantially different and unrelated purposes, in which case each area (with its own main or primary use) should be considered as a separate planning unit (see Burdle and Another v Secretary of State for the Environment and Another [1972] 3 All ER 240 and Thames Heliport plc v Tower Hamlets LBC [1997] 2 PLR 72). In a mall-type development, each shop unit will be a separate planning unit (Church Commissioners for England v Secretary of State for the Environment (1996) 7 P & CR 73).

(b)   The use of a planning unit may involve various (and possibly fluctuating) ancillary uses which do not need planning permission provided that they remain ancillary to, and retain their ancillary connection with, the primary use. For instance, where produce grown on an agricultural unit is sold on a limited scale from the farmhouse, this retail use is ancillary to the primary agricultural use; however, the ancillary status is lost if, for example, produce is subsequently bought in for the purposes of resale (see *Wood v Secretary of State for the Environment* [1973] 1 WLR 707, HL).

As the courts will not normally interfere with LPAs' decisions on questions of fact and degree, it will therefore be the SOS or one of his inspectors who will generally be the final arbiter of the question as to whether a particular change of use is material. Thus, their views in similar cases will be important, and guidance may be found in particular in relevant DCLG circulars, the NPPF and NPPG and in Ministerial Decisions.

Planning policy provides guidance to LPAs on how some change of use applications should be treated. This follows the Government's drive to stimulate the economy. The NPPF states that LPAs should

> normally approve planning applications for change to residential use and any associated development from commercial buildings (currently in the B use class) where there is an identified need for additional housing in that area provided that there are not strong economic reasons why such development would be inappropriate. (para 51)

This guidance has now been supplemented by a raft of legislation reducing the scope of changes of use that require express planning permission. There is now much greater flexibility to change uses by relying on 'permitted development rights' (see **4.2.3.2**).

4.2.2.1 Statutory clarifications

Section 55(3) and (5) of the Act declares the following to be material changes of use:

(a)   the use as two or more separate dwelling houses of any building previously used as a single dwelling house; and

(b)   (generally) the deposit of refuse or waste materials.

Certain changes of use are also expressly excluded from amounting to development. These are set out in s 55(2) and include the following:

(a)   The use of any building or other land within the curtilage of a dwelling house for any purpose incidental to the enjoyment of the dwelling house as such (s 55(2)(d)).

Factors to be considered in deciding whether the use is 'incidental to the enjoyment of the dwelling house as such' include the nature and scale of the use, and whether it is one which could reasonably be expected to be carried out in or around the house for domestic needs or incidental to the personal enjoyment of the house by its occupants: see *Ministerial Decision* [1977] JPL 116. Thus, for example, in *Wallington v Secretary of State for the Environment* [1991] JPL 942, CA, the keeping of 44 dogs as pets was held not to be an incidental use. Enjoyment of the dwelling house must be distinguished from the enjoyment of the occupier (ie the test for enjoyment is objective, not subjective).

(b)   The use of any land or buildings occupied with it for the purposes of agriculture or forestry (s 55(2)(e)).

(c)   In the case of buildings or other land which are used for a purpose of any class specified in the UCO 1987, the use of the buildings or other land for any other purpose of the same class (s 55(2)(f)). This very important exception is now considered in detail.

4.2.2.2 The Town and Country Planning (Use Classes) Order 1987

The UCO 1987 contains a list of use classes for the purposes of s 55(2)(f). Thus, a change of use within any such class does not, prima facie, amount to development (but see the UCO 1987 checklist at **4.2.2.3**). Each use class is identified by a letter and a number (thus A1 and A2 are different use classes).

Nothing in the UCO 1987 permits use as a theatre, amusement arcade, launderette, garage or motor showroom, taxi or hire-car business, hostel, or scrapyard, waste disposal installation, retail warehouse club, night club or casino (UCO 1987, art 3(6)). Note also that not all other uses come within the 1987 Order. The courts have consistently held that there is no justification for stretching the meaning of the wording of the classes and that other uses will therefore be outside the terms of the Order. Such uses are called 'sui generis'.

The classes are divided into four main groups as follows:

(a)   Group A: shopping area uses;
(b)   Group B: other business and industrial uses;
(c)   Group C: residential uses;
(d)   Group D: non-residential uses.

Note in particular the following nine use classes.

Class A1: shops

Use for all or any of the following purposes: retail sale of goods other than hot food; post office; ticket or travel agency; sale of cold food for consumption off the premises; hairdressing; direction of funerals; display of goods for sale; hiring out of domestic or personal goods; washing or cleaning of clothes on the premises; internet cafe. In all cases, however, the sale, display or service must be to visiting members of the public.

Class A2: financial and professional services

Use for the provision of financial services, professional services (other than health or medical services) or any other services (including use as a betting office) which it is appropriate to provide in a shopping area, where the services are provided principally to visiting members of the public. In the case of solicitors' and other professional offices, the crucial question is whether the firm principally serves visiting members of the public. In *Kalra v Secretary of State for the Environment* [1996] JPL 850, CA, the Court of Appeal held that the introduction of an appointment system did not of itself prevent a solicitor's office falling within Class A2.

Class A3: restaurants and cafes

Use for the sale of food and drink for consumption on the premises.

Class A4: drinking establishments

Use as a public house, wine bar or other drinking establishment.

Class A5: hot food takeaways

Use for the sale of hot food for consumption off the premises.

Class B1: business

Use for all or any of the following purposes, namely as an office other than a use within Class A2, for research and development of products or processes, or for any industrial process (being a use which can be carried out in any residential area without detriment to the amenity of that area.)

Class B2: general industrial

Use for the carrying out of an industrial process other than one falling within Class B1.

Class B8: storage or distribution

Use for storage or as a distribution centre.

Class C3: dwelling houses

Use as a dwelling house whether or not as a sole or main residence by: (a) a single person or by people to be regarded as forming a single household; or (b) not more than six residents living together as a single household, whether or not care is provided, other than a use falling within Class C4.

Class C4: houses in multiple occupation

Use of a dwellinghouse by not more than six residents as a 'house in multiple occupation'.

Wales

Note that, in Wales, Class A3 covers use for the sale of food and drink for consumption on the premises or of hot food for consumption off the premises. Classes A4 and A5 do not exist. Class B8 in Wales does not include use of a building or land for the storage of, or as a distribution centre for, radioactive material or radioactive waste.

4.2.2.3   UCO 1987 checklist

Although a change of use within a class does not amount to development, it does not necessarily follow that a change of use from one class to another will constitute development. Whether it will depends on the basic rule, ie is that change of use 'material'? However, *Palisade Investments Ltd v Secretary of State for the Environment* [1995] 69 P & CR 638, CA, suggests that it will be extremely rare for this not to be the case.

A change of use within a class may be accompanied by building operations which could amount to development in their own right (remember that development has two parts to it – see **4.2** above).

A change of use within a class may have been validly restricted by a condition attached to a previous planning permission, in which case permission will be needed to change to a use restricted by that condition.

4.2.3   Permitted development

Once it has been established that development is involved, the basic rule is that planning permission will be required. However, it is not always necessary to make an express application for planning permission, for the reasons given below.

4.2.3.1   Resumption of previous use

By s 57(2)–(6), certain changes of use do not require planning permission even though they may amount to development, for example the resumption of a previous lawful use after service of an enforcement notice or the expiration of a temporary planning permission.

4.2.3.2   The Town and Country Planning (General Permitted Development) Order 1995 (as amended)

By ss 59–61 of the Act, the SOS may provide by statutory instrument for the automatic grant of planning permission by means of development orders. The most important of these orders is the GPDO 1995. This lists, in Sch 2, numerous categories of development for which planning permission is automatically granted, ie although the activity amounts to development, there is not normally any need to make an express application for planning permission for it (but see the GPDO 1995 checklist at **4.2.3.3**). For further detail on the points made below, the Town and Country Planning (General Permitted Development) (Amendment) (England) Order 2013 (SI 2013/1101) (GPD(A)O 2013) should be consulted, particularly in relation to the limitation and conditions imposed on permitted development rights. The GPDO 1995 has been significantly amended by provisions in the GPD(A)O 2013, many of which came into force on 30 May 2013 (further amendments were made by GPDO amendment orders numbered 2, 3 and 4 during 2013). Note that further amendments to permitted development rights and use classes were proposed by the DCLG Technical Consultation on Planning 2014 (open for comment 31 July–26 September 2014). The outcome of this consultation is not known at the time of writing.

Similar principles will apply in relation to works to listed buildings. Following new provisions in the ERRA 2013, 'listed building consent orders' may be made which will grant listed building consent for specific categories of work, subject to conditions and limitations. This will remove the need to obtain an express grant of listed building consent except in cases where, as a matter of policy, that should be required.

As to the development permitted by the GPDO 1995, note in particular the following six categories:

Part 1: development within the curtilage of a dwelling house

Part 1 is divided into classes as follows:

- Class A: the enlargement, improvement or other alteration of the dwelling house;
- Classes B and C: additions or alterations to its roof;
- Class D: the erection of a porch;
- Class E: the provision within the curtilage of the dwelling house of any building, enclosure or pool for a purpose incidental to the enjoyment of the dwelling house as such, or the maintenance, improvement or alteration of such a building or enclosure;
- Classes F and G: the provision of a hard surface or a container for the storage of domestic heating oil; and
- Class H: the installation, alteration or replacement of a satellite antenna.

All of these classes of permitted development are, however, subject to certain restrictions, limitations or conditions (see below).

There may occasionally be problems in determining the extent of the 'curtilage' of the dwelling house. It is the small area forming part of the land on which the house stands and used for the purposes of the enjoyment of the house. Its extent is a question of fact and degree in each case. It is not necessarily synonymous with 'garden'.

Restrictions on Class A development (enlargement, improvement, etc) include:

(a)   a limit on the increase in the cubic content of the dwelling house;

(b)   height limits;

(c)   specified limits on distances from the rear wall of the original dwelling (which have been relaxed, provided specific conditions are met, by the GPD(A)O 2013 for a limited period but excluding dwellings on land in certain borough areas and on certain sites designated for nature protection) and to a neighbouring dwelling;

(d)   limits on extending beyond a wall which fronts a highway and forms either the principal elevation or a side elevation of the original dwelling house; and

(e)   limits on extending beyond a wall forming a side elevation of the original dwelling house.

Restrictions on Class E development (the provision of buildings within the curtilage, etc) include restrictions (a) and (b) above. Additional restrictions include:

(a)   the building must not have more than one storey; and

(b)   the development must not be situated within the curtilage of a listed building.

Note that for a dwelling house on 'article 1(5) land' (ie within a National Park, an area of outstanding natural beauty or conservation area) there are further restrictions.

Restrictions on Class H development (satellite antennae) include dish size, height and siting.

Part 2: minor operations

Part 2 permits:

(a)   the erection, construction, maintenance, improvement or alteration of a gate, fence, wall or other means of enclosure (Class A);

(b)   the construction of a means of access to a highway which is not a trunk or classified road (Class B);

(c)   the painting of the exterior of a building (Class C).

In Class A, any gates, fences, etc must be for the purpose of enclosure. They must not exceed 1 metre in height (2 metres in the case of a school) if they adjoin a highway, or 2 metres in any other case. Development within the curtilage of, or to enclosures surrounding, a listed building is not permitted.

In Class C, painting of the exterior is not permitted if it is for the purpose of advertisement, announcement or direction.

Part 3: changes of use

Part 3 permits certain changes of use within and between Classes A, B, C and D and others of the UCO 1987, including but not limited to:

(a)   from A3, A4 and A5 (food and drink) to A2 (financial and professional services);

(b)   from A2 to A1 (shops), provided the premises have a display window at ground level;

(c)   from A3, A4 and A5 directly to A1;

(d)   from B8 (storage and distribution) to B1 (business) and vice versa;

(e)   from B2 (general industrial) to B8 or B1;

(f)   from A4 (drinking establishment) and A5 (hot food takeaways) to A3 (restaurants and cafes);

(g)   from A1 or A2 to a mixed use including up to two flats alongside A1 or A2 respectively, and from A2 to a mixed use including A1 and up to two flats; and vice versa in each case;

(h)   for a limited time period, from B1(a) (offices) to C3 (dwelling houses), except if the building is on land in certain LPA areas that are excluded from the application of these rights or on certain other land (although note that the DCLG Technical Consultation on Planning 2014 proposed making this permitted change permanent and removing exemptions (the outcome of the consultation is not known at the time of writing));

(i)   from B1 (business), C1 (hotels), C2 (residential institutions), C2A (secure residential institutions) and D2 (assembly and leisure) to use as a state-funded school and vice versa; and

(j)   from an agricultural building to a flexible use falling within any of A1, A2, A3 (food and drink), B1 (business), B8 (storage and distribution), C1 (hotels) or D2 (assembly and leisure).

Permitted development rights within Class B of Part 3 have recently been relaxed so that the rights apply to floorspace of up to 500 square metres (an increase from 235 square metres).

In some cases, changes permitted under Part 3 are subject to obtaining prior approval from the LPA. The procedure to be followed is set out in section N of Part 3. The LPA can impose conditions or refuse to give approval, but planning permission is not required.

Part 4: temporary buildings and uses

Part 4 permits:

(a)   the provision of buildings, structures, plant, etc required temporarily in connection with authorised operations (Class A);

(b)   the use of open land for any purpose for not more than 28 days in any calendar year of which not more than 14 days may be used for holding a market or motor racing/trials (Class B);

(c)   the use of a building and any land within its curtilage as a state-funded school for a single academic year (Class C); and

(d)   various flexible uses for a single continuous period of up to two years (Class D).

In terms of limitation and conditions:

•   Class A rights are subject to conditions requiring removal of the buildings, etc or reinstatement of land at the end of the operations.

•   Class C rights apply only if the existing use of the site is specified in the Schedule to the UCO 1987. This means that 'sui generis' uses do not benefit from the rights conferred by Class C. Class C rights do not apply to listed buildings and building on certain, specified types of land. The use of the land must be approved by the relevant Minister and may be used only once in relation to a particular site. The land may not be used for any other purpose (including other D1 classes) and will revert to its previous use at the end of the academic year.

•   Class D rights apply to a maximum of 150 square metres of floorspace. At some point during the two-year period, there must be only one use ongoing from the list of flexible uses. Class D rights do not apply if they have already been exercised, in relation to certain types of buildings or certain types of land. A site will revert to its previous lawful use at the end of the period of flexible use.

The right to revert to the previous use of the land after the expiry of the temporary use is permitted by s 57(2) (see **4.2.3.1**).

Part 6: agricultural buildings and operations

Part 6 permits, inter alia, the carrying out on agricultural land of certain operations (in particular the erection, extension or alteration of buildings or excavation or engineering operations) which are reasonably necessary for the purposes of agriculture on that unit. These are subject to many exceptions and conditions.

Part 31: demolition of buildings

Part 31 permits any building operation consisting of the demolition of a building except where the building has been made unsafe or uninhabitable by the fault of anyone who owns the relevant land, or where it is practicable to secure health or safety by works of repair or temporary support. This is also subject to prior approval unless certain exemptions apply.

Part 41: office buildings

Part 41 permits the extension or alteration of an office building subject to various limitations and conditions. Until 30 May 2016, all buildings except those within a site of special scientific interest (SSSI) may be extended by up to 50% (measuring floorspace) or by an additional 100 square metres, whichever is less. Buildings that are within an SSSI currently benefit from the rights that will apply to all buildings from 31 May 2016: a 25% increase in floorspace is permitted, or an additional 50 square metres, whichever is less. Height restrictions apply and a minimum distance from the boundary must be maintained (except where alterations are being carried out). Listed buildings (and their curtilage) do not benefit from these rights. Alterations are not permitted on land designated for special protection under art 1(5) of the GPDO 1995 (eg in National Parks or a conservation area) ('article 1(5) land') and are only permitted at ground level. The materials used for extensions to buildings on article 1(5) land must be in keeping with those used for the building being extended.

Part 42: shops or catering, financial or professional services establishments

Part 42 permits the extension or alteration of a shop or financial or professional services establishment, subject to various limitations and conditions. Part 42 imposes the same floorspace limits as apply under Part 41 (in respect of time periods and exclusions). A height restriction of four metres also applies. Until 30 May 2016, in the case of residential buildings, article 1(5) land and development within an SSSI, a minimum distance of two metres from the boundary must be maintained. Listed buildings (and their curtilage) do not benefit from these rights. Alterations are not permitted on article 1(5) land. A number of other limitations apply.

The remaining Parts give permitted development rights to a number of bodies including, in particular, LPAs, statutory undertakers, highway authorities and educational institutions.

4.2.3.3 GPDO 1995 checklist

If the proposed development is permitted by the GPDO 1995, there should, prima facie, be no need to make an application for planning permission. However, before deciding, the following other matters should also be checked.

Limitations, etc

Confirm that all the limitations, restrictions and conditions imposed by the GPDO 1995 will be complied with. There are two categories of these. First, there is a general one in art 3(5), which applies to all the Parts in Sch 2 and which states that (subject to limited exceptions) the making or altering of an access to a trunk or classified road, or any development which obstructs the view of road users so as to cause them danger, is not permitted. Secondly, there are specific limitations, conditions, etc in almost all of the Parts of Sch 2 which must be observed (see above).

If the limitations, etc are not complied with then, as a general rule, the whole development will be unauthorised by the GPDO 1995 and not merely the excess. This, though, is subject to the LPA's power to under-enforce if it thinks fit (see **Chapter 6** and in particular **6.1**). If the excess is *de minimis* it can be ignored.

Where the development is (or as a result of case law on environmental impact assessment (EIA) forms part of) a wider development for which EIA is required, permitted development rights are not available and a planning application will be necessary (see art 3(10) of the GPDO 1995).

Conditions on existing planning permission

Check any existing planning permission to see whether it contains a condition excluding or restricting relevant permitted development rights. Such conditions can be imposed in appropriate cases (see **4.3.3**).

Article 4 direction

Ascertain by means of an appropriate inquiry of the local authority whether an Article 4 direction is in force which may affect the proposed development.

Article 4 of the GPDO 1995 empowers the SOS or an LPA (usually with the SOS's approval) to make a direction removing from the classes of permitted development under the GPDO 1995 any development specified in the direction as regards the area of land specified in it.

The making of an Article 4 direction will not affect the lawfulness of any permitted development commenced before the direction was made.

Compensation may be payable if an LPA introduces an Article 4 direction.

Special development orders

Check whether the land is in an area covered by a special development order (SDO).

Some SDOs restrict the provisions of the GPDO 1995 which would otherwise apply in the relevant area; others (especially those made for urban development areas) confer wider permitted development rights. It is therefore important to be aware of what SDOs exist and, where relevant, their provisions.

Local development orders and simplified planning zones

As part of the LDF (see **4.1.3.2**), the LPA is able to introduce local development orders (LDOs) and simplified planning zones (SPZs). Local development orders operate to give permitted development rights, but are granted at local rather than central government level. They can apply over the whole or part only of an LPA's geographical area. Whilst in the past they were rarely adopted, recent evidence suggests their introduction has become more widespread as a result of the Government's localism agenda. Local planning authorities have seen an opportunity to encourage investment in their areas in a difficult economic climate by introducing LDOs, which enable businesses to carry out development without express planning permission.

In practice, LDOs complement the introduction of SPZs. An SPZ is an area in which an LPA wishes to stimulate development and encourage investment. It operates by granting a specified planning permission in the zone without the need for a formal application or the payment of planning fees.

Neighbourhood development orders

The LA 2011 introduced a right for communities to draw up 'neighbourhood development orders', which permit development without the need for planning applications. The creation of neighbourhood development orders is led by parish and town councils or neighbourhood forums, which first need to apply to the LPA to be designated a 'qualifying body' to produce a neighbourhood development order.

The LA 2011 sets out the basic conditions for neighbourhood development orders, including that they must:

(a)   have appropriate regard to national policy and advice contained in guidance issued by the Secretary of State;

(b)   be in general conformity with the strategic policies contained in the development plan for the area; and

(c)   not breach, nor otherwise be incompatible with, EU and human rights obligations.

4.3 PLANNING PERMISSION

4.3.1 Types of planning permission

There are two types of planning permission: full and outline. Relevant law and procedures are set out in the DMPO 2010.

By the DMPO 2010, art 4, where the application is for permission to erect a building, the applicant may, if he wishes, apply for outline permission. By art 1 of the DMPO 2010, 'building' includes any structure or erection and any part of a building, and 'erection' includes 'extension, alteration or re-erection'.

If the applicant elects to submit an outline application, the application merely has to contain a description of the proposed development sufficient to indicate its major features (eg, for residential developments, the number and type of dwellings). A plan is also required of sufficient detail to identify the boundaries of the site and the nearest classified public highway.

These basic requirements have been supplemented by additional case law and regulations, which have defined the minimum thresholds of information that must be provided more precisely (see the DMPO 2010, art 4). However, the application need not contain the considerable amount of detail that is required for a full application for permission. Paragraph 193 of the NPPF highlights the need for LPAs to require only information that is proportionate to the nature and scale of development proposals and to keep requirements under review.

If outline planning permission is granted, it will be subject to a condition setting out certain matters for which the subsequent approval of the LPA is required. The only matters which can be so specified ('reserved matters') are defined in the DMPO 2010, art 2(1) as those concerned with access, appearance, landscaping, layout and scale of the development.

The effect of outline planning permission is that the LPA is committed to allowing the development in principle, subject to approval of any reserved matters and the discharge of any other planning conditions. This is because it is the grant of the outline permission which constitutes the grant of planning permission for the proposed development, ie no further planning permission is required. The LPA cannot revoke the outline permission except on payment of compensation (see revocation of planning permissions at **4.3.4.2**), neither can it impose additional conditions subsequently except as regards the reserved matters.

Application for approval of the reserved matters can be made in stages, but must be made within the timeframe specified in the decision notice, usually three years from the grant of the original outline permission but sometimes longer in the case of larger, multi-phase developments.

It is also common for developers to make outline planning applications and at the same time ask the LPA to approve certain details that could otherwise be reserved. This approach is known as making a 'hybrid' application. It is a useful way for a developer to retain flexibility over the development to be brought forward on a particular site and provide extra information on the impact of the development if, for example, it would affect the setting of a listed building.

4.3.2 The basis for decision

An application for planning permission is made initially to the LPA, unless an applicant is able to make an application direct to the SOS (see **4.1.2.1**). By s 70(1), the LPA may grant planning permission either unconditionally or subject to such conditions as it thinks fit, or it may refuse planning permission.

In reaching its decision the LPA must have regard to the provisions of the development plan, if it is relevant to the application, and to any other material considerations. The importance of this 'plan-led' principle was considered at **4.1.3**, and its importance should be acknowledged, as it is this test which will determine whether planning permission is granted at all and, if so, on what terms. Note the case of *Tesco Stores Limited v Dundee CC* [2012] UKSC 13 in which the Supreme Court confirmed that the courts have a role in deciding what planning policy actually means. In contrast to the predominant approach taken prior to that case, in which the court would ask itself whether or not the decision-maker had in interpreting policy adopted a reasonable meaning in each case, the court will now identify for itself the meaning of a policy. If the court decides that the LPA or SOS has not adopted the correct meaning of the policy, there will be an error of law which could result in the decision being quashed. *Tesco* has undoubtedly expanded the court's role in interpreting planning policy, which will be of particular importance in deciding whether or not to appeal or judicially review a refusal.

For considerations other than the development plan to be 'material', they must be relevant to the application and be planning considerations, ie relate to the use and development of land (see *Stringer v Minister for Housing and Local Government* [1971] 1 All ER 65). Matters which the courts have held to be capable of being 'material considerations' include:

(a)   a development plan which is in the course of preparation (see, eg, *Allen v Corporation of the City of London* [1981] JPL 685 and *Kissel v Secretary of State for the Environment and Another* [1994] JPL 819). The closer the new plan gets to adoption, the greater the weight that should be given to it;

(b)   the protection of private interests in a proper case and, in exceptional circumstances, personal hardship (see, eg, *Great Portland Estates plc v Westminster City Council* [1985] AC 661, HL);

(c)   financial considerations involved in the proposed development (see, eg, *Sovmots v Secretary of State for the Environment; Brompton Securities Ltd v Secretary of State for the Environment* [1977] 1 QB 411);

(d)   planning obligations (see **Chapter 5**);

(e)   retention of an existing use (see, eg, *London Residuary Body v Lambeth Borough Council* [1990] 2 All ER 309, HL);

(f)   the previous planning history of the site;

(g)   a real danger of setting an undesirable precedent (see, eg, *Anglia Building Society v Secretary of State for the Environment and Another* [1984] JPL 175);

(h)   planning policies of the DCLG (such as the NPPF and the remaining circulars and Planning Policy Statements (PPSs) that have not been superseded by the NPPF or the NPPG);

(i)   policies of other government departments where relevant (eg, transport, energy, etc);

(j)   policies of the LPA concerned (as evidenced in its own policy statements and non-statutory plans); and

(k)   environmental considerations. Likely environmental pollution from a proposed development is a material consideration, but it is not the function of the planning system to duplicate statutory pollution controls (see *Gateshead Metropolitan Borough Council v Secretary of State for the Environment* [1995] JPL 432, CA; and *Envirocor Waste Holdings v Secretary of State for the Environment* [1995] EGCS 60, QB).

Note that in making planning decisions, there is a duty on LPAs to have 'due regard' to the need to eliminate discrimination, harassment, victimisation and any other conduct prohibited under the Equality Act 2010, which consolidates and broadens the positive equality duties previously found in s 71 of the Race Relations Act 1976, s 49 of the Disability Discrimination Act 1995 and s 76A(1) of the Sexual Discrimination Act 1975 (see *R (on the application of Harris) v Haringey LBC* [2010] EWCA Civ 703).

The SOS has a new power to consider and determine certain planning applications in place of a poorly performing planning authority if the application made to him seeks permission for specific kinds of development. The general powers and duties that apply to LPAs in determining applications also apply in general terms to the SOS (see GAIA 2013, s 1 and Sch 1). In general, therefore, the functions conferred on the LPA will also be relevant to determinations made by the SOS, who will be subject to the same restrictions and guidance in exercising those functions.

4.3.3 Planning permissions subject to conditions

The power in s 70(1) for an LPA to impose such conditions as it thinks fit (see **4.3.2**) is supplemented by s 72(1), which provides that, without prejudice to the generality of s 70(1), conditions may be imposed on the grant of planning permission for the purpose of:

(a)   regulating the development or use of any land under the control of the applicant (whether or not it is land in respect of which the application was made), or requiring the carrying out of works on any such land, so far as appears to the LPA to be expedient for the purposes of or in connection with the development authorised by the permission; or

(b) requiring the removal of any buildings or works authorised by the permission, or the discontinuance of any use of land so authorised, at the end of a specified period, and the carrying out of any works required for the reinstatement of land at the end of that period.

Whether an applicant has 'control' of the relevant land is a question of fact and degree in each case.

The NPPF, para 203, sets out that LPAs 'should consider whether otherwise unacceptable development could be made acceptable through the use of conditions'.

4.3.3.1 Judicial restrictions on the power

The general power to impose conditions in s 70(1) is not as wide or unfettered as it appears, because over the years the courts have imposed restraints on it.

The leading case on judicial control of the power is *Newbury District Council v Secretary of State for the Environment; Newbury District Council v International Synthetic Rubber Co* [1981] AC 578, where Viscount Dilhorne (at p 599) said:

> The conditions imposed must be for a planning purpose and not for any ulterior one and ... they must fairly and reasonably relate to the development permitted. Also they must not be so unreasonable that no reasonable planning authority could have imposed them.

It is important to bear in mind that the majority of conditions imposed by LPAs on planning permissions do not fall foul of the test in *Newbury*. In the very few cases where a condition does fail, it will normally breach more than one of the elements in the test. This is because there are potentially considerable areas of overlap between the three elements in the test.

Planning purpose

There are many cases illustrating the first element of the above test (ie that conditions must be imposed for a planning purpose). For example, in *R v Hillingdon London Borough Council, ex p Royco Homes Ltd* [1974] 1 QB 720, outline permission for a residential development was granted subject to a condition that the dwellings should first be occupied by persons on the local authority's housing waiting list with security of tenure for 10 years. The court held that the principal purpose of the condition was to require the applicants to assume at their expense a significant part of the authority's statutory duties as a housing authority. The condition was therefore ultra vires.

'Fairly and reasonably related to the development permitted'

The second part of the test in *Newbury* is probably the most difficult one to understand and apply. In *Newbury* the facts were that planning permission was granted for a change of use of aircraft hangars to warehouses, subject to a condition requiring removal of the hangars at the end of 10 years. The House of Lords held that although this condition satisfied the first test, in that the removal of unsightly old buildings was a proper planning purpose, the condition was not sufficiently related to the change of use permitted by the permission and was therefore void.

'Manifestly unreasonable'

The final part of the test in *Newbury* is that the condition must not be manifestly unreasonable in the sense that no reasonable LPA would have imposed the condition in question.

Under this element, a condition may not require the applicant to pay money or provide other consideration for the granting of planning permission (but see **Chapter 5**, where a similar practical result can be achieved by means of a planning obligation). A condition may not require the ceding of land owned by the applicant for public purposes (eg a highway) either, even if the applicant consents.

Severability of void conditions

If the condition in question is fundamental to the permission (ie if the permission would not have been granted without the condition), the court will not sever the offending condition. (Most conditions are considered to be fundamental to their permissions.) Thus, if the condition is quashed, the whole permission will fail, ie the applicant will be left with no permission at all. A condition imposed by an LPA can be challenged by appealing the whole permission to the SOS, but this risks a refusal. It may therefore be better to apply for a modified permission under s 73 (see **4.4.3.1**).

4.3.3.2   Central Government Guidance on the Acceptability of Conditions

The NPPG contains a new section on the 'Use of Planning Conditions', which gives detailed guidance to planning authorities on the imposition of conditions (and which cancels most of the previous Circular 11/95).

The NPPG section on the Use of Planning Conditions and para 206 of the NPPF set out six criteria that conditions must satisfy, namely that they should be imposed only where they are:

(a)   necessary;

(b)   relevant to planning;

(c)   relevant to the development to be permitted;

(d)   enforceable;

(e)   precise; and

(f)   reasonable in all other respects.

These basic principles (which are clearly based on the court's criteria, above) are further explained, in particular in Appendix A to Circular 11/95 which is retained and contains model conditions.

The NPPG Use of Planning Conditions section sets out further guidance on key considerations for the LPA to take into account with respect to each of the six tests.

4.3.4   The effect of planning permission

4.3.4.1   General

By s 75(1) of the Act, without prejudice to the provisions of the Act on duration, revocation or modification (for all of which, see below), planning permission shall (except in so far as the permission otherwise provides) enure for the benefit of the land and of all persons for the time being interested in it. As a general rule, therefore, the benefit of planning permission runs with the land concerned and, once implemented (see **4.3.4.3**), runs forever. This is (as indicated) subject to contrary conditions in the permission, and it is possible for planning permission to be granted for a limited period or be made personal to the applicant, but this is rare and must be justified on planning grounds. Once a temporary permission lapses, the right to revert to the previous use of the land is permitted by s 57(2) (see **4.2.3.1**).

Note that any conditions attached to the planning permission will also run, ie will burden the relevant land.

It follows from the provisions in s 75(1) that the doctrine of abandonment cannot apply to express planning permissions (in other words, once implemented, the permission will not lapse if the activity ceases). Note, however, that once a permission has been fully implemented its effect is spent, ie it does not authorise the re-carrying out of that development. Thus if a building is destroyed, a new planning permission will be required to authorise its re-erection.

The grant of planning permission is effective for planning purposes only. At the time of writing, it does not confer, for example, listed building consent, building regulation approval or any consent required under any other enactment (except conservation area consent, see below); nor does it confer the right to break any enforceable covenant affecting the land.

The ERRA 2013 introduced changes which, from 1 October 2013, removed the need to obtain conservation area consent when demolishing unlisted buildings in a conservation area. Consent for demolition is instead conferred by the grant of planning permission for the development including the demolition of the building. The enforcement regime has been amended to take into account this change (see **Chapter 6**).

4.3.4.2 Revocation and modification of planning permissions

By s 97, the LPA may, if it thinks it expedient to do so, revoke or modify (to the extent the LPA considers necessary) any planning permission, provided that the LPA does so before the development authorised by the permission is completed.

4.3.4.3 Implementation

Although generally, once implemented, the benefit of a planning permission lasts forever, there are statutory time limits governing implementation itself. If the time limit expires without the development having been started, the permission effectively lapses. Any further development will be unauthorised and subject to possible enforcement proceedings.

For full permissions granted before 24 August 2005, this time limit is five years. For full permissions granted on or after 24 August 2005, the PCPA 2004 has reduced the default period to three years. In the case of outline permissions, the time limit for implementation is within two years of approval of the last of the reserved matters (see **4.3.1**).

Note also that the LPA may substitute longer or shorter time limits if it thinks it appropriate on planning grounds. In the current economic climate, LPAs have been encouraged to consider the desirability, in individual cases, of imposing a longer time limit. If an LPA does this, however, it must give its reasons for doing so in case the applicant should wish to appeal against this.

The Act (s 56) defines what steps must be taken to implement the permission. It provides that development is taken to be begun on the earliest date on which any of the following 'material' operations begin to be carried out:

(a)   any work of construction in the course of erection of a building;

(b)   any work of demolition of a building;

(c)   the digging of a trench for the foundations of a building;

(d)   the laying of an underground main or pipe to the foundations;

(e)   any operation in the course of laying out or constructing a road;

(f)   any material change in the use of any land.

If a planning permission is lawfully implemented, the permission will be preserved and will not expire. Consequently, there is much case law considering how a planning permission may be 'lawfully implemented'. The court's consideration has focused on two main issues.

The first issue is whether the works carried out are significant enough in themselves to 'implement' the permission lawfully. Works that are more than *de minimis* will be sufficient to implement a planning permission and can include, for example, merely digging a trench for the foundations of the building. A number of court decisions have confirmed that, in practice, the threshold of operation required to establish that development has begun is very low (see, for example, *Malvern Hills DC v Secretary of State for the Environment* [1982] JPL 439).

The second issue is whether the work carried out to implement the permission has been carried out 'lawfully'. This will turn on whether the 'pre-commencement conditions' listed on the permission have been discharged before any substantive works of development have been carried out. If all pre-commencement conditions are discharged, any kind of building work subsequently carried out on site will lawfully implement the development. Work carried out in breach of a pre-commencement condition may lawfully implement development if the condition is subsequently discharged.

4.3.4.4   Renewal of a planning permission

What if a developer cannot start the development within the time limit because of, for instance, financial problems? A planning permission may be renewed only if it was granted before 1 October 2010 and has not yet expired (although this procedure does require the issue of a replacement permission, and the LPA will consider any changes in policy in the meantime, so there is no guarantee that the permission will be renewed). In all other cases where a permission has expired without being implemented, the whole permission will lapse and a fresh application for planning permission will therefore have to be made.

4.3.4.5   Completion notice

Once a developer starts the development, there is generally no time limit in which the development must be completed. However, if the LPA is of the opinion that the development will not be completed within a reasonable period, it may serve a completion notice on the owner and any occupier of the land stating that the permission will cease to have effect at the expiration of a further period specified in the notice (being not less than 12 months after the notice takes effect). The notice is subject to confirmation by the SOS. Any part of the development carried out before a confirmed completion notice takes effect remains lawful and cannot be the subject of an enforcement notice requiring demolition (however unsightly). The service of completion notices is rare, however.

4.4   APPLICATION TO THE LOCAL PLANNING AUTHORITY

Application for planning permission is, in the first instance, made to the LPA, which will consider and determine the application in accordance with the principles referred to throughout this chapter. Note, as already mentioned, that the Government has now introduced a power for an applicant to make an application directly to the SOS, provided that the application is within a specified description and the SOS has designated the relevant LPA as performing inadequately in respect of making planning decisions. The criteria that must be met for an LPA to be designated are set out in guidance prepared by the DCLG published in June 2013. Adequacy will be judged on the basis of: (i) the speed with which applications for major development are dealt with by LPAs; and (ii) the quality of decisions, measured by the extent to which such decisions are overturned at appeal (as an indicator of the quality of the decisions made by LPAs). An assessment of the speed and quality of decisions will be made (and regularly reviewed) using the tests also found in the guidance.

In the case of 'nationally significant infrastructure projects' (such as, for example, in respect of power stations or gas pipelines exceeding a certain threshold in terms of scale), the PA 2008 requires applications for development consent to be made directly to the SOS. A recent extension to this regime introduced by the GAIA 2013 means that certain business or commercial projects now fall within the definition of a 'nationally significant infrastructure project'. However, these may only be determined by the SOS pursuant to a formal request from the applicant. This means that the vast majority of commercial and business projects remain likely to be considered and determined under the 1990 Act planning regime. The consideration of nationally significant infrastructure projects is outside the scope of this book.

4.4.1   Preliminary steps

It makes sense at this stage in the chapter to consider what steps should be undertaken in advance of applying to the LPA for permission. It is unusual for a solicitor to make this original application, but it is common for a legal audit to be undertaken prior to submission to ensure that all statutory requirements have been complied with. Further, should the LPA refuse planning permission (or impose adverse conditions), a solicitor may become involved in advising on any appeal. As an appeal takes the form of a total rehearing of the merits of the original application, the solicitor will therefore in effect need to review the matter as if from the outset at the appeal stage.

Steps to be taken include the following:

(a) Considering whether planning permission is required at all, ie do the proposals amount to development and, if so, are they permitted development (see **4.2** and **4.3**)?

(b) Undertaking a site visit. A site visit can be very valuable as it may:

  (i) clarify the client's maps, diagrams and plans;

  (ii) provide information about the immediate environment; and

  (iii) alert the solicitor to potential problems with the application.

(c) Obtaining copies of the relevant parts of the development plan and any non-statutory plans which may affect the proposed development. This could be vital in many cases because, for the application to stand a chance of succeeding, the development proposed will usually have to be in accordance with the development plan (see **4.1.3**).

(d) Investigating the title to the land concerned. This is necessary for two main reasons: first, to check whether the proposed development is in breach of an enforceable covenant affecting the land concerned; secondly, to identify any other 'owners' who will need to be given notice of the application (see further **4.4.2**).

(e) Obtaining the relevant application form from the LPA, which is in prescribed form, and obtaining the LPA's list of documents to be provided with a planning application (requirements may vary depending on the nature of the development to be permitted).

(f) Considering whether a pre-application discussion with the appropriate case officer might be beneficial. This is encouraged by DCLG in order to reduce uncertainty and delay in processing applications. Such discussions can be particularly helpful in the case of large-scale or potentially controversial development proposals, to enable the developer to find out in what respects the proposals may not be acceptable and in what ways chances of success can be improved; they also enable the LPA to advise the developer of probable objections to the development which, if remedied, should lead to a quicker determination.

Note that LPAs have no statutory duty to enter into such discussions, although in practice they do so regularly. It follows, therefore, that any advice, etc given in such discussions is merely informal and advisory, and ultimately cannot normally bind the LPA (see *Western Fish Products Limited v Penwith DC and Another* (1979) 38 P & CR 7).

A developer and LPA may use a Planning Performance Agreement (PPA) to agree a timeframe for pre-application discussions to take place and to fund provision of LPA resources to determine the application. A PPA may be completed by an LPA under its general powers under the Local Government Act 1972. An LPA also has the power to charge for pre-application discussions under s 93 of the Local Government Act 2003. As at 6 September 2012, the Government intended that the use of PPAs be increased to commit both applicants and authorities to a clear timetable for determining proposals.

(g) Considering whether there is a statutory requirement to carry out pre-application consultation under s 61W of the TCPA 1990. Currently the requirement to carry out pre-application consultation applies only to onshore wind farms with more than 2 turbines or taller than 15 metres. Note that this duty is separate from the duty on the LPA to publicise the application (see **4.4.2.3**).

4.4.2 The procedure

Procedure is governed mainly by ss 62 to 69 of the Act and the DMPO 2010.

4.4.2.1   What is submitted to whom?

The application form and such other documents, plans, drawings, etc as are prescribed by the LPA should be submitted (usually in triplicate) to the district planning authority, London borough or metropolitan district council or unitary council (as the case may be). The application will require the applicant to detail its proposals, but from 25 June 2013 a design and access statement (DAS) will be required only in limited circumstances. A DAS must be submitted with applications for 'major development', or applications for development to be carried out in a conservation area or to property designated as a World Heritage Site where one or more dwelling is provided, or where 100 square metres of floorspace or more would be created. A DAS need not be provided alongside applications for permission made under s 73 of the Act, for engineering or mining operations, for changes of use, for waste development or for applications to renew permissions (see **4.3.4.4**).

Whilst LPAs have a power to require submission of a number of documents, s 6 of the GAIA 2013 imposes a limit on this power. It must be reasonable to request the document(s) sought (having regard to the nature and scale of development in particular), and an applicant may be required to provide such document or evidence only if it is reasonable to think that the matter addressed in that document or evidence will be a material consideration in the determination of the application.

In addition, the Government has reduced the amount of detail that must be provided as part of an outline planning application. Since 31 January 2013 there is no longer a requirement to provide minimum information about layout and scale. Note, however, the need to provide sufficient information in order to be able to carry out a robust EIA (see below).

If the LPA is satisfied that the appropriate documents have been submitted, it will 'validate' the application, after which the LPA will commence the consultation process (see **4.4.2.2**). This step has previously been the subject of disputes between the applicant and an LPA. In some cases, LPAs have required an unreasonable number of documents or made unreasonable requests for additional information but have refused to validate the application until the additional information has been provided. Alongside the introduction of the 'reasonableness' criterion, the Government has also introduced changes – in force from 25 June 2013 – designed to avoid the impasse that has arisen in the past. The Town and Country Planning (Development Management Procedure) (England) (Amendment) Order 2013 (SI 2013/1238) provides a right of appeal for non-determination of applications where an applicant considers that an LPA is requiring particulars or evidence that do not meet the tests outlined above. The applicant must follow a prescribed procedure to make the application eligible for appeal using that power. The power to appeal on this basis does not apply to planning applications made prior to 25 June 2013.

In cases where the development to be permitted exceeds particular thresholds and where the impacts of the development are likely to have significant effects on the environment, an EIA must be undertaken and an environmental statement provided to the LPA as part of the application (see the Town and Country Planning (Environmental Impact Assessment) Regulations 2011 (EIA Regulations) (SI 2011/1824)). The environmental statement (ES) sets out the results of the EIA. If an ES should have been provided but has not been supplied, the LPA must not determine the planning application. The need to carry out the assessment and its scope are significant areas for legal challenge, and considerable care must therefore be taken to ensure that EIA is carried out in compliance with the EIA Regulations. This will include not only considering whether EIA is required but, if it is, the scope of the EIA to be undertaken. It is usual for an EIA to be carried out using a set of parameters, within which the development if carried out would be within the bounds of the EIA undertaken. The EIA process will need to take into account not only the legal requirement to provide specific information in detailed (and to a lesser extent, outline) applications, but also the need to prepare a robust EIA (and ES) that seeks to minimise the risk of judicial challenge. Note that the European Commission has consulted on changes to the European legislation which is transposed into UK law by the EIA Regulations and as a result has adopted a revised EIA Directive. The United Kingdom is required to transpose these amendments into its various jurisdictions by 2017.

The application must be accompanied by the appropriate fee. The fee will vary according to the type of application and the scale of development involved.

4.4.2.2 Notification of persons by the applicant

It is not necessary for the applicant to have any interest in the land that is the subject of the planning application. By the DMPO 2010, art 11, where the applicant is not the sole owner of the application site, he must give notice to all persons who are 'owners' or 'tenants' of the land.

'Owner' is defined by s 65(8) of the Act as meaning any person who owns the fee simple, or a tenancy granted or extended for a term certain of which not less than seven years remain unexpired.

'Tenant' is defined by the DMPO 2010, art 11(8) as meaning the tenant of an agricultural holding any part of which is comprised in the application site.

The application must also be accompanied by a certificate under art 12 of the DMPO 2010 and an agricultural holdings certificate. These certificates have to be given to certify compliance with the DMPO 2010, art 11.

4.4.2.3 Action by the LPA

By s 69, the LPA must enter certain particulars of the application in the register that it is required to keep by that section. The register is open to public inspection.

By the DMPO 2010, art 13, the LPA must publicise the application. This publicity may consist of a site notice, notifying neighbours, or a local advertisement, depending upon the type of development proposed.

4.4.2.4 Power to decline to determine applications

Section 70B of the TCPA 1990 (inserted by s 43 of the PCPA 2004) gives LPAs the power to decline to determine:

(a)   repeat planning applications;

(b)   overlapping planning applications.

Repeat planning applications are applications that are submitted repeatedly with the intention that, over time, opposition to a controversial proposed development is reduced and permission granted. This process may result in undesirable developments being built.

Section 70B allows the LPA to decline to determine an application which is similar to one refused by the authority or by the Secretary of State on appeal within the preceding two years, and where the LPA thinks there has been no significant change in the relevant considerations since such refusal. The LPA may also decline to determine an application where another application relating to the same or substantially the same land is still under consideration. These powers are not intended to prevent a new application being submitted that is similar to an earlier one but altered to address objections raised in relation to the earlier application.

4.4.2.5 The making of the decision

The decision should be made within eight weeks of the submission of the application or such longer period as may have been agreed in writing with the applicant (DMPO 2010, art 29). However, in the case of major developments, the time limit is 13 weeks, and if an EIA of the development is required, so an ES accompanies the application, then the period is 16 weeks. If no decision has been made in time, the applicant can appeal to the SOS.

The LPA should make its decision in line with the plan-led principle (see **4.1.3**).

If the LPA does not make its decision within the relevant time limit, this is treated as a deemed refusal of planning permission and entitles the applicant to appeal to the SOS.

Decisions are taken by members of the LPA at a committee meeting or by officers under delegated powers through the LPA's scheme of delegation (or 'standing orders').

4.4.2.6   Procedure after the decision

After making the decision, the LPA must register it in its planning register (s 69 of the Act and the DMPO 2010, art 36). In addition, the applicant must be given written notification of the decision and full reasons for each condition imposed, or a clear and precise statement of the full reasons for refusal, specifying all policies and proposals in the development plan which are relevant to the decision (see the DMPO 2010, art 31, as amended by the Town and Country Planning (Development Management Procedure) (England) (Amendment) Order 2013 (SI 2013/1238), which has effect from 25 June 2013 to reduce the amount of information that must be provided). If full reasons are not given, the decision could be challenged by judicial review or dealt with by way of appeal.

It is the written notification which constitutes the grant of planning permission (see *R v West Oxfordshire District Council, ex p CH Pearce Homes* [1986] JPL 523). Where a deed of planning obligations is required to be entered into as a prerequisite to the grant of planning permission, the notification may follow some time after a resolution to grant is made.

4.4.3   Amendments to planning permissions

If an LPA imposes conditions, it is open to the applicant to appeal. However, as the appeal takes effect as a total rehearing of the matter, it is possible that the original grant (admittedly subject to adverse conditions) might be reversed altogether, leaving the appellant worse off. A number of procedures are available to reduce this risk, and to give greater flexibility in relation to planning permissions that have been granted.

4.4.3.1   Section 73

Section 73 entitles a person to apply for planning permission to develop land without complying with conditions subject to which a previous planning permission was granted. Such an application must, however, be made before the previous permission expires.

The application has to be made in writing and give sufficient information to enable the LPA to identify the previous grant of planning permission and the condition or conditions in question.

The important feature of a s 73 application is that in determining the application, the planning authority may consider only the question of the conditions subject to which the permission should be granted, and thus may only:

(a)   grant unconditional permission;

(b)   grant permission subject to different conditions; or

(c)   refuse the application.

In the first two cases above, the applicant will then have the benefit of two permissions (ie the original one and the one obtained as a result of the s 73 application). In cases (b) and (c), the applicant can appeal to the SOS in the usual way. Thus, whatever happens on the s 73 application, the applicant will always retain the benefit of the original planning permission.

This is the only procedure available for challenging a condition where the time limit for appealing the grant of permission has passed.

Section 73 cannot be used to extend, or have the effect of extending, the time within which a development must be started or an application for approval of reserved matters must be made.

A streamlined procedure under s 73 also exists. This enables 'minor material' changes to be made to a planning permission. The procedure was introduced following the Killian Pretty Review, which recommended that 'Government should take steps to allow a more proportionate approach to minor material changes in development proposals after permission has been granted'. A minor material amendment is defined in the NPPG as including 'any amendment where its scale and/or nature results in a development which is not substantially different from the one which has been approved'. The guidance recommends that a developer seeking to rely on the streamlined procedure engages in pre-application discussions with the relevant LPA to determine that using the procedure is appropriate in the circumstances.

4.4.3.2 Section 73A

Section 73 applies only to applications for the removal, etc of a condition before it is breached. However, under s 73A, an application may be made for planning permission for, inter alia, development carried out before the date of the application in breach of a condition subject to which planning permission was previously granted.

Permission for such development may be granted to have effect from the date on which the development was carried out, thereby rendering it retrospectively lawful.

4.4.3.3 Section 96A

More recently, the Government has introduced a mechanism under s 96A of the Act that enables a person with an interest in the land to apply for approval of non-material changes to a planning permission. The scope of the power given to the LPA is necessarily limited. It may only make a change to the planning permission if it is satisfied that the change is not material. In deciding whether the change is material, the LPA must have regard to the effect of the change (cumulatively with any others approved under the section) on the planning permission originally granted. However, where the LPA is so satisfied, the procedure provides a quicker and more desirable route for a change to be permitted, which would formerly have to have been made under the s 73 procedure.

Unlike a s 73 application, a successful amendment under s 96A will not result in the grant of a new planning permission. Instead, it takes effect as a modification to the original permission. The applicant for a s 96A amendment must have an interest in the land that is the subject of the proposed modification.

4.5 APPEALS AGAINST ADVERSE PLANNING DETERMINATIONS

Where an LPA has:

(a) refused to grant planning permission; or

(b) granted planning permission subject to conditions to which the applicant objects; or

(c) refused approval of reserved matters on an outline permission; or

(d) refused an application or granted a permission subject to conditions under s 73 or s 73A; or

(e) failed to notify its decision within the prescribed period (normally eight weeks),

the applicant may appeal to the SOS. This right to appeal is subject to certain time limits, themselves dependent on the nature of the appeal (s 78; DMPO 2010, art 33). In the case of appeals not being brought by a householder, the time limit is six months from the date of the relevant notice from the LPA or expiry of the prescribed period.

4.5.1 Who may appeal?

Only the applicant may appeal; this is so even though the applicant may not be the owner of an interest in the land. Third parties have no right of appeal, and neither does the owner of the freehold have an independent right of appeal. However, third parties may challenge the decision by judicial review where there has been a procedural error; judicial review is not an appeal on the merits of the decision but a challenge to the way in which the decision was made. A third party who objects to the grant of planning permission may challenge the grant of that permission in the High Court within six weeks of the decision to grant planning permission.

The Ministry of Justice introduced a new Planning Court, as a separate part of the High Court, with effect from 6 April 2014, in which specialist planning judges hear planning cases – to speed up the system by freeing up the burdened court system and ensuring that the most appropriate judges hear planning cases.

The previous time limit for making a challenge by way of judicial review was three months. The six-week time limit applies to grounds of challenge arising after 1 July 2013 which are brought under 'the Planning Acts' (as defined by s 336). The change is intended to permit developers to commence development more quickly, since they may be reluctant to implement planning permission during the challenge period. This also brings the limit in line with the six-week period for bringing a statutory challenge to the grant of a planning permission by the SOS on appeal.

4.5.2   Initial procedure (DMPO 2010, arts 32, 33)

An appeal must be made on the form supplied by the DCLG.

As well as setting out the grounds of appeal, the appellant must indicate whether he would like the appeal to be determined by the written representations procedure, whether he wishes it to be heard by an inspector, or whether he wishes the appeal to be determined at a public inquiry (see **4.5.3**). Note, however, that it is PINS that will choose the procedure; it will not necessarily adopt the method desired by the appellant. The LPA's views as to the choice of procedure will also be taken into account. PINS's decision will be made in the light of published criteria approved by Ministers. These are as follows:

Criteria for Determining the Procedure for Planning Appeals

Written representations

If your appeal meets the following criteria, the most appropriate procedure would be written representations:

1.   the grounds of appeal and issues raised can be clearly understood from the appeal documents plus a site inspection; and/or

2.   the Inspector should not need to test the evidence by questioning or to clarify any other matters; and/or

3.   an environmental impact assessment (EIA) is either not required or the EIA is not in dispute.

Hearing

If the criteria for written representations are not met because questions need to be asked, for example where any of the following apply:

•   the status of the appellant is at issue, eg Gypsy/Traveller;

•   the need for the proposal is at issue, eg agricultural worker's dwelling; Gypsy/Traveller site;

•   the personal circumstances of the appellant are at issue, eg people with disabilities or other special needs;

the most appropriate procedure would be a hearing if:

1.   there is no need for evidence to be tested by formal cross-examination; and

2.   the issues are straightforward (and do not require legal or other submissions to be made) and you should be able to present your own case (although you can choose to be represented if you wish); and

3.   your case and that of the LPA and interested persons is unlikely to take more than one day to be heard.

Inquiry

If the criteria for written representations and hearings are not met because the evidence needs to be tested and/or questions need to be asked, as above, the most appropriate procedure would be a local inquiry if:

1. the issues are complex and likely to need evidence to be given by expert witnesses; and/or

2. you are likely to need to be represented by an advocate, such as a lawyer or other professional expert because material facts and/or matters of expert opinion are in dispute and formal cross-examination of witnesses is required; and/or

3. legal submissions may need to be made.

NOTE: Where proposals are controversial and have generated significant local interest, they may not be suitable for the written representation procedure. We consider that the LPA is in the best position to indicate that a hearing or inquiry may be required in such circumstances.

There is also an expedited process based on written representations where a householder is appealing through the Householder Appeals Service. This is dealt with on an electronic basis and covers appeals in relation to minor developments affecting existing dwellings, eg extensions, garages, etc.

The completed form, together with all relevant documents, must be sent to PINS in good time to reach it within the time limit. Copies of the form must also be sent to the LPA, together with copies of any documents sent to the Inspectorate which the LPA has not yet seen (DMPO 2010, art 33).

4.5.3 Types of appeal

4.5.3.1 Written representations

Under the written representations procedure the appeal is decided, as its name suggests, almost entirely on the basis of written representations submitted to PINS by the appellant, the LPA and any other interested parties. No oral evidence is permitted, and that includes evidence by way of video or audio tape; maps, plans and photographs are acceptable, however, and in many cases will be necessary. At some point before a decision is made, the inspector will visit the site either unaccompanied, if the site can be seen sufficiently well from a public road or place, or accompanied by the appellant or his representative and a representative from the LPA.

The procedure is governed by the Town and Country Planning (Appeals) (Written Representations Procedure) (England) Regulations 2009 (SI 2009/452). It is speedy and cost-effective, and is recommended by DCLG for the simpler or non-controversial cases. It is by far the most common appeal procedure in England, accounting for about 90% of current appeals (see Planning Inspectorate, Statistical Report: England 2011/2012; appeals received – Table 1.3). Because of its nature, it also offers less scope for third parties to influence the eventual decision.

Statement of case

The appellant's statement of case must be set out on the appeal form. As a general guide, the statement should:

(a) contain quotations from the development plan, the NPPF and other policy documents which support the appellant's case;

(b) consider each of the reasons given (where relevant) for the refusal, etc, and analyse and refute them by logical argument. In this part, any precedent (eg showing that the LPA has granted a similar application) should be mentioned, as should any policies of the LPA which contradict the LPA's reasons;

(c) justify the appellant's case. Here there should be a brief description of the development proposed, together with additional plans, photographs, etc if desired. The local environment may be described (although the inspector will visit the site). Any material considerations and special circumstances should be set out and any objections from third parties should be addressed; and

(d)   conclude with a general statement in support of the appellant's case.

4.5.3.2   Inquiry

This is the most formal of the appeal procedures and is reserved for larger and more controversial developments. Inquiries are usually held in LPA offices, village halls or community centres. The procedure is governed by the Town and Country Planning (Inquiries Procedure) (England) Rules 2000 (SI 2000/1624) and the Town and Country Planning (Determination by Inspectors) (Inquiries Procedure) (England) Rules 2000 (SI 2000/1625) as amended by the Town and Country Planning (Hearings and Inquiries Procedure) (Amendment) (England) Rules 2009 (SI 2009/455). Guidance as to the procedure to be followed can be found on the PINS website or in the NPPG online guidance.

These are often cases where expert evidence is presented and witnesses are cross-examined. An inquiry may last for several days, or even weeks. It is not a court of law, but the proceedings will often seem to be quite similar, and the appellant and the LPA usually have legal representatives. It is thus a much slower and more costly procedure.

PINS sets out the following guidance in its 'Guide to taking part in enforcement appeals proceeding by an inquiry' (July 2009):

> Inquiries are open to members of the public, and although there is no legal right to speak the Inspector will normally allow [local people to take part in the inquiry process]. Local knowledge and opinion can often be a valuable addition to the more formal evidence given by the appellant and the LPA.
>
> …
>
> At the inquiry opening, the Inspector will go through some routine matters, including asking who will be taking part in the inquiry. This is often called 'taking the appearances'. When the appellant and the LPA have given their details, the Inspector will ask if anyone else wants to speak. …
>
> …
>
> The appellant will usually be asked to make a brief opening statement first, to set the scene [and describe the nature of the proposal]. The LPA will then make their opening statement. Their witnesses will then give their evidence and the appellant can cross-examine them. After that the Inspector will normally ask if anyone who supports the proposal has any questions to put to the witnesses.
>
> The appellant will then call their witnesses, and the LPA can cross-examine them. After that the Inspector will normally ask if anyone who objects to the proposal has any questions to put to the witnesses.
>
> …
>
> The inquiry ends with closing speeches by those who have spoken at the inquiry, followed by the LPA and finally the appellant. This is normally followed by the Inspector visiting the appeal site. Because the inquiry is over, there can be no further discussion about the case during that visit.
>
> At the discretion of the Inspector, video, audio cassette, CD/DVD or electronic media files may be played at the inquiry. … The recording will become part of the inquiry evidence and will be retained.

The appeal form

In the appeal form, it is not necessary or desirable to give a full statement of case. Full grounds of appeal must, however, be included. Thus, the appellant must, as before, consider each of the LPA's reasons and analyse and refute them briefly. The entire case should be summarised by describing the development proposed, the environment and any special needs or circumstances, and by referring to any appropriate parts of the development plans and government policies. Any relevant previous decisions (whether by the LPA or on appeal) should be set out as being 'material considerations', and potential planning obligations should also be outlined.

It is important that the full grounds of appeal are stated and that nothing is omitted, as the appellant or his representative at the appeal will largely be bound by the grounds, and any omissions may cause adjournments and may have financial consequences (see **3.9**).

4.5.3.3 Hearing

This is less formal than a public inquiry. The hearing is an inquisitorial process led by the Inspector, who identifies the issues for discussion based on the evidence submitted and any representations made. The hearing may include a discussion at the site, or the site may be inspected, without discussion, on an accompanied or unaccompanied basis.

The procedure is governed by the Town and Country Planning (Hearings Procedure) (England) Rules 2000 (SI 2000/1626), as amended. The procedure is intended to save time and money for the parties. In essence, it will be an informal hearing before an inspector, who will try to stimulate a discussion on the main issues between the parties. It is not appropriate for complex or controversial appeals, but where it is appropriate it is quicker and more cost-effective than an inquiry.

4.5.4 Costs in appeals

By ss 320(2) and 322 of the Act, the SOS is given the powers under s 250(5) of the Local Government Act 1972 to award costs in planning appeals. Inspectors may now exercise the SOS's powers. There is power to make an award in all cases, irrespective of the procedure for deciding the appeal.

Detailed guidance on the exercise of power to award costs is contained in the NPPG online guidance. The basic principle is that, unlike in civil cases, costs do not 'follow the event', ie normally, each party will bear its own costs. Costs may be awarded against one party in favour of another, however, where:

(a)   a party has sought an award at the appropriate stage of the proceedings; and

(b)   the party against whom costs are sought has behaved unreasonably; and

(c)   this has caused the party seeking costs to incur or waste expense unnecessarily.

The Government intends to amend this guidance, to give PINS more power to initiate an award of costs in planning appeal proceedings 'where it is clear that an application has not been handled as it should have been with due process'.

4.5.5 Challenging the appeal decision

By s 284, the validity of an appeal decision may not be challenged in any legal proceedings. However, by s 288, a 'person aggrieved' may question the decision by appeal to the High Court if the decision was not within the powers of the Act, or if any relevant procedural requirements have not been complied with.

In certain limited cases, a challenge may alternatively be mounted by way of judicial review.

REVIEW ACTIVITY

1.   'When determining an application for planning permission, there are no criteria with which LPAs are required to comply.'

    Do you agree with this statement?

2.   An individual has bought a house for investment purposes. He plans to sub-divide the building and create three self-contained flats which he will then sell. The exterior of the building will be unaffected apart from the installation of a window in the roof (which is permitted by the GPDO).

    'He will not need planning permission for his proposals.'

Do you agree with this statement?

3. Would change of use from a clothing store to a bookshop require planning permission (ignore any building works that might need to be undertaken)?

4. What is the effect of an Article 4 Direction?

5. Does the GPDO give an individual who currently has permission for use of premises under use Class A2 an unqualified right to change to a use under use Class A1?

6. 'The longest an outline planning permission can last before implementation is three years.'

    Do you agree with this statement?

7. A full planning permission has been granted for the erection of an office block. Is there a time limit within which the office block must be completed?

8. On appeal against an adverse planning decision by an LPA, what is the basis on which the matter is heard?

9. What is the time limit within which an appeal against an adverse planning decision by an LPA must be made?

10. A farmer plans to convert a disused barn into a row of cottages. The LPA has granted planning permission and has imposed conditions limiting occupation to agricultural workers only. In the farmer's opinion, this outcome is better than nothing, but he would like to challenge the decision.

    How would you advise the farmer?

Answers to this Review activity may be found in Appendix 1.

CHAPTER 5

PLANNING OBLIGATIONS AND COMMUNITY INFRASTRUCTURE LEVY

5.1	Introduction	57
5.2	Planning obligations	58
5.3	Government policy	59
5.4	Unilateral undertakings	60
5.5	Modification and discharge of planning obligations	60
5.6	Community Infrastructure Levy	61
5.7	CIL and planning obligations	66
5.8	Practical points	67
	Review activity	68

5.1 INTRODUCTION

The limitations discussed in **Chapter 4** (see **4.3.3**) on what matters can be dealt with by way of a condition attached to a planning permission provide certainty and clarity. There will, however, be situations where these limitations prove problematic. An example might be where a development proposal gives rise to the need for additional infrastructure provision (such as roads or schools). A condition cannot be imposed requiring the developer to make a financial contribution towards this. The use of planning obligations in section 106 agreements under the TCPA 1990 (and previously their predecessors, usually referred to as section 52 agreements) provides an alternative means to secure mitigation measures when planning conditions cannot be used.

In simple terms, a planning obligation is a separate agreement or undertaking made by deed that runs alongside the planning permission and which can be used to deal with issues (such as contributions to infrastructure costs) that cannot be dealt with in the planning permission itself. The planning obligation will be treated as a 'material consideration' in determining whether the planning permission should be granted and on what terms (see **4.3.2**). Planning obligations have, however, been the subject of criticism for some time. First, there is an apparent lack of transparency (leading to a perception in some cases that developers can simply 'buy' planning permission by offering generous terms in the obligation). Secondly, because obligations tend to be negotiated on a case-by-case basis, it is difficult for LPAs to manage their infrastructure spending strategically and for developers to predict the costs of development. Thirdly, costs can fall disproportionately on developers promoting larger projects.

For these reasons among others, the PA 2008 and, subsequently, the Community Infrastructure Levy Regulations 2010 (SI 2010/948) (CIL Regulations) as amended by the Community Infrastructure Levy (Amendment) Regulations 2011, 2012, 2013 and 2014 (SI 2011/987, SI 2012/98, SI 2013/982 and SI 2014/395) introduced a new mechanism for developer contributions, the Community Infrastructure Levy (CIL). Since then, the charge has been adopted by a number of public authorities.

The introduction of CIL was intended to reduce the use of planning obligations, but the Government has already responded to its slow adoption across the country by confirming that it will extend the period in which planning obligations may continue to be used to fund infrastructure. This means that planning obligations and CIL will continue to operate side by side for the foreseeable future.

5.2 PLANNING OBLIGATIONS

The terms of each planning obligation will depend on the individual needs of the development proposal, but a model form of planning obligation (which may be accessed on the DCLG section of the Government's website and on The Law Society's website) is available as a starting point.

Unless stated otherwise, all references to section numbers in this chapter are to the TCPA 1990.

5.2.1 Meaning of 'planning obligation'

Any person interested in land in the area of an LPA may, by agreement or otherwise, enter into a planning obligation which may:

(a)   restrict the development or use of the land in a specified way; or

(b)   require specified operations or activities to be carried out in, on, over or under the land; or

(c)   require the land to be used in a specified way; or

(d)   require money to be paid to the LPA on a specified date or dates, or periodically (s 106(1)).

Note the following points:

(a)   'Person interested in land' means a person with any legal or equitable interest in the land.

(b)   'Agreement or otherwise' indicates that a planning obligation may be created either by agreement between the LPA and the developer, or by means of a unilateral undertaking offered by the developer or a combination of both (as to the potential use of unilateral undertakings, see **5.4**).

(c)   A planning obligation may impose both restrictive covenants (eg restricting the development or use of the land) and positive obligations (eg requiring works to be done or money to be paid). These covenants and obligations will then be enforceable against successors in title of the developer (see **5.2.4**).

(d)   A planning obligation may be unconditional or subject to conditions, and may impose restrictions and requirements either indefinitely or for a specified period. It may also provide that a person will be bound by the obligation only while he has an interest in the land (s 106(2) and (4)).

5.2.2 When can a planning obligation be used?

Pursuant to the CIL Regulations, reg 122, a planning obligation may only constitute a reason to grant planning permission if it is:

(a)   necessary to make the development acceptable in planning terms;

(b)   directly related to the proposed development; and

(c)   fairly and reasonably related in scale and kind to the proposed development.

This test was introduced by the CIL Regulations in April 2011. It enshrines in legislation a similar test previously found in Circular 05/05. Further restrictions on the use of planning obligations arise where an LPA has adopted the CIL as its principal mechanism for securing developer contributions. For further detail, see **5.7**. Planning obligations that do not meet these criteria cannot be reasons to grant planning permission but will still be lawful if agreed by the developer.

5.2.3 Formalities

A planning obligation must be made by a deed which states that it is a planning obligation for the purposes of s 106, and identifies the land and the parties concerned (including the interest of the developer). It is registrable by the LPA as a local land charge.

5.2.4 Enforceability

By s 106(3) and (4), a planning obligation is enforceable by the LPA against the original person entering into the obligation (the 'developer') and any person deriving title from that person.

Note the following points:

(a) The obligation will bind only the interest or estate of the developer and those deriving title from him. It cannot bind a superior title. Thus, for example, if a tenant enters into a planning obligation, it cannot bind the landlord of that tenant.

(b) A planning obligation cannot bind parties who have rights in the land existing at the time the obligation is entered into unless they consent to be bound by it. Thus, for example, existing mortgagees of the land will not be bound (unless they consent), so that if they subsequently sell under their statutory power, the purchaser will take the land free from the obligation which will be enforceable only against the original covenantor.

For these reasons, the LPA will generally insist on all parties with an interest in the relevant land entering into a planning obligation.

5.2.5 Enforcement by the LPA

Section 106 provides three main methods of enforcement, as follows:

(a) Injunction to restrain a breach of any restrictive covenant in the obligation (s 106(5)).

(b) By s 106(6), where there is a failure to carry out any operations required by a planning obligation, the LPA may enter upon the land, carry out the operations and recover its expenses from the person or persons against whom the obligation is enforceable.

(c) Any sums due under the planning obligation (including any expenses recoverable under s 106(6) above) may be charged on the land in accordance with regulations yet to be made (s 106(12)). Until regulations have been made, it is unclear whether such a charge will be registrable as a local land charge or as a private charge (and therefore registrable as a land charge or by notice, etc on the register of title).

5.3 GOVERNMENT POLICY

Government policy on planning obligations is currently set out in the National Planning Policy Framework (NPPF) and also in National Planning Practice Guidance (NPPG). Paragraphs 203–205 of the NPPF set out the following:

203. Local planning authorities should consider whether otherwise unacceptable development could be made acceptable through the use of conditions or planning obligations. Planning obligations should only be used where it is not possible to address unacceptable impacts through a planning condition.

204. Planning obligations should only be sought where they meet all of the following tests:

• necessary to make the development acceptable in planning terms;

• directly related to the development; and

• fairly and reasonably related in scale and kind to the development.

205. Where obligations are being sought or revised, local planning authorities should take account of changes in market conditions over time and, wherever appropriate, be sufficiently flexible to prevent planned development being stalled.

5.4 UNILATERAL UNDERTAKINGS

By s 106(1), planning obligations may be entered into 'by agreement or otherwise'; 'or otherwise' indicates that a fully enforceable obligation may be offered unilaterally by the developer. The rules as to the contents and formalities of such 'unilateral undertakings' are the same as those that apply to ordinary planning obligations entered into by agreement, except that the agreement of the LPA is not needed. They are also binding and enforceable in the same way.

The unilateral undertaking is designed to deal with the situation where the LPA and developer do not agree as to what should be covered by way of a planning obligation, and allows a developer to break the deadlock by offering what it believes to be acceptable terms in a unilateral undertaking. If the LPA refuses the developer's application, the developer can then appeal to the SOS against the refusal or deemed refusal of planning permission. At the appeal the unilateral undertaking will (subject to compliance with the CIL Regulations, reg 122) be taken into consideration by the inspector, which, if he considers it appropriate, may result in the grant of planning permission. Indeed, a unilateral undertaking (if given at the time of the original planning application) may dissuade the LPA from refusing planning permission in the first place.

5.5 MODIFICATION AND DISCHARGE OF PLANNING OBLIGATIONS

5.5.1 The power to modify or discharge

A planning obligation may be modified or discharged either by agreement between the LPA and the person(s) against whom it is then enforceable, or by application by such person to the LPA or an appeal to the SOS.

5.5.2 Application for modification or discharge

A person against whom a planning obligation is enforceable may, at any time after the expiry of five years from the date of the planning obligation, apply to the LPA for the obligation to have effect subject to such modifications as may be specified in the application, or to be discharged. Since 28 March 2013, an obligation entered into before 6 April 2010 may also be modified by application to the LPA (this temporarily allows more planning obligations to benefit from the opportunity of modification earlier than the expiry of five years) (s 106A(3)–(4)).

In addition, s 106BA currently entitles developers to apply to modify affordable housing requirements in a s 106 agreement relating to any scheme that is economically unviable due to the level of affordable housing required. If this is the case, the LPA must determine the application for modification so that the development becomes economically viable, including by modifying, replacing or removing the affordable housing requirement (or, if it is a lone requirement, discharging it). If the level of affordable housing required does not cause the development to be economically unviable, the LPA must determine that the affordable housing requirement remains in its current form. The developer may apply to modify an affordable housing requirement more than once under these provisions, but in relation to a second or subsequent application the mandatory duty will not apply. These new provisions only apply for a three-year period until 30 April 2016 (unless a later date is ordered by the SOS).

5.5.3 Determination of application by the LPA

In the case of an application made under s 106A, the LPA must notify the applicant of its decision within eight weeks or such longer period as may be agreed in writing between the parties. Where the application is refused, the notification must state clearly and precisely the LPA's full reasons for its decision and tell the applicant of his rights of appeal (see **5.5.4** below).

An application made to the LPA under s 106BA must be determined within 28 days (unless subordinate legislation is brought into force specifying a different period).

5.5.4 Appeal against determination (s 106B and s 106BC)

Where the LPA fails to reach a decision on a s 106A application in the eight-week period, or determines that the planning obligation shall continue to have effect without modification, the applicant may appeal to the SOS within six months of the date of the notice or deemed refusal, or such longer period as the SOS may allow.

The appeal procedure is closely modelled on that for ordinary planning appeals (see **Chapter 4**).

Where the LPA does not agree with the developer's revised proposal for affordable housing or does not determine the application for modification under s 106BA, there is a right of appeal to the SOS provided by s 106BC. This appeal must be made within six months of the deemed refusal or date of notice of the LPA's decision (unless regulations are made which prescribe a different time period).

5.6 COMMUNITY INFRASTRUCTURE LEVY

5.6.1 Fundamentals

The Community Infrastructure Levy (CIL) is a levy imposed on development in order to fund the provision of infrastructure. The purpose of CIL is to ensure that infrastructure necessary to support development within an area can be provided by the local authority. Infrastructure is widely defined in the CIL Regulations. It includes roads and transport facilities, educational facilities and recreational facilities.

The Government's continuing focus on economic growth, along with negative feedback from developers, has resulted in the CIL regime undergoing significant changes since it was first introduced, with a further review due in 2015 (whatever the outcome of the General Election). The Government has already made amendments, ranging from the rectification of errors in the formulae used to calculate CIL, to taking certain planning applications outside the scope of CIL liability all together. Many of these amendments have been made in response to feedback from developers who have provided valuable guidance to Government on how CIL has been working in practice. This section focuses on the arrangements relating to CIL contained in the current CIL Regulations in force at the time of writing.

5.6.1.1 Charging authorities

CIL is imposed by charging authorities. In England, these are district and metropolitan district councils, London borough councils, unitary authorities, national park authorities, the Broads Authority and the Mayor of London. In Wales, the county and county borough councils and the national park authorities have the power to charge CIL. In Greater London, the Mayor can charge CIL in addition to the LPA, meaning that a developer may be liable to pay two CIL charges: one imposed by the Mayor of London and one by the LPA for the area in which the development will be situated. No CIL will be payable if there is no CIL 'charging schedule' (which sets the rates payable) in force when planning permission is granted.

5.6.1.2 Rate payable

The rate payable will vary between charging authorities, which may apply different rates to different use classes of development and even different parts of their local area. For example, the Mayor of London has introduced a tiered CIL charge (so that more CIL is payable in more affluent boroughs) for the purpose of funding the Crossrail development in London. In contrast, Newark and Sherwood District Council in Nottinghamshire has applied different rates to different use classes of development in different areas across its district. Charging authorities may also set differential rates by reference to the scale of development as well as use (since 24 February 2014).

5.6.1.3   Calculating the area subject to a CIL charge

CIL is charged in pounds per square metre of gross internal area (GIA) on the net additional increase in floor space of any chargeable development. Chargeable development is the development authorised by the planning permission. There are minimum thresholds for liability which means that CIL will not be payable unless the GIA of the new build comprising the development is at least 100 square metres or a new dwelling is created.

In calculating the area in respect of which CIL payments will be charged, the GIA of existing buildings which are either to be demolished and redeveloped or which will be retained as part of the development on completion may be deducted from the GIA of the proposed development. The existing buildings must have been in lawful use for a continuous period of at least six months in the three years before the date on which planning permission first permits development where the use is not abandoned (this was extended in February 2014; previously the test was six months in the previous 12 months) (see **5.6.1.6**). The test was designed so that CIL is not required where infrastructure supporting a development is already in place. The levy will be payable in full if the previous use of the existing buildings has been abandoned, because the infrastructure required to support the development may not be in place in these circumstances.

The CIL Regulations do not adopt the definition of 'building' found in the TCPA 1990. They only set out what a building does not include. The result is that the meaning of 'building' for the purposes of the CIL Regulations is any building capable of having a GIA, except for buildings that people do not normally go into and buildings into which people go only intermittently for the purpose of inspecting or maintaining fixed plant or machinery (CIL Regulations, reg 6(2)).

5.6.1.4   Liability

The liability to pay CIL is triggered on the grant of most types of planning permission, including planning permission that is deemed granted under the Town and Country Planning (General Permitted Development) Order 1995 (as amended), permission granted under a neighbourhood development order and 'development consent' granted under the PA 2008. An important exception to CIL liability is where planning permission is granted for a limited period.

Following changes to the CIL regime made by the Government in 2012, planning permissions granted pursuant to a s 73 application no longer trigger CIL liability, except where they grant permission for an increase in floorspace or amend the proposed planning uses permitted.

Following the amendments made in 2014, new applications bringing forward only design changes to an existing scheme prior to or during its construction will not trigger a new full CIL liability for the whole development. The amount payable will be reduced by the levy already paid under the earlier permission.

5.6.1.5   Party liable to pay CIL

As with planning obligations, liability for payment of CIL runs with the land. Every person with a material interest in the land on the day planning permission first permits development (see **5.6.1.6**) is liable to pay CIL in proportion to the value of their land (where there is a chargeable development). However, the legislation envisages that in the normal course of events liability will be assumed by one person, and there is a procedure for this. Indeed, assumption of liability is a prerequisite to claiming certain exemptions and reliefs (see **5.6.2**). There is also provision allowing authorities to transfer liability to landowners in the event of non-payment. Lastly, there is provision for the transfer of liability between willing parties, and liability may be shared, although only on a joint and several basis. This means that any party may be pursued by the collecting authority in the event of non-payment.

5.6.1.6   Date on which rate payable is fixed

If CIL liability arises, the amount of CIL payable will be calculated on the date that planning permission first permits development. This date is a defined term in the CIL Regulations, and currently its meaning depends on the nature of the permission granted. If an outline planning permission is granted, the amount of CIL payable will be calculated on the date of final approval of the last reserved matter associated with the permission or relevant phase of development (if the planning permission allows phasing).

If a full permission is granted, the amount of CIL liability will be calculated on the date the last planning condition that must be discharged to allow development to commence is discharged for that permission or that phase (where the permission allows phasing). Where there are no pre-commencement conditions, the relevant time for calculating CIL for a full permission will be the date of the grant of the permission.

5.6.1.7   Figure

The figure payable will be set out by the charging authority in a notice in prescribed form. The figure will be indexed from the date the charging schedule came into effect until the date planning permission is granted. There is an appeal mechanism for resolving certain disputes, but this is limited in scope. The right to appeal must be exercised before a chargeable development is commenced.

If, when calculated, the CIL payable is less than £50 it is deemed to be zero.

5.6.1.8   Payment

Payment must be made to the collecting authority on commencement of the scheme in question.

Commencement is defined as the carrying out of a material operation in accordance with s 56(4) of the TCPA 1990. Payment of CIL may become due if planning permission is commenced by the demolition of buildings on the site (where demolition is not set out as a separate phase in the permission; see below).

Payment may be made in instalments where a charging authority has an instalment policy in place. A 60-day grace period for payment to be made is permitted in cases where a party has assumed liability for CIL. In London, special arrangements apply if either the Mayor or a London borough has an instalment policy in place.

The CIL Regulations allow payment of CIL in phases in respect of outline or full planning permissions where such permission requires or expressly permits development to be carried out in phases; each phase is treated as a separate phase of development. This enables a developer to manage its payments and does not require it to discharge its entire liability on commencement. These arrangements allow developers to avoid paying CIL in relation to site preparation (including demolition) works, where these are carried out as a separate phase. Liability to pay would arise only when a phase that involves erecting buildings (new floorspace) commences.

The CIL Regulations allow a charging authority to accept a payment in kind (eg, a developer transferring land to the charging authority as payment or part payment of CIL liability). In-kind payments can include provision of land or infrastructure (on-site or off-site), or a combination of both. The inclusion of infrastructure as an in-kind payment is intended to permit a developer to deliver infrastructure that it may be best placed to bring forward itself and reflect the cost in a reduction to the levy charge.

Under the current CIL Regulations, a charging authority may collect CIL on its own behalf and also on behalf of other charging authorities. The CIL Regulations also provide for the transfer of CIL collected by a charging authority to a third party in some circumstances. In England, where a development is in an area where a neighbourhood plan is in place or permission for it was granted by a neighbourhood development order, the charging authority must pass 25% of the CIL receipts to the parish council. In other circumstances, the charging authority must pass 15% of the CIL receipts to the parish council.

5.6.2 Exemptions and reliefs

As previously explained, CIL is a levy payable at a rate determined in accordance with the charging schedule(s) in effect in the area in which the development is located. This means that the principle and amount of liability cannot in general be disputed, and exemptions and reliefs are only available in the limited circumstances specified in the CIL Regulations.

Some exemptions and reliefs are available provided that certain conditions are met. If an exemption applies, CIL will not be chargeable. A relief may be applied at the charging authority's discretion. In all cases, the claimant must be an owner of a material interest in the relevant land that is earmarked for development in order to claim the exemption or relief.

5.6.2.1 Charitable exemption

An owner of a material interest in the relevant land will be exempt from liability to pay CIL in respect of chargeable development if that owner is a charitable institution and the chargeable development will be used wholly or mainly for charitable purposes (as defined in the CIL Regulations). The part of the development to be used for such purposes must be occupied by or under the control of a charitable institution. The owner cannot benefit from the exemption if its material interest is jointly owned with another person who is not a charitable institution.

5.6.2.2 Charitable reliefs

There are two discretionary charitable reliefs available.

The first of these may be applied in certain circumstances if the charitable exemption cannot be applied because to do so would amount to State aid.

The second relief relates to development held by a charitable institution as an investment (investment relief). An owner may be eligible for the investment relief if such relief has been made available by the charging authority in the area in which the development will be situated; the owner is a charitable institution; and the whole or greater part of the development will be held by the owner, or it and other charitable institutions, as an investment from which the profits will be applied for charitable purposes.

Neither relief can be applied if the owner of a material interest will occupy that part of the development and use it for ineligible activities (defined in the CIL Regulations).

5.6.2.3 Social housing relief

The CIL Regulations give full relief from paying the levy on a part of the chargeable development intended for social housing. In short, chargeable development that does or will comprise 'qualifying dwellings', in whole or in part, is eligible for the relief. Qualifying dwellings are those that are let by registered housing providers, social landlords or a local housing authority on a specified basis (eg, an assured tenancy), or occupied under shared ownership arrangements (provided certain terms are met).

In order to claim social housing relief, the claimant must own the land in respect of which the planning permission has been granted. It must also have assumed liability to pay CIL.

5.6.2.4 Exceptional circumstances relief

Exceptional circumstances relief is available only where a charging authority has chosen to make it available and where a planning obligation has been entered into in respect of the development, the value of which is greater than the CIL charge that would be payable, meaning that having to pay the CIL charge too would have an unacceptable impact on the economic viability of the development.

The Mayor of London has decided not to make this relief available. Other charging authorities have varied in their approach or decided to keep their position under review.

5.6.2.5 Management and recovery of exempted or relieved sums

The CIL Regulations contain provisions that manage liability in particular circumstances (eg, if land to which social housing relief has been applied is subsequently transferred to another party).

The amount by which any CIL liability has been reduced on application of an exemption or relief may be clawed back by the charging authority in certain circumstances (eg, where a social housing product later falls outside the definition of 'qualifying dwellings') for a period of seven years after commencement of the chargeable development to which the relief is applied.

5.6.3 Procedure

Strict procedures must be followed when paying CIL or in claiming an exemption or relief.

5.6.3.1 General

Assumption of liability must be made using a prescribed form. Where CIL is payable because planning permission has been granted under a general consent (such as the GPDO 1995), the collecting authority must be notified of that fact on a prescribed form. Various surcharges may be payable if procedural requirements are not complied with (see **5.6.4.1**).

5.6.3.2 Exemptions and reliefs

Claims for exemptions or reliefs must also be made on a prescribed form. Claims will lapse if the claimant carries out any activity that is inconsistent with such a claim (eg, commencing development before the claim is determined by the charging authority).

The CIL Regulations contain provisions on when and how an exemption or relief may be applied to reduce CIL liability. In general, the CIL charge should be calculated in full before an exemption or relief is applied.

5.6.4 Enforcement

The CIL Regulations impose serious penalties for non-compliance with the procedures relating to, or failure to make, payment of CIL to the collecting authority.

5.6.4.1 Surcharges and interest

Surcharges are payable in a number of circumstances, including where:

(a)   development has commenced without anyone assuming liability to pay CIL (£50, which increases to £500 if the CIL is to be apportioned between different interests);

(b)   a notice alerting a collecting authority to chargeable development having been permitted (eg, by the GPDO 1995) has not been served;

(c)   a notice of commencement of development has not been served (the lower of 20% of the chargeable amount payable in respect of that development or £2,500); or

(d)   notice has not been given by the appropriate party within the prescribed 14-day period when certain events occur (eg, where social housing products later fall outside the definition of qualifying dwellings).

Interest will be payable on any amount payable under the CIL Regulations that is not paid on the date it is due.

5.6.4.2   Penalties for non-payment of CIL and other amounts payable in respect of chargeable development

In circumstances where the collecting authority thinks it is expedient to do so, it may serve notice requiring a development to stop if an amount which is payable in respect of chargeable development has not been paid. The collecting authority must first serve a notice warning of its intention to serve a CIL stop notice. A CIL stop notice must be noted on the public register.

In cases where CIL remains unpaid, the collecting authority may pursue a number of ways to recover the sum. These include by levying distress (selling goods), which it may do if a liability order has been made by the magistrates' court in respect of the sum payable, or by application for a charging order. Where a collecting authority is unable to recover the sum by means of a charging order, a debtor may be committed to prison.

A person's liability to pay CIL on that person's death will lie with his executor, to be paid out of the estate.

5.7   CIL AND PLANNING OBLIGATIONS

One supposed advantage of the CIL regime is that it allows parties to identify, at an early stage, what contributions will be required and in what sums. However, because CIL charges are not calculated or capable of being calculated until the time planning permission first permits development, a developer will in practice be required to estimate its actual CIL liability. The time when CIL is calculated may be some way in the future (especially in the case of phased planning permissions), by which time a CIL charging schedule may have been amended or replaced.

The charging schedule should be prepared and consulted upon by the LPA alongside an up-to-date development plan; it must also be subject to examination in public before it can be adopted.

Ultimately, the Government hopes that the new system will replace the use of the planning obligation in the majority of cases. From the date of an LPA adopting its charging schedule or 6 April 2015, whichever is the earlier, use of the planning obligation will be more restricted. The date was extended from 2014 to 2015 to reflect initial inertia in adopting CIL and to allow authorities to respond to recent amendments to the CIL Regulations.

The CIL Regulations (as amended in 2014) also limit the use of Highways Agreements (made under s 278 of the Highways Act 1980) so that they cannot be used to fund infrastructure for which CIL is earmarked.

From the relevant date, a planning obligation may not constitute a reason for granting planning permission for development to the extent that the obligation provides for the funding or provision of relevant infrastructure. The CIL Regulations will also prevent use of more than five s 106 obligations to fund a specified piece of infrastructure.

However, for certain contributions, the s 106 obligation will remain the appropriate mechanism even under the CIL regime. This is the case for some site-specific impact mitigation requirements, and for all affordable housing. The charging authority may recalculate CIL when the provision of affordable housing is varied (since the 2014 amendments) (see **5.5.2**).

The relationship between CIL and s 106 obligations has attracted some critical comment from the developer community. The CIL Regulations require the charging authority to use CIL to fund infrastructure specified in the CIL charging schedule. However, the charging schedule may be changed at will by the charging authority. In addition, there is no obligation to bring forward any infrastructure within a particular period. This leaves developers with the risk that infrastructure necessary for their development may not be provided. Moreover, developers to date have not perceived much significant change in the way LPAs negotiate s 106 agreements to take account of CIL, which leaves developers in a difficult negotiating position and ultimately serves only to increase the financial burden for any development to bear. Charging authorities must produce the list of infrastructure to which CIL would be applied at an early stage so that it is available to scrutinise at the examination into a charging authority's draft CIL charging schedule.

5.8 PRACTICAL POINTS

In view of the law and guidance above, the following points should be borne in mind when drafting and negotiating a planning obligation.

5.8.1 By the LPA

(a) It is important that the title to the land is thoroughly investigated before the LPA enters into the planning obligation. All parties with a legal interest in the land should be made parties to it, including any persons with existing interests (such as a prior mortgagee); otherwise the obligation may not be enforceable against a successor in title to that interest.

(b) The future exercise of any of the LPA's statutory powers should not be fettered by the obligation. If this does occur and the obligation is later challenged in court, it could invalidate the planning obligation (see *Royal Borough of Windsor and Maidenhead v Brandrose Investments* [1983] 1 WLR 509, CA).

(c) The planning obligation should be executed either before, or simultaneously with, the grant of the planning permission, otherwise the developer may have the benefit of the permission without being bound by the obligation.

(d) The timing of related infrastructure agreements should be considered carefully. It will normally be preferable, where possible, to have all related agreements (eg agreements under the Highways Act 1980) executed at the same time as the planning obligation.

(e) Consideration should be given as to whether the obligation ought, in the circumstances of the case, to provide that liability under the obligation will cease once the owner of the interest parts with it. In the absence of such a provision, liability will continue against the original covenantor(s).

(f) If there is a disagreement about the inclusion of a particular term in the planning obligation, the LPA should consider whether it is within the guidance contained in the NPPF. If it is doubtful, or may be considered excessive, the LPA may find that the developer will appeal and offer a unilateral undertaking on the appeal (see further **5.6**).

(g) Consideration should also be given as to whether a clause should be included providing for payment of the LPA's costs in connection with the negotiation, drafting and execution of the planning obligation. If there is no such clause, the LPA will have to bear its own costs.

(h) Consideration should be given to any potential restriction in the CIL Regulations on the use of a s 106 agreement and to the amount of any CIL charge to be paid in respect of the proposed development.

5.8.2 By the developer

(a) The draft planning permission should be included in one of the schedules to the obligation so that it is clear from the terms of the obligation what conditions, etc will be attached to the planning permission.

(b) The developer should try to ensure that the terms of the obligation do not continue to bind after he has sold his interest to a successor. This is particularly important where positive covenants in the obligation are likely to continue well into the future and if lenders are involved in the transaction.

(c)   The developer should attempt to have a clause inserted to the effect that the planning obligation will be discharged or cease to have effect if the planning permission expires or is revoked, or if planning permission is later granted for some other development which is incompatible with that originally granted.

(d)   The obligation should not contain a covenant to comply with the conditions attached to the related planning permission. If there is such a covenant and the conditions on the planning permission are subsequently varied (under s 73 or s 73A, see **4.4.3**), or the permission lapses or is revoked, the conditions will continue to bind the land by virtue of the covenant in the planning obligation; such a covenant is in any case unnecessary since conditions can be enforced directly.

(e)   Covenants should be avoided which impose obligations (in particular, positive ones) which take effect as soon as the planning obligation is executed (as opposed to when the planning permission is implemented). There may be a gap of quite a few months, if not a few years, between the developer obtaining the permission and being in a position to implement it and, in some cases, the permission may never be implemented so the developer should not be bound to perform the obligations.

(f)   The developer should consider his potential CIL liability and whether he can lawfully restrict payment of planning obligations to reflect such liability.

REVIEW ACTIVITY

1.   An LPA intends to require a developer to contribute to the construction costs of a new roundabout that will be needed as a result of the developer's proposals. Could the LPA do this by way of a condition attached to the planning permission?

2.   Assume that the LPA intends instead to embody the obligation to contribute towards the cost of the roundabout mentioned in Question 1 in a planning obligation. What are the relevant factors to consider if acting for a developer?

3.   Do you think the LPA would be acting reasonably if the background to the situation in Question 1 is that local traffic is already busy and the roundabout is already really needed: the developer's proposal has merely made the need particularly pressing?

4.   The developer mentioned in Question 1 currently has an option to buy the land he wishes to develop. Does this mean that there needs to be another party to the planning obligation?

5.   What steps would you take to protect any additional party identified in answer to Question 4 in respect of the obligation to contribute towards the costs of the roundabout?

Answers to this Review activity may be found in Appendix 1.

ENFORCEMENT OF PLANNING CONTROL

6.1	Introduction	69
6.2	Definitions and time limits	69
6.3	Certificates of lawful use or development (ss 191–192)	70
6.4	Right of entry for enforcement purposes (ss 196A–196C)	72
6.5	Planning contravention notice (ss 171C–171D)	72
6.6	Breach of condition notice (s 187A)	73
6.7	Enforcement notice (ss 172–182)	74
6.8	Stop notice and temporary stop notice (ss 183–187 and ss 171E–171G)	78
6.9	Injunctions (s 187B)	80
6.10	Appeals against enforcement notices (ss 174–177)	80
	Review activity	82

6.1 INTRODUCTION

It is not generally an offence in itself to be in breach of planning control. It is only if an LPA takes enforcement action which is not complied with that an offence arises. There are exceptions to this rule, for instance where unauthorised works are done to a listed building, where there is a breach of a tree preservation order, or where an unlisted building in a conservation area is demolished without planning permission (or, prior to 1 October 2013, without conservation area consent). Even if an LPA becomes aware of a breach, it has discretion whether to act: it may choose not to do so. If it does, Pt VII of the TCPA 1990 (ss 171–196) gives wide powers as follows:

(a)   a right of entry;

(b)   service of a planning contravention notice;

(c)   service of a breach of condition notice;

(d)   service of an enforcement notice;

(e)   service of a stop notice; and

(f)   injunction.

Each of these powers will be considered in turn, but first it is necessary to set out some basic definitions and time limits which apply to enforcement generally, and to consider certificates of lawful use or development which can provide proof of immunity from enforcement action. (Unless stated otherwise, references in this chapter are to the TCPA 1990.)

6.2 DEFINITIONS AND TIME LIMITS

6.2.1 Definitions (s 171A)

For the purposes of the Act:

(a)   a 'breach of planning control' occurs when development is carried out without the requisite planning permission, or when any condition or limitation attached to a permission is not complied with;

(b)   'taking enforcement action' means the issue of an enforcement notice or the service of a breach of condition notice.

6.2.2   Time limits (s 171B)

The LPA can take enforcement action only if it does so within the appropriate time limits. There are two of these:

(a)   Where the breach of planning control consists of:

(i)   operational development carried out without planning permission; or

(ii)   a change of use of any building to use as a single dwelling house;

the LPA must take enforcement action within four years from the date on which the operations were substantially completed or the change of use occurred (as the case may be). Note the case of *Sage v Secretary of State for the Environment, Transport and the Regions* [2003] 1 WLR 983 for its commentary on the meaning of 'substantially completed'.

(b)   With all other breaches (ie any material change of use other than to use as a single dwelling house and any breach of condition or limitation attached to a planning permission) no enforcement action may be brought after the expiry of 10 years from the date of the breach.

As regards both of the above time limits, see the provisions of s 171B(4)(b) at **6.7.3**.

Provisions in the LA 2011 that came into force on 6 April 2012 affect the strict time limits set out above by amending the TCPA 1990. Section 171BA permits an LPA to take enforcement action for an apparent breach of planning control even if the periods specified in s 171B have expired. An LPA must apply to the magistrates' court for an order (a 'planning enforcement order') entitling the LPA to take such action. The order may be made by the court only if it is satisfied on a balance of probabilities that the apparent breach has been deliberately concealed, which is a term that is not defined. The enactment of these provisions follows cases such as *Welwyn Hatfield Council v the Secretary of State* [2011] 4 All ER 851 and *R (on the application of Fidler) v Secretary of State for Communities and Local Government* [2011] EWCA Civ 1159, where in each case the construction of a residential dwelling was concealed.

The ability of an LPA to take enforcement action outside the limits defined in s 171B is a factor that may need to be considered when advising the purchaser of a property.

6.3   CERTIFICATES OF LAWFUL USE OR DEVELOPMENT (ss 191–192)

Historically, expiry of the time limit for enforcement rendered the breach of planning control immune from enforcement but it did not make the development 'lawful'. This meant that rights (such as those given by the GPDO 1995) that depend on lawfulness (as opposed to mere immunity) could not be enjoyed. It is now provided that breaches become lawful if:

(a)   the relevant time limit for enforcement has passed; and

(b)   the use, operation or breach of condition is not being carried on in contravention of a current enforcement notice.

It will make a property more marketable if a seller is able to provide proof of such lawfulness to a buyer. The Act provides a mechanism to obtain proof that an existing or proposed use or development is lawful.

6.3.1   Existing development (s 191)

'Any person' (which could include a prospective buyer) who wishes to ascertain the lawfulness of any existing use, operation or breach of a condition or limitation may apply to the LPA specifying the land and describing the use, operations or other matter (s 191(1)) in question. This is a 'certificate of lawful existing use or development' (CLEUD).

6.3.1.1 Onus of proof

The onus of proof is on the applicant, who must prove the lawfulness on a balance of probabilities. The planning merits of the case (ie whether or not the development is desirable) are irrelevant; the sole question in issue is whether or not, as a matter of evidence and law, the use or development described in the application is lawful.

6.3.1.2 Issue of CLEUD

If the LPA is satisfied of the lawfulness at the time of the application of the use, etc, it must issue a certificate. In any other case it must refuse one; note, though, that a refusal merely indicates that the matter has not been proved on a balance of probabilities.

6.3.1.3 Effect of CLEUD

The lawfulness of any use, operations, etc for which a certificate is in force shall be conclusively presumed. Thus, no enforcement action may be brought in respect of the matters stated as lawful in the certificate.

6.3.2 Proposed development (s 192)

Any person who wishes to ascertain the lawfulness of any proposed use or operational development of land can apply to the LPA, specifying the land and describing the use or operations in question.

The lawfulness of any use or operations stated in the certificate shall be conclusively presumed unless there is a material change, before the proposed use or operations are started, in any of the matters relevant to the determination.

6.3.3 General provisions applying to certificates of lawful use or development

A certificate may be issued in respect of part only of the land or just some of the matters specified in the application (s 193(4)), or, with existing development, may be issued in terms which differ from those specified in the application (s 191(4)).

The LPA must enter prescribed details of any applications and decisions in its s 69 register (s 193(6)), and must notify the applicant of its decision within eight weeks or such longer period as may be agreed in writing between the parties (DMPO 2010, art 35).

6.3.3.1 Appeals

The applicant can appeal to the Secretary of State for Communities and Local Government (SOS) against a refusal, a refusal in part or a deemed refusal (ie where the LPA fails to determine the application within the relevant time). The time limit is six months from the date of notification of the decision or the deemed refusal.

A further legal challenge can be made to the High Court within six weeks of the decision of the SOS on procedural grounds rather than on the merits (see s 288 of the Act).

6.3.3.2 Offences

It is an offence for any person to procure a particular decision on an application by knowingly or recklessly making a statement which is misleading or false in a material particular, or (with intent to deceive) using a document which is false or misleading in a material particular or withholding any material information.

If a statement was made or a document was used which was false or misleading in a material particular, or if any material information was withheld (whether or not this was done knowingly or recklessly or with intent to deceive), the LPA may revoke the certificate.

6.4   RIGHT OF ENTRY FOR ENFORCEMENT PURPOSES (ss 196A–196C)

6.4.1   Right of entry without a warrant

Any person duly authorised in writing by the LPA may enter any land at any reasonable hour without a warrant to:

(a)   ascertain whether there is or has been any breach of planning control on that or any other land; or

(b)   determine whether any enforcement power should be exercised and, if so, how; or

(c)   ascertain whether there has been compliance with any enforcement power that has been exercised.

There must, however, be 'reasonable grounds' for doing so, ie entry must be the logical means of obtaining the information in question.

In the case of a dwelling house (which includes any residential accommodation in, say, a commercial building), 24 hours' notice of the intended entry must be given to the occupier. This requirement does not apply, however, to land or outbuildings in the curtilage of the house.

6.4.2   Power to enter under a warrant

A justice of the peace may issue a warrant to any person duly authorised as stated at **6.4.1** for any of the purposes listed above, if he is satisfied on sworn information in writing that:

(a)   there are reasonable grounds for entering for the purpose in question; and

(b)   admission has been refused, or it is reasonably apprehended that it will be refused, or it is an urgent case. Entry is deemed to be refused if no reply is received within a reasonable time to a request for admission.

Entry under a warrant must be at a reasonable hour (except in cases of urgency) and must be within one month from the date of issue of the warrant. Each warrant authorises one entry only.

6.4.3   Restrictions and offences

The person entering the land must produce his authority and state the purpose of his entry, if requested, and may take with him such other persons as may be necessary (eg policeman, expert, etc). On leaving the land, if the owner or occupier is not then present, he must ensure that the land is as secured against trespassers as when he entered.

Anyone who wilfully obstructs a person exercising a lawful right of entry is guilty of an offence.

6.5   PLANNING CONTRAVENTION NOTICE (ss 171C–171D)

A planning contravention notice (PCN) (rather than the right of entry) is the principal power available to an LPA for obtaining information needed for enforcement purposes.

6.5.1   Contents of a PCN

There is no prescribed form of PCN, although a model is suggested in the 'ensuring effective enforcement' section of the online National Planning Practice Guidance (NPPG).

Section 171C states that a PCN may require the person on whom it is served to give any information specified in the notice in respect of any operations, use or activities being carried out on the land and any matter relating to conditions or limitations attached to an existing permission. In particular, it may require the person served, so far as he is able, to:

(a)   state whether the land is being used as alleged in the notice, or whether alleged operations or activities are or have been carried out;

(b)   state when any use, operation or activity began;

(c)   give particulars of any person known to use or have used the land for any purpose, or to be carrying out or have carried out any operations or activities;

(d)   give any information he holds about any relevant planning permission, or to state why planning permission is not required;

(e)   state his interest (if any) in the land and the name and address of any person he knows to have an interest in the land.

A PCN may also give notice of a time and place at which the LPA will consider:

(a)   any offer from the person served to apply for planning permission, or to refrain from operations or activities, or to undertake remedial work; and

(b)   any representations he may wish to make about the notice.

If the notice states this, the LPA must give him the opportunity to make the offer or representations at that time and place.

By s 171C(5), a PCN must warn the person served that if he fails to reply, enforcement action may be taken and he may be deprived of compensation if a stop notice is served.

6.5.2   The person served

A PCN may be served on anyone who is the owner or occupier of the land to which the notice relates, or who has any other interest in it, or on anyone who is carrying out operations on the land or using it for any purpose (s 171C(1)).

It is an offence for any person served with a PCN to fail to reply to it within 21 days unless he has a reasonable excuse. The offence is a continuing one, even after conviction (s 171D(2)–(4)).

It is also an offence knowingly or recklessly to make a statement in a purported reply which is false or misleading in a material particular (s 171D(5)–(6)).

6.5.3   Effect of a PCN

Apart from the consequences mentioned above, service of a PCN does not affect the exercise of any other enforcement power available to the LPA.

6.6   BREACH OF CONDITION NOTICE (s 187A)

A breach of condition notice (BCN) is primarily intended as an alternative remedy to an enforcement notice where the LPA desires to secure compliance with conditions or limitations attached to an existing planning permission. It has the big advantage that, unlike an enforcement notice, there is no right of appeal against the service of such a notice (see **6.7.1**).

6.6.1   When and on whom a BCN may be served

Where there has been a breach of condition or limitation attached to an existing permission, the LPA may serve a BCN on any person who is carrying out or has carried out the development, or on any person having control of the land.

6.6.2   Contents of a BCN

The BCN must specify the steps which the LPA considers ought to be taken or the activities which ought to cease in order to secure compliance with the conditions, etc specified in the notice. Where, however, a notice is served on a person who has control of the land but who is not carrying (or has not carried) out the development, it can only require compliance with any conditions regulating the use of the land.

The notice must also specify a period for compliance, which must not be less than 28 days from the date of service of the notice.

6.6.3 Effect of a BCN

Unlike an enforcement notice, there is no right of appeal against service of a BCN.

If the person served has not remedied the breach by the time specified in the notice (or by the time specified in any further notice served by the LPA), he is guilty of an offence: the offence is a continuing one. It is a defence, however, for the person served to prove that he took all reasonable measures to ensure compliance with the notice or, if he was served as the person having control of the land, that he did not have control at the time he was served.

6.7   ENFORCEMENT NOTICE (ss 172–182)

6.7.1   Introduction

The enforcement notice was intended as the primary method of enforcement of breaches of planning control, and it is the most flexible in that it can be used to address any kind of breach. It is possible to appeal against the service of an enforcement notice, the detail of which is considered at the end of this chapter. For the moment it should be noted that if an enforcement notice is appealed, it ceases to be effective until the appeal is determined.

6.7.2   Issue of enforcement notice

By s 172(1), an LPA may issue an enforcement notice where it appears to the LPA that there has been a breach of planning control and that it is expedient to issue the notice having regard to the provisions of its development plan and any other material considerations. Issue of an enforcement notice is the most commonly used method of enforcement.

6.7.2.1   Prerequisites to issue

There must be an apparent breach of planning control and it must be expedient to issue an enforcement notice.

Apparent breach of planning control

There is no duty on the LPA to satisfy itself that there is a breach (see, eg, *Tidswell v Secretary of State for the Environment* [1977] JPL 104), although with the powers now available, in particular the right to serve a PCN (see **6.5**), it may be required to do some preliminary research before issuing an enforcement notice.

It must be expedient to issue an enforcement notice

The LPA should not automatically issue an enforcement notice whenever there appears to be a breach of planning control. It must consider its development plan and any other material considerations (which will include advice in the National Planning Policy Framework (NPPF) and NPPG). The provisions of the European Convention on Human Rights will also be relevant.

Paragraph 207 of the NPPF provides guidance to LPAs on this matter, accepting that enforcement action is important as a means of maintaining public confidence in the planning system and stating that enforcement action is discretionary and LPAs should act proportionately in responding to suspected breaches. The NPPG advises that, when deciding whether enforcement action should be taken, the LPA should have regard (where relevant) to the potential impact of the proposed action on the health, housing needs and welfare of those affected by the proposed action and those affected by the breach of planning control.

6.7.2.2   Challenging the issue or failure to issue

A decision to issue an enforcement notice cannot be challenged unless the decision was arbitrary or capricious (see, eg, *Donovan v Secretary of State for the Environment* [1988] JPL 118).

Equally, a decision not to issue an enforcement notice is not challengeable unless the decision is arbitrary or capricious (see *Perry v Stanborough (Developments) Ltd* [1978] JPL 36).

6.7.3 Time limits

An enforcement notice must be issued (though not necessarily served) within the relevant time limit as defined in s 171B. Failure to do so will render the breach lawful, subject to any action the LPA may take under s 171BA (see **6.2.2**).

However, by s 171B(4)(b), an LPA is not prevented from taking further enforcement action in respect of a breach of planning control if, during the four years prior to the new action being taken, the LPA has taken or purported to take enforcement action in respect of that breach. This would enable an LPA, for example, to serve another enforcement notice within four years of one which had been withdrawn or set aside on an appeal (see **6.7.8** and **6.10**).

6.7.4 Contents of an enforcement notice (s 173)

No statutory form is prescribed, but the notice must comply with the following:

(a)   it must state the matters alleged to constitute the breach of planning control in such a way as to enable the person served to know what those matters are, and must state the paragraph of s 171A(1) (development without permission or breach of condition/limitation – see **6.2.1**) within which, in the opinion of the LPA, the breach falls (s 173(1) and (2));

(b)   it must specify the steps to be taken or the activities to be discontinued in order to achieve wholly or partly the remedying of the breach or of any injury to amenity caused by the breach (s 173(3) and (4)). Examples of requirements that may be included are given in s 173(5)–(7) and include:

    (i)   alteration or removal of buildings or works,

    (ii)   carrying out of any building or other operations,

    (iii)   cessation of any activity except to the extent permitted by the notice,

    (iv)   modification of the contour of any deposit of refuse or waste,

    (v)   construction of a replacement building after unauthorised demolition;

(c)   it must state the calendar date on which the notice is to take effect, which must be at least 28 days from service of the notice (s 173(8));

(d)   it must state the period within which any steps specified in the notice are to be taken and may specify different periods for different steps (s 173(9));

(e)   it must state such additional matters as may be prescribed. These are set out in the Town and Country Planning (Enforcement Notices and Appeals) (England) Regulations 2002 (SI 2002/2682), regs 4 and 5, which require that the notice:

    (i)   states the reasons why the LPA considered it expedient to issue the enforcement notice. This is intended to enable appellants to direct their minds to relevant issues (see online NPPG),

    (ii)   specifies all policies and proposals in the development plan which are relevant to the decision to issue an enforcement notice; and

    (iii)   defines the precise boundaries of the site by reference to a plan or otherwise (see online NPPG).

The relevant regulations in Wales are the Town and Country Planning (Enforcement Notices and Appeals) (Wales) Regulations 2003 (SI 2003/394).

The notice must be accompanied by an explanatory note, which must include the following:

(a)   a copy of ss 171A, 171B and 172 to 177, or a summary of those sections including the following information—

    (i)   that there is a right to appeal to the SOS;

(ii)   details of how to make the appeal by sending notice to the SOS, including the deadlines;

(iii)   the grounds on which an appeal may be brought under s 174;

(iv)   the fee payable in relation to the deemed application for planning permission for the development alleged to be in breach of planning control in the enforcement notice (see **6.10.4.1** below);

(b)   notification that an appellant must submit a statement in writing specifying the grounds on which he is appealing and stating briefly the facts on which he proposes to rely, and that this must be submitted with the notice of appeal or within 14 days from the date on which the SOS sends a notice requiring this;

(c)   a list of the names and addresses of the persons on whom a copy of the enforcement notice has been served.

6.7.5   Service

6.7.5.1   Persons to be served

The enforcement notice must be served on:

(a)   the owner – this term is defined in s 336(1) as being the person (other than a mortgagee not in possession) who is entitled to receive a rack (ie full) rent, or who would be so entitled if the land were let; and

(b)   the occupier – this includes any person occupying by virtue of a lease or tenancy, but may also extend to licensees if their occupation resembles that of a tenant (see *Stevens v Bromley London Borough Council* [1972] 2 WLR 605, CA); and

(c)   any other person having an interest in the land, being an interest which, in the opinion of the LPA, is likely to be materially affected by the notice – this would include, in particular, known mortgagees.

6.7.5.2   Time for service

The notice must be served not more than 28 days after its issue and not less than 28 days before the date specified in the notice as the date on which it is to take effect. Failure to comply with these provisions is a ground for appeal to the SOS and, in general, is challengeable only in that way (s 285(1) and see *R v Greenwich London Borough Council, ex p Patel* [1985] JPL 851, CA; see also **6.10**).

6.7.6   Validity of notice

An error or defect in an enforcement notice may render it either a nullity or invalid.

6.7.6.1   Nullity

The notice will be a nullity only where there is a major defect on the face of it, for example where it does not state what the alleged breach is, what must be done to put it right or on what date the notice takes effect. The notice will also be a nullity if it does not fairly and reasonably tell the recipient what he must do to remedy the breach.

If the notice is a nullity it is of no effect. This is therefore a complete defence to any prosecution brought for non-compliance with it. In addition, there is technically no right of appeal to the SOS under s 174, although in practice, an appeal will normally be made at which the SOS may find as a preliminary issue that the notice is a nullity and that he therefore has no jurisdiction to hear the appeal. Any such finding may be challenged by the LPA by way of judicial review.

6.7.6.2   Invalidity

Other defects, errors or misdescriptions in an enforcement notice do not render it a nullity. In such a case, it can be challenged only by way of appeal under s 174 (see s 285 and **6.10**).

On a s 174 appeal, the SOS may correct such defects, etc, or vary the terms of the notice if satisfied that this will not cause injustice to either the appellant or the LPA (s 176(2)). This means that defects in a notice that might otherwise have resulted in its being quashed may be overcome and the notice upheld.

6.7.7 Effect of enforcement notice

An enforcement notice does not have to require restoration of the status quo, ie under-enforcement is possible. Where a notice could have required buildings or works to be removed or an activity to cease but does not do so, and the notice is complied with, then planning permission is deemed to have been given under s 73A (see **4.4.3**) for those buildings, works or activities (s 173(11)).

Similarly, where an enforcement notice requires construction of a replacement building and is complied with, planning permission is deemed to have been given (s 173(12)).

Where a notice has become effective and has not been complied with, the then owner is guilty of an offence. In addition, the LPA may enter the land and take the steps required by the notice, and recover its expenses of so doing.

6.7.8 Variation and withdrawal

The LPA may withdraw, or waive or relax any requirement of an enforcement notice whether or not it has become effective. If it does so, it must immediately notify everyone who was served with the enforcement notice, or who would have been served if it had been re-issued.

Note that the withdrawal of the notice (but not the waiver or relaxation of any requirement in it) does not affect the power of the LPA to issue a further enforcement notice in respect of the same breach.

6.7.9 Non-compliance with notice

6.7.9.1 Offences

Where the notice has become effective and any step required by the notice has not been taken or any activity required to cease is being carried on, the then owner is in breach and is liable on summary conviction to a fine of up to £20,000 or, on indictment, an unlimited amount. The court in assessing any fine must take into account any financial benefit or potential benefit accruing or likely to accrue as a result of the offence (s 179(1), (2), (8) and (9)). Note that the burden of proving ownership is on the prosecutor.

Any person (other than the owner) who has control of, or an interest in, the land must not carry on, or permit to be carried on, any activity required by the notice to cease. If he does so, he is guilty of an offence (s 179(4) and (5)).

Where a conviction for breach of an enforcement notice is secured, local authorities may also use the Proceeds of Crime Act 2002 to bring confiscation proceedings to recover an amount equivalent to the value of the benefit the offender has obtained from the criminal conduct. See *R v Del Basso and Another* [2010] EWCA Crim 1119.

6.7.9.2 Defences

It is a defence for the owner to show that he did everything he could be expected to do to secure compliance (s 179(3)).

It is also a defence for the person charged to show that he was not served with the enforcement notice, and that it was not entered in the s 188 register (in which LPAs are required to note all enforcement and stop notices) and that he did not know of the existence of the notice (s 179(7)).

It is no defence to show that the notice was defective because it failed to comply with s 173(2) (see **6.7.4**), although it would be a defence to show that the notice was a nullity (see **6.7.6.1**) or that the LPA exceeded its powers.

6.7.9.3   Action by the LPA

After any period for compliance with an enforcement notice has passed and the notice has not been fully complied with, the LPA, in addition to prosecuting, may enter the land and take any steps required by the notice. It may then recover any reasonable expenses incurred from the owner of the land at that time (s 178(1)).

Where the breach is a continuing one, the LPA may seek an injunction, whether or not after any conviction (s 187B, see **6.9**).

6.8   STOP NOTICE AND TEMPORARY STOP NOTICE (ss 183–187 AND ss 171E–171G)

6.8.1   Introduction

An enforcement notice cannot become effective earlier than 28 days after service, and its effect is suspended until final determination of any appeal (but subject to any court order to the contrary). As such, it may be many months before the LPA can take steps to enforce it other than by way of an injunction. In the meantime, local amenity may suffer detriment because of the continuing breach. Accordingly, the Act provides for the possibility of a stop notice to be served, to bring activities in breach of planning control to an end before the enforcement notice takes effect.

A stop notice cannot be served as a method of enforcement action in its own right, which effectively forces an LPA to serve an enforcement notice before doing so. The temporary stop notice procedure was introduced to deal with this issue. It is a free-standing form of stop notice but it lasts for no more than 28 days. This will give the LPA time to investigate the matter further and decide what, if any, action it wishes to take.

Stop notices and temporary stop notices will be considered in turn, but in both cases it should be noted that they cannot be used to stop use as a dwelling house or any activity that has been carried out for a period of more than four years at the date of the service of the notice.

6.8.2   Stop notice

6.8.2.1   General

Where an LPA considers it expedient to prevent, before the expiry of the period for compliance, any activity specified in the enforcement notice, it may serve a stop notice (s 183(1) and (2)). Details of this should be entered in the register of enforcement and stop notices kept under s 188.

6.8.2.2   Contents

The stop notice must refer to the enforcement notice and must have a copy of it annexed. It must also state the date on which it will take effect, being at least three days and not more than 28 days after service of the notice. An earlier date may be specified if the LPA considers that there are special reasons and a statement of those reasons is served with the notice (s 184(1)–(3)).

6.8.2.3   Service

A stop notice may be served with the enforcement notice or subsequently, but must be served before the enforcement notice takes effect (s 183(1) and (3)).

It must be served on any person who appears to have an interest in the land or to be engaged in any activity prohibited by the enforcement notice (s 183(6)).

Where a stop notice has been served, the LPA may also display a 'site notice' on the land concerned, stating that a stop notice has been served, giving its details and stating that any person contravening it may be prosecuted.

6.8.2.4 Offences

Any person who contravenes a stop notice (or causes or permits its contravention) after a site notice has been displayed or after he has been served with the stop notice is guilty of an offence which is punishable in the same way as for enforcement notices (including the taking into account of any financial benefit, see **6.7.9.1**).

It is a defence to prove that the stop notice was not served on him and that he did not know, and could not reasonably be expected to know, of its existence.

6.8.2.5 Withdrawal

By ss 183(7) and 184(7), the LPA may at any time withdraw a stop notice without prejudice to its power to serve another one. If it does withdraw a stop notice, it must serve notice of this on everyone who was served with the original stop notice and, if a site notice was displayed, display a notice of withdrawal in place of the site notice. Compensation may then become payable (see **6.8.2.6**).

6.8.2.6 Compensation

The LPA is liable to pay compensation in respect of any prohibition in a stop notice if:

(a)   the enforcement notice is quashed on any ground other than that in s 174(2)(a) (see **6.10.1**); or

(b)   the enforcement notice is varied other than under s 174(2)(a) so that the activity would no longer have fallen within the stop notice; or

(c)   the enforcement notice is withdrawn otherwise than in consequence of a grant of planning permission or of permission to retain or continue the development without complying with a condition or limitation attached to a previous permission; or

(d)   the stop notice is withdrawn.

No compensation is payable:

(a)   if the enforcement notice is quashed or varied on the ground in s 174(2)(a); or

(b)   in respect of any activity which, when the stop notice was in effect, constituted or contributed to a breach of planning control; or

(c)   in respect of any loss or damage which could have been avoided if the claimant had provided the information when required to do so under s 171C (ie a PCN, see **6.5**).

Compensation is payable to the person who, when the stop notice was first served, had an interest in or occupied the relevant land. The amount payable is that loss or damage which is directly attributable to the prohibition in the notice, and can include any sum payable for breach of contract caused by compliance with the stop notice.

Any claim must be made within 12 months of the date compensation became payable (ie the date on which the enforcement notice was quashed, varied, etc). In the event of a dispute as to the amount, the matter must be referred to the Lands Tribunal.

6.8.3 Temporary stop notice

A temporary stop notice may be served where the LPA thinks there has been a breach of planning control and that it is expedient that the activity or any part of it should be stopped immediately. Any person who contravenes a stop notice (or causes or permits its contravention) after a site notice has been displayed or after he has been served with the stop notice is guilty of an offence which is punishable in the same way as for enforcement notices (including the taking into account of any financial benefit, see **6.7.9.1**).

Compensation is payable by the LPA if a temporary stop notice is served in respect of any activity which is authorised by a planning permission or development order, or in respect of which a CLEUD (see **6.3**) is issued or if the LPA withdraws the notice. The latter is not available if the LPA grants planning permission in respect of the alleged breach.

6.9   INJUNCTIONS (s 187B)

An LPA may apply to the High Court or county court for an injunction if it considers it necessary or expedient to restrain an actual or apprehended breach of planning control. It may do this whether or not it has used, or proposes to use, any of its other enforcement powers under the Act.

Whether an injunction is granted and, if so, its terms are entirely a matter for the discretion of the court as the remedy is an equitable one. Thus, an LPA will need to show not only that the remedy is expedient and necessary, but also that it has taken into account all relevant considerations in coming to that decision, that there is a clear breach or a clear likelihood of a breach, and that the remedy is the most appropriate one in the circumstances of the case. (For good illustrations, see *Croydon London Borough Council v Gladden* [1994] JPL 723, CA, at 729ff; *Harborough District Council v Wheatcroft & Son Ltd* [1996] JPL B128; and *Hambleton District Council v Bird* [1995] 3 PLR 8.)

6.10   APPEALS AGAINST ENFORCEMENT NOTICES (ss 174–177)

6.10.1   Grounds of appeal

Section 174(2) lists seven grounds of appeal, as follows:

(a)   Planning permission ought to be granted, or any condition or limitation attached to an existing permission ought to be discharged (as the case may be) in respect of the matters alleged to be a breach of planning control in the enforcement notice.

(b)   The matters alleged have not occurred.

(c)   The matters, if they occurred, do not amount to a breach of planning control.

(d)   No enforcement action could be taken at the date the notice was issued as regards the matters alleged in it (ie the LPA was out of time, see **6.2.2**).

(e)   Copies of the enforcement notice were not served as required by s 172 (see **6.7.5**).

(f)   The steps required by the notice or the activities required to cease exceed what is necessary to remedy any breach of planning control or injury to amenity (as the case may be).

(g)   The period specified in the notice for the taking of steps, etc falls short of what should reasonably be allowed.

Note also the following points:

(i)   If ground (a) is expressly made a ground of appeal, the SOS may grant planning permission in determining the appeal, but this is the only circumstance in which he may do so (s 177(1C)).

(ii)   As regards ground (e), the SOS may disregard failure to serve any person if that failure has not caused substantial prejudice to that person or to the appellant (s 175(5)).

(iii)   Grounds (f) and (g) do not go to the validity of the enforcement notice and the SOS may vary the requirements of the original notice (s 176(1)).

6.10.2 Time limit (s 174(3))

Written notice of appeal (which can be by letter, although the standard form supplied by the DCLG is normally used) must be given to the SOS before the date on which the enforcement notice takes effect. There is no power for the SOS or the court to extend the time limit for appealing.

Note that if the notice is sent to the proper address by pre-paid post at such time that, in the ordinary course of post (two working days in the case of first-class post), it would have been delivered before the enforcement notice takes effect, the appeal will be in time even if it is delayed in the post (s 174(3)(b)).

6.10.3 Who may appeal? (s 174(1) and (6))

Any person having an interest in the land (whether served with the enforcement notice or not) may appeal, as may any person who was occupying the land under a licence at the time the notice was issued and continues to occupy the land when the appeal is brought.

6.10.4 Procedure

6.10.4.1 Documentation and fees to be submitted

By s 174(4), and reg 6 of the Town and Country Planning (Enforcement Notices and Appeals) (England) Regulations 2002, the applicant may submit with the notice of appeal a statement in writing specifying the grounds on which he is appealing and stating briefly the facts in support of those grounds. If he does not submit this with the appeal, he must do so within 14 days of being required to do so by notice from the SOS. It is important for the appellant to specify all the grounds on which he wishes to rely as amendments adding additional grounds are unlikely to be allowed subsequently.

As there is a deemed application for planning permission, whether or not the applicant also specifies ground (a), a fee is payable.

The fee is refundable in certain circumstances (eg if the appeal is allowed on grounds (b) to (e), or if the enforcement notice is quashed or found to be invalid).

6.10.4.2 Appeal forum

There are three possible procedures for the determination of an appeal: written representations, hearings and inquiries. PINS will decide which procedure an appeal should follow, but will take into account the views of the appellant and the LPA. Its decision will be based on indicative criteria issued by the SOS. See **Chapter 4** for detailed consideration of this topic.

6.10.4.3 Effect of appeal

Until the final determination or withdrawal of the appeal, the enforcement notice is of no effect. According to the Court of Appeal in *R v Kuxhaus* [1988] 2 WLR 1005, [1988] 2 All ER 705, CA, 'final determination' means when all rights of appeal have been exhausted, including appeals to the High Court under s 289.

6.10.4.4 Written representations and informal hearings

As mentioned above, the SOS may suggest these alternatives in appropriate cases, but they can be used only with the consent of both parties.

6.10.5 Costs

The SOS or his inspector has power to award costs in all cases, even where the appeal was by way of written representations or even where the inquiry was not held (ss 320 and 322).

6.10.6   Further appeals (s 289)

Further appeal to the High Court or the Planning Court, but on a point of law or procedure only, lies against any decision made by the SOS in proceedings on an enforcement appeal. No such appeal lies, though, under s 289 if the SOS declined to entertain the appeal or set the enforcement notice aside as being a nullity; in these cases the appropriate way to proceed is by way of judicial review.

REVIEW ACTIVITY

1.   An individual has completed building an extension on the rear of his house. Has he committed an offence under the law governing planning control?

2.   Assuming the same facts as Question 1, does the LPA have an automatic right to issue an enforcement notice in respect of any breach?

3.   Assuming the same facts as Question 1, how long would the individual have to respond to any planning contravention notice served by the LPA investigating the matter?

4.   Would your answer to Question 1 differ if the individual had completed the work five years ago?

5.   Assuming the same facts as in Question 4, how would you advise the individual should he decide to sell the house given that he is concerned that any breach of planning control might deter a purchaser?

6.   You are a planning enforcement officer at an LPA. You have received a report that a coffee shop has started operating as a wine bar. How might you confirm whether this is the case?

7.   It turns out that the coffee shop considered in Question 6 is indeed operating as a wine bar. There is a planning permission allowing the property to be used as a shop within use Class A1 but it is subject to a condition that no alcohol be served. What enforcement options are available?

8.   Assuming the same facts as for Questions 6 and 7, why can you not just serve a stop notice to force the owner to stop its activities?

9.   What is the time limit for appealing against the service of an enforcement notice?

10. A firm of accountants is operating in a property that has planning permission for any use within use Class A2. The property is in an area identified in the Local Development Framework as one where mixed retail and business use should be encouraged. An enforcement notice has been issued requiring the firm to cease trading within six weeks. What grounds of appeal do you think the firm could rely on should it decide to challenge the service of the enforcement notice?

Answers to this Review activity may be found in Appendix 1.

CHAPTER 7

ENVIRONMENTAL ISSUES

7.1	Introduction to environmental law	83
7.2	Environmental risk management	85
7.3	Contaminated land	87
7.4	Nuisance	95
7.5	Environmental Damage Regulations	98
7.6	Environmental permitting and regulation	99
7.7	Climate change law and energy performance	102
7.8	Regulatory Enforcement and Sanctions Act 2008	106
7.9	Asbestos	106
7.10	Japanese knotweed	108
7.11	Flood risks	108
7.12	Sentencing guidelines: environmental offences	108
7.13	Environment Tribunal	109
	Review activity	109

7.1 INTRODUCTION TO ENVIRONMENTAL LAW

Not long ago, environmental law might have been considered an alternative practice area. It is now an established specialisation, and remains one of the fastest expanding areas of law.

Environmental issues are also increasingly part of our socio-economic consciousness. Our choice of food is progressively informed by concerns not just of taste, but of sustainable farming and air miles. Our modes of transport are evaluated not just by time, but also by emissions. How we build, heat or cool our homes is regulated by increasingly strict standards of a low carbon existence. In the space of a generation, our global environmental awareness has moved from singular campaigns to save endangered species to the regulation of our everyday lives.

This recent emphasis is mostly due to anthropogenic climate change. The rise in extreme weather events and global warming now gain economic quantification as well as mainstream media and political coverage. The Stern Review on the Economics of Climate Change estimated a 5–20% detriment to GDP if we do not take action. Beyond output, though, climate change remains the greatest threat to our existence as a species.

Accordingly, the wealth of environmental laws and issues in practice and academia now encompasses planning and construction, health and safety, energy and projects, conservation, climate change, carbon markets, sustainable international development, corporate responsibility and human rights.

This chapter focuses on the core environmental issues that every property lawyer should be aware of, namely:

(a) *Environmental risk management* (see **7.2**). Any share or asset deal requires due diligence. Environmental liabilities could arise from various sources, including remediation of contaminated land, compliance with permit requirements and mitigating flood risks. Some risk management tools are universal, such as enquiries of the seller, contractual warranties and indemnities. However, environmental desktop studies, Phase I and II Reports, and environmental insurance are peculiar to this area of practice.

(b)   *Contaminated land* (see **7.3**). The Contaminated Land Regime is based on 'the polluter pays' principle and may impose retrospective liability. It remains a core environmental concern in property acquisition, particularly as an *innocent owner or occupier of contaminated land may be liable* if the original polluter cannot be found.

(c)   *Nuisance* (see **7.4**). Anything emanating from land may cause a nuisance – from methane emissions to oil spills – and liability may arise in tort (including under the rule in *Rylands v Fletcher*) or pursuant to statute.

(d)   *Environmental regulation and permitting* (see **7.6**). Most non-residential properties will require an environmental permit or exemption of some sort, whether it is a restaurant discharging waste or a factory emitting industrial pollutants. Failure to comply can lead to significant penalties and other tortious liabilities.

(e)   *Climate change and energy performance* (see **7.7**). This area represents the legal and practical ramifications of the universal drive towards reducing greenhouse gas (GHG) emissions. It includes the Carbon Reduction Commitment (CRC) Energy Efficiency Scheme, Energy Performance Certificates (EPCs) and Green Leases.

(f)   *Asbestos* (see **7.9**). Responsible for more cancer-related deaths than any product in history (so far), asbestos could be present in any UK building built before 2000. The responsible person (who could be the owner or occupier) must monitor and manage its existence.

This chapter also briefly discusses the Environmental Damage (Prevention and Remediation) Regulations 2009 (see **7.5**), the Regulatory Enforcement and Sanctions Act 2008 (see **7.8**), Japanese knotweed (see **7.10**), flood risks (see **7.11**), sentencing guidelines for environmental offences (see **7.12**) and the First-Tier (Environment) Tribunal (see **7.13**). It concludes with some review activities addressing the main environmental issues along with some related areas of property law.

Lastly, the author conducted a survey with the top dozen firms practising environmental law in England (as ranked by Legal 500), enquiring as to their current core practices and predictions for growth. The results are summarised in **Table 7.1** below. In such a dynamic area as environmental law, it is a challenge to keep abreast of all developments. However, the core principles of *sustainable development* and *the polluter pays* informs all of the law discussed below, and should be kept in mind while considering any advice on environmental liabilities, regulation or development. The last category in the table highlights the importance of good, fundamental practical legal research and reasoning skills.

Table 7.1   Environmental law: private practice survey

Main practice areas identified (in descending order):
(1)   Transactional due diligence/risk management
(2)   Contaminated land
(3)   Waste
(4)   Environmental regulation/permitting
(5)   Emissions trading

Number one predicted growth area:
(1)   Carbon/climate change

What partners look for in new recruits:
(1)   Analytical skills
(2)   Commercial acumen
(3)   Communication skills
(4)   Knowledge

7.2 ENVIRONMENTAL RISK MANAGEMENT

7.2.1 Introduction

As noted in **Table 7.1**, transactional risk management remains a core environmental practice for most corporate law firms. The first step in determining any environmental risks in a property deal is to make enquiries of the seller and the local authority (the latter using Standard Form CON29, see **8.1**). A prudent solicitor would almost always commission a desktop study as well, particularly for non-residential properties. Depending on the results, the buyer's solicitor may then consider a Phase I Report (including a site visit), or even a Phase II Report (including soil and groundwater tests) (see **7.2.3** below).

If significant risks or existing issues are identified, the buyer's solicitor may then consider a variety of tools to limit the buyer's potential liability. These may include, particularly for contingent risks:

(a) warranties, eg that the land is free of such risks;

(b) indemnities, ie that should a risk eventuate, the seller will pay for the resulting liability;

(c) an agreement on liabilities;

(d) environmental insurance, which *may* still be available for a known risk.

In addition, where the risk is more certain, the following methods may be pursued:

(e) positive obligations on either party (to address matters such as clean-up);

(f) carving out the land, so as to purchase only the 'non-risky' section, eg a 'pie-crust' lease;

(g) negotiate a price reduction;

(h) in the worst case scenario, decline the deal.

We shall look at enquiries, studies, reports, warranties, indemnities and insurance further below.

7.2.2 Enquiries of the seller

In addition to the standard queries made in a property transaction, a buyer should always request specific environmental information from the seller, such as details of any:

(a) historic, present or potential pollution incidents, hazardous substances, enforcement actions, or complaints by third parties in relation to environmental matters at the property; and

(b) environmental permits, licences, consents held or required for the property, or any activity at the property.

'Environmental matters' is obviously a loaded term. It could be defined very broadly, to encapsulate impacts on human health, ecosystems and property. Or it could be narrowly defined to specific liabilities, such as nuisance, contamination and regulated emissions. For this reason, much of the drafting of enquiries and contractual terms comprises comprehensive definitions. The operative questions and clauses, on the other hand, tend to be relatively brief. Precedent questions are usually adopted from firm databases or professional legal support providers, such as LexisPSL and Practical Law. A good lawyer will always tailor precedent questions to the specific transaction.

7.2.3 Enquiries of consultants

Almost every commercial property acquisition should include a desktop screening study in order to comply with The Law Society's Warning Card on contaminated land. Specialist environmental consultants provide basic desktop studies for around £150 (depending on the size of the property) – the turnaround time can be a matter of hours. As the name suggests, a desktop study does not entail a physical inspection but a trawl through databases and maps of present and historical land use, pollution incidents, flood risks, regulatory enforcement and neighbouring uses, amongst other things. Although some of the information is derived from public sources, such as the Environment Agency, the speed, breadth and analysis in consultants' reports warrants their use over free searches.

Where actual or potential liabilities have been identified in the desktop report, the consultant will normally recommend further action that can be taken to reduce or mitigate the risk, such as:

- making specific enquiries of a regulator;
- carrying out a site inspection (Phase I Report); or
- undertaking a detailed site investigation, including testing and analysis of the soil, water, etc (Phase II Report).

The results of the desktop study and the reports should clarify and quantify any concerns flagged by the enquiries or desktop study. If a major issue is identified at any stage, it may become a bargaining point or remedial condition of the transaction. Remediation may also be statutorily required (see **7.3.4**).

7.2.4   Warranties

In addition to standard transactional warranties, a buyer may wish to include specific promises from the seller in regard to environmental issues, such as:

> So far as the Seller is aware there are no known or likely hazardous substances present at the property, which are harmful to human health, the environment or would give rise to a nuisance claim.

> So far as the Seller is aware, in the last five years there have been no claims, litigation, or threatened actions in regard to environmental matters at the property.

> So far as the Seller is aware, they hold all requisite and current permits and licences required for the property and the activities carried on it.

> So far as the Seller is aware, they have complied with all Environmental, Health and Safety laws, including the conditions of any permit or licence required for the property and the activities carried on it.

The drafting of these clauses will also depend on whether it is a share or asset deal. The examples above would best suit an asset deal, as they refer specifically to the property in question. For a share deal, such a clause is often drafted simply as 'the Company holds', or 'has complied with', or 'is not subject to' the relevant environmental matter. This will have to be further carefully worded for properties formerly owned by the company.

Breach of warranty is actionable in contract law. The normal remedy would be damages. Again, the above are merely examples, which would be far more specific in practice and then hotly negotiated. If enquiries or reports showed a minor gap in information, a buyer might feel comfortable with a warranty alone.

7.2.5   Indemnities

Where the risk is higher, a buyer may try to extract an indemnity from the seller. Compared to a breach of warranty, an indemnity is effectively a safety net that if something happens – like regulatory action – the seller *will* cover all costs and indemnify the buyer (or vice versa). For example, an indemnity in regard to a former gas works site might state:

> The Seller agrees to indemnify the Buyer for all losses incurred as a result of any enforcement action or individual claim in regard to contaminated land or hazardous substances at, in, under or emanating from the property.

Understandably these are very hotly contested.

An option occupying the middle ground could be an agreement on liabilities (as provided for in the Contaminated Land Regime, see below at **7.3**), which requires even more sophisticated drafting.

7.2.6 Insurance

Environmental insurance in the UK has grown from a nascent to a competitive market in 20 years. There are several providers, which generally offer the following coverage, geared mostly towards contaminated land protection:

- up to £20 million protection
- up to 10 years
- for historical contamination and ongoing operations
- for remediation costs overrun (known as costcap/step loss policies)
- for contractors working on third-party sites.

Environmental insurance will usually cover on-site and off-site clean-up costs to the extent *required* by environmental law, as well as property damage. Typically the insurer will exclude cover for losses arising from known pollution conditions, though this is negotiable depending on the likelihood of enforcement action.

As this market develops, environmental insurance is increasingly seen as a valuable tool in risk management, for both buyer and seller. It can often be the last 'comfort' required for a risky site transfer.

7.3 CONTAMINATED LAND

7.3.1 Introduction

Contaminated land remains one of the single biggest environmental issues facing property lawyers in the UK. This is due to centuries of environmentally harmful progress: a legacy of the Industrial Revolution and often unsound agricultural, construction and development practices.

An estimated 25% of UK land is contaminated (R Pearman, 'Site remediation costs may fall to developers' *Contract Journal*, 12 July 2006). The degree of contamination may vary, but at its core the statutory definition of 'contaminated land' is that it poses a significant risk of harm to humans or the environment. This can severely impact a property acquisition, as liability for contamination can be extremely costly in many ways.

7.3.2 The risks in summary: legal and practical

Like most environmental liability, the core intention of the law is that 'the polluter pays'. The clean-up bill for dealing with something seemingly as innocuous as waste vegetables (causing methane emissions) could amount to millions of pounds (*Circular Facilities (London) Ltd v Sevenoaks District Council* [2005] EWHC 865 (Admin)).

The worrying addition of the Contaminated Land Regime (in force since 2000) is that if the original polluter cannot be found, the incumbent owner or occupier may be liable. Liability is strict and may be retrospective. Furthermore, s 157 of the Environmental Protection Act 1990 (EPA 1990) provides that where a company commits an offence with the consent, connivance or neglect of a director, secretary or similar officer, that person will also be personally liable.

Despite the headline issues, most contaminated land is dealt with by the planning regime, rather than by Pt IIA of the EPA 1990 (see **7.3.3**) (and to an even lesser degree, upon the relinquishment of environmental permits, see **7.6**). However, a client should be warned of the risks in any case. In 2000, given the risks of contaminated land, The Law Society saw fit to issue a (rare) Warning Card setting out what it regards as 'best practice' for solicitors in conveyances. The Warning Card states that, in relation to purchases, mortgages and leases, solicitors should advise the client of:

(a)   the potential liabilities associated with contaminated land; and

(b)   the steps that can be taken to assess and reduce the risk.

7.3.3 The Contaminated Land Regime

The Environment Act 1995 amended the EPA 1990 and introduced a new Pt IIA, dealing with contamination. In summary, Pt IIA requires local authorities to identify contaminated land and then require the responsible party to clean it up. A variety of exclusion and apportionment tests apply if there is more than one responsible person. In practice, a local authority is more likely to use a planning permission condition to ensure clean up, rather than the imposition of a statutory notice.

The Department for Environment, Food and Rural Affairs (Defra) reissued its Contaminated Land Statutory Guidance (Guidance) in April 2012. Although there were few substantial amendments, the Guidance is still of pivotal importance, particularly in elaborating on statutory definitions, exclusion tests and the apportionment of liability.

7.3.3.1 Local authority: duty to investigate and require remediation

Local authorities have a duty to investigate land in their area for contamination, and to notify the 'appropriate person' and any owners or occupiers (EPA 1990, s 78B).

With limited resources at councils' disposal, many have prioritised higher-risk sites, and most have used the planning regime rather than Pt IIA to ensure remediation. This is because development proposals will often require an environmental assessment, and then possibly a remediation scheme for any identified contamination, to ensure the property is suitable for the proposed use.

7.3.3.2 Contaminated land: significant harm and contaminant linkages

Overview

To determine whether land is contaminated, the local authority must establish a 'significant contaminant linkage' (Guidance, Section 3):

(a)   Is there significant harm, or a significant possibility of such harm?

(b)   Is there a contaminant linkage (a contaminant, a pathway and a receptor) or a significant possibility of such a linkage?

Both elements must exist before Pt IIA of the EPA 1990 is engaged, and the definition of both concepts is comprehensive.

Significant harm

There are four core definitions under Pt IIA. The specificity of these definitions is of paramount importance. Any italicised words appearing below were added by the author for emphasis:

(a)   'Contaminated land' is defined in s 78A(2) of the EPA 1990 as:

any land which appears to the local authority in whose area it is situated to be in such a condition, by reason of substances in, on or under the land, that (a) *significant harm* is being caused or there is a *significant possibility of such harm* being caused; or (b) significant pollution of controlled waters is being caused or there is a significant possibility of such pollution being caused.

(b)   'Harm' is defined (EPA 1990, s 78A(4)) as:

harm to the *health of living organisms* or other interference with the *ecological systems* of which they form part, and in the case of man, includes harm to his *property*.

The Guidance (Section 4) specifies that 'harm' to:

(i)   *human health* includes death, life-threatening diseases, serious injury, birth defects and the impairment of reproductive functions. In deciding if other health effects constitute significant harm, the local authority must consider the impact on health, quality of life, and the scale of harm (Section 4.1);

(ii)   *ecological systems* includes irreversible adverse change, or some other substantial adverse change, in the functioning of the ecological system. However, ecological systems comprise only recognised protected nature areas, eg SSSIs, National Nature Reserves, or Marine Nature Reserves (Section 4.3);

(iii) *property* includes crops, livestock and buildings, and includes substantial damage, disease and diminution in yield or value to these (Section 4.3).

(c) *'Significant possibility'* is defined depending on one of the four categories of human health affected, and separately again for ecological systems and property. Very broadly, the tests used include 'unacceptably high probability' (Section 4.19, Category 1: Human Health), and 'more likely than not to result' and 'reasonable possibility' (Section 4.33, Table 1: Ecological system effects). You should consult the Guidance for more detail.

(d) *'Controlled waters'* takes the meaning from s 104 of the Water Resources Act 1991, namely all territorial (to three nautical miles) coastal, inland and ground waters (EPA 1990, s 78A(9)).

Contaminant linkage

A contaminant linkage requires a contaminant, a pathway and a receptor. For example:

(a) rotting vegetation (a *contaminant* by methane emissions);

(b) building construction (creating drains and soil *pathways* for the contaminant); and

(c) housing residents (*receptors* who become ill due to the emissions).

These were the elements of the first major case under Pt IIA of the EPA 1990 (*Sevenoaks* – see **7.3.2** above).

The Environment Agency (EA) reports that the most prevalent *contaminants* in identified sites are:

(a) metals and metalloids;

(b) organic and inorganic compounds;

(c) ash (particularly in Wales).

The energy and waste industries are cited as the biggest sources of contamination (Reporting the Evidence, *Dealing with contaminated land in England and Wales: A review of progress from 2000– 2007 with Part 2A of the Environmental Protection Act*, Environment Agency 2007 ('the Report')).

Pathways, on the other hand, can be as simple as the air, earth, soil water table, or rivers and streams.

The main *receptor* concern is human beings, but note that it could also include buildings and livestock, or protected areas.

Figure 7.1 below illustrates some typical pollution linkages. Note that the term 'source' is often used instead of 'contaminant'. Removing one of the elements would break the chain, such that the land would no longer come under Pt IIA of the EPA 1990.

Figure 7.1   Contaminant linkages

(*Source:* Canterbury Regional Council, New Zealand)

Special Sites and further guidance

The authorities may also identify Special Sites (EPA 1990, s 78C) which, because of the level of harm or risk thereof, require notice to the Secretary of State and then regulation by the EA. The regime for dealing with such sites is not substantially different.

Note that within all these definitions there is often much data that must be scientifically assessed. The Guidance and further Defra and EA reports provide some certainty for this with the likes of Soil Guideline Values and Contaminated Land Exposure Assessment Models, from which consultants can make meaningful evaluations of risk. However, that is beyond the scope of this book.

7.3.3.3   Who is liable? Responsibility, exclusion and apportionment

Ultimately, if there is a risk of significant harm and a contaminant linkage, the relevant enforcing authority has a *duty* to require remediation (EPA 1990, s 78E).

Responsibility

While the local authority must notify all 'interested persons' (such as the site owner) of any contamination, s 78E also requires the local authority to identify and serve a *remediation notice* on each *'appropriate person'*, specifying what that person must do and the timeframe. Primarily this would cover the original polluter or knowing permitter of pollution (a 'Class A' person). If the original polluter cannot be found then the present owner or occupier (a 'Class B' person) would be the appropriate person. It is this element which understandably causes most concern.

A 'Class A' person is defined as:

> the person, or any of the persons, who *caused or knowingly permitted* the substance, or any of the substances, by reason of which the contaminated land in question is such land to be in, on or under that land. (EPA 1990, s 78F(2))

'Knowingly permitted' requires both knowledge of the substances, and the power to prevent them from being there (Hansard, HL Deb vol 565, coll 1495–501 (11 July 1995), at 1497).

A 'Class B' person is defined as 'the *owner or occupier* of the land for the time being' (EPA 1990, s 78F(4)). An *'owner'* means:

> a person (other than a mortgagee not in possession) who, whether in his own right or as trustee for any other person, is entitled to receive the rack rent of the land, or, where the land is not let at a rack rent, would be so entitled if it were so let. (EPA 1990, s 78A(9))

Hence this would cover a lessor.

Exclusion tests

Where the enforcing authority identifies two or more 'appropriate persons' within a liability group, those persons may take advantage of one of the following exclusion tests, provided in the Guidance (Sections 7(c) Class A Persons, and Section 7(e) Class B Persons). But note that a person will not be excluded if the effect is to exclude everyone in their group from liability (Guidance, Sections 7.32, 7.79). Only a summary of the tests is given below – see the Guidance for more detail; this is a particularly important area of the Contaminated Land Regime.

Class A person exclusion tests

The enforcing authority must apply these six tests sequentially, from 1 to 6 (Guidance, Section 7.3.2(b)).

A Class A person will be excluded from liability in the following circumstances:

- *Test 1: Excluded activities*

  The person's *supporting* or *advisory* role is of such limited scope and responsibility that even if the person could be said to have knowingly permitted contamination, he should still be excluded. The activities include lending, insuring, advising, licensing, consigning waste, consenting to activities or leasing land to the actual polluter.

- *Test 2: Payments made for remediation*

  The person made a sufficient payment for remediation to a responsible party, but remediation is not carried out properly or at all. A reduction in the purchase price due to estimated remediation costs could constitute such a payment. However, he must not retain control of the land.

- *Test 3: Sold with information*

  The person sold the land at arm's length and provided sufficient information to enable the buyer to be aware of the risk. Note that this was not successful in the case of R (*on the application of Redland Minerals Ltd*) *v* SSEFRA & *Others* [2010] EWHC 913 (Admin), which indicated that disclosure has to be full and exact. However, if the buyer is a large commercial organisation or public body, and the seller permits it to investigate the land, this will constitute constructive knowledge of that sufficient information. But this does not imply that the buyer 'caused or knowingly permitted' the presence of the contaminant.

- *Test 4: Changes to substances*

  The first person deposited substance A in, on or under the land. Another person in the liability group later introduced substance B, which reacts with substance A, creating a significant contaminant linkage. The first person will be excluded if he could not reasonably foresee that substance B would be introduced, and that it would cause such a chemical reaction, biological process, or radioactive decay, and took reasonable precautions against this.

- *Test 5: Escaped substances*

  The person is only liable due to the escape of substances from other land, caused or knowingly permitted by another member of the liability group. Although this has contaminated the land in question, the first person should be excluded.

- *Test 6: Introduction of pathways or receptors*

  The person caused or knowingly permitted the contaminant that created a significant contaminant linkage, but only because another person later introduced a pathway or receptor. The first person should be excluded. These were the facts of the *Sevenoaks* case (see **7.3.2**).

Class B person exclusion tests

A Class B person will be excluded from liability if:

(a)   he occupies the land under a licence with no marketable value; or

(b)   he pays a market rent with no beneficial ownership other than the tenancy itself.

The latter will normally exclude a tenant.

Apportionment of liability

If there is more than one appropriate person remaining within a class, liability is apportioned between them (Guidance, Section 7).

For *Class A appropriate persons* (Section 7(d)), the enforcing authority should apportion liability as summarised below:

(1)   Apportion according to relative responsibility (per steps 2–4 below), otherwise in equal shares.

(2)   Between a person who *caused the entry of a contaminant*, and one who *permitted its continued presence*, the two should share responsibility if the latter had the necessary 'means and opportunity' to deal with the contaminant.

However, the second person's responsibility should be relatively reduced to the extent that he did not have, or had insufficient, 'means and opportunity'. See Section 7.66 for more detail.

(3)   Between persons who *caused or knowingly permitted the entry of the contaminant*:

(a)   If there is a clear delineation of responsibility for remediation, liability should be apportioned according to that responsibility. This is particularly relevant if different persons were responsible for different areas of land, each requiring separate remediation.

(b)   If this is not clear, liability should be apportioned according to the relative amounts of contaminant referable to different persons.

(c)   If neither (a) nor (b) applies, apportionment will depend on a broader consideration of the appropriate persons' activities and periods of control.

See Sections 7.68–7.72 for more detail.

(4)   Between persons who have *knowingly permitted the continued presence of a contaminant*, liability should be apportioned according to their control in terms of:

(a)   time;

(b)   area;

(c)   means and reasonable opportunity to deal with the contaminant; or

(d)   combination of (a) to (c).

For *Class B appropriate persons* (Section 7(f)), liability is apportioned within this group:

(a)   to the Class B member who owns or occupies a particular area of land, where all or part of the remediation action clearly relates to it;

(b)   according to the capital values of the respective Class B members; or

(c)   equally, if the capital values of the Class B members cannot be ascertained.

See Sections 7.80–7.86 for more detail.

Agreement on liabilities

Finally, the appropriate persons may have agreed to divide responsibility for the contamination. If they provide the enforcing authority with a copy of this agreement on liabilities, the enforcing authority should give effect to it. It will not do this though if it would a place a party under hardship (EPA 1990, s 78P(2)).

7.3.3.4   Case law

Application of the provisions of the Contaminated Land Regime is not an exact science, as case law suggests. The three cases discussed below constitute appeals of a remediation notice, including one judicial review application. Despite the overriding policy that the 'original polluter pays', it appears that the definitions, exclusion and apportionment tests can obfuscate the identity of the polluter.

In the first appeal of a remediation notice under Pt IIA, *Circular Facilities (London) Ltd v Sevenoaks District Council* [2005] EWHC 865 (Admin), the previous owner had filled in clay pits with biodegradable waste, which created methane and carbon dioxide. Circular Facilities later redeveloped the site into a housing estate. The court held that this created the contaminant linkage (with construction pathways and human receptors) and so held the developer liable as the appropriate person. The matter was ultimately settled out of court, supposedly due to the costs already incurred by the Council.

In the second appeal case of R (*on the application of National Grid Gas plc) v Environment Agency* [2007] UKHL 30, a former gasworks operator left black coal tar pits on a site which was later redeveloped into a housing estate. The Environment Agency imposed liability on the statutory successor (National Grid Gas) of the original gas company, despite the fact that again it was the developer who introduced the pathways and receptors. The House of Lords held that the successor was not the appropriate person, primarily because it had not caused or knowingly permitted the contamination, nor inherited any contractual liability for such (as at the time no such liability existed). However, this leaves open the possibility that, with the right wording, a statutory successor could be held liable.

Finally, in the dismissed judicial review application of two related remediation notices, R (*on the application of Crest Nicholson Residential Ltd) v SSEFRA & Others* [2010] EWHC 561 (Admin) and R (*on the application of Redland Minerals Ltd) v SSEFRA & Others* [2010] EWHC 913 (Admin), Redland Minerals had operated a chemical production site from the 1950s to 1980, and then sold the site to a developer, Crest Nicholson, which undertook some testing and later attempted remediation. Redland argued that it should be excluded as it has sold the site to Crest *with information* (as to the presence of bromides on the land), but lost this point as the court found that Crest did not know about bromides which had already leached into groundwater. Secondly, in regard to apportionment, Redland had caused all the bromide and bromate to be on the land in the first place (and allowed them to filter to the lower strata). Crest brought no contaminants onto the site but accelerated their infiltration. The Secretary of State identified no simple quantitative causative mechanism to measure apportionment, and instead adopted a broad *evaluative judgement* as used by the inspector (reflecting the length of ownership, and use of the land). This was upheld by the Administrative Court.

These cases demonstrate the complexity of Pt IIA. Arguably the last case does indeed at least make the original polluter pay, and in *National Grid* the full potential extent of the retrospective aspect is evident. However, it is clearly a matter of the facts in each case, and it seems fairly harsh that Circular Facilities was liable when it was not the original polluter. The latest Statutory Guidance (April 2012) did not substantially amend the provisions on exclusion and apportionment.

7.3.3.5 Enforcement

Very few remediation notices have been served (only a dozen as of early 2013), as most contaminated land is addressed voluntarily or though planning permission. The regulator may also carry out works itself, at the expense of the 'appropriate person'.

Remediation notice

A remediation notice cannot be served in a number of circumstances, including the following:

(a)   the contamination is being or will be remediated voluntarily, and the enforcing authority is satisfied that this approach will adequately deal with the problem;

(b)   the act causing the contamination is licensed under another regime;

(c)   if the enforcing authority were to do the works itself, it would not recover the costs from the person concerned on grounds of hardship.

If none of these circumstances applies then the enforcing authority *must* serve a remediation notice on the appropriate person(s).

A remediation notice must specify what the recipient must do and the periods within which the work must be carried out.

Sanctions

Failure to comply with a remediation notice is an offence (EPA 1990, s 78M). The level of fine depends on whether an offender is an individual or a corporate entity. In the case of a company, the offender is liable in the magistrates' court to a fine not exceeding £20,000 and a further sum equal to one-tenth of the fine for each day after conviction. More importantly, the enforcing authority may seek an injunction in the High Court to secure compliance (EPA 1990, s 78M(5)). If an order is obtained and breached, the company and its officers may be held personally criminally liable (EPA 1990, s 157).

The Regulatory Enforcement and Sanctions Act 2008 (see **7.8**) may prove helpful to the regulator in decreasing the costs of enforcement.

Appeals

A person who has been served with a remediation notice may appeal to the magistrates' court (if the local authority is the enforcing authority) or to the Secretary of State (if the EA is the enforcing authority). The Contaminated Land (England) Regulations 2006 (SI 2006/1380) identify the grounds for appeal, which, along with other matters, include:

(a)   the enforcing authority failed to comply with the guidance notes (Guidance);

(b)   the enforcing authority acted unreasonably in determining that the appellant was an appropriate person;

(c)   disagreement with the requirements of what is to be done by way of remediation.

7.3.4 Planning and contaminated land

Despite the detail of Pt IIA, the National Planning Policy Framework (NPPF) makes clear that the main tool for dealing with contaminated land is the planning regime (greater detail was contained in the now replaced Policy Statements 23 and 10 (and Tan 21 (Wales)).

In fact, by 2007, local authorities estimated that approximately only 10% of contaminated sites were dealt with by Pt IIA (Report, p 3). Furthermore, a lack of resources meant that most local authorities had inspected less than 10% of their areas for contaminated land.

Most contaminated land is instead identified as a consequence of development or redevelopment. In such a case, when the developer applies for planning permission, it will find conditions attached requiring remediation of any contamination.

The Department for Communities and Local Government (DCLG) issued Model Planning Conditions for Contaminated Land in 2008 (effectively updating PPS 23), which require the developer to undertake and submit the following:

(a)   site investigation and risk assessment;

(b)   proposed remediation scheme;

(c)   remediation;

(d)   reporting of unexpected contamination;

(e)   long-term monitoring.

Development could not take place until conditions (a) to (d) were satisfied. The NPPF (March 2012) revoked these Model Conditions, but it is likely that councils will continue to use the same provisions.

7.3.5 Landlord and tenant issues

Landlords will be anxious to ensure that the tenant will be responsible for the clean-up of any pollution discovered during the term of the lease. It is doubtful whether clean-up works would fall within the tenant's general repairing covenant unless the pollution caused some physical damage to the building. Most modern commercial leases, however, deal expressly with environmental issues. Also, the tenant's covenant to comply with all statutory obligations may be broad enough to extend to requirements under environmental law. Furthermore, if there is a service charge in the lease, the landlord may be able to recover sums expended on the necessary clean-up. Even if this is not expressly mentioned in the list of services to be provided, the 'sweeping-up' clause may be wide enough to embrace such work.

7.3.6　Report: Review of the Contaminated Land Regime

The EA is under a statutory duty to provide 'from time to time ... a report on the state of contaminated land in England and Wales' (EPA 1990, s 78U). The most recent Report covered the period from 2000 to 2007, and some of its findings are summarised in **Table 7.2** below, as at March 2007. The last two statistics in the table again highlight what for many has become the core concern of the Regime.

Overall, rather than be burdened with a remediation notice, it is of course advisable to enter into a dialogue with the regulator and, if necessary, pursue voluntary remediation.

Table 7.2　Environment Agency: Summary of findings

> **Environment Agency,** *Dealing with contaminated land in England and Wales: A review of progress from 2000–2007 with Part 2A of the Environmental Protection Act*
>
> - Seven hundred and eighty-one sites had been determined under Pt 2A, including 35 Special Sites.
> - Fewer than 150 had been completely remediated in that time (this usually consists of excavation and off-site disposal of the contamination, although containment is also often used).
> - Remediation, backdated from initial identification, typically took months to years (typically many years), and often costs millions of pounds.
> - Twelve remediation notices have been served since the legislation was introduced (10 in England, including one for a Special Site, and two in Wales). Of those in England, there have been five appeals.
> - Conversely 281 remediation statements (which state what needs to be or has been done) were issued, demonstrating the high number of voluntary and planning-related options for dealing with contamination.
> - Over 90% of contaminated land in England and Wales had housing on it when the site was inspected.
> - *In the majority of sites, where appropriate persons were identified, it was the Class B owner or occupier who was ultimately liable.*

7.4　NUISANCE

7.4.1　Introduction

Private nuisance, public nuisance, statutory nuisance and the rule in *Rylands v Fletcher* combine to provide a wide ambit of potential liability for interference with land, people's enjoyment of it, or people's health. Liability is strict in each case; there is no requirement to establish carelessness on the part of the defendant. Remedies may lie in damages or injunction.

7.4.2　Private nuisance

7.4.2.1　Introduction

Private nuisance is the 'unlawful interference with a person's use or enjoyment of land, or of some right over or in connection with that land'. Private nuisance may cover anything from:

(a)　aircraft noise and turbulence affecting nearby residents (*Dennis v Ministry of Defence* [2003] Env LR 34); to

(b)　a particularly loud printing press affecting residents on Fleet Street (*Rushmer v Polsue and Alfieri Ltd* [1906] 1 Ch 234); to

(c) solvents from a leather works seeping into an aquifer (*Cambridge Water Company v Eastern Counties Leather plc* [1994] 2 AC 264). (Though note, in this case, that this was found not to be nuisance, as the claimant's case rested on changes to drinking water regulations which came into force long after the defendant's practices stopped. The claimants were successful under *Rylands v Fletcher*, though (see **7.4.5**)); to

(d) gas escaping from land and passing through a property in underground pipes (*Willis v Derwentside District Council* [2013] All ER (D) 70 (Apr)).

7.4.2.2 Standing

In *Hunter v Canary Wharf Ltd* [1997] 2 WLR 684, the House of Lords confirmed that only people with rights to the land affected have standing to bring a private nuisance action. In that case, the tenants and freehold owners in London's Docklands successfully sued the developers of Canary Wharf and the London Docklands Development Corporation in nuisance for dust from construction work and interference with television signals from the Canary Wharf Tower. However, some claimants (on behalf of children in the Docklands area) also took their case to the European Commission of Human Rights, claiming a breach of Article 8 of the European Convention on Human Rights (ECHR) (*Khatun v United Kingdom*, European Commission of Human Rights, 1 July 1998). The Commission held that Article 8 applied to all the claimants, whether they had property rights or not, and so would include the Docklands' children. Consequently, such people may have standing to bring claims in future cases, in light of the Human Rights Act 1998.

Many environmental matters, particularly emissions, can be the source of a nuisance claim, and so the breadth of legitimate claimants may be increased.

7.4.2.3 Interaction with planning permission

The case of *Coventry v Lawrence* [2014] All ER (D) 245 (Feb) ('Fen Tigers' case) concerned a claim in nuisance brought by a neighbour in relation to noise from a motorcross stadium and speedway. The activities and noise existed long before the claimant moved to the property. In summary, the Supreme Court held that:

- it was possible to obtain by prescription a right to commit what would otherwise be a nuisance by noise (however, the defendant had not established such a right in this case);
- it is no defence that the claimant had come to the nuisance;
- activities which give rise to a nuisance could constitute part of the character of the locality, but only to the extent that those activities did not constitute a nuisance;
- the mere fact that an activity had the benefit of planning permission was normally of no assistance to the defendant in a claim that the activity caused a nuisance; and
- the power to award damages in lieu of an injunction was a discretion, which should not, as a matter of principle, be fettered.

7.4.2.4 Interaction with environmental permitting

In *Barr and Others v Biffa Waste Services Ltd* [2012] EWHC Civ 312, a group of residents in a mixed use area successfully sued Biffa for odours emanating from its waste disposal site. Biffa was not entitled to rely on compliance with its Environmental Permit (see **7.6**), which did not expressly or impliedly authorise committing any nuisance. Biffa was therefore liable in nuisance for its odorous behaviour.

7.4.3 Public nuisance

Historically, public nuisance included a wide range of activities, from dumping sewage into a river to playing loud music in a public park. The Court of Appeal in *Corby Group Litigation v Corby District Council* [2009] EWHC 1944 referred to the following definition of public nuisance (at [686]):

A person is guilty of public nuisance ... who (a) does an act not warranted by law or (b) omits to discharge a legal duty, if the effect of the act or omission is to endanger the life, health, property, morals or comfort of the public, or to obstruct the public in the exercise or enjoyment of rights common to all her Majesty's subjects.

Although an established common law offence, public nuisance is used sparingly now. This is because most public nuisance activities are now addressed by statute. Furthermore, while the 'public' can mean a class of Her Majesty's subjects, in *Attorney-General v PYA Quarries Ltd* [1957] 2 QB 169, a case on dust and tremor nuisance by a quarry, Denning LJ also stated (at 191) that

a public nuisance is a nuisance which is so widespread in its range or so indiscriminate in its effect that it would not be reasonable to expect one person to take proceedings on his own responsibility to put a stop to it, but that it should be taken on the responsibility of the community at large.

Consequently, such a stand-alone claim would need both a large number of people to be affected and the omission of relevant statutory liability, which is unlikely in environmental law. However, public nuisance could still comprise part of a suite of claims. This was used in the *Corby* case, where the council was successfully sued in negligence, public nuisance, and under s 34 of the EPA 1990, for birth defects caused by its poor reclamation of a former steelworks site.

7.4.4 Statutory nuisance

7.4.4.1 Introduction

In statutory nuisance, the claimant does not need to have a property interest. Statutory nuisance is actionable pursuant to s 79 of the EPA 1990 and includes smoke, fumes, gases, dust, odours, insects, artificial light and noise emitted from premises which are 'prejudicial to health or a nuisance'. 'Nuisance' is given either its private or public nuisance meaning, whereas 'prejudicial to health' is assessed objectively, ie one would substitute the health of the average traveller on the Clapham omnibus.

7.4.4.2 Enforcement

Local authorities are under an express duty to inspect their areas periodically for statutory nuisance (EPA 1990, ss 79–80), and must serve an abatement notice on the person responsible for it. As in the Contaminated Land Regime, if that person cannot be found, the abatement notice will be served on the owner or occupier of the relevant premises. Otherwise, an aggrieved individual may seek an abatement order through the courts (EPA 1990, s 82) (see *McCaw v City of Westminster Magistrates' Court (D) and Middlesex SARL* [2008] EWHC 1504).

There is a defence of 'best practicable means' for some of the categories of public nuisance. Essentially this relies on the defendant showing that it did what is currently best practice (having regard to the local circumstances, current technical knowledge, and financial means) to prevent or counteract the nuisance.

7.4.5 The Rule in *Rylands v Fletcher*

The rule in *Rylands v Fletcher* [1868] UKHL 1 is essentially a subspecies of nuisance. As reformulated in *Transco v Stockport MBC* [2003] UKHL 61, the elements of liability are that:

(a) the defendant must bring or keep an exceptionally dangerous or mischievous thing on his land;

(b) he ought reasonably to have recognised that there is an exceptionally high risk of danger or mischief if that thing should escape, however unlikely an escape may be;

(c) his use of his land must, having regard to all the circumstances of time and place, be extraordinary and unusual;

(d) the thing must escape from his property into or onto the property of another;

(e) damages for death or personal injury are not recoverable;

(f)   an Act of God or the act of a stranger will provide a defence.

Traditionally the hardest element to satisfy was 'non-natural use'. However, in *Cambridge Water*, Lord Goff stated that

> the storage of substantial quantities of chemicals on industrial premises should be regarded as an almost classic case of non-natural use; and I find it very difficult to think that it should be thought objectionable to impose strict liability for damage caused in the event of their escape.

In light of this judgment, and considering the range of non-natural uses to be found on a given property (from solvents to industrial cleaning agents), the rule in *Rylands v Fletcher* continues to pose an environmental liability risk.

7.4.6   Trespass

Trespass requires an intentional or a negligent act which interferes directly with a person or his rights in land. The emphasis is on direct interference. In the case of *Esso Petroleum v Southport Corporation* [1956] AC 218, the defendant's tanker jettisoned oil into an estuary; the oil eventually polluted the foreshore. This was not an actionable trespass as there was no certainty the oil would end up on the foreshore – it was indirect. As with nuisance and the rule in *Rylands v Fletcher*, trespass is also a potential claim for environmental incidents.

7.5   ENVIRONMENTAL DAMAGE REGULATIONS

The Environmental Damage (Prevention and Remediation) Regulations 2009 (SI 2009/153) implement Council Directive 2004/35/EC ([2004] OJ L143/56) on Environmental Liability. The Regulations created the first ever duty to take *preventative* measures in the face of imminent environmental harm. The two main duties are:

13   Preventing environmental damage

(1)   An operator of an activity that causes an imminent threat of environmental damage, or an imminent threat of damage which there are reasonable grounds to believe will become environmental damage, must immediately—

(a)   take all practicable steps to prevent the damage; and

(b)   (unless the threat has been eliminated) notify all relevant details to the enforcing authority appearing to be the appropriate one.

14   Preventing further environmental damage

(1)   An operator of an activity that has caused environmental damage, or has caused damage where there are reasonable grounds to believe that the damage is or will become environmental damage, must immediately—

(a)   take all practicable steps to prevent further damage; and

(b)   notify all relevant details to the enforcing authority appearing to be the appropriate one.

Failure to comply with either duty is an offence.

The Regulations are based on the 'polluter pays' principle but are not retrospective (unlike Pt IIA of the EPA 1990) and apply only to operators of intensive environmental activities (listed in Sch 2), typically those requiring an environmental permit (see **7.6**), in addition to waste, mining and transport activities.

'Environmental damage' is specifically defined as damage to:

(a)   protected species or natural habitats, or a site of special scientific interest,

(b)   surface water or groundwater, or

(c)   land,

...

Environmental damage to land means 'contamination of land by substances, preparations, organisms or micro-organisms that results in a significant risk of adverse effects on human health'.

The emphasis is on the 'operator' identifying when there is an imminent threat or actual damage and taking immediate action. The operator will also be responsible for any remediation. This additional environmental duty on operators of industry could be seen as the prospective equivalent of Pt IIA of the EPA 1990.

The EA's first prosecution was of United Utilities in April 2010, for water pollution in Three Pools Waterway, Southport. United Utilities' faulty foul water pumps discharged sewage, causing the death of 3,000 fish. Remediation is ongoing, and may involve compensatory measures in addition to restocking the fish.

7.6 ENVIRONMENTAL PERMITTING AND REGULATION

7.6.1 Introduction

This is a vast area, covering permits and regulations for activities ranging from running a dry cleaners to dealing with radioactive substances.

The Environmental Permitting (England and Wales) Regulations 2010 (SI 2010/675) (EPR 2010) bring the licences previously managed under the main regulatory regimes (water discharges, waste, mining waste, radioactive substances, industries and installations) under the one system. Previously this constituted 41 different statutory instruments. These regimes now appear as schedules to the Regulations:

- Sch 7A (Part A installations: Industrial Emissions Directive);
- Sch 8 (Part B installations and Part B mobile plant);
- Sch 9 (waste operations);
- Sch 9A (materials facilities);
- Sch 10 (landfill);
- Sch 11 (waste motor vehicles);
- Sch 12 (waste electrical and electronic equipment);
- Sch 13A (waste incineration: Industrial Emissions Directive);
- Sch 14 (solvent emission activities);
- Sch 15A (large combustion plants: Industrial Emissions Directive);
- Sch 16 (asbestos);
- Sch 17A (titanium dioxide: Industrial Emissions Directive);
- Sch 18 (petrol vapour recovery);
- Sch 19 (waste batteries and accumulators);
- Sch 20 (mining waste operations);
- Sch 21 (water discharge activities);
- Sch 22 (groundwater activities);
- Sch 23 (radioactive substances activities).

7.6.2 Permit requirement

Principally, reg 12 of the EPR 2010 requires the following:

(1)   A person must not, except under and to the extent authorised by an environmental permit—

    (a)   operate a regulated facility; or

    (b)   cause or knowingly permit a water discharge activity or groundwater activity.

Regulation 7 defines 'operate a regulated facility' as:

(a)   operate an installation or mobile plant, or

(b)   carry on a waste operation, mining waste operation, radioactive substances activity, water discharge activity, groundwater activity, small waste incineration plant operation or solvent emission activity;

...

Table 7.3 below summarises the more common issues involving permitting and regulation.

Where possible, the regulator must enforce action under the Regulations, rather than under Pt IIA of the EPA 1990.

Table 7.3   Common offences and duties in environmental permitting and regulation

---

Industry and installations

Pollution prevention

It is an offence to operate a heavy industrial installation or listed activity without a licence (EPR 2010, regs 12 and 38). These include energy, mining, chemical or waste industries *and* lighter industries where emissions may be harmful. Together these are referred to as Part A(1) (regulated by the EA) and Part A(2) and Part B activities (regulated by local authorities). There are thresholds of activity before a permit is required.

Water

(1) Pollution

It is an offence, except pursuant to an environmental permit, to 'cause or knowingly permit a water discharge activity or groundwater activity' (EPR 2010, regs 12(1) and 38(1)).

A 'water discharge activity' includes the discharge or entry into inland freshwaters, coastal waters or territorial waters of any: (i) poisonous, noxious or polluting matter, (ii) waste matter, or (iii) trade effluent or sewage effluent (Sch 21).

A 'groundwater activity' includes the discharge of pollutants into groundwater (Sch 22).

(2) Abstraction

It is an offence to abstract or impound water without an abstraction or impoundment licence or in contravention of one (Water Resources Act 1991, ss 24 and 25).

(3) Trade effluent

It is an offence to discharge trade effluent to a public sewer without a consent or authorisation from the relevant water or sewerage undertaker (Water Industry Act 1991, s 118).

Waste

(1) Keeping or disposing

Pursuant to s 33 of the EPA 1990, it is an offence to treat, keep, or dispose of waste except in accordance with a permit (or pursuant to a permit holder's powers).

'Waste' is widely defined and includes batteries, residues from industrial processes, and oils.

(2) Waste operations and exemptions

Recycling centres, scrap metal and waste transfer sites etc will need an environmental permit for their waste operations (EPR 2010). Other non-waste businesses may need to register an exemption where they use or store waste below thresholds (EPR 2010, Schs 3 and 9).

(3) Duty of care

Section 34 of the EPA 1990 imposes a general statutory duty of care regarding waste. This includes preventing its escape, ensuring its transfer only to an authorised person (the fly-tipping offence) and keeping records of the transfer.

(4) Electricals

The Waste Electrical and Electronic Equipment Regulations 2013 (SI 2013/3113) impose a duty on producers, distributors and exporters of electrical and electronic equipment to reduce pollutants in and finance the collection, treatment and recovery of electrical equipment.

---

(5) *Recycling*

The Producer Responsibility Obligations (Packaging Waste) Regulations 2007 (SI 2007/871) create an obligation to recycle and recover for businesses that handle more than 50t of packaging waste and have a turnover of more than £2,000,000 pa.

Hazardous substances

These include corrosive, toxic and irritant substances, and biological agents as defined in the Control of Substances Hazardous to Health Regulations 2002 (SI 2002/2677) (COSHH 2002).

(1) *Storage*

Holding hazardous substances above prescribed control quantities without or in contravention of a consent is an offence (Planning (Hazardous Substances) Act 1990).

(2) *Exposure*

The COSSH 2002 impose a general duty to control or prevent exposure to such substances at work.

Figure 7.2 following reproduces an example provided by Defra of the number of regulated facilities that may be carried on at a given site.

Figure 7.2 Regulated facilities on a site

(*Source*: Defra Core Environmental Permitting Guidance 2010, updated March 2013)

7.6.3 Enforcement

The main offence under the EPR 2010 is similar to all environmental regulation and focuses on failing to hold or comply with an environmental permit where needed (regs 12 and 38). Under the EPR 2010 the regulator can also issue any of the following:

(a)   a revocation notice (reg 22);

(b)   an enforcement notice (reg 36);

(c)   a suspension notice, for serious pollution risks (reg 37);

(d)   a prohibition notice, in relation to a groundwater discharge (Sch 22, para 9);

(e)   an information requirement notice (reg 60).

It can also take steps to prevent or remedy pollution, and recover its costs from the operator (reg 57).

Failure to comply with such notices is an offence (reg 38), punishable by an unlimited fine and up to five years' imprisonment on indictment. Like most environmental liabilities, any offences by a body corporate, if committed with the consent, connivance or neglect of any of its officers, will mean they too are personally liable (reg 41).

Water pollution is a particular concern, and the enforcing authorities vigorously pursue offences, averaging more than 200 prosecutions a year in England and Wales (Defra, *Water Pollution Prosecutions 1990–2005*).

7.7   CLIMATE CHANGE LAW AND ENERGY PERFORMANCE

7.7.1   Introduction

This area of environmental law could be construed simply as part of environmental permitting and regulation (see **7.6** above). However, given the independent focus on climate change and energy efficiency, this chapter specifically discusses below the Kyoto Protocol, emissions trading and the UK's CRC Energy Efficiency Scheme, all of which cover the UK's most energy-intensive industries. In addition, the practical implication of the drive towards zero-carbon buildings is addressed by way of EPCs, Green Leases and the Green Deal.

7.7.2   Kyoto Protocol

Global warming has gradually become a well-recognised and highly regulated issue. The 1997 Kyoto Protocol to the United Nations Framework Convention on Climate Change set the world's first binding agreement on reducing carbon dioxide (and other harmful gases) emissions. The UK was bound to reduce its emissions by 12.5% below 1990 levels by the end of 2012. The UK planned to do this by a combination of encouraging and requiring energy efficiency, and reduced emissions. Although there are currently no further binding targets since 2012, the 18th Conference of the Parties at Doha resulted in an agreed timetable to adopt a universal climate agreement by 2015, and to continue the flexible mechanisms under Kyoto, discussed below.

There were three 'flexible mechanisms' under the Kyoto Protocol to achieve the previous targets: joint implementation (JI), the clean development mechanism (CDM) and emissions trading. The CDM enables developing nations to 'leapfrog' harmful industrial energy practices. Essentially, developed nations ('Annex I' countries) receive a credit towards their own targets by investing in cleaner technology in developing nations. These credits help fuel a carbon market for emissions trading. The most established market is the European Union Emissions Trading System (EU ETS).

7.7.3   EU ETS

7.7.3.1   Overview

The EU ETS (under Council Directive 2003/87/EC ([2003] OJ L275/32) establishing a scheme for greenhouse gas emission allowance trading) is integrated with the Kyoto Protocol and is now the world's largest GHG emissions trading scheme. Under the scheme, which began in January 2005, large emitters of GHGs in the EU must monitor and report their emissions. The scheme covers around 11,000 installations accounting for 45% of the EU's carbon dioxide emissions. These include energy generation activities, the production and processing of ferrous metals, mineral industries, and pulp and paper industries.

Each year, emitters are obliged to submit carbon allowances equivalent to their emissions. Allowances are allocated through permitting, are auctioned or are bought on the carbon market. If a permit holder exceeds its allowance, it will incur a penalty. However, if it improves its efficiency, it may have a surplus of allowances which can be sold on the carbon market to other permit holders. This is meant to incentivise cleaner technology and greater energy efficiency.

There was an over-allocation of allowances in Phase I (2005–07), which effectively nullified the price of carbon and meant that compliance was not difficult. The scheme is currently in Phase III (2013–20), and now includes the aviation industry (since 2012). International airline operators unsuccessfully challenged this inclusion before the Court of Justice of the European Union. However, the International Civil Aviation Organisation has since resolved that by 2016 it will implement global, market-based measures to reduce international aviation emissions, from 2020. In light of this, the European Commission has proposed amendments to the EU ETS, effectively exempting the non-EEA parts of flights – both retrospectively and up until 2020.

The EU ETS is implemented in the UK by the Greenhouse Gas Emissions Trading Scheme Regulations 2012 (SI 2012/3038), which require operators carrying out EU ETS activities to hold a Greenhouse Gas Permit.

7.7.3.2 Enforcement

There are civil penalties for failure to surrender sufficient allowances each year. The penalty is set by the EU ETS Directive, and is implemented across every Member State. Currently the penalty is set at €100 for every tonne of carbon dioxide in excess of allowances. The regulator can also issue surrender and revocation notices for those in breach.

7.7.4 Climate Change Act 2008

7.7.4.1 Introduction

The Climate Change Act 2008 made the UK the first country in the world to have a legally-binding, long-term framework to cut GHG emissions. The target is at least an 80% reduction of GHG emissions below 1990 levels by 2050.

The Act enables a vast range of measures to accomplish this, including a carbon-budgeting system (tied in with the EU ETS – see **7.7.3**) and domestic trading schemes. The CRC Energy Efficiency Scheme is an example of the last of these measures.

7.7.4.2 CRC Energy Efficiency Scheme

The CRC Energy Efficiency Scheme ('the CRC') is the UK's mandatory scheme to monitor and reduce energy usage by private and public sector organisations. Qualifying participants must submit allowances for their emissions in accordance with the CRC Energy Efficiency Scheme Order 2013 (SI 2013/1119).

The CRC's Initial Phase (Phase 2) runs from 1 April 2014 to 31 March 2019. Organisations that exceed their allowances will need to purchase credits from the Government or a trader, per t/CO_2.

The Government anticipates that while approximately 20,000 organisations will have to participate in the Scheme, at least by periodically disclosing their energy usage, some 5,000 of those organisations (public and private) will need to acquire allowances – primarily those with annual electricity bills in excess of £500,000.

The CRC has already undergone substantial amendment and is now essentially a trading scheme and an environmental tax. See LexisPSL, *The CRC Energy Efficiency Scheme*, for more detail.

7.7.5 Energy performance and green leases

7.7.5.1 Introduction

While around half the UK's CO_2 emissions come from industry, commerce and the transportation of goods (National Energy Foundation), the other half comes from buildings – mostly homes (Department of Communities and Local Government, *Building a Greener Future*, July 2007).

The recast Energy Performance of Buildings Directive (Council Directive 2010/31/EU) aims to improve the performance of both commercial and residential buildings in the EU. The principal requirements of the Directive are as follows:

(a)   Member States must set minimum energy performance requirements for buildings.

(b)   New buildings and large buildings subject to major renovations must meet the minimum energy performance requirements.

(c)   EPCs must be made available to prospective buyers and tenants whenever a building is constructed, sold or rented.

(d)   Display Energy Certificates (DECs) must be displayed in large buildings occupied by public authorities.

(e)   Boilers and air conditioning systems in buildings must be inspected on a regular basis (Articles 8 and 9).

These requirements are transposed in the UK by the Buildings Regulations 2010 (SI 2010/2214) and the Energy Performance of Buildings (England and Wales) Regulations 2012 (SI 2012/3118) (EPB Regulations 2012).

The Government wants to achieve an overall zero-carbon building requirement goal in three steps:

(a)   In 2010, a 25% improvement in the energy/carbon performance set in the Building Regulations 2010 (SI 2010/2214).

(b)   By 2013, a 44% improvement.

(c)   Finally, in 2016, a zero-carbon requirement.

7.7.5.2   Energy Performance Certificates

An EPC provides the asset rating of a building, from A to G, measuring its construction and services (by examining its insulation, boilers, radiators, glazing, etc). It also includes a recommendation report for energy efficiency improvement. An EPC must be supplied at the marketing, sale or rental of any property (EPB Regulations 2012, regs 6–7). If an EPC is not provided by a developer, the building control inspector cannot issue a completion certificate for the works. There are some exempt buildings though, eg places of worship and temporary buildings used for two years or less (reg 5).

Certificates are valid for 10 years (reg 9). See **Figure 7.3** below.

Figure 7.3   Energy Performance Certificate

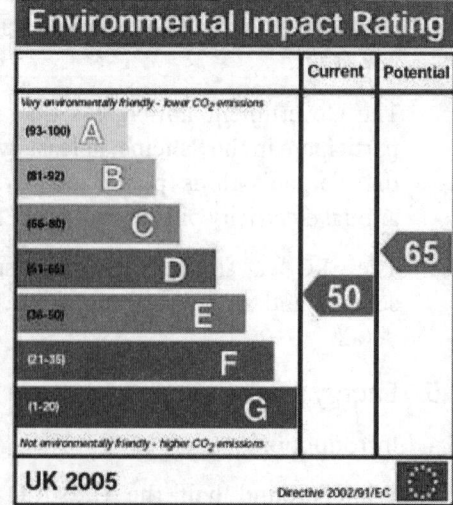

7.7.5.3   Display Energy Certificates

Any building in England and Wales occupied by a public authority, frequently visited by the public, with a floor area over 500m^2 also needs a DEC (EPB Regulations 2012, reg 10). This shows the *actual* energy use of the building (taken from meter readings), as well as its asset rating, and is valid for one year for buildings with a floor area of more than 1000m^2. For those between 500m^2 and 1000m^2 it is valid for 10 years.

7.7.5.4   Inspection of air-conditioning systems

Part 4 of the EPB Regulations 2012 imposes an obligation on those who have control of air-conditioning systems (with a maximum calorific output of more than 12kw) to ensure that the system is inspected at least every five years by an energy assessor.

The energy assessor must provide a written report of the inspection as soon as practicable after the inspection.

7.7.5.5   Enforcement and practical effect

Failure to comply with the Regulations can result in a penalty charge notice and a fine of up to £5,000.

The Government hopes that EPCs will encourage businesses and investors to support more energy-efficient construction and usage. In June 2013 the EU published a study indicating that better energy efficiency is rewarded in the market with higher rental and sales values.

However, given the rise of corporate social responsibility and public scrutiny of major organisations' environmental impact, improved energy efficiency is arguably also just good practice now. Furthermore, company directors are statutorily required to promote the success of the company, and in doing so 'must have regard to the impact of the company's operations on the community and the environment' (Companies Act 2006, s 172). See LexisPSL, *Mandatory Environmental Reporting*, for more detail. Hence, there are ethical, financial and fiduciary motivations to be more 'green' with energy usage.

7.7.5.6   Green Leases

With the ever-increasing awareness of environmental matters, some landlords and tenants are keen to enter into leases that actively promote a reduction in the building's impact on the environment.

Both landlord and tenant will enter into obligations to achieve this. For example, the landlord may covenant to:

(a)   achieve a specific energy rating throughout the term, with the tenant perhaps paying a reduced rent if that rating is not met;

(b)   for multi-let buildings, separately meter the water and electricity consumption of each tenant;

(c)   repair/modify buildings, plant and equipment so as to improve energy efficiency and to produce lower operating costs;

(d)   instigate a green management plan; this should not be too prescriptive, and should set targets rather than set out specific obligations;

(e)   ensure that all plant and equipment, particularly air-conditioning systems, operate to maximum efficiency; and

(f)   obtain an annual independent audit of the building's performance level.

Similarly, the tenant may be required to:

(a)   fit out or alter using recycled materials, or those that can be recycled (if practicable);

(b)   make all alterations energy neutral, or provide energy savings;

(c)   not partition in such a way as to make the air-conditioning system less efficient or that leads to a greater use of energy;

(d)   observe and perform the landlord's green management plan; and

(e)   yield up the premises with at least the same energy rating as applied at the beginning of the lease.

To facilitate the reduction of environmental impacts and help create an industry standard, the Better Buildings Partnership has released a Green Lease Toolkit. This contains best practice recommendations and model lease clauses.

7.7.6   Green Deal – Energy Act 2011

The Green Deal is an energy efficiency initiative to support microgeneration technologies in buildings. Energy improvement costs are funded by a charge on energy bills from accredited providers. Importantly, the liability to repay Green Deal finance rests with the bill payer and therefore attaches to the property rather than the owner. The register for Green Deal providers, assessors and installers launched on 28 January 2012.

7.8   REGULATORY ENFORCEMENT AND SANCTIONS ACT 2008

From April 2010 the EA and Natural England were given powers to impose administrative civil sanctions under the Regulatory Enforcement and Sanctions Act 2008 (RESA 2008). It is hoped that these will be used in place of criminal sanctions in appropriate circumstances. For example:

(a)   fixed or variable monetary penalties to address the financial benefits of non-compliance;

(b)   voluntary enforcement undertakings to remediate any harm to the environment;

(c)   compliance/restoration notices.

The aim is to prioritise compliance and the remediation of environmental harm, ahead of fines. This is a considerable new tool for environmental law regulators. The sanctions could prove popular next to the traditionally costly or disproportionate enforcement methods, particularly where an offender has an otherwise good record of compliance.

The EA issued its first civil sanction in July 2011, against Invensys for packaging waste offences. In addition to remedying its practices, the company will cover the cost of the Agency's investigation and future monitoring, and fund a community recycling initiative (a contribution of £21,000).

Again, it is too early to assess the impact of RESA 2008, but a client should be warned of the potential for the imposition of such sanctions (particularly monetary penalties) in addition to criminal liability, although, currently, it does not extend to environmental permitting offences.

7.9   ASBESTOS

7.9.1   Introduction

Asbestos remains the single greatest cause of work-related deaths in the UK. According to the Health and Safety Executive (HSE), at least 3,500 people in Great Britain die each year from asbestos-related cancer, as a result of past exposure.

Asbestos was used extensively as a building material in the UK from the 1950s through to the mid-1980s. It proved ideal for fireproofing and insulation, and so is likely to be found in roofing, floor tiles, around pipes (as insulation), and for wall and ceiling panels.

Although such use is now illegal, much asbestos remains in place. It is safe to assume that any building constructed before 2000 may contain asbestos. If it is in poor condition or damaged, asbestos fibres may become airborne, which is when they pose a significant risk.

7.9.2　Control of Asbestos Regulations 2012

The Control of Asbestos Regulations 2012 (SI 2012/632) impose a duty to identify and manage asbestos in non-domestic buildings. The duty could fall on the employer, owner or occupier of premises to conduct an asbestos survey and implement an Asbestos Management Plan (AMP).

7.9.2.1　Duty to manage asbestos in non-domestic premises

Regulation 4 imposes an obligation on the 'dutyholder' in 'non-domestic premises' to:

(a)　determine whether asbestos is present in a building, or is likely to be present (advice from the HSE is to assume that it is unless there is strong evidence to the contrary); and

(b)　manage any asbestos that is or is likely to be present (this requires an AMP, and the lack of one is also an offence).

Managing asbestos could include proper containment or even removal of it, which entails even further duties.

7.9.2.2　Definition of 'dutyholder'

The 'dutyholder' is defined in reg 4(1) as:

(a)　every person who has, by virtue of a contract or tenancy, an obligation of any extent in relation to the maintenance or repair of non-domestic premises or any means of access or egress to or from those premises; or

(b)　in relation to any part of non-domestic premises where there is no such contract or tenancy, every person who has, to any extent, control of that part of those non-domestic premises or any means of access or egress to or from those premises.

This broad definition could encompass owners, landlords, tenants, licensees and potentially managing agents.

Where there is more than one dutyholder, the relative contributions to be made by each in complying with the reg 4 duties are determined by the 'nature and extent of the maintenance and repair obligations' owed by each dutyholder.

7.9.2.3　Enforcement

Section 33(1)(c) of the Health and Safety at Work etc Act 1974 provides that it is an offence for a person to contravene any health and safety regulations. Similar to the EPA 1990, s 37 of the Health and Safety at Work etc Act 1974 provides that where an offence is committed with the consent or connivance of, or is attributable to any neglect on the part of, any director, manager, secretary or other similar officer, then that person (as well as the organisation) can be held criminally liable. If convicted on indictment in the Crown Court, the penalty for each offence is imprisonment for no more than two years and/or an unlimited fine.

The HSE enforces asbestos regulation rigorously. In transactional work, it is imperative that enquiries are made of assessments and current AMPs.

7.9.2.4　Landlord and tenant issues

In multi-let premises, the responsibility for maintenance of the common parts, services, external fabric and main structure of the building will generally lie with the landlord. The landlord will be a dutyholder, and will be required under reg 4 to arrange for asbestos surveys to be carried out and for copies of asbestos registers to be produced to each tenant.

Where a lease imposes repairing obligations on a tenant, the landlord should ensure that the tenant is aware of its obligations under reg 4 and be satisfied that the tenant has complied with those obligations.

7.10 JAPANESE KNOTWEED

7.10.1 Introduction

According to the EA, Japanese knotweed is the most invasive species of plant in Britain. It spreads extremely quickly, can grow 10cm a day, exists in almost any habitat and destroys native vegetation. It is now found in almost every county in the UK, particularly along rivers and railways and on brownfield sites.

7.10.2 Practical impact

The plant is an increasing problem for many developers. Japanese knotweed shoots can push through tarmac and damage pavements and building foundations. The presence of the plant on a development site can lead to significant delays and huge costs. Effective control of the plant using herbicides takes at least three years. Excavation offers rapid removal, but the costs are substantial, and the disposal at a licensed landfill site of a stand of Japanese knotweed measuring $1m^2$ will cost in the region of £27,000. Recent reports have indicated that the cost of dealing with Japanese knotweed on the Olympic site in east London could be around £70 million (Local Government Executive).

7.10.3 Liability

A developer that has Japanese knotweed on its site also faces the risk of criminal and civil liability. Under the Wildlife and Countryside Act 1981, for example, it is an offence to plant or otherwise cause the species to grow in the wild. Japanese knotweed is also classed as controlled waste under the EPA 1990, and must therefore be disposed of safely at a licensed landfill site, according to the Controlled Waste (England and Waes) Regulations 2012 (SI 2012/811).

The *Knotweed Code of Practice: Managing Japanese Knotweed on Development Sites*, produced by the EA towards the end of 2006 and updated in July 2013, provides advice and guidance in dealing with knotweed.

7.11 FLOOD RISKS

Flooding has become a major environmental risk in the past decade. Alongside global extreme weather events, the UK experienced devastating floods in 2007 and 2012. The combined damage caused exceeded £4 billion worth of insurance pay outs (Association of British Insurers (ABI)). The ABI agreed a Memorandum of Understanding with the Government to ensure flood insurance remains widely affordable and available. The Flood Re scheme, introduced in Pt 4 of the Water Act 2014, is intended to replace the ABI Statement of Principles from 2015. It provides a not-for-profit reinsurance scheme managed by the insurance industry, for households at significant risk of flooding.

Flooding risks are part of standard desktop studies and enquiries for sale. However, it is likely this area will also become more sophisticated as the risks increase.

7.12 SENTENCING GUIDELINES: ENVIRONMENTAL OFFENCES

The Sentencing Council for England and Wales' definitive guideline for environmental offences came into force on 1 July 2014. It covers sentencing for:

- the unauthorised deposit of waste (fly-tipping) under s 33 of the EPA 1990;
- illegal discharges to air, land and water under regs 12 and 38 of the EPR 2010;
- breach of the duty of care under s 34 of the EPA 1990;

- breach of an abatement notice under s 80 of the EPA 1990;
- offences committed under s 1 of the Control of Pollution (Amendment) Act 1989 (transportation of controlled waste without registering);
- restrictions on use of public sewers under s 111 of the Water Industry Act 1991; and
- offences under the Transfrontier Shipment of Waste Regulations 2007.

The Sentencing Council introduced these guidelines as it reports: 'There is limited guidance in the Magistrates' Court Sentencing Guidelines or in Court of Appeal authority. Research has also shown a lack of familiarity among magistrates with sentencing these types of offences.' See <http://sentencingcouncil.judiciary.gov.uk/about/environment.htm>.

7.13 ENVIRONMENT TRIBUNAL

As the breadth of environmental law grows, it arguably requires more sophisticated judicial resources. A First-Tier (Environment) Tribunal was created in May 2011. Its current jurisdiction is to hear appeals from regulators, such as under the RESA 2008. Since it heard its first case in November 2012 (against a remediation notice served by the Marine Management Organisation) the tribunal has received more than 400 appeals, with approximately one third allowed. As Lord Carnwath said: 'Making use of the new tribunals structure and expert resources could provide a low cost solution to what has long been seen as a gap in environmental law.'

REVIEW ACTIVITY

Below are four different scenarios, which cover many of the core environmental issues discussed above, as well as some related areas which a property lawyer may need to address. The first three cover general issues and liabilities, increasing with each scenario. The last covers the Contaminated Land Regime.

(1)   Operation of a dry cleaners

A client wants quick legal advice on what environmental liabilities he may face for operating a typical dry-cleaning business.

(2)   Mixed use inner-city redevelopment

A developer wishes to purchase and knock down a large inner-city building (built in the 1950s), and to build hundreds of new offices and residential units. During investigations it discovers that there is a lack of complete history on the site's use, but a small petrol station was in operation on part of the land until 10 years ago. During excavation the developer finds the remnants of an old Roman wall. What environmental issues are raised on these facts alone?

(3)   Sale of an aluminium and steel foundry

A PLC manufacturing giant wishes to purchase a large steel foundry, to add to its production capabilities. You know the site firsthand: it has been in use as a factory since the early 1900s and it is near a major river. What environmental issues would this raise, in addition to the typical activities and impact of a factory?

(4)   Contaminated land and appropriate persons

A partnership business, Alpha, operated a large paint factory from 1970–2008. Environmental reports show there was some chemical leakage in the factory basement during this period. Company Beta, a profitable car detailer, bought the property in 2008 after Alpha said, 'Do any investigations you want – it's a pretty dirty site.' Beta began reconstruction and foundation work for a premier car garage on site, before it suffered financially in the recession. PLC Gamma acquired the land in 2012 from Beta. Gamma had received comprehensive advice from both its investment bank, Delta, and its insurers, Epsilon. Knowing there was contamination on site, Gamma got a 10% discount on the sale price.

Assuming the land is contaminated under the Contaminated Land Regime, list the potential 'appropriate persons' for a remediation notice. Consider any exclusions and the apportionment test.

Answers to this Review activity may be found in Appendix 1.

CHAPTER 8

SEARCHES AND ENQUIRIES

8.1	Local search and enquiries	111
8.2	Planning matters	111
8.3	Drainage	112
8.4	Highways	112
8.5	Contaminated land	112
8.6	Commons registration	112
8.7	Enquiries of the seller	112
8.8	Flood searches	112
8.9	Survey and inspection	113
8.10	Investigation of title	113
	Review activity	114

A buyer of development land (or other commercial property) will make the same pre-contract searches and raise broadly similar pre-contract enquiries as a buyer of residential property. This part of the book does not intend to repeat sections of the Legal Practice Guide, *Property Law and Practice*; rather it focuses upon the particular concerns of a buyer of a development site at the pre-contract stage.

8.1 LOCAL SEARCH AND ENQUIRIES

The usual form of application for a search and enquiries should be submitted to the local authority in duplicate together with the fee. A plan should be attached so that the local authority can identify the land concerned.

In commercial transactions, consideration ought to be given to the possibility of raising the optional enquiries which are set out in form CON29O, in addition to the usual CON29R enquiries. An additional fee is payable in respect of each optional enquiry. These enquiries are designed to cover matters which are relevant only in particular kinds of transactions.

For example, on the acquisition of a development site, the buyer's solicitor ought to consider raising the optional enquiry relating to the location of public footpaths or bridleways which may cross the development site (since consent of the local authority would be required in order to divert them), and the optional enquiry relating to the location of gas pipelines to see if any run under or near the property (since this may affect development of the land). Prudent buyers will opt for safety by paying for replies to all of the optional enquiries.

In reviewing replies to CON29R enquiries, particular attention should be given to information relating to planning matters affecting the property and access to the site over adopted highways.

8.2 PLANNING MATTERS

The developer will want to know whether planning permission currently exists in respect of all or part of the site, or whether there have been any past applications for permission which have been unsuccessful. (The fact that an application for development was recently refused will be an important consideration for a developer.) He will also need to know what type of land use is currently indicated by the local planning authority in the development plans for the area in which the site is situated. Any existing or proposed tree preservation orders must be clearly pointed out to the developer.

8.3 DRAINAGE

It will be important for the developer to establish how foul and surface water currently drains away from the property to the public sewers (ie through main drains, private drains, or watercourses) so that he can estimate whether the current drainage system will be able to cope with foul and surface drainage from the developed site, or whether new drains will have to be constructed. If the site is vacant land, there are unlikely to be any drains serving it, and therefore he will need to know the location of the nearest public sewer where connection of newly-constructed drains may be made.

8.4 HIGHWAYS

The developer will need to know that immediate access to the site can be obtained from a public highway. He will need to know about each pavement and verge lying between the title boundary of the property and the public road, because if such land is in private ownership and is not publicly adopted, it may become a ransom strip if access is needed over it. The developer will also need to confirm that there are no new highways proposed in the vicinity of the site which would adversely affect the development. Some of this information is available from the CON29 Enquiries of the Local Authority, but the information revealed is not particularly detailed, so specific enquiries will have to be raised with the relevant highway authority.

8.5 CONTAMINATED LAND

There is a danger that a buyer of land will become liable to pay excessive clean-up costs in relation to contaminated land. See **Chapter 7** regarding contaminated land and suggested ways of reducing the risk.

8.6 COMMONS REGISTRATION

The need to raise CON29O optional enquiry 22 relating to the registration of the property in the commons register maintained by the county council will depend upon the type and location of the land being acquired, but the case of *G & K Ladenbau (UK) Ltd v Crawley and de Reya* [1978] 1 All ER 682 serves as a warning to all solicitors of the dangers of overlooking the necessity for raising such an enquiry in appropriate cases. In that case, solicitors were held to be negligent for not having carried out a commons registration search in respect of a site being acquired for a new factory development. If a rural site is being acquired, enquiry 22 should always be made. If an inner-city industrial site is being acquired for redevelopment, this enquiry might be inappropriate. However, between these two extremes there will be other cases where the buyer's solicitor is unsure as to whether or not such an enquiry is necessary, and in those cases it would therefore be prudent to raise enquiry 22.

8.7 ENQUIRIES OF THE SELLER

Pre-contract enquiries of the seller will be raised on one of the standard printed forms of enquiry, or on the buyer's solicitors' own word-processed form of enquiry. Additional enquiries may be raised as the buyer's solicitor considers appropriate. These may focus upon discovering further information about the planning status of the site, the location of public drains and highways, the suitability of the land for building purposes and possible past contamination of the land. Again, information regarding these matters is often discoverable from other sources, but that alone should not be a sufficient reason for the seller to refuse to provide answers.

8.8 FLOOD SEARCHES

In June 2009, the Environment Agency (EA) reported that 5.2 million properties were at risk of flooding. Under an agreement made in June 2008 between Defra and the Association of

British Insurers, cover is provided to existing and successor policy holders in areas where the flood risk is not significant (1.3% or less), and where it is significant (over 1.3%) so long as the EA has announced plans for flood protection measures that will reduce the risk below significant within five years. However, the 2008 agreement (recently extended until 2015) does not apply to commercial properties unless they are 'small businesses'. Negotiations are taking place between the Government and the insurance industry for a successor scheme, Flood Re, but it seems that the new scheme will not apply to commercial properties at all. A property without standard buildings insurance, including flood cover, is unlikely to be mortgageable and will therefore be difficult to sell.

The flood map on the EA's website and Land Registry's Flood Risk Indicator Online are not suitable for assessing the risk of flooding to a particular property, and the Land Registry's search does not deal with surface water flooding (which in 2007 accounted for 70% by value of property flood damage). Accordingly, many solicitors acting on the purchase of a commercial property will routinely order a flood report from a commercial provider, which will usually provide the EA floodplain data, the EA National Flood Risk Assessment (NaFRA) and data on surface water flooding, topography, groundwater flooding, historic floods, and dam and reservoir flooding. The report may also contain practical suggestions on flood resistance and flood resilience measures.

8.9   SURVEY AND INSPECTION

Even though the land may be vacant, the developer-client should be advised to commission a survey of the land. Primarily, his surveyor will be checking on the suitability of the land for building purposes, in terms both of land stability and means of access and drainage. However, a thorough environmental survey of the land should be conducted to ensure that the developer does not acquire land which could have a potential clean-up liability (see **Chapter 7**).

For a number of reasons, an inspection of the property must always be conducted before exchange of contracts in order to:

(a)   assist in establishing ownership of, or responsibility for boundary walls, hedges and fences;

(b)   discover the existence of public or private rights of way which may be evidenced by worn footpaths, stiles, or breaks in the hedgerows;

(c)   spot the presence of overhead electricity power lines which would prevent or impede development. If there are power lines, the land is likely to be subject to a written wayleave agreement between the landowner and the electricity company giving the company the right to maintain its supply across the land. A copy of the agreement should be requested from the seller;

(d)   discover the rights of persons in occupation of the land. Solicitors are accustomed to thinking only in terms of a contributing spouse as the type of person who has occupiers' rights. However, with a development site, it is not unknown for a solicitor to overlook the presence of several cows in the corner of a field, which is unremarkable if the seller is a farmer but could be serious if the cows are grazing by virtue of rights of common, or under an agricultural or farm business tenancy;

(e)   ensure that adjoining landowners do not enjoy the benefit of easements of light or air which would impede the buyer's proposed development.

8.10   INVESTIGATION OF TITLE

Title is almost invariably deduced and investigated at the pre-contract stage of the transaction.

A thorough investigation of title is required in the same way as in the case of residential property. The developer-client will be particularly concerned to ensure that the property enjoys the benefit of all necessary easements and rights of access (both for the purpose of developing and for future occupiers of the completed development) and drainage (for foul and surface water). He will also need to be satisfied that there are no covenants restricting the proposed development or use of the land; or if there are, that they will be released, removed or modified, or that appropriate insurance will be available, and that any easements which burden the property will not prevent or restrict the proposed development or use.

REVIEW ACTIVITY

Consider the development site in Canvey Island, Essex shown in the title plan below. If you were acting for the prospective buyer of this site, what searches and enquiries would you raise?

Answers to this Review activity may be found in Appendix 1.

CHAPTER 9

CONSTRUCTION PROJECTS

9.1	Introduction	115
9.2	Who will be involved? The design and construction team	115
9.3	Different forms of procurement	118
9.4	Duties owed to third parties	125
9.5	Protecting third parties	128
9.6	Dispute resolution	132
	Review activity	133

9.1 INTRODUCTION

Having completed the acquisition of a site which is physically capable of being developed, and which is not encumbered in a way which would impede development, and having obtained satisfactory planning permission and sufficient funds, the client will now want to obtain a building which will be completed within a satisfactory timescale, within budget and in accordance with his specified requirements.

9.2 WHO WILL BE INVOLVED? THE DESIGN AND CONSTRUCTION TEAM

9.2.1 The employer

The employer is the owner of the site who will employ various professionals to design and construct a building upon his land. For the purposes of this book, the employer is a client who has acquired a site with the aim of developing it, and who will grant leases of the completed development. This part of the book assumes that the client, whilst involved in commercial property, is not a member of the construction industry and will, therefore, need to employ other persons in connection with design and construction.

9.2.2 The building contractor

In a traditional building contract (see **9.3.2**), the building contractor is engaged by the employer to construct a building in accordance with plans and specifications prepared by the employer's architect (see **9.2.3**). The contractor (sometimes called the 'main contractor' or 'principal contractor') will enter into a building contract with the employer, although he may not necessarily carry out all, or indeed any, of the building works. Instead, the contractor may enter into sub-contracts with other builders or trade contractors who will carry out the work. These sub-contractors are likely to be specialists in particular areas of the construction industry, such as lift sub-contractors, cladding sub-contractors or mechanical and electrical sub-contractors, so that, in a large project, there may be several different sub-contractors who execute works on different parts of the development. Most traditional forms of building contract permit sub-contracting only with the prior written consent of the employer (to be given through the agency of his architect), and some building contracts require the sub-contractors to be engaged on specific terms and conditions acceptable to the employer, which may include the obligation on the sub-contractors to grant collateral warranties (see **9.5.1**) to the employer/lenders in relation to the works carried out under their sub-contracts.

There are many different standard forms of building contract used in the construction industry, and this chapter does not intend to provide a detailed analysis of the obligations of the employer and the main contractor. The basic obligations of the employer under most traditional forms of contract are to give up possession of the site to the contractor (to enable uninterrupted building works to commence), not to interfere with the execution of building works (as the contractor has an implied right to complete the works, as well as a duty to do so), to appoint an architect for the purposes of the contract (ie to supervise the execution of the works, in his role as designer of the works, and to certify when the building has been satisfactorily completed and therefore adjudged to have reached the stage of 'practical completion'), to nominate sub-contractors to carry out the works (unless the contractor is to select his own), and to pay the price payable to the contractor as and when the contract requires.

In return, the contractor agrees to complete the work set out in the contract in the form of the architect's plans and specifications. When the architect has issued a certificate of practical completion, the contractor becomes entitled to receive full payment of the contract price less an amount known as 'retention' monies, and the employer is able to resume possession of the site for the purpose of granting leases to his tenants. The retention monies are held until such time as any minor works still to be completed at practical completion, known as snagging items of work, are completed, whereupon the retention monies are released to the contractor and a 'final certificate' is issued. If the contractor does not complete the works on time, the employer will usually be able to levy liquidated damages for delay, the amounts of which the parties will have agreed at the outset of the project. Such damages must represent a 'genuine pre-estimate' of the losses likely to be incurred by the employer, otherwise there is a danger that they will be classified as penalties which are unenforceable under English law.

Obligations as to quality and fitness of the building materials are implied under s 4 of the Supply of Goods and Services Act 1982, and s 13 of that Act implies a term that the contractor will exercise reasonable care and skill to see that the works will be of satisfactory quality and reasonably fit for their intended purpose. However, notwithstanding his implied obligations, the building contract is likely to contain an express obligation to execute the works in accordance with a standard prescribed by the contract and in accordance with the employer's requirements and performance specifications. The 'fitness for purpose' implied term referred to above is often included as an express term of the contract and is heavily negotiated between the parties. Employers sometimes seek an obligation that the contractor will carry out the works so that completed project as a whole (rather than simply the works) is fit for purpose. Conversely, contractors often seek to exclude fitness for purpose obligations altogether, spurred on by their professional indemnity insurers, by stating that such risks are uninsurable. A compromise is commonly achieved by linking the obligation of the contractor back to the wording of the Act, with a clause in the contract being inserted stating that the liability of the contractor shall be to carry out the works (rather than the completed project as a whole) so that such works are reasonably fit for their intended purpose.

It should be noted that with all forms of procurement, save for construction management (see **9.3.4.2**), there is no privity of contract between the employer and the sub-contractors since it is the main contractor who engages their services. However, the main contractor should be made liable under the terms of the main contract in respect of the acts or omissions of the sub-contractors. As noted above, in major projects, collateral warranties (see **9.5.1**) are often sought by clients from a list of principal sub-contractors, ie those whose packages of work are particularly important by size, value or the nature of their particular expertise. A client may regard any sub-contractors' warranties beyond such principal sub-contractors as an added benefit, but will likely be relying on the strength of the main contractor's covenant in the event that a defect arises in the completed works.

9.2.3   The architect

In a traditional form of contract the architect is engaged by the employer to carry out various tasks in relation to the design of the building. Broadly speaking, the architect prepares plans and specifications of the works required by the employer from which the builders will take their instructions, and he will supervise the execution of those works by the building contractor (or sub-contractors) in accordance with the plans and specifications. When the architect is satisfied that the works required by the building contract have been completed, he will issue a certificate of practical completion. As noted at **9.2.2**, this triggers the release of payments to the contractor save for retention monies, which are released only when snagging has been completed. In some instances, where, for example, there are several sections of the works comprising a building contract, the architect may issue sectional completion certificates to reflect the completion of different phases of the project.

9.2.4   The quantity surveyor/cost consultant

The quantity surveyor or cost consultant is engaged by the employer (or by the architect on behalf of the employer) to estimate the quantities of the materials to be used and to set them into bills of quantities. What the quantity surveyor or cost consultant does is to measure the amount of work and materials which will be necessary to complete construction in accordance with the architect's plans and specifications. On the basis of his bills of quantities, building contractors will be able to work out the amount of their estimated cost of construction.

9.2.5   The engineers

In large construction projects, there may be a team of consulting engineers, including a structural engineer, engaged by the employer to give advice on structural design, and mechanical, electrical, heating and ventilating engineers, who give advice to the employer on matters within their areas of competence.

The architect, quantity surveyor and team of consulting engineers, as professional people, owe the employer a duty by contract to carry out the work required of them with reasonable skill, care and diligence. The standard of care expected is the standard of the ordinary skilled man exercising and professing to have that special skill. If any one of them falls below that standard, or below any higher standard of care set by the professional appointment under which he is engaged, he will be liable in damages for breach of contract.

9.2.6   The project manager

In addition to the consultants referred to above, clients will often engage a project manager on major projects to assist with managing the contractor and professional team to achieve a successful completion of the project. The role of the project manager will be to coordinate the other team members, ensure deadlines are met and oversee the project as a whole.

9.2.7   The construction, design and management coordinator

There is also an obligation on clients involved in major construction projects in the UK to engage a construction, design and management coordinator (a 'CDM coordinator'). The Construction (Design and Management) Regulations 2007 (SI 2007/320) (the CDM Regulations), which came into force on 6 April 2007 and which replaced the Construction (Design and Management) Regulations 1994 (SI 1994/3140), govern the relevant obligations of the client and team members. The CDM coordinator's function is to ensure that the project is carried out in accordance with applicable health and safety regulations. For example, the CDM coordinator will ensure that the contractor provides adequate welfare facilities for its workers on site and that the site is adequately protected with hoarding. There are also general duties on all team members to communicate, coordinate and cooperate effectively with one another. Breach of the CDM Regulations can lead to criminal as well as civil liability.

9.3 DIFFERENT FORMS OF PROCUREMENT

9.3.1 Introduction

The way in which risks and responsibilities are allocated between the parties on a construction project is determined by the procurement process and form of construction contract used. There are various industry bodies, one of which is the Joint Contracts Tribunal (JCT), which over the years have developed their own standard-form construction documents. These contain different terms and conditions depending upon what risks the employer or the contractor will be taking in relation to the project. As these industry bodies usually represent building contractors (rather than employers), it is usually necessary for lawyers acting for the employer to amend the standard terms and conditions to redress the balance of risk in favour of the employer.

The key elements of any building contract usually centre around time (ie when the project needs to be delivered), price (ie how much the project is going to cost) and quality (ie what standard of skill and care will be required, and whether that is appropriate for the intended use of the finished project, eg a high-tech city office or tower as opposed to a low-grade warehousing facility).

The relative importance attached to each of these critical factors will often determine the procurement process adopted and the form of building contract used. Many building projects require external funders in the form of commercial lenders to finance the construction of the project. In addition, in times of economic uncertainty many projects now involve a partnering or alliancing arrangement, whereby two or more project participants combine to form a consortium which is able to share the risks and rewards inherent in any building project. Such arrangements may take the form of binding commitments to each other and be documented contractually, or alternatively reflect a more aspirational, non-binding collaboration agreement or charter. Many of the industry bodies, including the JCT, have their own standard-form agreements. Bespoke partnering arrangements are also increasingly being adopted in the public sector, with an example being the use of framework agreements by local governments for utilities or infrastructure works. Under these types of agreement, several tendering contractors all sign up to a framework agreement (usually with no guarantee of work); when an individual works contract is required to be undertaken, the government entity then selects a contractor from the framework and enters into a separate call-off contract with the successful individual contractor. This has the perceived benefit for the client of providing a pre-selected panel of quality contractors ready to commence work quickly on an individual works contract, whilst the tendering contractors have the benefit of regular workflow from a financially sound client (albeit that no work is guaranteed to be forthcoming). Partnering arrangements often measure performance by use of key performance indicators (KPIs), which can be used successfully for the benefit of the project as a whole if parties collaborate in an open manner and in the spirit of mutual trust and co-operation. However, the take up of partnering agreements may be limited due to difficulties in being able to bring a successful claim against a party which has not met its obligations under the particular partnering arrangement.

The different forms of procurement are outlined below.

9.3.2 Traditional contract

A key feature of traditional procurement is that the design element and the construction of a project are separate. As noted at **9.2**, the building contractor is engaged to construct the project pursuant to the building contract, and the professional consultants are engaged to design the project under the terms of their professional appointments.

The typical structure of traditional procurement is set out in **Figure 9.1** below.

Figure 9.1   Structure of traditional procurement

Some advantages and disadvantages of a traditional contract are listed in **Table 9.1** below.

Table 9.1   Advantages and disadvantages of a traditional contract

	Time	Money	Quality
Advantages	More certainty in the construction period, as the design is completed and the contractor therefore has to build according to the detailed plans.	Greater certainty in the fixed lump-sum contract price as the design is fully developed prior to construction.	The detailed contract documents can specify the employer's exact requirements so should lead to better quality, with the construction phase starting only after the detailed design has been completed.
Disadvantages	Longer overall, because the employer needs to complete the design before the construction phase commences. Employer-driven changes to the project during construction phase may delay the project.	Additional design fees are paid to professional consultants. Employer-driven changes to the project during construction may increase costs.	The building contractor will be responsible for the works but will not be responsible for design (unless there is a contractor designed portion), and so the employer retains both the design risk itself and the interface risk with construction. The technical documents, forming part of the building contract, need to set out precisely the requirements of the employer. This places an additional burden on the employer.

9.3.3   Design and build contract

Under a design and build building contract, the building contractor is responsible for both the design and the construction of a project. The building contractor may appoint his own design team or sub-contractors to carry out design, but the building contractor is liable to the employer for the design (as well as construction) of the project.

In major construction projects where employers often seek an effective and complete risk transfer, the employer ordinarily appoints his own professional consultants to develop initial designs. After such designs have been developed, the employer, principal members of the design team (ie the architect and engineers) and the building contractor will enter into a 'novation' agreement. This tripartite agreement transfers both rights and responsibilities from the employer to the building contractor. The building contractor is then able to instruct the consultant previously engaged by the employer to complete the detailed design for the project, and also has direct rights against the consultant in the event that such designs developed under the appointment are deficient.

The typical structure of design and build procurement is set out in **Figure 9.2** below.

Figure 9.2   Structure of design and build procurement

Pre-novation (prior to construction)

Post-novation (during construction)

Some advantages and disadvantages of a design and build contract are listed in **Table 9.2** below.

Table 9.2   Advantages and disadvantages of a design and build contract

	Time	Money	Quality
Advantages	May be quicker than a 'traditional' contract because the employer needs to develop only outline designs.	Offers certainty by having a fixed lump-sum contract price.	The building contractor assumes a 'single point of responsibility' towards the employer rather than this being spread between the building contractor and design team.
Disadvantages	An employer who appoints and novates a team of professional consultants may take a similar total time to a traditional contract. Employer-driven changes to the project during construction phase may delay the project.	The 'single point of responsibility' assumed by the building contractor is likely to involve a price premium for the building contractor to take on this risk. Employer-driven changes to the project may significantly affect the final price paid.	Where the building contractor has single point responsibility for design and construction, there may be a temptation to drive down quality to save costs, as the building contractor's profit depends on meeting the building contract requirements at the lowest cost.

Design and build contracts are currently the most popular form of building contract, and are widely used on both simple structures and major projects.

9.3.4   Management contracting and construction management

The two forms of procurement referred to above are the most commonly used forms of procurement for building projects in the UK. However, other forms of procurement are available, one of which is called management contracting and the other of which is called construction management. These are usually adopted only by sophisticated developers on high-value projects, who are familiar with the procurement processes involved.

9.3.4.1   Management contracting

A management contractor is appointed by the employer and is similar to a professional consultant rather than a building contractor. The management contractor is responsible for managing the construction of the project.

The management contractor does not carry out the work itself, but instead appoints works contractors to carry out the work and any specialist design. The management contractor administers the works contracts. The employer looks to the management contractor to see that the work is carried out properly, but the management contractor has very limited liability to the employer for failure by the works contractors to carry out their works.

The typical structure of management contracting procurement is set out in **Figure 9.3** below.

Figure 9.3   Structure of management contracting procurement

Some advantages and disadvantages of management contracting are listed in **Table 9.3** below.

Table 9.3   Advantages and disadvantages of management contracting

	Time	Money	Quality
Advantages	May be quick: design and construction may progress in parallel as works contractors instructed on an ad hoc basis.	Shorter construction period and more flexible arrangements may allow the project to adapt to meet employer's needs.	Management contractor and design team can work together flexibly to meet employer's requirements.
Disadvantages	No certain construction period, and could be haphazard if works contractors not managed properly. The employer may have to claim delay damages from the management contractor and many works contractors if the requirements of the works contracts and management contract are not met.	No certain construction price. Number of different works contractors involved.	Overall responsibility for quality may be diluted between the professional consultants, the management contractor and the works contractors. No single point of responsibility for design and construction.

9.3.4.2   Construction management

The employer appoints a construction manager and the professional consultants. The construction manager is responsible for managing the construction of the project. The remaining professional consultants carry out the remaining design.

Where this form of procurement differs from management contracting (see **9.3.4.1**) is that whilst the construction manager arranges for the employer to appoint specialist trade contractors and administers the trade contracts, it is the employer who actually enters into the trade contracts themselves. The trade contractors carry out construction and any specialist design directly for the employer.

The typical structure of construction management procurement is set out in **Figure 9.4** below.

Figure 9.4   Structure of construction management procurement

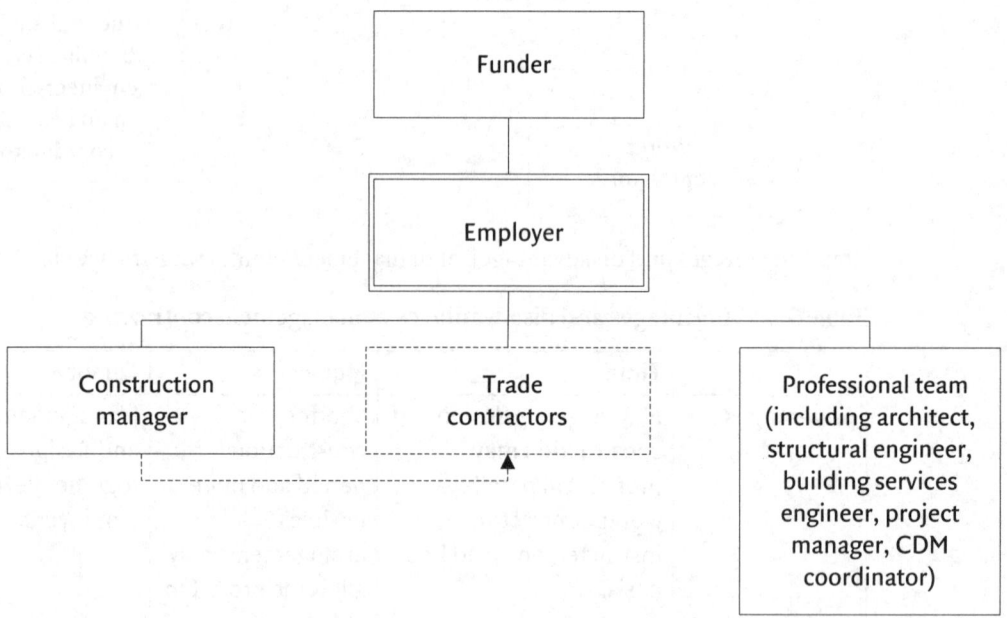

Some advantages and disadvantages of construction management are listed in **Table 9.4** below.

Table 9.4   Advantages and disadvantages of construction management

	Time	**Money**	**Quality**
Advantages	May be quick: design and construction may progress in parallel as works contractors instructed on an ad hoc basis.	Compared with management contracting, the construction manager may charge a fixed fee, rather than a percentage on the whole construction price.	Construction manager and design team can work together to meet employer's requirements. Flexible process can help meet employer's requirements.

	Time	Money	Quality
Disadvantages	No certain construction period and could be haphazard if works contractors not managed properly. The employer may have to claim delay damages from the many trade contractors if the requirements of the trade contracts and management contract are not met.	No certain construction price. Even with a construction manager, the client needs to be hands-on with the trade contractors, and this requires time, experience and resources.	Overall responsibility for quality may be diluted between professional consultants, the construction manager and the trade contractors. No single point of responsibility for design and construction.

9.3.5 Pricing mechanisms

Within the different forms of building contract, there is often flexibility as to how the price paid by the employer to the building contractor will be calculated. A 'lump-sum' contract gives the employer certainty as to what he will pay to the building contractor for the works described in the building contract, provided that the employer does not change his description of the works required to be carried out, or there are no grounds available to the building contractor to claim additional monies under the building contract.

Alternatively, certain building contracts have a guaranteed maximum price (GMP) mechanism in them for determining the price to be paid to the building contractor. This allows the employer to set a maximum price payable to the building contractor; it often includes financial incentives for the building contractor to achieve cost savings in relation to the works so that they cost less than the GMP and allow the contractor to benefit from any such cost savings.

Another way of calculating the price to be paid is found in a 'measurement' contract. Under a measurement contract, the employer pays the building contractor for expected levels of work carried out. Then, at given stages of the project or when the project is complete, the employer's professional consultants review the amount of work the building contractor has actually carried out. The building contractor or the employer makes any necessary balancing payment, if the building contractor has carried out more or less work than the parties originally expected.

There are also bespoke forms of building contract to cater for different types of contract. Major engineering contracts use their own bespoke forms of contract. Project finance transactions also have specific forms of contracts, as do projects carried out overseas, government projects and partnering or joint venture contracts. The key point to note here is that all projects place different values on the three critical objectives of time, cost and quality, and the relative importance attached to each of these factors will often determine the preferred method of procurement and the choice of contract.

9.4 DUTIES OWED TO THIRD PARTIES

9.4.1 Introduction

If the project results in the employer obtaining a completed building which turns out to be defective by reason of its design or the materials used, or by reason of the manner in which it was constructed, the employer is likely to have a claim for breach of contract against those members of the design and construction team who caused the defect. Contractual damages are assessed under the rule in *Hadley v Baxendale* (1854) 9 Exch 341, under which the claimant will be able to recover:

(a) losses arising naturally, according to the normal course of things, from the breach of contract; or

(b) such losses as may be reasonably be supposed to have been in the contemplation of the parties at the time they made the contract, as a probable result of the breach. This is likely to enable the employer to recover any costs incurred in carrying out remedial repairs, subject to the normal limitation rules under the Limitation Act 1980.

However, consider the position of a buyer from the employer who discovers a defect after completion of his purchase of the freehold; or that of a mortgagee of the freehold who discovers that the value of his security is seriously impaired because of a hidden design or construction defect; or that of a tenant of the building who enters into a lease on the basis of a full repairing covenant, which may oblige him to repair damage caused by such inherent defects. Traditionally, such third parties were unable to bring a claim for breach of contract as they did not have a contractual relationship with the employer's development team. Because of the rules of privity of contract, the practice arose of members of the development team giving a collateral warranty with such parties in order to enable them to bring a claim; as to collateral warranties, see **9.5.1**. In the absence of such a collateral warranty, and given the difficulties of a third party seeking a remedy in tort (see **9.4.3**), an alternative to collateral warranties can be found under statute (see **9.4.2**).

9.4.2 Contracts (Rights of Third Parties) Act 1999

The Contracts (Rights of Third Parties) Act 1999 came into force on 11 May 2000 and applies to contracts entered into on or after that date. It allows the parties to a contract to confer rights on third parties. A third party, such as a future tenant or mortgage lender, may enforce the contract as if he were a party to it, provided that the contract expressly provides that he may, or that it purports to confer a benefit on him. The third party must be expressly identified in the contract by name, as a member of a class or as answering a particular description, but need not be in existence when the contract is entered into.

In theory, therefore, this Act provides a mechanism whereby third parties would be able to enforce the contractual obligations of the employer's development team if, for example, the contract was stated to be for the benefit of 'all future tenants' of the building. Whilst the use of the Act has been promoted widely amongst City firms of solicitors, there has been some reluctance on the part of beneficiaries, in particulars funders, to accept it, many of whom seem to prefer the paper security of holding a document, ie in the form of a collateral warranty, rather than relying on the operation of the Act.

It still seems likely, therefore, that, for the time being at least, traditional forms of protection (eg tort or collateral warranties) will still need to be relied upon. However, the Act has great potential benefits, particularly for major projects, given the sheer number of interested third parties requiring rights. The use of the Act to grant third parties rights ought therefore to be promoted further as a way of minimising the paper trail that otherwise results in large-scale projects.

9.4.3 Liability in tort

In seeking to bring a claim in tort, the problem that the buyer, lender or tenant will encounter is that any loss they sustain as a result of faulty design, materials or workmanship is likely to be classified as pure economic loss and therefore generally irrecoverable in tort. For example, in the case of the freehold buyer, if he discovers after completion of his purchase that the foundations of the building have been laid in a negligent fashion, so that the building cannot be used without remedial works first being carried out, he can either execute the repairs himself (thereby incurring repair costs), or dispose of the defective building to someone else (probably at less than the purchase price) or simply abandon the property (thereby wasting the money paid for the building in the first place); but whichever course of action the buyer takes, the loss he incurs is purely economic, and only in limited circumstances will the courts allow the claimant to recover such loss in tort.

To establish a claim in negligence, the claimant will have to show that the defendant owed him a duty of care, that the defendant breached that duty and that the claimant suffered an actionable form of damage as a result. Following a series of House of Lords decisions in the late 1980s and early 1990s, it is safe to say that liability in the tort of negligence will arise only if there is a breach of one of two categories of duty. The first duty is based upon the decision in *Donoghue v Stevenson* [1932] AC 562, where liability will arise out of a lack of care which results in reasonably foreseeable damage to persons or to property (other than to the property which causes the damage). The second duty is founded upon the case of *Hedley Byrne & Co Ltd v Heller & Partners Ltd* [1964] AC 465 and is concerned with a lack of care which causes non-physical economic loss.

9.4.3.1 Liability for physical damage

The duty of care under *Donoghue v Stevenson* [1932] AC 562 is a duty to avoid physical injury to person or property. It imposes a duty upon the manufacturer of a product (eg a builder constructing a building) to take reasonable care to avoid damage to person or property through defects in the product. However, it does not impose a duty upon the manufacturer to ensure that the product itself is free from defects. Simply because the design or construction of the building is defective does not necessarily render the person who was responsible for the defect liable in damages, even if a duty was owed and the damage was foreseeable. The case would turn upon whether the claimant suffered a type of loss recognised by the courts as legally recoverable. Pure economic loss (eg the cost of repairing the defect, and the loss of profits while repairs are carried out) is not recoverable under *Donoghue v Stevenson* principles.

In *D&F Estates Ltd v Church Commissioners for England* [1989] AC 177, the House of Lords held that liability in tort arises only where there is some physical damage to the person or to some other property, and that damage to the building itself which merely reduces its value is pure economic loss and thus irrecoverable in tort (except under *Hedley Byrne v Heller* principles – see **9.4.3.2**). In *Murphy v Brentwood District Council* [1990] 2 All ER 908, the House of Lords reaffirmed its earlier decision and stated that the idea that component parts of the same building could amount to separate species of property (the 'complex structure' theory) – so that, for example, negligently laid foundations could be said to have damaged 'other' property when they led to cracks appearing in the walls – was not correct.

To give an example of what may be recoverable, consider the position where, after completion of his purchase of the freehold, a defectively-constructed roof collapses and causes personal injury to a buyer. The buyer may be able to recover damages in respect of his personal injuries and any economic loss arising out of those injuries (eg loss of earnings), but he will not be able to recover the cost of repairing the roof itself since that loss is pure economic loss.

9.4.3.2 Liability for economic loss

Economic loss is a term which can be used to describe any monetary loss. Pure economic loss is monetary loss which is not connected to physical injury to person or property. With one or two isolated and doubtful exceptions (see, eg, *Junior Books v Veitchi* [1983] 1 AC 520), pure economic loss is recoverable in tort only where, in a special relationship of close proximity, a duty of care is owed to avoid loss arising from a negligent misstatement. In *Hedley Byrne & Co Ltd v Heller & Partners Ltd* [1964] AC 465, the House of Lords decided that, in a relationship of close proximity, where a person was seeking information from one who was possessed of certain skills, a duty was owed by the latter to exercise reasonable care if he knew, or ought to have known, that reliance was being placed upon his skill and judgement. Put simply, the duty amounts to a duty to prevent pure economic loss arising from the making of a statement or the giving of advice. In the context of a building project, many statements are made and much advice is given, but proximity of the parties and reliance are the fundamental factors.

The extent of this duty was restated and redefined by the House of Lords in *Caparo Industries plc v Dickman* [1990] 2 AC 605. It is now the case that, in order for there to be the requisite degree of proximity between the parties for the duty to arise, the defendant (ie the person who made the statement or gave the advice) must have known (both in the preparation of what was said and in the delivery) that the statement would be communicated to an identified person or group of persons in connection with a transaction of a particular type, and that the recipient would be very likely to rely upon it.

While the employer, by reason of his contractual relationship with his professional advisers (eg the architect or structural engineer), might easily establish the requisite degree of proximity and show reliance upon the advice given, his tenant, buyer or the buyer's lender is unlikely to be able to show the requisite proximity (see *Hunt & Others v Optima (Cambridge) Ltd & Others* [2014] EWCA Civ 714). In other words, the pure economic loss that a third party suffers remains irrecoverable.

As a result of this inability to recover the cost of repairing damage to the building outside a contractual relationship, various devices have been utilised by buyers, their lenders, tenants and the employer's own financiers. These are examined further at **9.5**.

9.5   PROTECTING THIRD PARTIES

9.5.1   Collateral warranties

A collateral warranty is an agreement entered into (under hand or by deed) by someone engaged in the construction or design of a building, by virtue of which that person assumes a contractual duty of care for the benefit of someone who has an interest in seeing that the building is free from defects, but who does not otherwise have a contractual relationship with the warrantor. Collateral warranties are commonly required to be given by the consultants, the main contractor and the sub-contractors to the freehold buyer of the development, his lender, the employer's financiers and possibly (if negotiated) the tenant. The employer does not need warranties from either the building contractor or the design team as he is in direct contract with such parties under the building contract and professional appointments. However, he may require warranties from the sub-contractors with whom he has no direct contractual relationship as additional protection behind the main contractor's warranty, or may require warranties after the consultants have been novated to the contractor.

The key advantage of having collateral warranties is that they create the certainty of a contractual relationship, as opposed to the uncertainty that exists in tort. All the claimant would need to show in order to establish a claim is that the contractual duty contained in the warranty had been breached and that damage had ensued. Losses which can be described as purely economic will also be recoverable under contractual principles where the loss suffered as a result of the breach of warranty could reasonably be said to have been in the contemplation of the parties at the time the warranty was entered into.

Many of the standard building contracts and forms of consultancy appointment also contain suggested forms of collateral warranty. However, as with the terms of such contracts themselves, it is unlikely that well-advised employer/developer clients would accept these forms of collateral warranty as they often contain unacceptable limits of liability, once again driven by the requirements of the warrantor's professional indemnity insurers. For instance, standard forms of collateral warranty have been published by the British Property Federation, the Construction Industry Council and the Joint Contracts Tribunal, and have been approved by the relevant professional bodies. Such forms of warranty will not be sufficient if acting for employer/developer clients, who will require bespoke forms of collateral warranty without extensive limitation of liability provisions. This is an area where solicitors are involved extensively in the negotiation of acceptable forms, and where the market at the time the negotiation takes place can play a large part in resolving such negotiations.

A collateral warranty will normally contain the following provisions:

(a)   Confirmation that the warrantor (ie building contractor, sub-contractor or consultant) owes to the third party benefiting from the warranty a duty of care similar to that owed to the person employing him. The warrantor will already owe a duty of care to the person employing him, normally the developer, by virtue of being appointed under a contract by his employer to carry out the design or construction work. It will oblige the warrantor to use reasonable skill and care in the performance of his duties under the contract, and he will be negligent if he fails to do so.

(b)   Confirmation that deleterious materials will not be used in the development. A warranty given by the architect will confirm that such materials will not be specified for use in the development, and a warranty given by the building contractor will confirm that such materials will not be used in the development. The materials that are not to be used may be listed in the warranty, cross-referenced to the list appearing in the appointment, or the warranty may exclude the use of materials that do not comply with British Standards or are known to be deleterious. Listing deleterious materials in the warranty itself has been largely replaced by a general warranty not to use deleterious materials. This is because certain materials which appeared on the lists included in warranties were found not to be deleterious, and producers of such materials were able successfully to challenge the presence of such materials on the lists and bring claims for misrepresentation. A general warranty not to use deleterious materials is therefore thought to be a safer approach to avoid claims of this nature.

(c)   Confirmation that professional indemnity insurance cover will be maintained by the warrantor up to a specified amount for a specified period. The period will normally be either six years (if the warranty has been signed under hand) or 12 years (if the warranty has been entered into as a deed) from the date of issue of the certificate of practical completion in relation to the development. The beneficiary is usually entitled to request evidence that the relevant amount of professional insurance set out under the building contract/appointment is being maintained, and this can be provided in the form of a broker's certificate.

(d)   Confirmation that, on giving appropriate notification to the warrantor, the person to whom the warranty is given may 'step into the shoes' of the developer and, upon paying to the warrantor any outstanding fees or sums due, may instruct the warrantor under the terms of the contract as though the person to whom the warranty is given had in fact been the warrantor's employer. This step-in right is essential for any contracting purchaser of the completed development or any funder. If the employer becomes insolvent during the development process, it will be crucial for the contracting purchaser or funder to ensure that the development is completed properly, and the best way of achieving this is to instruct the team originally appointed to carry out the development. The right of step-in is not required or appropriate for a tenant, who will enter into a lease only when the building has been completed and the risk of insolvency of the employer has passed.

(e)   In the case of an architect or other person providing design material, an irrevocable, royalty-free licence to use that material in connection with the completion and subsequent maintenance of the development, with additional rights for the beneficiary to sub-licence if required. The copyright in the design material will normally remain with the designer but the person benefiting from the warranty will be able to use the material, though only to the extent that this is needed in connection with the development. This is critical, as the design material is likely to include details of how the major pieces of equipment or plant in the building operate.

(f)   There will be limitations/prohibitions on the assignment of the benefit of the warranty and often commercial caps on liability requested by the warrantor, who may also wish to state specifically that it shall be entitled to rely on any rights it has under the underlying consultancy appointment in defence of any claim made by the beneficiary of the warranty. This makes it vital for solicitors acting for the beneficiary of the warranty to undertake a specific review of the underlying building contract/professional appointment at this point, to ascertain whether or not there are similar caps on liability on which the warrantor will be able to seek to rely.

It is extremely unlikely that additional warranties will be offered by the building contractor or professional team after they have been engaged, over and above those required under their terms of contract, even if an additional fee for such warranties is provided to the building contractor or professional team. It is therefore essential that the professional/building contractor is contractually committed to provide whatever warranties are required on the particular project pursuant to the building contract or professional appointment.

9.5.2   Other methods

9.5.2.1   Assignment of rights

The employer may consider attempting to satisfy the demands of his financier, buyer or tenant for protection against latent defects by assigning whatever rights the employer may have (primarily under contract law) against the contractor and the consultants. An assignment is probably appropriate only if made in favour of a financier, a buyer or a tenant of the whole of the development site. However, even where a tenant takes a lease of the whole of a development site, a landlord will be reluctant to part with his contractual rights in case the tenant's lease is forfeited or disclaimed. If collateral warranties can be provided to the interested third party instead, the landlord will be able to retain its rights against the contractor and design team.

Building contracts and contracts for the engagement of consultants may contain prohibitions on the assignment of the benefit of the contract without consent; and it seems that, following the House of Lords decision in *Linden Garden Trust Ltd v Lenesta Sludge Disposals Ltd; St Martins Property Corporation Ltd v Sir Robert McAlpine & Sons Ltd* [1993] 3 WLR 408, most prohibitions will be effective, although each clause will have to be interpreted to discover its exact meaning.

9.5.2.2   Declaring a trust of rights

Declaring a trust of rights may be considered as an alternative to an outright assignment where the employer is retaining an interest in the property and therefore does not wish to part with valuable contractual rights. In this way the employer can retain the benefit of the rights he has against the contractor and consultants, but declares that he holds them upon trust for the benefit of himself and his tenants. Again, the effectiveness of a trust has not been tested in the courts and may fall foul of the rule that the party claiming damages must have suffered a loss: in a trust arrangement the party claiming damages may have suffered no loss, for example if the employer has sold the building to a purchaser for full value (see **9.5.2.6**), and therefore damages would be irrecoverable.

9.5.2.3   Latent defects insurance

With residential properties, buyers are anxious to ensure that a newly-constructed property is covered by the National House Building Council (NHBC) Buildmark scheme, or other equivalent insurance. In the commercial field, there are no such standard schemes. However, following the Building Users Insurance against Latent Defects Report (BUILD Report), published in 1988 by the National Economic Development Office, several of the leading insurance companies in the UK have introduced latent defects insurance in respect of commercial properties. This is a concept which is very familiar on the Continent, where latent defects insurance has been used for some time. There it is known as 'decennial liability' insurance, reflecting the period of 10 years during which such an insurance policy is usually valid.

Policies will vary from company to company (and, indeed, from development to development), but the essential elements are likely to be similar across the board. Latent defects insurance commonly provides cover against damage caused by defective design or construction works for a period of 10 years after practical completion of the development (or such longer period as may be agreed with the insurer). The beneficiary of the policy is covered against the cost of making good most (but not necessarily all) damage caused by a design or construction defect (although not other risks), and the policy may cover other items of economic loss such as loss of rent, or loss of use of the building while repairs are being carried out. The policy can be taken out to cover the employer (as initial owner of the building) and his financiers. Most policies will also automatically insure subsequent owners and occupiers, which will obviously be the desired aim from the employer's point of view. The premium is likely to be substantial (perhaps 1.5% of development costs) and often prohibitive.

The advantages of such a policy are that there is no need for the claimant under the policy to establish legal liability for the damage incurred, and there ought to be easy access to funds to finance repairing costs and, possibly, to cover other economic loss. The disadvantages are that, as with other policies, the insurance may be subject to excesses (meaning that the claimant might have to fund, say, the first £50,000 of a claim), there are often significant exceptions carved out of the policy, and the insurer will invariably require some element of supervision over the execution of the works from commencement, since the risk it is taking on will be considerable. Such insurance is not something which can be obtained after the construction process is complete, and in any event, at that stage of the project risks are generally known.

9.5.2.4   Limiting repair covenants

In a landlord and tenant relationship, the tenant should consider limiting the scope of his repairing covenant. The main problem for a tenant is that the landlord is likely to insist upon the tenant entering into a lease which contains a covenant by the tenant to repair the demised premises. Provided the damage amounts to disrepair, the usual repair covenant imposed by the landlord may oblige the tenant to repair damage which is caused by a defect in the design or construction of the building. While the tenant can commission a full structural survey of the premises prior to the grant of the lease in an effort to discover defects, the very nature of a design or construction defect makes it unlikely that it will manifest itself until some time after the building has been completed and the lease granted.

It is therefore suggested that, on the grant of a lease of a relatively new building, the tenant should attempt to limit the scope of his repairing covenant by excluding (either totally, or for a limited period of, say, three or six years after the grant of the lease) liability to repair damage caused by latent defects. Not only should the tenant seek to exclude such liability from his own covenant, but he also should make sure that no vacuum is left in the repairing obligations under the lease by insisting that the landlord assumes this liability. If this is not done, there is a risk that the property may remain in disrepair. The landlord will be anxious to avoid having to bear any repair costs in respect of the building, and so the limitation of the tenant's repairing obligations is a matter to be negotiated and will depend upon the relative bargaining strengths of the parties. It is most unlikely that the tenant would succeed in his negotiations if, in the agreement for lease, the tenant had insisted upon a degree of control and supervision over the execution of the landlord's works. The landlord would probably argue that the tenant had been given every opportunity before the lease was granted to discover defects and that he should, therefore, consider taking action against his professional advisers.

On the grant of a lease of part of a building, where the tenant would not ordinarily undertake repairing responsibilities in respect of the structure and external parts but would instead be expected to contribute via the service charge to the landlord's costs incurred in maintaining those parts, the tenant would seek to ensure that he was not obliged to contribute via the service charge to the landlord's costs of repairing damage caused by design or construction defects (either throughout the term, or for a limited period). Again, while the tenant could commission a full structural survey, design defects may not be apparent at the time of the survey, or may be hidden in some other part of the building to which the surveyor was unable to gain access.

9.5.2.5   Defect liability periods

In a landlord and tenant relationship, the tenant may seek the benefit of a defect liability period. If the landlord will not agree to exclude the tenant's liability for inherent defects in the lease, the tenant ought to press for the inclusion of a clause in the agreement for lease obliging the landlord to remedy any defects which appear within a short period of time following practical completion of the building. If the landlord agrees to the inclusion of a defects liability period, it is likely to mirror a similar clause in the building contract entered into with the contractor. Quite often, building contracts provide for the contractor to remedy any defects which manifest themselves within, say, the first six or 12 months after practical completion. By including a similar clause in the agreement for lease, the landlord is indirectly passing on the benefit of the clause to the tenant, but this should not be seen as an alternative to a limiting repair covenant.

9.5.2.6   Forced enforcement of remedies

A buyer, financier or tenant may seek the inclusion of a provision whereby the employer agrees to enforce his rights as original contracting party against the contractor or the consultants in respect of defects where loss or liability to repair would otherwise fall upon the former. Difficulties have arisen in this area, in that if the employer has received full market value on a sale of the property to a buyer, or has secured the inclusion of a full repairing covenant on the grant of a lease of the property to a tenant, he cannot be said to have suffered any loss upon which a claim could be maintained.

However, the House of Lords decision in the *Linden Garden* case (see **9.5.2.1**) has shown that in a commercial contract, where it was in the contemplation of the contracting parties that legal title to the property which formed the subject matter of the contract might be transferred to a third party before a breach had occurred, the original contracting party is taken to have entered into the contract for the benefit of himself and all persons who might acquire an interest in the property before the breach occurs. What this means is that, in certain circumstances, the employer may be able to recover damages for breach of contract in respect of loss incurred by his buyer, financier or tenant. This area is not without its complications, and the full ramifications of recent developments in this area have yet to be tested in full.

9.6   DISPUTE RESOLUTION

Disputes often arise in the construction context in relation to claims by the employer or end user that the works, materials or workmanship carried out by the contractor are defective, or the contractor may bring a claim for additional time to complete the works or additional monies for doing so.

Before briefly considering the different types of dispute resolution relevant to construction contracts, whatever the contract says, in the event of a dispute, the parties are not compelled to resort to the courts for the settling of their differences. They can choose instead to attempt to settle their differences amicably. The parties are likely to consider factors including the cost and expense of bringing a claim, and the uncertain and time-consuming nature of dispute resolution in determining whether to settle disputes through the courts rather than attempting to resolve disputes in a non-adversarial manner such as through conciliation, mediation or independent private enquiry.

The main adversarial methods of dispute resolution include adjudication, arbitration and litigation, and these are examined briefly below.

9.6.1 Adjudication

There is now a statutory right to adjudication which is designed to produce a decision that is at least temporarily binding on the parties. The right to adjudication is included within Pt II of the Housing Grants, Construction and Regeneration Act 1996, as amended by the Local Democracy, Economic Development and Construction Act 2009, which provides that any party to a construction contract has the right to refer any dispute arising under the contract for adjudication under a procedure complying with the Act. In order to satisfy the Act, the contract must include certain specific provisions, an important one of which requires the adjudicator to reach a decision within 28 days, or such longer period as both parties agree. If the parties do not explicitly lay down certain minimum provisions about the right to adjudication and the process thereof, an appropriate set of procedural rules will be implied, known as the Scheme for Construction Contracts (England and Wales) Regulations 1998 (SI 1998/649), as amended by the Scheme for Construction Contracts (England and Wales) Regulations 1998 (Amendment) (England) Regulations 2011 (SI 2011/2333).

9.6.2 Arbitration

The parties may also agree that any disputes arising in relation to the contract will be resolved by arbitration. The Arbitration Act 1996 sets out the procedural and evidential matters to be adopted in relation to the settling of disputes by arbitration. In addition, there are standard arbitration rules, published by arbitral institutions such as the Institution of Civil Engineers (ICE), the International Chamber of Commerce (ICC) and the London Court of International Arbitration (LCIA). These rules are often incorporated into the arbitration agreement and contain basic provisions for commencing the arbitration, establishing the arbitral tribunal and the procedures to be adopted prior to the award. International arbitration is commonly used as a choice of dispute resolution in relation to international construction contracts.

9.6.3 Litigation

In practice, many disputes of a construction nature are resolved finally by litigation, with construction and engineering cases of any appreciable size ordinarily tried in the Technology and Construction Court, which is a specialist subdivision of the Queen's Bench Division of the High Court. The advantages of litigation include the ability to join third parties in the proceedings and the ability to deal with legal complexities. These may be outweighed by the advantages of alternative forms of dispute resolution such as arbitration or adjudication, which are often preferred as cheaper, quicker and more commercially expedient ways of resolving disputes.

REVIEW ACTIVITY

Scenario

Your client, Land UK plc (LUK), a large property developer based in the UK, intends to build a new office tower in the City of London. LUK is taking out a bank loan to fund the development from the Royal Bank of England plc (R). The new tower is set to be a landmark, iconic building in the heart of the City, and LUK would like to engage an international architect to undertake the design of the tower. There will also be a number of other consultants, including structural and building services engineers, and the client will need to comply with UK health and safety legislation. In addition, the building will contain a large auditorium for board meetings, with a specialist acoustic engineering sub-contractor appointed to undertake its design and construction. The client has entered into a pre-let agreement with a major law firm, GoodLaw and Partners (G), who will be taking space on several floors of the building, one of which it intends to sub-let to an accountancy firm, HardSums and Partners (H).

Question

Consider what form of procurement your client might use to construct the tower, including the advantages and any disadvantages of such form of procurement, together with any rights each party involved in the transaction might require in the event that a defect arises in the building after its construction.

Answers to this Review activity may be found in Appendix 1.

CHAPTER 10

AN OUTLINE OF TAXATION OF COMMERCIAL PROPERTIES

10.1	Value added tax	135
10.2	Stamp duty land tax on leases	141
	Review activity	141

10.1 VALUE ADDED TAX

At the outset of any property transaction, it is essential to consider the impact of VAT legislation and to advise the client accordingly. The reader will already be aware of the basic principles of VAT, which dictate that VAT may be payable in respect of a supply of goods or services made in the course of a business. Whether VAT is payable depends upon a number of things, including whether the supplies in question are exempt, zero-rated or standard-rated. The reader will also be aware of the effects of such supplies, the payment and receipt of input and output tax, and the recovery of VAT incurred.

Supplies of goods and services made in relation to a property transaction may be grouped as follows:

(a) *Residential properties*

(i)   sale of a green field site – exempt (but subject to the option to tax);

(ii)   construction services – zero-rated;

(iii) civil engineering works – zero-rated;

(iv) professional services (eg legal and other professional fees) – standard-rated;

(v)   sale of a new house – zero-rated;

(vi) grant of a lease of a new house (for a term exceeding 21 years) – zero-rated.

(b) *Commercial properties*

(i)   sale of a green field site – exempt (but subject to the option to tax);

(ii)   construction services – standard-rated;

(iii) civil engineering works – standard-rated;

(iv) professional services – standard-rated;

(v)   sale of a new freehold building or the grant of an option to purchase such a building – standard-rated;

(vi) sale of an old freehold building – exempt (but subject to the option to tax);

(vii) the grant of a lease (for any length of term) – exempt (but subject to the option to tax);

(viii) the assignment of a lease – exempt (but subject to the option to tax);

(ix) the surrender of a lease – exempt (but subject to the option to tax by the person who receives the consideration);

(x)   repair, alteration and demolition works – standard-rated.

Rules relating to work carried out on listed buildings are not considered in this book, neither are the particular problems associated with premises of mixed use.

Some of the supplies listed above are exempt supplies but are subject to what is called the 'option to tax' (also known as the 'option to waive exemption'). This is dealt with more comprehensively at **10.1.3**. What the option means is that the person who makes the supply can voluntarily convert the supply from one which is exempt, and therefore gives rise to no VAT liability, into a standard-rated supply.

The VAT consequences arising in residential and commercial developments are now considered.

10.1.1 Residential developments

In a typical new residential development, the VAT consequences will not be too complicated. If, for example, a property company, ABC Ltd, buys a green field site, the seller is making an exempt supply to ABC Ltd which will not be subject to VAT unless the seller, being a taxable person, has elected to waive the exemption. In any event, if, as is often the case, the seller is a private individual, he is not likely to be selling the land in the course of a business, and the supply will therefore be outside the scope of VAT. Any construction services (such as work provided by builders and the provision of materials) and civil engineering works (such as the construction of the roads and sewers serving the development) supplied to ABC Ltd will be supplied at a zero-rate of VAT. It is therefore probable that the only significant VAT incurred by the property company in constructing the residential development will be in respect of professional fees paid to surveyors, solicitors, architects and selling agents for services supplied.

On completion of construction, ABC Ltd will dispose of the houses. The purchase price payable on the freehold sale of a newly-built house, or the premium (or rent) payable in respect of a lease of the house granted for a term exceeding 21 years, does not attract VAT because these supplies are zero-rated. However, when zero-rated supplies are made, while no VAT is paid for the supply, tax is deemed to be charged at a nil rate on the output (so that they are still technically regarded as taxable supplies) and therefore related input tax incurred can be recovered. What this means is that ABC Ltd will account to HM Revenue & Customs (HMRC) for output tax on supplies made (which will be nil), less input tax on related supplies received (ie the VAT paid on professional fees). This clearly leads to a deficit, which means that a refund of VAT will be due from HMRC. This process is sometimes known as 'recovering the VAT'.

A subsequent sale of a house (either freehold or leasehold) will be made by a private individual and will not, therefore, be made in the course of a business. In the event that the sale is made in the course of a business (eg by a relocation company), the supply would be exempt.

10.1.2 Commercial developments

In a typical new commercial development, the same process can be followed, with different VAT consequences. The sale of a green field site to a developer is again an exempt supply, subject to the option to tax. However, the provision of construction services and civil engineering works to a commercial developer is a standard-rated supply, which means that considerable VAT will be incurred in addition to VAT on the standard-rated supply of professional services.

Once the building has been completed, the developer may either sell the freehold, or grant a lease of it to a tenant. The sale of a 'new' or partially-completed building is a standard-rated supply. Value added tax must be charged in respect of the purchase price. In this context, a 'new' building is one which was completed within the three years preceding the sale, and 'completion' of a building takes place on the earlier of either the day upon which the certificate of practical completion was issued by the architect or the day upon which the building was completely occupied. The grant of a lease of all or part of commercial premises (whether new or old) is an exempt supply, subject to the right of the landlord to opt to tax the rents, premium and other sums payable under the lease. In both cases, whether the freehold sale or the grant of a commercial lease, the developer is able to charge VAT either because it is a standard-rated supply, or because the exemption has been waived. This means that output tax will be received to facilitate recovery of related input tax incurred.

Take, by way of example, a commercial development where the construction costs paid by the developer amount to £2 million (with VAT on a standard-rated supply of £400,000), the cost of roads and sewers amounts to £500,000 (with £100,000 VAT) and professional fees total £100,000 (with £20,000 VAT). The total input tax paid by the developer adds up to £520,000. If the developer, being a taxable person, is able to sell the 'new' freehold building for £4 million, he will have to charge VAT amounting to £800,000. This output tax can be set against related input tax incurred, resulting in only the difference (£280,000) having to be accounted for to HMRC. The developer suffers from cash-flow difficulties in that he is likely to incur the input tax some time in advance of receiving the output tax, but he is not left out-of-pocket. The same result will be achieved if, instead of selling the freehold, the developer chooses to grant a lease of the building and elects to charge VAT on the sums payable under the lease. The making of the election facilitates immediate recovery of related input tax.

10.1.3   The option to charge VAT

The election to waive exemption or, as it is more commonly called, the option to tax was introduced on 1 August 1989 in order to lessen the impact of the VAT charges on commercial developers. The purpose of the option to tax is to enable the commercial owner to convert what would otherwise be exempt supplies in respect of a particular property into supplies chargeable to VAT at the standard rate, so that the developer will be able to recover the input tax which he incurred when acquiring or developing the property.

The consequence of opting to tax is that all future grants in the property by the person who opts will be subject to VAT at the standard rate.

10.1.3.1   How is the election made?

As a preliminary to opting to tax, the owner must check that he is registered for VAT or the option will be meaningless. There is no prescribed form or procedure for opting to tax, neither is there any requirement to consult with or notify anyone who might be affected by the option. However, from a practical point of view, it is advisable that a landlord notifies his tenants, since it is the tenants who will bear the VAT. The one procedural requirement that must be followed when opting to tax is that written notice of the option must be given to HMRC within 30 days.

If an exempt supply (eg the grant of a lease) has been made by the person wanting to opt to tax in respect of the relevant property in the 10 years prior to the date on which the option is to take effect, consent of HMRC will be required before the option can be made, and consent will be granted only if HMRC is satisfied that the input tax which the person will be able to recover as a consequence of his opting to tax is fair and reasonable. It is therefore advisable for a landlord intending to opt to tax to do so before he grants a lease of his property. In all other cases, consent of HMRC is not required.

10.1.3.2   Who or what is affected?

The option to tax is personal, done on a property-by-property basis and, once made, it may be revoked only within six months of the option, where there has been a lapse of six years since any relevant interest in the property has been held, or after 20 years from the date of the option. The fact that the option is personal means that while a landlord who opts to tax would have to charge VAT on the rents payable by its tenants, its tenants would not, unless they too opted to tax, have to charge VAT to their sub-tenants, and the same applies to a buyer of the landlord's interest. As an exception to the general rule, an option to tax made by a company in respect of a property will bind other companies (in respect of that property) if they are in the same VAT group of companies at the time of the option, or joined the group later when the property affected was still owned by a group company.

The fact that the option to tax is made on a property-by-property basis means that a commercial owner can pick and choose which of its properties should be voluntarily standard-rated. Once made, the option to tax affects the whole of the property, or if that person owns an interest in only part of the property, it will affect the entirety of that part. Hence, an owner cannot choose to opt to tax in respect of the ground floor and not the upper two floors if he owns the entire building. What may appear to be separate buildings, but which are linked together internally or by covered walkways, are to be treated as one building. Therefore, if a shopping precinct is owned by one landlord (as is usually the case), an option to tax by that landlord will affect all of the shops in the precinct.

10.1.3.3 Should the option to tax be made?

The reason for opting to tax is to facilitate the recovery of related input tax incurred on the acquisition or development of the property. If no related input tax has been or is likely to be incurred, there is no reason why the option to tax should be made. If considerable input tax has been or will be incurred, consideration must be given to whether or not the option to tax should be made, but the person must have regard to the effect that the option will have on the persons to whom supplies are being made.

If a developer-landlord, having incurred VAT on acquisition or development costs, wants to opt to tax and charge VAT on the rents he will receive from his tenants, and those tenants make mainly standard-rated or zero-rated supplies in the course of their businesses (eg tenants of retail food stores, solicitors or surveyors offices), the tenants would not be adversely affected by a charge to VAT on rent, since there will be output tax (actual or deemed) to offset against the input tax. The tenants will be able to recover any VAT paid and will not end up out-of-pocket.

Tenants who make only exempt supplies in the course of their businesses (eg banks, building societies, insurance companies) will be hard hit by the option to tax. The VAT that these tenants have to pay on the rent will be irrecoverable, and will have to be borne as an overhead of the business. This could have the effect of frightening off a class of tenants whom the developer might have been hoping to attract to the development, or lead to their reducing the amount of rent that they would be prepared to pay.

10.1.3.4 Drafting points

Is the option to tax on its own sufficient to render VAT payable by the person who receives the supply? It is necessary to look at two principal relationships: seller and buyer; and landlord and tenant.

Seller and buyer

If a seller sells a 'new' commercial building (whether it is the first sale, or a subsequent sale of the still 'new' building) the seller is making a standard-rated supply, and so there will be mandatory VAT on the purchase price. The basic rule is that, unless the contrary appears, the purchase price stated in the contract is deemed to include VAT. It is therefore important that the seller includes a clause in the contract obliging the buyer to pay VAT in addition to the purchase price. Failure to do so will result in the seller having to account to HMRC for the VAT out of the purchase price received, which will mean that the seller will be left with considerably less than he anticipated, and his solicitor would no doubt be liable in negligence.

If the seller sells an old commercial building (ie one that is now more than three years old) then the supply which is being made is an exempt supply and the position is different. If the seller opts to tax *before* exchange of contracts then he converts the supply into a standard-rated supply and the above paragraph would then be applicable. The seller would have to make an express provision in the contract obliging the buyer to pay VAT in addition to the purchase price. If the option to tax is made *after* exchanging contracts then, under s 89 of the Value Added Tax Act 1994 (VATA 1994), the option to tax would operate as a change in the rate of tax from 0% to 20% (ie from an exempt to a standard-rated supply), and accordingly the seller could add VAT to the purchase price without the need for an express clause in the contract enabling him to do so. In this case, it is important that the buyer's solicitor ensures that the contract makes it clear that the purchase price is inclusive of VAT so that no hardship is felt by the buyer if the seller chooses to opt to tax after exchange. If the contract expressly excludes s 89, or the purchase price is expressly stated to be payable inclusive of VAT, the seller will be unable to add VAT to the purchase price.

Landlord and tenant

The grant of a commercial lease (of either an old or new building) is an exempt supply, unless the landlord has opted to tax. In respect of existing leases, s 89 of the VATA 1994 again operates, so that an option to tax by the landlord after the grant of the lease effects a change in the rate of VAT from 0% to 20%. The landlord does not need the benefit of an express clause in the lease, and can simply add VAT to the rent (and other sums payable under the lease) unless there is a clause in the lease (which would not usually be the case) expressly exonerating the tenant from liability to VAT on such payments, or excluding s 89.

If the option to tax is made before the grant of the lease, so that the supply is converted to a standard-rated supply from the outset, s 89 will not operate and the rent will be deemed to be payable inclusive of VAT. It is therefore essential that the landlord's solicitor ensures that the lease contains a covenant by the tenant to pay VAT on the rent (and the other sums payable under the lease). Whenever a lease is drafted, irrespective of whether advantage can be taken of s 89, there ought to be a covenant by the tenant to pay VAT in addition to the sums payable under the lease. This avoids problems for the landlord.

10.1.4 Other areas of concern

Value added tax is a far-reaching tax in the property world which can impact on other aspects of property transactions.

10.1.4.1 Reverse premiums and rent-free periods

A reverse premium is a payment made by the landlord to a prospective tenant as an inducement to him to enter the lease. Money is passing from landlord to tenant, and is the consideration for a supply being made by the tenant. This payment will be subject to VAT and the tenant should ensure that the terms of the contract allow this to be added to the payment. The landlord will not, however, be able to recover this VAT as input tax if, when granting the lease, he is making an exempt supply. So the cost to the landlord will be increased by 20%. The landlord could recover this VAT if he opted to tax in respect of the property, but this would also mean that he would have to charge VAT on the rent. This would then be a particular problem for exempt tenants, such as banks or insurance companies, as the VAT on the rent will not be recoverable, and they may wish to try to negotiate a lower rent to compensate for this.

Rent-free periods give rise to difficult VAT problems. It appears that if the rent-free period is being given because the tenant is carrying out work to the premises which will benefit the landlord, or simply because the landlord is trying to induce the tenant to enter into the lease (as an alternative to a reverse premium), then VAT at the standard rate will be payable on the amount of rent forgone. The tenant is making a supply to the landlord (ie is positively doing something) in consideration of a rent-free period. However, if the rent-free period is given simply because the state of the market means that it is part of the bargain negotiated between landlord and tenant (eg where it is given to allow the tenant some time in which to fit out the premises for his own benefit, or arrange sub-lettings), there will be no VAT on the rent-free period, since nothing is being done in return for it.

10.1.4.2 Surrenders

When a tenant surrenders his lease to the landlord, consideration may move in either direction, either because the tenant is desperate to rid himself of the liability to pay rent and perform the covenants, or because the landlord is anxious to obtain vacant possession. By virtue of the Value Added Tax (Land) Order 1995 (SI 1995/282), the supply made in either case is an exempt supply, subject to the option to tax by the person who receives the consideration.

10.1.4.3 Transfer of a going concern (TOGC)

Transferring a business can involve the sale of assets which would normally be taxable supplies (eg a building where there is an option to tax in place). However, provided certain conditions are met, where a taxable person transfers a business *as a going concern* to a taxable person, the transfer will not be treated as a supply of goods and services and no VAT will be chargeable. This is known as TOGC relief (VATA 1994, s 49), and the sale of an investment property which is let to one or more tenants can be treated as a TOGC for these purposes.

Briefly, the conditions are that the transferee must intend to use the assets to carry on the same kind of business as the transferor and that the transferee both exercises and notifies an option to tax (and does not revoke it) on or before the date of the supply.

There are detailed rules relating to a TOGC, but these are outside the scope of this book.

10.1.4.4 VAT on costs

Sometimes, a lease will oblige the tenant to pay the landlord's legal costs incurred on the grant of the lease. Often, a lease will oblige the tenant to pay the landlord's legal costs on an application for licence to assign, or alter or change use. The position as regards VAT on those costs is complicated by the approach of HMRC, which treats the payment of the landlord's legal costs, in either case, as part of the overall consideration for the grant of the lease. Hence, the VAT position depends upon whether the landlord has opted to tax.

If the landlord's solicitor charges his client £1,000 plus VAT for legal services provided on the grant of the lease, he will issue his client with a VAT invoice requiring payment of £1,000 plus VAT of £200. The landlord, having opted to tax in respect of this property, and making use of his VAT invoice, will be able to recover the input tax (£200) from the output tax which he will receive on the rents. If the lease contains a clause obliging the tenant to pay those legal costs, the landlord will look to the tenant for a reimbursement of the outstanding £1,000. However, since HMRC treats such a payment as part of the consideration for the grant of the lease, and since the landlord has opted to tax, the tenant must pay £1,000 plus VAT, the landlord must issue the tenant with a VAT invoice, and the landlord must account to HMRC for the VAT element received. The tenant may be able to recover the VAT which he has paid, depending on the nature of his business.

If the landlord has not opted to tax, the position is different. First, he will not be able to recover the VAT charged by his solicitor, since that VAT was incurred in relation to an exempt supply. Secondly, therefore, he will require the tenant to reimburse the full amount of costs and VAT (ie, £1,200), but because this reimbursement is treated as part of the consideration for the grant of the lease, and because the supply made by the landlord is an exempt supply, no VAT invoice can be issued to the tenant (as, in fact, there is no charge to VAT being made to the tenant), and the tenant will be unable to recover any part of the reimbursement.

The same principles are adopted where, during the term, the tenant exercises a right given to him under the lease and pays the landlord's legal costs (eg on an application for licence to assign pursuant to a qualified covenant (see **20.2.2**)).

10.2 STAMP DUTY LAND TAX ON LEASES

Stamp duty land tax (SDLT) will be assessed on any premium paid and also on the rent. It must be paid within 30 days of completion of the lease.

The amount of SDLT payable on the premium is assessed in the same way as on purchases of land. The normal reduced rates of duty are available.

In relation to the rental element of leases, SDLT is payable at a flat rate of 1% on the 'net present value' (NPV) of the total rent payable over the term of the lease. The NPV is calculated by discounting rent payable in future years by 3.5% per annum. Where the NPV of the total rent does not exceed £150,000, no duty will be payable. Stamp duty land tax will not be chargeable on the VAT element of consideration, provided the landlord has not opted to tax by the time the lease is granted.

Stamp duty land tax has now become an important factor in commercial leases as the amount of duty is directly related to the length of the term, ie the longer the lease, the more duty is potentially payable. Further, if the tenant remains in possession ('holds over') after the end of a fixed term under the provisions of Pt II of the Landlord and Tenant Act 1954 (see **Chapter 31**), a further charge to duty may arise. This will be payable by the current tenant.

REVIEW ACTIVITY

1. Which one of the following statements is correct?

    VAT is a tax levied on:

    (a) Land transactions.

    (b) The gain resulting from a disposal in an interest in land.

    (c) The supply of goods or services made in the course of a business.

    (d) Fixed plant and machinery within a commercial property.

2. Which of the following statements is correct?

    Provided the supplier is registered for VAT, input tax will be paid by a business where the supply made to it is:

    (a) Standard-rated.

    (b) Zero-rated.

    (c) Exempt.

    (d) Exempt but where the supplier has exercised the option to tax.

3. Which of the following statements is correct?

    Input tax may be recovered from HMRC provided that it was incurred by a business in making supplies that are:

    (a) Standard-rated.

    (b) Zero-rated.

    (c) Exempt.

    (d) Exempt but where the supplier has exercised the option to tax.

4. Set out below are the stages in a typical commercial property *development* transaction. For each stage, state whether the supply is standard-rated, zero-rated, exempt or exempt subject to the option to tax.

    (a) Sale to the developer of a green field site for development as a retail superstore.

    (b) Payment to the building contractor for constructing the superstore.

    (c) Grant of a lease of the superstore to a retail tenant.

    (d) Sale of the freehold interest in the superstore one year after construction, subject to the lease.

5.   In the circumstances set out in question 4, the developer of the retail superstore can recover the input tax paid on the construction costs.

True or false?

6.   Set out below are the stages in a typical commercial property *leasing* transaction. For each stage, state whether the supply is standard-rated, zero-rated, exempt or exempt subject to the option to tax.

(a)   Grant of a lease to an insurance company.

(b)   Payment of legal fees to the solicitors for negotiating the terms of the lease.

(c)   Payment to the building contractor for fitting out the property for the tenant's business.

(d)   Assignment of the lease to another tenant.

7.   In the circumstances set out in question 6, the insurance company tenant will be able to recover the input tax on the legal fees, fitting-out costs and (if the landlord opts to tax) the rents payable under the lease.

True or false?

Answers to this Review activity may be found in Appendix 1.

PART II

COMMERCIAL LEASES

CHAPTER 11

LANDLORD AND TENANT LAW

11.1	Introduction	145
11.2	Lease/licence distinction	145
11.3	Security of tenure	146
11.4	Liability of the parties on the covenants in the lease	146
	Review activity	147

11.1 INTRODUCTION

Given that over half of the UK's commercial property is rented by occupiers (*Property Data Report 2014*), having a comprehensive knowledge and understanding of commercial landlord and tenant law (and the ability to apply it) is essential for any commercial property lawyer. Without it, that lawyer is unable to advise a landlord or tenant client properly on the rights and obligations arising under a commercial lease. Consequently, this short chapter highlights three important principles which it is crucial to grasp.

11.2 LEASE/LICENCE DISTINCTION

Many of the statutory provisions discussed in Part II of this book apply only to a lease, not to a licence. A lease is an interest in land; a licence does not confer an interest but is merely a permission to enter another's land for a stipulated purpose(s) that would otherwise be a trespass. There have been many cases on the lease/licence distinction, but the leading decision remains *Street v Mountford* [1985] 2 All ER 289. That case concerned a residential tenancy, but the principles apply equally to commercial tenancies.

The House of Lords in *Street v Mountford* held that, as a general rule, an agreement to grant *exclusive possession* for a *term* at a *rent*, is a tenancy and the court will ignore any shams or pretences aimed at misleading the court. This general rule is subject to certain exceptions, for example a lack of intention to create legal relations or allowing into occupation pending the grant of a lease.

While payment of rent is not an essential component of a lease (*Ashburn Anstalt v Arnold* [1989] Ch 1; see also the Law of Property Act (LPA) 1925, s 205(1), which refers to a term of years absolute as being with or without a rent), exclusive possession is essential. There seems to have been a greater readiness by the courts to find that exclusive possession was *not* granted in commercial property cases than in residential cases.

One factor in determining exclusive possession is the degree of control exercised over the property by the owner. For example in *Esso Petroleum Co Ltd v Fumegrange Ltd* [1994] 46 EG 199, it was held that exclusive possession of a petrol station had not been granted because the landlord had retained extensive rights to control the operation and layout of the property, going beyond usual rights of access; in *National Car Parks Ltd v Trinity Development Co (Banbury) Ltd* [2001] EWCA Civ 1686, [2001] 28 EG 144, it was held that an agreement to occupy premises as a car park was a licence not a lease because the licensor had reserved rights to park for itself and regulated the conduct of the licensee's business.

The court will look at the agreement as a whole, and in construing any agreement, the terminology used by the parties is not decisive. A lease cannot be turned into a licence simply by labelling it as such. Conversely, *Clear Channel UK Ltd v Manchester City Council* [2005] EWCA Civ 1304 (where a right to erect advertising hoardings and display advertisements did not amount to exclusive possession of the land itself) suggests that it will be hard to persuade a court that an agreement amounts to a lease where substantial parties of equal bargaining strength and with the benefit of legal advice refer to that arrangement unequivocally as a licence.

11.3 SECURITY OF TENURE

A key reason to appreciate the lease/licence distinction is that a lease can entitle a business tenant to security of tenure under Pt II of the Landlord and Tenant Act (LTA) 1954, whereas a licence cannot. Where a business tenant has security of tenure, it means that:

(a) the business tenancy will automatically continue at the expiry of the contractual term on the same terms, until it is terminated in one of the ways specified in the Act; and

(b) the business tenant can apply to court for a new tenancy and the landlord may oppose that application only on certain statutory grounds (some of which involve the payment of compensation by the landlord to the tenant if the tenant's application is unsuccessful). If a new tenancy is granted, it will also benefit from security of tenure.

Whilst a licence, as mentioned above, will not attract protection of the LTA 1954, the danger of a licence where exclusive possession is given is that, despite the thrust of the decisions in the commercial cases cited above, it could later be construed as a lease and protection inadvertently obtained. Note that the parties can contract out of the 1954 Act, but certain formalities must be observed which are considered further in **Chapter 31**.

11.4 LIABILITY OF THE PARTIES ON THE COVENANTS IN THE LEASE

As the value of a commercial property investment depends partly on the financial strength of the tenants who occupy it and their correlative ability to pay the rent, a solicitor acting for a landlord must know the rules relating to liability and enforcement. Similarly, acting for a tenant client, a solicitor must know against whom a claim may be brought for, say, non-provision of services under the landlord covenants.

If the original parties remain the same throughout the term of the lease then they remain liable to each other for their performance (under the principles of privity of contract). If the identity of the parties changes during the course of the term then, on assignment, the liability of the parties and enforceability of covenants are somewhat more complex. The key to unlocking the complexity is the date of the lease.

The detailed rules relating to the enforceability of covenants are considered in **Chapter 14**. The following is intended as an outline only of the main issues involved.

11.4.1 Leases granted before 1 January 1996

11.4.1.1 Original tenant

Under the principles of privity of contract, if the original tenant assigns the lease, it will remain liable on its express covenants in the lease throughout the remaining term for any breach of covenant committed by its successors, unless the landlord agrees to the contrary. Note that a commercial lease will usually include a rent review clause (see **Chapter 18**) allowing an increase of the rent. So an original tenant could find itself pursued several years after an assignment for its successor's non-payment of rent at a level over which it had no control. It was this type of perceived unfairness that led to the then Government creating the new set of rules under the Landlord and Tenant (Covenants) Act 1995 (LT(C)A 1995).

11.4.1.2 Original landlord

In the same way, through privity of contract, the original landlord will remain liable on its express covenants to the original tenant for the whole term even if it assigns the reversion. Accordingly, an original landlord could find itself being pursued for a breach of covenant to provide services, even though it had long ceased to have any involvement in the property.

11.4.1.3 Tenant and landlord for the time being

The doctrine of privity of estate will apply, which means that a party is only liable for breaches of covenant (which touch and concern the land) committed during its ownership of the interest under the lease. Commonly, however, any assignee of the tenant's interest would have been required to enter into direct covenants with the landlord to perform the covenants in the lease, which would have the effect of making the assignee liable on the covenants in the lease for the whole term rather than just during its ownership.

11.4.2 Leases granted on or after 1 January 1996

11.4.2.1 Tenant

The effect of the LT(C)A 1995 is that once a tenant lawfully assigns the lease, it is automatically released from the tenant covenants in the lease. Liability for pre-assignment breaches continues. This applies to the original tenant and all successive tenants; but as succour to disgruntled landlords who lost their privity of contract rights (see **11.4.1** above), all outgoing tenants can be required to give a guarantee of their immediate assignee's performance: see **20.2.4.3**.

11.4.2.2 Landlord

The effect of the LT(C)A 1995 is that, unlike the tenant, a landlord is not automatically released when it assigns its interest but may apply to the tenant for a release (see **14.2.2**).

REVIEW ACTIVITY

NUFC Ltd (as landlord) let premises to AFC Ltd (tenant) under a lease dated 7 June 1992. AFC Ltd assigned the lease to THS Ltd in 1993. THS Ltd assigned the lease to TFA Ltd in 1997. TFA Ltd failed to pay last month's rent and NUFC Ltd wishes to recover the arrears.

1. Explain from whom NUFC Ltd can claim the arrears.
2. Explain the same position if the lease referred to above was dated 7 June 2001.

Answers to this Review activity may be found in Appendix 1.

CHAPTER 12

AGREEMENTS FOR LEASE

12.1	Introduction	149
12.2	A typical agreement	149
	Review activity	153

12.1 INTRODUCTION

In most commercial letting transactions, the parties proceed straight to the completion of the lease.

Generally, an agreement for lease will be used only where one (or both) of the parties cannot enter the lease immediately but requires the other to be bound to do so in the future. For example, where:

(a) the landlord has commenced, or is about to commence, constructing the premises. The landlord's aim is to ensure that, when construction has been completed, the tenant will be bound to complete the lease so that the rent will become payable to the landlord to provide income to offset its building costs;

(b) the landlord, at the request of the tenant, is carrying out substantial works of repair or refurbishment to the premises prior to the grant of the lease. The landlord may not be able to secure the funds to carry out the works without showing to the lender that the tenant is obliged to take the lease, and/or may not want to incur the expense of executing works without a commitment from the tenant to enter into a lease once the works have been carried out;

(c) the tenant is to carry out major works to the premises prior to the grant of the lease, in which case both parties will want the security of a binding commitment to enter into a lease upon completion of the works;

(d) third party consents are required before the lease can be granted or works can be carried out (for example, consent of a lender or a superior landlord).

In all such cases, the terms of the lease should be agreed in advance and a copy of the agreed form of lease annexed to the agreement for lease, which will be drafted by the landlord's solicitor. The agreement will also stipulate the nature of the works to be carried out to the premises, the time in which they are to be carried out and the manner in which they will be executed.

As there will be a delay between exchange and completion, the tenant's solicitor should consider protecting the agreement against the possibility of the landlord selling the reversion and defeating the tenant's interest. This is achieved in unregistered land by registering a Class C(iv) land charge and in registered land by registering a notice.

12.2 A TYPICAL AGREEMENT

In considering the terms of a typical agreement we shall assume that the landlord will be obliged to construct a building, the entirety of which will be let to the tenant under the agreed form of lease. (Many of the points raised will be equally applicable, or can be adapted, to a situation where it will be the tenant who is carrying out works to the premises.)

The basic thrust of the agreement will be that the landlord, as the owner of the site, will construct (or, by engaging building contractors, cause to be constructed) premises for occupation by the tenant. Once the premises reach a stage of 'practical completion' (see **12.2.1.3**) the tenant will be obliged to enter into the form of lease attached to the agreement. Rent will then become payable under the terms of the lease, giving the developer/landlord a return on its investment.

Common terms which are often the subject of negotiation are set out below.

12.2.1   Terms relating to the works

12.2.1.1   Landlord's obligations

The agreement must include a clear obligation on the landlord to carry out the works in accordance with detailed plans and specifications attached to the agreement for lease or in accordance with the (usually) standard form building contracts which the landlord has with its building contractors. Commonly the landlord will be obliged to ensure that the works are carried out with reasonable care and skill, and in accordance with all relevant statutory approvals (eg, planning permission, Building Regulations).

Often, during the course of a building project, variations are required for economic, architectural or aesthetic reasons, and the landlord will be keen to have flexibility under the agreement to make such changes. The tenant, however, must be careful not to give the landlord full rein, as that could result in the tenant having to take a lease of premises radically different from those originally planned. A possible compromise is for the agreement to provide for and define 'unacceptable variations' (eg, those that substantially affect the design, layout, nature, capacity or standard of construction, or prejudice the use of the premises to be demised) and 'permitted variations' (eg, those (not being an unacceptable variation) required by the local planning authority under the terms of any planning permission for the development of the site and any required by the landlord or required due to the unavailability of materials (provided the alterations required by the landlord or the unavailability of materials have been notified to the tenant and its consent obtained)).

12.2.1.2   Tenant's supervision

The landlord will want complete freedom to enable its builders to progress the development of the site without any interference from the tenant, and may be able to insist upon this in negotiations. However, the tenant may have sufficient bargaining strength to demand a degree of involvement, control and supervision, for example to allow the tenant's surveyor to inspect the works as they are being carried out, in order to make comments and representations to the landlord (or its architect), to point out errors in the works and any variations not permitted by the agreement.

12.2.1.3   Practical completion

The date upon which the building is completed will trigger the commencement of the lease (and therefore liability for rent). Accordingly, the landlord is interested in achieving completion as soon as possible in order to obtain rent, whereas the tenant may have an interest in delaying completion (if, unusually, it is not especially keen to gain possession). The tenant will not want the agreement to force it to complete the lease until the premises have been fully completed to its satisfaction and are ready for immediate occupation and use. However, the landlord will not want to give the tenant any scope for delaying the transaction on the basis of only one or two imperfections.

To resolve this tension, it is often agreed that a certificate of practical completion will be issued by the landlord's architect (as defined by the agreement). This will certify that the building has reached the stage of 'practical completion' for the purposes of the agreement and will trigger completion.

'Practical completion' usually occurs when the building works have been sufficiently completed to permit use and occupation for the intended purpose, even though there may be some minor matters outstanding ('snagging works').

Issues which will concern the tenant and upon which it will need to negotiate are whether it:

(a)   should have any control over who should act as the architect – the tenant may prefer an independent architect rather than the architect employed by landlord;

(b)   can insist upon the attendance of its own representative at the final inspection of the works to make representations to the landlord's architect, or to insist on a joint inspection for the purpose of issuing the certificate;

(c)   can object to and delay the issue of the certificate of practical completion if in its opinion the works have not yet been satisfactorily completed.

12.2.1.4   Completion date for the works

The landlord is likely to seek to resist being obliged to complete the building works within a fixed time-scale as delays are commonplace in the construction industry (eg, the new Wembley Stadium). However, the tenant is likely to press for the inclusion of a clause which requires the landlord to use its best (or reasonable) endeavours to ensure that the building is completed by a certain date (a long stop date) so that it is not kept from occupation indefinitely. The landlord may be prepared to accept such a clause, provided it is not liable for delays caused by matters outside the landlord's control (see **12.2.1.5** below).

12.2.1.5   Force majeure

It is usual for the agreement to include a 'force majeure' clause to ensure that the person executing the works will not be in breach of the requirement to complete the works by a certain date if the delay is caused by matters which are outside his control, such as adverse weather conditions, strikes, lock-outs or other industrial action, civil commotion, shortages of labour or materials, and others.

12.2.1.6   Penalties for delay

The agreement will provide for the lease to be completed within a specified number of days after the issue of the certificate of practical completion.

To discourage the tenant from delaying completion, and to compensate the landlord if it does, the agreement should stipulate a 'Rent Commencement Date' from which rent will become payable under the lease, regardless of whether the tenant has completed the lease. If the tenant delays completion beyond the Rent Commencement Date, it will still be bound to pay rent to the landlord on completion of the lease calculated from the earlier Rent Commencement Date.

The Rent Commencement Date is usually stated to be the day upon which the lease is due to be completed (ie, a certain number of days after the issue of the certificate of practical completion) or, if a rent-free period is being given to the tenant, a certain number of months after the day upon which completion is due.

If the landlord fails to complete the building by any long-stop date inserted in the agreement and cannot benefit from the *force majeure* clause, the tenant might be happy simply to await completion in the knowledge that rent will not become payable until then. However, the premises are usually required by the tenant for its immediate business needs. To incentivise the landlord to complete on time, the tenant should insist upon a liquidated damages clause providing for a daily rate of damages in the event of a delay. The landlord should ensure that the building contract entered into with its building contractors runs 'back-to-back' with the agreement for lease so that it may claim liquidated damages from its contractors. The tenant may want a further provision enabling it to terminate the agreement in the event of a protracted delay.

12.2.1.7   Damage before completion of the lease

If the premises are damaged before practical completion then the certificate will not be issued until the landlord has remedied the damage. If the premises are damaged after practical completion but before actual completion of the lease, the agreement ought to stipulate that the premises remain at the landlord's risk since the tenant is not yet entitled to possession. The landlord ought to maintain insurance cover until the premises are handed over, and the agreement may make this a requirement.

12.2.1.8   Defects in the works or materials after completion

If, after completion, the tenant discovers that there are defects in the design or construction of the premises, or in the materials used, then in so far as the defects amount to disrepair (see **19.4.1.3**) the tenant will be bound to remedy them under the usual repairing covenant in the lease. A pre-completion inspection by the tenant's surveyor may discover defects which can be addressed, but often the nature of a design or construction defect is such that it rarely manifests itself until some time after the lease has been completed. The tenant should therefore ask for some protection in the agreement (or in the lease itself) against the prospect of such liability for 'latent' or 'inherent' defects arising. There are several ways in which this may be done (see **9.5**).

12.2.2   Terms relating to the lease

12.2.2.1   Agreed form lease

Before the agreement is entered into, the final form of the lease into which the tenant will be required to enter must have been agreed between landlord and tenant. Full negotiations must have taken place regarding the terms of the lease. The agreed form of draft (a fair copy incorporating all agreed amendments) should be appended to the agreement, with an obligation in the agreement for the tenant to take a lease in that form on the date of actual completion.

12.2.2.2   Premises

The agreement will normally describe the premises by reference to the parcels clause (see **Chapter 15**) in the draft lease, which in turn may refer to plans attached to the agreement showing the exact extent of the premises. Plans will be essential where a lease of part is intended.

12.2.2.3   Other contractual terms

Conditions of sale

The terms of the agreement for lease ought to set out extensively the rights and obligations of the landlord and tenant, in which case there may be no need to incorporate a set of conditions of sale. However, they are usually incorporated to the extent they are applicable to the grant of a lease and are consistent with the other terms of the agreement.

Deduction of title and disclosure of incumbrances

If title is deduced to the tenant, the agreement will usually prohibit requisitions after exchange.

Non-merger

The usual conveyancing doctrine of merger applies to an agreement to grant a lease, but it is common practice to include a clause excluding the doctrine since many of the contractual obligations are intended to continue in operation post-completion.

In so far as they do continue in operation, they may be construed as landlord or tenant covenants of the tenancy and therefore as binding upon successors in title (see the definition of 'covenant' and 'collateral agreement' in s 28(1) of the LT(C)A 1995).

REVIEW ACTIVITY

1. The landlord and the tenant have entered into an agreement for lease under which the works to be carried out by the landlord include the erection of internal brick walls. The tenant has now been told by the landlord that it intends to use breeze block and plasterboard, instead of bricks, as they will be cheaper. This will reduce the floor area for the tenant's use, and the tenant is unhappy about this proposal. Acting for the tenant, what provisions should you have asked to have included in the agreement for lease to protect your client in this scenario?

2. The landlord carries out the works specified by the agreement for lease and is seeking to have practical completion certified by the architect. Acting for the tenant, what provisions should you have asked to have included in the agreement for lease to ensure your client has some control on the issue of the certificate?

Answers to this Review activity may be found in Appendix 1.

CHAPTER 13

LEASE CONTENTS

13.1	Introduction	155
13.2	The 2007 Code for Leasing Business Premises in England and Wales	155
13.3	Drafting leases	156
13.4	Prescribed clauses leases	157
13.5	The structure of the lease	158
	Review activity	162

13.1 INTRODUCTION

A commercial property practice will have its own commercial lease precedents, which it will adapt for use in each commercial letting in respect of which the firm is instructed on behalf of the landlord.

All leading commercial practices ensure that their office precedent is an 'institutional' lease, one which guarantees the landlord a 'clear rent' (ie the landlord takes the entire income without cost to itself) by imposing all the costs of repairing and insuring on the tenant. By granting an 'institutional' lease, the landlord should avoid any later difficulties on selling the freehold to an institutional investor (eg, an investment fund).

The 'institutional' lease is now often for a term of at least 10 years with a five-yearly upwards only rent review pattern, although shorter leases are common in recessionary times (the *Property Data Report* 2014 states that the average length of a new lease in mid-2013 was 4.5 years across all commercial sectors). The 'institutional' lease often has strict controls on alienation, inflexible service charge provisions and onerous provisions relating to restoration of the premises at the end of the term.

13.2 THE 2007 CODE FOR LEASING BUSINESS PREMISES IN ENGLAND AND WALES

Unsurprisingly, tenants do not consider the 'institutional' lease sufficiently flexible to meet their increasingly fluid business requirements. Whilst not wanting to jeopardise property investment, the Government has tried to address these tenant concerns over a number of years by the introduction of a voluntary Code of Practice. Initially launched in 1995 and then again in 2002 (after consultation with representatives of the property industry), the Code tried to introduce fairness and flexibility in leasehold transactions by advocating:

(a) wherever possible, giving tenants a choice of leasing terms, where this was practicable;

(b) the relaxation of alienation provisions;

(c) that restrictions, beyond the standard 'consent not to be unreasonably withheld', should be imposed only where necessary to protect the landlord's interests, and in particular that guarantees of the incoming tenant by the outgoing tenant under a new lease should be required only where the incoming tenant was of lower financial standing than the outgoing tenant.

There was a lacklustre response from landlords to the Code and it was found to have little impact on lease negotiations (University of Reading Report, *Monitoring the 2002 Code of Practice for Commercial Leases*, released in early 2005). In fact it was very much the norm for landlords to insist on a guarantee by outgoing tenants in all circumstances, as they had lost the benefits of privity of contract (see **11.4** and **Chapter 14**). So the Government tried again to encourage flexibility in the market, and a new version of the Code was published in March 2007 (the 2007 Code).

The 2007 Code offers three documents to improve leasing practice:

(a)   a 'Landlord Code', which clarifies what is expected from landlords;

(b)   a step-by-step 'Occupier Guide' for tenants that will take them through the leasing process, intended to help tenants avoid the pitfalls of bad contracts and to ensure that landlords operate to industry-agreed standards; and

(c)   'Model Heads of Terms', showing tenants at a glance what they are signing up to, which can also be used by all parties, their agents and solicitors during lease negotiations.

These documents are set out in full in **Appendix 3**. In addition, a lease prepared by the Practical Law Company (PLCProperty) to promote discussion of the 2007 Code is set out in **Appendix 4** ('the **Appendix 4** lease'). It is intended to be compliant with the 2007 Code and also the RICS Code of Practice for Service Charges (see **26.8**).

The recommended leasing practices include the following:

(a)   Landlords should price alternative rent review terms on a risk-adjusted basis (encouraging the parties to move away from upward only rent review clauses which enable landlords to ignore any downwards trend in the rental market) – see paragraph 4 of the Landlord Code.

(b)   Pre-conditions on break clauses should be restricted – see paragraph 3 of the Landlord Code.

(c)   If sub-letting is allowed, it should be at the market rent – see paragraph 5 of the Landlord Code.

(d)   At the time of lease negotiations, landlords should disclose known irregular events that would have a significant effect upon the amount of future service charges – see paragraph 6 of the Landlord Code.

(e)   Unless expressly stated in the heads of terms, tenants will only be obliged to give the premises back at the end of their lease in the same condition as they were in when the lease was granted – see paragraph 8 of the Landlord Code.

At the launch of the 2007 Code, the then Housing and Planning Minister, Yvette Cooper, said:

> The new code will mean all businesses get a better deal on commercial property leases ... My challenge to the industry is to make sure that it is used in all lease negotiations. We shall be keeping a close watch on the market to see that it makes a real difference ... We believe the new code should have a chance to work, but ... we have legal options if it does not succeed. Industry needs to take the lead here. We will keep an eye on the effect of the code and watch with interest to ensure that there is proper, accountable self-regulation so that legislation is not necessary.

Tough talking, but in July 2009 another report conducted by the University of Reading found a disappointing lack of awareness and use of the Code. Whether the current Government does decide to legislate remains to be seen.

13.3   DRAFTING LEASES

It is highly unlikely that you will have to draft a lease from scratch when acting for a landlord client as most firms have their own lease precedents, and even if they do not, there is a wealth of precedent available online and in hard-copy form. The techniques to be adopted in drafting a lease or adapting a precedent are outlined in the drafting section of the Legal Practice Guide, *Skills for Lawyers*, and are not repeated here.

When drafting a lease or adapting a precedent, bear in mind that the purpose of interpreting any legal contract is to discover the real intention of the parties, but that intention can be ascertained only from the wording of the contract itself and not from extrinsic evidence.

In construing a lease, the court is always reluctant to hold a clause void for uncertainty, so if the court can find a way to interpret the clause, it will. Equally, however, the court is generally unwilling to imply terms into a document which has been entered into after extensive negotiations between legally represented parties (although see the approach of the Court of Appeal in *Royal Bank of Scotland plc v Jennings and Others* [1997] 19 EG 152, where the rent review machinery broke down but the court chose to supplement it to make it work). Faced with an ambiguity, the court will usually adopt the literal approach to interpretation, unless this would lead to a result so absurd that, in the commercial reality of the situation in which the parties find themselves, they could not reasonably have intended it (see *Broadgate Square plc v Lehman Brothers Ltd* [1995] 01 EG 111 involving the construction of a rent review clause). The court will not examine the offending clause in isolation but will construe the lease as a whole, to see if some assistance can be gained from other parts of the deed, where similar words and phrases may have been used in other contexts. Ordinary and technical words of the English language will be given the meanings usually attributed to them by the lay person, unless the lease clearly directs some other meaning (eg, by use of a definitions or interpretation clause – see **13.5** below).

If, owing to a common mistake between the parties, the lease, as executed, does not embody the common intentions of the parties, the remedy of rectification may be available. This is, however, an equitable and discretionary remedy, and there is a heavy burden upon the claimant in a claim for rectification to show the existence of a common mistake. Rectification will not be awarded so as to prejudice a bona fide purchaser of the interest of either landlord or tenant who did not have notice of the right to rectify.

If there is a discrepancy between the executed original lease (signed by the landlord) and counterpart (signed by the tenant), the former prevails over the latter, unless the original is clearly ambiguous.

13.4 PRESCRIBED CLAUSES LEASES

To facilitate registration and electronic conveyancing, the Land Registration Act 2002 empowered Land Registry to prescribe a form of lease; but following consultation, Land Registry has decided against mandatory use of a prescribed form. However, the Land Registration (Amendment) (No 2) Rules 2005 (SI 2005/1982) dictate that prescribed clauses must be contained in certain leases. These leases ('prescribed clauses leases') are those that are dated on or after 19 June 2006, which are granted out of registered land and are compulsorily registrable. There are certain exceptions outside the scope of this book. Where they apply, a conveyancer's certificate or other evidence must be supplied with the application for registration.

13.4.1 Required wording

The wording required in a prescribed clauses lease must appear at the beginning of the lease, or immediately after any front cover sheet and/or front contents page. A new Sch 1A is inserted into the Land Registration Rules 2005 (SI 2005/1766) which sets out the required wording and gives instructions as to how the prescribed clauses must be completed. Land Registry Practice Guide 64 gives detailed guidance on use of the clauses. An example is in the **Appendix 4** lease.

13.5   THE STRUCTURE OF THE LEASE

13.5.1   Commencement, date and parties

It is customary to start the drafting of a document by describing the document according to the nature of the transaction to be effected; for example, a lease will commence with the words 'This Lease'. The date of the lease will be left blank until the date of actual completion is manually inserted on completion. The draft lease should then set out the names and addresses of each party to the lease (eg, landlord, tenant and any guarantors). You can see the layout in the **Appendix 4** lease.

13.5.2   Definitions

Every well-drafted document should contain a definitions section. If a word is to bear a specific meaning in a document, that meaning ought to be clearly defined at the start of the document. If certain phrases or words are likely to recur in the document, those phrases or words ought to be given a defined meaning at the start of the document. The use of a definitions clause in a legal document avoids needless repetition of recurring words and phrases, permitting a more concise style of drafting. If a word or phrase is to be defined in the definitions clause, the first letter of the defined term should be given a capital (upper-case) letter and every use of that word or phrase thereafter should appear in the same form.

Defined terms commonly used in commercial leases (and in the **Appendix 4** lease) are set out below.

'Insured Risks'

It is in both parties' interests to have the insured risks clearly defined as it governs (amongst other things) those risks against which the premises should be insured and liability for damage caused by an insured risk (see **24.2.4**). The risks commonly include fire, riot, malicious damage, flooding, storm and other risks commonly covered by a standard buildings insurance policy. To maintain flexibility, the landlord should retain the right to insure against other risks which it thinks are necessary. The tenant should insist on such discretion being exercised reasonably.

'Interest' (in the **Appendix 4** lease defined as **'Default Interest'**)

If the tenant delays paying rent or any other sums due to the landlord under the lease, the landlord will want to charge the tenant interest on the unpaid sums. The rate of interest may be set out in the definitions clause. It is usually agreed at 3–5% above the base lending rate of a nominated bank. The landlord usually stipulates that if the base rate of that bank should cease to exist, the interest rate under the lease will be a reasonably equivalent rate of interest.

'Premises' (in the **Appendix 4** lease defined as **'Property'**)

As the definition of the premises is inextricably linked to many of the tenant covenants (eg repair, alterations, etc), the definition should accurately define the premises demised by the lease with a full verbal and legal description set out either in the definitions clause (as in the **Appendix 4** lease) or in the parcels clause (see **13.5.4** and **Chapter 15**) or in one of the schedules to the lease.

'Term' (in the **Appendix 4** lease defined as **'Contractual Term'**)

It is possible for the term commencement date to be before, on or after (provided not more than 21 years from the date of execution) the date the lease is executed. Note that the term may continue after the expiry date as a result of the LTA 1954 (see **11.3**), which could extend the original tenant's liability if the term is defined as including any extension, holding over or continuation of the term.

'VAT'

Value added tax may be payable on the rent and other sums due under the lease. In defining 'value added tax', it should be made clear that 'VAT' also includes any tax replacing VAT, or becoming payable in addition to it, in case the fundamental principles of the tax are changed.

'Rent' (in the **Appendix 4** lease defined as **'Annual Rent'**)

Careful thought should be given as to what 'Rent' is to mean and, in the light of its definition, whether it is appropriate to use the term in every reference to rent in the lease. Usually a landlord will want to reserve service charge payments, insurance premiums and VAT as rent so that the same remedies for recovery of those sums will be available (eg, distress, forfeiture without the need to serve a s 146 notice under the LPA 1925), in which case 'Rent' should be defined to include those items. This may be seen in the **Appendix 4** lease.

It should also be made clear that 'Rent' means not only the original contractual rent but also any revised rent which becomes payable by virtue of the rent review clause, and any interim rent which becomes payable under s 24A of the LTA 1954 during a statutory continuation tenancy. In this manner, it is made clear that in a case where a tenant's liability continues after assignment, the liability relates to the payment of a rent which may be increased after the date the tenant assigns its interest in the premises (see **17.1**).

The term 'Rent' is not an appropriate term in every case under the lease. For instance, in the rent review clause, it is the annual rent which is to be reviewed from time to time during the term, not necessarily the 'Rent' as defined. Another example is that the landlord might be prepared to allow payment of the annual rent to be suspended for a period of time if there is damage to the premises by an insured risk, but may not wish to have suspended the payment of other sums (eg, service charge) which have been reserved as 'Rent'. A tenant may resist this given that it may not be benefitting from any services during the period of damage (see **17.5**).

On a lease of part, further definitions are likely to be included, for example:

'Building'

As the landlord may be entering into covenants in the lease to repair the structure and exterior of the building, it must be defined. There are likely to be other references to the 'Building' with regard to the provision of services and the grant and reservation of easements.

'Common Parts'

The tenant will be granted rights to use the 'Common Parts' of the 'Building', and their extent should be expressed clearly.

'Services/Service Charge'

The landlord will usually provide services and there will be a number of definitions included to provide for that (see the **Appendix 4** lease), although the detail of the provision of services is more often found in a schedule to the lease.

13.5.3   The interpretation clause

Certain words or phrases do not require a fixed definition for the purposes of the lease; rather, their meaning needs to be expanded or clarified to assist the reader in the interpretation and construction of the lease. Common examples of matters of interpretation are the following:

Joint and several liability (clause 40.1 in the **Appendix 4** lease)

The lease should make it clear that if the landlord or tenant is more than one person, the obligations placed upon those persons by the lease will be enforceable against either or all of them.

One gender to mean all genders (clause 1.8 in the **Appendix 4** lease)

Section 61 of the LPA 1925 applies in respect of all deeds executed after the 1925 Act came into force, so that any reference in a deed to the masculine will include the feminine, and vice versa. However, s 61 does not deal with the neuter (ie, 'it'), and it is therefore common to state, for the avoidance of doubt, that a reference to one gender includes all others.

References to statutes (clauses 1.20 and 1.21 in the **Appendix 4** lease)

Leases usually provide that unless a particular clause expressly provides to the contrary, a reference in the lease to a statute or to a statutory instrument is to be taken as a reference to the Act or instrument as amended, re-enacted or modified from time to time, and not restricted to the legislation as it was in force at the date of the lease.

Expanding the meaning of words or phrases (clauses 1.10 and 1.11 in the **Appendix 4** lease)

If a tenant covenant states that the tenant is prohibited from doing a certain act, the tenant will not be in breach of covenant if that act is done by a third party. It is therefore usual to state that if the tenant is required by the lease not to do a certain act, it may not permit or suffer the act to be done by someone else either. If a tenant covenant prohibits the carrying out of a certain act without the landlord's prior consent (not to be unreasonably withheld), it is usual to stipulate that the landlord's consent may not also be unreasonably delayed.

Rather than having to repeat the wording required to deal with these matters throughout the lease, both of these points may be dealt with concisely by using an appropriate form of wording in the interpretation clause at the beginning of the lease.

13.5.4 The letting

The letting is the operative part of the lease which will create the tenant's interest, define the size of that interest, reserve rent, impose covenants, and deal with the grant and reservation of rights and easements. The clauses are usually set out in the following logical sequence:

The operative words (clause 2.1 in the **Appendix 4** lease)

Sufficient words of grant should be used to show the intention of the landlord to grant an interest in favour of the tenant. The landlord usually either 'demises' or 'lets' the premises to the tenant.

The parcels clause (clauses 2.1, 2.2 and 3 in the **Appendix 4** lease)

A full description of the premises, including the rights to be granted to the tenant, should be contained in the parcels clause. Often, the description is removed to one of the schedules (see below) so that the parcels clause simply refers to 'the Premises' (which will be a defined term).

Exceptions and reservations (clause 2.2 and clause 4 in the **Appendix 4** lease)

Usually, the rights to be reserved for the benefit of the landlord are referred to only briefly in this part of the lease; they are set out extensively in one of the schedules.

The habendum (clause 2.1 in the **Appendix 4** lease)

The habendum deals with the length of term to be vested in the tenant and its commencement date.

The reddendum (clause 2.3 and clause 6 in the **Appendix 4** lease)

The reddendum deals with the reservation of rent (which may be varied from time to time by a rent review clause), the dates for payment and the manner of payment (ie, whether in advance or in arrear).

The covenants

Where the covenants on the part of landlord, tenant and guarantor are set out in separate schedules, the parties expressly enter into them in the operative part of the lease. Otherwise the covenants are set out in the main body of the lease under separate clauses (see the **Appendix 4** lease).

13.5.5 The provisos

Often grouped together under the heading of 'provisos' is a wide variety of clauses which cannot easily be dealt with elsewhere in the lease, as they are in the nature neither of covenants nor easements, and do not impose obligations on any party to the lease. They are clauses which have no common thread except that most of them are inserted into the lease for the landlord's benefit alone.

The **Appendix 4** lease has not grouped these provisos together, but many other commercial leases do. The provisos usually include the following clauses:

(a)   The proviso for re-entry (ie, the forfeiture clause) (see clause 39 in the **Appendix 4** lease). This is dealt with in greater detail in **Chapter 25**.

(b)   An option to determine the lease where the premises are damaged by an insured risk so that they are no longer fit for use or occupation, and where the landlord either cannot or, after a period of time, has not reinstated the premises (see **24.7**). See clauses 9.13 and 9.14 in the **Appendix 4** lease.

(c)   A rent suspension clause (see clause 9.12 in the **Appendix 4** lease), which provides that the rent (and, possibly, other sums payable by the tenant under the lease) should cease to be payable if the premises are rendered unusable by damage caused by an insured risk (see **24.6**).

(d)   A provision which states that the landlord does not, by reason of anything contained in the lease, imply or represent that the tenant's proposed use of the premises is a permitted use under planning legislation (see clause 41.3 in the **Appendix 4** lease).

(e)   A provision whereby the tenant acknowledges that it has not entered into the lease in reliance upon any statement made by or on behalf of the landlord (see clause 41.2 in the **Appendix 4** lease). This provision seeks to prevent the tenant from pursuing a remedy against the landlord in respect of a misrepresentation, but it will be subject to s 3 of the Misrepresentation Act 1967 (as amended by s 8 of the Unfair Contract Terms Act 1977) and will have to satisfy the test of reasonableness set out in the 1977 Act.

(f)   A provision regulating the method of service of notices under the lease (see clause 42 in the **Appendix 4** lease). On occasions during the lease, one party will want or need to serve a notice on the other under one of the provisions in the lease (eg, to implement a rent review clause, or to give notice of an assignment of the lease or as a preliminary step to the exercise of a right of re-entry). Whether or not a notice has been validly served will be an important issue and should, therefore, be a matter which is capable of conclusive determination. Accordingly, the lease should specify the method of service of notices, either by incorporating the provisions of s 196 of the LPA 1925 (as amended by the Recorded Delivery Service Act 1962) into the lease, or by expressly setting out the methods of service to be permitted by the lease. Section 196(3) provides that service may be effected by leaving the document at the premises, or at the person's last-known abode or place of business. Section 196(4) deems service to have been effected if the notice is sent by recorded delivery post, provided that it is not returned through the Post Office as undelivered. The importance of tenants having proper systems in place to deal with notices was emphasised in *Warborough Investments Ltd v Central Midlands Estates Ltd* [2006] PLSCS 139. In this case, a 'trigger' notice initiating a rent review (see **18.7.1**) was held validly served when left at the customer service desk of a supermarket.

(g)   Excluding compensation under the LTA 1954 (see clause 16 in the **Appendix 4** lease). The parties may agree that the tenant should not be entitled to compensation under s 37 of the LTA 1954 at the end of its lease (see **31.6.4**). If so, the lease must refer to this.

(h)   Excluding the tenant's security of tenure (see clause 44 in the **Appendix 4** lease). The parties may also agree that the security of tenure provisions contained in the LTA 1954, Pt II should not apply to the lease (see **31.1.6**). If that is the case, the lease should include a contracting-out provision in the provisos.

(i)   Options to break (see clause 45 in the **Appendix 4** lease). If either party is to enjoy the right to terminate the lease early by the exercise of an option to break (see **16.2**), the option is usually contained in this part of the lease.

13.5.6   Schedules

Some commercial leases are drafted to have a short main body, with the detail of the lease being placed in separate schedules. This can make the lease easier to read, and from the client's point of view it may make it easier to refer to the various provisions of the lease. If this is the case then, commonly, separate schedules will deal with (amongst other matters) the premises demised, any rights granted to the tenant, any exceptions reserving rights in favour of the landlord, rent review, service charge and tenant/landlord/guarantor covenants. (Examples of schedules dealing with service charges and guarantees may be seen in the **Appendix 4** lease.)

13.5.7   Execution

Following the main body of the lease and any schedules will be the execution clauses. The lease and its counterpart are deeds, and therefore the usual rules relating to the execution of deeds are applicable. A testimonium clause is not an essential part of a lease, but if one is included, it ought to appear immediately before the first schedule (see the wording before Schedule 1 in the **Appendix 4** lease). Attestation clauses are essential.

REVIEW ACTIVITY

Assuming all wording in parenthesis has been included, consider the **Appendix 4** lease:

1.   Will the landlord be able to recover the service charge from the tenant in the event that the property is damaged by an explosion?

2.   The landlord faxes the tenant a s 146 notice for non-payment of rent in anticipation of forfeiting the lease. Will this be a valid notice?

3.   A contractor of the tenant manages to cut an electricity cable during some repair works to the property. The tenant argues that it is not in breach of clause 28.3 as it did not cause the damage. What argument would you advance for the landlord?

Answers to this Review activity may be found in Appendix 1.

CHAPTER 14

THE PARTIES TO THE LEASE AND THEIR LIABILITIES

14.1	Introduction	163
14.2	The landlord	163
14.3	The tenant	165
14.4	The guarantor	168
	Review activity	173

14.1 INTRODUCTION

Following the date and commencement, the lease will set out details of the parties to the lease, namely the landlord, the tenant and any guarantor (who is also often referred to as a surety).

In respect of a corporate party, the lease should give the company's full name and either its registered office or its main administrative office, and the company's registration number. In respect of an individual party, the full name and postal address of the individual will suffice.

The purpose of this chapter is to examine the extent and duration of liability of the parties to a lease. The Landlord and Tenant (Covenants) Act 1995 (LT(C)A 1995) (which came into force on 1 January 1996) brought about considerable changes in this area. In particular, it abolished the concept of privity of contract in relation to leases which are defined as new leases for the purposes of the Act (see **14.2.2**). Accordingly, this chapter examines the law and practice both in relation to 'old leases' already in existence at the date when the Act came into force (the old regime) and in relation to those which are 'new leases' (the new regime).

14.2 THE LANDLORD

The landlord's primary purpose as a party to the lease is to grant to the tenant the leasehold interest that both parties intend, upon the terms agreed between them. These terms may require the landlord to enter into covenants with the tenant in order to ensure that the tenant peaceably enjoys occupation of the premises, and a certain quality of accommodation (see, more specifically, **Chapter 23**).

14.2.1 The old regime

14.2.1.1 The original landlord

By virtue of the principle of privity of contract, the original landlord, as an original contracting party, remains liable in respect of any covenants entered into in the lease, even after it has sold the reversion. The landlord protects itself against the possibility of being sued for a breach of covenant committed by its successor by obtaining from that successor an express indemnity covenant in the transfer of the reversion. Such a covenant is not implied at law.

If the landlord has granted a lease of an entire building, it is unlikely that it entered into many covenants with the tenant. If the landlord has granted a lease of part of a building, or of premises forming part of a larger commercial site, the landlord may have entered into covenants to provide services to the tenants. If this is the case, the landlord may have limited expressly the duration of its liability under the covenants to the time the reversion is vested in the landlord, rather than relied upon obtaining an indemnity covenant.

14.2.1.2   A successor to the reversion

The landlord's successor in title is bound during its period of ownership by all covenants imposed upon the landlord which have reference to the subject matter of the lease (see s 142(1) of the LPA 1925). At the same time, it takes the benefit of the tenant's covenants which have reference to the subject matter of the lease under s 141(1) of the LPA 1925. It will also take the benefit of any surety covenants contained in the lease, provided the lease makes it clear that a reference in the lease to the landlord includes its successors in title (P&A Swift Investments v Combined English Stores Group plc [1983] 3 WLR 313).

14.2.2   The new regime

14.2.2.1   The original landlord

When a landlord sells its reversionary interest in a new lease, there is no automatic release from its obligations. However, ss 6 and 8 of the Act provide a procedure whereby the assigning landlord can apply to the tenant to be released from its obligations under the lease. The outgoing landlord may serve a notice (in a prescribed form) on the tenant (either before or within four weeks after the assignment) requesting such release. If, within four weeks of service, the tenant objects by serving a written notice on the landlord, the landlord may apply to the county court for a declaration that it is reasonable for the covenant to be released. If the tenant does not object within that time limit, the release becomes automatic. Any release from a covenant under these provisions is regarded as occurring at the time when the assignment in question takes place. However, in the case of BHP Great Britain Petroleum Ltd v Chesterfield Properties Ltd [2001] EWCA Civ 1797, [2002] 2 WLR 672, the Court of Appeal held that the statutory release mechanism did not operate to release the landlord from those covenants which were expressed to be personal. In respect of such covenants, the original landlord would continue to be liable even after the assignment of the reversion had taken place.

Once a landlord is released under these provisions, it ceases to be entitled to the benefit of the tenant covenants in the lease as from the date of the assignment of the reversion. It would appear, however, that if the landlord does not apply for a release it will retain the benefit of the tenant covenants, even though it has sold on the reversion (see Wembley National Stadium Limited v Wembley (London) Limited [2007] EWHC 756 (Ch)).

There is an additional way for the original landlord to limit its liability following the House of Lords decision in Avonridge Property Co Ltd v Mashru [2005] UKHL 70. The House of Lords held that a provision expressly limiting the landlord's liability under the covenants to the time that the reversion was vested in it was valid. Such provisions appeal to landlords as they avoid the need to seek a release under the LT(C)A 1995. Tenants, however, should be very cautious in agreeing to such provisions when the landlord's covenants are of substantial value, eg to perform the covenants in the head-lease. If the reversion is transferred to a person unable to comply with the landlord's covenants, the tenant could be left without an effective remedy for breach of covenant.

14.2.2.2   A successor to the reversion

The landlord's successor becomes bound, as from the date of the assignment, by all of the landlord covenants in the lease (or any document collateral to it, such as an agreement for lease), except to the extent that immediately before the assignment they did not bind the assignor (eg, a covenant waived or released by the tenant). Personal covenants given by the landlord will not bind the landlord's successor (*BHP Great Britain Petroleum Ltd v Chesterfield Properties Ltd* [2001] EWCA Civ 1797, [2002] 2 WLR 672). In consequence, agreements for lease will often state that building obligations imposed on a developer landlord are personal to that landlord. This prevents a successor landlord assuming liability for inherent defects in the building that have arisen during the design or construction process.

In addition, the new landlord becomes entitled to the benefit of the tenant covenants in the lease, giving the new landlord the right to enforce covenants against the tenant, even though it was not an original party to the lease.

Sections 141 and 142 of the LPA 1925 do not apply in relation to new leases, so there is no need to enquire whether the relevant landlord or tenant covenant is one which 'has reference to the subject matter of the lease'.

Surety covenants are not tenant covenants for the purposes of the Act. However, their benefit will still pass to an assignee of the reversion in accordance with *P&A Swift Investments*. This is on the basis that the assignee has acquired the legal estate, and the surety covenants touch and concern that estate. In the same manner, the benefit of a former tenant's authorised guarantee agreement (see **20.2.4.3**) will pass to the assignee.

A successor who ultimately sells on its reversion can apply to be released from its obligations in the same way as the original landlord (see **14.2.2.1**). If at that time a former landlord is still liable on the lease covenants (because it did not obtain a release from the tenant when it assigned the reversion), it can make another application to the tenant to be released. It is probably the case that a provision of the kind used in *Avonridge* (see **14.2.2.1**) would also limit the liability of a successor landlord to the period of its ownership.

14.3   THE TENANT

The person to whom the lease is granted is known as the original tenant. The person to whom the tenant later assigns its lease is known as the assignee. The original tenant will be required to enter into many covenants in the lease regulating what can be done in, on or at the premises.

14.3.1   The old regime

14.3.1.1   The original tenant – privity of contract

Prior to the LT(C)A 1995, basic principles of privity of contract dictated that the original tenant, as an original contracting party, remained liable in respect of all of the covenants in the lease for the entire duration of the term, even after it assigned the lease. If, for example, the tenant was granted a 25-year term which it assigned at the end of the fifth year to an assignee who then failed to pay rent and allowed the premises to fall into disrepair, the landlord could choose to sue the original tenant for non-payment of rent and breach of the repairing covenant. It would not matter that since the assignment the rent had been increased under the rent review clause (unless the increase was referable to a variation of the lease terms agreed between the landlord and assignee – see s 18 of the LT(C)A 1995 and the case of *Friends Provident Life Office v British Railways Board* [1995] 1 All ER 336).

The effect of privity of contract becomes increasingly significant in recessionary times. If an assignee becomes insolvent, instead of pursuing a worthless claim against the assignee, the landlord will look to the original tenant for payment of rent.

Some protection is offered by s 17 of the LT(C)A 1995. This provides that if a landlord wishes to pursue a former tenant (and/or its guarantor) for a 'fixed charge' due under the lease (such as rent or service charge), the landlord must serve notice on the former tenant (and/or its guarantor). The notice must require payment of the outstanding sum and be served within six months of the sum falling due. The former tenant or its guarantor cannot be required to pay the outstanding sum if a s 17 notice is not served. Should a former tenant or its guarantor make full payment to the landlord of a sum demanded under a s 17 notice, it may call for an 'overriding lease' of the premises. This will make it the immediate landlord of the defaulting tenant. It can then seek to forfeit the defaulting tenant's lease and re-let.

14.3.1.2   For how long is the original tenant liable?

The original tenant's liability lasts for the entire duration of the contractual term. Once it has assigned its interest in the lease, the original tenant's liability will not extend into any continuation of that term that may arise under s 24 of the LTA 1954, unless there is an express provision in the lease to the contrary (*City of London Corporation v Fell* [1993] 49 EG 113). Often, however, the landlord's solicitor will have defined 'the Term' in the lease to include 'the period of any holding over or any extension or continuance whether by agreement or operation of law'. The effect of this will be to extend the original tenant's liability into the continuation term. The liability relates only to the contractual rent under the lease, and not to any interim rent fixed by the court under s 24A of the LTA 1954 unless the lease states otherwise (*Herbert Duncan Ltd v Cluttons* [1992] 1 EGLR 101).

14.3.1.3   The original tenant's need for an indemnity

As a result of the continuing nature of the original tenant's liability under the old regime, it is essential that, on an assignment of an old lease, the original tenant obtains an indemnity from the assignee against all future breaches of covenant (whether committed by the assignee or a successor in title). An express indemnity may be taken, but this is not strictly necessary since s 77 of the LPA 1925 automatically implies into every assignment for value a covenant to indemnify the assignor against all future breaches of covenant. If the lease is registered at Land Registry, Sch 12 to the Land Registration Act 2002 (LRA 2002) implies a similar covenant for indemnity into a transfer of the lease, whether or not value is given.

From a practical point of view, it should be noted that an indemnity from an assignee (whether express or implied) is worthless if the assignee is insolvent, and this may be the very reason why the landlord is pursuing the original tenant in the first place.

Where there has been a succession of assignments, and the original tenant finds that it is unable to obtain a full indemnity against its immediate assignee, the assignee in possession may be liable at common law to indemnify the original tenant who has been sued for breach of covenant (see *Moule v Garrett and Others* (1872) LR 7 Exch 101), but again the indemnity may be worthless owing to the insolvency of the defaulting assignee.

14.3.1.4   The assignee – privity of estate

By virtue of the doctrine of privity of estate, an assignee under the old regime is liable in respect of all of the covenants in the lease which 'touch and concern' the demised premises, for as long as the lease remains vested in that assignee.

An assignee cannot be sued for a breach of covenant committed prior to the lease being vested in it, save to the extent that the breach in question is a continuing breach (eg, breach of a covenant to repair) which effectively becomes the assignee's breach from the date of the assignment. If, at the time of the assignment there are arrears of rent, the landlord's claim to recover the arrears would be against the assignor, not the assignee. However, from a practical point of view, the landlord is unlikely to give its consent to an assignment (assuming the lease requires its consent) unless the arrears are cleared. Further, the assignee is unlikely to take the assignment while rent is in arrear because of the risk of forfeiture of the lease on account of the outstanding breach.

Under the doctrine of privity of estate, an assignee is not liable for breaches of covenant committed after it has parted with its interest in the premises (although it may still be sued in respect of breaches committed while it was the tenant). However, if it has given a direct covenant to the landlord to observe the tenant covenants throughout the term, it can be pursued under normal contractual principles for breaches by subsequent assigness (see **14.3.1.6**).

14.3.1.5   Covenants which touch and concern

Under the old regime, an assignee is liable only in respect of those covenants which touch and concern the demised premises. These are covenants which are not in the nature of personal covenants but have direct reference to the premises in question by laying down something which is to be done or not to be done at the premises, and which affect the landlord in its normal capacity as landlord or the tenant in its normal capacity as tenant. If the purpose of the covenant is to achieve something which is collateral to the relationship of landlord and tenant then the covenant does not touch and concern.

Nearly all of the covenants in a typical commercial lease will touch and concern the demised premises. In any event, as most landlords will require a direct covenant from an incoming assignee to observe the tenant covenants in the lease, the assignee will be liable under the direct covenant regardless of whether the covenants 'touch and concern' (see **14.3.1.6**).

14.3.1.6   Direct covenants

Landlords have never liked the limited duration of an assignee's liability under the doctrine of privity of estate. In practice, therefore, it is common for the landlord to try to extend the liability of an assignee under the old regime by requiring it, as a condition of the landlord's licence to assign, to enter into a direct covenant to observe the covenants in the lease for the entire duration of the term, thereby creating privity of contract between landlord and assignee. This covenant is usually contained in the formal licence to assign (see **27.2**). The landlord will always then have a choice between original tenant and present assignee as to whom to sue for a breach of covenant committed by the latter. Where intermediate assignees have entered into direct covenants in this manner, the landlord's options are increased.

If an assignee has given a direct covenant to the landlord, the extent of its continuing liability is governed by the *City of London v Fell* case, and the definition of 'the Term' in the lease in the same way as applies to the original tenant (see **14.3.1.2**).

14.3.1.7   The assignee's need for an indemnity

The assignee from the original tenant is likely to have given an indemnity covenant to the original tenant, either expressly or impliedly (see **14.3.1.3**). It therefore needs to obtain one from its assignee. An express indemnity may be taken, but s 77 of the LPA 1925 and Sch 12 to the LRA 2002 will operate in the same way as before.

14.3.2   The new regime

As stated above, the main purpose of the LT(C)A 1995 was to abolish privity of contract in leases, and it is therefore in the area of tenant liability that the Act has had the most significant impact.

14.3.2.1   The original tenant – privity of contract release

The basic rule is that a tenant under a lease which is a new lease for the purposes of the LT(C)A 1995 is only liable for breaches of covenant committed while the lease is vested in it. Thus, on assignment of the lease, the assignor is automatically released from all the tenant covenants of the tenancy (and it ceases to be entitled to the benefit of the landlord covenants). This means that while the outgoing tenant can be sued for breaches of covenant committed at a time when the lease was vested in that tenant, it cannot be sued for any subsequent breaches.

14.3.2.2   The assignee – liability on covenants

The basic rule applies equally to assignees. As from the date of assignment, an assignee becomes bound by the tenant covenants in the lease except to the extent that immediately before the assignment they did not bind the assignor (eg, they were expressed to be personal to the original tenant); but when it assigns the lease, it is automatically released from all of the tenant covenants. In addition, under the new regime an assignee will be liable on all the tenant covenants in the lease whether or not they 'touch and concern' the land.

In the same way that the assignee becomes bound by the tenant covenants, so too does the assignee become entitled, as from the date of the assignment, to the benefit of the landlord covenants in the lease.

14.3.2.3   Excluded assignments

Assignments in breach of covenant (eg, where the tenant has not complied with a requirement in the lease to obtain its landlord's consent before assigning) or by operation of law (eg, on the death or bankruptcy of a tenant) are excluded assignments for the purposes of the LT(C)A 1995. On an excluded assignment, the assignor will not be released from the tenant covenants of the lease, and will remain liable to the landlord, jointly and severally with the assignee, until the next assignment, which is not an excluded assignment, takes place.

14.3.2.4   Authorised guarantee agreement

To counterbalance the loss to the landlord of the benefits of the old privity regime, the LT(C)A 1995 allows the landlord to require an outgoing tenant, who will be released from liability under the Act, to enter into a form of guarantee (known as an 'authorised guarantee agreement' or 'AGA') whereby the outgoing tenant guarantees the performance of the tenant covenants by the incoming tenant (see **20.2.4.3**).

14.3.2.5   Indemnity covenants?

As an assigning tenant is not liable for the breaches of covenant committed by its successor, the LT(C)A 1995 has repealed s 77 of the LPA 1925 and Sch 12 to the LRA 2002 in relation to leases granted under the new regime. However, it should be noted that an outgoing tenant may remain liable to the landlord for an assignee's breaches of covenant under the terms of an AGA, and in such circumstances an express indemnity from the assignee should be obtained.

14.4   THE GUARANTOR

Much attention in practice is given to the financial status of the proposed tenant, and a consideration of what is called 'the strength of the tenant's covenant'. A tenant is said to give 'a good covenant' if it can be expected that the tenant will pay the rent on time throughout the term, and diligently perform its other obligations under the lease. An established, high-performing and renowned public limited company (such as one of the large retail food companies) will be regarded as giving a good covenant in the commercial letting market, whereas newly-formed public limited companies and many private companies, whose reputation, reliability and financial standing are unknown in the property market, will not be perceived as giving a good covenant. If the covenant is so bad that the landlord has reservations about the proposed tenant's ability to maintain rental payments throughout the term without financial difficulties, the landlord will consider not granting a lease to that tenant in the first place. However, in situations which fall between these two extremes, the landlord often requires a third party, known as a guarantor, to join in the lease to guarantee the tenant's obligations.

14.4.1   Practical points

The landlord's aim is to ensure that it receives the rent due under the lease on time throughout the term, either from the tenant or, if the tenant defaults, from the guarantor. Therefore, just as the landlord ought to investigate the financial status of its proposed tenant, so too it should investigate the status of the guarantor nominated by the tenant.

With private limited companies or newly-formed public limited companies (who, even with plc status, may be just as likely to be in breach as any other tenant), many landlords will ask for one or more of the company's directors to guarantee the tenant's performance of its obligations. However, the landlord should not necessarily be so blinkered in its approach, since other options may prove to be more fruitful.

Does a subsidiary company have a parent or sister company that can stand as guarantor? If the directors are not of sufficient financial standing, are the shareholders of the company in any better position to give the landlord the element of reliability it requires? Will the tenant's bank guarantee the obligation of its client?

The guarantor should be advised to seek independent advice, since there is a clear conflict of interests between tenant and guarantor. The conflict arises in that, on the one hand, the advice to be given to the tenant is that, without a guarantor, the tenant will not get a lease, while, on the other hand, the advice to give to the guarantor would be to avoid giving the guarantee. Further, in seeking to make amendments to the surety covenants in the lease on behalf of the guarantor, the solicitor may be prejudicing the negotiation of the lease terms between the landlord and his tenant-client, causing delay or disruption.

14.4.2 The extent of the guarantee

14.4.2.1 The old regime

The purpose of the guarantee is to ensure that the guarantor will pay the rent if the tenant does not, and will remedy or indemnify the landlord against any breaches of covenant committed by the tenant. Two points should be noted. First, it is usual for the landlord in drafting the lease to define 'the Tenant' to include the tenant's successors in title. This means that in guaranteeing the obligations of 'the Tenant', the guarantor has guaranteed the performance of future (and as yet unknown) assignees of the lease. Its liability would therefore extend throughout the duration of the lease (even after the original tenant had assigned the lease). Secondly, even if the guarantee was limited to a guarantee of the original tenant's obligations, an original tenant remains liable by virtue of privity of contract under the old regime to perform the covenants in the lease for its entire duration. Should, therefore, the landlord choose to sue not the assignee in possession but the original tenant, the guarantee would remain active.

Some guarantors under the old regime sought to limit the extent of their liability so that the guarantee applied only for so long as the lease remained vested in the tenant in respect of whom the guarantee was originally sought.

For guarantors who were unable to negotiate such a limitation, s 17 of the LT(C)A 1995 will offer some protection (see **14.3.1.1**).

14.4.2.2 The new regime

Abolition of the concept of privity of contract in leases applies equally to guarantors. Section 24(2) of the LT(C)A 1995 provides that where a tenant is released under the LT(C)A 1995 from the tenant covenants of the lease, the guarantor is also released. Any attempt to extend the liability of a guarantor beyond the duration of the liability of the tenant whose performance was guaranteed is likely to fall foul of the anti-avoidance provisions of s 25 of the LT(C)A 1995. This includes requiring the guarantor of an outgoing tenant directly to guarantee an incoming assignee's obligations (see *Good Harvest LLP v Centaur Services Limited* [2010] EWHC 330 (Ch)). However, s 25 would not preclude the guarantor from guaranteeing the outgoing tenant's AGA obligations and therefore indirectly guaranteeing the assignee (see *K/S Victoria*

Street v House of Fraser (Stores Management) Limited [2011] EWCA Civ 904). (Both these cases are discussed further at **20.2.4.3.**)

14.4.2.3   Guarantor's liability if tenant 'holds over'

Unless there is an express provision in the lease to the contrary, the liability of the guarantor will cease upon the contractual term date and will not continue during a statutory continuation tenancy under s 24 of the LTA 1954 (see *Junction Estates Ltd v Cope* (1974) 27 P & CR 482). However, it is common practice to define the lease term to include 'the period of any holding over or any extension or continuance whether by agreement or operation of law', and to prolong the guarantor's liability by requiring it to covenant with the landlord throughout 'the term' as so defined.

14.4.3   Discharge or release

The guarantor cannot unilaterally revoke its guarantee, but in certain cases, usually where the landlord acts to the prejudice of the guarantor, the conduct of the landlord might operate as a release.

14.4.3.1   Variations

If the landlord, without obtaining the consent of the guarantor, agrees with the tenant to vary the terms of the lease (eg, by substituting more onerous repairing obligations), the variation of the lease will operate to discharge the guarantor. A guarantor cannot stand as surety and be made liable for the tenant's default in the performance of terms different from those guaranteed to be performed, unless the guarantor has agreed to the variation. However, an immaterial variation of the lease which would not prejudice the guarantor (eg, by substituting less onerous repairing obligations) is not likely to discharge the guarantor, although authority appears to suggest that it is for the guarantor to decide whether or not it would be prejudiced by the proposed variation. In *Holme v Brunskill* (1877) 3 QBD 495, a surrender of part of the premises comprised in the lease (which might not appear in any way to prejudice the guarantor, particularly if the rent is reduced as a result), agreed without the consent of the guarantor, operated to discharge the guarantee. However, a variation which does not affect the terms of the (tenant's) principal contract will not affect the guarantor's secondary contract (see *Metropolitan Properties Co (Regis) Ltd v Bartholomew* [1995] 14 EG 143).

A surrender of the whole of the premises comprised in the lease will operate to end the liability of the guarantor as from the date of surrender, but not in respect of any breaches of covenant outstanding at that time.

Increasing the rent by exercising a rent review clause does not amount to a variation and so will not release the guarantor. This means that a guarantor may be guaranteeing the payment in future of an unknown level of rent (although see the protection given to guarantors of former tenants by s 18 of the LT(C)A 1995 and in the case of *Friends Provident Life Office v British Railways Board* [1995] 1 All ER 336).

Landlords should be aware that granting a permission to a tenant, for example to carry out works, can amount to a variation of the lease, if that permission allows for something prohibited in the original lease. So in *Topland Portfolio No 1 Ltd v Smiths New Trading Ltd* [2014] EWCA Civ 18, the landlord granted permission for the tenant to carry out substantial works to its premises by way of a Licence for Alterations. The tenant's guarantor was not a party to the Licence for Alterations and the type of work permitted by the Licence had been prohibited under the terms of the lease. The tenant subsequently went into administration and the landlord pursued the guarantor for rent arrears. Unfortunately for the landlord, since the Licence consented to something prohibited by the lease, the court considered that the Licence amounted to a variation of the lease. On that basis, as the guarantor had not been a party to the variation, it was released from its guarantee, leaving the landlord unable to recover the rent arrears.

In light of such case law, the safest course of action for landlords is to ensure any guarantor to the lease is also a party to any documentation granted supplemental to the lease.

14.4.3.2 'Giving time'

'Giving time' to the tenant may operate to discharge the guarantee. A landlord 'gives time' to a tenant if, in a binding way, it agrees to allow the tenant to pay rent late or not at all. It does not seem that a mere omission to press for payment (eg, due to an oversight, or perhaps to avoid a waiver of the right to forfeit the lease) will amount to the giving of time.

14.4.3.3 Release of co-guarantor

According to general principles of suretyship, if there is more than one guarantor, the release by the landlord of one of them operates as a release of all of them.

14.4.3.4 Death

The death of the tenant is not likely to bring an end to the guarantee, since the lease will vest in the tenant's personal representatives who, as the tenant's successors in title, will become 'the Tenant' under the lease, whose obligations are guaranteed by the guarantor. Under the new regime, such a vesting would be an excluded assignment, and so the guarantor would not be released. Further, the death of the guarantor will not necessarily bring an end to the guarantee since the guarantor's own personal representatives will remain liable under the guarantee to the extent of the deceased's assets passing through their hands. However, it is more common for the landlord to make provision for the possible death of the guarantor by obtaining a covenant from the tenant obliging him to find a suitable replacement.

14.4.3.5 Bankruptcy or liquidation

The bankruptcy or liquidation of the tenant will not operate to release the guarantor. On the bankruptcy of an individual tenant, the lease will vest in the trustee-in-bankruptcy who will become 'the Tenant' for the purposes of the lease (and such a vesting is an excluded assignment under the new regime). On the liquidation of a corporate tenant, the lease will remain vested in the company (unless the liquidator obtains an order under s 145 of the Insolvency Act 1986 (IA 1986)).

Even if the trustee or liquidator chooses to disclaim the lease, the disclaimer will not operate to end the guarantor's liability (see **32.9**).

14.4.4 Drafting points for the landlord

The landlord should ensure that the guarantor joins in the lease to give the covenants the landlord requires. A guarantee will be unenforceable if it is not in writing (see *Actionstrength Ltd v International Glass Engineering* [2003] 2 AC 541).

The two basic obligations of a guarantor are: (i) to pay the rent (and any other sums payable by the tenant under the lease) if the tenant does not pay; and (ii) to remedy, or to indemnify the landlord against loss caused by, any breaches of covenant committed by the tenant. The landlord will ensure that the guarantor is liable for the period in respect of which the tenant is liable under the lease and, possibly, under any AGA into which the tenant may enter. If the landlord wishes to extend the liability of the guarantor to cover the period of any AGA, it must ensure this is done by way of a sub-guarantee of the outgoing tenant's obligations in the AGA (see **20.2.4.3**). A direct guarantee of the incoming assignee's obligations will fall foul of the anti-avoidance provisions in s 25 of the LT(C)A 1995 (see *Good Harvest LLP v Centaur Services Limited* [2010] EWHC 330 (Ch)).

Several other provisions are usually required by the landlord:

(a)   A covenant from the tenant to provide a replacement guarantor should one of several unfortunate or undesirable events happen. For instance, if the guarantor is an individual who dies, or becomes mentally incapable (ie, a receiver is appointed under s 99 of the Mental Health Act 1983) or has a petition in bankruptcy presented against him (or is affected by other proceedings under the IA 1986 which the landlord considers serious enough to warrant substitution) the landlord will require the tenant to find a replacement of equivalent financial standing. If the guarantor is a company and a winding up commences (or, as above, it is affected by other adverse insolvency proceedings), again the tenant will be required to find a reasonably acceptable replacement.

(b)   A provision protecting the landlord against the tenant's trustee-in-bankruptcy or liquidator disclaiming the lease to bring the tenant's liability to an end. The effect of a disclaimer is dealt with at **32.10**. For present purposes it can be said that, whilst disclaimer does not end the liability of a guarantor, most landlords will nevertheless want the ability to require the guarantor to take a lease from the landlord in the event of disclaimer, for the full unexpired residue of the term then remaining.

(c)   A provision to deal with situations which might otherwise operate to release the guarantor. As part of the guarantor's covenants, the landlord will include a declaration that a release will not be effected by the giving of time to the tenant, or by a variation in the terms of the lease (although as a concession, the landlord might accept that a variation prejudicial to the guarantor will still operate as a release unless the guarantor has consented to it). The effect of stating in the lease that the guarantor will not be released 'by any other event which, but for this provision, would operate to release the surety' is doubtful.

14.4.5 Drafting points for the guarantor

If the guarantor has accepted the principle of giving a guarantee, it should make all efforts to minimise its liability. There are several provisions a guarantor can seek to negotiate:

(a)   A limit on the length of its liability. While the LT(C)A 1995 releases a guarantor to the same extent as it releases the tenant, the guarantor should try to ensure that it is not contractually bound to guarantee the tenant under any AGA (as to which, see **20.2.4.3**). This may prove difficult to negotiate if the covenant strength of the tenant is questionable.

(b)   An obligation on the landlord's part to notify the guarantor of any default by the tenant. One would expect the tenant to tell its guarantor if the tenant was experiencing difficulties in meeting its obligations under the lease. However, this might not always be the case, and in order to alert the guarantor to possible claims under the guarantee and, perhaps, to enable it to put pressure on the tenant, it could seek to include a covenant by the landlord to notify the guarantor in writing whenever the tenant falls into arrears with the rent, or otherwise breaches a covenant in the lease.

(c)   Participation in rent reviews. As the guarantor guarantees payment of future unascertained rents, it may try to persuade the landlord to allow it to play a part in the rent review process. This would necessitate amendments to the usual rent review clause and would not be attractive to the landlord. Further, the tenant would not be keen either to hand over the review negotiations to the guarantor, or to have it involved as a third party in the review process, and an assignee of the lease would certainly see it as an unattractive proposition.

(d)   An ability to demand an assignment of the lease from the tenant where the tenant is in default under the lease. This would enable the guarantor to minimise its liability by being able to call for an assignment and then assign the lease to a more stable assignee.

14.4.6 An assignee's guarantor

The above paragraphs have concentrated on the guarantee to be provided by the original tenant on the grant of the lease. However, as a condition of granting licence to assign the lease, the landlord may require the assignee to provide a suitable guarantor in respect of its obligations. This guarantor cannot be the person or company who guaranteed the obligations of the assignor (see *Good Harvest LLP v Centaur Services Limited* [2010] EWHC 330 (Ch) and *K/S Victoria Street v House of Fraser (Stores Management) Limited* [2011] EWCA Civ 904). Under the old regime, it will be the landlord's intention to fix the new guarantor with liability for the duration of the contractual term and beyond. Under the new regime, liability should not exceed the liability of the assignee.

REVIEW ACTIVITY

1. A tenant (T) took a lease in 1994 and assigned it for value in 2000. The original contractual term has now expired but the assignee is holding over under the LTA 1954. T has now received a letter from the current landlord saying the assignee has failed to pay the last quarter's rent and demanding it from T. Is T obliged to pay?

2. A landlord (L) grants a lease in 2010 and then sells on its freehold reversionary interest. It receives a letter from the current tenant alleging that the current landlord is insolvent and has failed to pay the insurance premiums for the building. The tenant is suggesting that L is liable for the insurance premiums. Is the tenant's assertion correct?

3. Your client has just purchased the freehold of an office block subject to a recently granted lease of the whole. The tenant has told your client that it has certain contractual obligations from the previous landlord contained in an agreement for lease that pre-dates the lease. One of the obligations is to repair any damage caused to the premises by inherent defects. Your client wishes to know if it is liable to comply with these obligations.

Answers to this Review activity may be found in Appendix 1.

CHAPTER 15

THE PARCELS CLAUSE

15.1	Purpose	175
15.2	Airspace and underground	175
15.3	Fixtures	175
15.4	Rights to be granted and reserved	176
	Review activity	177

15.1 PURPOSE

The purpose of the parcels clause is accurately and unambiguously to describe the property being let to the tenant (the 'demised premises'), so that it is clear what is included and what is excluded. This is important because key provisions in the lease, such as the tenant's repairing covenant, the landlord's insurance covenant and the controls on what alterations the tenant may carry out, are given in relation to the demised premises as defined in the lease.

Where the whole of a building is being let, the parcels clause will contain the same sort of description as in the case of the sale of freehold land, for example:

> the land and building at 25 High Street, Shaftesbury, Dorset SP7 8JE, shown red on the attached plan.

In most cases, a plan will be used, although if a lease is the grant of the whole of the landlord's registered title or the boundaries are clearly identifiable on the Ordnance Survey map, it may be possible to describe the demised premises adequately in words alone. However, where a lease of part only of a building is intended, the parcels clause needs more care and attention, and a plan will be essential. This chapter deals with the description of the demised premises in a lease of a whole building; see **Chapter 26** for the issues that arise on a lease of part of a building.

15.2 AIRSPACE AND UNDERGROUND

A lease of land includes the buildings on it, everything below the land, and the airspace above it to such a height as is necessary for the ordinary use and enjoyment of the land and buildings. However, the parties may limit the extent of the parcels clause by excluding the airspace above the roof. If there is such a limitation, this will prevent the tenant from adding extra floors by extending upwards, since to do so would be a trespass. The tenant should also appreciate that problems might be caused if it had to erect scaffolding above roof height to comply with its obligation to repair the roof; that would also amount to a trespass. The tenant should therefore ensure that it has any necessary right to enter the airspace above its building to the extent necessary to comply with its obligations under the lease. Without any limitation on the airspace the tenant will be free to extend upwards subject only to obtaining any necessary planning permission and consent under the alterations covenant.

15.3 FIXTURES

The point about a fixture is that it is part of the demised premises and prima facie belongs to the landlord. If an article is not a fixture it will be a chattel. Yet despite the apparent simplicity of the matter, it is not always easy to distinguish between the two, and over the years the courts have developed a test based on the degree of annexation of the item to the land and the purpose of annexation (see, eg, *Holland and Another v Hodgson and Another* (1872) LR 7 CP 328). However, the application of this test to a given set of facts is notoriously difficult, and for the avoidance of doubt, a prospective tenant should always compile a full inventory of the fixtures which are present at the start of the lease.

15.3.1 Repair of fixtures

If an article is a fixture, it is treated as part of the demised premises and the tenant will become responsible for its repair under its obligation to repair 'the demised premises'. This can have a significant impact on the tenant, bearing in mind that many business premises include expensive fixtures such as central heating and air-conditioning plant. For this reason the tenant should always inspect the condition of the fixtures before completion of the lease. If any defects are discovered, the tenant must make sure that it does not become liable to remedy those defects under its repairing obligation. This can be achieved by getting the landlord to do any necessary repairs before the lease commences, or by agreeing the state and condition of the fixtures with the landlord and ensuring that the covenant to repair does not require any higher standard than that existing at the start of the lease.

15.3.2 Removal of fixtures

The tenant may have the right to remove fixtures at the end of the lease depending upon whether they are 'landlord's fixtures', which cannot be removed, or 'tenant's fixtures', which the tenant is entitled to remove unless the lease provides to the contrary. Tenant's fixtures are those articles:

(a)   affixed by the tenant;

(b)   for the purpose of its trade; and

(c)   which are capable of removal without substantially damaging the building and without destroying the usefulness of the article (see *Peel Land & Property (Ports No 3) Ltd v TS Sheerness Steel Ltd* [2013] EWHC 1658 (Ch)).

The terms of the lease may require the tenant to yield up the demised premises at the end of the term together with all fixtures. Whether this excludes the tenant's right to remove tenant's fixtures depends on the form of wording used; very clear words will be required before the right is excluded. It has been held that an obligation to yield up the premises 'with all and singular the fixtures and articles belonging thereto' is sufficient to exclude the right (*Leschallas v Woolf* [1908] 1 Ch 641), and the tenant should resist such a clause. In the case of *Peel Land & Property (Ports No 3) Ltd v TS Sheerness Steel Ltd* [2014] EWCA Civ 100, a landlord successfully argued that a tenant's covenant not to make or suffer to be made any change or addition to the premises save in connection with the permitted purpose of steel making meant that a tenant could not remove a large number of pieces of equipment and plant installed by a former tenant in order to sell them.

Where the tenant is entitled to remove fixtures, it must make good any damage caused by their removal. As a general rule, the right exists only during the term.

15.4 RIGHTS TO BE GRANTED AND RESERVED

In many cases, the demised premises will be structurally independent and directly connected to all mains services. Where this is not the case, the tenant may need to be granted rights to enable it to use the demised premises to their full extent. For example, it may need the right to enter upon the landlord's adjoining property to comply with its obligation to repair; this may be particularly important where the walls of the demised premises are flush against the boundary. The tenant may also need the right to connect into services on the landlord's adjoining property.

From the landlord's point of view, it may need to reserve rights such as a right to enter the demised premises to view the state and condition or to repair. The service pipes and cables for the landlord's adjoining property may pass under or through the demised premises, and the landlord will thus need to reserve rights in respect of them.

REVIEW ACTIVITY

1. You act for Straudley Investments Ltd, the tenant under a lease of 67–81 Mortimer Street London for a term of 99 years from 1936. The parcels clause in the lease demises:

    'ALL THAT piece or parcel of ground with the messuages and buildings erected thereon situate and being on the south side of and numbered 67, 69, 71, 73, 75, 77, 79 and 81 in Mortimer Street ...'

    The landlord has erected a fire escape and a ventilation vent on the roof of the building without your client's consent. Can your client apply to court for a mandatory injunction requiring the landlord to remove the fire escape and ventilation vent on the grounds that the landlord is trespassing on its property?

2. You act for Ms Eileen Davies who is the tenant of top-floor premises at 13 Beechcroft Avenue London. The parcels clause in the lease demises all of the first-floor flat at 13 Beechcroft Avenue, as shown on the plan annexed to the lease, and the roof and roof space thereof. Your client wishes to carry out a loft conversion. The landlord is withholding his consent on the basis that the dormer windows that would be installed as part of the conversion involve a protrusion into the airspace above the roof and would therefore constitute a trespass by the tenant. Is your client entitled to a declaration from the court that the landlord is unreasonably withholding his consent to an improvement proposed by the tenant?

Answers to this Review activity may be found in Appendix 1.

CHAPTER 16

TERM

16.1	Introduction	179
16.2	Break clauses	180
16.3	Options to renew	181
16.4	Impact of SDLT	181
	Review activity	182

16.1 INTRODUCTION

The duration of a lease for a term of years must be fixed and certain before the lease takes effect. Thus, for example, a tenancy 'until the landlord requires the land for road widening' is void for uncertainty (*Prudential Assurance Co Ltd v London Residuary Body* [1992] 2 AC 386). This principle applies to all leases, including periodic tenancies. A provision that one party is unable to determine a periodic tenancy, or for it to be determined only in certain circumstances, is inconsistent with the concept of a periodic tenancy. If termination on the happening of an uncertain event is required by either party, this can be achieved by granting a long fixed term with a break clause exercisable only on the happening of the event in question (see **16.2**).

Most business tenancies will be for a fixed term, in which case the lease must specify the date of commencement of the term and its duration (eg 'for a term of ten years from and including the 29 September 2012'). There is no need for the commencement of the term to be the same date as the date of completion of the grant of the lease. It may be more convenient for the landlord, particularly when it is granting several leases in the same block, to choose one specific date from which the term of each will run. If this is an earlier date than completion then, unless the lease provides to the contrary, the tenant's rights and obligations will arise only on completion, not the earlier date. However, for the avoidance of doubt, the lease should expressly state the precise date from which the rent is to be payable.

In specifying the date when the term of the lease commences, it is important to avoid any ambiguity. It must be clear beyond doubt when the term expires (but see **Chapter 31** for the effect of the lease being protected under Pt II of the LTA 1954). The presumption is that if the term is stated to run 'from' a particular date, the term begins on the next day. If, however, the term is expressed to begin 'on' a particular date, that day is the first day of the term. To avoid any possible argument, it is always best to use clear words such as 'beginning on', 'beginning with' or 'from and including' (see *Meadfield Properties Ltd v Secretary of State for the Environment* [1995] 03 EG 128).

In recent years, various external pressures have affected the length of the term of commercial leases. The changes brought about by stamp duty land tax (SDLT) and Government pressure (see **13.5**) have resulted in shorter lease terms. For example, a 20-year lease at a rent of £250,000 per year will result in a payment of £50,000 in SDLT. Over the past few years, lease terms have fallen from the classic 25-year term of the past to less than 10 years, and even then many tenants are insisting on break clauses (see **16.2**) being included in the lease. In 2013, the average length of a new lease in the commercial property sector (including exceptional licences and short leases and the effect of break clauses) was just 4.5 years, compared with 8.7 years in 1999. Larger tenants had longer leases (5.2 years as opposed to 4.1 years for small and medium enterprises), and retail tenants had longer leases than office or industrial tenants (5.3 years as opposed to 4.5 years and 3.2 years respectively). Short, flexible lease terms are often the order of the day and in 2013 the proportion of new leases with terms of 1–5 years was 81%. (The figures quoted are taken from the *Property Data Report 2014*.)

16.2 BREAK CLAUSES

16.2.1 Who may operate break clauses and when?

Either party or both parties may be given an option to determine the lease at specified times during the term, or on the happening of certain specified events. For example, the tenant may be given the option to determine a 15-year lease at the end of the fifth and tenth years, or if it is prevented from trading due to the withdrawal of any necessary statutory licences. The landlord may be given an option to determine if, at some future date, it wishes to redevelop the premises or to occupy them for its own business purposes (although if the lease is protected by Pt II of the Landlord and Tenant Act 1954, the exercise of the option may not necessarily entitle the landlord to recover possession; see **16.2.4** and **Chapter 31**).

Some options to break are expressed to be personal to the original tenant in order to prevent their being exercised by successors in title following an assignment. Indeed, a break clause can be personal and incapable of being exercised by successors in title even where no limiting words such as 'only' or 'personal' are used (see *Gemini Press Ltd v Cheryl Lindsay Parsons* [2012] EWHC 1608 (QB)). However, in *Brown & Root Technology v Sun Alliance* [1997] 18 EG 123, the court held that following the assignment of a registered lease to the tenant's parent company, the option was still exercisable by the original tenant until the assignment was completed by registration. It was only on registration of title that the legal estate vested in the assignee; until then the assignor remained the tenant and thus retained the ability to exercise the option.

16.2.2 How are break clauses exercised?

The break clause must be exercised in accordance with its terms. Thus, it must be exercised at the correct time and in the correct manner.

If there are any pre-conditions to the exercise of the break clause, they must be complied with strictly. Consequently, the tenant should be wary of any provision in the lease making compliance with tenant covenants a pre-condition to the exercise of the break clause. In such a case, even a trivial, immaterial breach of covenant on the part of the tenant may prevent it from exercising the option validly (see *Avocet Industrial Estates LLP v Merol and Another* [2011] EWHC 3422 (Ch), where the tenant was deprived of the break because it had not paid negligible amounts of default interest on past arrears, and *Bairstow Eves (Securities) Ltd v Ripley* [1992] 2 EGLR 47, an analogous case concerning an option to renew which the tenant was unable to exercise because of a failure to decorate in the last year of the term despite the fact that it had decorated just before the beginning of the last year). If the landlord will not agree to the pre-condition being removed altogether, the tenant should modify it so that it requires 'substantial' or 'material' compliance (see, eg, *Bairstow Eves (Securities) Ltd v Ripley* (above) and *Fitzroy House Epworth Street (No 1) v The Financial Times Ltd* [2006] EWCA Civ 329), although this still leaves open the possibility of dispute and litigation.

Particular care should be taken by the tenant where the break right is conditional on performance of the tenant's covenants and the break date falls between rent payment days. If, as is common, the rent is payable quarterly in advance, the tenant must pay the full quarterly rent on the rent payment date before the break date, regardless of the fact that it will not be in occupation for the whole quarter (see *Marks and Spencer plc v BNP Paribas Securities Services Trust Company (Jersey) Ltd* [2014] EWCA Civ 603). Where the break date falls between rent payment dates, the tenant should try to include in the lease an express term allowing recovery of the rent where the break right is lawfully exercised by the tenant.

Any notice requirements for the exercise of the break clause must also be complied with strictly because, unless the lease states to the contrary, time is of the essence in a break clause (*United Scientific Holdings v Burnley Borough Council* [1978] AC 904). However, if an incorrect date is specified in the break notice, the court may be prepared to declare the notice valid if it would be obvious to a reasonable recipient of the notice with knowledge of the lease that the person serving it had made a mistake so that the reasonable recipient would not have been misled (*Mannai Investment Co Ltd v Eagle Star Life Assurance Co Ltd* [1997] AC 749). Subsequent cases have shown that the courts will adopt a similar approach when dealing with other errors in break notices. However, it must always be borne in mind that each case will turn on its own facts (see, eg, the contrasting cases of *Lemmerbell Ltd v Britannia LAS Direct Ltd* [1998] 3 EGLR 67 and *Havant International Holdings Ltd v Lionsgate (H) Investments Ltd* [1999] EGCS 144).

While there is some degree of latitude permitted in relation to the requirement to convey the meaning of a break notice, the requirement to serve it in the correct form or in accordance with a condition has been more strictly interpreted. For example, the doctrine in *Mannai* will not save a notice which is served in a manner different to that required by the lease. In *Hotgroup plc v Royal Bank of Scotland plc* [2010] EWHC 1193, the tenant's break was conditional on service of nine months' notice on the landlord and the landlord's managing agent; the tenant served correctly on the landlord but not on the agent. In *Claire's Accessories v Kensington High Street* [2001] PLSCS 112, the notice was held to be invalid because the landlord had served it at the tenant's premises rather than at its registered office. In *Friends Life Ltd v Siemens Hearing Instruments Ltd* [2014] EWCA Civ 382, the lease stated that the break notice must be 'expressed to be given under section 24(2) of the Landlord and Tenant Act 1954', and when the tenant served a break notice which did not refer to s 24(2), the notice was held to be invalid.

16.2.3 Effect of exercise of option on sub-tenants

The effect of the exercise of an option in a head-lease may be to terminate any sub-lease granted. This is dealt with further at **30.4**.

16.2.4 Relationship with the LTA 1954, Pt II

The landlord must be aware of the interrelationship with Pt II of the LTA 1954 and may wish to give thought to drafting the circumstances giving rise to the exercise of the option in line with the requirements of s 30(1)(f) or (g) of that Act (see **31.5**). This is desirable because the exercise of the option may not necessarily entitle the landlord to recover possession as it must also, where necessary, comply with the provisions of the 1954 Act (see **31.2**). Further, where necessary, regard should be had to the relationship between the notice required under the break clause and the notice provisions of the 1954 Act.

16.3 OPTIONS TO RENEW

Options to renew are not often found in business leases because most tenants are protected under Pt II of the Landlord and Tenant Act 1954 and will, therefore, have a statutory right to a new tenancy which the landlord may oppose only on certain grounds (see **Chapter 31**).

16.4 IMPACT OF SDLT

Because the amount of SDLT payable will increase with the length of the lease (see **10.2**), a tenant may find it preferable to take a short lease with an option to renew rather than a long lease with a break clause. A tenant will pay less SDLT on a five-year term with an option to renew than on a 10-year term with a right to break after five years. If the break clause is exercised, there will be no refund of SDLT paid in relation to the final five years of the term. Obviously, if a five-year lease is taken and this is renewed, extra SDLT will be then be payable, but it will be payable only if and when the lease is renewed.

REVIEW ACTIVITY

1. A lease contained an option to break the lease after 10 years. The 10-year term commenced on 24 June 1984. The tenant served a notice which purported to determine the lease on 23 June 1994. Was the notice to determine the lease valid?

2. A tenant entered into two leases, each for a term of 10 years from and including 13 January 1992. The leases were each subject to a break clause permitting the tenant to determine the lease by giving not less than six months' notice to the landlord, such notice to expire on the third anniversary of the term commencement date. What date should have been specified as the date of termination in the break notices?

3. A landlord granted a lease of a warehouse to two tenants (T1 and T2) for a term of 10 years. At the relevant time, T2 was dormant and a wholly-owned subsidiary of T1. The lease contained a break clause and the solicitors sent a break notice to the landlord, but only T1 was named as the tenant. Was the notice to determine the lease valid?

4. A lease for a term of six years granted the tenant an option to renew the term for a further six years by giving notice not more than 12 months and not less than nine months before the term date, 'if the tenant shall pay the rents hereby reserved and perform and observe all the covenants and obligations herein on the tenant's part contained until the term date, ...'. The tenant gave the requisite notice and kept the premises in a good state of repair, but in breach of covenant failed to paint and decorate in the last year of the term. Did the landlord have to grant the tenant a renewal of the lease?

Answers to this Review activity may be found in Appendix 1.

CHAPTER 17

RENT

17.1	Introduction	183
17.2	Amount	184
17.3	Time for payment	184
17.4	Other payments reserved as rent	184
17.5	Suspension of rent	184
17.6	Interest	184
17.7	VAT	185
	Review activity	185

17.1 INTRODUCTION

One of the primary purposes in granting the lease is to enable the landlord to receive income in the form of rent. However, the payment of rent by the tenant is not essential to the landlord and tenant relationship, and it is not uncommon, when property is difficult to let, for landlords to grant rent-free periods to tenants as an inducement for them to take the lease or to allow the tenant to fit out the premises. According to figures quoted in the *Property Data Report 2013*, the average rent-free period allowed to tenants of commercial property in 2011 was 8.8 months.

The lease must contain a covenant by the tenant to pay the rent. In certain rare situations the tenant may have the right to deduct sums from the rent payable. For example, the tenant has the right to deduct those sums allowed by statute and, where the landlord is in breach of its repairing obligation, the tenant seemingly has an ancient right to undertake the repairs itself and deduct the expense from future payments of rent (see **28.2**). In addition, the tenant may be able to exercise a right of set-off and deduct an unliquidated sum for damages where the landlord is in breach of covenant and the tenant has thereby suffered a loss. Landlords often seek to counter the tenant's right to make deductions by stating in the covenant to pay rent that rent is to be paid 'without deduction'. However, this will not prevent a tenant from making a deduction authorised by statute, nor from exercising its right of set-off (see *Connaught Restaurants Ltd v Indoor Leisure Ltd* [1993] 46 EG 184). To exclude the tenant's right of set-off, very clear words must be used.

The covenant to pay rent is usually followed by a covenant by the tenant to pay all taxes, rates, assessments and outgoings imposed on the demised premises; this will include business rates and water rates. For the avoidance of doubt, the tenant should make it clear that this obligation does not extend to any taxes payable by the landlord arising out of the receipt of the rent or due to any dealing by the landlord with the reversion.

Unless the lease is contracted out of the security of tenure provisions in Pt II of the LTA 1954, in the definitions clause of the lease the landlord should seek to define 'Rent' as also including any 'interim rent' which may become payable under s 24A of the LTA 1954 (see **31.4**). If this were not done and a guarantor's or former tenant's liability was stated by the lease to extend into the statutory continuation (under s 24), it would remain liable only for the contractual rent during that period and not for any interim rent which the current tenant might be ordered to pay as part of any future renewal proceedings under the 1954 Act (*Herbert Duncan Ltd v Cluttons* [1992] 1 EGLR 101).

17.2 AMOUNT

The amount of rent must be certain. However, the actual amount need not be stated as long as some means are provided by which the exact amount can be ascertained. For example, the rent may be fixed at £25,000 per annum for the first five years of a 10-year lease and then at 'such revised rent as may be ascertained'. Provided the means of ascertaining the new rent are clearly stated, this is a valid method of dealing with the rent. Such rent review clauses are dealt with in **Chapter 18,** where consideration is also given to the different methods of assessing the revised rent.

17.3 TIME FOR PAYMENT

The lease should set out the following:

(a) The date from which the rent is payable and the date of the first payment. It is usual to state that the first payment, or an apportioned part of it, is payable on the date of the lease unless a rent-free period is to be given.

(b) The payment dates, otherwise, in the case of a tenancy for a fixed term of years, there is authority for the proposition that the rent will be payable yearly. It is common practice in business leases to make the rent payable on the usual quarter days, ie, 25 March, 24 June, 29 September and 25 December.

(c) Whether rent is to be payable in advance or in arrears. Unless the lease provides that the rent is to be payable in advance, which is usual, the general law provides that rent is payable in arrears.

In modern commercial leases, provision is often made for the payment of rent by way of direct debit or standing order to minimise the risk of delay.

17.4 OTHER PAYMENTS RESERVED AS RENT

It is common for leases to provide for the tenant to make other payments to the landlord, such as a service charge or reimbursement of insurance premiums paid by the landlord. Landlords will often require the lease to state that such sums are payable as additional rent. Historically, the advantage to the landlord was that if the tenant defaulted, the remedy of distress would be available (a remedy which could be used only for non-payment of rent and not for breaches of other covenants), although this is no longer a factor now that distress has been abolished and Commercial Rent Arrears Recovery enacted (see **29.1.1.3**). It is still the case that the landlord will be able to forfeit the lease for non-payment of sums defined as rent without the need to serve a notice under s 146 of the LPA 1925 (see **25.4.1**).

It is also possible for any VAT payable on the rent to be reserved as additional rent.

17.5 SUSPENSION OF RENT

In the absence of any contrary provision in the lease, the rent will continue to be payable even if the premises are damaged or destroyed and so cannot be used by the tenant. The contractual doctrine of frustration will apply to leases only in exceptional circumstances (see *National Carriers Ltd v Panalpina (Northern) Ltd* [1981] AC 675). From the tenant's point of view, therefore, it should insist on a proviso that the rent is suspended if the premises become unfit for use. If the lease contains a service charge, provision should also be made for this to be suspended as otherwise it too would continue to be payable. This issue is considered further at **22.7**.

17.6 INTEREST

Unless there is provision to the contrary, interest cannot be charged by the landlord on any late payment by the tenant of rent or other sums due under the lease (unless judgment is obtained against the tenant for such amounts). It is therefore usual for a lease to provide that interest is payable by the tenant on any late payment of money due under the lease (from the due date to the date of actual payment). If, as is usual, the rate of interest is geared to the base rate of a named bank (eg, 4% above the base rate of Barclays Bank plc), a problem may arise if that bank no longer fixes a base rate. It is therefore sensible to provide for an alternative rate should this situation arise. For the tenant's protection, this should be stated to be 'some other reasonable rate as the landlord may specify'. Without the addition of the word 'reasonable' the tenant would have no right to dispute any new rate it thought excessive.

From the landlord's point of view, it is preferable for the lease to state that the interest rate is to apply 'both before and after any judgment'.

17.7 VAT

The implications of VAT on business leases have been discussed in **Chapter 10**. The landlord should include an appropriate clause entitling it to add VAT to the rent and other payments due from the tenant, by providing that the rent and other sums are payable exclusive of VAT.

REVIEW ACTIVITY

Consider the extract from a draft commercial lease of office premises below (adapted from the lease prepared by the Practical Law Company – see **Appendix 4**) and answer the following questions:

1. Why are all the monetary payments due under the lease listed in clause 2.3?

2. Can you think of any disadvantage to the landlord of reserving all the monetary payments as additional rent?

3. In clause 3, when are the quarterly instalments of rent due, and why is it necessary to state that there must be four equal payments payable in advance?

4. The payments are to be made by banker's standing order. Can you think of any disadvantage to the landlord inherent in this method?

5. When is the first payment due?

6. What is the purpose of clause 4?

Answers to this Review activity may be found in Appendix 1.

THIS LEASE is dated [ ]
Parties
(1) ABC LIMITED incorporated and registered in England and Wales with company number [ ] whose registered office is at [address] (**Landlord**).
(2) MNO LIMITED incorporated and registered in England and Wales with company number [ ] whose registered office is at [address] (**Tenant**).
(3) XYZ LIMITED incorporated and registered in England and Wales with company number [ ] whose registered office is also at [address] (**Guarantor**).
Agreed terms
1. **Interpretation**
1.1 The definitions and rules of interpretation set out in this clause apply to this lease.
   Annual Rent: rent at an initial rate of £100,000 per annum and then as revised pursuant to this lease and any interim rent determined under the 1954 Act.
   Rent Commencement Date: the date which is 6 calendar months after the date of this lease.

2.   Grant

2.1   At the request of the Guarantor, the Landlord lets with full title guarantee the Property to the Tenant for the Contractual Term.

2.2   The grant is made together with the ancillary rights set out in clause [ ], excepting and reserving to the Landlord the rights set out in clause [ ], and subject to the Third Party Rights.

2.3   The grant is made with the Tenant paying the following as rent to the Landlord:

(a)   the Annual Rent and all VAT in respect of it;

(b)   the Service Charge and all VAT in respect of it;

(c)   the Insurance Rent;

(d)   all interest payable under this lease; and

(e)   all other sums due under this lease.

3.   The Annual Rent

3.1   The Tenant shall pay the Annual Rent and any VAT in respect of it by four equal instalments in advance on or before the usual quarter days. The payments shall be made by banker´s standing order or by any other method that the Landlord requires at any time by giving notice to the Tenant.

3.2   The first instalment of the Annual Rent and any VAT in respect of it shall be made on the Rent Commencement Date and shall be the proportion, calculated on a daily basis, in respect of the period from the Rent Commencement Date until the day before the next usual quarter day.

4.   No deduction, counterclaim or set-off

The Annual Rent and all other money due under this lease are to be paid by the Tenant or any guarantor (as the case may be) without deduction, counterclaim or set-off.

CHAPTER 18

THE RENT REVIEW CLAUSE

18.1	The need for review	187
18.2	Types of rent review clause	187
18.3	The dates for review	189
18.4	Working out the open market rent	190
18.5	The assumptions	191
18.6	The disregards	197
18.7	The mechanism for determining the rent	199
18.8	The late review	200
18.9	Recording the review	200
	Review activity	201

18.1 THE NEED FOR REVIEW

Most commercial property leases exceeding five years in length will contain provisions requiring the parties to review the annual rent payable under the lease. With such leases it is difficult to set a rent at the outset of the term that both parties are satisfied will remain appropriate throughout the life of the lease. The effects of inflation, changes in the value of the rental property market or the tenant's circumstances can be reflected in the rent at review, depending on the type of rent review used.

18.2 TYPES OF RENT REVIEW CLAUSE

There are various ways in which rent may be varied during the term.

18.2.1 Fixed increases

This type of review provides for the rent to increase to a fixed amount at the review date. For example, in a lease for a 10-year term, the rent might be set at £10,000 for the first three years of the term, £15,000 for the next three years, and £20,000 for the remainder of the term. This sort of clause would be very rare since the parties to the lease would be placing their faith in the fixed increases proving to be realistic. If the parties have not been realistic then the tenant may pay more or the landlord receive less than on comparable properties.

18.2.2 Index-linked clauses

This type of review looks to increase or decrease the rent in line with an index reflecting changes in the value of money. In practice, the index favoured by practitioners is the Retail Prices Index (RPI). This is published by the Office of National Statistics and used as the domestic measure of inflation in the UK. Although changes in the RPI do not necessarily reflect changes in the property market, they do allow rents to change in line with inflation. Such clauses are usually relatively simple to operate. They generally involve multiplying the old rent by the relevant RPI increase since the date of last review. Due to their relative simplicity, they may be considered appropriate for lower-value property or in shorter leases where the parties would still like the rent to be reviewed. They may also be used where the property is very unusual and the comparable evidence used in assessing the open market rent (OMR) is not available (see **18.2.4**).

18.2.3   Turnover rents

A turnover rent is one which is geared to the turnover of the tenant's business, and can therefore be considered by the landlord only where turnover is generated at the premises. A turnover rent would be impractical in the case of office or warehouse property, but would be appropriate for retail premises.

There are various methods of calculating a turnover rent. Probably the most common is where the tenant pays a 'base rent' plus a 'top up rent' based on the turnover of the business. The 'base rent' is usually a percentage of OMR (typically somewhere between 70% and 80%). The 'top up rent' is typically between 7% and 15% of the tenant's trading turnover.

The main advantage of a turnover rent is that both parties have an interest in ensuring the success of the business operated from the premises. For example, the landlord of a shopping centre will have an added incentive to ensure the shopping centre attracts as many customers as possible, as this will encourage visitors to the shops within it and, it is hoped, increase their turnover. This, in turn, will lead to increased rent for the landlord.

On the downside, if the business operated from the premises fails to thrive, the landlord will share in the pain! The landlord will also need to consider whether it is happy for the turnover provisions to continue on an assignment of the lease, since the identity of the tenant in a turnover rent lease is crucial. Underletting is usually prohibited in a turnover rent lease. Thought will also need to be given to what happens if the tenant ceases to trade from the premises, either temporarily or permanently.

18.2.4   Open market rent review

An OMR review clause requires the rent to be revised in accordance with changes in the property market.

The most common form of OMR review clause will provide that at every rent review date (eg every fifth anniversary of the term) the parties should seek to agree upon a figure that equates to what is then the current OMR for a letting of the tenant's premises. The aim of the exercise is to find out how much a tenant in the open market would be prepared to pay, in terms of rent per annum, if the tenant's premises were available to let in the open market on the relevant review date. This agreement is achieved either by some form of informal negotiated process between the landlord and the tenant, or (less commonly) by the service of notices and counter-notices which specify proposals and counter-proposals as to the revised rent. If agreement cannot be reached, the clause should provide for the appointment of an independent valuer who will determine the revised rent. The valuer will be directed by the review clause to take certain matters into account in conducting his valuation, and to disregard others, and he will call upon evidence of rental valuations of other comparable leasehold interests in the locality.

There are two forms of OMR review clause that practitioners are likely to come across:

(a)   the upwards only rent review; and

(b)   the upwards/downwards rent review.

18.2.4.1   The upwards only rent review

In an upwards only rent review, the rent on review will be the higher of the rent currently being paid and the open market valuation. In other words, the rental level will never go down. It can either go up, if the open market revaluation is higher than the rent currently being paid, or remain static. The benefits for the landlord are obvious. It is protected against the vagaries in the property market and will never receive less annual rent than the figure agreed at the outset. It can also benefit from any increase in rental levels identified in the open market revaluation. The tenant's position is less advantageous. It will never get the benefit of a fall in rental levels but is subject to any increases in rental levels that may occur. Clearly there is a risk to the tenant that in a falling market it may end up paying far more than competitors in similar premises are paying. Its premises are said to be over-rented. Despite these risks, upward rent reviews are still demanded by institutional landlords and often accepted by tenants. Threats by the Government to legislate in this area have been met with attempts by the property industry to self-regulate. The 2007 Code for Leasing Business Premises provides as follows:

4 Rent Review

Rent reviews should be clear and headline rent review clauses should not be used. Landlords should on request offer alternatives to their proposed option for rent review priced on a risk-adjusted basis. For example, alternatives to upward only rent review might include up/down reviews to market rent with a minimum of the initial rent, or reference to another measure such as annual indexation.

Where landlords are unable to offer alternatives, they should give reasons.

Leases should allow both landlords and tenants to start the rent review process.

There is little evidence to suggest that landlords have taken much heed of the Code in this regard, and it seems upward only rent reviews will still be the most frequently encountered type of rent review in practice.

18.2.4.2 The upwards/downwards rent review

In an upward/downward rent review clause, the revised annual rent will be the OMR as determined in accordance with the lease. The annual rent will therefore reflect any increases or decreases in rental levels that have occurred since the start of the lease or the previous rent review. This is clearly an advantage to the tenant, but it means that the landlord cannot guarantee the amount of rent that will be generated by the lease. Sometimes, to protect itself against dramatic falls in rental levels, the landlord might provide in the lease that the rental level can never fall below a certain figure (often the initial annual rent figure).

18.3 THE DATES FOR REVIEW

18.3.1 How often should the rent be reviewed?

Most commercial property leases require the rent to be reviewed once every five years. Sometimes in a lease of less than 10 years the rent might be reviewed on a three-yearly basis.

18.3.2 The rent review dates

The tenant should ensure the dates for review are clearly set out in the lease. Usually the review dates are linked to the term commencement date (eg the fifth anniversary of the term commencement date). If this is the case, the tenant should ensure that the term commencement date does not start earlier than the date of the lease itself. Sometimes the term commencement date is backdated to enable the landlord to have all leases in a shopping centre or business park end on the same date (even though the leases have been completed on different dates). If the term commencement date has been backdated then the rent review date will be brought forward and the tenant will not enjoy the certainty of the initial rent figure for as long as it should.

Some leases specify actual dates for the rent review (eg 25 March 2020). This is probably best avoided, as it can give rise to valuation difficulties if on review the valuer is asked to value a hypothetical lease containing the same rent provisions as the actual lease (see **18.5.7**).

18.3.3 The penultimate day rent review

When specifying the rent review dates, the landlord may provide for the rent to be reviewed on the penultimate day of the term. Whilst it may seem strange to review the rent just before the lease is due to expire, there is of course the possibility of the lease continuing under the Landlord and Tenant Act 1954 (LTA 1954). By inserting a penultimate date review the landlord gives itself the possibility of obtaining an increased rent during the period of any holding over. Tenants' solicitors usually delete such penultimate day reviews, preferring instead for the parties to rely on the interim rent provisions in s 24A of the LTA 1954 (see **31.4**). These provisions can result in a more favourable review for the tenant, not least because the rent can go down on an interim rent application. This might lead one to conclude that a landlord will fight quite hard to retain a penultimate day review. However, since 2004, tenants as well as landlords have had the ability to apply for an interim rent under the 1954 Act. This now means that even if the lease contains a penultimate day review, the rent determined under it can, after one day, be replaced by the rent determined under an interim rent application made by the tenant. So in reality, the penultimate day review will now be of use to the landlord only if the tenant fails to make an interim rent application.

18.4   WORKING OUT THE OPEN MARKET RENT

As already discussed in **18.2.4**, most modern rent review provisions require the parties to agree what the OMR of the premises would be if they were being let on the rent review date. This task requires the parties to think hypothetically, since in reality the premises are not available to let as they are occupied by the tenant. So the lease will usually direct the parties to assume that a hypothetical letting of the premises is taking place on the review date and that a hypothetical market exists in which such letting can take place.

18.4.1   Defining the OMR

Different phrases are used by different clauses to define the rent to be ascertained, although in broad terms it is the OMR of the premises at the rent review date. Both landlord and tenant are usually happy to define this as the rent at which the premises 'might reasonably be expected to be let in the open market' at the relevant review date. This wording follows that in s 34 of the LTA 1954, and is therefore considered by most practitioners to be unlikely to be subject to adverse interpretation. Most tenants would want to avoid the use of the expression 'the best rent at which the premises might be let' since this might allow the valuer to consider the possibility of what is known as a special purchaser's bid. If, by chance, the market for a hypothetical letting of the premises contains a potential bidder who would be prepared to bid in excess of what would ordinarily be considered to be the market rent, the 'best' rent would be the rent which the special bidder would be prepared to pay. For example, if the premises which are the subject matter of the hypothetical letting are situated next to premises occupied by a business which is desperate to expand, the 'best' rent might be the rent which that business would be willing to pay.

18.4.2   Comparables

The parties will look at what rents similar premises in similar areas are fetching at the review date. These 'comparables' give the parties an idea of the rent that might be achieved if the premises were available to let in the market at the review date.

18.4.3   Instructions to the valuer

The parties seeking to agree the OMR, or the valuer determining it in the event of dispute, will also need instructions about what matters should be assumed about this hypothetical lease and what issues should be disregarded. For example, what happens if the tenant has carried out substantial improvements to the premises? Should those be taken into account when fixing the revised rent, or should they be ignored? What are the terms of the hypothetical lease? Are they the same as the actual lease, or are there to be differences? The instructions on these issues normally take the form of a set of 'assumptions' and 'disregards' in the lease, which are discussed in further detail in **18.5** and **18.6** below respectively.

18.5 THE ASSUMPTIONS

It is not possible to set out an exhaustive list of assumptions that can appear in a lease. It is important that the advice of a rent review surveyor is sought as to the impact on valuation of a particular set of assumptions and disregards before the lease is agreed. This is a much litigated area where significant sums can turn on the interpretation of a particular clause. The following are, however, fairly typical of the type of assumptions that will be encountered in practice.

18.5.1 The parties are to assume that the premises are available to let 'in the open market by a willing lessor to a willing lessee'

The purpose of this assumption is to create a market in which the letting can be valued. It means that the valuer must assume there are at least two hypothetical people who are prepared to enter into the hypothetical lease. The valuer must assume they are 'willing', ie neither of them is being forced to enter the arrangement or is affected by difficulties which might affect their position in open market negotiations. This wording prevents a tenant arguing, for example, that the letting market is completely dead and therefore the open market value of the premises is zero.

18.5.2 The parties are to assume that the premises are available to let 'as a whole or in parts (whichever shall produce the higher rental)'

The valuer is directed by this assumption to calculate two different rental figures. The first is the rental value if the premises are let as a whole. The second directs the valuer to calculate the cumulative rental value if the premises were to be let off in parts. It may be, for example, that small areas of space are in greater demand than larger areas, thus making smaller units (on a square foot by square foot basis) more expensive. The cumulative rental figure could, therefore, result in a higher open market valuation. Is this fair on the tenant, even though clearly to the tenant's disadvantage? In a rent review negotiation a tenant will usually accept this assumption only if the alienation provisions allow the tenant to sub-let in parts. The tenant could then, in theory, achieve any higher rental figure itself by sub-letting different parts of its demise (for example, on a floor by floor basis).

18.5.3 The parties are to assume that the premises are available to let 'with vacant possession'

If this assumption were not included, the valuer might have to take into account the fact that the tenant is still occupying the premises at the review date. The tenant could then argue that the rent a hypothetical bidder would be prepared to pay would be very low. After all, the hypothetical tenant would not be able to occupy the premises itself if the actual tenant was still in occupation. To avoid this argument, most rent review clauses of this type include an assumption that vacant possession is available for the hypothetical letting, ie it assumes that the actual tenant has moved out.

There are two issues to be aware of with such an assumption:

(a) sub-tenancies; and

(b) rent-free periods for fitting out.

18.5.3.1 Sub-tenancies

The assumption of vacant possession requires the valuer to ignore the effect on rent of any sub-tenancies in existence at the rent review date. The effect on the OMR of this will depend upon whether those sub-tenancies are high or low yielding. Lucrative sub-tenancies would undoubtedly increase the OMR if the valuer were to take them into account. The converse would be true of low yielding sub-tenancies. If either party wished to ensure that the effect on rent of sub-tenancies would be taken into account, the assumption of vacant possession would need to be amended to refer to vacant possession of only those parts of the premises not sub-let at the date of review.

18.5.3.2   Rent-free periods for fitting out

The assumption of vacant possession means that the tenant is deemed to have moved out of the premises and, as all vacating tenants would do, to have removed and taken its fixtures too. In respect of shop premises, this might mean that all of the shop fittings must be assumed to have been removed, leaving nothing but a shell behind. (Of course in reality the premises are still fully fitted out, but for hypothetical valuation purposes the tenant's fixtures are assumed to have gone.)

The tenant can argue that a hypothetical tenant bidding in the open market for these premises might demand a rent-free period in order to fit out the premises. The idea is that the rent-free period will compensate the hypothetical tenant for the cost of fitting out and the lost trade during the fit-out period. Such rent-free periods for fitting out often last between three and six months, depending on the extent of the fit-out needed.

If a rent-free period is granted at the start of the lease, it simply means the tenant will not start paying rent until the rent-free period has expired. When considering rent-free periods in the context of rent review, however, the situation is not as straightforward, as the valuer will be directed to determine an annual rental figure and will not be able to award a rent-free period.

If the valuer thinks a hypothetical tenant would have obtained a rent-free period in the market place, the valuer will need to 'spread' that rent-free period over the review period. This will reduce the amount of rent payable per annum. For example, imagine the valuer finds that the rent for the next five years should be £100,000 per annum, but that an incoming tenant would obtain a rent-free period of six months in order to fit out the premises. This is a saving to the tenant of £50,000, which the valuer will spread over the five-year review period. This would mean a £10,000 reduction per annum, ie an OMR of £90,000 rather than the £100,000 that would have been the OMR in the absence of the vacant possession assumption.

This result may not seem particularly fair on the landlord. After all, the premises will in reality be fitted out, and the actual tenant who will be paying this reviewed rent may well have had a rent-free period at the commencement of the term in order to carry out the fitting-out works. Why should the tenant in effect get another rent-free period at review (in the form of discounted rent) to compensate it for a notional fit out it does not actually need to do?

There are ways round this for the landlord when drafting the lease. It could include an assumption that the premises are fitted out (see **18.5.9**). Alternatively (or in addition), it could include an assumption that there is to be no discount or deduction made to the annual rent to represent a rent-free period for fit-out works that the hypothetical tenant would have been given (see **18.5.8**).

18.5.4   The parties are to assume that the premises are available to let 'without a fine or a premium'

This assumption is directing the valuer to assume that no capital sum is passing between the parties on the grant of the hypothetical lease. In reality, it is not uncommon for a capital sum to be given by one party to the other on the grant of the lease.

18.5.4.1   The reverse premium

A reverse premium is paid by the landlord to the tenant. The reasons for such a payment vary. It might be to induce a particularly attractive tenant to take the lease. However, it might also be that the rental level set by the landlord is higher than the market can actually support, and so to make the lease more appealing the landlord offers to pay the tenant a capital sum up front. Without such capital sum, the tenant may not be prepared to pay rent as high as the landlord wants. The landlord may prefer to keep the rent high (as it could be used as a comparable for similar units) and pay the inducement (or reverse premium).

18.5.4.2 Premiums

Sometimes, the tenant may pay a premium to the landlord for the lease in addition to an annual rent. This may be because the premises are particularly attractive to the tenant (for example, in a prime location). Or it may be because the landlord prefers to receive a capital sum up front, in return for which it will offer a lower annual rent.

18.5.4.3 The effect of premiums on rent

It can be seen from the illustrations above that the payment of a premium can distort the amount of annual rent that is paid by the tenant – increasing it where the tenant receives consideration and decreasing it where the landlord receives consideration.

To avoid such distortions on review, it is common for the rent review to assume that no 'fine or premium' (ie capital sum) is being paid for the hypothetical letting.

18.5.5 The parties are to assume that the premises are available to let 'for a term equal to the contractual term commencing on the relevant review date'

It is usual for the rent review clause to specify the length of the hypothetical lease. Often this will be the same as the original contractual term. So, in a 15-year lease with a five-year review pattern, the term of the hypothetical lease at the five-year review is 15 years, despite the fact that the actual lease has only 10 years left to run. On first glance this may appear to the disadvantage of the tenant, as it is tempting to assume that a longer hypothetical term will result in a higher OMR. This is not necessarily the case, however. In certain markets a tenant may prefer a shorter term, as it may not wish to commit itself to the premises for a long period of time. So sometimes a short-term lease can be worth more in rental terms than a longer-term lease.

Of course, at the time the lease is being negotiated it is very difficult to work out whether a shorter- or longer-term lease will command a higher rent. Whilst the advice of a rent review surveyor may be sought, this advice can only ever be speculative. For this reason the parties may agree the length of the hypothetical lease term should equal the unexpired residue of the actual lease at the date of the review. So, in our example, at the first review a 10-year term is assumed and at the second review a five-year term is assumed. This at least reflects reality.

18.5.6 The parties are to assume that the premises are available to let 'for any use falling within Class [A2 or B1] of the Town and Country Planning (Use Classes) Order 1987'

It is not uncommon to find that the valuer will be directed to assume a specified hypothetical use for the premises. This is often wider than the actual permitted use within the lease, meaning in effect the valuer is ignoring the restrictions on use within the actual lease. So the landlord is 'having its cake and eating it'. On the one hand, it is able to restrict the way the tenant can actually use the premises (eg by requiring the tenant to covenant not to use the premises for anything other than offices within Class A2). On the other hand, it is not penalised at review for imposing such restrictions (eg because the valuer must assume the premises can be used for either Class A2 or Class B1). Such an extended hypothetical use should be strongly resisted by the tenant, since it would find itself paying on review for a freedom it did not in fact enjoy. A compromise would be to widen the user covenant within the actual lease to match the use specified in the assumption.

18.5.7   **The parties are to assume that the premises are to be let 'otherwise on the terms of this lease other than as to the amount of the annual rent but including the provisions for review of the annual rent, and other than the provision in this lease for a rent-free period'**

The valuer is directed to assume the hypothetical lease will be on the same terms as the actual lease, except for:

(a)   any variations stipulated elsewhere in the rent review provisions. This would cover, for example, a hypothetical term that differed from the actual contractual term in the lease (see **18.5.5**);

(b)   the amount of the annual rent specified in the lease. As the aim of the review exercise is to vary the amount of rent, it is clear that the rent initially reserved by the lease must not be incorporated into the hypothetical letting. But what about the rent review provisions? In the specimen wording above the valuer is directed to assume that the hypothetical lease will contain provisions for review of the annual rent. This is very important for the tenant, as most practitioners take the view that a lease without rent review provisions would be more attractive to a tenant and therefore command a higher rent. This is because the tenant would have certainty at the outset of the lease that its rent would remain the same for the duration of the term, protecting it against uplifts in rent in a rising market. So a hypothetical lease with no rent review provisions would command a higher rent than one with rent review provisions (unless the hypothetical term were less than five years, when no rent review provisions would be expected). An example of the dramatic impact this may have can be found in *National Westminster Bank plc v Arthur Young McClelland Moores & Co* [1985] 1 WLR 1123. In this case the provisions of a rent review clause were interpreted in such a way as to exclude from the hypothetical letting the rent review provisions. This alone led to the annual rent being increased from £800,000 to £1.209 million, instead of £1.003 million if the rent review clause had been incorporated. Courts today tend to shy away from interpreting a rent review clause in such a way as to exclude a provision for review from the hypothetical letting. In the absence of clear words directing the rent review clause to be disregarded, the court will give effect to the underlying purpose of the clause and will assume that the hypothetical letting contains provisions for the review of rent. However, the tenant must always check carefully that the review clause is not expressly excluded from the hypothetical letting, since the court would be bound to give effect to such clear words;

(c)   any rent-free period granted in the actual lease. The tenant may have been granted a rent-free period at the outset of the lease to allow it to fit out the premises or as an inducement to enter the lease. The landlord, if it has granted such a rent-free period at the outset of the lease, will not want the hypothetical lease to have such a rent-free period. After all, the tenant will have already had the benefit of the actual rent-free period at the outset of the lease. The landlord will be concerned that the valuer will 'spread' the amount of the hypothetical rent-free period over the remaining rental period and thereby effectively discount the annual rent at review. Whilst a tenant will not normally object to the valuer ignoring any rent-free period actually granted at the outset of the lease, it will need to think more carefully about provisions that seek to ignore rent-free concessions that are being granted in the market place at the time of the rent review. The tenant must avoid ending up with a headline rent (see **18.5.8**).

18.5.8   **The parties are to assume 'the willing lessee has had the benefit of any rent-free or other concession or contribution which would be offered in the open market at the relevant review date in relation to fitting out works at the premises'**

This assumption assumes the hypothetical tenant has already had a rent-free period for fitting out purposes and will not therefore need a further rent-free concession in the form of discounted rent. It is included to counteract problems associated with an assumption that the property is available to let with vacant possession (see **18.5.3.2**). It is generally acceptable to a tenant who in reality will not need to fit out at review and who may well have had a rent-free period at the commencement of the lease.

However, the tenant must be careful with this type of assumption to ensure it is limited to rent-free periods for fitting-out purposes. Rent-free periods for fitting-out purposes are typically for a period of between three and six months. However, in practice it is not uncommon to find rent-free periods in excess of six months. These are granted by a landlord to induce the tenant to take the lease at a rental level it might otherwise not be prepared to pay. These rent-free concessions granted as inducements have a distorting effect on rent in much the same way as the payment of reverse premiums (see **18.5.4**). Take, for example, a premises with a rental of £200,000 per annum, where the tenant was granted a rent-free period of 12 months. The rental figure that will appear in the lease, and which the parties would quote if asked the annual rent, is £200,000 per annum (the 'headline rent'). However, if you take into account the 12-month rent-free period, in reality the tenant will be paying only £800,000 over a five-year period, equating to an 'effective' annual rent of £160,000.

At rent review the tenant will wish to ensure that the valuer, when looking at comparables, is not looking at 'headline' rental figures which are artificially inflated. It should therefore ensure that the lease does not assume that the willing or hypothetical tenant has received the benefit of a rent-free period (other than in respect of fitting out) which it may be the practice to give incoming tenants at the time of the review. Similar wording or provisions aiming to achieve a headline rent should be avoided. An example of such wording can be found in *Broadgate Square plc v Lehman Brothers Ltd* [1995] 1 EGLR 97, where the OMR was defined as 'the best yearly rent which would reasonably be expected to become payable after the expiry of a rent free period of such length as would be negotiated in the open market between a willing landlord and a willing tenant upon a letting of the premises'. This case was one of a number of 'headline rent' cases, suggesting that while the courts will lean against a headline rent construction, they will not be able to do so in the face of clear, unambiguous language. In the *Broadgate* case itself, the Court of Appeal determined that the OMR in the lease should be the rent payable once any rent-free period had expired (ie a headline rent). This resulted in a total rent in excess of £12 million for Nos 1 & 2 Broadgate. If the rent for the two premises had been discounted to reflect inducement rent-free periods, it would have totalled less than £9.3 million.

18.5.9 The parties are to assume that the premises 'may lawfully be used, and are fitted out and equipped so that they are ready to be used, by the willing lessee (or any potential undertenant or assignee of the willing lessee) for any purpose permitted by this lease'

This assumption is intended to ensure that no discount is made by the valuer from the annual rent to reflect the fact that an incoming tenant would ordinarily expect a rent-free period in order to carry out its fit-out works. If it is assumed the premises are fitted out then no such rent-free period is necessary.

The tenant will be concerned that an assumption that the premises are 'fitted out and equipped' may result in a rentalisation of any fitting-out works actually carried out while it has been occupying the premises. A hypothetical tenant would certainly pay more for premises that had already been fitted out and did not require further work by the tenant. Whilst a disregard of tenant's improvements might seem to deal with the tenant's concern, it is not entirely clear how this would sit with a 'fitted out' assumption. Words such as 'fitted out and equipped' should therefore be avoided by the tenant. The landlord's concerns about rent-free periods can be dealt with by including an assumption along the lines set out at **18.5.8**.

18.5.10 The parties are to assume 'the [landlord and the] tenant [have/has] fully complied with [its/their] obligations in the lease'

This is really two separate assumptions combined in one sub-clause.

18.5.10.1 Tenant's compliance

Without such an assumption, a tenant in breach of, for example, its repairing obligations could argue that the OMR of the premises should be reduced because the premises are in disrepair. After all, no hypothetical tenant will pay as much for premises in a poor state of repair as for those in full repair. This would clearly be unfair, as the tenant would be benefiting from its own wrongdoing. Most leases therefore contain this assumption; and in its absence, the courts have shown a willingness to imply it in any event (see *Family Management v Grey* (1979) 253 EG 369).

18.5.10.2 Landlord's compliance

Some leases also contain an assumption that the landlord has complied with its covenants. If the landlord were to be in breach of its obligations at the rent review date then, like a breach of the tenant's obligations, this would generally have a depressing effect on the OMR. If, for example, the landlord has failed to insure the building, a hypothetical tenant would consider the letting less attractive and be prepared to pay less rent for it. Tenants often resist this assumption. They argue that if the landlord is in breach of its covenants, it should suffer the consequences of such failure on review. The prospect of a negative impact on the rent review might well encourage the landlord to comply with its obligations. The landlord could point out that if it is in breach of its covenants, the tenant will be able to pursue other remedies for such breaches. It might consider the tenant sufficiently protected by these remedies without the need for the landlord to be penalised at review for a breach. The breach may be very minor or temporary, and it would be unfair to penalise this with a rent reduction that lasted until the next review. The extent to which this point is worth arguing between landlord and tenant really depends upon the extent of the landlord's covenants. The parties may consider compromising by accepting an assumption that the landlord's covenants have been complied with (other than in respect of material breaches).

18.5.11 The parties are to assume that 'if the premises, or any means of access to it or any service media serving the premises, has been destroyed or damaged, it has been fully restored'

The landlord needs this assumption to protect itself against a reduction in OMR arising through insured damage. If, for example, a fire causes serious damage to the premises shortly before the review date, it may well be impractical for the landlord to complete reinstatement by the review date. In the absence of this assumption, the valuer would therefore be valuing a fire-damaged building. This might result in the tenant paying a lower rent than would have otherwise been the case. Would this be a fair result? The tenant does, of course, have to suffer the consequences of damaged premises. However, this should only be temporary if the landlord is under an obligation to reinstate. Further, most leases contain a clause suspending the payment of rent during any period which the premises cannot be occupied as a result of insured damage. So, provided the rent suspension provisions are adequate, the tenant should not be prejudiced by accepting this assumption, although it might be advised to ensure it refers only to destruction or damage by insured risks.

18.5.12 The parties are to assume that 'no work has been carried out on the premises or any other part of the building that has diminished the rental value of the premises'

As a general premise, it seems fair that if the tenant has carried out works that have diminished the letting value of the premises then those works should be ignored at review. For example, if the tenant requires business-specific building works that another tenant would find unappealing, why should a landlord's rental income be prejudiced by the carrying out of those works? What, however, if the tenant is forced by statute to carry out those works? Perhaps disability discrimination legislation or fire regulations require the tenant to carry out works that reduce the lettable space, or render the premises less aesthetically pleasing. A tenant will often suggest that work it is required by statute to carry out, as opposed to work it has carried out voluntarily, should not be ignored if it has reduced the OMR of the premises.

18.5.13 The parties are to assume 'the willing lessee and its potential assignees and undertenants shall not be disadvantaged by any actual or potential election to waive exemption from VAT in relation to the premises'

If the landlord has opted to tax in respect of VAT then VAT will be payable on the annual rent under the lease. Most leases will require such VAT to be paid by the tenant. Provided the tenant itself makes taxable supplies, it will be able to recover the VAT it pays on the rent by offsetting it against the VAT it charges on its taxable supplies. If the tenant makes only exempt supplies, however, it will not be able to recover the VAT it pays on rent, which will be an additional cost to it. Tenants who make exempt supplies and are therefore unable to recover VAT include banks, building societies and insurers. These types of tenants pay 20% more rent, in real terms, than other tenants, due to their inability to recover VAT. This gives rise to the question whether such tenants, when considering renting premises, would pay less than other types of tenant to reflect the additional VAT expense that they incur. If this might be the case, should a valuer, when assessing a hypothetical letting, take into account such potential discounted bids in determining the OMR? If a premises particularly lent itself to occupation by exempt suppliers, this might result in the valuer determining a lower OMR than for premises where this was not the case. To guard against this, the landlord will often insert an assumption that the tenant will not suffer if the landlord opts to tax. It is sometimes phrased that it will be assumed that the tenant can recover any VAT charged on rents. The result is the same. Any inability to recover VAT by the actual or hypothetical tenants is ignored. The tenant should try to delete such a provision on the basis that the valuer should be directed to look at the reality of the situation, and if there would be exempt suppliers in the hypothetical market, the discounted bids that such tenants might make should be used as comparable evidence. To date, however, there has been no evidence of a 'two-tier' market (of exempt and non-exempt suppliers) with differing bid levels.

18.6 THE DISREGARDS

As with the assumptions discussed in **18.5** above, it is not possible to set out an exhaustive list of the disregards that may appear in a lease, and the advice of a rent review surveyor should always be sought before agreeing any particular form of wording. The following are examples of typical disregards that occur in leases of commercial premises.

18.6.1 The parties are to disregard 'any effect on rent of the fact that the tenant or any authorised under-tenant has been in occupation of the premises'

It is standard to disregard any effect on rent of the tenant's occupation. If this were not done, the landlord could argue at review that the actual tenant would bid more for the premises than other hypothetical tenants to save the trouble and expense of securing new premises. The tenant should ensure that the disregard extends to sub-tenants and any other type of occupier that may be permitted by the lease terms.

18.6.2 The parties are to disregard 'any goodwill attached to the premises by reason of any business carried out there by the tenant or by any authorised under-tenant or by any of their predecessors in business'

Goodwill generated by a business in the form of a regular flow of customers is a valuable asset. It therefore follows that a tenant will pay more for premises with established goodwill attached to the business than for one without. Since the goodwill will have been generated by the tenant, it seems unfair that the landlord should benefit from it at review. The tenant should ensure that the lease contains a disregard of goodwill generated by the tenant or any under-tenant (or their predecessors). While case law suggests that a valuer will imply such a disregard where occupation is disregarded (*Prudential Assurance Co Ltd v Grand Metropolitan Estate Ltd* [1993] 32 EG 74), it is good practice to do it expressly.

18.6.3 The parties are to disregard 'any effect on rent attributable to any physical improvement to the premises carried out after the date of this lease, by or at the expense of the tenant or any authorised under-tenant with all necessary consents, approvals and authorisations and not pursuant to an obligation to the landlord'

If the tenant carries out works to the premises that improve them, the premises are likely to be more valuable in the letting market. If the lease does not disregard the improvements, the valuer will take them into account when assessing the OMR. In consequence the tenant will end up paying for them twice: first, it will bear the cost of the works when they are carried out; secondly, it may end up paying more rent at review to reflect the increased letting value of the premises in consequence of the improvements. This would clearly be unfair on the tenant, and so it must ensure improvements are disregarded.

While most landlords have no objections to this in principle, differences in opinion can arise over exactly what improvements are to be disregarded. The following should be considered:

(a) *Works not carried out by the current tenant.* The tenant should ensure that improvements made by its predecessors in title or by any under-tenant are also disregarded.

(b) *Works carried out before the lease commenced.* The tenant must consider whether any works were carried out before the lease commenced. It is not uncommon for tenants to be granted access to the premises under the terms of an agreement for lease to carry out fitting-out works. If the lease disregards only works carried out after commencement of the lease (as in the specimen disregard above), such works would be rentalised at review.

(c) *Works the tenant was obliged to carry out.* A disregard of improvements will often be drafted so as to exclude from its remit improvements that the tenant is obliged to carry out. The specimen disregard above does exactly this. This is to ensure the tenant cannot seek to disregard repair works. However, it may also catch other works the tenant carries out to comply with statute, such as works carried out to comply with disability discrimination legislation. This is because the lease will normally contain a tenant's covenant to comply with statute, and therefore the tenant has a contractual obligation to the landlord to undertake works required by statute. This is clearly not ideal from the tenant's perspective, and it should seek to ensure that the disregard of improvements does cover works required by statute.

It is also wise to check any agreements for lease or licences for alterations to ensure that permissions to carry our works are not phrased as obligations to the landlord to undertake those works. If they are, the danger is the works will be excluded from the remit of the disregard. However, the courts have indicated that in order to exclude works carried out under a licence for alteration from a disregard of improvements, they would expect very clear words to that effect in the licence itself. (See the judgment of Dillon LJ in *Historic Hotels Ltd v Cadogan Estates* [1995] 1 EGLR 117.)

18.6.4 The parties are to disregard 'any statutory restriction on rents or the right to recover them'

The above disregard requires the valuer to ignore any legislation that may be introduced by the Government restricting rent levels. Such restrictions may be introduced in times of high inflation as a counter-inflationary measure, although they have not been used since the early 1970s. The landlord is concerned that the valuer would be obliged to set a reduced OMR if such legislation were in force. This would then last until the next rent review, even though the legislation might be repealed at an earlier point. The tenant, of course, will not wish to pay a rental level higher than that of competitors whose rent levels are restricted by legislation, and it should seek to delete such a disregard. A compromise may be to agree to delay any rent review until such time as any statutory restrictions are removed. Nevertheless, the tenant will need to be aware of the risk that at the end of any such restrictions, rents could rise rapidly.

18.7 THE MECHANISM FOR DETERMINING THE RENT

The following issues should be considered:

18.7.1 Is time of the essence?

Nearly all modern leases provide that the revised rent may be agreed in writing at any time between the parties. However, some older leases provide for the rent review process to be instigated by the service of a notice setting out the landlord's proposals for the revised rent. Such initial notices are often referred to as 'trigger notices'. The amount set out in the initial notice can be as exorbitant as the landlord wishes. The lease will then provide for the tenant to serve a counter-notice within a specified time period, setting out its proposals. The existence of time periods for the serving of this counter-notice raises the question of whether time is of the essence. The parties should ensure that the lease expressly states the position. In the absence of any 'contrary indications', there is a presumption that time is not of the essence (*United Scientific Holdings Ltd v Burnley Borough Council* [1977] 2 All ER 62). However, contrary indications have been found in a number of cases (*First Property Growth Partnership v Royal & Sun Alliance Services Ltd* [2002] EWHC 305 (Ch), [2002] 22 EG 140; *Starmark Enterprises Ltd v CPL Distribution Ltd* [2001] 32 EG 89 (CS); *Central Estates Ltd v Secretary of State for the Environment* [1997] 1 EGLR 239). Care must therefore be taken if the lease is silent on the issue.

If time is of the essence, a failure to respond to the landlord's trigger notice within the time periods stipulated in the lease could mean the tenant is fixed with the rent proposed by the landlord in the trigger notice, no matter how outrageous the level. In consequence, such trigger notice provisions should be avoided, and the tenant should look for provisions that stipulate that the revised rent will be such amount as the landlord and tenant shall agree between them.

18.7.2 Appointment of a valuer

The lease must provide a mechanism by which the parties can settle the review if they are unable to reach agreement through negotiation. Most leases provide for appointment of an independent valuer to determine the rent in the absence of agreement. The tenant should ensure that such a valuer has to be agreed upon by both parties (not just appointed by the landlord). The lease should also contain a mechanism for appointing such a valuer in the absence of agreement. Most leases provide that if the parties are unable to agree upon the appointment, it shall be made by the President of the Royal Institute of Chartered Surveyors following an application by either party.

18.7.3 Capacity of the valuer

The lease should stipulate the capacity in which the valuer is to act. Is he to act as an arbitrator, or as an expert? There are considerable differences between the two.

(a)   An arbitrator seeks to resolve a dispute by a quasi-judicial process, whereas an expert imposes his own expert valuation on the parties.

(b)   The arbitrator is bound by the procedure under the Arbitration Act 1996, which deals with hearings, submission of evidence and the calling of witnesses. An expert is not subject to such external controls and is not bound to hear the evidence of the parties. Whilst an arbitrator decides on the basis of the evidence put before him, an expert simply uses his own skill and judgement.

(c)   There is a limited right of appeal to the High Court on a point of law against an arbitrator's award, whereas an expert's decision is final and binding unless it appears that he failed to perform the task required of him.

(d)   An arbitrator is immune from suit in negligence, whereas an expert is not. Using an expert tends to be quicker and cheaper and is, therefore, often provided for in lettings of conventional properties at modest rents. Where there is something unorthodox about the premises, which might make it difficult to value, or where there is a good deal of money at stake in the outcome of the review, an arbitrator is to be preferred so that a fully-argued case can be put.

The tenant should resist any provision allowing the landlord to determine the capacity of the valuer at the time of his appointment, as this may lead to a more expensive arbitration that the tenant does not consider necessary. There is usually no reason why the capacity of the valuer can not be agreed upon when the lease is being negotiated.

18.7.4   The costs of the valuer's determination

If the valuer is to act an expert, it is usual for the lease to stipulate who will pay his costs. The tenant should avoid provisions that pass the entire cost to the tenant. It should look for the costs to be shared equally.

If the valuer is to act as an arbitrator, it will be for him to determine who pays his costs and expenses.

18.8   THE LATE REVIEW

The lease will contain rent review dates from which any revised rent will be payable. The lease will need to specify what is to happen if the revised rent has not been determined by the review date, as this is a common situation.

Most leases will provide that that the tenant should continue to pay rent at the current level until the rent review is complete. Once the outcome of the review is known, unless the rent has remained the same, balancing payments will need to be paid. As most leases contain upward only rent review provisions (see **18.2.4.1**), this will usually involve the tenant in making up the shortfall, being the amount by which the previous rent differs from the reviewed rent for the period from the rent review date until the date of determination. Most leases provide for interest to be paid by the tenant on the shortfall. This is to compensate the landlord for the late arrival of the increase. The tenant should look out for the following:

(a)   The tenant should ensure the rate of interest is not penal, as there is no reason to assume it will be the tenant's fault that the rent review has not been concluded by the rent review date.

(b)   The tenant should avoid provisions that require it to pay interest on the whole of the shortfall from the rent review date. Interest should be payable only from the date each instalment of the rent fell due to be paid (which in most leases will be the usual quarter days).

(c)   If the lease has an upward/downward rent review (see **18.2.4.2**), similar provisions for making balancing payments of any overpayment together with interest should apply to the landlord.

18.9   RECORDING THE REVIEW

Most leases provide that once the rent has been determined, the landlord will prepare a memorandum recording the agreement reached for signature by both parties. This memorandum is then kept with the lease. The tenant should ensure that each party bears its own costs in the preparation and completion of this memorandum.

REVIEW ACTIVITY

1.   Imagine you have received a draft lease in the form set out at **Appendix 4**. The proposed Contractual Term is 15 years and the rent will be reviewed in the fifth and tenth years. The hypothetical lease term inserted into the square brackets at clause 7.5(a)(v) is 15 years. How will you advise a prospective tenant client on clause 7.5(a)(v)?

2.   Read clause 7.2 of the lease at **Appendix 4**. You will see there are two alternative sets of wording contained in square brackets. Assume you are acting for a tenant and receive a draft of this lease containing the following clause 7.2:

The amount of Annual Rent shall be reviewed on each Review Date to equal:

(a)   the Annual Rent payable payable immediately before the relevant Review Date (or which would then be payable but for any abatement or suspension of the Annual Rent or restriction on the right to collect it); or, if greater;

(b)   the open market rent agreed or determined pursuant to this clause.

Would the draft of clause 7.2 that you have received be compliant with the 2007 Code for Leasing Business Premises?

Answers to this Review activity may be found in Appendix 1.

CHAPTER 19

REPAIR

19.1	Introduction	203
19.2	Tenant's covenant to repair	204
19.3	Definition of the subject matter of the covenant	204
19.4	Extent of liability	204
19.5	Tenant's concerns and amendments	208
19.6	Enforcement of covenant by landlord	209
19.7	Covenant to yield up in repair	209
19.8	Decorating	209
19.9	Landlord's covenant to repair	210
	Review activity	210

19.1 INTRODUCTION

The commercial landlord's objective, on anything more than a short-term letting, will be to obtain a 'clear rent' (ie the landlord takes the entire income without any cost to itself) by imposing a 'full repairing' lease so that the tenant ends up paying the cost of any repairs, regardless of who carries them out. How the landlord achieves this depends on the nature of the premises being let:

(a) *Whole of a building*

Examples of this include a warehouse or an entire office block. In this situation, the landlord will usually impose a full repairing covenant on the tenant for the entire building.

(b) *Part of a multi-occupied building*

Examples of this include one unit in a shopping mall or one floor in an office block. In this situation, the landlord will usually make the tenant responsible for internal non-structural repairs of its part of the building, whilst itself taking responsibility for the remainder of the building (the exterior, structure and common parts, eg the circulation areas of a shopping mall). The landlord will recover the costs of complying with its obligation from the various tenants of the building, usually through the service charge provisions. The particular issues associated with a lease of part of a building, including repair and service charges, are dealt with in **Chapter 26**.

In the absence of a comprehensive code of implied obligations (the nature of which is not dealt with in this book), it is imperative that the responsibility for repairs is dealt with expressly in the lease. However, even though most leases do contain express terms, there is a glut of illustrative cases on disputes over the extent of liability for repair arising out of the:

(a) meaning of 'repair';

(b) scope of the repair covenant;

(c) standard of repair required.

Please note that each of the cases turns on its own specific facts, lease clauses, premises and works of repair, and many are in the non-commercial property sector; so although guidance can be taken from them, in practice the circumstances of each particular case are crucial.

To explore the disputed areas listed above and other issues on repair, we are going to use clause 26 (the example clause) of the lease set out in **Appendix 4** ('the **Appendix 4** lease'), which is reproduced at **19.2** for convenience.

19.2   TENANT'S COVENANT TO REPAIR

26.   REPAIRS

26.1   The Tenant shall keep the Property clean and tidy and in good repair [and condition] [except that the Tenant shall not be required to put the Property into any better state of repair or condition than it was in at the date of this lease as evidenced by the schedule of condition initialled by the parties to this lease and annexed to this lease].

26.2   The Tenant shall not be liable to repair the Property to the extent that any disrepair has been caused by an Insured Risk, unless and to the extent that:

(a)   the Landlord's insurance has been vitiated or any insurance proceeds withheld in consequence of any act or omission of the Tenant, any person deriving title under the Tenant or any person at the Property or on the Common Parts with the actual or implied authority of the Tenant or any person deriving title from the Tenant; or

(b)   the insurance cover in relation to the disrepair is excluded, limited or unavailable.

19.3   DEFINITION OF THE SUBJECT MATTER OF THE COVENANT

As you can note from the example clause in **19.2**, the tenant's covenant will apply to the subject matter of the lease, and so a clear definition of the subject matter will be required. In the example clause, the defined term is 'Property', but other terms are commonly used such as 'premises' or, often in older leases, 'the demised premises' or 'the demise'.

Without a clear definition, the obvious risk (particularly on a lease of part of a building where the responsibility for repairs is to be divided between the parties) is that there may be a dispute as to who is responsible for repairing each part of the building. See **26.2**, where the definition of the subject matter of a lease of part is dealt with in more detail.

An issue which could arise in the context of defining the subject matter, particularly on a lease of a whole building, is the question of responsibility for site contamination. If the site on which the building stands is subsequently discovered to be contaminated, could the tenant be required to remove the contamination under a repairing covenant? There may be a problem for a landlord in persuading the court that a repairing covenant can be extended to the soil as well as the buildings. In the absence of judicial guidance, the matter should be dealt with expressly in the lease. The landlord could expressly include the remediation of site contamination in the tenant's repairing covenant. Where appropriate, given the nature of the premises, the tenant could exclude any possible liability by expressly excluding the sub-soil from the definition of the subject matter, and excluding remediation of contaminated land from the usual tenant's covenant in the lease to comply with all statutory obligations (for an example of a clause obliging the tenant to comply with statutory obligations see clause 32 of the **Appendix 4** lease) which, depending on the wording used, may be broad enough to extend to requirements under environmental law.

19.4   EXTENT OF LIABILITY

In examining the extent of the tenant's liability, a number of important matters arise.

19.4.1   Meaning of repair

19.4.1.1   Disrepair

Under an obligation to repair, the tenant will incur liability only if the landlord can show that the premises have 'deteriorated from some previous physical condition' (*Post Office v Aquarius Properties Ltd* [1987] 1 All ER 1055) so that they are in 'a condition worse than it was at some earlier time' (*Quick v Taff-Ely Borough Council* [1986] QB 809).

There needs to be damage to the subject matter of the covenant. In *Quick v Taff-Ely Borough Council*, a landlord covenanted to keep in repair the *structure and exterior* of a dwelling which became virtually unfit for human habitation due to condensation. However, damage was caused only to *furnishings and decoration* and not to the structure or exterior, and so the landlord was under no obligation to make good.

In *Post Office v Aquarius Properties Ltd*, the basement of a building regularly flooded due to a defect in the structure of the building which had existed since construction. Incredibly, no damage to the building (eg to the plaster on the walls, to the flooring or to electrical installations) had been caused by the flooding, and the defect itself had not worsened. As the landlord could not show damage, the tenant was not under any obligation to repair.

It is clear from other cases that if damage had been done to the building when the water entered, this would have constituted disrepair and the tenant would have been liable for the repair (see comments on inherent defect liability at **19.4.1.3**).

19.4.1.2   To keep in repair means to put in repair

If the premises are in disrepair at the date of the lease, a covenant *to keep* in repair (as in the example clause) will require the tenant first to *put* the premises into repair (*Payne v Haine* (1847) 153 ER 1304) and then to *keep* them in repair (according to their age, character and locality) (*Proudfoot v Hart* (1890) 25 QBD 42).

The tenant may perceive this obligation to put premises into repair as onerous. See **19.5** for tenant's amendments in this respect.

19.4.1.3   Inherent defects

As with all kinds of disrepair (see **19.4.2** below), it will be a question of degree, having regard to the nature of the premises, whether what the tenant is being asked to do can properly be described as repair or, to the contrary, whether it would involve giving back to the landlord something wholly different from that which it was demised (*Ravenseft Properties Ltd v Davstone (Holdings) Ltd* [1980] QB 12).

So, contrary to previous belief, a tenant can be required to repair *damage* caused by 'inherent defects' (ie defects in design or construction of the building) under a covenant to repair. Liability for damage caused by an inherent defect may require not only repair of the damage, but also eradication of the defect itself if this is the only realistic way of carrying out the repairs (*Ravenseft Properties Ltd v Davstone (Holdings) Ltd*).

If, however, the inherent defect has not caused any damage to the premises, they are not in disrepair and accordingly the tenant is not liable on its covenant (*Post Office v Aquarius Properties Ltd* [1987] 1 All ER 1055).

The possibility that they may have to put right defects in the building, which have occurred through no fault of their own and which pre-date their occupation, is deeply worrying for tenants. See **19.5** below for tenant's amendments (and **9.5.2.4** for further comment on inherent defects).

19.4.2   Scope of repair

In the example clause, the tenant is under an obligation to 'repair'. Do the works which the tenant is being asked to carry out fall within that obligation, or are they more properly classified as works of renewal or improvement, for which the tenant is not responsible under a covenant to repair?

19.4.2.1   Factors to consider

Several factors to consider have evolved from the many authorities which can help in deciding the question of whether the works fall within the scope of a covenant to repair. Three particular factors are set out below, which can be approached separately or concurrently as the circumstances of the case may demand, but all are to be 'approached in the light of the nature and age of the premises, their condition when the tenant went into occupation, and the other express terms of the tenancy' (*McDougall v Easington DC* (1989) 58 P & CR 201, CA).

Whether the works go to the whole or substantially the whole of the structure, or only to a subsidiary part?

It was said in *Lurcott v Wakeley & Wheeler* [1911] 1 KB 905 that:

> Repair is restoration by renewal or replacement of subsidiary parts of the whole. Renewal, as distinguished from repair, is the reconstruction of the entirety, meaning by the entirety not necessarily the whole but substantially the whole ...

It will be a question of degree in each case whether the work to be done can properly be described as repair, involving no more than renewal or replacement of defective parts, or whether it amounts to renewal or replacement of substantially the whole. In *Lurcott v Wakeley*, the rebuilding of a defective wall of a building was held to be within the tenant's covenant to repair because it was the replacement of a defective part rather than the replacement of the whole. However, the tenant may be required to replace part after part until the whole is replaced.

Whether the effect of the works is to produce a building of a wholly different character from that which had been let?

This is commonly thought to be the overriding factor, in that the tenant cannot be required to give back something wholly different from that which it took.

In *Lister v Lane & Nesham* [1893] 2 QB 212, where the tenant was held not to be liable for the cost of rebuilding an old house built on muddy soil which had become unsafe due to poor foundations, Lord Esher MR said:

> A covenant to repair ... is not a covenant to give a different thing from that which the tenant took when he entered into the covenant. He has to repair that thing which he took; he is not obliged to make a new and different thing ...

As indicated previously in **19.4.1.3**, it will always be a question of degree whether what the tenant is asked to do will involve simply repair or giving back to the landlord a wholly different thing from what it took (*Ravenseft Properties Ltd v Davstone (Holdings) Ltd* [1980] QB 12).

What is the cost of the works in relation to the previous value of the building, and what is their effect on the value and lifespan of the building?

In deciding whether the tenant is being asked to give back to the landlord a wholly different thing from that demised, guidance may sometimes be found by considering the proportion which the cost of the disputed work bears to the value or cost of the whole premises.

It must be stressed, however, that decided cases can do no more than lay down general guidelines, and each case will turn on its own facts.

19.4.2.2   Repair v improvement/renewal/replacement

In the same way that the tenant need not renew the entire premises under a covenant to repair, a covenant to repair does not impose any obligation on the tenant to improve them. A tenant may sometimes be concerned that its landlord is trying to get it to upgrade or improve the premises under the guise of carrying out repairs.

The distinction is not always easy to make, but Lord Denning stated in *Morcom v Campbell-Johnson* [1955] 3 All ER 264 that:

> if the work which is done is the provision of something new for the benefit of the occupier, that is, properly speaking, an improvement; but if it is only the replacement of something already there, which

has become dilapidated or worn out, then, albeit that is a replacement by its modern equivalent, it comes within the category of repairs and not improvements.

Repair (as indicated at **19.4.2.1**) can include the renewal or replacement of subordinate parts.

19.4.3   Standard of repair

19.4.3.1   Generally

The standard of repair required is determined to be such as 'having regard to the age, character and locality ... would make it [the premises] reasonably fit for the occupation of a reasonably minded tenant of the class likely to take it' (*per* Lopes LJ in *Proudfoot v Hart* (1890) 25 QBD 42). The age, character and locality by which repair is judged is that which existed at the time the lease was granted, so even if the locality now attracted a superior or inferior class of tenant, the standard required from the tenant would be neither higher nor lower than at the date of the lease (*Anstruther-Gough-Calthorpe v McOscar and Another* [1924] 1 KB 716).

It follows that:

(a)   the standard required would be different for a brand new purpose-built shopping centre than for your local parade of shops (*Proudfoot v Hart*, where the standards required for Spitalfields and Grosvenor Square in London were contrasted);

(b)   the premises need not be kept in perfect repair (*Proudfoot v Hart*, where Esher LJ stated that the property need not be 'put into perfect repair. It need only be put into such a state of repair as renders it fit for the occupation of a reasonably minded tenant of the class likely to take it').

In *Commercial Union Life Assurance Co v Label Ink Ltd* [2001] L & TR 29, a case which involved a leaking roof, the tenant's covenant was to keep the premises in 'good and substantial repair and condition'. The judge in this case stated that 'good and substantial does not mean pristine or even perfect repair' and that 'substantial' fell short of a requirement for perfection. It was considered that the expert evidence about the works needed to comply with the covenant was based on 'a standard of perfection: what a pristine building should look like, not what was required by a covenant to keep, what had been a pristine building, in good and substantial repair'.

19.4.3.2   Clause wording

In drafting the repairing obligation, it is possible to restrict or widen its scope from that imposed by a covenant to repair.

Additional adjectives and verbs

In the example clause, the word 'repair' is qualified by the addition of the word 'good'. Other qualifying word(s) commonly seen in practice are 'sufficient', or 'good and substantial' or 'tenantable'.

It was uncertain whether additional qualifications would strengthen (or potentially limiting words such as 'tenantable' dilute) the tenant's repair obligation. Scrutton LJ, commenting in *Anstruther-Gough-Calthorpe v McOscar and Another* [1924] 1 KB 716, suggested that they would not add anything to the word 'repair', there being 'no substantial difference in construction between 'repair', which must mean 'repair reasonably and properly', and 'keep in good repair' or 'sufficient repair' or 'tenantable repair'; but Atkin LJ held a dissenting view, stating that 'effect should be given to every word used'.

The more recent case *Credit Suisse v Beegas Nominees Ltd* [1994] 11 EG 151, determined that it *was* the court's duty to give a full and proper effect to each word used.

In any event, the same words could be used in two separate leases but be given a different meaning due to the age, character and condition of the premises in question. So, to avoid being under a less or more onerous obligation than that intended, the landlord and tenant should give careful consideration to each word used.

Good condition

In *Welsh v Greenwich London Borough Council* [2000] PLSCS 149 (which involved a short-term residential lease, so a court might take a different view in a commercial context), the Court of Appeal held that a reference to keeping the premises in 'good condition' in the repairing obligation was a significant addition and would extend the obligation to defects which had not caused any damage to the structure of the premises (on the facts, damage caused by condensation). See tenant's amendments at **19.5**.

Renew or improve

The landlord can extend the liability of the tenant by the use of clear words which make the tenant liable to renew, or improve or even rebuild the demised premises (see, eg, *Credit Suisse v Beegas Nominees Ltd* [1994] 11 EG 151, where it was held that the verbs 'amend' and 'renew' were capable of going outside the verb 'repair').

However, a landlord should always bear in mind that imposing onerous provisions could mean that it is penalised on any rent review.

19.5   TENANT'S CONCERNS AND AMENDMENTS

A tenant's broad concerns are reflected in the 2007 Code for Leasing Business Premises, which provides:

> **7   Repairs**
>
> Tenants' repairing obligations should be appropriate to the length of term and the condition of the premises.
>
> Unless expressly stated in the heads of terms, tenants should only be obliged to give the premises back at the end of their lease in the same condition as they were in at its grant.

From what has been said above, the tenant may be concerned to reduce its liability, and there are a number of ways in which it may seek to do so:

(a)   If the premises are in disrepair at the commencement of the lease, a tenant may seek to limit its obligation to put premises into repair by reference to a schedule of condition with appropriate photographic evidence, which should be prepared by a surveyor, agreed by the parties and annexed to the lease (see the wording in parenthesis in the example clause). This should also mean that the tenant never has to give anything back to the landlord which is better than that which was given to it.

(b)   The tenant may be alarmed at the prospect of having to repair inherent defects. For that reason, tenants of new buildings will often seek to limit their liability, by excluding from their obligation liability for defects caused by design or construction faults, at least for a specified period of time. From the tenant's point of view, the landlord should covenant to repair damage caused by these defects (see **9.5.2.4**).

(c)   In most leases the landlord will insure the premises against a number of stated risks. The tenant should always insist that its repairing covenant does not render it liable to repair damage caused by a risk against which the landlord has or should have insured (see clause 26.2 of the example clause). The landlord should not object, since it should be able to claim on the insurance policy. However, the landlord will insist that the tenant remains liable if the insurance is avoided because of an act or omission of the tenant or someone at the premises with the tenant's consent (see the example clause and **24.5.1**). The tenant may also want to address the position relating to damage caused by uninsured risks (see **24.8**).

(d)   The tenant may seek to dilute the wording of the covenant by excluding the various words designed to strengthen the obligation (eg, 'good', 'substantial') or to extend the obligation (eg, 'rebuild', 'reconstruct', 'replace'), or by the rejection of any obligation to keep in good 'condition' as well as repair.

(e)   Although this is rarely acceptable to commercial landlords, the tenant could also try to qualify the covenant by excluding 'fair wear and tear', so excluding the normal effects of time and weather and of normal and reasonable use of the premises.

19.6   ENFORCEMENT OF COVENANT BY LANDLORD

The tenant's covenant to repair is often followed by a covenant to permit the landlord to enter the premises, usually upon reasonable notice, to ascertain their state and condition (for an example of such a clause, see clause 35 of the **Appendix 4** lease). As you can see, that well-drafted clause further includes:

(a)   a provision for the landlord to serve a notice of disrepair on the tenant if it is found to be in breach of its repairing obligation;

(b)   a right for the landlord, if the tenant had not commenced the works within a specified time, to enter the premises to carry out the repairs, at the tenant's expense;

(c)   the expenses incurred by the landlord acting under such a power being recoverable 'as a debt'. This is an attempt to avoid the restrictions imposed by the Landlord and Tenant Act 1927 (LTA 1927) and the Leasehold Property (Repairs) Act 1938 on the recovery of damages, as opposed to a debt, for disrepair (see **29.1.2.1**).

Note that if the landlord reserves the right to enter the premises to carry out repairs in default, it will, in certain circumstances, become liable under the Defective Premises Act 1972.

The landlord may be able to forfeit the lease for breach of the tenant's covenant to repair (for an example of a clause allowing this, see clause 39.1(b) of the **Appendix 4** lease). See **Chapter 25** for more detail on the right to forfeit.

The landlord may bring a claim for damages in respect of the tenant's breach of a repairing covenant, but this may be limited by the operation of the Leasehold Property (Repairs) Act 1938 (see **29.1.2.1**).

19.7   COVENANT TO YIELD UP IN REPAIR

The tenant will often enter into a covenant to yield up the premises in repair at the end of the term (for an example of such a clause, see clause 29 of the **Appendix 4** lease). The usual form of covenant requires the tenant to yield up in the repair required under the terms of the lease and to remove any alterations made if required by the landlord. A tenant should ensure that the requirement must be reasonably made and that it is given notice in advance of the requirement (see clause 29.2 of the **Appendix 4** lease).

19.8   DECORATING

Because some doubt exists as to the amount of decoration required by a covenant to repair, the matter is best dealt with expressly in the lease (see clause 27 of the **Appendix 4** lease).

The usual form of covenant requires the tenant to decorate the premises at specified intervals during the term, and during the last year of the term.

The obligation to decorate in the last year could require the tenant to decorate in two consecutive years depending on when the lease is terminated (eg, in a 10-year lease with a decorating obligation every three years). The tenant may therefore wish to provide that the obligation to decorate in the last year shall not apply if it has decorated in the previous, say, 18 months.

The landlord may also wish to retain some control by requiring the tenant to obtain consent (not to be unreasonably withheld) before any change in the colour scheme is made. Some covenants in older leases specify the materials to be used. Unfortunately, the materials specified are sometimes inappropriate to the type of building concerned and its method of construction, so more modern covenants simply require the tenant to carry out its obligation 'in a good and workmanlike manner with good quality materials'.

On the grant of a lease of part of a building, the exterior decoration would normally be undertaken by the landlord who would recover his expenses under the service charge.

19.9 LANDLORD'S COVENANT TO REPAIR

The only common situation in which a landlord will covenant to repair is on the grant of a lease of part of a building, where the landlord will covenant to repair the exterior, structure and the common parts, and will be able to recover his expenditure under the service charge provisions. A landlord's covenant to repair will be subject to the same rules of construction as a tenant's covenant so, for example, the landlord need not carry out works so as provide the tenant with something wholly different from that originally demised.

REVIEW ACTIVITY

1.   Consider the amendments that you might make to the example clause if you were acting for a tenant on the grant of a 10-year lease of one floor of an old office building. The office premises have been left in a poor state by the previous tenant.

2.   Consider the amendments that you might make to the example clause if you were acting for a tenant on the grant of a 10-year lease of a newly-constructed warehouse which was built on a brown field site.

Answers to this Review activity may be found in Appendix 1.

CHAPTER 20

ALIENATION

20.1	Dealings with the premises	211
20.2	Restrictions on alienation	213
20.3	Seeking consent from the landlord	217
20.4	Notice of assignment or sub-letting	220
20.5	Virtual assignments	221
	Review activity	221

20.1 DEALINGS WITH THE PREMISES

The term 'alienation' refers to the tenant's ability to deal with the lease. Unless the lease contains some restriction, the tenant will be free to deal with its interest in any way it wishes.

There are various ways in which a tenant may seek to deal with its premises. It may seek to divest itself of the entirety of its interest by assigning the lease. Alternatively, it might retain its own lease and create a new interest through sub-letting (otherwise known as under-letting). It might also seek to mortgage the lease or grant licences for third parties to occupy the premises, or it might seek to share possession of the premises. Complete freedom like this is unlikely to prove acceptable to the landlord for a number of reasons, and thus a fair balance between the competing concerns and aims of both parties will have to be reached. In consequence, each side must understand the concerns of the other and the type of restriction that may be appropriate for each type of potential dealing.

20.1.1 Assignment

Assignment involves the tenant transferring the whole or part of its leasehold estate to another party. From the tenant's point of view, the lease may become a burden if it is unable to assign it freely when it no longer has any use for the premises. This situation may arise, for example, where the premises have become surplus to the tenant's requirements, or because they are no longer suitable for the tenant's needs. The tenant would also be in difficulty if its business venture failed and it could no longer afford the rent. However, from the landlord's point of view, close control over assignment is essential, because without it the landlord may find its premises occupied by an unsatisfactory tenant, and the value of its reversionary interest may be reduced. The assignee will become responsible for the rent and the performance of the other covenants in the lease, and the landlord will want to ensure that it is of good financial standing. The identity and status of any potential assignee is, therefore, important to the landlord for financial reasons. Further, there may be estate management reasons why the landlord will wish to exercise some control over assignees, for example where the landlord owns the adjoining premises.

20.1.2 Sub-letting

When a tenant sub-lets, it retains its own lease and creates a new lease carved out of its term in favour of a third party. There are several situations in which a sub-letting of the premises, or part of it, may be appropriate (see **28.2**).

The landlord will want the ability to control sub-letting, because in certain circumstances the head tenancy may cease to exist and the sub-tenant will become the immediate tenant of the landlord. This could happen, for example, on the surrender of the head-lease or on the forfeiture of the head-lease followed by the sub-tenant's successful application for relief. A similar situation could arise at the end of the contractual term if the head-tenant does not apply (or is unable to apply) for a new tenancy under Pt II of the Landlord and Tenant Act 1954 (LTA 1954) but the sub-tenant does; the sub-tenant may be granted a new tenancy of its part against the head-landlord. In all these situations the landlord would want to be sure that the sub-tenant was able to pay the rent and perform the covenants, and will therefore wish to have some control over the identity and status of any proposed sub-tenant.

20.1.3 Parting with/sharing possession

Most leases contain covenants prohibiting the tenant from either parting with possession or sharing occupation of the premises. 'Parting with possession' and 'sharing occupation' are, however, two different things.

A covenant preventing the tenant from *parting with possession* of the premises prevents the tenant from doing anything that means it will no longer have legal possession of the premises. Such a covenant will prevent both assignment and sub-letting, but will go further than that. For example, it has been held to prevent parting with possession of the premises to a purchaser pending completion of an assignment (*Horsey Estate Limited v Steiger* [1899] 2 QB 79). It will not, however, prevent the tenant from allowing another person to use the premises, provided the tenant retains legal possession. It will not, therefore, prohibit a tenant from granting a licence of the premises to another, unless the licence confers exclusive possession on the licensee (see *Street v Mountford* [1985] AC 809). In practice, of course, it can be very difficult to grant a third party rights of occupation without allowing exclusive possession.

Covenants which prohibit the tenant from *sharing possession* of the premises will prevent the tenant from granting licences. Such a prohibition will prevent the tenant from sharing occupation of the premises with a group company member. It will also prevent the sort of concession arrangements frequently made by retailers, whereby another business is allowed to promote its products or services within the tenant's store. The tenant should therefore try to resist an absolute prohibition against sharing possession, unless there is no possibility of the tenant or any future tenant wishing to share with a group company or grant concessions.

20.1.4 Dealings with part

Landlords often impose much stricter control on dealing with part only of the premises because of the estate management problems which dealings of part can create. For example, if assignment of part were permitted, there would need to be an apportionment of rents and other outgoings under the lease. It is therefore usual for rack rent leases of commercial premises to prohibit any dealings with part other than, possibly, sub-letting.

When considering whether to permit sub-letting of part, the landlord will bear in mind that a sub-tenant can in certain circumstances become the immediate tenant of the head-landlord (see **20.1.2**). If a number of sub-leases have been granted, a landlord who had let a building as a whole to a single tenant could, at some future date, be faced with the estate management problems associated with having a number of different tenants, each with a lease of a different part of the building. Further, if the tenant was allowed to grant a sub-lease of part only of the premises, this could lead to the division of the premises into commercially unattractive units. If the landlord inherited tenancies of part, it might have difficulty in re-letting any part that became vacant, if that part is no longer attractive to the market.

For these reasons, landlords often prohibit sub-letting of part only of the premises, as well as other dealings with part. In considering the acceptability of any such prohibition, the tenant will need to have regard to the nature of the premises. The design of some premises does not lend itself to sub-division. However, other premises (eg office blocks) can often be sub-let with relative ease (say, by sub-letting one or more floors). Clearly a prohibition on sub-letting part would prevent the tenant from disposing of a surplus of space. It also reduces its ability to deal with the premises flexibly if it wishes to dispose of them as a whole. For example, if at the time the tenant comes to dispose of the premises the market is demanding smaller units, the tenant's chances of disposing of the premises will be increased if it can divide the premises up into smaller units. A tenant should therefore consider carefully a complete prohibition on sub-letting part.

Sometimes a landlord can be persuaded to agree to sub-letting of part if the extent of the parts to be sub-let is specified (eg not less than one complete floor of the demise) and the sub-tenancy is excluded from the LTA 1954. (The latter requirement will ensure that the landlord can, if it wishes, require the sub-tenant to vacate the premises at the end of the contractual term of the sub-lease.)

20.1.5 Charging or mortgaging

A tenant may wish to mortgage or charge its leasehold interest in the premises. This is usually done by way of either a fixed or a floating charge. A fixed charge may be taken where the lease has some capital value, or where the premises are critical to the success of the tenant's business. Often, however, rack rent leases of commercial premises do not have a capital value. In addition, the forfeiture provisions within the lease may make it unattractive as security. Fixed charges over commercial leasehold property are not, therefore, a common way of raising finance.

The lease may, however, be caught by a floating charge granted by a corporate tenant over all its assets and undertaking. Such floating charges are often granted by a company borrower when raising finance. They do not fix upon the assets in question unless and until certain events specified in the charge arise. These are usually events of default or insolvency.

If the tenant wants to grant either a fixed or a floating charge, it will need to check the provisions of its lease to see what is permitted. It will also need to be aware of any floating charges already in existence at the time the lease is granted, as these normally cover future assets of the company.

Most leases will contain restrictions on charging, as the landlord will be concerned that, if the tenant defaults on the mortgage, the lender may take possession of the premises or exercise its power of sale. The lender under a legal charge also has a right to relief against forfeiture in much the same way as a sub-tenant.

20.2 RESTRICTIONS ON ALIENATION

For the reasons mentioned in **20.1** above, it is common for the landlord to impose restrictions on dealing. Such restrictions may be absolute or qualified.

20.2.1 Absolute covenants against dealings

An absolute covenant means that the tenant cannot carry out the specified dealing without being in breach of covenant. An example would be 'not to assign or sub-let the whole or any part of the premises'. This type of covenant would prevent an assignment of whole, an assignment of part, a sub-letting of whole and a sub-letting of part. While the landlord may be prepared to waive the covenant in a given case, the tenant will be entirely at the mercy of its landlord, who may refuse consent quite unreasonably subject only to the restrictions imposed by the Equality Act 2010. Also, if the covenant is absolute, the landlord is not obliged to give any reason for its refusal.

An absolute covenant against all dealings is unusual in business leases, except in very short-term leases or to the extent that it prohibits dealings with part of the premises (see **20.1.4**). Any wider form of absolute restriction should be resisted by the tenant; and if, exceptionally, there is such a restriction, the tenant should make sure its presence is reflected in the rent it has to pay.

20.2.2   Qualified covenants against dealings

A qualified covenant prohibits alienation by the tenant without the landlord's consent. An example would be 'not to assign or sub-let the whole or any part of the premises without the consent of the landlord'. Sometimes, the covenant will state that the landlord's consent is not to be unreasonably withheld; this is known as a fully qualified covenant. An example would be 'not to assign or sub-let the whole or any part of the premises without the consent of the landlord, such consent not to be unreasonably withheld'. However, even if these words are not expressly stated, they will be implied by s 19(1)(a) of the Landlord and Tenant Act 1927 (LTA 1927). This provides that a covenant not to assign, underlet, charge or part with possession of the premises or any part thereof without the landlord's licence or consent, is subject to a proviso that such licence or consent is not to be unreasonably withheld. In other words, a qualified covenant against dealings will be converted into a fully qualified covenant by the operation of s 19(1)(a). The section has no application to the operation of an absolute covenant, where the landlord remains free to refuse its consent quite unreasonably.

20.2.3   What is usually permitted and prohibited?

In practice the form of covenant found in a rack rent commercial property lease will contain elements of both the absolute and qualified restrictions. It will usually cover all types of potential dealing, as if a specific dealing is not referred to it will not be prohibited or restricted. So, for example, a restriction on assignment will not be broken by a sub-letting of the premises. Neither will a covenant against sub-letting prevent the tenant from granting licences. Similarly, a covenant against sub-letting 'the demised premises' will not be broken by a sub-lease of part only (*Cook v Shoesmith* [1951] 1 KB 752). If such restrictions are intended, they must be dealt with expressly.

The precise terms of the covenant will of course vary from transaction to transaction, but it is common to find that a lease will:

(a)   prohibit absolutely dealings in relation to part only of the premises, unless the premises lend themselves to subdivision (see **20.1.4**);

(b)   prohibit absolutely dealings which stop short of an assignment, sub-letting or charging of the whole, eg parting with possession or sharing occupation of the premises (see **20.1.3**);

(c)   prohibit without the landlord's prior written consent assignments, charges or sub-lettings of the whole.

Such a clause attempts to strike a balance between both landlord and tenant. It will allow the tenant to assign, charge or sub-let the whole of the premises subject to obtaining the landlord's prior consent (and the landlord will not be able to unreasonably withhold its consent). This should meet the tenant's main concern of being unable to divest itself of the lease should its circumstances change. At the same time, it will allay the landlord's fears by imposing an absolute prohibition on dealings with part only of the premises. Whether or not the tenant considers the balance to be a fair one will depend on the facts of the transaction. The tenant will need to bear in mind the issues discussed in **20.1.3** and **20.1.4** when deciding whether a total prohibition on dealings with part and sharing occupation is acceptable.

20.2.4   What detailed requirements will apply to assignments?

20.2.4.1   Leases granted before 1 January 1996

Prior to the Landlord and Tenant (Covenants) Act 1995 (LT(C)A 1995), the landlord knew that the original tenant would be liable throughout the term of the lease even if it had assigned it on. Whilst this did not stop the landlord being concerned with the identity of any assignee, it meant the landlord had a safety net if such assignee failed to comply with the lease covenants. In consequence, leases granted prior to 1 January 1996 (often referred to as 'old leases') tend to have less stringent requirements relating to assignment than those granted after that date. Such leases will, however, invariably require the assignee to enter into a direct covenant with the landlord to perform the covenants in the lease. This will make the assignee liable on the covenants in the lease during the whole term, rather than just during the currency of its ownership. There may also be additional requirements, such as the assignee providing guarantors or a rent deposit, although this will vary from lease to lease.

20.2.4.2 Leases granted on or after 1 January 1996

For tenants entering into leases on or after 1 January 1996 (often referred to as 'new leases') the position changed. Such tenants are automatically released from liability under the lease once they assign it on. This is subject to two significant caveats. First, the LT(C)A 1995 specifically states that nothing in the statute prevents the tenant from entering into an authorised guarantee agreement (AGA), whereby the outgoing tenant guarantees the performance of the tenant's lease covenants by the incoming assignee (see **20.2.4.3**).

Secondly, the LT(C)A 1995 inserted s 19(1A) into the LTA 1927. Section 19(1A) operates only in relation to qualified covenants against assigning in commercial leases granted on or after 1 January 1996. The consequences of s 19(1A) are as follows:

(a) the landlord can stipulate in the lease conditions which need to be satisfied, or circumstances which must exist, before the landlord will give its consent to the assignment;

(b) if the landlord withholds its consent on the grounds that the specified circumstances do not exist, or that the specified conditions have not been satisfied, then the landlord will not be unreasonably withholding its consent;

(c) if the landlord withholds its consent on grounds other than those specified, s 19(1)(a) of the LTA 1927 will apply in the usual way (see **20.2.2** and below).

The nature and type of condition to be satisfied (or circumstances which must exist) are left to the parties to decide, but s 19(1C) of the LTA 1927 envisages their falling into two categories: those which can be factually or objectively verified; and those where the landlord has a discretion.

Factual conditions or circumstances might include a requirement that the proposed assignee is a publicly-quoted company on the London Stock Exchange or has pre-tax net profits equal to three times the rent, or a requirement that the assignor enter into an AGA (see **20.2.4.3**) or that the assignee procure guarantors.

Discretionary circumstances or conditions are those which cannot be verified objectively, and a judgement or determination will have to be made as to whether they have been satisfied. This type of condition will be valid only if either it provides for an independent third-party reference (in the event of the tenant disagreeing with the landlord's determination), or the landlord commits himself to making a reasonable determination. Typical examples of discretionary circumstances or conditions might include a provision that the proposed assignee must, in the opinion of the landlord, be of equivalent financial standing to the assignor and, should the tenant not agree, the matter is to be referred to an independent third party; or a provision that the assignee must not, in the reasonable opinion of the landlord, be in competition with other tenants in the same development.

The tenant must consider the impact of each circumstance and condition carefully before agreeing to its inclusion in the lease. For example, a blue-chip tenant who accepts a condition requiring any assignee to be of equivalent financial standing, will finds its pool of potential assignees severely restricted (effectively it will contain only other blue-chip companies). This may result in the tenant being unable to assign the lease. It will be too late for the tenant to argue at the time of an assignment that this condition is unreasonable if it has been included in the lease. It can help to remind the landlord during lease negotiations that restrictions on alienation will generally have a downward effect on rent at review, as the lease is less marketable. As a result, the trend in recent years has been away from long lists of circumstances and conditions. Indeed, it is not uncommon to find that the only precondition for assignment is the provision of an AGA. Even where this is the only condition, the tenant should consider whether it is appropriate for the provision of an AGA to be an absolute requirement in *all* circumstances. What, for example, if the tenant is assigning to someone of greater covenant strength? In such circumstances the landlord would not be disadvantaged in any way by the assignment, and so is it fair that it can require the tenant to enter into an AGA (see **20.2.4.4**)?

It should be noted that by virtue of s 19(1)(a) of the LTA 1927, the landlord can always refuse to give consent on grounds not listed in the lease, if it is reasonable to do so. So a failure to list a circumstance or condition in the lease will not prevent its being relied upon if it is a reasonable ground for refusal to the application in question.

20.2.4.3   Authorised guarantee agreements

Although the LT(C)A 1995 has abolished privity of contract in relation to leases caught by the Act, an outgoing tenant may sometimes be required to guarantee its immediate assignee's performance of the obligations contained in the lease. This is achieved by the outgoing tenant entering into an AGA with the landlord. The landlord may require an AGA from an outgoing tenant where:

(a)   the lease provides that the consent of the landlord (or some other person) is required to the assignment;

(b)   such consent is given subject to a condition (lawfully imposed) that the tenant is to enter into the AGA. For example, the requirement of an AGA may be one of the conditions which the parties had previously agreed had to be satisfied before the landlord was prepared to give its consent to an assignment (see **20.2.4.2**);

(c)   the assignment is entered into by the tenant pursuant to that condition.

The terms of the guarantee are left to the parties, provided that the purpose of the LT(C)A 1995 is not frustrated. For typical terms, see **27.3.1** and the specimen at **Appendix 5**.

Whilst it is clear an outgoing tenant can be required to enter into an AGA, the position regarding any guarantor of the outgoing tenant has been less certain. Can the landlord validly ask the guarantor of the outgoing tenant to guarantee the obligations of the incoming tenant? In the absence of confirmation on the point from either the Act itself or case law, landlords in practice have been doing one of two things. The first is to require the outgoing tenant's guarantor to guarantee the obligations of the *assignee* in the AGA (sometimes referred to as a 'direct guarantee'). The second is to require the outgoing tenant's guarantor to guarantee the *outgoing tenant's* guarantee (sometimes referred to as a 'sub-guarantee'). Unfortunately for landlords, in the case of *Good Harvest Partnership LLP v Centaur Services Ltd* [2010] EWHC 330 (Ch), the High Court held that direct guarantees are invalid and questioned the validity of sub-guarantees (without ruling on the latter point). So any direct guarantee from an outgoing tenant's guarantor of an incoming assignee will be unenforceable. The validity of sub-guarantees, however, has been considered further in *K/S Victoria Street v House of Fraser (Stores Management) Limited* [2011] EWCA Civ 904. The Court of Appeal held that a sub-guarantee of the outgoing tenant's AGA obligations by the outgoing tenant's guarantor would be lawful, whilst upholding the decision of the High Court in *Good Harvest* regarding direct guarantees. (See also **14.4.2**.)

Where a lease contains an assignment clause requiring a direct guarantee as a condition of the landlord's consent, the requirement for a direct guarantee should be severed, leaving, in most cases, an assignment provision operating as a qualified covenant against assignment (*Tindall Cobham 1 Ltd & Others v Adda Hotels (an unlimited company) & Others* [2014] EWCA Civ 1215).

20.2.4.4   The 2007 Code for Leasing Business Premises

In relation to assignments, the 2007 Code for Leasing Business Premises ('the 2007 Code') provides:

> Leases should ... not refer to any specific circumstances for refusal, although a lease would still be Code compliant if it requires that any group company taking an assignment, when assessed together with any proposed guarantor, must be of at least equivalent financial standing to the assignor (together with any guarantor of the assignor).
>
> Authorised Guarantee Agreements should not be required as a condition of the assignment, unless at the date of the assignment the proposed assignee, when assessed together with any proposed guarantor:
>
> •   is of lower financial standing than the assignor (and its guarantor); or
>
> •   is resident or registered overseas.
>
> For smaller tenants a rent deposit should be acceptable as an alternative.

So, a 2007 Code-compliant lease would not contain an absolute requirement that the tenant enter into an AGA. This requirement would be appropriate only where the landlord was being asked to accept an assignee of reduced covenant strength. In addition, the 2007 Code recommends that the lease does not contain any other specific circumstances for refusal, except for one dealing with group company assignments. This is to address the concern of landlords that the lease might be passed from a parent company to a much weaker subsidiary, in order ultimately to divest the parent company of the lease liabilities. A landlord clearly would wish to prevent such dilution of the tenant's covenant strength. In consequence, sometimes leases prohibit absolutely group company assignments. The 2007 Code recommends something less than that, which would allow the tenant to make a group company transfer, but only where the covenant strength is not weakened.

20.2.5   What detailed provisions will apply to sub-lettings?

Since there is a risk that the landlord may inherit a sub-tenant (see **20.1.2**), the lease will usually contain detailed provisions prescribing what terms any permitted sub-lease must contain. For example, the lease may contain the following:

(a)   a prohibition on the sub-tenant doing any act inconsistent with the terms of the sub-lease;

(b)   a requirement that the sub-tenant enter into a direct covenant with the head-landlord;

(c)   a requirement that the sub-lease prohibit any further dealings other than an assignment of whole;

(d)   a requirement that the sub-lease contain similar rent review provisions to the head-lease;

(e)   restrictions on the level of rent that can be charged under the sub-lease.

As with assignment, the tenant should check any such requirements carefully before agreeing to them. For example, a tenant should avoid any provision requiring it to sub-let at no less than the rent currently payable under the head-lease. If rents have fallen since the rent was last reviewed under the head-lease, this will make it virtually impossible to sub-let lawfully. The 2007 Code recommends in paragraph 5 that the tenant should be allowed to sub-let at the market rent at the time of the sub-letting. A requirement that any sub-lease be excluded from the LTA 1954 should also be resisted, as it would limit the pool of potential sub-tenants who would be interested in the premises. If such a restriction does have to be accepted then the lease should not be prescriptive about the terms of the sub-lease (see paragraph 5 of the 2007 Code).

20.3   SEEKING CONSENT FROM THE LANDLORD

Whether the landlord can refuse consent will depend upon whether the landlord has made use of s 19(1A) of the LTA 1927 or, if not, its reasonableness in the circumstances of the case.

The landlord should also be mindful of its statutory obligations under the Landlord and Tenant Act 1988 (LTA 1988) (see **20.3.4**) and s 144 of the Law of Property Act 1925 (LPA 1925) (see **20.3.6**).

20.3.1 Applications for consent to assign

The landlord can lawfully withhold consent to assign if:

(a)   the lease contains an absolute prohibition on assignment; or

(b)   a circumstance or condition listed in the lease under s 19(1A) of the LTA 1927 has arisen (see **20.2.4.2**); or

(c)   it is otherwise reasonable to do so under s 19(1)(a) of the LTA 1927 (see **20.3.3**).

20.3.2 Other applications for consent

Section 19(1A) of the LTA 1927 has no application to covenants against sub-letting, charging or mortgaging, and does not apply in relation to leases granted before 1 January 1996. In consequence, the landlord can lawfully withhold its consent to such applications if:

(a)   the lease contains an absolute prohibition against the dealing in question; or

(b)   it is reasonable to do so under s 19(1)(a) of the LTA 1927 (see **20.3.3**).

20.3.3 Section 19(1)(a) of the LTA 1927

Where the lease contains a qualified covenant against dealings, even if the lease says otherwise, the landlord cannot unreasonably withhold consent to an application to deal with the lease. Whether the landlord is acting reasonably in such cases has to be judged from the circumstances existing at the time of the landlord's decision.

The Court of Appeal laid down a number of guidelines on the issue of the landlord's reasonableness under s 19(1)(a) in *International Drilling Fluids Ltd v Louisville Investments (Uxbridge) Ltd* [1986] 1 All ER 321. The case concerned an application to assign, and the Court held that:

(a)   the purpose of a fully qualified covenant against assignment is to protect the landlord from having its premises used or occupied in an undesirable way, or by an undesirable tenant or assignee;

(b)   a landlord is not entitled to refuse its consent to an assignment on grounds which have nothing whatever to do with the relationship of landlord and tenant in regard to the subject matter of the lease;

(c)   it is unnecessary for the landlord to prove that the conclusions which led it to refuse to consent were justified, if they were conclusions which might be reached by a reasonable man in the circumstances;

(d)   it may be reasonable for the landlord to refuse its consent to an assignment on the ground of the purpose for which the proposed assignee intends to use the premises, even though that purpose is not forbidden by the lease;

(e)   in general a landlord is bound to consider only its own relevant interests when deciding whether to refuse consent to an assignment of a lease. However, it would be unreasonable for a landlord not to consider the detriment which would be suffered by the tenant if consent were to be refused, if that detriment would be extreme and disproportionate in relation to the benefit gained by the landlord;

(f)   subject to the above propositions, it is, in each case, a question of fact, depending on all the circumstances, whether the landlord's consent to an assignment is being withheld unreasonably.

The following are examples of situations where consent has been held to have been reasonably withheld:

(a)   where the proposed assignee's references were unsatisfactory (*Shanley v Ward* (1913) 29 TLR 714);

(b)   where there was a long-standing and extensive breach of the repairing covenant by the assignor and the landlord could not be reasonably satisfied that the assignee would be in a position to remedy the breach (*Orlando Investments v Grosvenor Estate Belgravia* [1989] 2 EGLR 74);

(c)   where the assignee would be in a position to compete with the landlord's business (*Whiteminster Estates v Hodges Menswear* (1974) 232 EG 715);

(d)   where the assignment would reduce the value of the landlord's reversion. However, this will not be a reasonable ground for withholding consent if the landlord has no intention of selling the reversion (*Ponderosa International Development v Pengap Securities* [1986] 1 EGLR 66 and *FW Woolworth v Charlwood Alliance Properties* [1987] 1 EGLR 53);

(e)   where the proposed assignee intends to carry on a use detrimental to the premises, or a use inconsistent with the landlord's 'tenant mix' policy (see *Moss Bros Group plc v CSC Properties Ltd* [1999] EGCS 47);

(f)   where the assignee would, unlike the assignor, acquire protection under Pt II of the LTA 1954 (*Re Cooper's Lease* (1968) 19 P & CR 541);

(g)   where the terms of a sub-lease, when read together with a collateral agreement proposed between tenant and sub-tenant, did not mirror the terms of the lease (*Allied Dunbar Assurance v Homebase Ltd* [2002] 2 EGLR 23). In this case the lease required any sub-lease to mirror its terms, and the court held that the landlord was therefore entitled to see any collateral agreement between the tenant and sub-tenant.

The following are examples of situations where consent has been held to have been unreasonably withheld:

(a)   where the landlord has refused consent in an attempt to obtain some advantage for himself. See, for example, *Bates v Donaldson* [1896] 2 QB 241 and *Re Winfrey and Chatterton's Agreement* [1921] 2 Ch 7, where the landlord's refusal to grant consent to an assignment on the grounds that he wanted possession of the premises himself was held unreasonable. See also *Norwich Union Life Insurance Society v Shopmoor Ltd* [1999] 1 WLR 531, where, on an application to sub-let the premises, the landlord refused consent because the underlease rent was to be less than the market value. This was not prohibited by the terms of the lease, but the landlord argued that it would adversely affect the reversionary value of *neighbouring* properties it owned. The landlord did not make any argument that it would affect the reversionary value of the premises, and the court held this to be a case of the landlord seeking a collateral advantage unconnected with the demised premises;

(b)   where there are minor breaches of the repairing covenant (*Farr v Ginnings* (1928) 44 TLR 249);

(c)   where premises had been on the market for 18 months, the rent was significant and the slight harm to the landlord would be outweighed by prejudice to the tenant (*Footwear Corporation Ltd v Amplight Properties* [1999] 1 WLR 551).

An issue which has been before the court on more than one occasion is whether the landlord would be acting unreasonably in refusing consent where it anticipated a breach of the user covenant by the assignee. In *Ashworth Frazer Ltd v Gloucester City Council* [2002] 05 EG 133, the court considered that the correct approach is to examine what the reasonable landlord would do when asked to consent in the particular circumstances. It would usually be reasonable for a landlord to withhold consent where an assignee proposed to use the premises in breach of the terms of the lease. However, there could be circumstances where the refusal of consent on this ground alone would be unreasonable (although the court did not say what these circumstances might be). In other words, each case will be looked at on its own merits in light of what a reasonable landlord would do.

Under the provisions of the Equality Act 2010, any discrimination in withholding consent for the disposal of the demised premises on grounds of race, sex or disability is generally unlawful.

20.3.4 Delays in obtaining consent

The LTA 1988 further strengthens the position of a tenant seeking consent to deal with its lease. The Act applies where the lease contains a fully qualified covenant against alienation (whether or not the proviso that the landlord's consent is not to be unreasonably withheld is express or implied by statute). It applies to assignment, sub-letting, charging and parting with possession of the premises. When the tenant has made written application for consent to such a dealing, the landlord owes a duty, within a reasonable time:

(a)   to give consent, unless it is reasonable not to do so. Giving consent subject to an unreasonable condition will be a breach of this duty; and

(b)   to serve on the tenant written notice of its decision whether or not to give consent (see LTA 1988, s 1(3)(b), and *Footwear Corporation Ltd v Amplight Properties Ltd* [1999] 1 WLR 551), specifying in addition:

　(i)   if the consent is given subject to conditions, the conditions; or

　(ii)   if the consent is withheld, the reasons for withholding it.

The burden of proving the reasonableness of any refusal or any conditions imposed is on the landlord. The sanction for breach of this statutory duty is liability in tort for damages. The LTA 1988 does not specify what is to be regarded as a reasonable time, nor when refusal of consent is to be deemed reasonable. Again, this Act has to be read in the light of s 19(1A) of the LTA 1927. The operation of the LTA 1988 and relevant case law is considered further in **Chapter 27**.

20.3.5 What if consent is refused?

If, having applied for consent to assign or sub-let, the tenant thinks its landlord is being unreasonable in its refusal to give such consent, the tenant has a number of options available. These are dealt with at **27.1**.

20.3.6 Restrictions on requiring payment for consent

In the case of a qualified covenant against dealings, s 144 of the LPA 1925 implies a proviso that no fine or similar sum of money shall be charged for giving consent to assignment, sub-letting or parting with possession, unless the lease expressly provides for this. However, this does not prevent a landlord from requiring its tenant to pay a reasonable sum for legal and other expenses incurred in connection with the grant of consent.

20.4 NOTICE OF ASSIGNMENT OR SUB-LETTING

There is no common law obligation for a tenant to give its landlord notice of any dealing with the lease, but a well-drafted lease will provide for this so that the landlord knows at any given time in whom the lease is vested and whether any sub-lease has been granted.

The clause should specify the occasions on which the covenant is to operate (eg assignment, sub-letting, mortgage). The tenant is usually required to pay a registration fee to the landlord with each notice served. When negotiating the lease the tenant should ensure such registration fee is not excessive.

In the case of assignment, it will fall to the assignee to give notice (and pay any registration fee prescribed by the lease), since it will be its interest that will be jeopardised by the breach of covenant involved in failing to give notice.

20.5 VIRTUAL ASSIGNMENTS

The usual leasehold covenants preventing assignment, etc without the landlord's consent often prove inconvenient to tenants, eg on the sale of leasehold portfolios, where time is tight and consents would have to be obtained from a multiplicity of landlords. To deal with this, a handful of large city law firms acting for tenants with a large property portfolio developed a device that became known as the 'virtual assignment'.

A virtual assignment is an arrangement under which all the economic benefits and burdens of a lease are transferred to a third party, but without any actual legal (or equitable) assignment of the lease itself or any change in the occupation of the premises. Thus, as far as the landlord is concerned, the virtual assignor remains the legal tenant and the tenant avoids the need to seek the landlord's consent to the assignment. However, as between the parties to the virtual assignment, responsibility for the premises passes to the virtual assignee. The virtual assignee then acts as agent for the virtual assignor in all dealings connected with the property. This means it will be collecting rent from sub-tenants and paying it to the landlord, even though the assignor remains legally the tenant.

The question is whether such an arrangement is in breach of the terms of the lease. In *Clarence House Ltd v National Westminster Bank plc* [2009] EWHC 77 (Ch), the High Court held that although the virtual assignment did not amount to an assignment, sub-letting or declaration of trust, it was a breach of a provision in the lease preventing parting with or sharing of possession. On appeal, the Court of Appeal overturned the High Court decision (see *Clarence House Ltd v National Westminster Bank plc* [2009] EWCA Civ 1311). It was held that the appellant had not shared or parted with possession by entering into the virtual assignment, since there were sub-tenants in possession of the premises in question and the virtual assignee collected rents only as agent of the virtual assignor. While the Court accepted that being in receipt of the rents could amount to 'possession', it did not in this case, just as it would not have if the virtual assignor had appointed a managing agent to collect the rent on its behalf. This was despite the fact that the contract between the virtual assignor and virtual assignee entitled the virtual assignee to keep the rents once they were collected.

Some landlords may feel uncomfortable with this type of arrangement being possible. It puts a third party right in the middle of the landlord and tenant relationship, and if that third party gets into financial difficulty, may affect the ability of the tenant to pay the rent. In consequence, some draftsmen have already been adapting their precedents to prohibit virtual assignments. The effect this type of restriction may have on rent review, however, remains unclear. It will of course still be possible to effect a virtual assignment under standard alienation provisions drafted prior to this case. It should be borne in mind, though, that the cases where a virtual assignment would be appropriate are limited. If the virtual assignee were to have taken occupation, or have been entitled to take occupation of the premises itself, it seems clear there would have been a breach. Given the limited circumstances in which it is therefore likely to be appropriate, the issue of the virtual assignment is unlikely to be a cause for concern for the vast majority of landlords and tenants.

REVIEW ACTIVITY

Imagine your client has taken a lease of two upper floors of an office building in the form set out in **Appendix 4**. Read clauses 20 to 23 of the lease and answer the following questions:

1. Is the tenant allowed to sub-let one of the two floors it occupies in the event it no longer requires as much space?

2. On an assignment, can the landlord always insist that the outgoing tenant enters into an AGA?

3.   If the tenant wishes to assign the lease to a group company, in what circumstances can the landlord withhold its consent?

Answers to this this Review activity may be found in Appendix 1.

CHAPTER 21

USER

21.1	The need for a user covenant	223
21.2	The permitted use	224
21.3	The extent of the landlord's control	226
21.4	Ancillary clauses	227
21.5	Impact of competition legislation on user covenants	228
	Review activity	229

21.1 THE NEED FOR A USER COVENANT

There are several ways outside the terms of the lease in which the tenant's use of the premises may be restricted:

(a) *Planning legislation.* The tenant may not be able to carry out any building or other operations at the premises, and it will not be able to make a material change in the use of the premises without obtaining planning permission from the local planning authority. Generally, there is no implied warranty by the landlord that the tenant's use of the property is an authorised use under the planning legislation. It is, therefore, for the tenant to satisfy itself that planning permission is available for the use intended.

(b) *Covenants affecting a superior title.* There may be restrictive covenants affecting the landlord's reversionary title (or if the landlord is itself a tenant, affecting a superior title) which bind the tenant and prevent it from carrying out certain activities at the premises. Despite being restricted by statute as to the evidence of title it can call for, the tenant should always press the landlord for evidence of all superior titles.

(c) *Common law restraints.* The law of nuisance may prevent the tenant from using the premises in a such a way as to cause disturbance to a neighbour.

While these restraints operate to exert some degree of control over the tenant, they do not provide the landlord with any remedy should the tenant act in breach. A user covenant (together with several ancillary clauses) will therefore be required to give the landlord the desired level of control.

21.1.1 The landlord's concerns

There are various financial and estate management reasons why a landlord will wish to control use of the premises by the tenant:

(a) to maintain the value of the landlord's interest in the premises;

(b) to maintain the rental value of the premises;

(c) to avoid damaging the reputation of the premises by immoral or undesirable uses;

(d) to maintain the value of adjoining premises owned by the landlord;

(e) to avoid the tenant competing with other premises of the landlord in the vicinity;

(f) to maintain a good mix of different retail uses in a shopping precinct owned by the landlord.

The landlord has to be careful when drafting the user covenant to ensure that it does not restrain the tenant's use of the premises any more than is strictly necessary for the landlord's purposes, since a tight user covenant may have an adverse impact from the landlord's point of view on rental values both initially and at rent review. The wider the scope of the user covenant, the more attractive would be a letting of the premises on the open market and, therefore, the higher the rental value may be, both initially and at review. The tighter the covenant, the less attractive would be a letting of the premises on the open market (since the number of potential bidders for this letting would be restricted by the narrowness of the user covenant) and, therefore, the lower the rental value would be. The landlord is not able to argue at rent review that the valuer should assess the revised rent on the basis that the landlord might be prepared to waive a breach of the user covenant in order to permit a more profitable use (thereby increasing the rental value of the tenant's interest), nor is it allowed to vary the lease unilaterally in order to gain a benefit at review (see *Plinth Property Investments Ltd v Mott, Hay & Anderson* [1979] 1 EGLR 17 and *C&A Pension Trustees Ltd v British Vita Investments Ltd* [1984] 2 EGLR 75).

The landlord will therefore need to perform a balancing act between control of the tenant and good estate management on the one hand, and maximisation of rental values on the other. It is usually the case that if the premises are in a shopping centre or office block owned by the landlord, or the landlord owns adjoining property, the landlord will require greater control over the use. The chances of operating a successful shopping centre improve with the right mix and balance of uses. The landlord may seek valuation advice to get the right balance between control and rental income.

21.1.2 Tenant's concerns

From the tenant's point of view, a narrow user covenant ought to be avoided since, although the clause would work favourably for the tenant on rent review, its ability to dispose of the premises at some stage in the future will be hampered in that it will only be able to assign or sub-let to someone who is capable of complying with the covenant and who does not require any greater flexibility.

Additionally, the tenant must have regard to its own future use of the premises. There is a risk that the nature of the tenant's business may change to such a degree that it is taken outside the scope of the user covenant and, therefore, finds itself in breach. The tenant must ensure that sufficient flexibility is built into the covenant to permit future diversification of the tenant's business. However, it should not allow the landlord to insert a covenant that is wider than is strictly necessary for its purposes, since this may penalise the tenant at rent review by increasing the rental value of the tenant's interest. Once again a balancing act is required.

The user clause usually contains a principal covenant by the tenant governing the permitted use of the premises, followed by a range of ancillary clauses prohibiting or controlling a range of other activities.

21.1.3 The 2007 Code for Leasing Business Premises

The 2007 Code provides:

8 Alterations and Changes of Use

Landlords' control over alterations and changes of use should not be more restrictive than is necessary to protect the value, at the time of the application, of the premises and any adjoining or neighbouring premises of the landlord.

21.2 THE PERMITTED USE

There are several ways in which the permitted use can be defined in the lease. First, the landlord may be prepared to permit a wide range of uses by broadly stipulating the type of use to be permitted on the premises, for example, use as offices, or as a retail shop, or for light industrial purposes. This would give the tenant a large degree of flexibility and enable it to diversify its business operations within the broad range permitted.

Alternatively, the landlord may choose to restrict the tenant to a very narrow range of uses by defining the permitted use by reference to the nature of the business to be carried on at the premises, for example use as offices for the business of an estate agency, or as a retail shop for the sale of children's footwear, or as a factory for the manufacture of computer software. This would give the tenant no flexibility to diversify and would hamper the tenant in any efforts to assign its lease, or sub-let the premises to someone who was not in the same line of business.

As a third possibility, the landlord may adopt an approach which is mid-way between the first two by restricting the tenant's use of the premises to a class of similar uses by, for example, defining the permitted use as offices for the business of a solicitor, accountant, architect or other professional person. If the landlord intends permitting the tenant to use the premises for one of a number of similar uses, it may consider defining the use by reference to the Town and Country Planning (Use Classes) Order 1987 (SI 1987/764) (as amended).

In all cases, how strictly the user covenant operates will depend on whether it is expressed in absolute, qualified or fully qualified terms (see **21.3**).

21.2.1 Making use of the Town and Country Planning (Use Classes) Order (UCO)

It is often considered desirable that the permitted user is linked to available planning permission. For example, if planning permission is available for any office use within Class B1 of the UCO, then the landlord, being quite happy for the premises to be used for any such office purposes, may choose simply to prohibit any use other than B1 office use. However, if this approach is to be adopted, the landlord should check carefully to ensure that there are no uses which could conceivably fall within the definition of B1 office use which the landlord would consider to be unattractive. The same principle is more clearly demonstrated if the lease prohibits any use other than as a retail shop within Class A1. This is a very wide-ranging class of uses and there are likely to be several types of shop uses within that class which the landlord would not be prepared to tolerate at the premises.

If the landlord is to make use of the UCO in the user covenant, it should ensure that the lease clearly states that any reference to the UCO is intended to refer to the Order as enacted at the time the lease was granted. The danger is that at some stage during the term the UCO could be amended to bring within the class of use permitted by the lease a use which the landlord considered to be undesirable, thereby converting that use into a permitted use under the lease.

21.2.2 A covenant that names the tenant

It is sometimes difficult to define the type of business to be carried on by the tenant at the premises because of its peculiar nature, and so the landlord feels inclined to restrict use of the premises to the tenant's particular business. This is a dangerous approach to adopt, and it can lead to problems for the tenant (in terms of his ability to dispose of the premises) and can give rise to complicated valuation problems at rent review (*Sterling Land Office Developments Ltd v Lloyds Bank plc* (1984) 271 EG 894 and *Post Office Counters Ltd v Harlow District Council* [1991] 2 EGLR 121).

If the user covenant restricts the use of the premises to, for example, the offices of a particular company which is named in the lease, this would effectively prevent an assignment or sub-letting by the original tenant, even if the lease otherwise anticipated alienation (*Law Land Co Ltd v Consumers Association Ltd* (1980) 255 EG 617).

If the user covenant, without specifically naming the tenant, restricts use of the premises to 'the tenant's business', problems of interpretation will arise. Does the clause refer to the original tenant, or the current tenant? Does it refer to the business being conducted at the outset or the business being conducted from time to time? The danger from the landlord's point of view is that if, as is usually the case, the lease defines 'the Tenant' to include its successors in title, such a clause is likely to be construed by the court as permitting whatever business is currently being carried on by whoever is then the tenant. In other words, the landlord will have lost control. If reference is made to 'the tenant's business as a solicitor', does that mean that only the original tenant can comply with the covenant, or can an assignee? Would sub-letting be impossible since a sub-tenant, not being a tenant under the lease, would inevitably be in breach?

In view of these complications, it is advisable to avoid the use of covenants which either name the tenant, or refer to the tenant's business without sufficient clarity.

21.2.3   A positive or negative covenant?

If the covenant is positive, it will require the tenant 'to use the premises for the purposes of [the named permitted use]'. The benefit from the landlord's point of view is that non-use (eg, because of a temporary shut-down during a recession) will amount to a breach of covenant. This will entitle the landlord to damages (but not usually specific performance or an injunction) should the landlord suffer loss (see **29.1.3**). Loss can arise where a shopping centre loses what practitioners call an 'anchor tenant'. An anchor tenant may be, say, a large supermarket, whose presence generates a flow of customers for other shops in the shopping centre. If the anchor tenant leaves, it will reduce the number of shoppers in the shopping centre, thereby affecting the profitability of other shops in the centre and resulting eventually in an adverse effect on the value of the landlord's reversion. The tenant ought to resist a positive covenant as it can make it costly to cease trading from unprofitable or unsuitable premises.

Most user covenants are negative, obliging the tenant 'not to use the premises other than for the purposes of ... [permitted purpose]', in which case a breach is committed by the tenant only if he uses the premises for a purpose not authorised by the landlord. A negative user covenant is not breached by non-use.

Neither form of covenant will be breached if the tenant uses the premises for a purpose ancillary to the permitted use. For example, use of some rooms in a shop for storage purposes where the user covenant permits the retail sale of books, magazines and periodicals would not amount to a breach.

21.3   THE EXTENT OF THE LANDLORD'S CONTROL

The principal covenant may be absolute, qualified or fully qualified.

21.3.1   Absolute covenants

An absolute covenant gives the landlord absolute control over any change in the use of the premises in that it permits the tenant to use the premises for the purpose of the permitted use and no other. The tenant will not be able to use the premises for a use falling outside the scope of the covenant without obtaining from the landlord a waiver of the tenant's breach, or getting the landlord to agree to a variation of the lease. If the permitted use is narrowly defined, the tenant should be advised to resist an absolute covenant, unless it is sure that it will not want to assign or sub-let the premises, or diversify its business. If the permitted use is sufficiently widely defined (eg, use as offices only) then an absolute covenant should not unduly concern the tenant.

21.3.2   Qualified covenants

A qualified covenant allows the tenant to alter the use of the premises from a permitted use to some other use with the landlord's prior consent, which is usually required to be given in writing. However, such a covenant gives the tenant little extra comfort than is afforded by an absolute covenant since, unlike qualified covenants relating to alienation and improvements, there is no statutorily implied proviso that the landlord's consent is not to be unreasonably withheld. This means that, despite the additional wording added to the covenant, the tenant is still at the mercy of the landlord who may decline the request for a change of use for whatever reason it chooses. The only benefit from the tenant's point of view of a qualified covenant is derived from s 19(3) of the LTA 1927 which states that, provided the change of use will not entail any structural alterations to the premises (which would not often be the case), the landlord is not allowed to demand as a condition of giving consent the payment of a lump sum or an increased rent (as to which, see *Barclays Bank plc v Daejan Investments (Grove Hall) Ltd* [1995] 18 EG 117). However, s 19(3) does allow the landlord, as a condition of giving consent, to insist upon the payment of reasonable compensation in respect of damage to or diminution in the value of the premises or any neighbouring premises belonging to the landlord (which might occur if a valuable use of the premises is abandoned), and the payment of expenses incurred in the giving of consent, such as legal and surveyor's fees. Of course, the commercial reality for many tenants is that if they want a change of use, they will often end up offering a premium for a Deed of Variation, even though it is not lawful for the landlord to require its payment.

Section 19(3) does not apply to agricultural or mining leases.

21.3.3 Fully qualified covenants

A fully qualified covenant allows the tenant to change the use of the premises from a permitted use to some other use with the prior consent (in writing) of the landlord, whose consent is not to be unreasonably withheld. Most covenants of this kind will also stipulate (either in the wording of the covenant, or in the interpretation section of the lease) that the landlord cannot unreasonably delay giving consent. Should the landlord, in the tenant's opinion, be guilty of an unreasonable refusal of consent, the tenant may, if certain of its ground, change the use of the premises without the landlord's consent. However, this course of action carries a risk, and therefore most tenants would prefer to follow the safer course of action which is to apply to the court for a declaration that the landlord is acting unreasonably, and then proceed without the landlord's consent. The question of the landlord's reasonableness is ultimately left in the hands of the court. The only potential drawbacks of such a clause for the tenant are that, without an express provision in the lease, there is no obligation on the landlord to provide the tenant with reasons for refusing consent (making it difficult for the tenant to assess whether it has a good chance of success in its application for a declaration) and there is no positive duty upon the landlord to give consent along the lines of the statutory duty imposed by the LTA 1988 in respect of alienation covenants, which means that the tenant does not have a remedy in damages if it suffers loss as a result of an unreasonable refusal.

Section 19(3) of the LTA 1927 applies equally to fully qualified covenants.

21.4 ANCILLARY CLAUSES

It is usual for the landlord to impose many other covenants upon the tenant which also impact upon user, obliging the tenant:

(a) to comply in all respects with the Planning Acts (as defined in the definitions section of the lease). It is important for the landlord to have the benefit of this covenant since enforcement action for a breach of planning control committed by the tenant could be taken against the landlord, resulting in a possible fine;

(b) not to apply for planning permission, or to carry out acts of development at the premises. This covenant may be absolute, qualified or fully qualified. The landlord will not want the tenant to have freedom to change the authorised use of the premises as this may result in an existing profitable use being lost, thereby reducing the value of the premises. Although, as owner of the reversion, the landlord may be able to raise objections at the application stage, it would prefer to be able to veto the application under the terms of the lease in the first place. It should be noted that such a covenant may restrict the tenant's ability to alter or change the use of the premises even if elsewhere in the lease such action is more freely permitted;

(c)   where the landlord has consented to an application for planning permission, and development has commenced, to fully implement all permissions obtained before the end of the term in accordance with any conditions attached to the permission;

(d)   not to cause a nuisance, annoyance or inconvenience to the landlord or the tenants of adjoining premises. Whether an activity amounts to a nuisance is to be determined on the basis of ordinary tortious principles. An annoyance is anything which disturbs the reasonable peace of mind of the landlord or an adjoining occupier, and is a wider concept than nuisance. The concept of inconvenience is probably wider still;

(e)   not to use the premises for any immoral or illegal use (since such uses may tarnish the reputation of the building and reduce its value);

(f)   not to carry out any dangerous activities, or bring any noxious or inflammable substances onto the premises. The landlord's primary purpose behind this covenant is to preserve the premises. One consequence of a breach by the tenant might be an increase in the insurance premium for the premises, and although the tenant is likely to be obliged to pay the increased premium by virtue of the insurance covenant, the landlord would not want the level of insurance premiums to rise;

(g)   not to overload the premises in any way. The landlord is simply trying to preserve the premises with this covenant;

(h)   not to allow anyone to sleep or reside at the premises;

(i)   not to allow any licence which benefits the premises to lapse (eg, gaming licences, liquor licences). If the premises consist of a betting shop, the value of those premises will depend to a large extent on the continued existence of a betting office licence. The tenant will therefore be obliged by the landlord to maintain and, where necessary, renew the licence.

The tenant's solicitor will need to consider any and all of these ancillary clauses carefully. Without sufficient knowledge of the client's business, it is easy to miss a potential breach. For example, if your client is a retailer, might it sell fireworks at certain times of the year? Fireworks would potentially breach a restriction on the sale of inflammable items. Also, beware restrictions on the sale of alcohol. Again, if you act for a retailer, you should check whether there is any possibility of the sale of products containing alcohol. Even though it may not be the client's core business, many retailers will sell gift items at certain times of the year that include alcohol.

21.5   IMPACT OF COMPETITION LEGISLATION ON USER COVENANTS

Section 2 of the Competition Act (CA) 1998 prohibits any agreement which may affect trade within the UK and which prevents, restricts or distorts competition within the UK. Since April 2011 this prohibition has applied to land agreements (including leases) between businesses. The Act cannot be excluded and operates retrospectively but will only catch covenants which have an 'appreciable effect' on the market affected by the agreement. An agreement is exempt from the prohibition under s 9 of the CA 1998 if it either contributes to the improvement of production or distribution or promotes technical or economic progress. However, in either case, to fall within the exemption the agreement must:

•   allow consumers a fair share of the resulting benefit; and

•   not impose restrictions which are not indispensable to the attainment of those objectives; and

•   not eliminate competition in respect of a substantial part of the products in question.

It is for the person or company claiming the benefit of the exemption to prove that the conditions of it are satisfied.

The Office of Fair Trading has issued detailed guidance on the application of the CA 1998 to land agreements. This suggests that, in most leases, permitted user clauses (ie those specifying permitted uses) and restricted user clauses (those specifying uses that are not permitted) would be unlikely to restrict competition. This would include clauses restricting the lines of business that could be carried out by a tenant in order to achieve a good 'retail mix' and ensure the attractiveness of a shopping centre. However, a covenant by a landlord not to permit another business of the same type as the tenant to open in its shopping centre or restricting use where the landlord is active in a related market do have the potential to restrict competition and therefore be prohibited.

To date, there has been only one case that has considered the interaction of the CA 1998 Act with leasehold user covenants. The claimant in *Martin Retail Group Ltd v Crawley Borough Council* (CC (Central London), 24 December 2013) operated a newsagents from a parade of shops and on expiry of its lease sought a renewal lease with an extended user provision allowing for the sale of alcohol and convenience goods. The parade of shops already included a small supermarket selling such items and so the landlord objected to the proposed user and suggested a clause which specifically prohibited the sale of such items.

This dispute was referred to the County Court as a preliminary issue to the tenant's application for renewal of its lease under the Landlord and Tenant Act 1954. The court did not need to determine the issue of whether the user clause would be restrictive of competition, as the landlord conceded that this was the case. The judge did, however, comment that this concession was rightly made as the clause would restrict the sale of convenience goods on the parade. Interestingly, the relevant market was identified as within a relatively short walking distance from the parade. The issue for the court to determine, therefore, was whether the clause satisfied the conditions for exemption. The court was not satisfied that, as a matter of fact, the distribution of goods was improved or economic progress promoted through the existence of a number of different retailers, rather than via a supermarket or number of similar retailers, as the landlord had argued. On the evidence, it was not accepted that the community would benefit from the proposed restrictions, nor had the landlord proved the indispensability of them. The proposed user clause clearly provided a means of eliminating competition in convenience goods on the parade, contravening s 2 of the CA 1998. The court was not satisfied that the agreement fell within the s 9 exemption.

This case may cause some alarm for landlords who routinely impose restricted user covenants on tenants. However, it must be remembered that no argument was actually held on the issue of whether the user clause contravened s 2, as this was conceded by the landlord. In addition, the failure to persuade the court that the provision ought to fall within the s 9 exemptions, seems primarily to have resulted from the paucity of evidence presented by the landlord. Finally, a key factor in the court's decision seems to have been the determination that the relevant market was within a short walking distance from the parade and the absence of other nearby convenience stores.

REVIEW ACTIVITY

1. Which one of the following statements is correct?
    The user covenant in the lease at **Appendix 4** contains:
    (a) an absolute covenant;
    (b) a qualified covenant;
    (c) a fully qualified covenant.

2. Your client has a lease in the form of the lease at **Appendix 4**. The client informs you that it is changing the nature of its business, which will now involve members of the public visiting the property. The client has been advised by a planning consultant that its use

will be class A2 for the purposes of the Town and Country Planning (Use Classes) Order 1987. What provisions in the lease will affect this proposed change of use?

Answers to this Review activity may be found in Appendix 1.

CHAPTER 22

ALTERATIONS

22.1	Introduction	231
22.2	Lease controls	232
22.3	Restrictions outside the lease	235
22.4	Compensation for improvements	236
22.5	The 2007 Code for Leasing Business Premises	236
	Review activity	236

22.1 INTRODUCTION

A tenant will often wish to be able to make alterations to the premises, either immediately at the start of the lease (eg, fitting-out works at shop premises to enable it to start trading, or to erect partitioning in an open-plan office) or during the term of the lease to suit its changing business needs. A tenant will be concerned that the proposed restrictions in the lease are flexible enough to allow it to carry out its plans, that they will not affect assignability and that it will not suffer at rent review if the provisions are too flexible.

A landlord, however, usually wants to restrict the tenant's ability to make alterations for a number of reasons:

(a) to maintain the rental and capital value of the premises by preserving the character, reputation, appearance and physical integrity of the premises;

(b) to ensure that at the end of the lease the tenant gives back premises which are substantially the same as those demised to the tenant at the beginning;

(c) to ensure the landlord does not inadvertently become responsible for any breach by the tenant of the external restrictions which impact on alterations (see **22.3**).

The extent to which the landlord will want to restrict the tenant's ability will depend on the following:

(a) *The nature of the premises*

For example, in a letting of a large warehouse, or factory or other industrial premises, the landlord may require absolute control only over alterations affecting the structure and exterior of the premises, leaving the tenant free to do more or less as it pleases on the inside, as the landlord will know that the state of the interior will not affect its rental or capital interest. However, in a shopping parade, in order to maintain the general appearance of the parade and the quality of the development, and therefore its rental and capital value, the landlord may feel that it wants to have a very tight control over all alterations, inside and out.

In office leases, where the initial design of the building is open-plan, the landlord often allows the tenant to erect internal partitioning walls without having to obtain the landlord's prior consent, as long as the tenant notifies the landlord and agrees to remove them at the end of the term if the landlord so requires.

(b) *The length of the proposed term*

In a short-term letting (three years or less) the landlord is likely to want tight control over the tenant's ability to make alterations, in which case an absolute prohibition against all alterations may be appropriate.

However, in a longer-term letting (10 years or more), where the tenant may need to adapt the premises during the term to suit its changing business needs, or may anticipate the possibility of assigning the lease to an assignee who may wish to make alterations, the landlord will usually be prepared to allow the tenant a greater degree of freedom. Severe restrictions on a longer-term letting would give the landlord problems at the outset in securing a letting of the premises, and later on at rent review where the restrictive alterations covenant may be taken into account to reduce the rental value of the premises.

(c)   *The type of alterations*

The landlord may allow the tenant unrestricted freedom to carry out non-structural alterations or additions, for example the partitioning in an open-plan office mentioned above, which do not affect the rental or capital value of the landlord's interest.

In most cases the landlord will impose an absolute covenant against structural alterations, for the simple reason that the structure, being such a fundamental part of the building, should not be tampered with by the tenant.

22.2   LEASE CONTROLS

22.2.1   Alterations clause

As with other covenants, the covenant against alterations may be absolute (completely prohibited), qualified (prohibited unless the landlord consents) or fully qualified (prohibited unless the landlord consents, such consent not to be withheld unreasonably). The alterations clause may be a mixture, so that some alterations are completely prohibited, some are prohibited unless consent is obtained and some may be carried out without consent.

For example, a typical lease of office premises might contain the following alterations clause:

12.1   The Tenant shall not make any alteration to the Property except those expressly permitted by this clause.

12.2   The Tenant shall not make any internal non-structural alterations without the prior written consent of the Landlord.

12.3   The Tenant may erect internal demountable partitioning without the consent of the Landlord provided that the Tenant makes good any damage to the Property caused and within one month of completion of the alterations the Tenant provides the Landlord with a copy of 'as built' drawings.

In all cases, the landlord must first consider the type of premises involved, and the length of term proposed.

22.2.1.1   Absolute covenants

Subject to certain exceptions mentioned below, if the lease contains an absolute covenant against the making of any alterations or a particular type of alteration (for example in clause 12.1 of the typical office lease, set out at **22.2.1**, structural alterations are absolutely prohibited), the landlord will have total control over the tenant. The tenant can always ask the landlord for permission to make the prohibited alteration, but the landlord can simply refuse. If the landlord did agree then this could be by way of a one-off waiver of the proposed breach of covenant, or by a permanent variation of the lease (by deed of variation).

There are statutory exceptions to the landlord's absolute control. For example, the tenant can obtain a court order to enable it to carry out works required by some statutory bodies (eg a fire authority ordering the tenant to install a fire escape). In addition, the tenant of business premises can (although rarely does) use the provisions of the LTA 1927 (see **22.4**) to enable it to carry out works in the face of an absolute covenant.

The tenant should be advised to argue against an absolute covenant except, perhaps, where the covenant relates only to structural or external alterations (in which case the tenant may agree that it is reasonable that it should not be allowed to tamper with the structural parts of the building), or where the letting is for a short term and the tenant is confident that it will not need to alter the premises in the future to accommodate changes in its business, and that it will not need or want to assign the lease during the term. However, the longer the term, the more the tenant should ensure that it has sufficient flexibility to alter the premises.

22.2.1.2 Qualified covenants

A qualified covenant against alterations prohibits alterations to the premises by the tenant without the landlord's prior consent (which is usually required to be given in writing). An example of this is clause 12.2 of the typical office lease set out at **22.2.1**.

Other than in mining and agricultural leases, s 19(2) of the LTA 1927 implies into a qualified covenant against making *improvements* a proviso that the landlord's consent is not to be withheld unreasonably. Improvements are works carried out which increase the value or usefulness of the premises seen through the tenant's eyes (*Lambert v FW Woolworth & Co Ltd (No 2)* [1938] 2 All ER 664). There will therefore be few occasions where the landlord can argue that s 19(2) would not apply.

22.2.1.3 Fully qualified covenants

As said in **22.2.1.2** above, s 19(2) of the LTA 1927 converts a qualified covenant against alterations into a fully qualified covenant in so far as the alterations are *improvements*. To avoid any argument that the tenant's works are not improvements, most tenants will insist on converting a qualified covenant into a fully qualified covenant expressly by adding to the qualified covenant drafted by the landlord the words 'such consent not to be unreasonably withheld or delayed'.

22.2.1.4 Landlord's consent

Where landlord's consent is required, it will usually be given by deed in a document known as a licence for alterations or licence for works. The licence is usually negotiated between the landlord's solicitors and tenant's solicitors, and once agreed it will be produced in original and counterpart (or in duplicate) for signature by the landlord and the tenant.

The licence will often impose conditions on how the works are to be carried out to protect the landlord in respect of its concerns set out in **22.1** above. Common conditions are that the tenant must comply with statute in carrying out the works, obtain all necessary consents, carry out the works in a good and workmanlike manner, using good quality materials, comply with approved plans and specifications, and reinstate the premises to their previous condition at the end of the term. See **22.2.2** below.

Where s 19(2) of the LTA 1927 applies, or where there is a fully qualified covenant in the lease, consent from the landlord cannot be withheld unreasonably. The tenant must have supplied the landlord with all the information necessary for the landlord to reach an informed decision (*Kalford Ltd v Peterborough City Council* [2001] EGCS 42). If that has been done then a landlord will be acting reasonably in refusing consent only where its reasons follow the general principles laid down in *International Drilling Fluids Ltd v Louisville Investments (Uxbridge) Ltd* [1986] Ch 513 (see **Chapter 20**). This effectively means that the refusal must have something to do with the relationship of landlord and tenant, and must not involve the landlord simply seeking a collateral advantage outside the landlord and tenant relationship.

Section 19(2) allows the landlord to be compensated for damage to or reduction in the value of the premises or adjoining premises owned by the landlord, and to have its properly incurred legal and other (eg surveyor's fees) expenses met. It is therefore not reasonable for the landlord to refuse consent simply because the works will reduce the value of the reversionary interest.

Where the tenant thinks that the landlord is unreasonably withholding consent, the tenant could seek a declaration from the court that the landlord is acting unreasonably (coupled with an application for a declaration that the tenant can proceed with the alterations without any further need to seek the landlord's consent) or, with more risk, it could proceed with the works without consent and then use the landlord's alleged unreasonable withholding of consent as a defence to any claim for breach of covenant brought by the landlord.

The tenant is not, however, entitled to damages in respect of an unreasonable refusal of consent.

22.2.2   Other lease clauses

The landlord is likely to include many other covenants in the lease which will affect the tenant's ability to carry out alterations to the premises. For example:

(a)   *Reinstatement*

Section 19(2) of the LTA 1927 enables the landlord to impose a reinstatement obligation on the tenant in the case of an improvement which does not add to the value of the premises, where it is reasonable to do so.

The lease, however, usually contains an express reinstatement provision in any event for all alterations and additions (if requested by the landlord), so that it is less likely to be viewed as an unreasonable condition in giving consent. The tenant is likely to want to qualify an absolute obligation to reinstate by requiring that any such request be reasonable.

By obliging the tenant to reinstate the premises at the end of the term, the landlord may be able to avoid paying compensation to the tenant for improvements (see **22.4**) as, if the improvements have been removed, there is nothing to which the compensation requirement can attach.

(b)   *Access to inspect*

The lease may contain an express right to inspect a tenant's works to ensure that it is carrying them out properly. This should avoid any argument that a condition to that effect in the licence for alterations is an unreasonable one.

(c)   *Waste*

The doctrine of waste may operate to prevent the tenant from altering the premises. Waste is any act which changes the nature of the premises, and can be voluntary, permissive, ameliorating or equitable. If required, reference should be made to textbooks on land law for a more detailed consideration of the doctrine of waste. It is common to find a prohibition on waste (save to the extent that it might otherwise be permitted in the lease) in the alterations covenant.

(d)   *Electrical supply and installations*

Many landlords impose a covenant on the tenant not to tamper with the electrical supply or installations, especially in a lease of part of a building.

(e)   *Planning applications*

The landlord will want to control the tenant's ability to make applications for planning permission with an absolute, qualified or fully qualified covenant.

(f)   *Signs and advertisements*

The landlord will usually require a qualified covenant by the tenant not to display any signs or advertisements at the premises, to guard against a proliferation of signs or advertising hoardings giving the premises an unsightly appearance which might reduce the value of the landlord's interest in the building. The landlord may require control over the size or type of sign or advertisement.

(g)   *Decoration*

The decorating covenant may control the manner in which the tenant may alter the premises since it is likely to dictate that the tenant is not to change the colour of the premises (either inside or outside, or both) without the landlord's prior consent.

(h)   *No nuisance*

There will usually be a covenant imposed on the tenant not to do anything that would causes a nuisance or an annoyance to other tenants or owners or occupiers of adjoining properties, which may act as a control on how the tenant is able to carry out any works (eg, noise, times).

(i)   *Rent review*

See **Chapter 18** for the treatment of alterations and improvements at rent review.

If the tenant secures an alterations covenant that is too flexible, in that it gives the tenant extensive freedom to alter and improve the premises as it sees fit, the rental value of the letting may be increased at review as a result. On the other hand, if the landlord secures a very restrictive covenant, it may be penalised at review.

22.3   RESTRICTIONS OUTSIDE THE LEASE

As with user covenants, there are external restraints, outside the scope of the lease, which may prevent the tenant from altering the premises, or may at least regulate the way in which they are carried out. For example:

(a)   *Planning legislation*

Any alterations falling within the definition of 'development' within s 55 of the TCPA 1990 will require planning permission.

(b)   *The Building Regulations*

Works to be carried out by the tenant may have to comply with the Building Regulations.

(c)   *Covenants affecting a superior title.*

The tenant's proposed works may be prohibited by the terms of a covenant affecting the landlord's reversion (which may either be the freehold title, or a leasehold title if the landlord is itself a tenant), or may require the consent of the current beneficiary of the covenant.

(d)   *The common law*

The tenant will have to ensure that any works it carries out at the premises do not give rise to a cause of action in the tort of nuisance. The tenant will also have to ensure that it will not, in executing its works, infringe an easement benefiting an adjoining property (eg, a right to light or air over the tenant's premises).

(e)   *Fire legislation*

The tenant will have to bear in mind any requirements of the fire authority in regard to fire safety.

(f)   *Environmental legislation*

If the tenant's works are more than just minor works, the tenant must have regard to environmental legislation regarding noise and other kinds of pollution.

(g)   *Equality Act 2010*

Where reasonable, a landlord may have to waive or modify an absolute prohibition on alterations to allow the tenant to carry out 'reasonable adjustments' so that a disabled person is not put at a substantial disadvantage in the building under the Equality Act 2010. Such alterations, however, would still be subject to the landlord's consent which may be reasonably withheld, which will depend on the circumstances in question.

The landlord may 'have to carry out' reasonable adjustments in respect of any common parts. It is likely to want to pass on any costs incurred to its tenants through the service charge. The landlord will need to ensure that the service charge provision allows for this.

On rent review the tenant will be concerned to ensure that any works it carries out to comply with statute, including those pursuant to the 2010 Act, are disregarded (see **18.6.3**).

22.4 COMPENSATION FOR IMPROVEMENTS

Under Pt I of the LTA 1927 (as amended by Pt III of the LTA 1954), the tenant may claim compensation for improvements which at the end of the term 'add to the letting value of the holding'. The concept is fair in that the tenant will be returning to the landlord an asset that has increased in value as a result of the tenant's expenditure.

In addition, the LTA 1927 provides a mechanism whereby the tenant may obtain permission for improvements it would like to carry out to the premises even in the face of an absolute covenant.

In order to be entitled to compensation on quitting, the tenant must have obtained prior authorisation from the landlord to make the improvements by using a statutory procedure, and it must claim within the statutory time limits. It does not matter that the covenant in the lease is absolute, or is qualified and the landlord has reasonable grounds to withhold consent.

The amount of compensation payable to the tenant is a sum deemed to be either the additional value of the premises directly resulting from the improvements, or the reasonable cost (as at the date of termination of the tenancy) of carrying out the improvement.

Although the parties cannot contract out of the provisions relating to compensation for improvements, it is a procedure that is rarely relevant in practice given that most leases will contain a requirement to reinstate.

22.5 THE 2007 CODE FOR LEASING BUSINESS PREMISES

The 2007 Code provides:

8   Alterations and Changes of Use

Landlords' control over alterations and changes of use should not be more restrictive than is necessary to protect the value, at the time of the application, of the premises and any adjoining or neighbouring premises of the landlord.

Internal non-structural alterations should be notified to landlords but should not need landlords' consent unless they could affect the services or systems in the building.

Landlords should not require tenants to remove permitted alterations and make good at the end of the lease, unless reasonable to do so. Landlords should notify tenants of their requirements at least six months before the termination date.

REVIEW ACTIVITY

1.   You are acting for a landlord of a multi-let office block. You have received a letter from a tenant's solicitor stating that the tenant wishes to carry out works. The tenant has a lease of the first floor of the office block (with six years left to run). The lease is in the form set out in **Appendix 4** (assume all bracketed wording in clause 28 has been incorporated). The proposed works are:

      (a)   to fix an aerial to the exterior of the Building (ie the office block);

      (b)   to erect internal partitioning; and

      (c)   to drill holes in an internal structural wall of the Property (ie that part of the Building demised to the tenant and defined in the lease) in order to hang the modern art collection of the tenant.

      Advise the landlord whether the tenant is entitled to carry out the proposed works.

2.   Consider the lease in the form set out in **Appendix 4** (assume all bracketed wording has been incorporated) and advise how it is compliant with the 2007 Code.

Answers to this Review activity may be found in Appendix 1.

CHAPTER 23

THE LANDLORD'S COVENANT FOR QUIET ENJOYMENT

23.1	Nature of the covenant	237
23.2	Negotiating the covenant	237
23.3	Acts constituting a breach	238
	Review activity	238

23.1 NATURE OF THE COVENANT

The landlord is under an *implied* obligation to give the tenant 'quiet enjoyment' of the premises. This means that the landlord must ensure that there is no interference with the tenant's use and enjoyment of the premises. However, most leases will contain an *express* covenant for quiet enjoyment by the landlord. The inclusion of an express covenant makes the obligation clearer to the parties (who may not know about the implied covenant) and helps to establish the status of the arrangement as a lease rather than a licence. It also gives each party the opportunity to modify the implied covenant in its favour.

23.2 NEGOTIATING THE COVENANT

This example of an express covenant appears in the lease set out in **Appendix 4**:

> The Landlord covenants with the Tenant that, so long as the Tenant pays the rents reserved by and complies with its obligations in this lease, the Tenant shall have quiet enjoyment of the Property without any interruption by the Landlord or any person claiming under the Landlord except as otherwise permitted by this lease.

The tenant will want to extend the protection of the covenant by making the following amendments:

> The Landlord covenants with the Tenant that, ~~so long as the Tenant pays the rents reserved by and complies with its obligations in this lease~~, the Tenant shall have quiet enjoyment of the Property without any interruption by the Landlord or any person claiming under the Landlord <u>or by any person with title paramount</u> except as otherwise permitted by this lease.

The tenant will argue that there are more appropriate ways to deal with breaches of the tenant's covenants in the lease (including forfeiture) than disturbing the tenant's quiet enjoyment, particularly where there is a dispute as to whether a breach has actually taken place. The tenant will also want to extend the protection offered by the covenant to include the acts of those with a superior title.

The landlord will want to resist these amendments. It is reasonable to expect the tenant to comply with its covenants and it would be dangerous to take on liability for a superior landlord over which it has no control. Even if the inserted words do not appear, the landlord should check the definition of 'landlord' in the lease to see that it does not include superior landlords.

The landlord may also prefer not to take on liability for the actions of those claiming under it:

The Landlord covenants with the Tenant that, so long as the Tenant pays the rents reserved by and complies with its obligations in this lease, the Tenant shall have quiet enjoyment of the Property without any interruption by the Landlord ~~or any person claiming under the Landlord~~ except as otherwise permitted by this lease.

The tenant will argue that the landlord should take responsibility for its employees, agents and tenants as it has some control over them. Moreover, the covenant only extends to the *lawful* acts of those claiming under the landlord since, if they are *unlawful* (eg trespass), the tenant will have its own remedies against the person committing the act. This means that there is no breach of the covenant in the event of an interruption by an adjoining tenant which is unauthorised by the landlord.

23.3 ACTS CONSTITUTING A BREACH

The covenant will provide the tenant with a remedy in the case of unlawful eviction or where there is substantial interference with the tenant's use or enjoyment of the demised premises. While this is a question of fact in each case, the following situations have given rise to a breach:

(a)   Where the landlord erected scaffolding on the pavement in front of a shop which blocked the access to the shop (*Owen v Gadd* [1956] 2 QB 99). This illustrates that it is not necessary for there to be any physical intrusion into the demised premises provided that there is physical interference with the enjoyment of the premises.

(b)   Where the demised premises were flooded due to the landlord's failure to repair a culvert on his adjoining land (*Booth v Thomas* [1926] Ch 397).

(c)   Where the landlord carried out work to the building in a manner which caused prolonged and substantial interference to the tenant by reason of 'dust, noise, dirt ... deterioration of common parts ... general inconvenience ... and water penetration' (see *Mira v Aylmer Square Investments Ltd* [1990] 1 EGLR 45). If the landlord is under an obligation to repair the premises, it must take all reasonable precautions to prevent disturbance (*Goldmile Properties Ltd v Lechouritis* [2003] EWCA Civ 49, [2003] 15 EG 143).

It used to be thought that the word 'quiet' in the covenant did not refer to the absence of noise and that some direct and physical interference was required before the landlord incurred liability under it. However, in the case of *Southwark London Borough Council v Mills and Others; Baxter v Camden London Borough Council* [1999] 3 WLR 939, the House of Lords held that no such limitation exists. The fact that the tenant was complaining of noise from adjoining premises in the block due to poor sound insulation did not in itself preclude a claim for breach of the covenant for quiet enjoyment. However, it was also held that the covenant applies only to the subject matter of the lease at the date of the grant. If, at that date, the premises already suffer from poor soundproofing qualities, the covenant is one not to interfere with the tenant's use or enjoyment of premises with that feature.

The covenant for quiet enjoyment is closely linked with the landlord's implied obligation not to derogate from its grant. This requires a landlord not to do anything which substantially interferes with the use of the demised premises for the purpose for which they were let. (See **29.2.2.2.**)

> ## REVIEW ACTIVITY
>
> 1.   You act for a tenant under a lease containing an express covenant for quiet enjoyment. The landlord wants to enter the premises and carry out an environmental investigation that involves drilling boreholes and taking samples from under the ground. The landlord says that it is entitled to do this as the lease contains a right for the landlord to enter for the purpose of making a survey. Your client has refused the landlord entry to

drill boreholes and take samples. If the landlord does so, will your client have a remedy for breach of the covenant of quiet enjoyment?

2.   You act for a landlord who has recently carried out repairs to the outside of the building pursuant to its repairing covenant under the lease. Although your client took all *reasonable* steps to minimise the disruption and loss of profit caused to the tenant's restaurant business, the tenant is suing for damages for breach of the express covenant of quiet enjoyment because your client did not take all *possible* steps to minimise disruption and loss of profit. Will the tenant have a remedy for breach of the covenant of quiet enjoyment?

Answers to this Review activity may be found in Appendix 1.

CHAPTER 24

INSURANCE

24.1	Introduction	241
24.2	The obligation to insure	242
24.3	The obligation to pay for the insurance	244
24.4	Compliance with the terms of the insurance	245
24.5	The obligation to reinstate	245
24.6	Rent suspension	247
24.7	Termination	248
24.8	Damage by uninsured risks	249
24.9	Additional provisions	250
24.10	Insurance by the tenant	250
	Review activity	250

24.1 INTRODUCTION

There is no implied obligation on either party to insure the premises demised by the lease. However, it is very important to both parties and their lenders that their respective interests are fully protected, and it is therefore essential for the lease to make express provision for insurance.

There are a number of important issues which will need to be addressed by the draftsman. These include not only imposing an obligation to insure, but also specifying what will happen if damage does occur: Who will reinstate? Will the tenant continue to pay rent? Should the lease be terminated? As with any lease negotiation, there will be some areas that prove contentious between the parties. This chapter highlights some of those areas and identifies issues of which the parties should be particularly aware. The 2007 Code for Leasing Business Premises ('the 2007 Code') also contains recommendations as to how some of these difficult issues should be dealt with. It provides as follows:

9 Insurance

Where landlords are insuring the landlord's property, the insurance policy terms should be fair and reasonable and represent value for money, and be placed with reputable insurers.

Landlords must always disclose any commission they are receiving and must provide full insurance details on request.

Rent suspension should apply if the premises are damaged by an insured risk or uninsured risk, other than where caused by a deliberate act of the tenant. If rent suspension is limited to the period for which loss of rent is insured, leases should allow landlords or tenants to terminate their leases if reinstatement is not completed within that period.

Landlords should provide appropriate terrorism cover if practicable to do so.

If the whole of the premises are damaged by an uninsured risk as to prevent occupation, tenants should be allowed to terminate their leases unless landlords agree to rebuild at their own cost.

Unless specifically drafted to be compliant with the 2007 Code, many leases will not contain such obligations, and the tenant will have to amend the lease if it wishes the landlord to be bound by such obligations. For an example of a lease that complies with the 2007 Code, see **Appendix 4** to this book.

24.2   THE OBLIGATION TO INSURE

24.2.1   Who is to insure?

In a lease of commercial premises, it is common practice for the landlord to take out the insurance cover. On a lease of part of a building (eg one unit in a shopping centre, or a suite of offices in a block) it is more appropriate for the landlord to arrange insurance for the whole building, including any car parks, pedestrian areas, etc, as in this way only one policy is needed. Further, all the common parts of the building will be covered under the same policy and there is no danger of any parts of the building being left uninsured. On the grant of a lease of the whole of a building, either party could be made to insure, but the landlord will usually wish to assume the responsibility rather than face the risk of the tenant failing to comply with its covenant to insure. While the landlord would be able to sue the tenant for breach of covenant, the tenant may have insufficient funds to satisfy the judgment.

If the landlord takes out the insurance before completion of the lease, the tenant should ask to see a copy of the policy so that it can satisfy itself as to the amount and terms of cover. As the tenant has a continuing interest in the insurance of the premises, it should also impose an obligation on the landlord in the lease to produce evidence of the terms of the policy and of payment of the premiums, at any time during the term of the lease.

24.2.2   What is to be insured?

On the grant of a lease of the whole of a building, it is quite clear that the insurance and reinstatement obligations will need to apply to the whole of that building.

On the grant of a lease of part, the insurance and reinstatement obligations should also apply to the whole of the building of which the premises form part. The building will often provide access or contain services essential to useful occupation of the premises. Even if it does not, most tenants would consider it undesirable to occupy premises in a damaged building, even if their premises were undamaged.

In the case of either a lease of whole or a lease of part, if the building is on an estate or business park owned by the landlord, the tenant should check that the insurance and reinstatement obligations apply to any other essential common parts. It would clearly be unacceptable to the tenant if, for example, the building it occupied were reinstated but the estate roads needed to access that building were not.

24.2.3   In whose name?

Where the landlord is to insure, the tenant should consider amending the lease to require the insurance to be effected in the joint names of the landlord and tenant. This will be to the tenant's advantage because the insurance company will not allow the policy to lapse unless both parties have been given notice. It will also ensure that the proceeds of the policy will be paid out to both parties jointly, and thus give the tenant some control over how they are spent.

Another advantage to the tenant is that insurance in joint names may prevent subrogation. This is the right of the insurer to step into the shoes of the insured and pursue any claims that the insured has against third parties to recover the loss. This means that, where the tenant is not named on the policy, if the landlord had a cause of action against the tenant arising out of some default on the tenant's part which caused the damage, the insurers would be able to pursue that claim. If, however, the insurance is in the joint names of the landlord and tenant, subrogation may not be possible, depending on the intentions of the parties (see the judgment of Rix LJ in *Tyco Fire & Integrated Solutions (UK) Ltd v Rolls Royce Motor Cars Ltd* [2008] EWCA Civ 286).

However, even in those cases where the insurance is in the landlord's name alone, the tenant may still be able to prevent subrogation occurring where it can be shown that the insurance has been taken out for the mutual benefit of both parties (eg see *Mark Rowlands Ltd v Berni Inns*

Ltd [1986] 1 QB 211, where the tenant agreed to reimburse the landlord the premiums paid; see also *Lambert v Keymood Ltd* [1997] 43 EG 131).

Whether the landlord agrees to the insurance being in joint names depends to a large extent on the nature of the tenant's interest in the premises. If the tenant occupies only part of the property that is insured, the landlord should not agree to the insurance being in joint names. It would be impractical to have more than one tenant named as a joint insured, and in any event, the landlord will be reluctant to share control of the insurance monies with a tenant who does not occupy the whole of the insured property. Institutional landlords will often have block insurance policies under which their whole portfolio of properties is insured. In those circumstances joint insurance will not be possible.

If, however, the tenant occupies the whole of the insured property and it is not insured under a block policy, in theory there is nothing to stop the insurance being in joint names. However, the landlord will be conscious of the fact that it has the more valuable interest in the premises and that it has the obligation to reinstate. It may therefore still be reluctant to agree to joint insurance.

If the landlord objects to insurance in joint names, the tenant should ensure that the lease provides that its interest will be 'noted' on the landlord's policy. This will mean the tenant will be notified of any claim or of any event that might invalidate the insurance. It might also be possible for the landlord to obtain a non-subrogation clause for the benefit of the tenant in the insurance policy.

24.2.4 Risks and losses covered

The lease should contain a comprehensive definition of the risks against which the insured party is to insure. A definition of 'insured risks' will typically include fire, lightning, explosion, impact, storm, tempest, flood, overflowing and bursting of water tanks or pipes, riot, civil commotion and many other risks commonly included in a buildings insurance policy. To give the landlord flexibility, at the end of the definition there should be a 'sweeping-up' provision along the lines of 'and such other risks as the landlord may from time to time reasonably consider to be necessary'.

It is important that the tenant carefully checks the definition of insured risks. If a risk is not insured against, the cost of any damage caused by it will usually be borne by the tenant, either under the repairing obligation or through the service charge provisions. The tenant must therefore make sure that the definition of insured risks includes all risks normally covered by a comprehensive buildings insurance policy. It should look out for any provisions allowing the landlord to vary the list of insured risks or be relieved from the obligation to insure against them.

24.2.4.1 Terrorism

Consideration also needs to be given to the issue of insurance cover against terrorist acts. The 2007 Code provides that 'the landlord should provide appropriate terrorism cover if practicable to do so'. However, such cover is no longer provided automatically by all insurers of commercial properties following a series of terrorist incidents in London in the early 1990s linked to the troubles in Northern Ireland. Cover can still be obtained, however, through a Government-backed scheme called Pool Re. This was set up in 1993 in response to the withdrawal of terrorist cover by the insurance industry.

The landlord and the tenant must therefore decide whether they think cover against terrorism is necessary. This will depend on the location of the property and the nature of the occupier and its business. It will also, of course, depend on the cost of obtaining such insurance. If it is required, it should be referred to in the list of insured risks. If it is not specified, an obligation to insure against 'explosion' may be sufficient to cover it (as it was in *Qdime Ltd v various leaseholders at Bath Building (Swindon)* [2014] UKUT 0261 (LC)), but this is uncertain. If there is no requirement to insure against terrorism, any damage caused in consequence of it would then be an uninsured loss. Both parties to the lease need to be aware of who is responsible for such uninsured loss (see **24.8**).

24.2.4.2   Flood

Certain properties are at a greater risk of flooding than others, and there has recently been a significant increase in extreme flood events in the UK. Concern exists that those properties in areas with a high flood risk may become either uninsurable for flood damage or insurable only at great cost. At present, the insurance industry has an arrangement with the Government which means that flood insurance is available for most homes and small businesses even where there is a high flood risk. Whilst this arrangement formally expired in June 2013, the insurance industry has agreed to continue abiding by it until a new arrangement can be formalised. The new arrangement (anticipated to become effective in June 2015) will see the development of a not-for-profit fund – known as Flood Re – to ensure that flood insurance remains affordable and available to homeowners at high flood risk. However, this fund will not be available for certain types of property, including commercial property, nor will it be available to the owners of blocks of flats and buy to let property. These types of property will be subject to premiums based on their individual risk of flooding.

If the tenant occupies premises at high risk of flood, it should therefore be advised to consider the risk that insurance premiums (which it will normally pay for via the insurance rent) may become very high at some point during the lease term. If the risk is such that, at some point, insurance for flooding cannot be obtained at all, any damage caused as a result of flooding would constitute uninsured loss (see **24.8**). As with terrorism, the parties must be advised as to how such uninsured loss is dealt with.

24.2.4.3   Loss of rent

Most leases will also allow the landlord to insure against loss of rent for a specified period, usually three or five years. The landlord will wish to carry such insurance, as in most leases the tenant's obligation to pay rent will be suspended if the premises cannot be occupied due to damage caused by insured risks (see **24.6**).

24.2.5   The sum insured

The tenant should ensure the landlord is obliged to insure the premises for their full reinstatement value. This will mean the landlord will have adequate funds to replace the building should it be totally destroyed. Care must be taken to ensure that site-clearance costs, professional fees, and fees for any necessary planning applications and any VAT are also covered. As to the actual amount of cover, specialist advice will be needed and the insuring party should consult experienced insurance brokers. The tenant, if it has obtained a covenant from the landlord to insure for the full reinstatement value, will have a claim for breach of covenant if the policy proceeds are inadequate due to the landlord underinsuring. A successful claim would mean the landlord would have to make up any shortfall from its own resources.

24.3   THE OBLIGATION TO PAY FOR THE INSURANCE

Where the landlord has insured the premises, there will be a covenant in the lease requiring the tenant to reimburse the cost of insurance to the landlord. This sum is likely to be reserved as rent in order to give the landlord better remedies for recovery. If the premises are part of a larger building which the landlord has insured, recovery can either be through the service charge provisions or, alternatively, there may be a separate covenant by the tenant to reimburse an apportioned part of the premium. The tenant must ensure that the apportionment of the premium between the tenants is fair, particularly if the business of some of the tenants involves hazardous activities which lead to an increase in the premium.

It should be noted that a covenant by the tenant to reimburse premiums that the landlord 'shall from time to time properly expend' does not impose an obligation on the landlord to shop around for a reasonable level of premium (see *Havenridge Ltd v Boston Dyers Ltd* [1994] 49 EG 111). The 2007 Code does provide that 'the insurance policy terms should be fair and reasonable and represent value for money' (see **24.1**). However, for this to bind it must be specifically provided for in the lease.

In addition to reimbursement of the buildings insurance, the landlord will usually also require the tenant to reimburse it for the cost of insuring against loss of rent. This will protect the landlord if the rent payments by the tenant are suspended (see **24.6**).

24.4 COMPLIANCE WITH THE TERMS OF THE INSURANCE

Anyone who has ever read an insurance policy will know there are usually various requirements that need to be complied with for the insurance to be effective. Most leases will require that the tenant complies with these requirements. This is another reason for the tenant to ensure that the lease requires the landlord to supply a copy of the insurance policy. Further, the lease will often provide that the tenant must not invalidate the policy. A failure to comply with, for example, a requirement to service a security alarm, may lead to a policy being invalidated in the event of theft from the premises. In these circumstances, the tenant would then be left to bear the loss.

Being entitled to sight of the policy obviously means that the tenant has the information to enable it to comply with its requirements. However, what if the tenant is unhappy with the requirements or terms of the policy? In an ideal world, the tenant would ensure that the lease stipulated that the terms of the insurance policy were subject to its approval. This qualification may be possible where the tenant is a tenant of whole. However, a landlord will resist such a provision where the tenant occupies part only, as seeking approval of more than one tenant to the terms of a policy becomes administratively cumbersome, if not impractical, in the event of disagreement between the tenants. Nonetheless, even a tenant of part should seek to ensure that it is obliged to comply only with the reasonable requirements of the insurer of which it has received written notice. It should also ensure that the landlord is obliged to place the insurance with a reputable and substantial insurer. This will minimise the risk of unusual terms and conditions. The 2007 Code does provide that the insurance should 'be placed with reputable insurers' (see **24.1**).

The tenant should also be wary of any excess payable under the insurance policy. The terms of the lease may require the tenant to bear the cost of such excess. This could be quite an onerous liability if the landlord accepts a large excess in return for a lower premium. The tenant should resist such a requirement, or restrict it to reasonable excesses of the kind usually imposed by insurers.

If the tenant sells combustible or flammable goods (eg lighter fuel, fireworks), it should be aware of any restriction on the storage of such items in the lease and insurance policy, and qualify such provisions accordingly.

24.5 THE OBLIGATION TO REINSTATE

If the premises are damaged or destroyed, the lease should contain provisions dealing with who will be liable for their repair and reinstatement.

24.5.1 Will the tenant's repairing covenant apply?

Since the tenant will be paying for the insurance taken out by the landlord, it should ensure that it is not obliged to repair the premises if they are damaged by one of the insured risks. It is common practice to exclude from the tenant's repairing covenant liability for damage caused by an insured risk. However, this exclusion will not usually apply if the insurance policy has been invalidated, or the insurance proceeds are not fully paid out by reason of the act or omission of the tenant (or some other person who was at the premises with the tenant's authority). The landlord may also attempt to stipulate that the exclusion will not apply to damage caused by insured risks for which it has not been able to obtain insurance on reasonable terms. The tenant should be wary of this exclusion as it passes the responsibility for uninsured losses to the tenant (see **24.8**).

24.5.2   Who will reinstate?

If the insurance is in the joint names of landlord and tenant, the proceeds of the policy will be paid to both of the insureds, who have equal control over the application of the proceeds and therefore the reinstatement of the premises. However, where the policy is in the sole name of the landlord, unless the lease provides to the contrary, there is no obligation on the landlord to use the proceeds of the policy to reinstate the premises. In those cases where the tenant is under an obligation to pay the cost of the insurance, it has been held that the landlord may be presumed to have insured on behalf of the tenant as well as itself, and thus the tenant can require the proceeds to be laid out on reinstatement (*Mumford Hotels Ltd v Wheler and Another* [1964] Ch 117).

Nonetheless, in any event, it is good practice for the lease to contain an express obligation on the party obliged to insure, to apply the proceeds of insurance in reinstating the premises. This will usually be the landlord. The landlord should make it clear that any insurance money in respect of loss of rent is not to be applied in the reinstatement of the premises, as this is to compensate it for the loss of the tenant's rent when the rent suspension clause is operating (see **24.6**).

From the tenant's point of view, it should pay particular attention to the wording of the covenant, which is often an obligation just to lay out the insurance monies received in respect of damage to the premises in their reinstatement. There are two potential issues with this. First, such an obligation does not deal with the situation where the insurance proceeds are insufficient to cover the entire cost of reinstatement. Although the landlord might be in breach of covenant for underinsuring the premises, the tenant should nevertheless press for a covenant by the landlord to make up the difference. The second potential issue with a simple obligation to lay out the insurance monies in reinstating the premises is that it does not deal with the situation where the landlord delays (or indeed fails altogether) to make a claim on the insurance. The tenant should insert an obligation to make such a claim promptly.

An alternative way around both of these issues is to impose on the landlord an absolute covenant to reinstate (unconnected to and regardless of any insurance pay out). Where this latter form of covenant is chosen, the landlord should qualify the absolute nature of its obligation to reinstate by providing that it is not liable in the event that the policy is invalidated, or where the proceeds are irrecoverable by reason of the act or omission of the tenant (or anyone at the premises with the tenant's consent). If the landlord accepts an obligation to make up any shortfall in the proceeds of the insurance then, again, this obligation should exclude any shortfall arising from the act or omission of the tenant (or anyone at the premises with the tenant's consent).

In any event, the landlord would not want to be liable to reinstate the premises for so long as circumstances beyond the landlord's control contrive to prevent it from doing so (eg strikes, lock-outs, shortages of materials, a failure to obtain planning).

The tenant should look out for any provision allowing the landlord to vary the premises on reinstatement. Whilst it is useful for the landlord to have flexibility to reflect changes in building practices, the tenant does not want reinstated premises that are unsuitable for its needs. Any such provision should therefore be amended to require the landlord, as a minimum, to provide premises that are of a similar size and no less suitable for the tenant than the original premises. The tenant should also consider requesting a landlord's covenant to provide collateral warranties (see **9.5.1**) in the event the premises require a complete rebuild.

24.6 RENT SUSPENSION

24.6.1 What is rent suspension?

Unless the lease is frustrated, rent continues to be payable by the tenant where the premises are damaged, even if the damage is extensive. It is therefore common to include a provision in the lease that if the premises are damaged by an insured risk, and become unfit for occupation or use by the tenant, the rent (or a fair proportion of it, depending on the extent of the damage) should cease to be payable. This is often referred to by practitioners as 'rent suspension' or 'rent cesser'. The landlord does not usually lose out by including such a provision, as it will usually insure against loss of rent when it takes out buildings insurance (see **24.2.4**).

24.6.2 When will rent suspension apply?

A tenant of part of a building should ensure that the rent suspension provisions apply if any part of the building is damaged so as to render the premises unusable. For example, a tenant would not want to pay rent for undamaged premises on the fifth floor of the building if all the staircases and lifts leading to the premises were unusable. A tenant of the whole of a building should give consideration as to whether it has any essential services or rights running over any other land of the landlord. If it does, the rent should be suspended in the event that such essential services are damaged or destroyed, Provided the landlord owns and controls the land over which such services or rights run, it will not usually object to such a provision.

The lease will usually provide for suspension of rent only if the damage results from an insured risk, so that the tenant will remain liable for rent where the premises become unusable as a result of damage by uninsured risks. Again, it is therefore important that the tenant examines the defined list of insured risks to ensure that they are adequate. Otherwise, it will not benefit from rent suspension where it was expecting to, and may also be left with an unexpected repair bill (see **24.8**).

Thought will need to be given as to whether rent will be suspended when damage arises as a result of a risk that the landlord has been unable to insure against, such as terrorism. The 2007 Code envisages that rent will be suspended where such uninsured loss arises (see **24.1**). However, the landlord may be reluctant to accept this given that it is unlikely to receive loss of rent insurance where damage is caused by an uninsured risk (see **24.8**).

The landlord will want to qualify the rent suspension further by stipulating that rent continues to be payable where the landlord's insurance policy has been invalidated by the act or omission of the tenant (or someone at the premises with the tenant's consent). Without this qualification, the landlord would not receive rent or loss of rent insurance proceeds.

24.6.3 How long will rent suspension last?

The suspension will continue for such period as is specified in the lease. It is usual for the rent to become payable as soon as the premises have been reinstated and are again fit for use and occupation, for the purpose permitted by the lease. It should be noted that there is a subtle difference between premises being fit for occupation *and* use, and the premises being fit for occupation *or* use. The tenant should ensure that the premises have to be fit for occupation *and* use, as premises can sometimes be occupied without being usable for the purposes of the tenant's business.

The lease will often specify a maximum period of rent suspension. This is usually the period for which the landlord has loss of rent insurance, and is therefore normally either three or five years. The problem for the tenant is that the rent suspension will end on the expiry of this three- or five-year period, even if the premises have not been fully reinstated. One way of dealing with this is to insist that there be no time limit on the rent suspension. Practitioners sometimes refer to this as an 'unlimited rent cesser'. The other method is to insert in the lease an option for the tenant to end the lease if the premises have not been reinstated by the end of the rent suspension period (see **24.7**).

24.6.4   Will other payments be suspended?

The tenant should also press for a similar suspension in respect of other payments under the lease, such as the service charge and insurance rent. If the premises are damaged and the tenant is unable to occupy them, it will not be able to take advantage of the services provided by the landlord. In addition, it will probably have to relocate while the premises are reinstated, and will have to pay service charge and insurance rent for the alternative premises.

The landlord may try to argue against suspension of these additional sums. If damage is occasioned to the tenant's premises alone, this is not likely to reduce significantly the level of services provided to the rest of the tenants. The landlord may therefore argue that it is not prepared to suffer any reduction in the amount of service charge income. It will also have to continue to insure the premises, even while the tenant is not in occupation.

One way forward may be for the landlord to insure against loss of service charge in the same way as it insures against loss of rent. Some policies do cover loss of service charge as well as loss of rent. This may extend to insurance rent, depending on the wording of the policy. Much will depend on the bargaining strength of the tenant and the landlord's willingness to be dictated to on the terms of its insurance policy. Institutional landlords in particular will resist the suspension of these sums if their loss is not insured, as they generally require FRI (full repairing and insuring) leases with clear rents. A tenant who has business interruption insurance cover may be able to recover the increased costs arising from operating alternative premises, depending on the wording of its policy.

24.7   TERMINATION

Although the doctrine of frustration is capable of applying to leases (*National Carriers Ltd v Panalpina (Northern) Ltd* [1981] AC 675), it will do so only in exceptional circumstances. Accordingly, unless the doctrine applies, the lease will continue notwithstanding any accidental damage to the premises, and the loss will fall on the party obliged to repair. As a result, the lease will need to specify the circumstances (if any) in which the lease can be terminated following damage or destruction.

24.7.1   By the tenant

If the premises are damaged or destroyed by an insured risk so as to be unfit for occupation or use, the tenant will be faced with the possibility of relocating its business during the reinstatement period. Ideally, in such circumstances, the tenant would be able to end the lease of the damaged premises, leaving it free to take up a lease of new premises on a permanent basis. To do this the tenant would need a break clause in the lease of the damaged premises operable in these circumstances.

If the landlord agreed to this, however, it would be left with no tenant and potentially no loss of rent insurance (because once the lease is gone, no rent is contractually payable on it). For these reasons the landlord will usually require the tenant to reoccupy the premises once they have been reinstated. The problem for the tenant is it does not know how long such reinstatement might take.

Most landlords will not accept an obligation to reinstate within any particular timescale, as there are too many factors that may cause delay. Planning permission may prove difficult to obtain, there maybe historic contamination that has to be dealt with of which the parties were unaware when the site was originally developed, or there may be delays in the building programme caused by weather or shortage of materials or labour. Rather than have complex clauses in the lease to deal with these possibilities, the parties often agree that the landlord will reinstate the premises as soon as reasonably practicable. This creates a lack of certainty for the tenant, who does not know how long it will be left operating out of temporary premises.

On possible solution is for the tenant to have an option to end the lease in the event that the premises have not been reinstated within a particular time period. This time period is usually identical to the loss of rent insurance period. The option to end the lease then deals with two possible problems – the lack of a time-specific reinstatement obligation and a limited rent suspension.

24.7.2 By the landlord

For the reasons explored above, the landlord will not usually want the lease to be terminated where damage or destruction by an insured risk occurs. However, if reinstatement proves impossible (eg because planning permission cannot be obtained), the landlord will need the ability to end the lease and its reinstatement obligations. The landlord will usually insert into the lease a provision allowing it to terminate the lease in these circumstances.

The landlord should always bear in mind that the tenancy may be protected by Part II of the LTA 1954, and consequently the lease would need to be terminated in accordance with the provisions of that Act (see **Chapter 31**).

24.7.3 Who retains the insurance monies?

If reinstatement is not possible (or the parties do not desire it), in the absence of an express provision in the lease it is unclear to whom the insurance proceeds will belong, and it will be left to the court to ascertain the intention of the parties by looking at the lease as a whole.

For this reason the lease will often provide that following termination in the circumstances discussed above, the landlord will retain the insurance monies. The tenant may consider this unfair – after all, it is usually the tenant who will have reimbursed the landlord for the insurance premium. The tenant should try to insert a provision that the insurance monies will be shared between the landlord and tenant according to the values of their respective interests in the premises. The tenant would need to be aware that this may result in its receiving nothing, as a lease where an open market rent is paid on a quarterly basis often has no capital value. The landlord may also resist the amendment using this argument. Further, if reinstatement still remains a possibility, payment of a portion of the insurance monies to the tenant will leave the landlord with a reduced fund from which to reinstate.

24.8 DAMAGE BY UNINSURED RISKS

Historically, the risk of damage caused by an uninsured risk has been carried by the tenant. The landlord would not be obliged to reinstate the property, there would be no rent suspension and the terms of the tenant's repairing covenant would probably be wide enough to require it to carry out the necessary remedial work.

However, in recent years tenants have become more aware of the potential financial consequences of accepting such provisions. Should, for example, terrorism cover become unavailable for a particular type of property, a tenant who accepted the responsibility for uninsured losses would find itself in an unenviable position if its premises were destroyed by a terrorist act. Despite the fact that it might have a short-term lease with little time left to run, it could be left paying the cost of rebuilding the premises while continuing to pay rent on it.

Lawyers for both landlords and tenants now tend to be more attuned to the issue of uninsured losses. The problem is, of course, that the risk has to be borne by one party or the other for such losses, despite no one being at fault for the loss having arisen.

Given that it is the landlord who has the long-term capital interest in the premises, the view might be taken that the landlord is the more appropriate party to bear the risk of such losses. Whilst an institutional landlord in particular may be resistant to this, the 2007 Code does take this line. Indeed, para 9 of the 2007 Code contains a number of recommendations in respect of uninsured risks, namely:

> If the whole of the premises are damaged by an uninsured risk so as to prevent occupation, tenants should be allowed to terminate their leases unless landlords agree to rebuild at their own cost.
>
> Landlords should provide appropriate terrorism cover if practicable to do so.
>
> Rent suspension should apply if the premises are damaged by an uninsured risk other than where caused by a deliberate act of the tenant.

24.9 ADDITIONAL PROVISIONS

Certain other covenants on the part of the tenant are commonly included in relation to the insurance of the premises:

(a)   to pay any increased or additional premiums that become payable by reason of the tenant's activities at the premises;

(b)   to pay the cost of annual valuations for insurance purposes (which the tenant should specify must be reasonable and proper);

(c)   to insure and reinstate any plate glass at the premises. Some retail tenants prefer to pay the cost of plate glass replacement themselves rather than insure against it. If this is the case, a requirement in the lease to insure plate glass will need to be amended so that it does not apply to the tenant in question.

24.10 INSURANCE BY THE TENANT

If, exceptionally, the tenant covenants to insure the premises, the landlord must make sure that its interest as landlord is fully protected. The landlord will have concerns similar to those expressed above on behalf of the tenant, and so will wish to ensure:

(a)   that insurance is taken out in the joint names of the landlord and tenant, with insurers to be approved by the landlord;

(b)   that the insurance is taken out on terms to be approved by the landlord (eg as to the basis of cover, the risks insured, the amount and any excesses);

(c)   that in the event of damage or destruction, the tenant covenants to reinstate the premises.

There will not usually be a rent suspension clause if the tenant assumes the insuring obligation.

REVIEW ACTIVITY

Imagine your client has taken a lease of two upper floors of an office building in the form set out in **Appendix 4**. The ground-floor reception area of the Building is seriously damaged by a flood. There is an excess on the landlord's insurance policy of £5,000. Read clause 9 of the lease at **Appendix 4** and answer the following questions:

1.   Will your client be obliged to pay rent and other sums whilst the reception area is repaired?

2.   Who will have to bear the cost of the excess?

3.   What will happen if the reception area has not been reinstated after three years?

Answers to this Review activity may be found in Appendix 1.

CHAPTER 25

FORFEITURE

25.1	Introduction	251
25.2	Express reservation of the right	251
25.3	Waiver of the right to forfeit	252
25.4	Strict procedural rules and relief against forfeiture	252
25.5	Additional rules in special cases	255
25.6	Position of sub-tenants and mortgagees on forfeiture	257
25.7	The 2007 Code for Leasing Business Premises	257
	Review activity	257

25.1 INTRODUCTION

Forfeiture is the right of the landlord to retake possession of the premises and so prematurely end the lease on the happening of certain specified events. Forfeiture is primarily a remedy rather than a method of termination (for which see **Chapter 30**) albeit that the result of a successful forfeiture will be the termination of the lease.

A landlord should think carefully before it proceeds to forfeit the lease. In a rising market the landlord should have no difficulty in subsequently re-letting the premises, possibly at a higher rent. However, in a falling market, re-letting the premises may not be so easy and the landlord may be left with an empty property on its hands for a long time, leading to a loss of income and a potential detrimental effect on any adjoining property of the landlord (eg, other shops in a parade or shopping mall).

The right is enforced in one of two ways: by court order or peaceable re-entry. Landlords are sometimes reluctant to adopt peaceable re-entry because it is an offence to use or threaten violence (Criminal Law Act 1977, s 6) to achieve re-entry where the landlord knew that there was someone on the premises opposed to the entry. In addition, it may be that peaceable re-entry could be the subject of a successful challenge to the ECtHR under Pt II of Sch 1 to the Human Rights Act 1998 (protection of property).

The right to forfeit is restricted in a number of ways, which are discussed below.

25.2 EXPRESS RESERVATION OF THE RIGHT

The right to forfeit is not automatic; it only exists where the lease expressly includes such a right (or where, rarely, the lease is made conditional upon the performance of the tenant's covenants or where the tenant denies the landlord's title).

The right is typically expressed as a proviso and is sometimes referred to as a 'right of re-entry'. The events commonly specified as giving rise to the right can be seen in clause 39 of the **Appendix 4** lease (briefly non-payment of rent, breach of other covenant or condition, events of insolvency).

The landlord's intention is to give itself as many opportunities as possible to forfeit the lease where the tenant is in financial difficulty. You can see from clause 39 of the **Appendix 4** lease that, in some insolvency proceedings, the landlord gives itself two attempts at forfeiting the tenant's lease (eg, once on the presentation of the petition in bankruptcy and once on the making of the bankruptcy order) in case the landlord inadvertently waives its right to forfeit on the first occasion (see below).

A tenant should resist the inclusion of some of the less serious events (eg, the mere presentation of the petition) or those insolvency events which are designed to cure insolvency (eg, administration proceedings, voluntary arrangements, liquidations for the purpose of restructuring). Further, if the tenant's lease has sufficient capital value to provide security for a loan (though this may be unlikely), the tenant should try to restrict the landlord's right to forfeit in those circumstances.

25.3 WAIVER OF THE RIGHT TO FORFEIT

Once a landlord knows of the breach (or existence of the specified event) giving rise to a right to forfeit, if it does something to recognise the continued existence of the lease, it will be deemed to have waived the right to forfeit (albeit without prejudice to its ability to pursue its other remedies).

Knowledge of the breach can be actual or imputed where the premises are managed by an agent.

Waiver can be express or implied. It is judged objectively, without regard to motive or intention. The most common way a landlord acknowledges the continued existence of the lease is by accepting or demanding rent falling due after the right to forfeit has arisen. That will amount to waiver notwithstanding a clerical error by the landlord's agent (*Central Estates (Belgravia) Ltd v Woolgar (No 2)* [1972] 1 WLR 1048), receipt of rent paid under a standing order or that the rent is demanded or received 'without prejudice to the landlord's right to forfeit' (*Segal Securities Ltd v Thoseby* [1963] 1 QB 887). However, banking of a cheque covering both payment to avoid a bankruptcy order and payment to discharge arrears of rent and then returning the sum to discharge the arrears did not amount to waiver (*Osibanjo v Seahive Investments Ltd* [2008] EWCA Civ 1282).

Other examples of conduct which have been held to amount to waiver are: suing on provisions in the lease, serving notices under the lease provisions, granting licences to assign/sublet and levying distress.

Waiver of the right to forfeit operates only in respect of past breaches of covenant. Where the landlord waives it in respect of a 'once and for all' breach (eg, breach of a covenant against sub-letting, against alterations or payment of rent for a particular rent period), the right to forfeit is lost for ever. If, however, the breach is of a continuing nature (eg, breach of a repairing covenant or user covenant), the right to forfeit, though waived on one occasion, will arise again, as the property continues to be in disrepair or used for an unauthorised purpose.

25.4 STRICT PROCEDURAL RULES AND RELIEF AGAINST FORFEITURE

Even if the landlord has a right to forfeit, it must exercise it; the lease does not end automatically on the happening of the particular event specified in the forfeiture clause. The right must be exercised in accordance with strict procedural rules, which are different for non-payment of rent than breach of any other covenant. Even where the strict procedural rules have been complied with, there is yet one further limitation on forfeiture in that the tenant may obtain relief from forfeiture.

25.4.1 Forfeiture for non-payment of rent

25.4.1.1 Procedural rules

The landlord is required to make a formal demand for the rent, but this requirement is usually negated in the lease by providing for forfeiture if the tenant is, for example, 21 days or more in arrears 'whether the rent is formally demanded or not'. The forfeiture clause in the lease should be checked to confirm the position (see the **Appendix 4** lease).

There is also no need for a formal demand if at least half a year's rent is in arrears and the goods available on the premises for recovery are insufficient to cover the arrears (Common Law Procedure Act 1852, s 210 (High Court) and County Courts Act 1984, s 139(1)).

If the rent falls into arrears, the landlord may proceed to forfeit either by court proceedings or by peaceable re-entry. See **Figure 25.1** below for a summary of the process.

Figure 25.1 Forfeiture by landlord for breach of tenant's covenant in lease: payment of rent

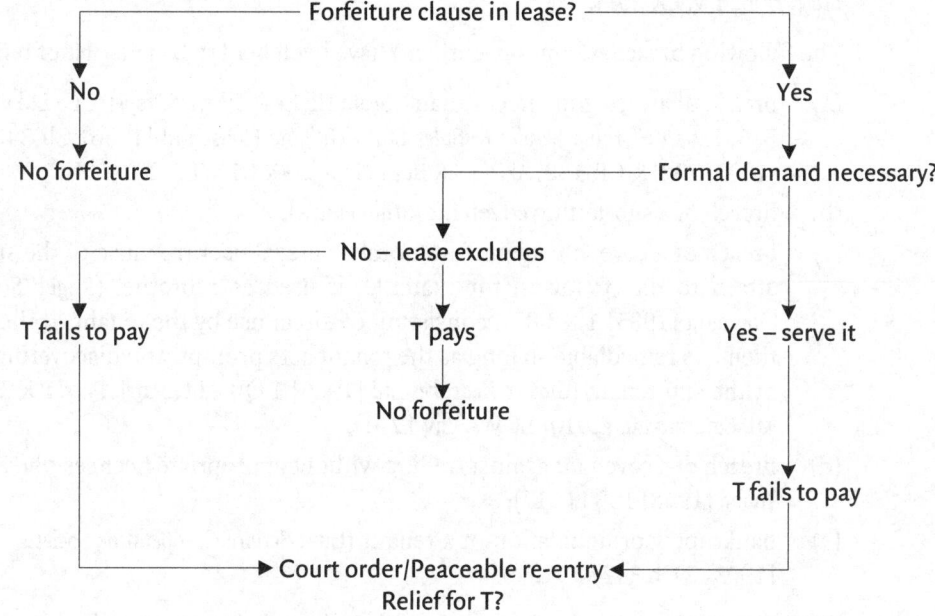

25.4.1.2 Relief from forfeiture for non-payment of rent

As **Figure 25.1** indicates, the tenant can apply to court for relief from forfeiture which, if granted, will mean that the tenant continues to hold under the existing lease.

Where the landlord is proceeding by way of court action, those proceedings will be stayed if the tenant pays all the arrears plus the landlord's costs before the hearing. In certain cases, the tenant may also apply for relief within six months from the landlord's recovery of possession, although the rules differ between the High Court and county court.

Where the landlord is proceeding by way of peaceable re-entry, the tenant may still apply to the court for relief. Again, the tenant will have to pay the arrears and must, as a general rule, apply within six months of re-entry by the landlord (although in exceptional circumstances the court may be prepared to grant relief outside this period: *Thatcher v CH Pearce & Sons (Contractors) Ltd* [1968] 1 WLR 748).

25.4.2 Forfeiture for breach of other covenants

25.4.2.1 Procedural rules

Before a landlord is able to forfeit for a breach of covenant, other than for the payment of rent, the landlord must serve a notice on the tenant under s 146 of the LPA 1925 which must:

(a) specify the breach

(b) require it to be remedied within a reasonable time, if it is capable of being remedied

If the breach is remediable, the notice must require its remedy; otherwise the notice will be invalid.

Whether a breach is remediable is a question of fact in each case. The distinction is not always easy to make, but the modern courts seem to have arrived at a test of whether the breach causes irreparable harm (described as the 'mischief' in *Savva v Hussein* (1997) 73 P & CR 150) to the landlord rather than whether the breach itself is capable of remedy. Only if the harm suffered by the landlord cannot be put right by the tenant remedying the breach and paying compensation to the landlord will a breach be considered irremediable (*Expert Clothing Service & Sales Ltd v Hillgate House Ltd* [1986] Ch 340).

The majority of breaches should be capable of remedy, and a practical rather than technical approach must be taken to the question whether a breach is remediable or not (*Akici v LR Butlin Ltd* [2006] 1 WLR 201).

The following breaches (amongst others) have been held to be *incapable* of remedy:

(a)   breach of an assignment covenant (*Scala House & District Property Co Ltd v Forbes* [1974] QB 575; *Expert Clothing Service & Sales Ltd v Hillgate House Ltd* [1986] Ch 340; *Savva v Hussein* (1997) 73 P & CR 150; *Akici v LR Butlin Ltd* [2006] 1 WLR 201);

(b)   breach of a sub-letting covenant (*Scala House*);

(c)   breach of a covenant against immoral or illegal user (because of the stigma that would attach to the premises, for example, if used as a brothel (*Rugby School (Governors) v Tannahill* [1935] 1 KB 87)) consisting of direct use by the tenant. If the use is not direct then it is remediable so long as the tenant acts promptly on discovering the relevant use by the sub-tenant (*Glass v Kencakes Ltd* [1966] 1 QB 611; *Patel, Patel v K & J Restaurants Ltd, MP Catering Ltd* [2010] ECWA Civ 1211);

(d)   breach of a covenant against trading without appropriate licences (*Bickerton's Aerodromes v Young* (1958) 108 LJ 217);

(e)   bankruptcy or liquidation of a tenant (*Civil Service Co-operative Society v McGrigor's Trustee* [1923] 2 Ch 347).

The following breaches (amongst others) have been held to be *capable* of remedy:

(a)   breach of a covenant against parting or sharing with possession, at least where it falls short of creating or transferring a legal interest (*Akici*);

(b)   breach of a covenant to reconstruct premises by a stated date – remedied by the tenant carrying out the work within a reasonable time (*Expert Clothing*);

(c)   breach of a covenant against making alterations and erecting signs – remedied by their removal (*Savva*).

If the landlord is in any doubt about whether a particular breach can be remedied, the notice should require the tenant to remedy the breach 'if it is capable of remedy'.

What is a 'reasonable' period for compliance is a question of fact in each case (*Hopley v Tarvin Parish Council* (1910) 54 JP 209). *Albany Holdings Ltd v Crown Estate Commissioners* [2003] EWHC 1480 held that a period of one month would normally be sufficient. However, where the work to remedy a breach would take longer than one month to carry out, a longer period may be necessary.

(c)   require the tenant to pay compensation for the breach, if the landlord so requires

If this is lacking, the notice is not, however, invalidated (*Lock v Pearce* [1893] 2 Ch 271).

If the tenant does not comply with the requirements of a valid s 146 notice, the landlord may proceed to forfeit the lease by court proceedings or peaceable re-entry. See **Figure 25.2** below for a summary of the process.

Figure 25.2 Forfeiture by landlord for breach of tenant's covenant in lease

25.4.2.2   Relief from forfeiture for breach of covenant (other than non-payment of rent)

As **Figure 25.2** indicates, the tenant may be able to seek relief from forfeiture. If the landlord takes court proceedings, the tenant may seek relief at any time before the landlord actually re-enters the premises; no relief can be granted afterwards. However, if the landlord re-enters peaceably, the tenant can seek relief even after the landlord has re-entered, though the court will take into account all the circumstances, including any delay by the tenant in seeking relief (*Billson v Residential Apartments Ltd* [1992] 1 AC 494).

In deciding whether or not to grant relief, each case will turn on its own facts, and the courts have refused to lay down any rigid rules on the exercise of their discretion (*Hyman v Rose* [1912] AC 623). The court will have regard to the conduct of the parties, the nature and seriousness of the breach, the value of the property and the extent of damage caused by the breach, the loss that the tenant will suffer if relief is not granted and all other relevant circumstances.

Relief is usually granted where the breach has been remedied and is unlikely to re-occur and where to grant it would not damage the landlord's interests. Clearly, the landlord should not be able to forfeit for any trivial breaches or breaches of minor covenants that would not damage the landlord's interests.

Where a breach is irremediable then the court is less likely to grant relief. In the context of immoral user causing a stigma to the premises, it is likely that relief would be refused, but there are cases where relief has been granted (eg, in *Patel* where, given the nature of the surrounding area, there would be no stigma attached to the premises and possession would result in a substantial windfall to the landlord).

In the context of breach of covenant to assign or sub-let, the courts may grant relief (*Scala House*) unless the assignment or sub-letting resulted in the assignee or sub-tenant acquiring statutory protection that the tenant would not have had (*Leeward Securties v Lilyheath* (1983) 17 HLR 35).

If relief is granted, it will be granted on such terms as the court thinks fit (LPA 1925, s 146(2)), such as compensation or an injunction to restrain further breach.

25.5   ADDITIONAL RULES IN SPECIAL CASES

25.5.1   Breach of a tenant's repairing covenant

If a lease was originally granted for a term of seven years or more and has at least three years unexpired, the provisions of the Leasehold Property (Repairs) Act 1938 (LP(R)A 1938) apply. These provide that when a landlord serves a notice under s 146 of the LPA 1925 prior to forfeiture, it must include a statement of the tenant's right to serve a counter-notice within 28 days. If the tenant does so, the landlord may proceed with its claim (ie forfeiture) only if it receives the leave of the court. See **Figure 25.3** below. Leave will be granted only in the specified circumstances set out in s 1(5) of the LP(R)A 1938 (eg that the value of the reversion has been substantially diminished) (see **29.1.2.1**).

Figure 25.3 Forfeiture by landlord for breach of tenant's covenant in lease: repair covenant

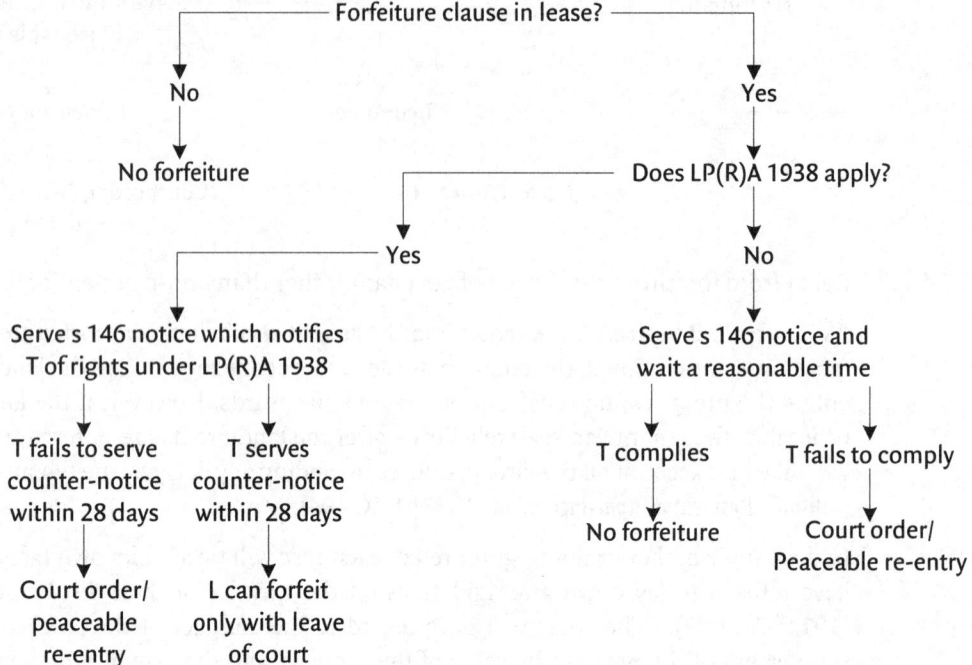

25.5.2   Internal decorative repairs

Where the s 146 notice relates to internal decorative repairs, the tenant has a special right to apply to the court for relief under s 147 of the LPA 1925. This is separate from the general right to apply for relief under s 146. If the court is satisfied that the notice is unreasonable (having regard to all the circumstances of the case, including the length of the unexpired term), it may wholly or partially relieve the tenant from liability. The court has no power to award relief under s 147 if (inter alia) the notice relates to repairs required under an express covenant to put the property in a decorative state of repair which has never been performed, or if it relates to any matter necessary or proper to keep the property in a sanitary condition, or for the maintenance or preservation of the structure, or to any covenant to yield up the premises in a specified state of repair at the end of the term.

25.5.3   Tenant's bankruptcy or liquidation

A lease will usually give the landlord the right to forfeit upon the tenant's bankruptcy (or liquidation) or having the lease taken in execution. If the landlord wishes to forfeit, it needs only serve a s 146 notice and the tenant may only apply for relief during the first year following the bankruptcy or taking in execution. However, there is an important exception to this rule. If, during that first year, the trustee or liquidator sells the lease, the s 146 protection lasts indefinitely. Without such an exception, it would be difficult for the trustee or liquidator to find a buyer for the lease because of the risk of forfeiture taking place after the expiration of the first year without the service of a s 146 notice and with no right to seek relief.

For further detail on the impact of insolvency events on the landlord's right to forfeit, see **32.7.2**.

25.5.4   Particular premises

Exceptionally, there is no need for the landlord to serve a s 146 notice following bankruptcy, liquidation or taking in execution, and the tenant has no right to apply for relief, if the lease is of agricultural land, mines or minerals, a public house, a furnished house or any premises where the personal qualifications of the tenant are important for the preservation of the nature or character of the premises or on the ground of neighbourhood to the landlord (see *Hockley Engineering Ltd v V & P Midlands Ltd* [1993] 1 EGLR 76 for meaning) or anyone holding under it.

25.6   POSITION OF SUB-TENANTS AND MORTGAGEES ON FORFEITURE

If the head-lease is forfeited, this will automatically end any sub-lease. This is unfair to sub-tenants who stand to lose their interest through no fault of their own. Under s 146(4), a sub-tenant can apply to the court for relief and the court may make an order vesting, for the whole term of the head-lease or any less term (but not longer than that remaining under the sub-lease), the property comprised in the head-lease or any part of it in the sub-tenant. The court can impose any conditions as to payment of rent, costs, expenses, damages, compensation, giving security, or otherwise, as the court in the circumstances of each case may think fit.

Lenders (whether by sub-demise or legal charge) are classed as sub-tenants for the purposes of s 146(4) and can apply for relief from forfeiture of the lease, but only if arrears and costs are paid within six months of the landlord's re-entry (see *United Dominion Trust Ltd v Shellpoint Trustees* [1993] EGCS 57).

25.7   THE 2007 CODE FOR LEASING BUSINESS PREMISES

The 2007 Code provides:

> 10   Landlords should handle defaults promptly and deal with tenants and any guarantors in an open constructive way

Tip 34 of the Occupier Guide advises tenants to make sure the forfeiture provisions are clear, allow enough time to pay, and enable tenants to restructure without necessarily making the lease vulnerable to forfeiture.

See the **Appendix 4** lease, which complies with the 2007 Code.

REVIEW ACTIVITY

Mercurial Ltd ('the landlord') owns two-storey office premises in a somewhat run-down area of east London. Two years ago, the landlord granted a lease of the ground floor to Tiempo Trading Ltd ('Tiempo') and a lease of the first floor to Grantham solicitors ('Grantham'). Both leases were for a term of 10 years and were granted in the form of the **Appendix 4** lease.

Six months ago, the landlord consented to a sub-letting of the ground floor by Tiempo to Escorta Ltd. Recently, following a complaint by Grantham, the landlord discovered that the sub-tenant is using the ground floor premises as a brothel.

The landlord has also just checked its bank account to discover that Grantham has not paid the quarter's rent which was due four weeks ago.

Explain to the landlord whether it can forfeit the lease of the ground floor and/or the lease of the first floor, and in each case the procedure which must be followed. In addition, explain whether the tenant can apply for relief against forfeiture and on what conditions relief might be granted.

Answers to this Review activity may be found in Appendix 1.

CHAPTER 26

LEASE OF PART

26.1	Introduction	259
26.2	Defining the demised premises	259
26.3	Rights granted and reserved	259
26.4	Repairs	260
26.5	Service charges	261
26.6	Sinking and reserve funds	266
26.7	Insurance	266
26.8	RICS Code of Practice for Service Charges	266
	Review activity	267

26.1 INTRODUCTION

The purpose of this chapter is not to deal with every single issue of relevance on the lease of part of a building; some can be dealt with only in the context of particular clauses. The reader will therefore find references to leases of part elsewhere in this book. However, there are some important issues which can be dealt with separately, and by drawing these together in this chapter, particularly the service charge provisions, the reader will become aware of the special considerations which apply whenever a lease of part of a building is contemplated.

26.2 DEFINING THE DEMISED PREMISES

It is important that the lease fully and accurately identifies the boundaries of the property to be let. This is particularly important bearing in mind that the tenant's liability to repair is often co-extensive with the demise; if it has to repair the 'demised premises', it must be clear where they start and finish. The following are some of the matters which will need consideration:

(a) *Walls.* It must be clear which walls fall within the demise and which outside. The demise often excludes the structural walls and outer half of the internal non-structural walls dividing the demised premises from the other parts of the building. The plaster finishes of such walls are often within the demise.

(b) *Floors, ceilings and roofs.* These often fall outside of the demise. However, floor and ceiling finishes and coverings, false ceilings and floor screeds are often within the demise.

(c) *Windows.* In a lease of part, windows in the exterior walls normally fall outside the demise.

(d) *Conducting media (such as pipes and cables) and plant (such as air conditioning units and boilers).* Those that exclusively serve the premises are usually demised to the tenant. Those that serve the premises and other parts of the building are normally excluded from the demise.

Practitioners often refer to leases of part that deal with the demise as described above as 'internal only' demises.

26.3 RIGHTS GRANTED AND RESERVED

As far as easements are concerned, the tenant will usually need to be granted rights over the parts of the building retained by the landlord or let to other tenants. The following are some of the rights that will need considering:

(a)   rights over staircases, lifts, landing areas and corridors;

(b)   rights over estate roads and footpaths and rights to use shared car parks;

(c)   rights over shared facilities such as bin stores, sign boards and toilets;

(d)   rights to use shared conducting media;

(e)   rights of access onto retained parts of the building to carry out repairs to the premises.

The landlord will need to be satisfied that such rights do not unduly restrict its use of the remainder of the building. The case of *B&Q plc v Liverpool and Lancashire Properties Ltd* [2000] EGCS 101 illustrated the way in which rights granted to tenants may hinder the landlord's future development proposals. In that case the tenant successfully applied for an injunction against the landlord, preventing the latter from constructing a 3,500 square foot extension to one of the units on its retail park. The extension would have reduced the area of a service yard used by B&Q. B&Q had been granted rights over the service yard in its lease, and although the yard could still be used if the extension went ahead, the fact that it was rendered 'materially less convenient' than before was sufficient for the tenant to succeed.

The landlord will, of course, wish to reserve certain rights over the property being let. These will often include rights of access to carry out repairs and to run services through the service media on the demise. More contentiously, they may also include rights to re-route accesses and service media, to erect scaffolding and to extend or alter other parts of the landlord's estate. The tenant will need to consider the possible impact on its business before unconditionally accepting such reservations. If possible, the tenant's solicitor should obtain a qualification to such reservations that no interference is caused to the tenant's use and occupation of the premises or the rights granted to it.

26.4 REPAIRS

It is usual, in a large multi-occupied building, to make the tenant responsible for repair of the internal non-structural parts of the demised premises and the landlord responsible for repair of the remainder of the building. This can be achieved by creating an 'internal only demise' (see **26.2**) which the tenant covenants to repair. The landlord then covenants to repair all other parts of the landlord's property excluding the demised premises (and sometimes the internal parts of other lettable units). These retained areas for which the landlord assumes responsibility are often referred to as the common parts. Any expense incurred by the landlord in complying with its obligations for the common parts will usually be recoverable under the service charge provisions (see **26.5**).

For the repairing obligations to work effectively, great care must be exercised in drafting the definitions of the demised premises and the common parts (see **26.2**). If the tenant has taken an internal only demise, it must ensure the definitions and obligations work to oblige the landlord to repair all other parts of the building and estate. This would include the structural parts of the building, such as the roof, main load bearing walls and foundations. It may also include entrances, staircases, corridors and lifts, together with shared conducting media, and external areas (including any landscaped areas, forecourts, roadways and fences). The landlord may resist accepting responsibility for other units capable of being let, as the tenants of such units would be responsible for their repairs.

In considering repairing obligations, practitioners must also appreciate the precise meaning of certain words and phrases which have been judicially defined in a plethora of case law. Thus, for example, 'structural repairs', 'main walls', 'external walls' and 'exterior' have all been judicially considered; reference should be made to one of the standard works on landlord and tenant law for a more detailed analysis of such technicalities.

26.5   SERVICE CHARGES

As discussed at **26.4,** in a lease of part, the landlord will often be responsible for the repair of all parts of the building and estate other than the internal only demises let to the tenants. There may also be other services provided by the landlord (see **26.5.1**). The landlord will want to recover the costs of providing these services from the tenants. It could charge a higher inclusive rent to cover its anticipated costs, but the landlord then runs the risk of inflation or unexpected outgoings making its estimate incorrect. The inclusive rent method is unpopular with institutional landlords and lenders who prefer a 'clear lease', where the rent will always represent the landlord's clear income from the property and the landlord is reimbursed for the expenditure on the provision of services by means of a service charge which fluctuates annually according to the actual costs incurred.

From the landlord's point of view, it is necessary to decide whether the service charge should be reserved as additional rent. The advantages of reserving it as rent have already been considered (see **17.4**).

26.5.1   Services to be provided

Tenants need pay for the provision only of those services specified in the lease. There is no presumption that a landlord should receive full recovery of its maintenance and repair costs from a tenant (see *Campbell v Daejan Properties Ltd* [2012] EWCA Civ 1503). If there is no provision for the tenant to pay for a particular cost, the landlord cannot recover its expenditure. Therefore, when drafting the service charge provisions, the landlord's solicitor will aim to include all the expenditure the landlord may lay out on the building. The tenant's solicitor will need to check that each item of expenditure listed in the lease is reasonable and appropriate. Tenants' solicitors will often seek express provisions in the lease that only expenditure reasonably and properly incurred by the landlord is recoverable.

This can be a very contentious area for the parties. Whilst both parties wish to have a well-serviced building, the tenant will want this at the lowest possible cost to it. It will not wish to pay for services it perceives as unnecessary or disproportionately expensive when compared to benefit.

Some common items of expenditure and the issues that can arise in relation to them are set out below.

26.5.1.1   Repairs and decoration

The landlord will want to recover all its expenses in performing its repairing obligation. Leases will often allow the recovery of expenses for inspecting, cleaning, maintaining, repairing and decorating the common parts and any other parts of the building for which the landlord is responsible. Usually the lease will also allow for the recovery of similar expenditure in relation to plant and equipment, service media and landlord's fittings. This will often include potentially expensive items of plant, such as air conditioning, security and heating systems and fire alarms.

Whether the landlord can go beyond 'repair', and rebuild or carry out improvements, is a question of construction of the relevant clause, but the tenant must be aware of the danger of having to contribute to work which would be outside a simple covenant to 'repair', for example the replacement of defective wooden window frames with modern double-glazed units. A tenant that accepts that it will pay the landlord's costs in 'renewing' or 'replacing' items for which the landlord is responsible, risks the landlord deciding to upgrade the property at the tenant's cost. If such an upgrade were to be carried out towards the end of the lease term, the tenant would bear the cost without experiencing the benefit of the works. It is therefore wise for the tenant's solicitor to specify that the costs of renewal and replacement are only recoverable where the item in question is beyond economic repair.

Another concern of the tenant is that the clause may require its contribution to expenditure incurred by the landlord in remedying inherent defects in the building, for example those caused by a design defect or through the use of defective materials. The tenant should seek to expressly exclude such costs.

The landlord should pay particular attention to the wording of the service charge provision. In *Northways Flats Management Co v Wimpey Pension Trustees* [1992] 31 EG 65, the clause required the landlord, before carrying out the work, to submit details and estimates to the tenants. The court held that this was a precondition to the recovery of the service charge and, since it had not been complied with, the landlord was unable to recover its expenditure.

26.5.1.2   Heating, air conditioning, etc

The landlord will wish to recover its costs in supplying heating, lighting, air conditioning and hot and cold water to the common parts of the building and possibly the demised premises as well. This will include the costs of maintaining the plant, equipment and service media associated with such services. Sometimes, the landlord will restrict the provision of heating, air conditioning and lighting to certain times. The tenant must ensure it is happy with such restrictions. The landlord should also ensure that it is not liable to the tenant for any temporary interruption in supply due to a breakdown.

26.5.1.3   Staff

The landlord will wish to recover its costs in employing staff in connection with the management of the building such as receptionists, maintenance staff, caretakers and security personnel. This will include the cost of any equipment or uniform provided to such staff, together with their wages, taxes, national insurance contributions and any other benefits they receive. The clause should also extend to any staff employed by the managing agents for the purpose of providing services at the building. From the tenant's point of view, it should guard against having to pay the full-time wages of staff who are not wholly engaged in providing the services. The tenant should also consider whether such staff are necessary and appropriate.

26.5.1.4   Managing agents

Most modern leases allow the landlord to recover the cost of employing managing agents to manage the building and services. A company owned by the landlord can be employed as managing agent provided such an arrangement is not a sham (*Skilleter v Charles* [1992] 13 EG 113). If the landlord performs its own management services, the service charge will usually enable it to recover its reasonable costs for this. In the absence of an express provision, it is unlikely such management costs can be recovered.

The tenant must make sure that the amount of fees recoverable is reasonable and may want some restriction placed on them in the lease. There is clearly a danger, where the landlord performs the management services itself, that the tenant is overcharged. The tenant will not want the landlord to profit out of the service charge. The tenant should also seek to ensure it does not pay the costs of the managing agent in performing additional duties such as rent collection. Attempts by the landlord to charge a notional rent for premises within the building used in connection with the management of the building should also be resisted.

26.5.1.5   Other common items of expenditure

Other common items of expenditure include:

(a)   refuse removal;

(b)   maintenance of signage and sign boards;

(c)   window cleaning and cleaning of common parts;

(d)   fire prevention equipment;

(e)   insurance (although sometimes this is dealt with outside the service charge provisions);

(f)   security equipment (such as CCTV);

(g)   maintenance of car parks and landscaped areas;

(h)   costs in complying with statute and insurers' requirements;

(i)   borrowing costs to fund major expenditure;

(j)   outgoings payable by the landlord;

(k)   advertising and promotion costs, in the case of a shopping centre;

(l)   legal and other professional fees (in particular those incurred in the preparation and auditing of the service charge certificate and accounts (see **26.5.4.3**)).

Each of these items can be contentious. The landlord may, for example, be keen to have the landscaped areas regularly replanted, but a tenant with a unit that does not adjoin such areas may not wish to pay for such a service. The tenant's solicitor will need to check each item of expenditure listed as recoverable is appropriate. The tenant's solicitor may wish to specify that such expenditure is only recoverable if reasonably and properly incurred for the benefit of the tenant. Obviously, any such qualifications the landlord accepts bring with them the risk that the tenant will argue certain expenditure is irrecoverable.

26.5.1.6   'Sweeper' clause

No matter how comprehensive the landlord thinks it has been in compiling the list of services to be provided, it is advisable to include a 'sweeper' clause to take account of any new services to be provided over the lifetime of the lease. However, careful drafting of such a clause is required as the courts construe them restrictively (see *Mullaney v Maybourne Grange (Croydon) Ltd* [1986] 1 EGLR 70). From the tenant's point of view, it should guard against the clause being drafted too widely. The sweeper should only allow the landlord to provide services not contemplated when the lease was granted; it should not be used to cover something left out in error. The draft lease should require the landlord to act reasonably and in accordance with the principles of good estate management before being able to recover expenditure under the sweeper clause. The tenant's solicitor may require the sweeper clause to specify that any service provided under it be of some benefit to the tenant.

26.5.2   Landlord's covenant to perform the services

The services to be provided often fall into two categories: essential services which the landlord should be obliged to provide (eg, heating and lighting the common parts and repairing and maintaining the structure) and other non-essential services which it has discretion to provide. From the tenant's point of view, it must make sure that, in return for paying the service charge, the landlord covenants to provide the essential services. Without such an express provision, it is by no means certain that one would be implied, leaving the tenant with no remedy if the services were not provided (see, however, *Barnes v City of London Real Property Co* [1918] 2 Ch 18).

The tenant would also be ill-advised to leave non-essential services within the absolute discretion of the landlord. Whilst, for example, maintenance of adjacent landscaped areas may not be 'essential', if poorly maintained the tenant may find that its trade is detrimentally affected. It is wise, therefore, for the tenant to provide that the landlord's discretion must be exercised reasonably and in the interests of the tenants of the building.

From the landlord's point of view, it may wish to restrict the covenant so that the landlord is liable to use only 'reasonable endeavours' or 'best endeavours' to provide the services, rather than be under an absolute obligation to do so. In any event, the covenant should be limited so that the landlord is not liable to the tenant for failure to provide the services due to circumstances outside its control, such as industrial action. The tenant's solicitor will need to advise his client that if it accepts such qualifications, there may be circumstances in which the tenant has no remedy against the landlord for a failure to supply the services.

Turning to the standard of the services, the tenant's solicitor should seek an express provision that the services be provided in an efficient and economical manner and to a reasonable standard, rather than a standard the landlord considers adequate. The Supply of Goods and Services Act 1982 provides that, where a service is provided in the course of a business, there is an implied term that the supplier will carry out the service with reasonable care and skill, but it is obviously better for the tenant to deal with the matter expressly. As a general rule, the obligation to provide the services is independent of the obligation to pay for them. Therefore, in the event of non-payment by the tenant, the landlord cannot withdraw services (and in any event it is unlikely that the landlord could withdraw services from one tenant alone). Tenants should be wary of any clause that links provision of the services to payment of the service charge. In the event of a legitimate dispute over the service charge, the ability of the landlord to withdraw services from the tenant may well compel the tenant to pay the disputed sum.

26.5.3   The tenant's contribution: basis of apportionment

In addition to setting out the items which can be charged to the tenant, the clause must deal with how the total cost is to be apportioned between the tenants in the building. It can be difficult to decide on an appropriate basis of apportionment. In many buildings, not all occupiers will benefit from the services to the same extent. For example, a tenant on the ground floor of a shopping centre will not benefit from the provision of lifts and escalators to upper floors.

The following are some commonly used methods of apportionment:

(a)   *According to floor area.* This can be a relatively simple method, depending on the nature of the building, but some method of measurement will have to be agreed.

(b)   *According to anticipated use of services.* This can be difficult to assess and depends on the nature of each tenant's business and its location within the building.

(c)   *As a fixed percentage.* This provides certainty for both parties but is inflexible. Further, the landlord must make provision for any future enlargement of the building which would necessitate a recalculation of the percentages.

In older leases, the service charge may be apportioned by reference to rateable value. This can be arbitrary since rateable values can vary for reasons which bear no relationship to the amount of services consumed, such as value and location. It is therefore no longer recommended by the RICS as an appropriate method for calculating service charge apportionments.

Each method has its own advantages and disadvantages, and reference should be made to one of the standard works on the drafting of business leases for further consideration of the matter. Whatever method is adopted, the tenant will want to ensure that it does not become liable for any un-let units or units occupied by the landlord for its own purposes; the landlord should be required to pay the service charge for these. The tenant's solicitor should also ensure that if special service charge concessions have been given to individual occupiers, the tenant is not left to make up the shortfall via its own service charge contribution. Again, this should be borne by the landlord.

26.5.4   Payment of the charge

26.5.4.1   Advance payments

Typical service charge provisions stipulate that the service charge is to be paid by the tenant periodically in advance (usually on rent days). Advance payment is necessary because otherwise the landlord would have to fund the provision of work and services out of its own resources and recoup its expenditure from the tenants later. The amount of the advance payment may give rise to disputes between the parties unless the tenant can be sure such amount is not excessive. There are different ways of calculating the service charge, for example it may be based on the previous year's actual expenditure or on an estimate of the likely expenditure in the current year. If the latter method is adopted, the tenant should insist on the amount payable being certified by, for example, the landlord's surveyor, and that the payment is to be made only upon receipt of such a certificate (see **26.5.4.3**).

The tenant may wish to consider a requirement that the landlord is to pay the advance payments into a separate account to be held on trust in order to avoid the problems which may arise if the landlord becomes insolvent. All interest earned should be credited to the service charge account.

26.5.4.2 Final payments and adjustments

At the end of the year, the service charge provisions will, typically, require the landlord to prepare annual accounts showing its actual expenditure in the year (see **26.5.4.3**). Where advance payments have been made, an adjustment will be necessary to correct any over- or underpayment. In the case of underpayment, the tenant will be required to pay this amount within a specified time. If there is an overpayment, the lease may provide for its refund to the tenant or, more usually, it will be credited to the following year's payments. The tenant's solicitor should consider requiring the landlord to notify it of any significant variation between budgeted and actual expenditure, as soon as the landlord becomes aware of such a variation.

26.5.4.3 Certification of amounts due

At the end of the service charge year, most leases will provide for the tenant to be provided with two items. The first is a service charge statement or certificate. This usually provides a summary of service costs and sets out the calculation of the service charge. The second item is the service charge accounts on which the statement is based.

Most tenants will want some reassurance that the service charge statement and accounts are accurate. In consequence, many leases will set out requirements for such statements and accounts.

As far as the service charge statement goes, it is common to find a requirement that this be 'certified' as a true and accurate record of the landlord's expenditure incurred in accordance with the lease. The lease will need to specify who can carry out such certification. This should be an appropriately qualified accountant or surveyor. Some leases allow such a person to be an employee of the landlord, although the tenant may not find this acceptable. The tenant should be aware, however, that if the lease provides for the certification to be done by an independent third party, the charges payable by that third party will normally be paid by the tenant via the service charge.

Turning to the service charge accounts, some leases require that the service charge accounts be 'audited'. This will require an external review of the accounts by a registered auditor, which can be a costly and time-consuming process. It has the benefit of additional reassurance to the tenant, but this will need to be weighed against the additional cost which is likely to be passed back to the tenant via the service charge. An alternative (and generally less costly) option is to have the accounts examined by an independent accountant, who should check that the correct figures have been extracted from the accounting records maintained by the manager and that entries in the accounting records are supported by receipts. Although cheaper, there will still be a cost involved in this and the parties should consider whether the expenditure involved justifies the cost.

The landlord will be keen to avoid challenges by the tenant to the service charge certificate. If the certificate is said to be 'final and conclusive as to the facts stated', its finality is likely to be upheld by the courts. If the lease makes the expert's certificate conclusive on matters of law, for example as to the construction of the lease, there are conflicting views on its validity. It may be that it will be upheld if the expert is given the exclusive right to determine the issue and the lease is clear on the party's intention to exclude the jurisdiction of the courts (see *National Grid Co plc v M25 Group Ltd* [1999] 08 EG 169 and *Morgan Sindall v Sawston Farms (Cambs) Ltd* [1999] 1 EGLR 90). From the tenant's perspective, statements that the certificate is final and binding should be avoided as this may leave the tenant without any way of challenging its service charge. One option may be to make provision for disputes about the service charge to be dealt with by alternative dispute resolution (ADR). This can provide a quicker and more cost effective way of dealing with disputes than court action.

26.6   SINKING AND RESERVE FUNDS

The object of sinking and reserve funds is to make funds available when needed for major items of irregular expenditure. A sinking fund is a fund established for replacing major items such as boilers and lifts which may only be necessary once or twice during the lifetime of the building. A reserve fund is established to pay for recurring items of expenditure such as external decoration which may need attending to, not annually, but perhaps every four or five years. The estimated cost of such decoration will be collected over each five-year period so that tenants are not faced with a large bill every five years.

The advantage of such funds is that money is available to carry out these major works when needed without any dramatic fluctuations in the service charge payable from one year to another. However, the creation of such a fund needs careful thought, and many difficult questions will need to be addressed at the drafting stage. Who is to own the fund? Is it to be held absolutely or on trust? What is to happen to the fund when the landlord sells the reversion? What will be the position upon termination of the lease? (See *Secretary of State for the Environment v Possfund (North West) Ltd* [1997] 39 EG 179.) Further, there may be considerable tax disadvantages. Such matters are beyond the scope of this book, but the parties will need specialist advice on them.

26.7   INSURANCE

On a lease of part of a building in multi-occupation, the landlord will usually insure the whole building and recover the premium from the tenants under the service charge provisions or in a separate insurance clause. Insurance is dealt with in **Chapter 24**.

26.8   RICS CODE OF PRACTICE FOR SERVICE CHARGES

Unfortunately, disputes over service charges in commercial properties are commonplace. Tenants regularly complain that they have been charged for services or items that should not have been charged at all, that they are bearing too high a percentage of the costs relative to other tenants and/or that, in relation to properly incurred expenditure, they have been charged an uncompetitive price. Because of such problems, the RICS publishes a guidance note for surveyors: the Code of Practice on Service Charges in Commercial Property ('the Code'). This is aimed primarily at surveyors who administer the services on a day-to-day basis as managing agents and represents best practice for the operation of a service charge. The second edition came into effect in October 2011 and, whilst aimed primarily at surveyors, it states as a key aspiration 'increased engagement with the legal profession'. Whilst the Code cannot override leases, it is the hope of the RICS that as leases are renewed or new leases are granted, they will be drafted to reflect best practice on service charges set out in the Code. With existing leases, the Code advises that the lease should, as far as possible, be interpreted by surveyors in a way that is consistent with the Code. Whilst the Code is not binding on lawyers or their clients, it is a useful reference point as to best practice.

The Code sets out 26 core principles in section 1. For example, services are to be procured on an appropriate value-for-money basis, owners should not profit from the provision or supply of services, and all costs are to be transparent (core principles 1, 2 and 3). There must be timely and regular communication between the managing agent and the tenants, and there are time limits by which service charge budgets and statements of actual expenditure must be produced (core principles 23 and 24). In the event of dispute, either party should be able to refer the matter to ADR rather than to the court (core principle 21). Detailed guidance on how to achieve the core principles is given in section 2 of the Code.

The existence of the Code gives those negotiating and approving leases on behalf of tenants strong grounds for resisting any service charge terms not complying with the Code. The Code may also provide assistance when surveyors and lawyers are asked to advise on whether particular services or types of expenditure properly fall within a service charge. The 2007 Code for Leasing Business Premises (see **13.2**) provides:

> **6 Service Charges**
>
> Landlords must, during negotiations, provide best estimates of service charges, insurance payments and any other outgoings that tenants will incur under their leases.
>
> Landlords must disclose known irregular events that would have a significant impact on the amount of future service charges.
>
> Landlords should be aware of the RICS 2006 Code of Practice on Service Charges in Commercial Property and seek to observe its guidance in drafting new leases and on renewals (even if granted before that Code is effective).

Both PLC and the City of London Law Society publish leases complying with the 2007 Code for Leasing Business Premises. An example of such a lease is contained in **Appendix 4**.

REVIEW ACTIVITY

Read clause 8 of the **Appendix 4** lease. Answer the following questions and identify the relevant lease clauses that support your answer:

1.   Will the tenant have to pay for upgrades to the plant in the building that it does not consider necessary?

2.   Will the landlord be able to recover its expenditure from the tenant if it decides to provide a new service to the building not envisaged when the lease was granted?

3.   What can the tenant do if it is unhappy with the level of expenditure shown in the service charge certificate and certified accounts?

Answers to this Review activity may be found in Appendix 1.

CHAPTER 27

SELLING THE LEASE

27.1	Applications for consent to assign	269
27.2	The landlord's licence	271
27.3	Authorised guarantee agreements	272
	Review activity	272

27.1 APPLICATIONS FOR CONSENT TO ASSIGN

27.1.1 The lease provisions

It will nearly always be the case that the lease will restrict the tenant's right to assign the lease. There may be an absolute covenant against assignment, in which case the tenant is absolutely prohibited from assigning the lease. The landlord may (or may not) agree to waive the breach in a particular case but the tenant will be entirely at the mercy of the landlord. An assignment in breach of an absolute covenant will be effective, but the lease will be liable to forfeiture by the landlord because of the breach of covenant. More commonly, there will be a qualified covenant, ie, not to assign without the landlord's prior written consent. In the case of a qualified covenant against assignment, s 19(1)(a) of the LTA 1927 implies a proviso that, notwithstanding any contrary provision, the landlord's licence or consent is not to be unreasonably withheld. The reasonableness of the landlord's refusal of consent has been dealt with earlier in this book (see **20.3**), and it will be recalled that if the parties have specified for the purposes of s 19(1A) of the LTA 1927 conditions to be satisfied, or circumstances to exist, before consent is to be given, a refusal of consent on the grounds that they are not satisfied, or they do not exist, is not an unreasonable withholding of consent.

27.1.2 The consequences of failing to obtain consent

Assuming the alienation covenant is qualified, the first step is for the tenant to make written application to the landlord for consent to assign. If the landlord consents, the tenant can proceed with the assignment. If the landlord unreasonably refuses consent, the tenant can proceed to assign and will not be deemed in breach of covenant. The danger for the tenant is in knowing whether the landlord's refusal is unreasonable or not, because if the landlord's refusal turns out to have been reasonable, the landlord will have the right to forfeit the lease. Further, for the purposes of the LT(C)A 1995, the assignment will be an excluded assignment, meaning that the assignor will not be released from the tenant covenants in the lease. Alternatively, the tenant may pursue the safer course of action by seeking a court declaration that the landlord is acting unreasonably in withholding consent, but this may prove costly and time-consuming. A further problem, prior to the passing of the LTA 1988, was that the tenant could not, in the absence of an express covenant by the landlord, obtain damages if the landlord withheld consent unreasonably.

27.1.3 The landlord's statutory obligations

As discussed at **27.1.1,** by virtue of s 19(1)(a) of the LTA 1927, the landlord is under an obligation not to unreasonably withhold consent in relation to a qualified covenant against alienation. Additionally, s 1 of the LTA 1988 (which only applies to qualified covenants) provides that where the tenant has made written application to assign, the landlord owes a duty, within a reasonable time:

(a)   to give consent, unless it is reasonable not to do so. Giving consent subject to an unreasonable condition will be a breach of this duty; and

(b)   to serve on the tenant written notice of its decision whether or not to give consent, specifying in addition:

(i)   if the consent is given subject to conditions, the conditions; or

(ii)   if the consent is withheld, the reasons for withholding it.

Usually the landlord will wish to see a bank reference, audited accounts (eg, for the last three years) and, if appropriate, trade references for the proposed assignee, and these should accompany the tenant's application. If the landlord needs any further information to enable it to process the application, it should request this from the tenant.

27.1.3.1   To respond within a 'reasonable time'

The LTA 1988 does not define what amounts to a reasonable time and each case will turn on its own facts. However, in *Go West Ltd v Spigarolo* [2003] EWCA Civ 17, [2003] 07 EG 136, the judge commented:

> I find it hard to imagine that a period of ... almost four months could ever be acceptable, save perhaps in the most unusual and complex situations ... it may be that the reasonable time ... will sometimes have to be measured in weeks rather than days; but, even in complicated cases, it should be measured in weeks rather than months.

In *Blockbuster Entertainment Ltd v Barnsdale Properties Ltd* [2003] EWHC 2912, a landlord who was asked for consent on 28 May and gave it on 15 July was held to have unreasonably delayed in giving that consent. Similarly, in *Mount Eden Land Ltd v Folia Ltd* [2003] EWHC 1815, the judge, while emphasising that each case turned on its own facts, thought that a period of four to five weeks was 'generous'. At the other end of the scale, in *E.ON UK plc v Gilesports Ltd* [2012] EWHC 2172 (Ch), the court considered 11 working days too short a period.

It should be noted that the landlord will not be under an obligation to respond at all if the tenant has failed to make its application in accordance with the provisions of the lease. So, in *E.ON UK plc v Gilesports Ltd* (above), the court held that service of the tenant's application by e-mail did not trigger the landlord's statutory duty to consider the application. The lease did not provide for service of applications or notices by e-mail, and the fact the landlord had actually received the e-mail application was considered irrelevant.

27.1.3.2   Not to withhold consent unreasonably

As to whether the landlord is unreasonably withholding its consent, this is left to the general law (see **20.3.3**). The burden of proving the reasonableness of any refusal or any conditions imposed is on the landlord, and the sanction for breach of the statutory duty is liability in tort for damages. As a result of the Act, landlords must give careful consideration to the financial consequences of having delayed or refused consent unreasonably, and they should set up efficient procedures to ensure that each application for consent is dealt with expeditiously and in accordance with the Act.

In considering whether or not to give consent, the landlord does not owe earlier tenants a duty of care to ensure that the assignee is of sufficient financial standing. If the assignee turns out to be unsatisfactory, the landlord will still be able to serve a default notice on those former tenants who may still be liable to the landlord (according to whether it is an 'old' or 'new' lease for the purposes of the LT(C)A 1995) (*Norwich Union Life Insurance Society v Low Profile Fashions Ltd* (1992) 21 EG 104). In such a situation, the earlier tenants may then be able to secure an overriding lease under the provisions of the LT(C)A 1995 (see **29.1.4**).

The landlord's solicitor, on receiving the tenant's application to assign, will often seek an undertaking from the tenant's solicitor to pay the landlord's legal and other costs of dealing with the application and preparing the licence (plus VAT). This is acceptable, provided the costs for which the undertaking is required are reasonable (see *Dong Bang Minerva (UK) Ltd v Davina Ltd* [1996] 31 EG 87). Care should be taken in drafting the undertaking to make it clear whether the obligation to pay the landlord's costs applies in the event of the licence not being granted; this may be a requirement of the lease in any case.

27.1.4 Superior landlord's consent

If may be that the landlord is itself a tenant and the applicant for consent is the sub-tenant. If this is the case and the head-lease requires the head-landlord's consent to the assignment, the LTA 1988 imposes the following:

(a) a duty on the immediate landlord to pass on a copy of the application to the head-landlord within a reasonable time.

(b) a similar duty to that contained in s 1 on the head-landlord towards the sub-tenant.

27.2 THE LANDLORD'S LICENCE

If the landlord is prepared to give its consent to the assignment, a licence to assign will usually be prepared by the landlord's solicitor in which the landlord will formally grant its consent. The landlord and his advisers must take care to ensure that correspondence entered into prior to completion of the licence does not amount to consent for the purposes of the lease. In several cases that have come before the court, correspondence from the landlord or his advisers indicating the landlord's agreement to the proposed assignment has been held to amount to consent. This has been so even where the correspondence has been marked 'subject to contract' or 'subject to licence' (see *Next plc v National Farmers Union Mutual Insurance Co Ltd* [1997] EGCS 181), or where the consent has been described as 'in principle' and subject to completion of a formal licence (see *Aubergine Enterprises Ltd v Lakewood International Ltd* [2002] EWCA Civ 177). The landlord will, however, be protected if the lease requires that consent be given by deed.

If the tenant and assignee are to enter into covenants in the licence then all three (ie, landlord, tenant and assignee) will be parties to the licence, which will be in the form of a deed. Often the licence will be prepared in triplicate, so that on completion each party receives a signed and dated part. The licence will include various covenants and conditions such as:

(a) A direct covenant by the assignee to the landlord to observe and perform the covenants in the lease. If the lease to be assigned is a 'new lease' for the purposes of the LT(C)A 1995, this covenant should be limited to the period the assignee is actually the tenant (see **14.3.2.2**). However, in an old lease, a covenant by the assignee to observe and perform the covenants in the lease for the entire duration of the term would be permitted and is usual (see **14.3.1.4**).

(b) A covenant by the tenant:

(i) to pay the landlord's costs and expenses in dealing with the tenant's application;

(ii) not to allow the assignee to take up possession until the assignment has been completed.

(c) That the licence extends only to the transaction specifically authorised.

(d) That the licence is not to act as a waiver of any breach committed by the tenant prior to the date of the licence.

(e) That the licence shall cease to be valid unless the assignment is completed within, say, two months. This is because, although the proposed assignee is now acceptable to the landlord, the assignment might otherwise be delayed to a time when the assignee is of a poorer financial standing.

(f)   In a new lease, the landlord will probably require the assignor to enter into an AGA (see **20.2.4.3**). As to the lawfulness of such a requirement, see **27.3**.

27.3   AUTHORISED GUARANTEE AGREEMENTS

It is currently standard practice for a landlord to insist on an outgoing tenant entering into an AGA on an assignment of a new lease, guaranteeing that the assignee will perform the covenants in the lease. This is often a requirement set out in the lease in accordance with s 19(1A) of the LTA 1927, in which case it must be complied with. If it is not set out in the lease, it would be lawful to require an AGA provided that this was reasonable in the circumstances.

As noted (at **20.2.4.4**), the 2007 Code for Leasing Business Premises provides that an AGA should not be an automatic requirement on an assignment; it is necessary only if the proposed assignee is of a lower financial standing than the assignor, or is resident or registered overseas. Assignors should therefore cite the 2007 Code to landlords insisting on an AGA, but may well find that most landlords will not be sympathetic and will still insist on the guarantee.

As to the position of the guarantor of an outgoing tenant requested to enter an AGA, see **20.2.4.3**.

27.3.1   Content of an authorised guarantee agreement

A specimen AGA is set out in **Appendix 5**. It will typically contain covenants by the assignor:

(a)   guaranteeing that the assignee will perform the tenant's covenants in the lease;

(b)   promising to perform such covenants if the assignee does not;

(c)   promising to take a new lease if the liability of the assignee is disclaimed on insolvency (see **32.9**).

It should be ensured that the assignor's liability does not extend beyond that of the assignee; and it should be provided that on the assignee being released from liability under the LT(C)A 1995 (see **14.3.2**), so is the assignor.

27.3.2   LTA 1954 considerations

If the AGA does contain a provision that the outgoing tenant will take a new lease in the event of a disclaimer ((c) in **27.3.1** above) then the provisions of the LTA 1954 need to be considered. If the original lease is contracted out of the LTA 1954, it is likely the landlord will want any new lease granted to the outgoing tenant following disclaimer to be similarly contracted out. However, to contract out after 1 June 2004, the landlord is required to serve notice (in the prescribed form) prior to the tenant becoming bound to take the lease. As it is the AGA that obliges the tenant to take a new lease, it is suggested that the notice should be served prior to the AGA being entered into (see **31.1.6**).

REVIEW ACTIVITY

1.   In what circumstances would clauses 6.2.4 and 6.3 of the specimen AGA at **Appendix 5** be included?

2.   You act for a client that wishes to assign its lease. It is in the form of the lease at **Appendix 4**. The client informs you the landlord has provided a letter of consent to the proposed assignment. On this basis, the client instructs you to complete the assignment. You see the landlord's letter which is signed and does confirm the landlord's consent to the assignment. It is, however, headed 'subject to licence'. What should you advise the client about the letter of consent?

Answers to this Review activity may be found in Appendix 1.

CHAPTER 28

SUB-LEASES

28.1	The nature of a sub-lease	273
28.2	Reasons for sub-letting	273
28.3	Consent to the sub-letting	274
28.4	Liability to the head-landlord	275
28.5	Drafting the sub-lease	275
	Review activity	278

28.1 THE NATURE OF A SUB-LEASE

A sub-lease (like any other lease) is an estate in land. It is called a sub-lease (or sometimes an underlease) as it is carved out of and derives from another leasehold estate (often referred to as the head-lease). The sub-lease must be for a shorter term than the head-lease from which it is granted (although in practice it is often shorter by only a couple of days) or the transaction will amount to an assignment.

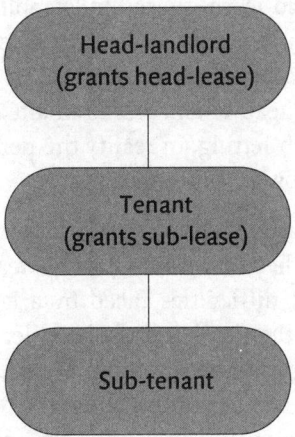

28.2 REASONS FOR SUB-LETTING

There are many reasons why a tenant may want to grant a sub-lease of all or part of the premises demised by the head-lease. It may be that the tenant finds that it has surplus accommodation which is not required for the purpose of its business; therefore, instead of leaving that part vacant (thereby wasting money), the tenant may try and cut its losses by finding a sub-tenant. Indeed, the tenant may well seek to create space for a sub-letting in the knowledge that the current market would lead to the sub-tenant paying a rent per square foot in excess of what the tenant is paying to the head-landlord, thereby enabling the tenant to make a profit.

On other occasions, the tenant may be sub-letting the premises as an alternative to assigning the lease. There are several reasons for this. It may be because the head-landlord is more willing to grant consent to sub-letting than to assignment, as its direct relationship with the tenant remains. Alternatively, if the tenant has any concerns about the covenant strength of the sub-tenant, it may wish to retain control of the premises by sub-letting rather than assigning. If the tenant assigns and the assignee defaults, the tenant would have to claim an overriding lease to regain control of the premises (see **29.1.4**). The tenant may also anticipate a need to reoccupy the premises at some point in the future. By granting a fixed-term sub-lease excluded from the Landlord and Tenant Act 1954 (LTA 1954), the tenant can then reoccupy the premises for the balance of the head-lease reversionary term. Finally, when rents are falling, the tenant may find it difficult to assign: it may not find a tenant willing to take on the lease when lower rents are being offered on similar premises currently being let. In that case, it may be that the only alternative for the tenant is to sub-let at a rent lower than that of the head-lease and cover the shortfall itself. There can be difficulties in doing this if the head-lease controls the sub-lease rental level (see **28.5.2**).

28.3   CONSENT TO THE SUB-LETTING

28.3.1   Restrictions on sub-letting

Where the tenant proposes to grant a sub-lease of all or part of the premises, it must have regard to the terms of its own lease, and in particular to the terms of the alienation covenant which is likely to control or regulate sub-letting. The prospective sub-tenant must also ensure any restrictions in the head-lease are complied with. If they are not, then the head-lease is at risk of forfeiture (see **Chapter 25**). If the head-lease is forfeited, then any sub-lease granted from it will fall too.

There are two main reasons why a head-landlord will wish to control sub-letting, even though, on the face of it, its relationship with the head-tenant remains unchanged. First, it is possible the head-landlord may end up with the sub-tenant as his direct tenant. This can occur if the head-lease is forfeited and the sub-tenant (whose sub-lease would also come to an end on forfeiture of the head-lease) successfully applies for relief from forfeiture. It can also occur if the head-lease is surrendered or disclaimed or, at the end of the sub-lease term, if the sub-tenant applies for a new lease under the LTA 1954 but the head-tenant does not. Secondly, whilst legally the head-tenant will remain liable to perform the head-lease covenants, regardless of the sub-letting, in reality the performance of many of the head-lease covenants will be undertaken by the sub-tenant.

As a result, most leases of commercial property will strictly regulate sub-lettings. Indeed, it is quite common for head-leases to bar sub-leases of part altogether. This is because of the estate management difficulties faced by a landlord with a building occupied by different tenants. Usually, at the very least, the head-lease will require the tenant to obtain the consent of the head-landlord before granting any sub-lease (whether of whole or part). Often, the head-lease will also be prescriptive about the terms of the sub-letting and require the terms of the sub-lease to match (or be at least as onerous as) the head-lease. It should be noted, however, that s 19(1)(a) of the LTA 1927 and s 1 of the LTA 1988 apply to qualified covenants against sub-letting. In consequence, where required, consent cannot be unreasonably withheld or delayed.

28.3.2   Licences to sub-let

Most head-landlords will require formal consent to the sub-letting to be given in the form of a licence to sub-let. This is a tripartite document entered in to by the head-landlord, tenant and sub-tenant.

The usual condition of granting consent is that the sub-tenant is to enter into a direct covenant with the head-landlord to perform the covenants in both the sub-lease and the head-lease. The latter covenant usually excludes the head-lease covenants to pay rent and only applies in so far as the head-lease covenants relate to the sub-let premises. Ordinarily, there is no privity of contract or estate between a head-landlord and a sub-tenant, but the direct covenant creates a contractual relationship. This enables the head-landlord to sue the sub-tenant for any breaches of either the head-lease (other than for non-payment of rent) or the sub-lease.

28.4   LIABILITY TO THE HEAD-LANDLORD

Ordinarily, there is neither privity of contract nor privity of estate between a head-landlord and a sub-tenant and, therefore, the head-landlord is unable to sue a sub-tenant in respect of any breaches of the terms of the head-lease. There are, however, three methods by which the head-landlord may acquire such a right to sue.

28.4.1   Under the common law

A sub-tenant may be bound by those restrictive covenants in the head-lease of which it had notice when it took its sub-lease. As the sub-tenant is entitled to call for production of the head-lease on the grant of its sub-lease (LPA 1925, s 44), the sub-tenant will be deemed to have notice of the contents of the head-lease even if it does not insist on its right to inspect it. This will not, however, assist the head-landlord with the enforcement of positive covenants.

28.4.2   By a direct covenant

As discussed at **28.3.2**, it is common practice for a direct covenant with the head-landlord to be given in the licence to sub-let. This covenant will make the sub-tenant liable to the head-landlord in contract. However, a new direct covenant will need to be obtained on each and every assignment of the sub-lease from the proposed assignee.

28.4.3   Use of the Contracts (Rights of Third Parties) Act 1999

As an alternative to requiring the sub-tenant to enter into a direct covenant with the head-landlord, use could be made of the Contracts (Rights of Third Parties) Act 1999. Under the provisions of this Act, a non-contracting third party (such as the head-landlord) has the right to enforce a contract term if the contract expressly provides that it may or, subject to contrary intention, if the term purports to confer a benefit on that party. In the context of sub-leases, the tenant's covenants in the sub-lease could be expressed to be for the benefit of both the landlord and head-landlord. This would enable the head-landlord to sue the sub-tenant for any breach of the sub-lease, despite not being a party to the sub-lease. An advantage of this method is that, as each of the sub-tenant's covenants would be a 'tenant's covenant' for the purpose of the Landlord and Tenant (Covenants) Act 1995, they would automatically bind any assignee of the sub-tenant. In consequence, the head-landlord could, on assignment of the sub-lease, sue the sub-tenant's assignee without the need to take a direct covenant from the assignee. Despite this advantage, practitioners still tend to pursue a direct covenant (from both the original sub-tenant and any assignee) as it is a tried and tested method.

28.5   DRAFTING THE SUB-LEASE

In drafting the sub-lease, the tenant should bear in mind the following matters.

28.5.1   The term

The tenant should ensure that the term of the sub-lease is at least one day shorter than the unexpired residue of its head-lease term, since a sub-lease for the whole residue of the head-lease term will take effect as an assignment of that term. Not only will this be contrary to the tenant's intention, it will also probably breach the alienation covenant in the head-lease, as the landlord will have given its consent to a sub-letting, but not an assignment. In *Allied Dunbar Pension Services Ltd v Baker* [2001] All ER (D) 46, the High Court refused to grant rectification to a tenant who had granted a sub-lease for a term due to expire on the same day as the term of the head-lease. The court considered it plain that the parties had intended the sub-lease to expire on the same day as the head-lease. It was irrelevant that the tenant had not realised that by making the expiry dates of the sub-lease and head-lease coincide, it was effectively assigning its interest.

In taking up possession, the sub-tenant will be in occupation for the purpose of a business and may, therefore, enjoy security of tenure under Pt II of the LTA 1954 (see **Chapter 31**). The tenant may want to consider excluding the sub-letting from the protection of the Act so that it can be sure to resume occupation at the end of the sub-lease. Indeed, it may be a requirement of the alienation covenant in the head-lease that any sub-leases are to be contracted out of the LTA 1954, so that if the tenant's interest is terminated in circumstances which result in the sub-tenant becoming the immediate tenant of the head-landlord, the head-landlord will be guaranteed possession at the end of the sub-lease.

28.5.2 The rent

The tenant will want to ensure that the rent to be paid by the sub-tenant is as high as the market will currently allow, and if the sub-lease is to be granted for anything longer than a short term, the tenant will want to review the rent from time to time. Careful attention must again be paid to the alienation covenant in the head-lease which might dictate the terms upon which any sub-lettings are to be granted.

In the past, it was common for the head-landlord to include several requirements in the head-lease:

(a)   that any sub-letting by the tenant be granted at a rent equal to the greater of the rent payable under the head-lease and the full open market rent for the premises;

(b)   that any sub-letting be granted without the payment of a premium; and

(c)   that any sub-letting contain provisions for the review of rent (in an upwards direction only) which match the head-lease review provisions in terms of frequency, timing and basis of review.

The reason head-landlords sought to impose such conditions was that, at some future date, the head-lease might determine (eg by reason of surrender), leaving the sub-tenant as the head-landlord's immediate tenant upon the terms of the sub-lease. However, if the tenant, at the grant of its head-lease, had agreed to the restrictions described in (a) and (b) above, it could find it difficult to arrange a sub-letting, particularly at times when rents were depressed and potential sub-tenants would only pay a rent lower than the head-lease rent. One popular way around this was for the tenant to enter into a side letter or collateral agreement with the proposed sub-tenant in which the tenant agreed to reimburse the sub-tenant the difference between the head-lease rent and the current market rent. However, the case of *Allied Dunbar Assurance plc v Homebase Ltd* [2002] EWCA Civ 666, [2002] 27 EG 144 ruled that this was not a valid way of avoiding restrictions in the head-lease preventing sub-letting below the head-lease rent. The result of this was to render sub-leases containing such restrictions inalienable in times of falling rents. Whilst clearly problematic for the tenant, this also caused problems for the head-landlord. First, a lease that cannot in reality be disposed of will not be valued highly when it comes to rent review. Secondly, the practical effect of an inalienable lease may be the insolvency or financial difficulty of the tenant, leading to non-payment of rent. In consequence, many institutional head-landlords no longer require sub-lettings to be at the higher of the head-lease rent or open market rent. Note that the 2007 Code for Leasing Business Premises requires that if sub-letting is allowed, the rent should be the market rent as at the time of sub-letting.

If the sub-tenant is prepared to pay the same rent as that payable under the head-lease, it should be wary of an obligation in the sub-lease which simply requires it to pay the rents payable from time to time under the head-lease. Such a provision would give the sub-tenant no input into any negotiations for the review of rent during the term, and is likely to give little incentive to the tenant to argue with any vigour against the head-landlord at review, since it knows that whatever figure is agreed, it will be paid by the sub-tenant.

If the head-landlord has opted to tax for VAT purposes, so that VAT is payable by the tenant, the option in no way affects the sub-lease rents. It would, therefore, be wise for the tenant to opt to tax in respect of these premises so that VAT can be charged to the sub-tenant, although careful consideration must always be given to the effect of opting to tax.

28.5.3 The covenants

In drafting the sub-lease, the tenant will attempt to mirror the provisions of the head-lease. The tenant should be careful not to allow the sub-tenant scope to do anything at the premises which is forbidden under the provisions of the head-lease.

Particular attention should be paid to:

(a) *Alienation.* It is unlikely that the head-lease will allow any further sub-letting of the premises. Care should, therefore, be taken to impose appropriate restrictions in the sub-lease. There ought to be an absolute covenant against sub-letting (or sharing or parting with possession of the premises), with a qualified covenant against assigning the sub-lease.

(b) *Repair.* The same repairing obligation as affects the tenant (or an even tighter one) ought to be imposed upon the sub-tenant. In interpreting a repair covenant, regard is to be had to the age, character and locality of the premises at the time the lease was granted. If there has been a considerable lapse of time between the grant of the head-lease and the grant of the sub-lease, different standards of repair might be required by the respective repair covenants, leading to a possible residual repair liability on the part of the tenant. The sub-tenant's obligation will be to repair 'the premises'. The tenant must make sure that 'the premises' are defined in the sub-lease to include all of the premises demised by the head-lease or, if a sub-letting of part is contemplated, that the division of responsibility is clearly stated.

(c) *Insurance.* In all probability, the head-landlord will be insuring the premises, with the tenant reimbursing the premium. The sub-lease should, therefore, provide that the sub-tenant reimburses the premiums paid by the tenant (or a proportionate part if a sub-lease of part is contemplated).

(d) *Decoration.* The tenant should ensure that the sub-lease obliges the sub-tenant to decorate the premises as frequently as, at the times and in the manner required by the head-lease.

28.5.4 Rights of access

The tenant may resist attempts to extend the usual covenant in the sub-lease for quiet enjoyment to cover liability for the acts and omissions of someone with a title paramount (eg, the head-landlord). If the tenant did so, it would be in breach of the covenant if the head-landlord disturbed the sub-tenant's occupation by exercising a right of entry contained in the head-lease. However, in any case, to avoid a possible dispute, the tenant should ensure that, in reserving rights of entry onto and access over the sub-let premises, those rights are reserved for the benefit of the tenant and head-landlord.

28.5.5 Covenant to observe head-lease

Despite imposing broadly similar covenants in the sub-lease to those contained in the head-lease, the tenant will also want to include a sweeping-up provision obliging the sub-tenant to perform all of the covenants in the head-lease (other than those relating to the payments of rent) in so far as they affect the sub-let premises, and to indemnify the tenant against liability for breach. The sub-tenant might prefer, however, to enter into a negative obligation not to cause a breach of the head-lease covenants. Either way, the result will be that the sub-tenant's solicitor will need to conduct a careful review of the head-lease terms in addition to those of the sub-lease. Care must be taken on a sub-lease of part to ensure that a correct division of liability is made between tenant and sub-tenant in respect of the head-lease covenants.

28.5.6 Other drafting points

When drafting and negotiating the sub-lease, the following additional points may be borne in mind:

(a) Where there is to be a direct covenant in the licence to sub-let, it is important for the sub-tenant to remember that it will not work both ways, and so the sub-tenant does not have any means of enforcing a breach of covenant by the head-landlord. The sub-tenant should consider insisting upon a covenant by the tenant in the sub-lease obliging the tenant to enforce a breach of covenant by the head-landlord as and when required by the sub-tenant. The sub-tenant is likely to concede that it should bear the cost of any such action.

(b) The usual covenant for quiet enjoyment will not impose liability on the tenant in respect of the acts or omissions of the head-landlord. The sub-tenant may consider extending the usual covenant. See, however, **28.5.4**.

(c) The sub-tenant should ask the tenant to covenant with it to pass on to it any notices received from the head-landlord (eg LPA 1925, s 146 notices).

(d) The sub-tenant should explore the possibility of having its interest noted on the head-landlord's insurance policy. It should ask for details of the policy and ensure that provision is made to enable the policy to be produced to it from time to time. The provision referred to at (a) above should enable the sub-tenant to force the tenant to require the head-landlord to reinstate the premises if they are damaged by an insured risk.

REVIEW ACTIVITY

1. Imagine that several years ago your client entered into a lease in the form set out at **Appendix 4**, but with an annual rent of £100,000. Your client now wishes to sub-let the whole of the premises and has found a prospective sub-tenant. The sub-tenant is only prepared to take a sub-letting at an annual rent of £80,000. Is this permissible under the terms of the lease?

2. Would the client referred to in Question 1 be entitled to grant a sub-lease protected by Part II of the LTA 1954?

3. What is the purpose of clause 21.5(d) of the **Appendix 4** lease?

Answers to this Review activity may be found in Appendix 1.

CHAPTER 29

REMEDIES FOR BREACH OF COVENANT

29.1	Landlord's remedies	279
29.2	Tenant's remedies	284

29.1 LANDLORD'S REMEDIES

Before the landlord takes any steps against a defaulting tenant, it should first consider whether any other party is also liable. For example, are there any sureties or guarantors, is the original tenant under a continuing liability, or did any of the previous assignees give the landlord a direct covenant on assignment upon which they may still be liable? The reader will recall that the ability of the landlord to proceed against some of these other parties is affected by the Landlord and Tenant (Covenants) Act 1995 (LT(C)A 1995). These issues have been dealt with earlier in the book.

Before proceeding against a former tenant or its guarantor for a 'fixed charge', that is:

(a) rent; or

(b) service charge; or

(c) any liquidated sum payable under the lease; or

(d) interest on such sums,

the LT(C)A 1995, s 17 requires the landlord to serve a notice of the claim (usually referred to as a 'Default Notice') upon the former tenant or its guarantor, as the case may be, within six months of the current tenant's default (there is no requirement to serve a notice also on a former tenant before serving a notice on that tenant's guarantor (*Cheverell Estates Ltd v Harris* [1998] 02 EG 127)). Failure to serve a valid notice will mean that the landlord is unable to recover that sum from the former tenant or guarantor concerned. This requirement applies to all leases and not just those granted after the commencement of the LT(C)A 1995.

The Court of Appeal, in *Scottish & Newcastle plc v Raguz* [2007] EWCA Civ 150, had held that a s 17 notice had to be served by a landlord where a rent review date had passed without the new rent having been assessed, whether or not there were actually any arrears outstanding. The House of Lords ([2008] UKHL 65) reversed that decision. Should the delayed fixing of the new rent result in an increased amount being payable (which would be backdated to the review date), this would normally be due as a lump sum on the date specified in the lease. The landlord would then have six months from that date to serve a s 17 notice should it not be paid by the current tenant.

Where the landlord does proceed against a former tenant or its guarantor, that person may be able to regain some control over the property by calling for an overriding lease (see **29.1.4**).

In addition to considering whether there are other parties that it can pursue, the landlord should check whether it has another fund from which to meet the sums that are due, for example a rent deposit. If so, then it should first check that the contractual terms of that deposit permit deduction of the relevant amount and that the necessary preconditions (perhaps due notice) have been satisfied.

29.1.1   For non-payment of rent

Only six years' arrears of rent are recoverable, whether by claim or distress (Limitation Act 1980).

29.1.1.1   By claim

If the tenant, or one of the parties mentioned above, is liable for the rent, the landlord may pursue its normal remedies for recovery through the High Court or county court. As to the choice of court and type of proceedings, see the Legal Practice Guide, *Civil Litigation*.

29.1.1.2   Bankruptcy and winding up

If the sum owed to it exceeds £750, the landlord can consider starting insolvency proceedings against the tenant, in the hope that this will bring pressure to bear and the tenant will pay the debt rather than face insolvency. This approach has risks, though. If the tenant does not pay and the insolvency proceeds, the landlord may rank as only one of the unsecured (ordinary) creditors. These may not well not receive payment in full.

If the landlord wants to start insolvency proceedings (bankruptcy for an individual tenant, liquidation for a corporate tenant), it will first have to serve a statutory demand for payment of the debt. More details of insolvency processes are given in **Chapter 32**.

29.1.1.3   Commercial Rent Arrears Recovery

Part 3 of the Tribunals, Courts and Enforcement Act 2007 (TCEA 2007) contains provisions which replace the ancient common law remedy of distress with a more limited, court-based system called Commercial Rent Arrears Recovery (CRAR). CRAR allows a landlord of commercial property (where the tenancy is in writing) to instruct an enforcement agent to take control of the tenant's goods and sell them to recover the amount of the rent arrears. Rent, for these purposes, means the pure income rent plus any VAT and does not include sums in respect of services, repairs or insurance, even if such sums are reserved as rent in the lease.

The new procedure for CRAR is set out in Sch 12 to the TCEA 2007. Under CRAR, the landlord has to serve an enforcement notice on the tenant before seizing the goods. The minimum period of notice is currently at least seven clear days, unless a court orders a shorter period in circumstances where it thinks that the tenant will use the notice period to dispose of the goods. The landlord then needs to authorise (in writing) an enforcement agent to carry out CRAR on its behalf. The enforcement agent (an individual holding a certificate issued by a judge) may then take control of and sell the chattels in order to recover the rent arrears.

Under s 77 of the TCEA 2007, the tenant must be in arrears of rent before the enforcement notice is served, the amount of the rent arrears must be certain or capable of being calculated with certainty, and the net unpaid rent (ie the rent less interest, VAT or any sums owing to the tenant) must be equal to or exceed an amount prescribed in regulations, currently an amount equal to seven days' rent. These requirements must be met at the time the enforcement notice is given and when the enforcement agent takes control of the goods. If they are not, then CRAR cannot be exercised. The sale of goods cannot take place until at least seven clear days have passed since the goods were removed, unless delay would cause the goods to be unsaleable, or their value would be extinguished or substantially reduced. The tenant must be given at least seven clear days notice of the date, time and place of the sale, and the sale must be by public auction unless a court orders otherwise. If the CRAR provisions are breached, the tenant can bring a claim against the enforcement agent or the landlord, and the court can either return the goods to the tenant or award damages for loss suffered by the tenant because of the breach.

29.1.1.4   Collecting the rent from a sub-tenant

If the premises have been sub-let, the superior landlord can serve notice on the sub-tenant under s 81 of the TCEA 2007, requiring the sub-tenant to pay its rent to the superior landlord until the arrears are paid off. The sub-tenant should pay the rent to the superior landlord after the expiry of 14 clear days from the date when the notice was served on it.

29.1.1.5   Forfeiture

Forfeiture for non-payment of rent is dealt with at **25.4.1**.

29.1.2   Breach of tenant's repairing covenant

From a practical point of view, and as a first step, the landlord, exercising its right of entry in the lease, should enter onto the demised premises with its surveyor to draw up a schedule of dilapidations. This should be served on the tenant with a demand that the tenant comply with its repairing obligation. If the tenant remains in breach of its obligation to repair the demised premises, the landlord has various remedies available to it.

29.1.2.1   Claim for damages

The measure of damages

The landlord may bring a claim for damages against the tenant either during the term or after its expiry. Section 18 of the LTA 1927 limits the maximum amount recoverable in all cases by providing that the damages cannot exceed the amount by which the value of the reversion has been diminished by the breach. It follows that the cost of repairs will be irrecoverable to the extent that it exceeds this statutory ceiling.

Where proceedings are commenced during the term of the lease, the reduction in the value of the reversion will be influenced by the length of the unexpired residue of the term. The longer this is, the less the reduction should be.

In proceedings commenced at or after the end of the lease, the court may be prepared, at least as a starting point, to accept the cost of repairs as evidence of the measure of damages, subject to the ceiling imposed by s 18 (see *Smiley v Townshend* [1950] 2 KB 311). For examples of how this has been applied, see *Ultraworth Ltd v General Accident Fire and Life Assurance Corporation* [2000] 2 EGLR 115 (a case where the diminution in the value of the reversion was unaffected by the tenant's breach of the repairing obligation) and *Ravensgate Estates Ltd v Horizon Housing Group Ltd* [2007] All ER (D) 294 (where the landlord was planning to redevelop, so the full cost of repairs was not awarded). The correct approach is set out in *Van Dal Footwear v Ryman Ltd* [2009] EWCA Civ 1478.

If a sub-tenant is in breach of a repairing covenant in the sub-lease, the measure of damages is the reduction in value of the intermediate landlord's reversion. If the sub-tenant knows of the terms of the superior tenancy, the intermediate landlord's liability to the superior landlord will be relevant in assessing these damages.

Section 18 of the 1927 Act further provides that no damages are recoverable for failure to put or leave the premises in repair at the termination of the lease, if the premises are to be pulled down shortly after termination or if intended structural alterations would render the repairs valueless. To benefit from this provision the tenant must show that the landlord had a firm intention (to pull down or alter) at the end of the lease.

It is important to appreciate that s 18 applies only to claims for damages by the landlord and has no application where the sum owed by the tenant is in the nature of a debt. If, therefore, the tenant covenants to spend £x per year on repairs, but fails to do so, the landlord may recover the deficiency as a debt without regard to the statutory ceiling in s 18. This is the reason behind the clause in many leases, which permits the landlord to enter and carry out repair work that the tenant has failed to do (the *Jervis v Harris* clause, discussed in more detail at **29.1.2.2**).

The need for leave to sue

If the lease was granted for seven years or more and still has at least three years left to run, the Leasehold Property (Repairs) Act 1938 lays down a special procedure which the landlord must follow before being able to sue for damages (or forfeit the lease) for breach of the tenant's repairing covenant. Where the Act applies, it requires the landlord to serve a notice on the tenant under s 146 of the LPA 1925. Apart from the normal requirements of such a notice (see **30.5.3**), it must in addition contain a statement informing the tenant of its right to serve a counter-notice within 28 days claiming the benefit of the Act. If such a counter-notice is served, the landlord cannot proceed further without leave of the court, which will not be given unless the landlord proves (and not just shows an arguable case):

(a)   that the immediate remedying of the breach is required for preventing substantial diminution, or for complying with any Act or by-law, or for protecting the interests of occupiers other than the tenant, or for the avoidance of much heavier repair costs in the future; or

(b)   that there are special circumstances which render it just and equitable that leave be given.

Even if the landlord makes out one of the grounds, the court still has a discretion to refuse leave, but this should be exercised only where the court is clearly convinced that it would be wrong to allow the landlord to continue. The court may, in granting or refusing leave, impose such conditions on the landlord or tenant as it thinks fit. The relevant date for determining whether the grounds are established is the date of the hearing; see *Landmaster Properties Ltd v Thackeray Property Services* [2003] 35 EG 83.

The Act does not apply to breach of a tenant's covenant to put premises into repair when the tenant takes possession or within a reasonable time thereafter.

29.1.2.2   Self-help

If the tenant is in breach of its repairing obligations, can the landlord enter the demised premises, carry out the necessary works and recover the cost from the tenant? In the absence of a statutory right or an express provision in the lease, the landlord has no general right to enter the demised premises even where the tenant is in breach of its obligations. Indeed, the tenant may be able to obtain an injunction to restrain the landlord's trespass. For that reason most leases will contain an express right for the landlord to enter the demised premises and carry out any necessary repairs at the tenant's expense, in default of the tenant complying with a notice to repair. In the case of *Jervis v Harris* [1996] Ch 195, the court accepted the landlord's argument that his claim against the tenant to recover this expenditure was in the nature of a debt claim rather than one for damages. Thus, the landlord was able to evade the statutory restrictions in the 1927 and 1938 Acts, mentioned above.

Enforcing a *Jervis v Harris* clause (either to do the works or to recover all the money expended) can be very tricky. For example, the tenant may refuse the landlord entry to the building. The landlord will have to seek an injunction to compel the tenant to give access, and *Creska Ltd v Hammersmith and Fulham London Borough Council (No 2)* (1999) 78 P & CR D46 shows that the court may refuse such an injunction (in that case the circumstances were most unusual – the proposed repair works were of no benefit to the tenant, there was a long unexpired residue of the lease, and the tenant was willing to deposit monies in an escrow account to do the repairs at the end of the lease). Alternatively, the tenant may argue that the works being done do not qualify as repairs (but something more extensive, lying outside the ambit of the clause) or have been done at too great a cost.

29.1.2.3   Specific performance

In *Rainbow Estates Ltd v Tokenhold Ltd* [1999] Ch 64, the court held that, in principle, there is no reason why the equitable remedy of specific performance should not be available to enforce compliance by a tenant with its repairing obligation. However, other remedies are likely to be more appropriate, and the court stressed that specific performance will be awarded only in exceptional circumstances. In this case there was no alternative remedy for the landlord – unusually, the lease contained no forfeiture clause, nor a provision allowing the landlord to enter and carry out the repairs itself.

29.1.2.4   Forfeiture

The landlord may be able to forfeit the lease for breach of the tenant's covenant to repair; forfeiture is dealt with in **Chapter 25**.

29.1.3   Breaches of other covenants by the tenant: an outline

29.1.3.1   Damages

Damages for breach of covenant are assessed on a contractual basis, the aim being to put the landlord in the same position as if the covenant had been performed. The general principle is that the landlord may recover as damages all loss which may be fairly and reasonably considered as arising in the natural course of things from the breach, or such as may be reasonably supposed to have been in the contemplation of both parties, at the time of entering into the lease, as the probable result of that breach (*Hadley v Baxendale* (1854) 9 Exch 341). In the majority of cases the damages will be equal to the diminution in the value of the reversion.

The breach of some particular covenants will now be considered.

Covenant to insure

The landlord usually assumes responsibility for insurance. If, however, the tenant has covenanted to insure, there will be a breach of covenant if the premises are uninsured or underinsured at any time during the term. If the premises are damaged during the period of default, the measure of damages will be the cost of rebuilding (*Burt v British Transport Commission* (1955) 166 EG 4).

Covenant against dealings

There is little authority on the measure of damages obtainable by a landlord where, for example, the tenant has assigned the lease without consent. However, the landlord will probably be entitled to compensation for the fact that its new tenant is less financially sound than the assignor and the value of its reversion is thus reduced.

User covenant

Damages may be awarded for breach by the tenant of a positive covenant to keep the premises open. For example, if the anchor tenant, in breach of covenant, closes its shop premises in a shopping centre, it may have such an adverse effect on the profitability of the other shops in the centre that the landlord may be forced to offer rental concessions to the other tenants. The landlord should be compensated for this loss by an award of damages; but there may be difficult problems in quantifying the amount of the damages. If the landlord can prove that its financial loss arises wholly from the tenant's breach, there should be no difficulty for the landlord. However, it may be the case that the centre was already in decline long before the tenant ceased trading, so that the defaulting tenant's breach merely contributed to the already falling profitability of the centre (see, generally, *Transworld Land Co Ltd v J Sainsbury plc* [1990] 2 EGLR 255).

29.1.3.2 Injunction

In certain circumstances, the landlord may be able to obtain an injunction against the tenant. An injunction is an equitable remedy and thus at the discretion of the court, which may award damages instead. In an appropriate case the landlord may be able to obtain an interim injunction pending the full hearing. There are two types of injunction:

(a) *Injunctions prohibiting a breach of covenant.* The landlord may consider the use of such an injunction to prevent, for example:

    (i)   an assignment in breach of covenant;

    (ii) the carrying out of unauthorised alterations;

    (iii) an unauthorised use.

(b) *Mandatory injunctions.* These injunctions compel the tenant to do something to ensure the performance of a covenant. The court is cautious in its grant of mandatory injunctions.

Standard works on landlord and tenant law contain a more detailed consideration of the subject of injunctions.

29.1.3.3 Specific performance

Like the injunction, this is an equitable remedy and is therefore discretionary. The House of Lords confirmed that specific performance is not available against a tenant who is in breach of its 'keep open' covenant (*Co-operative Insurance Society Ltd v Argyll Stores (Holdings) Ltd* [1997] 23 EG 137).

29.1.3.4 Forfeiture

Often the landlord's most effective remedy will be to commence (or threaten to commence) forfeiture proceedings against the tenant with a view to ending the lease. This remedy is dealt with at **30.5**.

29.1.4 Right of former tenant or its guarantor to an overriding lease

If a former tenant, or guarantor, is served with a notice by the landlord requiring payment of a fixed charge (see **29.1**), the LT(C)A 1995 allows it to call for an overriding lease within 12 months of payment. For example, L granted a lease to T in 1980. The lease is now owned by A which fell into arrears with its rent. L served notice on T requiring T to pay this sum. T duly made full payment and now claims an overriding lease from L. This will be a head-lease 'slotted in' above the lease of the defaulting tenant. The lease of the defaulting tenant moves one step down the reversionary line and becomes a sub-lease. Thus, T will become the immediate landlord of A and in the event of continued default by A can decide what action to take against A, eg forfeiture of the occupational lease (sub-lease). Under the overriding lease, T now has some control over the premises for which it is being held liable. The same situation would arise in leases granted on or after 1 January 1996 where the former tenant had been required under an authorised guarantee agreement to guarantee the performance of its immediate assignee, and that assignee is now in default (see **20.2.4.3**).

The terms of the overriding lease will be on the terms of the defaulting tenant's lease (with consequential adjustments to add a small reversionary period).

Before deciding to call for an overriding lease, a former tenant (or guarantor) should be made aware that it may become liable for landlord's covenants (eg repairing obligations).

29.2 TENANT'S REMEDIES

29.2.1 Breach of an express covenant

In general, a breach by the landlord of one of its covenants in the lease will entitle the tenant to bring a claim for damages. The measure of damages will usually be the difference between the value of the tenant's interest in the premises with the covenant performed and the value with the covenant broken. In certain circumstances, the tenant may seek a more appropriate remedy, such as specific performance or an injunction.

Particular attention should be paid to the landlord's repairing covenant.

29.2.1.1 Breach of landlord's repairing covenant

Unless the lease is of part of a building, it is unusual for the landlord to enter into a covenant to repair. Even where the landlord has assumed the responsibility for repairs, it will generally be liable only if it has notice of disrepair. If the landlord fails to carry out the repairs for which it is liable, the tenant has various remedies available to it. These include the following.

Claim for damages

The tenant's normal remedy will be to bring a claim against its landlord for damages for breach of covenant. Section 18 of the LTA 1927, which restricts a landlord's claim for damages (see **29.1.2.1**), is not relevant to a tenant's claim. Here, damages will be assessed by comparing the value of the premises to the tenant at the date of assessment with their value if the landlord had complied with its obligation. The tenant will also be entitled to damages for consequential loss such as damage caused to the tenant's goods. If the disrepair was such that the tenant was forced to move into temporary accommodation, the cost of this should also be recoverable, provided the tenant had acted reasonably to mitigate its loss.

Self-help

Subject to notifying the landlord and giving it a reasonable opportunity to perform its covenant, the tenant is entitled to carry out the repair itself and deduct the reasonable cost of so doing from future payments of rent (*Lee-Parker v Izzet* [1971] 1 WLR 1688). If the landlord sues the tenant for non-payment of rent, the tenant will have a defence (see **17.1**).

Specific performance

The tenant, unlike the landlord, may be able to obtain an order of specific performance. The granting of the order is entirely at the discretion of the court, and being an equitable remedy it will not be granted if damages are an adequate remedy. Further, there must be a clear breach of covenant and must be no doubt over what is required to be done to remedy the breach.

Appointment of receiver

In the tenant's claim against the landlord for breach of covenant, the tenant may seek the appointment of a receiver to collect the rents and manage the property in accordance with the terms of the lease (including the performance of the landlord's covenants). The court has this power whenever it appears just and convenient to make such an appointment (Senior Courts Act 1981, s 37). The power has been exercised not only where the landlord had abandoned the property, but also where it has failed to carry out urgently needed repairs in accordance with its covenant (see *Daiches v Bluelake Investments Ltd* [1985] 2 EGLR 67).

The tenant must nominate a suitably qualified person to act as receiver, for example a surveyor; and before agreeing to act, the potential appointee should ensure that the assets of which he will have control will be sufficient to meet his fees, or that he obtains an indemnity in respect of them from the applicant.

A receiver may also be appointed where the landlord collects a service charge from the tenants but fails to provide the services it has promised.

29.2.2 Breach of an implied covenant

29.2.2.1 Covenant for quiet enjoyment

Most leases will contain an express covenant by the landlord for quiet enjoyment (see **Chapter 23**). In the absence of an express covenant, one will be implied arising out of the relationship of landlord and tenant. The implied covenant extends only to interruption of or interference with the tenant's enjoyment of the demised premises by the landlord or any person lawfully claiming under it; it does not extend to acts done by anyone with a title superior to that of the landlord. Express covenants are often similarly restricted, in which case the only significant difference between the express and the implied covenant is that under an express covenant the landlord will remain liable throughout the term granted (unless, under a 'new lease', the landlord is released on assignment under the LT(C)A 1995), whereas under an implied covenant the landlord's liability operates only during the currency of its ownership of the reversion.

The covenant will provide the tenant with a remedy in the case of unlawful eviction, or where there is any substantial interference with the tenant's use and enjoyment of the premises either by the landlord or by the lawful (rightful) acts of anyone claiming under it. The acts likely to amount to a breach of the covenant are discussed at **23.2**. The normal remedy will be damages, assessed on a contractual basis, to compensate the tenant for the loss resulting from the breach.

29.2.2.2   Derogation from grant

A landlord is under an implied obligation not to derogate from its grant. This covenant complements the covenant for quiet enjoyment, and sometimes the two overlap. The landlord will be in breach of its obligation if it does anything which substantially interferes with the use of the demised premises for the purpose for which they were let. Having given something with one hand, the landlord cannot take away its enjoyment with the other. The principle is often used to prevent the landlord from using its retained land in a way which frustrates the purpose of the lease. Thus, it has been held to be a derogation from grant for a landlord to grant a lease for the purpose of storing explosives and then to use its retained land in such a way as to render the storage of explosives on the demised premises illegal (*Harmer v Jumbil (Nigeria) Tin Areas Ltd* [1921] 1 Ch 200; see also *Petra Investments Ltd v Jeffrey Rogers plc* [2000] 3 EGLR 120, a case concerning the landlord's ability to alter the original concept of a shopping centre, and *Platt v London Underground* [2001] 20 EG 227, where the landlord closed off the entry to the station and reduced footfall past the unit). Similarly, if the landlord uses machinery on its retained land which by reason of vibration affects the stability of the demised premises, there will be a breach of the implied covenant. However, there will be no derogation from grant where the landlord's use of the adjoining land merely makes the user of the demised premises less attractive, for example by letting the adjoining premises to a business competitor of the tenant (*Port v Griffith* [1938] 1 All ER 295 and *Romulus Trading Co Ltd v Comet Properties Ltd* [1996] 2 EGLR 70; but see also *Oceanic Village Ltd v Shirayama Shokusan Co Ltd* [2001] All ER (D) 62 (Feb), in which the High Court was prepared, exceptionally, to find the landlord in breach of the obligation in such circumstances).

Until the decision in *Chartered Trust plc v Davies* [1997] 49 EG 135, it was generally believed that it was insufficient to amount to derogation from grant for a landlord to stand back while tenant A, in breach of covenant, committed acts of nuisance against tenant B thus driving tenant B out of business. Just because the landlord failed to take action against tenant A to prevent the nuisance did not, so it was thought, amount to a repudiation of B's lease. However, the Court of Appeal held that inaction by the landlord in these circumstances may amount to derogation from grant. The implications of this decision will be felt most where, as in the instant case, the landlord has retained management control of a shopping centre and is responsible for the common parts. If, in breach of covenant, one of the tenants does something in the common parts which adversely affects another tenant, the landlord will have to consider acting to enforce the lease obligations or else run the risk of being found to have derogated from grant (see also *Nynehead Developments Ltd v RH Fibreboard Containers Ltd and Others* [1999] 9 EG 174).

CHAPTER 30

METHODS OF TERMINATION

30.1	Introduction	287
30.2	Expiry	287
30.3	Notice to quit	287
30.4	Operation of break clause	288
30.5	Surrender	288
30.6	Merger	289
	Review activity	289

30.1 INTRODUCTION

There are a number of ways at common law in which a lease may be ended. Before looking at these in detail, it is important to appreciate that if the tenant enjoys the protection of the security of tenure provisions under Pt II of the LTA 1954, the lease may be ended only in one of the ways specified by that Act (for which see **Chapter 31**).

In addition, forfeiture is a way in which a lease may come to an end, and this is considered in detail in **Chapter 25**.

The methods of termination to be considered here are:

(a)   expiry (effluxion of time);

(b)   notice to quit;

(c)   operation of break clause;

(d)   surrender;

(e)   merger.

30.2 EXPIRY

A fixed-term tenancy will terminate automatically at the end of that term; there is no need for either party to take any steps at all. If the tenant remains in possession beyond the expiry date with the landlord's consent, it holds over as a tenant at will (ie, on terms that either party may end the tenancy at any time). A tenant at will may become an implied periodic tenant by the payment and acceptance of rent.

30.3 NOTICE TO QUIT

A periodic tenancy will not end by effluxion of time but may be determined by service of a notice to quit by either party. There are many technical rules surrounding the drafting and service of such notices and reference should be made to one of the standard works on landlord and tenant law for a consideration of these. What follows is only intended as a reminder of some of the more important rules.

In the absence of contrary agreement, the minimum length of notice required is as follows:

(a)   yearly tenancy: half a year's notice (or two quarters if the tenancy expires on a quarter day);

(b)   monthly tenancy: one month's notice;

(c)   weekly tenancy: one week's notice.

Not only must the length of notice be correct, it must also expire at the end of a completed period of the tenancy. In the case of a yearly tenancy, this means that the notice must expire on the anniversary of the commencement of the tenancy or on the day before the anniversary. For example, with a yearly tenancy beginning on 1 January in one year, the notice should expire on 1 January or 31 December in any subsequent year. A similar rule applies to other periodic tenancies.

At common law, no particular form of notice is required but it must be unambiguous and, for the avoidance of doubt, in writing.

As a general rule, unless the lease provides to the contrary, a notice to quit must relate to all of the land in the lease and not just part.

30.4 OPERATION OF BREAK CLAUSE

A fixed-term tenancy may contain a provision, known as a break clause, for the tenancy to be terminated by either landlord or tenant before it has run its full term. An example of a break clause is at clause 45 of the **Appendix 4** lease. According to the *Property Data Report 2014*, the proportion of commercial leases in 2012 with break clauses was 31%.

The right to break will usually be at a particular time (eg at the end of the fifth year of a 10-year lease) or on the happening of a specified event.

The exercise of a break clause is often subject to conditions that must be met (see clause 45.2 of the **Appendix 4** lease – payment of rent, no occupation, no sub-leases). Another common condition is that the right is subject to the tenant having complied with its covenants, which will be construed strictly, so a tenant may find a minor or trivial breach will prevent it from exercising the right to break. The exact wording of the break clause should be examined to see whether any such conditions have to be satisfied at the date when the notice is served or at the date when the notice expires.

Normally a break right must be exercised strictly in accordance with its express terms, conditions and procedures (confirmed by the Court of Appeal in the recent case of *Friends Life Ltd v Siemens Hearing Instruments Ltd* [2014] EWCA Civ 382). However, minor errors in the formalities required may be allowed following the case of *Mannai Investment Co Ltd v Eagle Star Life Assurance Co Ltd* [1997] AC 749, which held that if a notice could be unambiguously understood to be an effective notice by a reasonable recipient then the errors may not render the notice invalid.

Conditional break rights and the formalities required to break a lease are dealt with further at **16.2.2**.

If a head-lease is terminated by the exercise of a break right, any sub-lease which has been created will also end. If the underlease term would have expired after the break date, the sub-tenant may have a claim against the tenant for derogation from grant (*Barrett v Morgan* [2000] 2 AC 264). However, if the sub-tenant is protected under Pt II of the LTA 1954, it would have the right to apply for a renewal lease.

30.5 SURRENDER

Surrender occurs where a tenant yields up its lease to its immediate landlord who accepts the surrender. It is a consensual arrangement. The lease is said to merge in the landlord's reversion and is extinguished.

Surrender can be express or by operation of law. An express surrender of a lease exceeding three years must be made by deed (LPA 1925, s 52). Surrender by operation of law occurs where the parties act in an unequivocal way which is inconsistent with the continuance of the lease. There are many examples of conduct where a surrender by operation of law has been inferred, including:

(a)   The parties agree a new lease to commence during the currency of the existing lease.

(b)   The tenant gives up possession and returns the key to the landlord, and the landlord accepts this as surrender (but if the key is merely left with the landlord, this in itself will not amount to surrender unless the landlord accepts it as surrender, for example by re-letting the premises (see *Arundel Corporation v The Financial Training Co Ltd* [2000] 3 All ER 456)).

Examples of conduct where a surrender by operation of law *has not been inferred* include:

(a)   where a third party occupant is negotiating a lease (*QFS Scaffolding Limited v Sable and Another* [2010] EWCA Civ 682);

(b)   where the landlord failed to demand rent and service charge when it knew the tenant no longer wanted the lease (*Belcourt Estates Ltd v Adesina* [2005] EWCA Civ 208).

In *Artworld Financial Corporation v Safaryan* [2009] 23 EG 94 it was held a surrender had occurred due to the cumulative effect of the landlord's conduct, even though the landlord's individual acts (accepting the keys from the tenant, redecorating, allowing occupation by a third party related to the landlord) might not have supported that effect.

A provision in a lease protected under Pt II of the LTA 1954 which requires the tenant to offer to surrender the lease before seeking consent to assign is void under s 38 of the LTA 1954 (*Allnatt London Properties Ltd v Newton* [1984] 1 All ER 423, and see **31.1.5**).

A surrender will release the tenant from any future liability under the lease but not in respect of past breaches. A well-advised tenant should therefore seek a release from all breaches.

The surrender of a head-lease will not terminate any sub-lease (*Mellor v Watkins* (1874) LR 9 QBD 400). The sub-tenant will become the immediate tenant of the head-landlord on the terms of the sub-lease (LPA 1925, s 139). Sometimes, a head-tenant will agree to surrender its head-lease with a view to taking a new fixed term from its landlord; this may happen where the head-lease is coming to the end of its fixed term. In this situation, any new head-lease granted following the surrender will be subject to the sub-lease (LPA 1925, s 150).

30.6   MERGER

Merger occurs where a tenant acquires its immediate landlord's reversion or a third party acquires both the lease and the immediate reversion. In such a case the lease will end. However, merger will take place only where the person acquiring both the lease and immediate reversion holds both estates in the same capacity and intends merger to take place.

As with surrender, merger of a lease will not affect the position of any sub-tenant (LPA 1925, s 139).

REVIEW ACTIVITY

Complete the grid below by placing a cross in the relevant column.

	Sub-lease survives	Sub-lease does not survive
Surrender		
Merger		
Break exercised		
Forfeiture		

Answers to this Review activity may be found in Appendix 1.

CHAPTER 31

THE LANDLORD AND TENANT ACT 1954, PART II

31.1	Introductory matters	291
31.2	Termination under the Act	296
31.3	The application to court	300
31.4	Interim rents	301
31.5	Grounds of opposition	303
31.6	Compensation for failure to obtain a new tenancy	307
31.7	The renewal lease	308
31.8	The order for the new lease	310
31.9	Procedural flowchart – s 25 notice	311
	Review activity	311

31.1 INTRODUCTORY MATTERS

31.1.1 The protection of the Act

The principal Act conferring security of tenure on business tenants and regulating the manner in which business tenancies can be terminated is the LTA 1954 (statutory references in this chapter are to this Act, unless otherwise stated). The protection given to tenants covered by Pt II of the Act is twofold. First, a business tenancy will not come to an end at the expiration of a fixed term, nor can a periodic tenancy be terminated by the landlord serving an ordinary notice to quit. Instead, notwithstanding the ending of the contractual term, the tenancy will be automatically continued under s 24 until such time as it is terminated in one of the ways specified in the Act. Secondly, upon the expiration of a business tenancy in accordance with the Act, business tenants normally have a statutory right to apply to court for a new tenancy and the landlord may only oppose that application on certain statutory grounds. Any new tenancy granted will also enjoy the protection of the Act.

Selected extracts from the Act are set out in **Appendix 6**.

31.1.2 The application of the Act

Section 23(1) provides that

> this ... Act applies to any tenancy where the property comprised in the tenancy is or includes premises which are occupied by the tenant and are so occupied for the purposes of a business carried on by him or for those and other purposes.

This involves a number of elements.

31.1.2.1 There must be a 'tenancy'

Tenancy includes an agreement for a lease and an underlease (even an unauthorised one). However, licences are not protected. The lease/licence distinction is further considered at **11.4**. In view of the danger for landlords in inadvertently creating a protected tenancy, the use of licences as a means of avoiding the Act needs very careful consideration. Certain tenancies are specifically excluded from the protection of the Act and these are dealt with at **31.1.3**.

31.1.2.2   The premises must be occupied by the tenant

Occupation need not be by the tenant personally. It has been held that occupation may be sufficient where it is conducted through the medium of a manager or agent provided that such representative occupation is genuine and not a sham arrangement. Similarly, s 23(1A) and (1B) provides that the Act will apply where an individual is the tenant but the premises are then occupied by a company in which the tenant has a controlling interest. 'Controlling interest' is defined by s 46(2). There are also special rules as to occupation in ss 41, 41A and 46 where a tenancy is held on trust, vested in partners as trustees, or held by one member of a group of companies but occupied by another member of the same group.

Occupation need not be continuous provided that the 'thread of continuity' of business user is not broken (*Hancock & Willis v GMS Syndicate Ltd* (1982) 265 EG 473 and *Flairline Properties Ltd v Hassan* [1997] 1 EGLR 138). In *Pointon York Group plc v Poulton* [2006] EWCA Civ 1001, it was held that parking a car in a car parking space during normal business hours could amount to occupation for the purposes of the LTA 1954.

Problems may arise where a business tenant sub-lets part of the property to a business sub-tenant. In such a situation, they cannot both qualify for protection in respect of the sub-let part; there can be no dual occupation for the purposes of the Act. In normal circumstances, it will be the sub-tenant who enjoys the protection of the Act, although in an exceptional case the head-tenant may reserve sufficiently extensive rights over the sub-let part that it remains the occupier (see *Graysim Holdings Ltd v P&O Property Holdings Ltd* [1995] 3 WLR 854). The case of *Pointon York Group plc v Poulton* [2006] EWCA Civ 1001 shows the problems landlords can face due to the rule that any sub-lease must of necessity be shorter than the head-lease out of which it is granted. In this case, the head-tenant moved back into occupation in the short period between the end of the sub-lease and the later ending of the head-lease and was thus enabled to claim the protection of the Act. It is arguable that a landlord cannot serve a s 25 notice at a time when the tenant is not in business occupation, and so in situations like the *Poulton* case the landlord would not be able to serve the s 25 notice until the tenant actually took up occupation. Since the landlord must give at least six months' notice (see **31.2.1.1**), this would seriously delay the landlord's ability to obtain possession or grant a renewal lease at an increased rent.

31.1.2.3   The premises must be occupied for the purposes of a business carried on by the tenant

'Business' is widely defined in s 23 to include a 'trade, profession or employment and includes any activity carried on by a body of persons, whether corporate or unincorporate'. Where the business is carried on by an individual, it must amount to a trade, profession or employment; but where it is carried on by a body of persons (corporate or unincorporate) 'any activity' may suffice. Thus, it has been held that the organising of a tennis club and the activities of the governors in running a hospital, both amounted to a business use (*Addiscombe Garden Estates v Crabbe* [1958] 1 QB 513 and *Hills (Patents) Ltd v University College Hospital Board of Governors* [1956] 1 QB 90). This does not mean, however, that the Act will apply whenever the tenant is a body of persons; the 'activity' must be correlative to the conceptions involved in the words 'trade, profession or employment'.

Two problem areas may arise with this requirement.

(a)   The demised premises will sometimes be used for two purposes, only one of which is a business user. For example, the letting may consist of a shop on the ground floor with living accommodation above. Does the Act still apply? In cases of mixed user the Act will apply provided the business activity is a significant purpose of the occupation and not merely incidental to the occupation of the premises as a residence (*Cheryl Investments Ltd v Saldhana* [1978] 1 WLR 1329 and *Gurton v Parrot* [1991] 1 EGLR 98). In the example mentioned, the Act is likely to apply. If, however, a residential tenant occasionally brought work home with him, this would not result in his tenancy being protected under the Act.

(b) The business user may be in breach of a covenant of the lease. How does that affect the tenant's rights? If the lease merely forbids a specific business use (eg, not to use the shop as a newsagents), or any use except the business use specified (eg, not to use the premises for any purpose other than as a newsagents), a business use in breach of such a provision will not deprive the tenant of the protection of the Act. However, s 24(3) does exclude from protection any tenancy where the use of the premises for business purposes is in breach of a general prohibition preventing all business use (eg, not to carry on any business, trade, profession or employment) although if the landlord had consented to or acquiesced in the breach, the Act would still apply.

31.1.3 Exclusions from the Act

Apart from those tenancies which fail to satisfy the requirements of s 23, there are other tenancies which are not protected by the Act. These include:

(a) Tenancies at will. In *Javad v Aqil* [1991] 1 WLR 1007, a prospective tenant who was allowed into possession while negotiations proceeded for the grant of a new business lease was held, on the facts, to be a tenant at will, and thus excluded from protection. A similar decision was reached in *London Baggage Co (Charing Cross) Ltd v Railtrack plc* [2000] EGCS 57, where a tenant holding over after the expiry of its lease, pending the negotiation of a new lease, was held to be a tenant at will. (See also *Barclays Wealth Trustees (Jersey) Ltd v Erimus Housing Ltd* [2014] EWCA Civ 303, where it was held that the inference of a tenancy at will, rather than a periodic tenancy, is even stronger where a periodic tenancy would have security of tenure but the intended new lease is to be contracted out.)

(b) Tenancies of agricultural holdings: these have their own form of protection under the Agricultural Holdings Act 1986.

(c) A farm business tenancy.

(d) Mining leases.

(e) Service tenancies. These are tenancies granted to the holder of an office, appointment or employment from the landlord and which continue only so long as the tenant holds such office, etc. For the exclusion to apply the tenancy must be in writing and express the purpose for which it was granted.

(f) Fixed-term tenancies not exceeding six months. These tenancies are excluded unless the tenancy contains provisions for renewing the term or extending it beyond six months, or the tenant (including any predecessor in the same business) has already been in occupation for a period exceeding 12 months (see *Cricket Ltd v Shaftesbury plc* [1999] 3 All ER 283).

(g) 'Contracted out' tenancies (see **31.1.5**).

31.1.4 Two important definitions

31.1.4.1 The competent landlord

It is between the tenant and the competent landlord that the procedure under the Act must be conducted. It is important, therefore, that the tenant identifies its competent landlord and deals with that landlord. Where a freeholder grants a lease, there is no cause for concern as the tenant's competent landlord can be no other than the freeholder. However, where the tenant is a sub-tenant, the statutory definition of competent landlord means that the sub-tenant's immediate landlord may not be its competent landlord. Using s 44 of the Act, the sub-tenant must look up the chain of superior tenancies for the first person who either owns the freehold or who has a superior tenancy which will not come to an end within 14 months. The following examples may assist:

As the first example involves a sub-letting of the whole of the premises, T will not be in occupation, and will not, therefore, enjoy the protection of the Act. This means that the head-lease will come to an end on its contractual expiry date, with the result that as soon as the head-lease has entered the last 14 months of its contractual term, ST's competent landlord will be the freeholder. However, in the second example, because it is a sub-letting of part only, then provided T occupies the remaining part for business purposes, the head-lease will be protected. Therefore, it will not expire by effluxion of time. So even if the head-lease has entered the last 14 months of its contractual term, the sub-tenant's competent landlord will still be T (unless, eg, the freeholder has served an appropriate notice terminating the head-lease within 14 months, see **31.2.1**).

It is therefore very important for sub-tenants to identify their competent landlord, and this can be done by serving a notice on their immediate landlord under s 40 of the Act seeking information about the landlord's interest. A s 40 notice should always be served by a sub-tenant before taking any other steps under the Act. The prescribed form is set out in **Appendix 2**.

31.1.4.2 The 'holding'

The definition of the holding is important because the tenant's right to a new lease normally extends to only that part of the premises known as the 'holding'. Further, many of the landlord's grounds of opposition refer to the holding. This term is defined in s 23(3) of the Act as being the property comprised in the current tenancy excluding any part which is not occupied by the tenant or a person employed by the tenant for the purposes of the tenant's business. In practice, in the majority of cases, it is correct to describe the holding as comprising all the premises originally let except those parts which the tenant is currently sub-letting.

31.1.5 Contracting out – before 1 June 2004

As a general rule, s 38(1) forbids any contracting out of the Act. This means that any agreement purporting to exclude or modify the tenant's security of tenure is void. However, under s 38(4) of the Act the court was empowered to make an order excluding the security of tenure provisions, provided certain conditions were satisfied:

(a)   The proposed letting must have been for a term of years certain. Care must be taken not to fall foul of this requirement. In *Nicholas v Kinsey* [1994] 16 EG 145, a tenancy for 12 months and thereafter from year to year was held to be outside it. More controversially, in *Newham London Borough Council v Thomas-Van Staden* [2008] EWCA Civ 1414, the landlord had granted its tenant a lease for a term beginning on 1 January 2003 and ending on 28 September 2004. The lease defined this period as 'the Term, which expression shall include any period of holding over or extension of it whether by statute or at common law or by agreement'. The Court of Appeal decided that was not for a 'term of years certain', as required by the legislation, because the term had been defined to include a subsequent indefinite period. This again rendered the contracting out void.

(b)   There must have been a joint application to court by both parties.

(c)   The lease entered into must have been substantially the same as the draft lease attached to the court order (*Receiver for Metropolitan Police District v Palacegate Properties Ltd* [2001] 2 Ch 131).

Further, and most importantly, the court's approval must have been obtained before the tenancy was granted (*Essexcrest Ltd v Evenlex Ltd* [1988] 1 EGLR 69).

These provisions have now been changed with regard to leases entered into on or after 1 June 2004. However, the old rules will still be relevant in the case of a dispute between the parties to a contracted-out lease granted before this date if the tenant were to claim that the contracting-out procedures were not correctly followed and that the lease does have security of tenure. Equally, any potential purchaser of the landlord's reversion to a contracted-out lease will need to check carefully that the correct procedures were followed in order to avoid as far as possible any such claim by a tenant.

31.1.6   Contracting out – on or after 1 June 2004

The new rules no longer require a court order, but still require the proposed letting to be for a term of years certain. Instead the landlord must serve a notice on the tenant in the prescribed form and the tenant (or someone duly authorised by the tenant) must sign a declaration that it has received the notice and accepts the consequences of the agreement to contract out. If the notice is served within the 14 days prior to the grant of the tenancy, the tenant must make a statutory declaration as to this before an independent solicitor. The prescribed form of notice contains a 'health warning' advising the tenant that it is giving up the right to security of tenure and advising it to seek advice not only from a solicitor or surveyor but also from its accountant. The 'instrument creating the tenancy', ie, normally the lease, must then contain reference to the exclusion agreement, the notice and the declaration. The prescribed form of notice is set out below:

IMPORTANT NOTICE

You are being offered a lease without security of tenure. Do not commit yourself to the lease unless you have read this message carefully and have discussed it with a professional adviser.

Business tenants normally have security of tenure – the right to stay in their business premises when the lease ends.

If you commit yourself to the lease you will be giving up these important legal rights.

*   You will have **no right** to stay in the premises when the lease ends.
*   Unless the landlord chooses to offer you another lease, you will need to leave the premises.
*   You will be unable to claim compensation for the loss of your business premises, unless the lease specifically gives you this right.
*   If the landlord offers you another lease, you will have no right to ask the court to fix the rent.

It is therefore important to get professional advice – from a qualified surveyor, lawyer or accountant – before agreeing to give up these rights.

If you want to ensure that you can stay in the same business premises when the lease ends, you should consult your adviser about another form of lease that does not exclude the protection of the Landlord and Tenant Act 1954.

If you receive this notice at least 14 days before committing yourself to the lease, you will need to sign a simple declaration that you have received this notice and have accepted its consequences, before signing the lease.

> **But if you do not receive at least 14 days' notice, you will need to sign a 'statutory' declaration. To do so, you will need to visit an independent solicitor (or someone else empowered to administer oaths).**
>
> Unless there is a special reason for committing yourself to the lease sooner, you may want to ask the landlord to let you have at least 14 days to consider whether you wish to give up your statutory rights. If you then decided to go ahead with the agreement to exclude the protection of the Landlord and Tenant Act 1954, you would only need to make a simple declaration, and so you would not need to make a separate visit to an independent solicitor.

It is clear that the Government anticipated that the 14-day 'ordinary' notice would be the one most used. However, in practice, the statutory declaration procedure is the one most used. This is largely because solicitors are reluctant to serve the notice until the form of the lease has been finalised – and once it has been finalised, parties do not want to have to wait 14 days before the tenant can take up occupation and start paying rent.

The reason for the reluctance stems from a lack of clarity in the new procedure. Under the old law, it had been held (see **31.1.5**) that the lease entered into must be in substantially the same form as the one approved by the court for contracting out. It was not made clear under the new provisions whether a similar rule might apply. What if the contracting-out notice was signed and then the terms of the lease were substantially renegotiated. Would that original notice still be valid? In order to avoid any possible problems, it is usual practice for the notice not to be signed until the terms of the lease have been substantially agreed.

Another problem to bear in mind with the procedure is the position of any guarantors. It is not unusual in a guarantee agreement to find a covenant by the guarantor that it will enter into a new lease of the premises if the tenant should become insolvent and the liquidator should then disclaim the lease. If it is intended that such lease is also to be contracted out of the Act, notice must be served on and signed by the guarantor before it is legally obliged to take that lease, ie before it signs the guarantee agreement, not before the lease itself is granted. Similar principles must be applied where an outgoing tenant is entering into an AGA (see **20.2.4.3**). It is likely that this will require the tenant to take a new lease on disclaimer.

31.1.7 Continuation tenancies

A business tenancy protected by the Act will not come to an end on the expiry of the contractual term. Instead, s 24 continues the tenancy on exactly the same terms (except those relating to termination) and at exactly the same rent until it is terminated in accordance with the Act. However, the landlord may be able to obtain an increased rent by asking the court to fix an interim rent under s 24A (see **31.4**).

If the tenant ceases occupation of the premises on or before the contractual termination date then one of the qualifying conditions for the Act to apply is no longer fulfilled (see **31.1.2**). In these circumstances a fixed-term tenancy will come to an end by effluxion of time and no continuation tenancy will arise (see s 27(1A), confirming the decision in *Esselte AB v Pearl Assurance plc* [1997] 1 WLR 891; see also *Surrey County Council v Single Horse Properties Ltd* [2002] EWCA Civ 367, [2002] 1 WLR 2106). In this situation the tenant will not incur any further liability for rent (the tenant may also choose to serve a s 27 notice in these circumstances, see **31.2**).

31.2 TERMINATION UNDER THE ACT

A tenancy protected under the Act will not end automatically at the expiration of a lease for a fixed term, nor, if it is a periodic tenancy, can it be ended by an ordinary notice to quit given by the landlord. Instead, such a tenancy can only be terminated in one of the ways prescribed by the Act:

(a)   By the service of a landlord's statutory notice (a 's 25 notice').

(b)   By the tenant's request in statutory form (a 's 26 request').

(c)   Forfeiture (or forfeiture of a superior tenancy).

(d)   Surrender. To be valid the surrender must take immediate effect.

(e)   For a periodic tenancy, by the tenant giving the landlord a notice to quit, unless this was given before the tenant has been in occupation for a period of one month.

(f)   Where the lease is for a fixed term, by written notice under s 27 of the Act. Where there is at least three months before the contractual expiry date, the tenant can serve a notice under s 27(1), terminating the tenancy on or after the contractual expiry date. As noted above, s 27(1A), confirming the case of *Esselte AB v Pearl Assurance plc* [1997] 1 WLR 891, provides that if a tenant ceases to occupy the premises for business purposes on or before the contractual expiry date, the lease will come to an end by effluxion of time and a s 27 notice is not needed. However, *Esselte* (and s 27(1A)) must now be read in the light of subsequent cases (*Bacchiocci v Academic Agency Ltd* [1998] 1 WLR 1313 and *Sight and Sound Education Ltd v Books etc Ltd* [1999] 43 EG 61) which have created uncertainty over the period of absence required before it can be established that the tenant has ceased occupation for the purposes of the Act. In light of these cases it may be safer for a tenant to proceed by service of a s 27 notice (see also *Arundel Corporation v The Financial Training Co Ltd* [2000] 3 All ER 456 which, again, emphasises the desirability of a s 27 notice). Where the tenancy is already continuing, or where there is less than three months left to the contractual expiry date, the tenant can serve a notice under s 27(2) giving the landlord not less than three months' notice of the date of termination.

It is the first two of the above methods, the s 25 notice and s 26 request, which are the usual methods of terminating a protected business tenancy.

31.2.1   Section 25 notices

31.2.1.1   Form

If such a notice is to be effective, it must be in the prescribed form and be given to the tenant by the competent landlord not less than six months, nor more than 12 months, before the date of termination specified in it. The prescribed forms are contained in the Landlord and Tenant Act 1954, Part II (Notices) (England and Wales) Regulations 2004 (SI 2004/1005), although a form 'substantially to the like effect' can be used instead. Two slightly different forms are prescribed: one for use where the landlord does not oppose the grant of a new tenancy; and one for use where it does. The forms are set out in **Appendix 2**.

A tenant will often seek to attack the validity of its landlord's notice on the ground that it is not in the correct form. The task of the court in these circumstances is to ascertain whether the notice served is substantially the same as the prescribed form. In doing this, any omission from the notice of matters irrelevant to the tenant's rights or obligations may not affect the validity of the notice. However, if the court decides that the notice is not the same as, or substantially to the same effect as, the prescribed form, it is irrelevant that the recipient did not suffer any prejudice: the notice will be invalid (*Sabella Ltd v Montgomery* [1998] 09 EG 153).

In *Smith v Draper* [1990] 2 EGLR 69, it was held that a landlord who had served what turned out to be an invalid notice, could withdraw it and serve a second valid notice.

31.2.1.2   Content

The notice must comply with the following requirements:

(a)   The notice must state the date upon which the landlord wants the tenancy to end. The specified termination date must not be earlier than the date on which the tenancy could have been terminated at common law, and, as mentioned above, the notice must be given not less than six months, nor more than 12 months, before this specified termination date.

For a periodic tenancy or a fixed term with a break clause, the specified termination date cannot be earlier than the date upon which the landlord could have ended the tenancy with an ordinary common law notice. If there is a break clause, it would appear that a separate contractual notice is unnecessary provided the s 25 notice states a date for termination no earlier than the date the break clause would operate (*Scholl Manufacturing Ltd v Clifton (Slim-Line) Ltd* [1967] Ch 41). If the tenancy is for a fixed term without a break clause, the specified termination date cannot be earlier than the last day of the contractual term. If, however, the contractual tenancy has already expired and the tenancy is being continued under the Act, the s 25 notice need only comply with the six–12-month rule mentioned above.

(b)   The notice must state whether or not the landlord will oppose an application to court by the tenant for the grant of a new tenancy and, if so, on which statutory ground(s). The tenant has the right to apply to court for a new tenancy but the landlord can oppose that application on one or more of the seven grounds of opposition set out in s 30 of the Act (see **31.5**). If this is the landlord's intention, it must state in the s 25 notice the ground(s) upon which it intends to rely. As there is no provision in the Act allowing the landlord to amend its notice, the choice of ground(s) is a matter which must be given very careful consideration.

It will not be in every case that the landlord states a ground of opposition. Often the landlord will be quite happy with the tenant's presence and is seeking to end the current tenancy simply with a view to negotiating a new tenancy upon different terms, for example, at an increased rent. In this type of situation the landlord should consult a valuer and obtain expert advice before proceeding further. Where the landlord is not opposing the grant of a new tenancy, the landlord's notice must set out its proposals for the new tenancy, including the property to be comprised in it (ie, all or part of the property contained in the existing tenancy), the rent to be payable and the other terms proposed.

(c)   The notice must relate to the whole of the premises contained in the lease. A s 25 notice cannot relate to part only of the demised premises (*Southport Old Links Ltd v Naylor* [1985] 1 EGLR 66 and see also *M&P Enterprises (London) Ltd v Norfolk Square Hotels Ltd* [1994] 1 EGLR 129).

(d)   The notice must be given and signed by, or on behalf of, the landlord. If there are joint landlords, all their names must be given (*Pearson v Alyo* [1990] 1 EGLR 114).

31.2.2   Section 26 requests

Rather than wait for the landlord to serve a s 25 notice, the tenant can sometimes take the initiative and request a new tenancy from its landlord under s 26 of the Act. However, the tenant must remember that the sooner there is a new tenancy, the sooner the new rent will be payable, which may be higher than the rent payable under the old tenancy. Nevertheless, there are situations where the service of a request by the tenant has tactical advantages for it.

Not all tenants can request a new tenancy. A request cannot be served if the landlord has already served a s 25 notice. Further, a request is only possible where the tenant's current lease was granted for a term of years exceeding one year (or during its continuance under s 24). This will exclude both periodic tenants and those with fixed terms of one year or less; although these tenants still enjoy security of tenure.

31.2.2.1   Form

To be valid, the request must be in the prescribed form as laid down in the Landlord and Tenant Act 1954, Part II (Notices) (England and Wales) Regulations 2004 (SI 2004/1005) and served on the competent landlord. As with the s 25 notice, a form 'substantially to the like effect' can be used instead. The prescribed form is set out in **Appendix 2.**

31.2.2.2 Content

The request must comply with the following requirements:

(a)   It must state the date on which the new tenancy is to begin. The current tenancy will terminate on that date. This date must not be more than 12 months nor less than six months after the making of the request, and cannot be earlier than the date on which the tenancy would have expired by effluxion of time or been brought to an end by notice to quit given by the tenant.

(b)   It must give the tenant's proposals as to:

(i)   the property to be comprised in the new tenancy, which must be either the whole or part of the property comprised in the current tenancy;

(ii)   the proposed new rent (this issue requires the advice of a valuer);

(iii)   the other terms of the tenancy (eg, as to duration).

(c)   The request must be signed by or on behalf of all the tenants.

A landlord who is unwilling to grant a new tenancy must, within two months of receipt of the request, give notice to the tenant that it will oppose any application to court for a new lease stating on which statutory ground(s) of opposition it intends to rely. This is effected by means of a landlord's counter-notice (see **31.2.3**).

As with a s 25 notice, the landlord must choose its ground(s) of opposition with care because it will be confined to those stated in its counter-notice.

If the tenant serves a valid s 26 request and then fails to apply to court for a new tenancy within time (see **31.3**), it will not be allowed to withdraw it and serve a new one with a view to complying with the time limit the second time since the effect of the s 26 request was to fix the date of termination of the tenancy (*Stile Hall Properties Ltd v Gooch* [1979] 3 All ER 848).

31.2.2.3 Reasons for making a request

Usually a tenant is best advised not to make a request because it is not always in a tenant's interest to bring its current tenancy to an end. However, there are some situations in which it might be advisable. For example:

(a)   If the rent payable under the current tenancy is more than that presently achievable in the open market. In a falling market like this the landlord is unlikely to serve a s 25 notice, as it is in its interests to let the existing tenancy continue under the Act. Therefore, the tenant should give careful consideration to ending the current tenancy and obtaining a new one at a reduced rent.

(b)   If, as is more often the case, the current rent is less than the present market rent, it is in the tenant's interest to prolong the tenancy for as long as possible. In this case the tenant may be able to make what is sometimes called a pre-emptive strike. Say the lease is contractually due to expire on 30 September. In the previous March the landlord is considering serving a s 25 notice with a view to bringing the tenancy to an end on 30 September and negotiating a new tenancy at an increased rent. If the tenant knows or suspects the landlord's plans, it can, before the landlord has acted, serve a request specifying sometime in the following March as the date for the new tenancy. The tenant has thus achieved an extra six months at the old rent.

(c)   If the tenant has plans to improve the premises, it may prefer the certainty of a new fixed term as opposed to the uncertainty of a statutory continuation.

(d)   If the tenant has plans to sell the lease, a buyer would prefer the security of a new fixed term rather than the uncertainty of a statutory continuation.

31.2.3   Counter-notices

31.2.3.1   The tenant's counter-notice

Under the procedure applicable prior to 1 June 2004 both landlord and tenant had to serve a counter-notice following receipt of a s 26 request or a s 25 notice respectively. However, the requirement for a tenant to serve a counter-notice on receipt of a s 25 notice has now been abolished. The requirement for a landlord to serve a counter-notice remains, however.

31.2.3.2   The landlord's counter-notice

The service of a s 26 request by the tenant will require a counter-notice by the landlord if it wishes to oppose the tenant's application to court for a new tenancy. This must state any ground(s) of opposition that the landlord intends to rely on to oppose the tenant's application (see **31.5**). If the landlord fails to serve a counter-notice within two months of receipt of the tenant's request, it will lose its right to raise any ground of opposition to the tenant's application to court for a new tenancy although it will be allowed to raise issues relating to the terms of the new tenancy.

A landlord who has served a counter-notice stating that it will not oppose the tenant's application for a new tenancy will be bound by that decision. Similarly, the landlord cannot later amend its stated grounds of opposition.

There is no prescribed form of counter-notice but it should be unequivocal and in writing.

31.2.4   Service of notices and requests

Notices and requests given under the Act require service. Section 23(1) of the LTA 1927 provides for personal service or by leaving the notice at the last known place of abode (which includes the place of business of the person to be served; *Price v West London Investment Building Society* [1964] 2 All ER 318), or by sending it through the post by registered or (as now applies) recorded delivery. Service on a company may be effected at its registered office (s 1139 of the Companies Act 2006). The effect of complying with one of the methods of service laid down in the LTA 1927 is that there is a presumption of service so that it does not matter that the recorded delivery letter may not have been received by the intended recipient because it went astray in the post. Other methods of service may be effective (eg, the ordinary post) if in fact the notice is received by the person to whom it has been given. But the risk is that the letter may be lost in the post, in which case, notice will not have been given. The question also arises as to the date on which the notice is treated as having been served. In *Railtrack plc v Gojra* [1998] 08 EG 158, it was held that if the registered or recorded delivery method is used (both being methods laid down in the LTA 1927), the notice (or request) is served on the date on which it is posted. This decision was confirmed by the Court of Appeal in *CA Webber Transport Ltd v Railtrack plc* [2004] 1 WLR 320. When, however, notice is sent through the ordinary post, it is served on the date it would have been delivered in the ordinary course of post.

31.3   THE APPLICATION TO COURT

31.3.1   The need for an application

It will become apparent after service of a s 25 notice or counter-notice to a s 26 request, whether or not the landlord is willing to grant a new tenancy. Where a s 25 notice has been served, the contents will have told the tenant whether or not the landlord intends to oppose its application. If the tenant initiated the termination procedure with a s 26 request, the landlord will have responded with a counter-notice if it is not prepared to grant a new tenancy.

Either the landlord or the tenant may apply to the court (although, of course, one cannot make an application if the other has already done so). It will usually be the tenant who will apply to the court. Even if the landlord has stated that it is prepared to grant a new tenancy, the tenant will lose its entitlement unless an application is made to the court within the prescribed time limits (see **31.3.2**), or the parties have entered into a legally-binding contract for a new lease. Where the landlord is opposing the grant, there is obviously little possibility of such an agreement and so an application must be made.

The landlord will normally only apply to the court where it is opposing the grant and wants an order determining the tenancy on one of the s 30 grounds to be made as quickly as possible. It could wait for the tenant to apply for a new tenancy, but making its own application would mean the matter could be brought before the court as soon as possible. A tenant who fears it will lose in court may delay making its own application for as long as possible in order to gain an extra few weeks or months in the premises. The landlord can only make such application if it has served a s 25 notice opposing renewal or served a counter-notice to a tenant's s 26 notice to that effect.

Where a landlord is not opposing the grant, it can again apply to the court for the grant of that new lease, again in order to have the matter determined as soon as possible. Otherwise, a tenant may delay its own application for as long as possible in order to enjoy the benefit of the more favourable terms of the old lease for as long as possible.

Unless the parties have already entered into a binding lease, the tenant must always apply to court at the appropriate time otherwise it will lose the right to a new tenancy.

31.3.2   The application

Applications may be commenced in either the High Court or, as is more usual, in the county court.

The application must be made within the 'statutory period'. This is defined in s 29A(2) to mean a period ending, where the landlord served a s 25 notice, on the date specified in its notice; and, where the tenant made a s 26 request, a period ending immediately before the date specified in its request.

However, where the tenant has made a s 26 request, the court cannot entertain an application which is made before the end of the period of two months beginning with the date of the making of the request, unless the application is made after the landlord has served its counter-notice.

31.3.3   Agreements extending time limits

By s 29B the parties can by written agreement extend the time limit for applications and they may do so any number of times. The only provisos are that the first agreement to extend must be made prior to the end of the statutory period and any subsequent agreement must be made before the expiry of the period of extension agreed in the previous agreement.

Following the tenant's application to court it is advisable to protect the application by registration of a pending land action under the Land Charges Act 1972. This will make the tenant's application binding on a buyer of the reversion. Where the landlord's title is registered, the application may be an overriding interest under the Land Registration Act 2002, Sch 3, but it would nevertheless be prudent to register a unilateral notice against the reversionary title.

31.4   INTERIM RENTS

31.4.1   The need for an interim rent

Where the tenant validly applies to court for a new tenancy, its current tenancy does not terminate on the date specified in the s 25 notice or s 26 request. Instead, the Act provides that the current tenancy will be continued until three months after the proceedings are concluded. If the tenancy were to continue at the old rent, there would be an incentive for tenants to delay proceedings as much as possible, because the longer the current tenancy lasts, the longer the old rent (which was usually below current market rents) remains payable. This is unfair to landlords, particularly in those cases where, due to the effects of inflation, there is a substantial difference between the old contractual rent and the rent achievable in the open market. So, under s 29A of the Act, the court may, on the application of either party, determine an 'interim rent' to be substituted for the old contractual rent until such time as the current tenancy ceases.

The interim rent will be payable from the earliest date for the termination of the existing tenancy that could have been specified in the s 25 notice or s 26 request that was served to bring the tenancy to an end. So a tenant who serves a s 26 request but states a commencement date for the new tenancy 12 months after service when the contractual termination date is only six months away (and so it could have served six months' notice) will find that the interim rent will be payable from that earlier date. Either landlord or tenant can apply for an interim rent. Normally, it will be the landlord who will apply as the interim rent is likely to be higher than the existing rent which may have been fixed several years previously. However, in times on falling property values, it might be advantageous for the tenant to apply if the current market rent will be below that being paid under the lease.

31.4.2 Amount

The interim rent will normally be the same as the rent payable under the new tenancy, ie, an open market rent assessed as set out at **31.7.3**. However, this will not be the case where there is a significant movement in the market (upwards or downwards) in the intervening period or where the terms of the new tenancy are so different from the terms of the old one to make a substantial difference in the rent. (Bear in mind here that normally the new lease will be on very similar terms to the old lease; see **31.7.4**.) Nor will this be the case where the landlord opposes the grant of a new tenancy. In both cases, the following provisions apply:

(a)   Section 24A requires the court to assess the interim rent on the basis of a yearly tenancy, while the rent payable under the new lease is usually assessed on the basis of a term of years. Market rents under yearly tenancies are usually less than under fixed terms, since the latter guarantee tenants a more substantial period of occupation.

(b)   The court is obliged to have regard to the rent payable under the current tenancy. This is so that the court can exercise a discretion to 'cushion' the tenant from too harsh a blow in moving from the old out-of-date contractual rent to the new rent (see *English Exporters (London) Ltd v Eldonwall Ltd* [1973] Ch 415). However, a 'cushion' does not have to be provided in every case. The court has a discretion which it may use to specify the full market rent, especially in those cases where the tenant has already benefited from a low contractual rent for a long time (see, eg, *Department of the Environment v Allied Freehold Property Trust Ltd* [1992] 45 EG 156).

31.4.3 Avoiding s 24A

While the introduction of interim rents has been a step in the right direction for landlords, many still feel that the application of the 'cushion' can produce unfairness. Accordingly, the landlord may wish to avoid s 24A altogether by including a penultimate day rent review in the lease. This would revise the contractual rent just before the contractual term expired. In such a case the harshness of changing from the old rent to the new rent would be suffered during the contractual term without the imposition of any 'cushion'. Tenants, on the other hand, will wish to resist such a clause.

Another way of avoiding s 24A would be for the landlord, at the lease-drafting stage, to make it clear that the contractual rent review provisions are to continue to apply notwithstanding the ending of the contractual term. Careful drafting would be required to achieve this but the case of *Willison v Cheverell Estates Ltd* [1996] 26 EG 133 indicates that this is another possibility for the landlord.

31.5 GROUNDS OF OPPOSITION

When the landlord serves its s 25 notice or counter-notice in response to the tenant's s 26 request, it must, if it is intending to oppose the grant of a new tenancy, set out one or more of the seven grounds of opposition in s 30 of the Act. The landlord can rely only on the stated ground(s); no later amendment is allowed.

If the landlord has stated a ground of opposition and the tenant's application proceeds to a hearing, a 'split trial' will usually be ordered with the question of opposition being dealt with first as a preliminary issue. Only if the ground is not made out will the terms of the new tenancy be dealt with.

The statutory grounds of opposition are all contained in s 30(1) of the Act and, as will be seen, some of the grounds ((a), (b), (c) and (e)) confer a discretion on the court whether or not to order a new tenancy even if the ground is made out.

31.5.1 Ground (a): tenant's failure to repair

The landlord can oppose the tenant's application for a new tenancy on the ground of the tenant's failure to repair the holding. To succeed, the landlord will have to show that the tenant was under an obligation to repair or maintain the holding and that the tenant is in breach of that obligation. Problems can arise where the repairing obligation is divided between the landlord and tenant, for example, where the landlord is responsible for the exterior and the tenant for the interior of the premises. In such cases, an inspection will be necessary to determine the party in breach. The ground only applies to failure to repair the holding, and not to the disrepair of another part of the demised premises not forming part of the tenant's holding (eg, where the tenant has sub-let part and it is that part which is in disrepair).

This is one of the discretionary grounds and the landlord is only likely to succeed if the tenant's breaches are both serious and unremedied at the date of the hearing.

As an alternative, the landlord may be able to commence forfeiture proceedings to terminate the tenancy, this being one of the permitted methods of termination under the Act. This remedy may be available throughout the term and while the tenant may apply for relief, this will usually only be granted if the tenant rectifies the breach.

31.5.2 Ground (b): persistent delay in paying rent

The requirement of 'persistent delay' suggests that the tenant must have fallen into arrears on more than one occasion. However, the rent need not be substantially in arrears nor need the arrears last a long time. Indeed, there need not be any arrears at the date of the hearing; the court will look at the whole history of payment (see *Hazel v Akhtar* [2002] EWCA Civ 1883, [2002] 07 EG 124). Again, this is one of the discretionary grounds and the court is entitled to take into account the likelihood of future arrears arising should a new tenancy be ordered. The tenant should, therefore, consider offering to provide a surety for any new lease ordered.

31.5.3 Ground (c): substantial breaches of other obligations

Discretionary ground (c) requires other substantial breaches by the tenant of its obligations in the lease, or some other reason connected with the tenant's use or management of the holding. Ground (c) is rarely encountered in practice. Any breach of an obligation may be relied upon by the landlord (eg, breach of the user covenant) but the breach must be substantial and this will be a question of fact and degree. In *Youssefi v Mussellwhite* [2014] EWCA Civ 885, the Court of Appeal found that the tenant's failure to allow access to the property and its failure to open a business were substantial breaches of the lease.

The ground also extends to reasons connected with the tenant's use or management of the holding and this has been held to include carrying on a use in breach of planning control (see *Fowles v Heathrow Airport Ltd* [2008] EWCA Civ 1270). In *Horne & Meredith Properties v Cox*,

Billingsley [2014] EWCA Civ 423, a tenant was denied a new tenancy because his conduct in bringing litigation against the landlord for alleged obstructions to a right of way granted by the lease had 'grossly exceeded any reasonable balance' and he was 'a legal menace'.

31.5.4   Ground (d): alternative accommodation

The landlord must have offered and be willing to provide or secure alternative accommodation for the tenant. The accommodation must be offered on reasonable terms having regard to the terms of the current tenancy and all other relevant circumstances. Further, the accommodation must be suitable for the tenant's requirements (including the requirement to preserve goodwill), bearing in mind the nature and type of its business and the location and size of its existing premises. It seems that offering the tenant part only of its existing premises may qualify as alternative accommodation.

This ground, unlike the three previously mentioned, is not discretionary. If the landlord proves the requirements of the ground, the court must refuse the tenant's application.

31.5.5   Ground (e): current tenancy created by sub-letting of part only of property in a superior tenancy

Ground (e) is the least used ground because the necessary requirements are seldom fulfilled. It only applies where the current tenancy was created by a sub-letting of part of the property in a superior tenancy, and the sub-tenant's competent landlord is the landlord under the superior tenancy. The competent landlord will succeed if it can show that the combined rents from the sub-divided parts of a building are substantially less than the rent to be obtained on a single letting of the whole building, and that it requires possession to let or dispose of the whole.

This is the last of the discretionary grounds.

31.5.6   Ground (f): demolition or reconstruction

Ground (f) is the most frequently used ground. The landlord must show that on termination of the tenancy:

(a)   it has a firm intention;

(b)   to demolish or reconstruct the premises in the holding (or a substantial part of them), or to carry out substantial work of construction on the holding (or part of it); and

(c)   that it could not reasonably do so without obtaining possession of the holding.

Each of these elements is considered in turn.

31.5.6.1   The landlord's intention

The landlord must prove a firm and settled intention to carry out relevant work. It has been said that the project must have 'moved out of the zone of contemplation ... into the valley of decision' (per Asquith LJ in *Cunliffe v Goodman* [1950] 2 KB 237, approved in *Betty's Cafes Ltd v Phillips Furnishing Stores Ltd* [1959] AC 20). Not only must the landlord have made a genuine decision to carry out relevant work, it must also show that it is practicable for it to carry out that intention. This will be a question of fact in each case but the landlord's position will be strengthened if it has:

(a)   obtained (or shown a reasonable prospect of obtaining) planning permission and building regulation approval (if necessary);

(b)   instructed professional advisers;

(c)   prepared the necessary drawings and contracts;

(d)   obtained quotations and secured finance; and

(e)   obtained the consent of any superior landlord (if necessary).

Where the landlord is a company, intention is normally evidenced by a resolution of the board of directors. Similarly, local authority landlords should pass an appropriate resolution and have it recorded in their minutes.

The landlord's intention must be established at the date of the hearing (*Betty's Cafes Ltd v Phillips Furnishing Stores Ltd*, above). It is thus irrelevant that the s 25 notice (or s 26 counter-notice) was served by the landlord's predecessor who did not have the necessary intention. See also *Zarvos v Pradhan* [2003] 2 P & CR 9 where a landlord failed at the hearing because the judge was not satisfied that it would be able to finance the project. The landlord appealed and by the time of the appeal has received assurances from its bank that finance would be available. The Court of Appeal refused to allow the landlord to adduce this evidence at the appeal as this would be unfair to the tenant.

If the court is not satisfied that the landlord's intention is sufficiently firm and settled at the date of the hearing, a new tenancy will be ordered. In such cases, however, the court, in settling the terms of the new tenancy, may take into account the landlord's future intentions, and limit the duration of the new tenancy so as not to impede development later when the landlord is able to fully establish intention and the ability to carry it out (see **31.7.2**).

31.5.6.2 The nature of the works

The landlord must prove an intention to do one of six things:

(a)   Demolish the premises comprised in the holding (see *Coppin v Bruce-Smith* [1998] EGCS 45).

(b)   Reconstruct the premises comprised in the holding. For the works to qualify as works of reconstruction it has been held that they must entail rebuilding and involve a substantial interference with the structure of the building but need not necessarily be confined to the outside or loadbearing walls (*Romulus Trading Co Ltd v Henry Smith's Charity Trustees* [1990] 2 EGLR 75).

(c)   Demolish a substantial part of the premises comprised in the holding.

(d)   Reconstruct a substantial part of the premises comprised in the holding.

(e)   Carry out substantial work of construction on the holding. It has been held that such works must directly affect the structure of the building and must go beyond what could be more properly classified as works of refurbishment or improvement (*Barth v Pritchard* [1990] 1 EGLR 109).

(f)   Carry out substantial work of construction on part of the holding.

31.5.6.3 The need to obtain possession

The landlord must show that it could not reasonably execute the relevant work without obtaining possession of the holding. This means the landlord must show that it needs 'legal' (not just 'physical') possession of the holding. It has to show that it is necessary to put an end to the tenant's interest, and this may not always be the case. Accordingly, if the lease contains a right of entry for the landlord which is sufficiently wide to enable it to carry out the relevant work, its ground of opposition will fail. In such a situation, the tenant will be able to argue that the work can be carried out under the terms of the lease and there is thus no need to end it.

Even if the lease does not include a right of entry, the landlord may still fail in its opposition if the tenant is able to rely on s 31A of the Act. This provides that the court shall not find ground (f) to be established if the tenant will either:

(a)   agree to a new lease which includes access and other rights for the landlord, which enable the landlord to reasonably carry out the relevant work without obtaining possession and without substantially interfering with the use of the holding for the tenant's business; or

(b)   accept a new lease of an economically separable part of the holding with, if necessary, access rights for the landlord.

31.5.7   Ground (g): landlord's intention to occupy the holding

Ground (g) is another frequently used ground. The landlord must prove that on the termination of the current tenancy it intends to occupy the holding for the purposes, or partly for the purposes, of a business to be carried on by it, or as its residence. There are a number of elements to this ground which will be considered in turn.

31.5.7.1   The landlord's intention

As with ground (f), the landlord's intention must be firm and settled, and many of the matters discussed at **31.5.6** will be equally relevant here. Therefore, not only must the landlord be able to show a genuine intention to occupy the holding, it must also show that it has a reasonable prospect of being able to do so. It is, therefore, necessary for the court to take into account, for example, whether planning permission would be required to use the premises for the landlord's business and, if so, whether it would be likely to be granted. In some cases, the court has accepted as evidence of intention to occupy, an undertaking to do so given by the landlord. Such an undertaking is not conclusive but it is a relevant consideration when the court is determining the issue (see, eg, *London Hilton Jewellers Ltd v Hilton International Hotels Ltd* [1990] 1 EGLR 112). As with ground (f), the landlord's intention must be shown to exist at the date of the hearing.

The court will not assess the viability of the landlord's proposed business venture provided its intention to occupy is genuine. Thus, the court has held the ground to be established even where they thought the landlord's business plans to be ill thought out and likely to fail; its intention was nevertheless genuine. See, for example, *Dolgellau Golf Club v Hett* [1998] 2 EGLR 75, CA, but also the contrasting case of *Zarvos v Pradhan* [2003] EWCA Civ 208, where possession was refused as the landlord could not establish a reasonable prospect of being able to raise finance.

31.5.7.2   The purpose of occupation

Occupation must be for the purpose of the landlord's business or as its residence. The landlord need not intend to occupy all the holding immediately, provided that within a reasonable time of termination it intends to occupy a substantial part of the holding for one of these purposes.

The wording of this ground refers to a business to be carried on by the landlord. However, the landlord need not physically occupy the premises and it will be sufficient if occupation is through a manager or agent provided that the arrangement is genuine. Further, the ground is still available where the landlord intends to carry on the business in partnership with others. Where the landlord has a controlling interest in a company, any business to be carried on by the company, is treated as a business carried on by the landlord. The landlord has a controlling interest for this purpose, either if it beneficially holds more than half of the company's equity share capital, or if it is a member and able, without consent, to appoint or remove at least half of the directors (s 30(3)). Where the landlord is a company in a group of companies, it may rely on ground (g) where another member of the group is to occupy the premises (s 42). If the landlord is a trustee, he may be able to rely on an intention to occupy by a beneficiary (s 41).

31.5.7.3   The five-year rule

The most important limitation on the availability of this ground of opposition is the 'five-year rule' in s 30(2) of the Act. A landlord cannot rely on ground (g) if its interest was purchased or created within five years before the end of the current tenancy, ie, the termination date specified in the s 25 notice or s 26 request. However, the restriction only applies if, throughout those five years, the premises have been subject to a tenancy or series of tenancies within the protection of the Act.

The idea behind the provision is to stop a landlord buying a reversion within five years of the end of the lease, and then using this ground to obtain possession for himself at the end of the term. Thus, a landlord will not be able to rely on this ground if it purchased the premises subject to the tenancy within the last five years. However, the restriction does not apply where a landlord buys premises with vacant possession, grants a lease, and then seeks to end the lease within five years relying on this ground.

The wording of the provision refers to the landlord's interest being 'purchased' and this is used in its popular sense of buying for money (*Bolton (HL) Engineering Co Ltd v Graham & Sons Ltd* [1957] 1 QB 159). Thus, it will not cover a freeholder who has accepted the surrender of a head-lease without payment, and then seeks to use this ground against the sub-tenant.

Finally, a landlord who is unable to rely on ground (g) because of this restriction, may be able to rely on ground (f) if it intends to demolish or reconstruct the premises. This remains so even if the landlord then intends to use the reconstructed premises for its own occupation.

31.6 COMPENSATION FOR FAILURE TO OBTAIN A NEW TENANCY

On termination, a tenant may be entitled to compensation for any improvements it has made. Additionally, if the tenant is forced to leave the premises it may lose the goodwill which it has built up and it will be faced with all the costs of relocation. This is particularly unfair to those tenants that are forced to leave the premises through no fault of their own, ie, if the landlord establishes one of the grounds of opposition (e), (f) or (g). In certain circumstances, therefore, the tenant may be entitled to compensation for failing to obtain a new tenancy where the landlord establishes one of these 'no fault' grounds.

31.6.1 Availability

Compensation is only available on quitting the premises in one of the following situations:

(a)   Where the landlord serves a s 25 notice or counter-notice to a s 26 request stating one or more of the grounds of opposition (e), (f) or (g) but no others, and the tenant either:

(i)   does not apply to court for a new tenancy or does so but withdraws its application; or

(ii)   does apply to court for a new tenancy, but its application is refused because the landlord is able to establish its stated ground.

(b)   Where the landlord serves a s 25 notice or counter-notice to a s 26 request specifying one or more of the grounds (e), (f) or (g) and others; the tenant applies to court for a new tenancy but the court refuses to grant a new tenancy solely on one or more of the grounds (e), (f) or (g). Here the tenant must apply to court for a new tenancy and ask the court to certify that a new tenancy was not ordered solely because one of these three 'no fault' grounds has been made out.

31.6.2 Amount

The amount of compensation is the rateable value of the holding multiplied by the 'appropriate multiplier' which is a figure prescribed from time to time by the Secretary of State, and is currently 1. In some cases, the tenant will be entitled to double compensation.

31.6.3 Double compensation

Sometimes the appropriate multiplier is doubled. This happens when the tenant or its predecessors in the same business have been in occupation for at least 14 years prior to the termination of the current tenancy. These provisions are summarised in the illustration below.

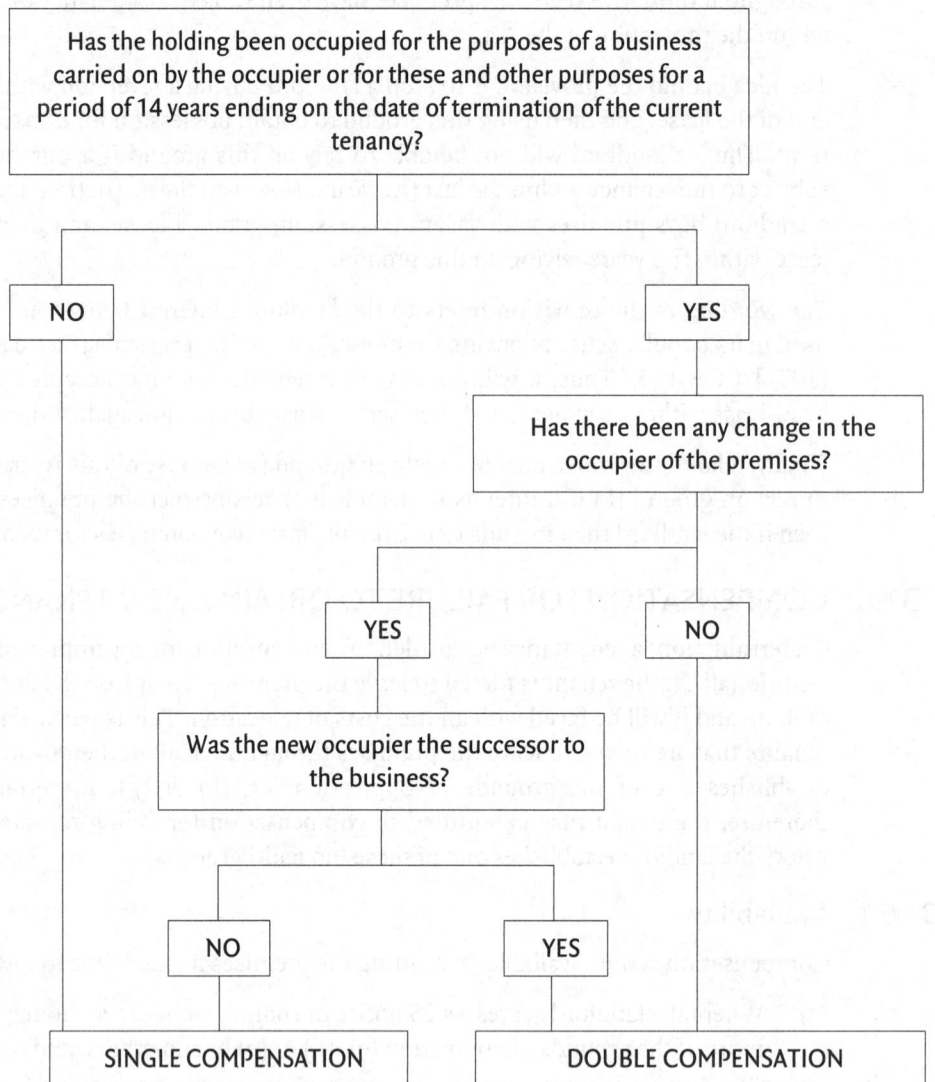

31.6.4 Contracting out

In some situations the tenant's right to compensation can be excluded by agreement between the parties. This agreement is often in the lease itself. However, s 38(2) of the Act provides that where the tenant or its predecessors in the same business have been in occupation for five years or more prior to the date of quitting, any agreement to exclude or reduce the tenant's right to compensation is void.

31.7 THE RENEWAL LEASE

If the tenant follows all the correct procedures and properly applies to court for a new tenancy, the court will make an order for a new lease in two situations:

(a)   if the landlord fails to make out its s 30 ground of opposition; or

(b)   if the landlord did not oppose the tenant's application for a new tenancy.

The terms of this new lease are usually settled by agreement between the parties and it is only in default of such agreement that the court will be called upon to decide the terms. In either event, any new lease will also enjoy the protection of the Act.

The court has jurisdiction over the premises, duration, rent and the other terms.

31.7.1 The premises

The tenant is entitled to a new tenancy of the holding only as at the date of the order. This term was defined in **31.1.4.4**, and excludes any part of the premises which have been sub-let. However, the landlord (but not the tenant), has the right to insist that any new tenancy to be granted shall be a new tenancy of the whole of the demised premises including those parts sub-let.

The court may grant a new lease of less than the holding under s 31A, where the landlord establishes ground (f), the redevelopment ground, but the tenant takes a new lease of an 'economically separable part' of the holding (see **31.5.6**).

The new lease may also include appurtenant rights enjoyed by the tenant under the current tenancy.

31.7.2 The duration

The length of any new lease ordered by the court will be such as is reasonable in all the circumstances but cannot exceed 15 years (often it is much less than this). In deciding this issue the court has a very wide discretion and will take into account matters such as:

(a)   the length of the current tenancy;

(b)   the length requested by the tenant;

(c)   the hardship caused to either party;

(d)   current open market practice;

(e)   the landlord's future proposals.

It may be that the landlord was unable to rely on ground (f) because it could not prove that its intention to demolish or reconstruct was sufficiently firm and settled at the date of the hearing (see **31.5.6**). If, however, the court is satisfied that the landlord will be able to do so in the near future, it may order a short tenancy so as not to impede development later. Similarly, if the premises are shown to be ripe for development, the new lease may be granted subject to a break clause (*National Car Parks Ltd v The Paternoster Consortium Ltd* [1990] 15 EG 53). In the same way, where the landlord has narrowly missed being able to rely on ground (g) because of the five-year rule, the court may be prepared to grant a short tenancy.

31.7.3 The rent

The amount of rent to be paid is the greatest source of disagreement between the parties and specialist valuation advice will be essential. If the question of rent comes before the courts, they will assess an open market rent having regard to the other terms of the tenancy. However, in assessing the rent the court is obliged to disregard certain factors which may otherwise work to the detriment of the tenant, ie:

(a)   Any effect on rent of the fact that the tenant or its predecessors have been in occupation. The classic landlord's argument would be that the tenant, being a sitting tenant, would pay more in the open market for these premises simply to avoid relocation. This would inflate an open market rent and is thus to be disregarded.

(b)   Any goodwill attached to the holding due to the carrying on of the tenant's business. The tenant should not have to pay a rent assessed partly on the basis of goodwill it generated.

(c)   Any effect on the rent of improvements voluntarily made by the tenant (certain conditions must also be satisfied).

(d)   Where the holding comprises licensed premises, any addition in value due to the tenant's licence.

Where the premises are in disrepair due to the tenant's failure to perform its repairing obligation, conflicting views have been expressed on whether the court should disregard this in setting the rent of the new tenancy. One view is that the premises should be valued in their actual condition. This will probably produce a lower rent but the landlord may be able to sue the tenant for breach of its repairing obligation.

The other view is that the premises should be valued on the basis that the tenant has complied with its obligation, thus preventing the tenant benefiting from its own breach. This view is supported by cases such as *Crown Estate Commissioners v Town Investments Ltd* [1992] 08 EG 111.

In *Fawke v Viscount Chelsea* [1980] QB 441, the premises were in disrepair because the landlord was in breach of his repairing obligation. The court decided that the premises should be valued in their actual condition and, therefore, fixed a new rent which was below open market value but which increased once the landlord had complied with his obligation.

Under s 34(3), the court has power to insert a rent review clause in the new lease whether or not the previous lease contained such a provision. The frequency and type of review is at the discretion of the court which may be persuaded by the tenant to make provision for downward revisions as well as upward (see *Forbuoys plc v Newport Borough Council* [1994] 24 EG 156).

As to the effect of the LT(C)A 1995, see **31.7.4**.

Finally, the court does have power to require the tenant to provide guarantors.

31.7.4   Other terms

It will only fall to the court to decide other terms in the absence of agreement between the parties. In fixing the other terms the court must have regard to the terms of the current tenancy and all other relevant circumstances. For that reason, the terms will be much the same as before. The leading case in this area is *O'May v City of London Real Property Co Ltd* [1983] AC 726 which held that if one of the parties seeks a change in the terms, it is for that party to justify the change. Further, the change must be fair and reasonable and 'take into account, amongst other things, the comparatively weak negotiating position of a sitting tenant requiring renewal, particularly in conditions of scarcity' (per Lord Hailsham in *O'May*). Therefore, the tenant should be on its guard against any attempt by the landlord to introduce more onerous obligations into the new lease (eg, a more restrictive user covenant). In the *O'May* case the landlord was, in effect, trying to transfer the responsibility for the repair and maintenance of office premises to the tenant. This would have increased the value of the reversion by more than £1 million but the House of Lords held that the landlord was not entitled to do this. Notwithstanding the effect of the *O'May* case, variations may be made in the renewal lease to reflect the changes introduced by the LT(C)A 1995. The renewal lease will, of course, be subject to the provisions of that Act. This will often mean that under the current lease (granted before 1 January 1996) the original tenant was liable for the entire duration of the term through privity of contract; whereas for the renewal lease, privity of contract will not apply. This change is one of the circumstances to which the court must have regard in fixing the rent and other terms of the new lease. For example, the landlord may wish to alter the terms of the alienation covenant to balance the effect of the loss of privity of contract (see *Wallis Fashion Group Ltd v General Accident Life Assurance Ltd* [2000] EGCS 45; and **20.2.4.2**).

31.8   THE ORDER FOR THE NEW LEASE

Any new lease ordered by the court will not commence until three months after the proceedings are 'finally disposed of'. This is when the time for appeal has elapsed, and for appeals to the Court of Appeal the time limit is four weeks from the date of the order. The tenant continues to occupy under its old tenancy during this period. Either party may appeal.

If the court makes an order for a new tenancy upon terms which the tenant finds unacceptable (eg, as to rent), the tenant may apply for revocation of the order within 14 days. In such a case, the existing tenancy will continue for such period as the parties agree or the court determines as necessary to enable the landlord to re-let the premises.

31.9 PROCEDURAL FLOWCHART – s 25 NOTICE

The flowchart below shows the stages and time limits following service of a landlord's s 25 notice opposing the grant of a new tenancy.

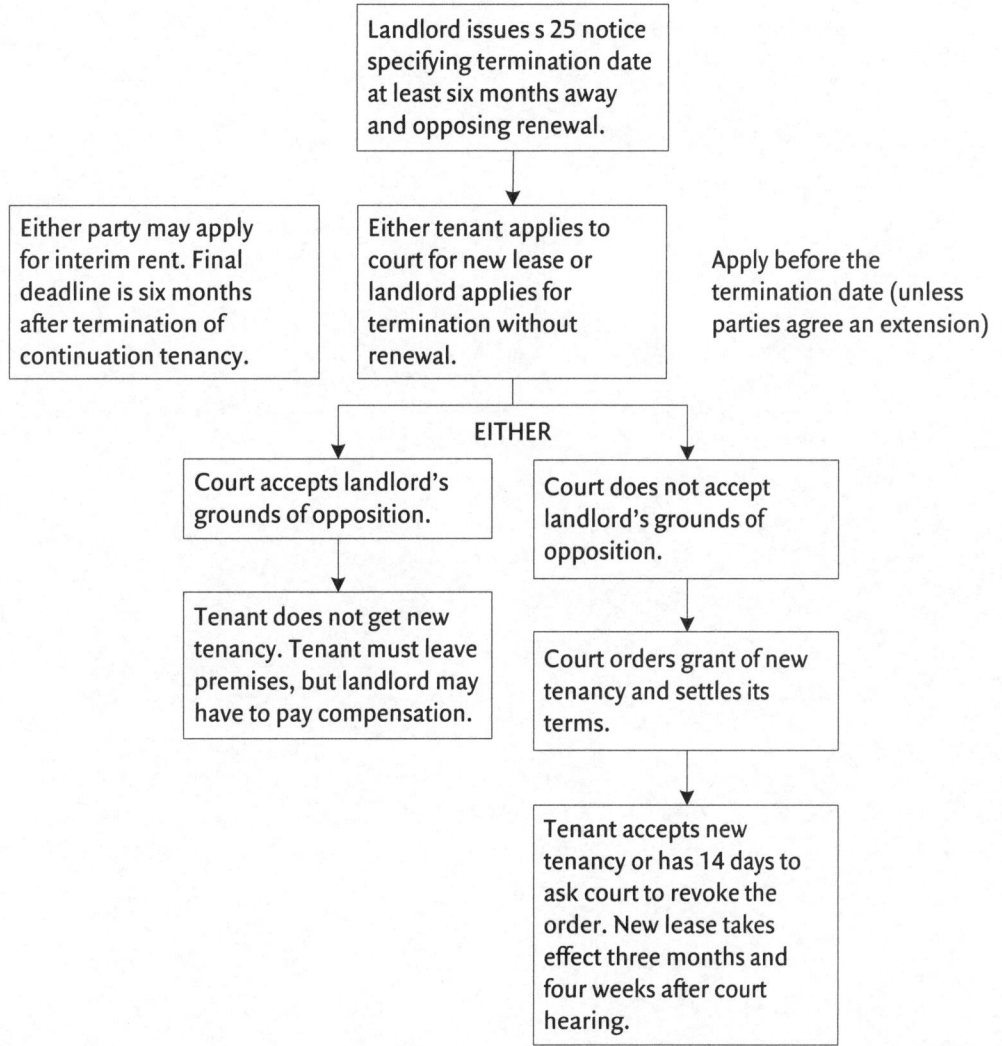

REVIEW ACTIVITY

1. When does the Act apply?
2. What are the consequences of the Act applying?
3. How can a landlord let premises without giving a business occupier security of tenure?
4. How can a secure tenant that wants to leave its business premises at the end of the contractual term bring its tenancy to an end?
5. How can a secure tenant that wants to stay in its business premises after the expiry of the contractual term request a new lease?
6. How can a secure sub-tenant of business premises identify its competent landlord for the purposes of the Act?
7. How can a landlord obtain vacant possession of premises occupied by a secure tenant?
8. How can a landlord ensure that a secure tenant that wants to stay in the premises enters into a new lease, rather than continuing the old one?

Answers to this Review activity may be found in Appendix 1.

PART III

PROPERTY AND INSOLVENCY

CHAPTER 32

Insolvency and its Effect on Commercial Property

32.1	Why insolvency matters	315
32.2	Measures to reduce the perceived risk of insolvency	315
32.3	Always establish the type of insolvency regime	316
32.4	Identify the type of contract	318
32.5	Different types of insolvency regime	318
32.6	Setting aside transactions which have already been completed	323
32.7	The effect of a tenant becoming insolvent	325
32.8	Requiring the insolvency official to pay rent	332
32.9	Requiring the insolvency official to observe the lease covenants	333
32.10	Disclaimer and its effects	334

32.1 WHY INSOLVENCY MATTERS

If one party (X) to an existing contract becomes insolvent, this will cause the other party (Y) significant problems. X is likely to breach its obligations, and may pull out of the contract altogether. Completed transactions to which X is a party may be reversed by the court. Y's normal remedies for breach will be restricted either as to what Y can do, or how quickly it can act. All this may put Y in breach of its own obligations to others (for example, an insolvent tenant's failure to pay rent will reduce the landlord's income stream, which may mean it defaults on its mortgage payments; similarly, in a chain of related sales, if one buyer becomes insolvent and fails to complete, buyers higher up the chain may well not have sufficient funds to complete their own purchases). This is why, before entering into the contract, Y should always check X's financial track record and resources (by taking references, establishing its credit rating and looking at its accounts).

Also, when X becomes insolvent, it usually loses the ability to deal with its assets. Even if it retains legal ownership, any purported disposition by X (without the involvement of its insolvency official or the court) may well be void. This is why Y should always check that a party with whom it proposes to enter into a contract is not insolvent. Ways to do this are discussed at **32.3**. If entering into a contract with an insolvency official, Y will usually find that the contractual terms will need to be modified.

The Insolvency Act 1986 (as amended) is the primary source of insolvency legislation. In this chapter, it is referred to as the 'IA 1986'. The Insolvency Rules 1986 are also relevant, but it should be noted that these are currently being updated and new rules are due in 2015.

32.2 MEASURES TO REDUCE THE PERCEIVED RISK OF INSOLVENCY

If X's financial strength is in doubt, Y may still be willing to contract with X if additional financial reassurance is provided. If X subsequently becomes insolvent, Y should then have meaningful ways to ensure performance of the contract (or at very least, payment of damages for breach) without becoming embroiled in the insolvency process. These could include:

(a)   requiring another person (with a better financial track record) to enter into the contract at the outset, either as joint covenantor with X or as guarantor for X. This could include requiring the existing tenant (who wishes to assign to X) to act as guarantor by way of an authorised guarantee agreement (AGA);

(b)   requiring X to obtain a bank bond or guarantee. Here the bank agrees to perform the obligations, or pay damages, if X is in breach. Usually, the bank's liability is capped at a specified amount;

(c)   (where the contract is the grant of a new lease, or the assignment of an existing lease to X) requiring X to deposit cash in a rent deposit, held either by a neutral party or (more likely) by the landlord (see **14.5**);

(d)   drafting the contract to include a right for Y to rescind if X becomes insolvent or is likely to do so. At least Y is then free to do a different deal with someone else. A forfeiture clause in a lease, which is triggered by an insolvency event, is very similar to this. For more details on forfeiture, see **Chapter 25**;

(e)   keeping a close eye on X's financial and trading performance, so that Y picks up very quickly any signs of impending insolvency. This might include watching for press announcements of the loss of a major contract, reacting quickly to late payments of rent by the tenant or investigating the background to a request from an occupation tenant to pay rent monthly rather than quarterly.

If X becomes insolvent, Y should always check whether it can take advantage of any of these measures (as they may be quicker or more productive than pursuing X for performance or damages).

32.3 ALWAYS ESTABLISH THE TYPE OF INSOLVENCY REGIME

When Y first becomes aware of X's insolvency or likely insolvency, it is critical to establish precisely which type of insolvency regime is involved. Y's range of remedies will vary considerably from one regime to another, and the terminology can be misleading. For example, being told 'the receivers have gone in' might refer to a receiver under the LPA 1925 (a 'LOPA receiver'), an administrative receiver or the Official Receiver, acting either as liquidator or as interim trustee in bankruptcy. The range of insolvency regimes is set out in **Table 32.1** below, and a more detailed explanation of the types of regime and their consequences is given in the appropriate part of **32.5**.

Table 32.1   The alternative insolvency regimes

Where X is an individual	Where X is a company
Law of Property Act Receiver (a LOPA receiver, or sometimes called a fixed charge receiver)	Law of Property Act Receiver (a LOPA receiver, or sometimes called a fixed charge receiver)
Individual Voluntary Arrangement (IVA)	Company Voluntary Arrangement (CVA)
–	Administrative Receivership
–	Administration
Bankruptcy (either on X's own petition or that of a creditor)	Liquidation • Compulsory • Voluntary (triggered by creditors) • Voluntary (triggered by members) (Liquidation is also known as winding up)

32.3.1 How to check which insolvency regime applies

Y can check which insolvency regime applies by following these guidelines:

(a) *Voluntary arrangements (CVA or IVA).* Once a CVA has been agreed, it should be registered at Companies House and thus be discoverable by a company search. An IVA that has been agreed should be registered on the Insolvency Service register, and this can be searched on-line. Also the supervisor of the voluntary arrangement must give notice to all X's known creditors, so Y (if it is X's landlord) may find out that way. An interim order (for an IVA) can be discovered only by asking the local court.

(b) *Appointment of a receiver where X is a company.* This will be registered at Companies House (regardless of whether this is a LOPA receiver, or an administrative receiver). All business correspondence has to state that a receiver has been appointed, and an administrative receiver also has to notify all known creditors promptly after his appointment.

The appointment of either receiver cannot be noted on the title to any registered property belonging to X which is affected by the receivership, but this will not matter, as the debenture or charge under which the receiver is appointed will have been noted on the title already. However, the receiver may wish to ensure that any notices which are served by Land Registry will reach him. He may therefore wish to register his own address as an additional address for service.

(c) *Administration order.* This should show up as an entry in the Companies House file, but to find out about any recent administration order that has not yet been registered at Companies House, Y should telephone the Central Registry of Winding Up Petitions and the county court for the area where X's registered office is situated. A notice of the administrator's appointment may be entered on the registers of title of any property that is affected by the administration, but absence of such a notice is not conclusive as no application for this entry may have been made.

(d) *Voluntary liquidation.* The winding-up resolution must be registered at Companies House within 15 days, so will be revealed by a company search. A notice of the liquidator's appointment may be entered on the registers of title of any property that is affected by the liquidation, but absence of such a notice is not conclusive as no application for this entry may have been made.

(e) *Compulsory liquidation.* The winding-up order will be registered at Companies House 'forthwith', so will be revealed by a company search. To be sure that there are no more recent applications/orders for compulsory liquidation, Y should telephone the Central Registry of Winding Up Petitions (which covers petitions for compulsory liquidation, whether submitted in the High Court or the county court). A notice of the liquidator's appointment may be entered on the registers of title of any property that is affected by the liquidation, but absence of such a notice is not conclusive as no application for this may have been made.

(f) *Bankruptcy.* The register of bankruptcy orders can be searched on-line at the Insolvency Service. Bankruptcy petitions are recorded at the debtor's local county court, the Royal Courts of Justice or the Central London County Court (sometimes at more than one of these). These registers can be inspected in person. Both bankruptcy petitions and orders are ultimately also recorded at the Land Charges Department as pending actions (and can be searched using Form K16). Details may also have been entered on the register of title for X's properties as the court is supposed to notify the Land Registry when a bankruptcy petition is issued (Insolvency Rules 1986, r 6.13).

32.3.2 The insolvency official

Each of the insolvency regimes listed at **32.3.1** is implemented by a different person (the supervisor (nominee) of a voluntary arrangement, a LOPA receiver, an administrative receiver, an administrator, a liquidator, or a trustee in bankruptcy). For convenience, in this chapter, all of these individuals are called 'insolvency officials'.

32.4   IDENTIFY THE TYPE OF CONTRACT

It is equally important to know what type of contract exists between X and Y, as this can also affect the remedies available to Y when X becomes insolvent. For example, it may be:

(a)   an existing lease;

(b)   an agreement for lease (lease not yet granted);

(c)   a recently completed transfer;

(d)   an exchanged contract for sale which has yet to complete;

(e)   an existing freehold restrictive covenant;

(f)   a pure contract, with no property interest at all – such as a contractual licence to occupy;

(g)   a new sale contract or lease into which the insolvency official is proposing to enter with Y as part of the process of realising X's assets.

32.5   DIFFERENT TYPES OF INSOLVENCY REGIME

32.5.1   Voluntary arrangements (CVAs and IVAs)

Voluntary arrangements can arise under ss 1 to 7 of the IA 1986 (for companies) or ss 252 to 263 of the Act (for individuals). They are a statutory compromise agreement between X (who is insolvent) and the majority of its creditors. Where X is a company, the arrangement is known as a CVA; where X is an individual, it is known as an IVA.

The aims of a voluntary arrangement are for the general creditors to agree to proposals which secure them better payments than would be the case under a formal insolvency distribution, but which reduce the overall burden on X by giving it longer to pay its debts or by reducing the amount it has to pay. A voluntary arrangement can compromise both existing and future debts (such as rent that will become due under a lease). A voluntary arrangement rarely lasts for more than five years. The distribution of assets in accordance with the agreed arrangement is supervised by a licensed insolvency practitioner (called 'the nominee').

A voluntary arrangement cannot include proposals which would adversely affect the rights of secured creditors or preferential debtors, unless they consent. Interestingly, a voluntary arrangement can propose changes to third-party liabilities (usually the release from liability of guarantors or former tenants who have given an AGA). Such proposals have been challenged successfully on grounds of unfair prejudice (see **32.5.1.1**) in recent cases.

The advantage of a CVA/IVA is that it avoids the more formal insolvency regime. This is particularly important where X would be prohibited (by the rules of his professional organisation) from practising, or would have to give up his other directorships, if he was declared bankrupt. It may be less expensive than the alternative insolvency regimes and can be more flexible.

32.5.1.1   Approval of the voluntary arrangement

A voluntary arrangement requires the consent of 75% or more in value (not numbers) of the creditors who attend the initial meeting to discuss the proposals. A CVA also has to be approved by at least 50% of X's members by shareholding (or more if the constitution of X so prescribes). Creditors who oppose the arrangement can challenge its terms on grounds that they cause them unfair prejudice. They must do so quickly (within 28 days). The IA 1986 does not define unfair prejudice, but recent case law has upheld claims by landlords that a CVA should be revised on this ground. (See *Prudential Assurance Company Ltd & Others v PRG Powerhouse Ltd & Others* [2007] EWHC 1002 and *Mourant & Co Trustees Ltd v Sixty UK Ltd (in administration)* [2010] EWHC 1890, where the CVA proposed stripping some landlords of their rights to pursue the guarantor of the leases for rent arrears. In both *Powerhouse* and *Mourant*, the original terms of the CVA were held to offer the landlord inadequate compensation for being deprived of its rights against the guarantors.)

32.5.1.2 Moratorium

Unless X is a 'small company' and particularly requests this, there is no moratorium to prevent Y seeking to enforce its remedies during the period leading up to formal approval of the CVA. A small company is one which satisfies two of three criteria (these relate to turnover, balance sheet assets and number of employees) and is not one of the types of company which are disqualified (by the IA 1986) from being 'small companies'. For more detail on how the small company moratorium works, see **Flowchart 3** at **32.7.2**.

There are very complex moratorium arrangements in an IVA (IA 1986, ss 252 and 254). More details are given in **Flowchart 1** at **32.7.2**.

The moratorium provisions apply only up to the point that the CVA/IVA is approved. After that, X may dispose of property only in accordance with the terms of the approved voluntary arrangement.

32.5.2 Receivership

Receivership occurs where a person is appointed (by the holder of a mortgage or charge) to realise the charged assets (either taking income from them, or selling them) in order to secure repayment of the debt due from the borrower. Thus receivership is only available to lenders who hold security. In a property context, the most likely varieties of receiver will be a LOPA receiver or an administrative receiver (less frequently encountered now). The rules which govern what such a receiver can do (and thus how these operate to affect other parties such as Y) differ significantly from those applicable to other types of insolvency official (administrators, liquidators or trustees in bankruptcy).

Table 32.2 below indicates how these two types of receiver differ.

Table 32.2   The differences between a LOPA receiver and an administrative receiver

Law of Property Act Receiver (also called a fixed charge receiver)	Administrative Receiver
Can be appointed if X is an individual or a company.	Can be appointed only if X is a company
Appointed by a lender with a fixed charge over the property as security. It is unusual for a rack rent lease to be used as security (since it often has no capital value), so a LOPA receiver is more likely to be appointed in respect of freehold land or long leases granted for a premium.	Appointed by a lender who has a floating charge over the whole or substantially the whole of X's undertaking and • that floating charge was executed on or before 15 September 2003; or • that floating charge was executed after that date but falls into one of the limited categories which continue to qualify for administrative receivership (such as PPI and other projects loans).
Appointed either under the terms of the mortgage, or under the default power in s 101 of the LPA 1925, in circumstances where the mortgagee's power of sale has arisen.	Appointed under the terms of the floating charge, as expanded by s 28 of the IA 1986 and following.
Receiver acts only in relation to the charged asset (the particular property).	Receiver acts in relation to the class of assets covered by the floating charge.
Need not be a licensed insolvency practitioner.	Must be a licensed insolvency practitioner.

Law of Property Act Receiver (also called a fixed charge receiver)	Administrative Receiver
The LOPA receiver can always collect the income of the property. Usually the mortgage expands these powers to include sale and letting of the property. The aim is for the LOPA receiver to realise enough from the asset to allow repayment of the debt, though he must use reasonable endeavours to secure the market value of the asset. He is not interested in maximising the amount which other classes of creditor will recover.	The administrative receiver's powers depend on the mortgage, but these are expanded by statutory powers of sale, granting and surrendering leases, and carrying on X's business (because the floating charge is over all of X's undertaking). The aim is for the administrative receiver to realise enough from the assets to allow repayment of the debt, though he must use reasonable endeavours to secure the market value of the asset. He is not interested in maximising the amount which other classes of creditor will recover.
Legal title to the assets remains in X	
The LOPA receiver *cannot* <ul><li>disclaim the charged property (whether onerous or not);</li><li>ignore any obligations that bind the charged property, eg restrictive covenants, leases or easements. He must observe these, negotiate to escape from them or modify them, or run the risk that X is sued for breach. The LOPA receiver has no personal liability to observe these obligations.</li></ul>	The administrative receiver *cannot* <ul><li>disclaim any assets (whether they are onerous or not);</li><li>ignore any obligations that bind the property asset, eg restrictive covenants, leases or easements. He must observe these, negotiate to escape from them or modify them, or run the risk that X is sued for breach. The administrative receiver has no personal liability to observe these obligations.</li></ul>
The LOPA/administrative receiver acts as agent of X (IA 1986, s 44)	
If the LOPA/administrative receiver enters into a new contract, he will be personally liable on that contract (unless the terms of the contract state otherwise, as they usually will).	
The appointment of a LOPA/administrative receiver does not impose a moratorium on actions against X by other creditors or contracting parties. Thus Y can seek to enforce any contract that it has with X.	

32.5.3 Bankruptcy

Bankruptcy is applicable only to an insolvent individual (X). A licensed insolvency practitioner (generally one selected by the creditors) is appointed to act as the trustee in bankruptcy, to collect in the realisable assets belonging to X, convert them to cash and distribute this to the creditors. Once this process is complete, X is released from any of the debts he incurred up to the date of bankruptcy if they have not been fully settled in the bankruptcy.

A bankruptcy order is made by the court following presentation of a bankruptcy petition. The rules are complex, but in essence, a petition can be lodged by X (on grounds that he is unable to pay his debts), or by a unsecured creditor of X who is owed more than £750 and can demonstrate that X cannot pay this debt or has no reasonable prospect of doing so.

32.5.3.1 Effect of bankruptcy

Once the trustee in bankruptcy is appointed, X's assets vest in him automatically. Where this includes leasehold property, this automatic assignment does not need the consent of the landlord. It is an 'excluded assignment' for the purposes of the Landlord and Tenant (Covenants) Act 1995.

Once the assets have vested in the trustee in bankruptcy, X loses the ability to dispose of them, so Y should not enter into new contracts with X in relation to his property. Y should deal only with the trustee in bankruptcy. However, there is limited protection, in the case of registered land, under s 86 of the Land Registration Act 2002, where Y, in good faith, buys the property from X for value without knowing there has been a bankruptcy petition or order and without these having been registered (as a notice or restriction) against the title to the property (see *Pick v Chief Land Registrar* [2011] EWHC 206).

32.5.3.2 Powers of trustee in bankruptcy

The trustee in bankruptcy has a wide range of powers (detailed in the IA 1986), enabling him to manage the assets and eventually sell them. The trustee in bankruptcy must observe any existing restrictions and covenants which affect existing properties vested in him in this way (eg registered restrictive covenants affecting the property). This includes paying rent on existing leases (see **32.8.2.3**). However, the trustee is not obliged to implement any outstanding contracts (such as sale or purchase contracts), though he may choose to do so if this is consistent with proper realisation of X's assets. If the trustee considers the properties or contracts to be onerous, he can disclaim them (in the same way as a liquidator, but not other insolvency officials). For more details about disclaimer and its effect, see **32.10**.

32.5.3.3 Restrictions placed on the bankrupt

During the bankruptcy process there are restrictions both on what X can do and on the action its creditors may take against X to recover sums due to them or secure performance of obligations. These restrictions include the following:

(a) Between presentation of the bankruptcy petition and the vesting of the property in the trustee in bankruptcy, any purported disposition of that property by X is void (IA 1986, s 284(1)) unless it is:

  (i) made with the court's permission or subsequent ratification; or

  (ii) a disposition of registered land to a purchaser acting in good faith, for value and without notice of the presentation of the petition (see **32.5.3.1**).

(b) Between presentation of the bankruptcy petition and making the bankruptcy order the court can, if asked, stay any action or legal process brought against X or its property (IA 1986, s 285(1)).

(c) Once the bankruptcy order has been made, unsecured creditors may not enforce a remedy against X or its property, or bring any action or legal proceedings against X, unless they have the leave of the court to do so (IA 1986, s 285(3)). Secured creditors are not affected by this restriction (IA 1986, s 285(4)).

32.5.4 Administration

Administration is applicable only to an insolvent company (X). It is intended to provide an opportunity to rescue X from insolvency (perhaps selling it as a going concern). If this is impossible, the administration will focus instead on realising X's assets in a manner that produces a better result for the creditors as a whole than they would achieve in a liquidation. The administrator will seek to ensure that secured and preferential debts are cleared in full.

32.5.4.1 Appointment of the administrator

The administrator may be appointed by the court (on the request either of a director of X or of a creditor) or directly (without court involvement) by resolution of X in general meeting, or by resolution of its directors or by the holder of a floating charge (dated on or after 15 September 2003) over the whole or substantially the whole of X's assets. The administrator must be a licensed insolvency practitioner.

32.5.4.2   Powers and duties of the administrator

The administrator has powers and duties as set out in the IA 1986. These are designed to equip the administrator to manage X's business and property, with a view to rescuing X from insolvency. The administrator will put forward proposals as to which assets should be sold and which retained, which debts should be compromised and at what level, which contracts (to which X is a party) will be performed by X and which the administrator proposes should be terminated, and whether and how X should continue to trade. The administrator is an officer of the court, so must act fairly.

An administrator cannot disclaim any property of X, neither can he simply repudiate contracts into which X has entered. He must negotiate their termination, or allow X to be in breach of them and let the other party pursue what remedies it may have for that breach.

The administrator acts as X's agent and has no personal liability on the contracts into which X has already entered, or new ones into which it enters during the course of the administration. X's property does not vest in the administrator, so if the administrator wishes to dispose of properties, he does so in X's name. Once X is in administration, the directors lose their ability to determine the disposal of the properties.

Administration usually lasts for no more than one year. If the company is still insolvent at that point, the administration will generally change either to a CVA or to liquidation.

32.5.4.3   Moratorium

Whilst X is in administration, a statutory moratorium applies (IA 1986, Sch B1, para 43). This prevents both forfeiture by peaceable re-entry and any 'legal process' against X without the consent of the administrator or the court. Such consent was given in *Lazari GP Ltd v Jervis* [2012] EWHC 1466, when a landlord of one the properties previously used by Game Retail (UK) Ltd successfully applied to forfeit the lease rather than assign it to the buyer of the business. The moratorium also restricts X's creditors from seeking specific performance by X of its contracts with them (perhaps a contract to purchase land), suing for damages in lieu of performance, or seeking repayment of debts owed to them by X (such as a landlord trying to recover rent arrears). Similarly, those creditors cannot issue a petition to put X into liquidation, and the restriction on legal process means that a tenant will need consent before it can apply for a new lease under Pt II of the LTA 1954 where its landlord is in administration (*Somerfield Stores Ltd v Spring (Sutton Coldfield) Ltd* [2009] EWHC 2384). While consent will sometimes be given, the delay and uncertainly means that the moratorium can be very frustrating for creditors.

32.5.5   Liquidation

Liquidation is also applicable only to companies (not individuals). They are usually (but not always) insolvent (see **32.5.5.1**). Where X is insolvent but cannot be rescued, liquidation is appropriate. All X's assets must be realised (converted into cash) for distribution to its creditors (or shareholders if there is a surplus). In such circumstances, the unsecured creditors may receive very little towards the debt or damages for breach of contract owed to them by X.

32.5.5.1   Types of liquidation

A voluntary liquidation is started by a resolution of X's shareholders (members). Usually they pass such a resolution because X is insolvent, and in this case X's creditors must approve the resolution and choice of liquidator. This is a creditors' voluntary liquidation. Sometimes, the shareholders wish to wind up the company even though it is solvent (a members' voluntary liquidation). No court order is needed to confirm a voluntary liquidation.

Alternatively, compulsory liquidation occurs where the court makes an order following presentation of a winding-up petition against X because it cannot pay its debts. Such a petition is often lodged by a creditor (who must be owed at least £750, though it would seem that, unlike a bankruptcy petition, this need not be on an unsecured basis).

32.5.5.2 Powers and duties of the liquidator

The liquidator deals with realisation of X's assets and distribution of the proceeds, but X's assets do not vest in him. The liquidator must be a licensed insolvency practitioner. He has wide-ranging powers and duties as set out in the IA 1986, but may need approval for some actions, depending on whether the liquidation is voluntary or compulsory.

Unlike other insolvency officials, a liquidator (and a trustee in bankruptcy) has the ability to disclaim any property or other assets belonging to X that are considered to be onerous. Section s 178(3)(a) of the IA 1986 allows the liquidator to disclaim an unprofitable contract. A contract is not unprofitable just because it is financially disadvantageous. The liquidator has to balance the benefit to the creditors from complying with the contract against the liability which the contract imposes on the company. Contracts which impose obligations on X, either to do things or to pay money, would generally be onerous. This would include contracts in which X agrees to take a new lease or purchase property, or existing leases where X is the tenant. It might also include a sale agreement where X is the seller (perhaps where the sale price is rather low). Disclaimer terminates X's rights and obligations under the contract and is possible regardless of whether there is a termination clause in the contract. It is very rare for freehold property to be considered onerous, as it usually has a positive value. However, if the obligations associated with its ownership are extensive and costly, it could be disclaimed as onerous. For more on disclaimer see **32.10**.

32.5.5.3 Moratorium

Unlike administration, no moratorium applies in a voluntary liquidation. Thus creditors, and other parties (such as Y) to contracts into which X entered (but of which it is now in breach) can take enforcement action, unless the liquidator obtains a court order (under s 112 of the IA 1986) to prevent this.

In a compulsory liquidation, once the winding-up order is made by the court, Y cannot take any action or proceedings against X or its property without the consent of the court. Also, from the earlier point when the winding-up petition is presented, any purported disposition by X of its property is void, unless made with the court's permission or subsequent ratification.

32.6 SETTING ASIDE TRANSACTIONS WHICH HAVE ALREADY BEEN COMPLETED

One of the surprising implications of insolvency is that certain kinds of insolvency official (liquidators, administrators and trustees in bankruptcy) can ask the court to set aside completed transactions (potentially resulting in the return of the property or an award of damages against Y as the current owner). This power is designed to prevent some creditors 'getting in first', to the detriment of the remainder.

The two most important categories of completed transaction which can be set aside are transactions at an undervalue and preferences. **Table 32.3** below shows the essential features of both. There are other rules which operate in different circumstances to set aside dealings with insolvent companies (eg the 'anti-deprivation' principle), but these are not discussed further here.

Table 32.3   Transactions at an undervalue and preferences

Transactions at an undervalue	Preferences
IA 1986, s 238 (insolvent companies). IA 1986 s 339 (insolvent individuals).	IA 1986, s 239 (insolvent companies). IA 1986 s 340 (insolvent individuals).
X was a party to a completed transaction (either direct with Y, or with a predecessor in title of Y).	Y is one of X's creditors or a guarantor of X's debts.
X (or someone at X's direction) received substantially less than the value of the property disposed of in the transaction (perhaps it was a gift, or only nominal consideration was paid).	X does something which has the effect of putting Y in a better position than it would have been if X were subject to a formal insolvency process (gave a 'preference' to Y direct or to someone else with Y's agreement and benefiting Y as a result)
X's intention in entering into the undervalue transaction is irrelevant.	X must do this with the *desire* to produce the effect of putting Y in a better position. Where Y is connected to X in some way, this desire is presumed to exist.
X subsequently goes into administration or liquidation (companies), or becomes bankrupt (individuals). Other forms of insolvency process cannot take advantage of this process.	
The completed transaction took place within: • the 2-year period leading up to the start of the administration or liquidation (where X is a company); • the 5-year period leading up to the bankruptcy (where X is an individual).	The preference was given within: • the 2-year period leading up to the start of the administration, liquidation or bankruptcy, where Y is connected to X; or • the 6 months leading up to that point, where Y is not connected to X.
At the time of the transaction, or immediately after and in consequence of the transaction, X is in practice insolvent (ie cannot pay its debts, even if it is not yet subject to any formal insolvency process). Where X is an individual, this requirement does not apply in the 2 years immediately before the bankruptcy – it applies only during the earlier part of the 5-year period	At the time of the giving the preference, or immediately after and in consequence of giving it, X is in practice insolvent (ie cannot pay its debts, even if it is not yet subject to any formal insolvency process).
Where X is a company, the transaction, even if at an undervalue and completed during the 2-year period, will not be at risk of being reversed if X can show that it entered into the transaction in good faith, for the purposes of carrying on its business, and at the time of the transaction there were reasonable grounds for believing that the transaction would benefit the company. There is no equivalent escape clause if X is an individual.	No equivalent.
The administrator, liquidator (with various consents from creditors and shareholders) and the trustee in bankruptcy (as appropriate) can ask the court to set the transaction aside. The court can make such order as it sees fit, including ordering the return of the property or payment of damages. However, it can refuse to make the order, even if the criteria to do so are satisfied (eg *Claridge* [2011] EWHC 2047 (Ch), a bankruptcy case).	

Transactions at an undervalue	Preferences
If Y was the other party to the undervalue transaction with X, Y cannot argue (as a defence to any such court order) that it did not know: • X was insolvent or in danger of becoming so; or • the value Y was giving was significantly less than market value.	If Y was the party given the preference, it cannot argue (as a defence to any such court order) that it did not know: • X was insolvent or in danger of becoming so; or • X had the desire to give Y a preference.

If Y is not the other party to the undervalue transaction/preference, but is a successor in title to the party that was, then Y may be protected from any such court order to return the property or pay damages (IA 1986, ss 241/342). Protection is available where Y:

• acted in good faith when it entered into its own transaction; and

• gave value for its own transaction.

Y will be presumed *not* to act in good faith if, at the time of its own transaction, either:

• Y was connected to the party to whom X transferred at an undervalue or to whom X gave the preference; or

• Y had notice of both the previous undervalue transaction/preference *and* the fact that X had since entered into administration, liquidation or bankruptcy.

If Y can prove otherwise then the protection will once more apply.

If Y gave no value for its own transaction then it cannot benefit from this protection.

This is why, when investigating title, if there is evidence of an undervalue transaction it is necessary to carry out either a company search or a land charges (bankruptcy) search against the company or individual that was the 'donor' under that transaction (X), to see if they subsequently went into administration, liquidation or became bankrupt.

32.7 THE EFFECT OF A TENANT BECOMING INSOLVENT

32.7.1 The range of remedies available to a landlord

Where an insolvent tenant (X) fails to pay its rent or perform its obligations, the landlord may want to pursue all or any of the following remedies:

(a) sue for unpaid rent (proceedings);

(b) exercise commercial rent arrears recovery (CRAR) rights – see **29.1.1.3**;

(c) divert to itself the rent due from a sub-tenant to X (under s 81 of the Tribunals, Courts and Enforcement Act (TCEA) 2007) (a 's 81 TCEA notice');

(d) sue for specific performance (proceedings);

(e) sue for damages for breach of covenant (proceedings);

(f) forfeit the lease on grounds either of insolvency or breach (for more details see **30.5**);

(g) start insolvency proceedings (perhaps a petition for bankruptcy or compulsory liquidation) in order to bring pressure to bear;

(h) force a trustee in bankruptcy or liquidator, acting for X, to decide whether to disclaim the lease or not, so that (if they do disclaim) at least Y is free to re-let.

(i) persuade the insolvency official to surrender the lease

In some cases the insolvency official may be personally liable to pay the rent, or the rent may qualify as an expense of the insolvency (see **32.10.5**). This gives the landlord an extra remedy.

As indicated in **32.2**, the landlord should also consider whether it has meaningful remedies against third parties (for example, guarantors, or through a rent deposit or a performance bond from a bank). Bear in mind, if X is subject to a voluntary arrangement, the obligations of those third parties may have been amended (see **32.5.1**).

32.7.2 The restrictions on exercise of these various remedies

To illustrate how the various principles outlined in **32.5** impact on the landlord's remedies against the tenant, see **Flowcharts 1 to 6** below. Consult the correct flowchart for the insolvency regime that affects X. Note that CRAR and s 81 TCEA notices can only be used where there is a written lease of commercial property.

Flowchart 1   Where an individual tenant (X) is subject to an IVA

Flowchart 2   Where an individual tenant (X) is bankrupt

Yes = ⟶   No = - -►

Landlord can exercise all the remedies as normal. ◄- - - Has the bankruptcy petition been filed in respect of X?

Has the bankruptcy order been made?

With leave of the court, the landlord can bring any of the following proceedings:

• for unpaid rent;
• for specific performance;
• for damages for breach of contract;
• CRAR for a maximum of six months' rent.

The court may refuse leave where the landlord is seeking a remedy for a debt provable in the bankruptcy (IA 1986, s 285(3)).

The landlord can do the following without leave of the court:

• serve a s 81 TCEA notice;
• forfeit by peaceable re-entry;
• seek a court order for possession (forfeiture) (*Christina Sharples v Places for People Homes Ltd* [2011] EWCA Civ 513).

However, the court may stay proceedings for possession (IA 1986, s 285(1)).

The landlord can serve notice on the trustee in bankruptcy requiring confirmation of whether it plans to disclaim the lease (IA 1986, s 316).

The landlord can bring any of the following proceedings (but they may be stayed by the court (IA 1986, s 285(1))):

• for unpaid rent;
• for specific performance;
• for damages for breach of contract;
• for forfeiture.

The landlord can do the following without leave of the court:

• serve a s 81 TCEA notice.

The landlord cannot yet serve notice on the trustee requiring confirmation of whether it plans to disclaim the lease, because the trustee is not yet appointed.

Flowchart 3   Where a corporate tenant (X) is subject to a CVA

Yes = ──▶   No = --▶

Have the CVA proposals been approved by creditors and shareholders? ──▶ Terms of the CVA govern what landlord can do.

Is X a 'small company' because it satisfies at least two of the following tests?

- Turnover of less than £5.6m
- Balance sheet assets under £2.8m
- Fewer than 50 employees

Do the CVA proposals include a request for the moratorium? --▶ Landlord can exercise all the remedies as normal.

Have those proposals been lodged with the court?

There is a moratorium which lasts from the date the proposals are lodged with the court until the date of the meeting to approve the CVA (or 28 days if shorter). During this period, the landlord cannot:

- petition or pass a resolution to wind X up, or make an administration application;
- forfeit by peaceable re-entry unless it does so with the leave of the court;
- exercise CRAR without the leave of the court;
- take any steps to enforce security without the leave of the court;
- commence or continue any other proceedings or legal process (including for outstanding rent, breach of covenant or specific performance) without the leave of the court.

The landlord may be able to serve a s 81 TCEA notice without leave of the court.

Once a CVA is approved, what the landlord can do is governed by the terms of that CVA.

Disclaimer (and forcing the insolvency official to decide whether to disclaim) is not relevant here.

Flowchart 4 Where a corporate tenant (X) is in administration

Yes = ⟶   No = ⇢

Has an application been made to court for an administration order.

Have the relevant documents been filed at court?

Has a resolution been passed for an out-of-court administration?

Interim moratorium applies until the administration order is made or dismissed, or the administrator is appointed (for out-of-court administration).

Landlord can do any of the following with prior leave of the court.

- bring proceedings for unpaid rent;
- bring proceedings for specific enjoyment;
- bring proceedings for damages for breach of contract;
- bring forfeiture proceedings;
- forfeit by peaceable re-entry;
- exercise CRAR.

Landlord can also, without the leave of the court, serve a s 81 TCEA notice (though this may be challenged).

All remedies can be exercised as normal.

Has an administration order been made or the administrator appointed?

Long-term moratorium replaces interim moratorium.

Same restrictions apply, but either the consent of the administrator or leave of the court will be sufficient.

Disclaimer is irrelevant here – administrators cannot disclaim.

Flowchart 5   Where a corporate tenant (X) is in voluntary liquidation

Yes = ⟶   No = ⇢

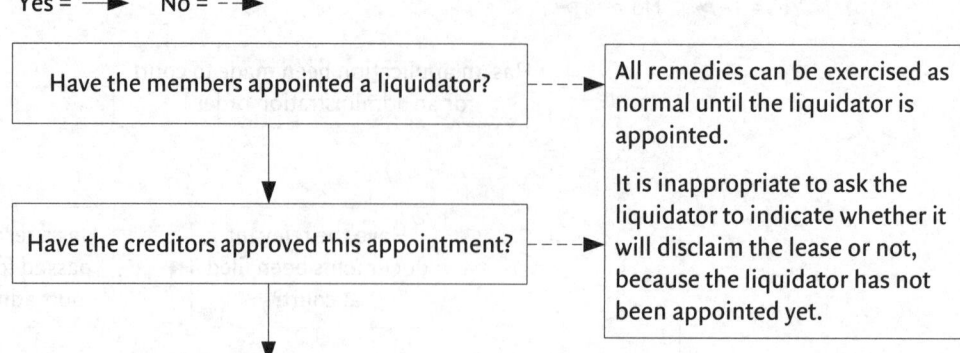

Have the members appointed a liquidator?

All remedies can be exercised as normal until the liquidator is appointed.

It is inappropriate to ask the liquidator to indicate whether it will disclaim the lease or not, because the liquidator has not been appointed yet.

Have the creditors approved this appointment?

Liquidator has been appointed.

There is no moratorium.

Landlord can make use of the following procedures without leave of the court or the liquidator. However, if he does so, the liquidator can ask the court to stay the proceedings:

- proceedings for unpaid rent;
- proceedings for specific enjoyment;
- proceedings for damages for breach of contract;
- forfeiture proceedings or forfeiture by peaceable re-entry.

Landlord can take the following action without leave of the court or the liquidator, and the liquidator *cannot* apply for a stay or otherwise stop such action:

- serve notice requiring the liquidator to decide whether it will disclaim the lease or not (IA 1986, s 178).

At the time of writing it is not clear whether a s 81 TCEA notice requires court permission.

Flowchart 6   Where a corporate tenant (X) is in compulsory liquidation

Yes = ⟶   No = --▶

Has a petition been presented to court for compulsory liquidation? ----▶ All remedies except CRAR can be exercised as normal.

Has a winding-up order been made? ----▶ All remedies except CRAR can be exercised as normal, but most can be stayed by the court (on the application of the company or a creditor) (IA 1986, s 126.

CRAR proceedings are void, but once the winding up order has been made, the landlord can seek the leave of the court to exercise CRAR.

It is inappropriate to ask about the liquidator's intention to disclaim the lease, because the liquidator has not yet been appointed.

Liquidator has been appointed.

Landlord can use the following procedures only with prior leave of the court or the liquidator (IA 1986, s 130):

• proceedings for unpaid rent;
• proceedings for specific enjoyment;
• proceedings for damages for breach of contract;
• forfeiture proceedings;
• exercise CRAR.

Landlord can take the following action without leave of the court or the liquidator, and the liquidator *cannot* apply for a stay or otherwise stop such action:

• forfeit by peaceable re-entry (this may be challenged);
• serve notice requiring the liquidator to decide whether it will disclaim the lease or not (IA 1986, s 178).

At the time of writing it is not clear whether a s 81 TCEA notice requires court permission.

32.7.3 Recovering the premises – forfeiture and its drawbacks

The forfeiture clause in most leases includes insolvency events as a trigger for possible forfeiture. These usually include the appointment of an administrator, a liquidator or a trustee in bankruptcy, but can extend to voluntary arrangements or the appointment of a receiver. Usually the preliminary steps in those insolvency processes (such as lodging a petition for winding up, rather than just the making of the winding-up order) are enough to give the landlord the right to forfeit.

Where the landlord can insist that a third party/source pays the rent and performs the covenants (perhaps a guarantor or a rent deposit), it may prefer to keep the lease alive, for once it has been forfeited these remedies will generally cease with it. One exception may be if the guarantee states that the guarantor will take a replacement lease if the original is forfeited. The landlord may also be reluctant to forfeit if it will be difficult to find a replacement tenant quickly, or if the cost of the necessary incentives to achieve a re-letting will be prohibitive or if the bill for rates whilst the property stands empty is unaffordable.

If the landlord decides to forfeit on an insolvency ground, it must serve a notice on the tenant under s 146 of the LPA 1925. However, the insolvency ground is irremediable, so the tenant need not be given a reasonable time to remedy the breach. The greatest source of delay in forfeiture is likely to be the need for consent from the court or the insolvency official to allow forfeiture (either by proceedings or by peaceable re-entry). Consult **Flowcharts 1 to 6** for further details of what consent is required and when. The main case to consider whether such consent should be given for forfeiture proceedings is *Re Atlantic Computer Systems plc* [1990] EWCA Civ 20.

Even if forfeiture is permitted and achieved, X or its insolvency official can apply for relief from forfeiture. The court has a wide discretion to permit this, and can set terms for doing so (eg requiring X to pay off the arrears or remedy the breach of covenant).

For more details on forfeiture, see **30.5**.

32.8 REQUIRING THE INSOLVENCY OFFICIAL TO PAY RENT

32.8.1 Rent arrears for the period leading up to the insolvency event

These must be claimed for by the landlord in the insolvency.

32.8.2 Rent/service charge arising after the start of the insolvency

Whether these are payable in full depends on the type of insolvency.

32.8.2.1 Voluntary arrangements

The terms of the CVA/IVA will determine whether X is liable for the ongoing rent in full or in part, or not at all. The supervisor of the CVA/IVA is not liable personally to pay these sums.

32.8.2.2 Receiver

The tenant company remains liable for the rent and service charge, and the receiver may choose to require the tenant company to pay those sums or it may not. The receiver is not personally liable to pay these sums (even if it chooses to direct the tenant company to pay them). Moreover, the receiver can collect in sub-lease rents and account for these to the mortgagee even if the main lease rent is not being paid.

If the ongoing rent is not paid, the tenant company will be in breach and the landlord will have its normal remedies, which may include forfeiture, diverting any sub-lease rents under s 81 of the TCEA 2007 (or any law which supersedes this) or commencing more formal insolvency proceedings (such as bankruptcy or liquidation). The unpaid rent will usually rank as an unsecured claim in such an insolvency. For more details on remedies, see **32.7.1** and **Chapter 29**.

32.8.2.3 Bankruptcy

The lease becomes vested in the trustee in bankruptcy, who will be personally liable on the covenants in the lease. The trustee should therefore pay the rent and other sums that fall due whilst the lease is vested in him. Generally the trustee will try to bring his liability for rent and other payments to an end by assigning, surrendering or disclaiming the lease.

If the trustee disclaims the lease, the landlord cannot sue the trustee for rent arrears accruing for the period prior to the disclaimer. Instead the landlord will have to submit a claim in the bankruptcy for that sum, as an unsecured creditor, and may well recover only part of the debt. It is possible (but not yet established by case law) that where the trustee has been using the let premises for the purpose of realising the assets (perhaps continuing to trade X's business from them pending sale of that business as a going concern), the landlord's claim for rent arrears (for the period from the making of the bankruptcy order to the date of disclaimer) might be treated as an expense of the bankruptcy and therefore more likely to be paid in full.

32.8.2.4   Administrator or liquidator

Rent and other sums need not be paid by an administrator or a liquidator as they are not personally responsible for the contracts into which X has entered. However, if they choose to occupy the property (or part of it) for the purposes of the administration or winding up, then they may be liable to pay both rent and service charge that fall due during that period (as an expense of the administration or liquidation). What qualifies as use for such purposes was considered in *Sunberry Properties Limited v Innovate Logistics Ltd (in administration)* [2008] EWCA Civ 1261. If the rent and service charge qualify as expenses of the administration or liquidation, they will be settled as a priority debt in the insolvency (ahead of the remuneration of the insolvency official) and, therefore, should be paid in full.

There have been many cases on which rent and service charges must be paid and for what periods, but the law was recently clarified, with the leading cases (*Leisure Norwich (II) Ltd v Luminar Lava Ignite Ltd & Others* [2012] EWHC 951 (Ch) and *Goldacre (Offices) Ltd v Nortel Networks (UK) Ltd (in administration)* [2009] EWHC 3389 (Ch)) being overruled by the case of *Pillar Denton Ltd and Others v Jervis and Others* [2014] EWCA Civ 180 (24 February 2014). This case related to the administration of the Game group of companies.

The Court of Appeal held that an administrator (or a liquidator) must make payments at the rate of the rent for the duration of any period during which he retained possession of the premises for the benefit of the administration, and that the rent would be treated as accruing from day to day. The period of beneficial possession was to be determined as a question of fact.

This is a welcome simplification of the previous law, but there may be a time during which administrators allege they have paid too much and landlords argue they are due more than under the previous rules, and it will be interesting to see how these issues are resolved.

32.9   REQUIRING THE INSOLVENCY OFFICIAL TO OBSERVE THE LEASE COVENANTS

The insolvency official acting for an insolvent corporate tenant is not personally liable to perform the other covenants in the lease (for example, to carry out repairs, make good dilapidations at the end of the lease, or observe the user covenant). The insolvency official is merely the agent of the tenant (which continues to exist). By contrast, a trustee in bankruptcy acting for an insolvent individual tenant is personally liable to perform the lease covenants.

Where the tenant remains liable to observe the lease covenants and fails to do so, the landlord will have its normal remedies, subject to any relevant restrictions on their exercise. For more details of those restrictions, see **32.7.2**.

32.9.1   Voluntary arrangements (CVA or IVA)

The tenant is still bound to perform the covenants in the lease (though the extent of the obligation to perform them may be varied by the CVA or IVA terms). The nominee (see **32.5.1**) is not personally liable.

32.9.2   Receiver

The tenant company remains liable as tenant under the lease. The receiver can control whether the tenant will discharge its obligations under the lease. The receiver is not personally liable.

32.9.3   Administrator

The tenant company remains liable as tenant under the lease. The administrator will not be personally liable, although he will control whether the tenant discharges its obligations under the lease. If the administrator has chosen to continue to occupy and trade from the property for the purposes of the administration, then he will have a powerful incentive to observe the lease covenants, in order to avoid the risk of the landlord applying for leave to forfeit the lease. It is possible (by analogy with the *Nortel* case – see **32.8.2.4**) that any debts due to the landlord from the tenant, arising as a result of its failure to comply with the lease covenants during the period of occupation for the purposes of administration, may qualify as a priority debt, as being an expense of the administration.

32.9.4   Liquidator

The tenant company remains liable as tenant under the lease. The liquidator will not be personally liable. If the liquidator has continued to trade from the premises (rather than disclaiming the lease, or leaving the premises empty) or wishes to sell the lease (because it has some capital value) then he will have an incentive to observe the lease covenants, in order to avoid the risk of the landlord applying for leave to forfeit the lease. It is very unclear whether debts arising due to failure to observe the covenants of the lease during such period would be recoverable as a priority debt in the liquidation, as an expense of the liquidation.

32.9.5   Trustee in bankruptcy

The lease vests in the trustee in bankruptcy, who is therefore bound to observe all its provisions, unless he chooses to disclaim (see **32.10**). The trustee can claim (from the bankrupt's estate) reimbursement for any costs incurred in complying with the lease. The tenant will also remain bound (as the statutory assignment to the trustee in bankruptcy does not release the tenant from liability, under the Landlord and Tenant Covenants Act 1995).

32.10   DISCLAIMER AND ITS EFFECTS

32.10.1   Who can disclaim?

Only trustees in bankruptcy (IA 2006, s 315) and liquidators (IA 2006, s 178) can disclaim property.

32.10.2   What is disclaimer?

The insolvency official, by notice filed in court, renounces future involvement by X in the contract, or future ownership by X of the property (as appropriate). Copies of that notice have to be served on the other people who may be interested in the disclaimed property, or who will remain under an obligation in relation to it despite the disclaimer. This gives them the chance to decide whether they want to apply for an order vesting the disclaimed property in them. For more on vesting orders see **32.10.7**.

Where X is a tenant, and the insolvency official wishes to bring liability under the lease to an end, it may prefer to do so by methods other than disclaimer. It may be possible to terminate the lease by notice to quit (a periodic tenancy), or by exercising a break right. The landlord may be willing to take a surrender of the lease (particularly if there are sub-leases, as this will be a more reliable way for the landlord to take over those sub-leases). Alternatively, the insolvency official may choose to do nothing, fail to pay the rent or observe the provisions of the lease, and hope that the landlord takes the initiative and chooses to forfeit the lease.

32.10.3   What can be disclaimed?

Any property which the insolvency official considers to be onerous can be disclaimed. Onerous property is defined (IA 1986, s 178(3)) as property which is either unsaleable or not readily saleable, or which might give rise to a liability to pay money or perform any onerous act. This will include:

Leasehold property

(a)   a lease where X is the tenant (because a tenant has a range of obligations which involve paying money or doing things);

(b) a lease where X is the landlord, if the obligations which the landlord must discharge (perhaps carrying out repairs) may cost more than it can recover from the tenants. This is rarely done where X is the freeholder, as well as the landlord, because disclaimer of the lease requires disclaimer of the underlying freehold interest too, and this usually has some value.

Sale contracts

(c) a sale contract or agreement for lease where X is the buyer/tenant, if that contract is unprofitable (see **32.5.5.2**);

(d) a sale contract or agreement for lease where X is the seller/landlord and the contract is unprofitable (perhaps because it imposes on X obligations beyond the mere transfer of the property for the agreed price – for example to carry out extensive repair works).

In each case, disclaimer of the contract must be accompanied by disclaimer of the property to which it relates (so, in the case of a sale contract where X is the seller, the freehold or leasehold property it covers). This is unlikely where the freehold property has value.

Freehold property

Freehold property is rarely encumbered with such extensive obligations that it will be onerous, so disclaimer of freehold property is very unusual.

32.10.4 Is consent needed for disclaimer?

In most cases consent is not needed to disclaim (there are a few situations where a trustee in bankruptcy will need the consent of the court to disclaim, but these are beyond the scope of this book).

32.10.5 When can the onerous property be disclaimed?

The insolvency official can disclaim whenever he wishes, as long as he does so before the insolvent party is discharged from bankruptcy (where X is an individual) or finally dissolved (where X is a company).

If the insolvency official delays, the other party to the contract is left in limbo, not knowing whether the contract will be observed. That other party can force the pace, by serving on the insolvency official a notice to elect whether or not to disclaim (IA 1986, s 316(1) or s 178(5)). The insolvency official then has 28 days to serve notice of disclaimer. If no notice is served in time:

(a) the trustee in bankruptcy is deemed to have adopted the contract and will be personally liable to perform it;

(b) the liquidator is still not personally liable to perform the contract, but (at least in the case of a lease) may be taken to have retained the premises for the benefit of the liquidation, in which case rent and other payments due under the lease will rank as expenses of the liquidation and be payable as a priority debt (*ABC Coupler and Engineering Co Ltd (No 3)* [1970] 1 All ER 650).

32.10.6 Effect of disclaimer

32.10.6.1 On the insolvent party (X) and the insolvency official

The disclaimer releases X from its obligations (and rights) under the contract from the date of the disclaimer. It also releases the insolvency official from any such liability.

32.10.6.2 On the other party to the contract

The other party to the disclaimed contract will be left with a claim in the insolvency for the damages or losses it suffers as a result of the contract not being performed by X. In some circumstances it may be able to secure performance by a third party and will not, therefore, suffer any loss (see **32.10.6.3**).

Where it is a lease that is disclaimed, the landlord will be entitled to retake possession. However, it should not do so if it wishes to require a third party to take on the responsibility for the lease (see **32.10.6.3**).

32.10.6.3   On third parties

Disclaimer does not (unless this is necessary in order to release X from its obligations) affect the liabilities and rights of any third party (IA 1986, s 178(4)). For example, if X has agreed, jointly with Z, to purchase a property from Y, X's insolvency official can disclaim the purchase contract but Y may still seek specific performance against Z. This comes up most often in the context of a lease where there is a guarantor for X, or possibly previous tenants who are still liable to perform the lease (either as original tenant under a pre-1996 lease, or under an AGA for a more recent lease). All will remain liable to the landlord under the guarantee arrangements, despite the disclaimer, unless the terms of the guarantee state that it terminates on disclaimer (*Hindcastle v Barbara Attenborough Associates* [1997] AC 70 and *Doleman v Shaw* [2009] EWCA Civ 283).

In such circumstances, the landlord can, despite disclaimer, still sue the guarantor or former tenant for the rent or performance of the lease covenants. If (as is usual) the guarantee clause provides for this, the landlord can, alternatively, require the guarantor or former tenant to take up a replacement lease.

The landlord must be careful not to retake possession of the premises following disclaimer, if it wishes to be able to pursue such remedies against third parties. If the landlord does retake possession, this will be treated rather as if it had successfully forfeited the lease, which brings the lease to an end, and with it the liability of the guarantors and former tenants (see *Hindcastle*, above, and *Active Estates Ltd v Parness* [2002] EWHC 893).

32.10.6.4   On sub-tenancies

Sub-tenants are a special variety of third party where a lease is disclaimed, and the rules are very complex. In simple terms, disclaimer of the head-lease brings to an end the obligations which X had as landlord of the sub-leases and the subtenants' rights against and obligations to X. However, it does not:

(a)   terminate the sub-tenants' interests in the property (so disclaimer differs from forfeiture in this respect);

(b)   substitute the superior landlord as landlord of the sub-leases (as would occur if X's lease had been surrendered).

There is privity neither of contract nor estate between the superior landlord and the sub-tenant. In effect, the disclaimed head-lease is treated as still being in existence, unless and until the superior landlord chooses to forfeit it (for default in rent payments or performance of other conditions). If that forfeiture is successful then the sub-lease will be forfeit too (assuming the sub-tenant does not obtain relief from forfeiture). Until that point, the sub-tenant has a continued right to possession (not under the sub-lease but under a *sui generis* set of rights).

This means that if the sub-tenant continues, in practice, to pay the rent and observe the covenants of the disclaimed head-lease, the superior landlord may have no grounds for forfeiture. If the sub-tenant pays more rent (under the head-lease) than it was obliged to do under the sub-lease, it can claim in the insolvency for the difference.

32.10.7   Vesting orders

Where a third party (perhaps a guarantor, former tenant or sub-tenant) ends up paying the rent under X's disclaimed lease, it may want to apply for a vesting order. Likewise, a mortgagee of X's disclaimed property may want to apply for a vesting order. If successful, the lease or property will be transferred to the third party. This gives that party control over the property, and thus the ability to ensure performance of relevant covenants and to sell or assign the property, in order to bring their liability to a close.

The court has discretion over whether to make a vesting order and on what terms. Generally it will require the person in whom the property is vested to be subject to the same obligations (in relation to that property) as X was before the disclaimer. If more than one person applies for a vesting order, the court applies an established pecking order in deciding who should succeed (sub-tenants come higher up this order than guarantors, former tenants or the landlord itself). If the landlord applies for a vesting order (so as to be sure that the lease is under his control), the court will give people higher up the pecking order (such as sub-tenants) the chance to take the vesting order instead. If they do not take up this opportunity reasonably quickly, they will lose the right to apply for a vesting order at a later date.

If the vesting order is granted, ownership of the lease or other property transfers automatically. There is no need for a conveyance, an assignment or a transfer.

A party seeking a vesting order must apply for it within three months of becoming aware of or being notified of the disclaimer. This period can be extended by the court.

Review Activity Answers

Chapter 1

1. The three main types of commercial property are offices, retail and industrial.

2. Renting avoids the need to find or borrow the purchase money at the outset and means that capital is not tied up in the building.

3. Investors hope to make an income by letting the property to tenants and a capital gain as the property rises in value.

4. Developers hope to make a profit by selling the completed development for more than it cost to purchase and develop the original site.

5. An investor may join with another investor to spread the financial risk and/or make it easier to obtain funding for the development. It may join with a developer to gain specialist expertise in areas such as project management, planning, environmental remediation and construction. It may join with a prospective buyer of the completed development to give the buyer some input into design and construction, and thereby strengthen the buyer's commitment to the purchase.

6. Contractual joint ventures and joint venture partnerships have no separate legal personality so they are 'tax transparent' and pay no tax in their own right. Tax is paid only once the profits and gains have reached the joint venture parties. An SPV, being a separate legal entity, pays tax in its own right, and tax is charged again when the SPV dividends are paid to the joint venture parties, hence the term 'double taxation'.

7. Both an SPV and an LLP, as legal entities separate from the joint venture parties, offer limited liability for losses incurred in the development. Traditional partnerships and contractual joint ventures have unlimited liability, and a traditional partner is also liable for the defaults of its partners.

8. Which joint venture structure is most efficient in terms of SDLT depends on the stage of the development. At the outset, a contractual joint venture is the more efficient, as the necessary transfer of the property into the joint venture partnership or SPV gives rise to a charge to SDLT. On the eventual sale of the developed property, an SPV offers the possibility of selling the shares with 0.5% stamp duty instead of the property with 4% SDLT.

Chapter 2

There are potential risks to Western if the issues raised are not addressed prior to the release of the loan. The issues raised are best dealt with in the loan agreement in conditions precedent. Conditions precedent must be satisfied prior to the release of the loan and, accordingly, unless Western is satisfied with the position, the loan will not proceed.

(a) *Subsidence*

Unit 3 may be suffering from subsidence. If so, the building may require significant and expensive remedial works, which are not included in the development budget. Ross may need to borrow further monies from Western. This may impact on the loan-to-value ratio, and Ross may struggle to meet the interest obligations under an increased loan. Any remedial works may delay the development which may affect the period of the loan. If the development is delayed, the institutional investor may no longer be interested in buying the property and Ross would need to find another buyer for the completed development. This may delay the repayment of the loan.

Condition precedent – Western is in receipt of a satisfactory structural engineer's report in respect of Unit 3 confirming that the movement to the property is long-established settlement and there is no subsidence.

(b) *Right of way*

If the dispute with the owner of Unit 4 cannot be resolved, the extension cannot be built. Resolving the dispute may require litigation, which would be expensive and time-consuming. This drain on Ross's resources and management time may affect Ross's ability to pay the capital and interest due under the loan. The alternative would be to proceed without the extension, but the project may be viable only with the extension. The institutional investor may no longer be interested in purchasing Unit 3 if it cannot be extended.

Condition precedent – The dispute relating to the right of way with the owner of Unit 4 is resolved to Western's satisfaction.

(c) *Flooding*

The recent flooding may make it difficult to insure Unit 3 against the risk of flooding. If this risk is not covered, Ross may find it difficult to let the property. Tenants may be unwilling to accept the risk that they may be faced with expensive remedial works and clean-up costs if the flooding recurs, unless the lease provides that the landlord will be responsible for uninsured risks. The institutional investor would object to any such term in the lease, as it would expect there to be no circumstances in which it would be required to make any expenditure. If the property cannot be let/sold, this will affect Ross's ability to repay the loan.

Condition precedent – Western is satisfied with details of the fully comprehensive insurance policy, which includes the risk of flooding, and which will be put in place on completion of the acquisition of Unit 3.

Chapter 3

1. A call option combined with a non-returnable fee and/or overage.

    Both a put option and a right of pre-emption would give all the decision-making power to the seller, who would presumably trigger the relevant provisions immediately as there is an alternative buyer already in the wings. ABC must offer the seller an immediate incentive not to sell to the rival developer whilst not committing itself to buy the land. The incentive could take the form of a non-returnable fee and/or the offer of an overage payment if and when the barn conversion takes place. Either (or both) of these could be incorporated into a conditional contract or a call option. However, although it would be possible to draft a contract conditional upon the obtaining of funding on acceptable terms, it would be very difficult to agree a test of acceptability. A call option would avoid these drafting difficulties and is obviously preferable for ABC as there would be no commitment to buy. It should be borne in mind, however, that the seller is likely to demand a high option fee/overage payment for the grant of a call option, to reflect the fact that it is passing up the chance to sell to the rival developer with no certainty that ABC will ever buy the land.

2. A right of pre-emption.

    A call option would not serve any useful purpose as the housing association might never be in a position to exercise it, and in the meantime MBC will be prevented from selling to anyone else. Similarly, the housing association is presumably not in a position to enter into a put option; and even if it does, it may not be able to comply with the obligation to complete if and when MBC exercises the put option. It will be difficult to draft a contract conditional upon the housing association getting sufficient funding to allow it to proceed, as the sources and amount of its funding will be variable from year to year. A right of pre-emption might be suitable here as it does not commit the housing association to a purchase it may not be able to afford but gives MBC a way of imposing a timetable on the decision-making process.

Chapter 4

1. The statement is incorrect. The basis on which LPAs are required to make decisions on whether to grant planning permission (and on what terms) is set out in s 38(6) of the Act. In simple terms, decisions should be made in line with the terms of the development plan unless material considerations indicate to the contrary. (See **4.1.3.**)

2. The statement is incorrect.

    First, permitted development rights under the GPDO amount to the grant of planning permission in any event (albeit that such permission is granted 'automatically' by the order rather than as a result of an express application). Secondly, the conversion of a building into more than one dwelling house is a material change of use and so will require planning permission. (See **4.2.2.1.**)

3. Subject to there being a condition preventing this within any planning permission allowing the current use, change of use from one A1 shop use to another A1 shop use would not amount to development. (See **4.2.2.1** and **4.2.2.2.**)

4. An Article 4 Direction removes permitted development rights given under the GPDO (to the extent stated in the relevant Direction). This will mean that an individual will have to make an express application for planning permission should it wish to carry out an activity amounting to development that is the subject of such a Direction. (See **4.2.3.3.**)

5. When seeking to rely on the permitted development rights granted by the GPDO it should be remembered that the rights are not unqualified. In the case of a change of use from a use within use class A2 to a use within use class A1, the change is only permitted if there is a display window at ground level. (See **4.2.3.2.**)

6. The statement is not correct. An outline planning permission will typically require that approval of reserved matters be obtained within three years of the grant of the permission. Implementation must take place within two years of approval of the last of such reserved matters. In this way, an outline planning permission potentially has a life span of up to five years before implementation. (See **4.3.1** and **4.3.4.3.**) But this is merely the default position. The LPA can specify whatever time limits it chooses, within reason.

7. In the case of a full planning permission, implementation of the permission must usually be commenced within three years of grant. The meaning of 'commenced' is set out in s 56 of the Act and includes such steps as digging a trench for foundations and any work of demolition in connection with the development. The erection of the building does not have to be completed within the three year period. (See **4.3.4.3** and **4.3.4.5.**)

8. An appeal against an adverse planning decision by an LPA is a total rehearing of the matter and so an Inspector must put himself in the position he would be in if he were the LPA making the decision in the first instance. This is different to many appeals (such as from the High Court to the Court of Appeal) where the appeal is made on a point of law and points of evidence cannot generally be considered. (See **4.4.1.**)

9. In most cases, the time limit is six months from the date of the LPA's notice of decision or its failure to determine. (See **4.5.**)

10. The danger for the farmer is that if he appeals against the decision, it is possible that an Inspector would refuse the application altogether (see Question 8) and so the farmer would be worse off than is the case currently.

    A way round this is for the farmer to submit a fresh application for planning permission under s 73 of the Act. If refused, he can appeal against the refusal in respect of that application. This will leave the original planning permission intact. (See **4.4.3.1.**)

Chapter 5

1. It is not possible to require the payment of money as a condition attached to planning permission. Such a requirement could be imposed by way of a planning obligation. (See **4.3.3** and **5.1**.) The LPA may alternatively wish to fund such work through CIL, if this kind of infrastructure is specified in its infrastructure list. The LPA may alternatively consider accepting provision of certain infrastructure as a payment in kind towards a CIL payment (see **5.6.1.8**).

2. Planning obligations can require the payment of money. The general land law principle that only the burden of restrictive covenants can bind successors in title does not apply to planning obligations. The burden of both positive and restrictive covenants contained in a planning obligation can be enforced against successors in title. (See **5.2**.) The LPA may also consider using CIL contributions to cover such work, but must consider the interaction of CIL and planning obligations (see **5.7**).

3. The Government's policy on planning conditions and obligations is set out in the NPPF (see **5.3**). Planning conditions should only be used where they are necessary, relevant to planning and to the development to be permitted, enforceable, precise and reasonable in all other respects. If there is already a need for the roundabout, a requirement to contribute towards it would not necessarily be directly relevant to the development to be permitted, so may be considered an unreasonable requirement. However, contributions towards infrastructure improvements may also be made by way of a highways agreement or a CIL payment, depending on what types of infrastructure the LPA decide to fund through CIL (although it is up to the LPA to choose what to spend CIL on and the roundabout would not be set out as the reason for charging CIL, which would depend on the existence of a charging schedule and other matters set out in this chapter). The LPA may alternatively accept provision of certain infrastructure as a payment in kind towards a CIL payment.

4. The LPA will generally insist on all parties with an interest in the relevant land entering into a planning obligation (see **5.2.4**). In light of this, the current freehold owner of the land in question will need to be made a party to the planning obligation. (See **5.2**.)

5. The owner of the land will be keen to ensure that it does not take on any unnecessary liability. It would, in particular, be keen to ensure there was no obligation to pay until the development linked to the planning obligation has been commenced. It would also wish to have its liability limited to its period of ownership. (See **5.4**.)

Chapter 6

1. First, it does not follow from the question that there is a breach of planning control at all. The works could be permitted by an express application or under permitted development rights under the GPDO. Even if there is a breach of planning control, it is not an offence in itself to be in breach. It is only if the LPA takes enforcement action that this can occur (such as failing to comply with a planning contravention notice). (See **Chapter 4** generally and **6.1**.)

2. The LPA does not have an automatic right to issue an enforcement notice. There must be an apparent breach of planning control and the service of the notice must be expedient having regard to the provisions of the development plan and other material considerations. (See **6.7.2**.)

3. Once served with a planning contravention notice, it is an offence not to reply to it within 21 days without reasonable excuse (See **6.5.2**.)

4. Enforcement action must be taken within four years in the case of building and other operational development (and change of use to a dwelling house). Once this time limit has passed, the LPA is unable to take enforcement action. On the facts of Question 4, therefore, the extension would be immune from being the subject of enforcement action.

5. A Certificate of Lawful Use or Development could be obtained in the circumstances envisaged in Question 4. This would act as proof that the development is lawful. (See **6.3.**)

6. There are various information gathering tools available to an LPA in respect of possible breaches of planning control. In particular, LPAs have a right of entry to ascertain whether there has been a breach of planning control and a planning contravention notice could be served requiring information about the use to which a relevant property is being put. (See **6.4** and **6.5.**)

7. The LPA could serve a breach of condition notice (given the nature of the breach in question). It could also consider serving an enforcement notice (and associated stop notice: see Question 8). One major advantage of the service of a breach of condition notice is that, unlike an enforcement notice, it cannot be appealed against. There are defences to being prosecuted for being in contravention of a breach of condition notice, but they are more limited than the grounds of appeal in respect of the service of an enforcement notice. Further, if an enforcement notice is appealed, its effect is suspended until the appeal has been heard. (See **6.6** and **6.7.**)

    The LPA could always choose not to enforce at all. (See **6.1.**)

8. A stop notice cannot be served in isolation and instead depends upon an enforcement notice having first been issued. A stop notice cannot be served once the enforcement notice has taken effect. (See **6.8.2.**)

9. Notice of appeal against the service of an enforcement notice must be given to the DCLG before the date on which the relevant enforcement notice takes effect. (See **6.10.2.**)

10. There are seven grounds of appeal. (See **6.10.1.**)

    On the facts, ground (c) (no breach of planning control) might be relevant. The firm's use of the property could be within use class A2 in any event and so there would be no breach of planning control at all. (See **4.2.2.2.**)

    If the firm's use of the property does amount to a breach of development control, ground (a) (planning permission should be granted) might be relevant. The facts indicate that under the plan-led principle which governs when planning permission should be granted, the use stands a good chance of being granted. (See **4.1.3.1.**)

    Ground (g) might also be relevant as six weeks is a very short time limit within which to cease to operate.

    Note that other grounds might also be relevant would but the above are particularly relevant from the facts.

Chapter 7

Scenario 1

As always, you would need to ascertain the size of the operation and its environment. In particular, what equipment or chemicals does it use, and are there other shops or even residences nearby? However, a 'typical' dry-cleaner may need to consider:

*   use of harsh chemicals – hazardous substances regulation applies;

*   smell and noise – potential nuisance claims from neighbours;

*   emissions and waste – environmental permit or exemption may be required.

Scenario 2

You would need to consider the following:

*   Building constructed in 1950s – asbestos removal probably required.

- Petrol station previously on site – contaminated land regime/PPS 23 planning condition for assessment and remediation of, say, any leaks from underground storage tanks.

- Roman wall on site – protection of archaeological sites; special building consent and preservation requirements.

- Limited information on previous use – transactional risk management (enquiries and warranties from seller) and possibly insurance needed for contingent risks.

- Mixed use commercial/residential planned – requirement to provide affordable housing under planning regime.

Scenario 3

This would raise the following environmental issues:

- Buildings on site since 1900 – asbestos management plan required.

- Long site history of industrial use and a nearby river – contaminated land and water pollution liability.

- Industrial chemicals and solvents used – hazardous substances and Control of Major Accidents Hazards Regulations, and potentially any *Rylands v Fletcher* claim.

- Produces substantial waste – waste management regulations.

- Strong burning smells and smoke – nuisance and statutory nuisance issues.

- Heavy industry activity – requires environmental permit(s).

- Depending on activity use – caught by the EU ETS, so needs requisite allowance (could trade on the carbon market).

- Substantial fire risks – higher duties of assessment, training and monitoring under the Fire Safety Order.

- Heavy energy use – Climate Change Levy Agreement still in force, and now also caught by the Carbon Reduction Commitment Energy Scheme.

- Purchase from another plc – transactional risk management, complex indemnities and agreement on liabilities, consideration of s 172 of the Companies Act 2006.

- Environmental Damage Regulations applicable due to questionable standard of machinery and hazardous substances containment – need to take precautionary measures.

Scenario 4

Each party – Alpha, Beta, Gamma, Delta, Epsilon – could constitute a Class A appropriate person, as each caused or knowingly permitted the significant contaminants. Gamma could also be a Class B person, as the present owner or occupier.

However, for the Group A persons, Alpha may be excluded as it sold the property with information to Beta (Test 3), mostly by allowing it to undertake extensive investigations. Alpha may also be excluded under Test 6, if the only reason there is a significant contaminant linkage is because Beta introduced pathways or receptors with its construction work.

Beta, though, may also be excluded, as it effectively paid for the remediation when it sold the property at a discount to Gamma, reflecting the cost of the contamination (Test 2). It is likely that Test 3 would also exclude Beta.

Delta and Epsilon may have known of the contaminants during their due diligence, but will likely both be excluded for committing only lending and insuring activities for Gamma (Test 1).

Gamma is unlikely to be able to use an exclusion, either as a Class A or Class B appropriate person.

If, however, none of Alpha, Beta or Gamma is excluded, the enforcing authority should consult the Guidance on apportionment of liability. Between Alpha (allowing the entry of the substance) and Beta (permitting its continuation), it is likely that Beta's liability should diminish as it arguably had less means and opportunity (it went bust) to deal with the contamination. Likewise, between Beta and Gamma (both knowing permitters), it is possible that Gamma may not receive a substantially reduced apportionment, as it is likely to have more means as a PLC.

Chapter 8

1. Usual searches:
    (a) A search of the local land charges register on form LLC1.
    (b) Enquiries of the local authority on form CON29R, paying particular attention to the replies to enquiries 1 (planning consents and refusals), 2 (are the access roads maintainable at public expense) and 3.12 (notices in relation to the remediation of contaminated land).
    (c) Optional enquiries of the local authority on form CON29O, all enquiries to be raised except those relating to parks and countryside, houses in multiple occupation, food safety notices and hedgerow notices. Particular attention should be paid to the replies to enquiries 5 (public rights of way) and 19 (environmental and pollution notices).
    (d) Water and drainage enquiries.
    (e) Enquiries of the seller, paying particular attention as to by what right access is gained to the site and whether any maintenance contributions are required.
    (f) Chancel repairs liability search.
    (g) Survey (ground conditions only as site has no buildings).
2. Additional searches:
    (a) Inspection of the property.
    (b) Full environmental survey as the land is clearly in an industrial area.
    (c) Flooding report. Apart from the risk of surface water flooding, the name suggests proximity to river or coastal water.
    (d) Highways search, particularly as it is clear that parts of the site do not immediately abut the road.
    (e) Public index map search, to try to find out who owns the land between the site and the access road.
    (f) Note that a coal mining search is not indicated as Canvey Island is not listed in the *Coal Authority Gazette for England and Wales* as a place where a mining search is required.

Chapter 9

There is no simple right or wrong answer in these circumstances. However, suggested points you should consider are as follows:

*   In considering the most appropriate form of procurement, you ought to consider the type of building and nature of the project, ie 'landmark', 'iconic' and the relevant importance of each of the different factors of time/cost/quality. The facts suggest that design is going to be an important consideration as 'an international architect' is being engaged.
*   You should also consider the pros and cons of different forms of procurement, eg traditional, design and build, and even construction management. While the importance of design is usually associated with using traditional procurement, you could also consider the possibility of design and build with novation, which would allow the client to employ the architect and control the conceptual design for the building,

prior to the architect (and other consultants) being novated to the contractor, to ensure single point responsibility for the client.

- You should also set out the consultancy appointments to be entered into, which should include the CDM coordinator (as the building must comply with health and safety legislation). In addition, a project manager is almost certainly required for a large development of this nature.

- You should set out details of those parties requiring collateral warranties/third party rights, ie the client (if design and build), R, G and H. Details of the warrantors providing the collateral warranties/third party rights, ie the different consultants and key sub-contractors (especially the specialist acoustic engineering sub-contractor) should also be set out. Note that warranties/third party rights may be given to G in respect of each floor it is letting (to enable G to assign the benefit of that warranty to H whilst retaining warranties for its other floors), rather than for the whole of its letting.

- Other forms of protection in the event of a defect arising may also be considered, eg defects liability insurance.

Chapter 10

1. (c)

    Value added tax is charged on any supply of goods or services made in the United Kingdom where it is a taxable supply made by a taxable person in the course or furtherance of a business carried on by him.

    In general terms, SDLT is levied on land transactions, CGT on the gain resulting from a disposal of an interest in land, and capital allowances are a form of tax relief that a buyer of commercial property may be entitled to claim on any fixed plant and machinery.

2. (a) and (d)

    Input tax is not paid when the supply is zero-rated or exempt.

3. (a), (b) and (d)

    In order to recover input tax, the business must make 'taxable' supplies, ie supplies that are standard or zero-rated, or where the option to tax has been exercised. A zero-rated supply is a taxable supply, albeit with VAT chargeable at the zero rate.

    When it makes a taxable supply, the business will charge output tax from which it will deduct input tax paid by it, so that it pays only the balance to HMRC.

4. The sale of the green field site to the developer and the grant of the retail lease are both exempt, subject to the option to tax. The payment to the building contractor and the freehold sale of the superstore (being a 'new' building) are both standard-rated.

5. True. The input tax can be recovered if the developer makes a taxable supply by opting to tax the rent due under the retail lease. Alternatively, the developer will be making a taxable supply when it sells the 'new' freehold superstore.

6. The grant and assignment of the lease are both exempt subject to the option to tax, the legal fees and fitting out costs are both standard-rated.

7. False. The insurance company tenant will *not* be able to recover the input tax as it makes only exempt supplies in the course of its business. The irrecoverable VAT will have to be borne as an overhead of the business.

Chapter 11

1. This is an 'old' lease granted prior to 1 January 1996. NUFC Ltd can claim against AFC Ltd, who remains liable to pay the rent throughout the entire term. NUFC Ltd can also claim the arrears from TFA Ltd, who is liable for breaches during its occupation. NUFC Ltd cannot claim the arrears from THS Ltd unless, on the assignment to TFA Ltd, THS

Ltd was required to give a direct covenant to NUFC Ltd to perform the covenants in the lease.

2. This is a 'new' lease granted after 1 January 1996. NUFC Ltd can claim against TFA Ltd. NUFC Ltd can also claim against THS Ltd, but only if THS Ltd guaranteed the performance of TFA Ltd as its immediate assignee.

Chapter 12

1. The tenant's solicitor should have asked to have included a provision dealing with 'unacceptable variations' and 'acceptable variations'. 'Unacceptable variation' should have included any variation which would reduce the capacity of the demise or standard of the works. Sometimes the parties will agree a percentage of leeway in capacity (usually not more than 10% difference either way), with a provision for joint measurement of the premises before practical completion is certified. The tenant's solicitor should also have asked to have included a right to supervise the works so that the tenant or its surveyors could point out any 'unacceptable variations'.

2. The tenant's solicitor should have asked to have included provisions relating to:

    (a) a pre-completion inspection by the tenant's representative to identify major defects and snagging works;

    (b) the attendance of the tenant's representative at the final inspection of the works to make representations to the landlord's architect or to carry out a joint inspection for the purpose of issuing the certificate;

    (c) the tenant's ability to object to and delay the issue of the certificate of practical completion if in its opinion the works have not yet been satisfactorily completed.

    Note that the tenant may also have a remedy against the architect for improper issue of the certificate (see **9.4**).

Chapter 13

1. Yes. Under clause 9.12, if the building (defined as including the property) is damaged (other than by deliberate damage – defined as damage caused deliberately by the tenant) by an insured risk (defined as including explosion) then payment of the annual rent (defined as rent at the initial rate on grant of the lease) or a fair proportion of it shall be suspended for a specified time. The definition of annual rent does not include the service charge.

2. Yes. Under clause 41 a notice given pursuant to the lease may be sent by fax.

3. Clause 1.10 states that an obligation on the tenant not to do something includes an obligation not to agree to or suffer that thing to be done and an obligation to use best endeavours to prevent that being done by another person.

Chapter 14

1. T is the original tenant of an 'old lease' governed by the old regime. T therefore remains liable throughout the term of the lease, even if it has assigned it on. T is consequently obliged to pay the rent if the definition of 'the Term' in the lease includes the period of any holding over. If it does not then T's liability ended on the expiry of the contractual term. If T is obliged to pay, T may be able to recover the sum from the assignee if it has an indemnity from the assignee. Under the old regime, an indemnity is implied into every assignment for value. Of course, if the assignee is in financial difficulty, it may not be worthwhile T's pursuing the assignee.

2. The lease is a 'new lease' governed by the new regime. L would not have been automatically released from the landlord's covenants when the reversion was sold on. There are two ways in which it may escape liability. First, if L served a notice on the

tenant requesting a release before or within four weeks of the sale, and the tenant did not object to the request, L will have been released. Secondly, if no notice was served, L will need to check the drafting of the lease. If the covenants were expressed to be binding only while the reversion was vested in L then it will have no liability. If L had not served a notice requesting a release and the lease does not limit L's liability for the landlord's covenants, L will be liable. On the assumption that L obtained an indemnity covenant from the buyer on the sale of L's reversionary interest, L may have a claim against the buyer. However, if the current tenant's assertion of insolvency is correct, the buyer is unlikely to be worth pursuing.

3. As the lease will be a new lease, all 'landlord covenants' will transmit automatically. This includes covenants not only in the lease but also in any 'collateral agreement'. Section 28 of the LT(C)A 1995 defines 'collateral agreement' to include agreements made before the date of the tenancy. Unless, therefore, the obligations in the agreement for lease are expressed to be personal to the previous landlord, they will constitute 'landlord covenants' and will bind your client.

Chapter 15

1. Yes, a demise of a whole building will prima facie include the roof and airspace above the building, even if this is not expressly mentioned in the demise. These are the facts of *Straudley Investments Ltd v Barpress Ltd* [1987] 1 EGLR 69. Counsel for the landlord argued that the upper surface of the roof and the airspace above the roof were not part of the premises demised to the tenant. However, the Court of Appeal held that the terms of the lease were 'crystal clear' that the roof did pass under the demise, and granted the tenant the mandatory injunction it sought.

2. Yes. These are the facts of *Davies v Yadegar* [1990] 1 EGLR 71. Counsel for the landlord sought to draw a distinction between a unitary building (where the demise would have included the airspace above the roof) and a building divided into flats (where it would not). The Court of Appeal rejected that distinction and said that the demise includes the airspace above the roof. Therefore, there was no trespass and the tenant was entitled to the declaration.

   The position would have been different if the flats had been divided horizontally and the landlord had retained the roof and roof space (see **Chapter 26** for the considerations which apply to a lease of part).

Chapter 16

1. Yes. These are the facts of *Meadfield Properties Ltd v Secretary of State for the Environment* [1995] 03 EG 128. The landlord argued that the term of 10 years started immediately after midnight on 24 June 1984, so that the lease could only be determined on 24 June 1994. However, it was held that a term stated to start on a certain date will start at the beginning of that day rather than at the end. Consequently, the term started on 24 June 1984 and terminated at the last moment of 23 June 1994, so the tenant's notice to determine the lease on 23 June 1994 was valid.

2. 13 January 1995. In fact, the tenant in the case of *Mannai Investment Co Ltd v Eagle Star Life Assurance Co Ltd* [1997] AC 749 specified 12 January 1995, but the House of Lords held that the notices were valid because it would have been obvious to the landlord, as a reasonable recipient with knowledge of the lease's terms and date of the third anniversary, that the tenant wanted to determine the leases on the third anniversary date but had made an immaterial error in wrongly describing the date as '12' rather than '13'.

3. No. These are the facts of *Prudential Assurance Co Ltd v Exel UK Ltd* [2009] EWHC 1350 (Ch), and the court held that the notice was invalid as it would not unambiguously have

been understood to be an effective notice by a reasonable recipient. Because it was known that T2 was a tenant under the lease, there would have been real doubt as to whether the notice had been served on T2's behalf. Indeed, there was some evidence that the omission of T2 from the notice was not accidental.

4.   No. These are the facts of *Bairstow Eves (Securities) Ltd v Ripley* [1992] 2 EGLR 47. The tenant argued that the condition precedent should be regarded as satisfied unless at the term date there were breaches for which substantial damages would be recoverable. The judge at first instance agreed with the tenant, but the Court of Appeal rejected the tenant's argument and agreed with the landlord that the condition precedent – requiring performance and observance of the tenant's covenants until the term date – was not satisfied.

Chapter 17

1.   All the monetary payments due under the lease have been reserved as rent under clause 2.3 because it makes it easier for the landlord in terms of the remedies it can exercise if the tenant fails to pay. First, under current law the landlord can exercise the remedy of distress for non-payment of rent (when the remedy of distress is replaced by CRAR (see **29.1**) this will no longer be the case). Also, no s 146 notice needs to be served on the tenant in relation to a failure to pay rent.

2.   Where a sum is reserved as rent, a notice under s 17 of the LT(C)A 1995 must be served on any former tenant or guarantor of a former tenant before the landlord can recover rent from that person. The s 17 notice has to be served within six months of the default. Section 17 applies to service charge and other fixed charges anyway, but if acting for the landlord, it may be worth considering not reserving as rent 'all other sums due under this lease' which are not easily ascertainable.

3.   The quarterly instalments are due on the usual quarter days which are 25 March, 24 June, 29 September and 25 December. These dates, originally linked to religious festivals, have been the traditional dates for rent payment going back many centuries. It is necessary to state that the payments must be equal because the quarters are not of equal length. It is necessary to state that the payments are in advance because if the lease is silent, the payments are due in arrears.

4.   If the rent is paid automatically, there is a danger that a landlord who is aware of a breach of covenant will accept rent from a defaulting tenant and thereby waive the right to forfeit in respect of that breach (see **30.5.1**).

5.   The first payment is not due until the Rent Commencement Date, which is six months after the grant of the lease. Thus the tenant has a six-month rent-free period. It may have been given this to allow time for fitting out the premises ready for occupation and/or as an effective discount on the rent to encourage it to take the lease.

6.   The purpose of clause 4 is to stop the tenant making deductions from the rent when, for example, it is owed money by the landlord or feels it should not have to pay the amount demanded. For the landlord, the lease is an investment product, and it is important that the rent is 'clear', ie as fixed and certain as possible.

Chapter 18

1.   If the lease is completed in the form set out at **Appendix 4**, then on review the valuer will assume the hypothetical lease term is 15 years. In reality, by the second review date, only five years of the lease will be left. The effect of this on the open market rent will depend on whether longer or shorter terms are favoured in the market at the date of review. It is therefore sensible to seek the advice of a rent review surveyor on the length of the hypothetical lease term before agreeing the draft lease. However, this advice will be speculative, since the surveyor cannot judge with any certainty what length of lease will

be most valuable in the market at the date of review. In consequence, the rent review surveyor may advise having a hypothetical term that equals the unexpired residue of the term. This at least reflects the reality of the situation at the date of review and is therefore fair to both parties.

2.   In the form received, the rent will be reviewed on an upwards only basis. Whilst the 2007 Code does not specifically prohibit upwards only rent reviews, it does say that landlords should, on request, provide for alternative mechanisms. You would need to ask your client whether alternatives were requested when the heads of terms for the lease were negotiated. If not, and the client did not agree during initial negotiations to an upwards only rent review, you should request alternatives. If the landlord is unable to give them, it should explain why.

Chapter 19

1.   If the premises are in disrepair at the beginning of the lease, a tenant may be concerned not to be obliged to repair the premises to a higher standard, so would include the provision for a schedule of condition (see **19.5**).

      A tenant might resist the inclusion of the words 'good' and 'condition', as potentially imposing a more onerous obligation on the tenant (see **19.4**).

2.   The tenant may be alarmed by the prospect of having to repair inherent defects, and so an exclusion of liability for defects caused by design or construction faults should be included, at least for a specified period (see **9.5.2.4**).

      A tenant might resist the inclusion of the words 'good' and 'condition', as potentially imposing a more onerous obligation on the tenant (see **19.4**).

      A tenant might seek to exclude liability for historic contamination (see **19.3**).

Chapter 20

1.   No, the tenant cannot sub-let only one floor. Clause 21.2 prohibits sub-lettings of part.

2.   No, the landlord cannot always insist on the outgoing tenant entering into an AGA. Clause 20.3 provides that the landlord can require an AGA only in the circumstances set out in clause 20.3(a) or (b).

3.   Under clause 20.6 the landlord can withhold its consent if, in the reasonable opinion of the landlord, the incoming group company tenant is of a lower financial standing than the outgoing tenant and any guarantor. In assessing this, the landlord must take into account any guarantor proposed by the incoming tenant. Under clause 20.7 the landlord reserves the right to refuse consent in any other circumstances where it is reasonable to do so.

Chapter 21

1.   The user covenant is contained in clause 30.1. It states that the tenant shall not use the property for any purpose other than the Permitted Use. 'Permitted Use' is defined at clause 1.1 as offices within Class B1. This is therefore an absolute covenant – there is no mechanism provided in the lease for the use to be changed.

2.   Clause 30.1 allows the premises to be used only as Class B1 offices. In addition, clause 32.4 states that the tenant shall not apply for planning permission for the property. The proposed change of use will require planning permission, as it constitutes a material change of use and is not permitted by the GPDO. To proceed with its change of use the client will therefore require a Deed of Variation from the landlord varying clauses 30.1 and 32.4. The landlord will have complete discretion as to whether or not to enter into such a Deed of Variation. If it is not willing to do so, the tenant will not lawfully be able to implement the proposed use.

Chapter 22

1. The approach to be taken would be to analyse and categorise the nature of the works, and then read and apply the relevant lease clause to the facts:

    (a) Affixing the aerial to the exterior of the building would involve external structural works. The tenant is not entitled to carry these works out as they are works outside the demised premises (clause 1.1 definition of 'Property').

    (b) The erection of internal partitioning is likely to be non-structural work (although any plans or specifications would need to be checked to ensure this). As non-structural alterations, under clause 28.2 the tenant would be able to carry out the works without the consent of the landlord, provided that the tenant makes good any damage caused and provides plans and specifications immediately following completion of the alterations.

    (c) This is a structural alteration. If the interior structural walls were demised (clause 1.1 definition of 'Property') then, under clause 28.1, the tenant is not entitled to make the alteration without the landlord's consent (not to be unreasonably withheld). The tenant will be entitled to make the alteration unless the landlord can show that it is reasonable for it to refuse consent. The landlord under clause 28.5 must determine the application within 15 working days of receiving all information as specified. If the tenant is able to carry out these works, it will have to reinstate the Property under clause 29.2 if reasonably required by the landlord and having been given six months' notice of that requirement.

    If the interior structural walls were not demised then the comments in (a) above would apply.

2. It is compliant with the Code for Leasing Business Premises in that no consent is required for internal non-structural alterations unless they could affect the services or systems (clause 28.2 and 28.3); where consent is not required, the tenant is to notify the landlord under clause 28.2; reinstatement is to be required only where it is reasonable and there is a notification requirement of six months (clause 29.2).

Chapter 23

1. Yes. These are the facts of *Heronslea (Mill Hill) Ltd v Kwik-Fit Properties Ltd* [2009] EWHC 295. In that case it was held that the landlord was not permitted to enter the premises to carry out a 'survey' that involved drilling boreholes and taking samples because the proper interpretation of 'survey' under the lease meant a survey of, not under, the premises.

2. No. These are the facts of *Goldmile Properties Ltd v Lechouritis* [2003] EWCA Civ 49, in which it was held that the landlord's obligation to repair co-existed with the tenant's right to quiet enjoyment, so the landlord should take all reasonable precautions, not all possible precautions, before causing a disturbance by carrying out repairs. Moreover, the repair covenant was for the benefit of both parties, and it would have been apparent to both parties when they agreed to the lease that the tenant's enjoyment of the premises might occasionally be less quiet by reason of the landlord having to carry out necessary repairs.

Chapter 24

1. Clause 9.12 is a rent suspension clause. One of the circumstances in which it applies is if the Common Parts are damaged so as to make the Property inaccessible or unusable. So the tenant needs to show that the Property cannot be accessed or cannot be used in consequence of the damage to the reception area. If it can show this then the Annual Rent will be suspended. The rent suspension will end once the Property is reusable or

after three years (whichever event occurs first). Only the Annual Rent is suspended, and so Insurance Rent, Service Charge and other outgoings will continue to be payable by the tenant.

2.   Clause 9.1(b)(i) states that the landlord's obligation to insure is subject to any excess imposed by the landlord's insurer. Clause 9.4(b) states that the tenant will pay (on demand) a reasonable proportion of any excess. The landlord and tenant will have to agree between them what 'reasonable proportion' of the £5,000 the tenant should pay.

3.   If the reception area has not been reinstated after three years, the tenant can determine the lease with immediate effect under clause 9.14. If it does not, the rent suspension clause at 9.12 will cease to operate and the tenant will have to pay Annual Rent again. As flood falls within the definition of Insured Risks in clause 1.1, the landlord should, if it was available, have obtained insurance against it in accordance with clause 9.1. The landlord should then, subject to obtaining any required planning permission, have repaired the damage (clause 9.10). The tenant may therefore have a claim for damages against the landlord for breach of clause 9.10.

Chapter 25

Lease of ground floor – Tiempo

There is likely to be a breach of clause 30.4 of the lease, which entitles the landlord to exercise its right to forfeit in clause 39(1)(b).

As this is a breach (other than non-payment of rent), the landlord must serve a s 146 notice to give the tenant an opportunity to rectify the breach. The notice must specify the breach, requiring the breach to be remedied (if it is capable of being so) within a reasonable time and requiring the tenant to pay compensation (if the landlord so requires).

The breach is of a covenant against illegal user, which would generally be classed as an irremediable breach and so the landlord would not need to require it to be remedied in the notice. However, the breach is not by the tenant's direct use, so it is remediable so long as the tenant acts promptly on discovering the sub-tenant's use (*Glass v Kencakes Ltd* [1966] 1 QB 611; *Patel, Patel v K & J Restaurants Ltd, MP Catering Ltd* [2010] ECWA Civ 1211).

If there is any doubt as to whether it is remediable or not then the landlord should require it to be remedied 'if it is capable of being remedied'.

The landlord must give the tenant a reasonable time to remedy the breach and may then proceed to forfeit by peaceable re-entry or court proceedings. Successful forfeiture will bring both the lease and the sub-lease to an end.

The tenant (and sub-tenant) can apply for relief against forfeiture which may be granted where the breach has been remedied and is unlikely to re-occur and where to grant it would not damage the landlord's interests.

Where a breach is irremediable then the court is less likely to grant relief. If the illegal use causes a stigma to the premises, it is likely that relief would be refused, but if there is no stigma because of the area (on the facts it is run down but this may be countered by the fact there is a firm of solicitors in the area) then relief may be granted (eg in *Patel*).

Lease of first floor – Grantham

Grantham has breached clause 6 (obligation to pay rent) on the relevant payment dates in the lease (the quarter days). Clause 39.1(a) entitles the landlord to forfeit the lease if the rent is in arrears for 21 days. On the facts the tenant has been in arrears for four weeks. The landlord need not serve a formal demand as this has been negated in clause 39.1(a). There is no need to serve a s 146 notice as the breach is of a covenant to pay rent.

The landlord is therefore entitled to forfeit the lease by peaceable re-entry or court proceedings. Successful forfeiture will bring the lease to an end. However, Grantham will be entitled to apply for relief against forfeiture. It is likely that relief would be granted if Grantham pays the arrears and the court is satisfied that the breach is unlikely to re-occur.

Chapter 26

1.   Clause 2.3 of the lease reserves the service charge as rent, and clause 8.8(b) obliges the tenant to pay the service charge. Clause 8.7 specifies that the landlord shall not charge any of the excluded costs as part of the service charge. 'Excluded costs' is defined in clause 1.1 as the costs set out in para 3 of Sch 3. By virtue of para 3(e)(v) of Sch 3, the landlord will not be able to recover the cost of replacing the plant unless:

 (a)   it is beyond economic repair; or

 (b)   the expenditure is necessary for the purposes of good estate management and following the analysis of reasonable options and alternatives.

 If the landlord considers the expenditure is necessary, upon request from the tenant, it must provide evidence justifying the cost.

2.   Clause 2.3 of the lease reserves the service charge, and clause 8.8 obliges the tenant to pay the service charge. 'Service charge' is defined in clause 1.1 as a fair and reasonable proportion of the service costs. The service costs are defined in para 2 of Sch 3 and include the costs of providing the services. The services are defined in para 1 of Sch 3, and sub-paragraph (q) is a sweeper clause. The landlord can therefore recover the cost of providing a new service via the service charge if it is for the benefit of the tenants and occupiers of the building. However, the landlord must have acted reasonably and in accordance with the principles of good estate management in deciding to provide it.

3.   Clause 8.8(f) provides that the tenant has a right to reasonably challenge the expenditure by referring the matter to alternative dispute resolution (ADR). If the tenant does decide to make such a referral then each party will pay its own costs of the ADR. Under clause 8.8(g), the tenant is also allowed a reasonable period in which to raise enquiries in respect of the certified accounts. The landlord is obliged to respond promptly and efficiently to any such enquires and allow the tenant to see any relevant paperwork and documentation it requests. Further, under clause 8.8(h), if the tenant requests, the landlord must agree to an independent audit of the service costs, although the tenant would bear the cost of such an audit.

Chapter 27

1.   These clauses should be included if the original lease under which the AGA is required is excluded from the LTA 1954. If the original lease is disclaimed following the insolvency of the assignee, the landlord has the right under clause 6.1 of the AGA to require the outgoing tenant to take a new lease. For the new lease to be excluded from the LTA 1954, the relevant notice must have been served prior to the tenant being committed to the new lease. This will be prior to the AGA being entered into. Clause 6.2.4 reflects an intention to exclude any new lease, and clause 6.3 recites the fact that the correct procedure has been followed. Of course, for these clauses to be effective, the correct procedure must in fact have been followed – see **31.1.6**.

2.   Clause 20.1 states that the tenant must not assign the lease without the consent of the landlord. Whilst the case of *Next plc v National Farmers Union Mutual Insurance Co Ltd* [1997] EGCS 181 indicates that consent can be given effectively without a formal licence (and even if correspondence is marked 'subject to licence'), this is subject to the terms of the lease. Clause 42.5 of the lease stipulates that consent under the lease must be given by deed unless the circumstances in paragraphs (a) and (b) apply. So in this case, unless

the landlord's letter expressly waives the requirement for a deed, a Licence to Assign in the form of a deed will be required.

Chapter 28

1. Clause 21.1 of the lease provides that the tenant shall not sub-let the whole of the property except in accordance with clause 21 nor without the consent of the landlord. Clause 21.5(b) provides that any sub-letting shall be at the open market rent of the premises at the date the property is sub-let. If, therefore, £80,000 is the current market rent payable for the premises then this would be permissible, subject to the landlord's consent and compliance with the remainder of clause 21.

2. No. Clause 21.5(a) provides that any sub-lease must contain an agreement that the sub-letting will be excluded from the protection of the LTA 1954. To ensure this agreement is effective, clause 21.4 requires the tenant to supply the landlord with a certified copy of the notice and declaration needed to exclude the sub-lease from Part II of the LTA 1954.

3. Clause 21.5(d) requires that any sub-letting contains a covenant by the sub-tenant to observe the tenant's covenants in the sub-lease. That covenant must be expressed to be enforceable by the head-landlord, thereby taking advantage of the Contracts (Rights of Third Parties) Act 1999. This should allow the head-landlord to sue the sub-tenant for a breach of its covenants in the sub-lease, even though there is no privity of contract or estate between the head-landlord and sub-tenant.

Chapter 30

	Sub-lease survives	Sub-lease does not survive
Surrender	x	
Merger	x	
Break exercised		x
Forfeiture		x

Chapter 31

1. The Act applies when there is a tenancy of premises occupied for business purposes which has not been excluded from the protection of the Act. Many lawyers use 'TOBE' to help them remember this.

2. When the Act applies, the tenancy will not come to end on the contractual expiry date but will automatically continue until terminated in one of the ways permitted by the Act. Moreover, the tenant is entitled to apply to court for a new tenancy and the landlord may oppose this only on certain limited grounds.

3. A landlord can let premises without giving a business occupier security of tenure by the following means:

   • a tenancy at will (these are specifically excluded from the protection of the Act);

   • a licence rather than a lease (a licence is not a tenancy for the purposes of the Act);

   • a fixed-term tenancy not exceeding six months (these are specifically excluded from the protection of the Act);

   • a fixed-term tenancy of any length, but contracted out of the protection of the Act by following the prescribed procedure.

4. A secure tenant who wants to leave its business premises at the end of the contractual term can bring its tenancy to an end by moving out before the contractual expiry date (so it is no longer in occupation) or by serving a s 27(1) notice on the landlord not less than three months before the contractual expiry date.

5. A secure tenant who wants to stay in its business premises after the expiry of the contractual term can request a new lease by serving a s 26 request on its competent landlord and applying to court within the statutory period (which must be before the date specified in its request). If the competent landlord has already served a s 25 notice, the tenant can still request a new lease by making an application to court before the date specified in the s 25 notice.

6. A secure sub-tenant of business premises can identify its competent landlord for the purposes of the Act by serving a s 40 notice on its immediate landlord to see whether that landlord's tenancy has at least 14 months to run.

7. A landlord can obtain vacant possession of premises occupied by a secure tenant by:

    •   serving a s 25 notice stating one or more of the statutory grounds for opposition and succeeding in proving at least one of those grounds at the subsequent court hearing;

    •   giving counter-notice to the tenant's s 26 request stating that the landlord wishes to oppose the tenant's application to court for a new tenancy on one or more of the statutory grounds and succeeding in proving at least one of those grounds at the subsequent court hearing;

    •   accepting a surrender of the lease, if the tenant is willing (or can be incentivised) to surrender;

    •   forfeiting the lease, provided that the tenant is in default of its obligations under the lease and does not obtain relief from forfeiture.

8. A landlord can ensure that a secure tenant which wants to stay in the premises enters into a new lease, rather than continuing the old one, by serving a s 25 notice on the tenant stating that the landlord does not wish to oppose the tenant's application to court for a new tenancy and applying to court for the grant of a new lease. The landlord may also want to consider making an application to court for interim rent.

Prescribed forms of notice under the Landlord and Tenant Act 1954

Form 1

LANDLORD'S NOTICE ENDING A BUSINESS TENANCY WITH PROPOSALS FOR A NEW ONE

Section 25 of the Landlord and Tenant Act 1954

IMPORTANT NOTE FOR THE LANDLORD: If you are willing to grant a new tenancy, complete this form and send it to the tenant. If you wish to oppose the grant of a new tenancy, use form 2 in Schedule 2 to the Landlord and Tenant Act 1954, Part 2 (Notices) Regulations 2004 or, where the tenant may be entitled to acquire the freehold or an extended lease, form 7 in that Schedule, instead of this form.

To: (*insert name and address of tenant*)

From: (*insert name and address of landlord*)

1. This notice applies to the following property: (*insert address or description of property*).

2. I am giving you notice under section 25 of the Landlord and Tenant Act 1954 to end your tenancy on (*insert date*).

3. I am not opposed to granting you a new tenancy. You will find my proposals for the new tenancy, which we can discuss, in the Schedule to this notice.

4. If we cannot agree on all the terms of a new tenancy, either you or I may ask the court to order the grant of a new tenancy and settle the terms on which we cannot agree.

5. If you wish to ask the court for a new tenancy you must do so by the date in paragraph 2, unless we agree in writing to a later date and do so before the date in paragraph 2.

6. Please send all correspondence about this notice to:

Name:

Address:

Signed: Date:

*[Landlord] *[On behalf of the landlord] *[Mortgagee] *[On behalf of the mortgagee]

*(*delete if inapplicable*)

SCHEDULE

LANDLORD'S PROPOSALS FOR A NEW TENANCY

(*attach or insert proposed terms of the new tenancy*)

IMPORTANT NOTE FOR THE TENANT

This Notice is intended to bring your tenancy to an end. If you want to continue to occupy your property after the date specified in paragraph 2 you must act quickly. If you are in any doubt about the action that you should take, get advice immediately from a solicitor or a surveyor.

The landlord is prepared to offer you a new tenancy and has set out proposed terms in the Schedule to this notice. You are not bound to accept these terms. They are merely

suggestions as a basis for negotiation. **In the event of disagreement, ultimately the court would settle the terms of the new tenancy.**

It would be wise to seek professional advice before agreeing to accept the landlord's terms or putting forward your own proposals.

NOTES

The sections mentioned below are sections of the Landlord and Tenant Act 1954, as amended, (most recently by the **Regulatory Reform** (Business Tenancies) (England and Wales) Order 2003).

Ending of tenancy and grant of new tenancy

This notice is intended to bring your tenancy to an end on the date given in paragraph 2. Section 25 contains rules about the date that the landlord can put in that paragraph.

However, your landlord is prepared to offer you a new tenancy and has set out proposals for it in the Schedule to this notice (section 25(8)). You are not obliged to accept these proposals and may put forward your own.

If you and your landlord are unable to agree terms either one of you may apply to the court. You may not apply to the court if your landlord has already done so (section 24(2A)). If you wish to apply to the court you must do so by the date given in paragraph 2 of this notice, unless you and your landlord have agreed in writing to extend the deadline (sections 29A and 29B).

The court will settle the rent and other terms of the new tenancy or those on which you and your landlord cannot agree (sections 34 and 35). If you apply to the court your tenancy will continue after the date shown in paragraph 2 of this notice while your application is being considered (section 24).

If you are in any doubt about what action you should take, get advice immediately from a solicitor or a surveyor.

Negotiating a new tenancy

Most tenancies are renewed by negotiation. You and your landlord may agree in writing to extend the deadline for making an application to the court while negotiations continue. Either you or your landlord can ask the court to fix the rent that you will have to pay while the tenancy continues (sections 24A to 24D).

You may only stay in the property after the date in paragraph 2 (or if we have agreed in writing to a later date, that date), if by then you or the landlord has asked the court to order the grant of a new tenancy.

If you do try to agree a new tenancy with your landlord remember:

- that your present tenancy will not continue after the date in paragraph 2 of this notice without the agreement in writing mentioned above, unless you have applied to the court or your landlord has done so, and
- that you will lose your right to apply to the court once the deadline in paragraph 2 of this notice has passed, unless there is a written agreement extending the deadline.

Validity of this notice

The landlord who has given you this notice may not be the landlord to whom you pay your rent (sections 44 and 67). This does not necessarily mean that the notice is invalid.

If you have any doubts about whether this notice is valid, get advice immediately from a solicitor or a surveyor.

Form 2

LANDLORD'S NOTICE ENDING A BUSINESS TENANCY AND REASONS FOR REFUSING A NEW ONE

Section 25 of the Landlord and Tenant Act 1954

IMPORTANT NOTE FOR THE LANDLORD: If you wish to oppose the grant of a new tenancy on any of the grounds in section 30(1) of the Landlord and Tenant Act 1954, complete this form and send it to the tenant. If the tenant may be entitled to acquire the freehold or an extended lease, use form 7 in Schedule 2 to the Landlord and Tenant Act 1954, Part 2 (Notices) Regulations 2004 instead of this form.

To: (*insert name and address of tenant*)

From: (*insert name and address of landlord*)

1. This notice relates to the following property: (*insert address or description of property*)

2. I am giving you notice under section 25 of the Landlord and Tenant Act 1954 to end your tenancy on (*insert date*).

3. I am opposed to the grant of a new tenancy.

4. You may ask the court to order the grant of a new tenancy. If you do, I will oppose your application on the ground(s) mentioned in paragraph(s)* of section 30(1) of that Act. I draw your attention to the Table in the Notes below, which sets out all the grounds of opposition.

*(*insert letter(s) of the paragraph(s) relied on*)

5. If you wish to ask the court for a new tenancy you must do so before the date in paragraph 2 unless, before that date, we agree in writing to a later date.

6. I can ask the court to order the ending of your tenancy without granting you a new tenancy. I may have to pay you compensation if I have relied only on one or more of the grounds mentioned in paragraphs (e), (f) and (g) of section 30(1). If I ask the court to end your tenancy, you can challenge my application.

7. Please send all correspondence about this notice to:

Name:

Address:

Signed: Date:

*[Landlord] *[On behalf of the landlord] *[Mortgagee] *[On behalf of the mortgagee]

(*delete if inapplicable*)

IMPORTANT NOTE FOR THE TENANT

This notice is intended to bring your tenancy to an end on the date specified in paragraph 2.

Your landlord is not prepared to offer you a new tenancy. You will not get a new tenancy unless you successfully challenge in court the grounds on which your landlord opposes the grant of a new tenancy.

If you want to continue to occupy your property you must act quickly. The notes below should help you to decide what action you now need to take. If you want to challenge your landlord's refusal to renew your tenancy, get advice immediately from a solicitor or a surveyor.

NOTES

The sections mentioned below are sections of the Landlord and Tenant Act 1954, as amended, (most recently by the **Regulatory Reform** (Business Tenancies) (England and Wales) Order 2003).

Ending of your tenancy

This notice is intended to bring your tenancy to an end on the date given in paragraph 2. Section 25 contains rules about the date that the landlord can put in that paragraph.

Your landlord is not prepared to offer you a new tenancy. If you want a new tenancy you will need to apply to the court for a new tenancy and successfully challenge the landlord's grounds for opposition (see the section below headed '*Landlord's opposition to new tenancy*'). If you wish to apply to the court you must do so before the date given in paragraph 2 of this notice, unless you and your landlord have agreed in writing, before that date, to extend the deadline (sections 29A and 29B).

If you apply to the court your tenancy will continue after the date given in paragraph 2 of this notice while your application is being considered (section 24). You may not apply to the court if your landlord has already done so (section 24(2A) and (2B)).

You may only stay in the property after the date given in paragraph 2 (or such later date as you and the landlord may have agreed in writing) if before that date you have asked the court to order the grant of a new tenancy or the landlord has asked the court to order the ending of your tenancy without granting you a new one.

If you are in any doubt about what action you should take, get advice immediately from a solicitor or a surveyor.

Landlord's opposition to new tenancy

If you apply to the court for a new tenancy, the landlord can only oppose your application on one or more of the grounds set out in section 30(1). If you match the letter(s) specified in paragraph 4 of this notice with those in the first column in the Table below, you can see from the second column the ground(s) on which the landlord relies.

Paragraph of section 30(1)	Grounds
(a)	Where under the current tenancy the tenant has any obligations as respects the repair and maintenance of the holding, that the tenant ought not to be granted a new tenancy in view of the state of repair of the holding, being a state resulting from the tenant's failure to comply with the said obligations.
(b)	That the tenant ought not to be granted a new tenancy in view of his persistent delay in paying rent which has become due.
(c)	That the tenant ought not to be granted a new tenancy in view of other substantial breaches by him of his obligations under the current tenancy, or for any other reason connected with the tenant's use or management of the holding.

Paragraph of section 30(1)	Grounds
(d)	That the landlord has offered and is willing to provide or secure the provision of alternative accommodation for the tenant, that the terms on which the alternative accommodation is available are reasonable having regard to the terms of the current tenancy and to all other relevant circumstances, and that the accommodation and the time at which it will be available are suitable for the tenant's requirements (including the requirement to preserve goodwill) having regard to the nature and class of his business and to the situation and extent of, and facilities afforded by, the holding.
(e)	Where the current tenancy was created by the sub-letting of part only of the property comprised in a superior tenancy and the landlord is the owner of an interest in reversion expectant on the termination of that superior tenancy, that the aggregate of the rents reasonably obtainable on separate lettings of the holding and the remainder of that property would be substantially less than the rent reasonably obtainable on a letting of that property as a whole, that on the termination of the current tenancy the landlord requires possession of the holding for the purposes of letting or otherwise disposing of the said property as a whole, and that in view thereof the tenant ought not to be granted a new tenancy.
(f)	That on the termination of the current tenancy the landlord intends to demolish or reconstruct the premises comprised in the holding or a substantial part of those premises or to carry out substantial work of construction on the holding or part thereof and that he could not reasonably do so without obtaining possession of the holding.
(g)	On the termination of the current tenancy the landlord intends to occupy the holding for the purposes, or partly for the purposes, of a business to be carried on by him therein, or as his residence.

In this Table 'the holding' means the property that is the subject of the tenancy.

In ground (e), 'the landlord is the owner an interest in reversion expectant on the termination of that superior tenancy' means that the landlord has an interest in the property that will entitle him or her, when your immediate landlord's tenancy comes to an end, to exercise certain rights and obligations in relation to the property that are currently exercisable by your immediate landlord.

If the landlord relies on ground (f), the court can sometimes still grant a new tenancy if certain conditions set out in section 31A are met.

If the landlord relies on ground (g), please note that 'the landlord' may have an extended meaning. Where a landlord has a controlling interest in a company then either the landlord or the company can rely on ground (g). Where the landlord is a company and a person has a controlling interest in that company then either of them can rely on ground (g) (section 30(1A) and (1B)). A person has a 'controlling interest' in a company if, had he been a company, the other company would have been its subsidiary (section 46(2)).

The landlord must normally have been the landlord for at least five years before he or she can rely on ground (g).

Compensation

If you cannot get a new tenancy solely because one or more of grounds (e), (f) and (g) applies, you may be entitled to compensation under section 37. If your landlord has opposed your application on any of the other grounds as well as (e), (f) or (g) you can only get compensation if the court's refusal to grant a new tenancy is based solely on one or more of grounds (e), (f) and (g). In other words, you cannot get compensation under section 37 if the court has refused your tenancy on *other* grounds, even if one or more of grounds (e), (f) and (g) also applies.

If your landlord is an authority possessing compulsory purchase powers (such as a local authority) you may be entitled to a disturbance payment under Part 3 of the Land Compensation Act 1973.

Validity of this notice

The landlord who has given you this notice may not be the landlord to whom you pay your rent (sections 44 and 67). This does not necessarily mean that the notice is invalid.

If you have any doubts about whether this notice is valid, get advice immediately from a solicitor or a surveyor.

Form 3

TENANT'S REQUEST FOR A NEW BUSINESS TENANCY

Section 26 of the Landlord and Tenant Act 1954

To (*insert name and address of landlord*):

From (*insert name and address of tenant*):

1. This notice relates to the following property: (*insert address or description of property*).

2. I am giving you notice under section 26 of the Landlord and Tenant Act 1954 that I request a new tenancy beginning on (*insert date*).

3. You will find my proposals for the new tenancy, which we can discuss, in the Schedule to this notice.

4. If we cannot agree on all the terms of a new tenancy, either you or I may ask the court to order the grant of a new tenancy and settle the terms on which we cannot agree.

5. If you wish to ask the court to order the grant of a new tenancy you must do so by the date in paragraph 2, unless we agree in writing to a later date and do so before the date in paragraph 2.

6. You may oppose my request for a new tenancy only on one or more of the grounds set out in section 30(1) of the Landlord and Tenant Act 1954. You must tell me what your grounds are within two months of receiving this notice. If you miss this deadline you will not be able to oppose renewal of my tenancy and you will have to grant me a new tenancy.

7. Please send all correspondence about this notice to:

Name:

Address:

Signed: Date:

*[Tenant] *[On behalf of the tenant] (*delete whichever is inapplicable*)

SCHEDULE

TENANT'S PROPOSALS FOR A NEW TENANCY

(attach or insert proposed terms of the new tenancy)

IMPORTANT NOTE FOR THE LANDLORD

This notice requests a new tenancy of your property or part of it. If you want to oppose this request you must act quickly.

Read the notice and all the Notes carefully. It would be wise to seek professional advice.

NOTES

The sections mentioned below are sections of the Landlord and Tenant Act 1954, as amended, (most recently by the **Regulatory Reform** (Business Tenancies) (England and Wales) Order 2003).

Tenant's request for a new tenancy

This request by your tenant for a new tenancy brings his or her current tenancy to an end on the day before the date mentioned in paragraph 2 of this notice. Section 26 contains rules about the date that the tenant can put in paragraph 2 of this notice.

Your tenant can apply to the court under section 24 for a new tenancy. You may apply for a new tenancy yourself, under the same section, but not if your tenant has already served an application. Once an application has been made to the court, your tenant's current tenancy will continue after the date mentioned in paragraph 2 while the application is being considered by the court. Either you or your tenant can ask the court to fix the rent which your tenant will have to pay whilst the tenancy continues (sections 24A to 24D). The court will settle any terms of a new tenancy on which you and your tenant disagree (sections 34 and 35).

Time limit for opposing your tenant's request

If you do not want to grant a new tenancy, you have two months from the making of your tenant's request in which to notify him or her that you will oppose any application made to the court for a new tenancy. You do not need a special form to do this, but the notice must be in writing and it must state on which of the grounds set out in section 30(1) you will oppose the application. If you do not use the same wording of the ground (or grounds), as set out below, your notice may be ineffective.

If there has been any delay in your seeing this notice, you may need to act very quickly. If you are in any doubt about what action you should take, get advice immediately from a solicitor or a surveyor.

Grounds for opposing tenant's application

If you wish to oppose the renewal of the tenancy, you can do so by opposing your tenant's application to the court, or by making your own application to the court for termination without renewal. However, you can only oppose your tenant's application, or apply for termination without renewal, on one or more of the grounds set out in section 30(1). These grounds are set out below. You will only be able to rely on the ground(s) of opposition that you have mentioned in your written notice to your tenant.

In this Table 'the holding' means the property that is the subject of the tenancy.

Paragraph of section 30(1)	Grounds
(a)	Where under the current tenancy the tenant has any obligations as respects the repair and maintenance of the holding, that the tenant ought not to be granted a new tenancy in view of the state of repair of the holding, being a state resulting from the tenant's failure to comply with the said obligations.
(b)	That the tenant ought not to be granted a new tenancy in view of his persistent delay in paying rent which has become due.
(c)	That the tenant ought not to be granted a new tenancy in view of other substantial breaches by him of his obligations under the current tenancy, or for any other reason connected with the tenant's use or management of the holding.
(d)	That the landlord has offered and is willing to provide or secure the provision of alternative accommodation for the tenant, that the terms on which the alternative accommodation is available are reasonable having regard to the terms of the current tenancy and to all other relevant circumstances, and that the accommodation and the time at which it will be available are suitable for the tenant's requirements (including the requirement to preserve goodwill) having regard to the nature and class of his business and to the situation and extent of, and facilities afforded by, the holding.
(e)	Where the current tenancy was created by the sub-letting of part only of the property comprised in a superior tenancy and the landlord is the owner of an interest in reversion expectant on the termination of that superior tenancy, that the aggregate of the rents reasonably obtainable on separate lettings of the holding and the remainder of that property would be substantially less than the rent reasonably obtainable on a letting of that property as a whole, that on the termination of the current tenancy the landlord requires possession of the holding for the purposes of letting or otherwise disposing of the said property as a whole, and that in view thereof the tenant ought not to be granted a new tenancy.
(f)	That on the termination of the current tenancy the landlord intends to demolish or reconstruct the premises comprised in the holding or a substantial part of those premises or to carry out substantial work of construction on the holding or part thereof and that he could not reasonably do so without obtaining possession of the holding.
(g)	On the termination of the current tenancy the landlord intends to occupy the holding for the purposes, or partly for the purposes, of a business to be carried on by him therein, or as his residence.

Compensation

If your tenant cannot get a new tenancy solely because one or more of grounds (e), (f) and (g) applies, he or she is entitled to compensation under section 37. If you have opposed your tenant's application on any of the other grounds mentioned in section 30(1), as well as on one or more of grounds (e), (f) and (g), your tenant can only get compensation if the court's refusal to grant a new tenancy is based solely on ground (e), (f) or (g). In other words, your tenant cannot get compensation under section 37 if the court has refused the tenancy on *other* grounds, even if one or more of grounds (e), (f) and (g) also applies.

If you are an authority possessing compulsory purchase powers (such as a local authority), your tenant may be entitled to a disturbance payment under Part 3 of the Land Compensation Act 1973.

Negotiating a new tenancy

Most tenancies are renewed by negotiation and your tenant has set out proposals for the new tenancy in paragraph 3 of this notice. You are not obliged to accept these proposals and may put forward your own. You and your tenant may agree in writing to extend the deadline for making an application to the court while negotiations continue. Your tenant may not apply to the court for a new tenancy until two months have passed from the date of the making of the request contained in this notice, unless you have already given notice opposing your tenant's request as mentioned in paragraph 6 of this notice (section 29A(3)).

If you try to agree a new tenancy with your tenant, remember:

▪ that one of you will need to apply to the court before the date in paragraph 2 of this notice, unless you both agree to extend the period for making an application.

▪ that any such agreement must be in writing and must be made before the date in paragraph 2 (sections 29A and 29B).

Validity of this notice

The tenant who has given you this notice may not be the person from whom you receive rent (sections 44 and 67). This does not necessarily mean that the notice is invalid.

If you have any doubts about whether this notice is valid, get advice immediately from a solicitor or a surveyor.

Form 4

LANDLORD'S REQUEST FOR INFORMATION ABOUT OCCUPATION AND SUB-TENANCIES

Section 40(1) of the Landlord and Tenant Act 1954

To: (*insert name and address of tenant*)

From: (*insert name and address of landlord*)

1. This notice relates to the following premises: (*insert address or description of premises*)

2. I give you notice under section 40(1) of the Landlord and Tenant Act 1954 that I require you to provide information—

(a)   by answering questions (1) to (3) in the Table below;
(b)   if you answer 'yes' to question (2), by giving me the name and address of the person or persons concerned;
(c)   if you answer 'yes' to question (3), by also answering questions (4) to (10) in the Table below;
(d)   if you answer 'no' to question (8), by giving me the name and address of the sub-tenant; and
(e)   if you answer 'yes' to question (10), by giving me details of the notice or request.

TABLE

(1)	Do you occupy the premises or any part of them wholly or partly for the purposes of a business that is carried on by you?

(2)	To the best of your knowledge and belief, does any other person own an interest in reversion in any part of the premises?
(3)	Does your tenancy have effect subject to any sub-tenancy on which your tenancy is immediately expectant?
(4)	What premises are comprised in the sub-tenancy?
(5)	For what term does it have effect or, if it is terminable by notice, by what notice can it be terminated?
(6)	What is the rent payable under it?
(7)	Who is the sub-tenant?
(8)	To the best of your knowledge and belief, is the sub-tenant in occupation of the premises or of part of the premises comprised in the sub-tenancy?
(9)	Is an agreement in force excluding, in relation to the sub-tenancy, the provisions of sections 24 to 28 of the Landlord and Tenant Act 1954?
(10)	Has a notice been given under section 25 or 26(6) of that Act, or has a request been made under section 26 of that Act, in relation to the sub-tenancy?

3. You must give the information concerned in writing and within the period of one month beginning with the date of service of this notice.

4. Please send all correspondence about this notice to:

Name:

Address:

Signed: Date:

*[Landlord] *[on behalf of the landlord] *delete whichever is inapplicable

IMPORTANT NOTE FOR THE TENANT

This notice contains some words and phrases that you may not understand. The Notes below should help you, but it would be wise to seek professional advice, for example, from a solicitor or surveyor, before responding to this notice.

Once you have provided the information required by this notice, you must correct it if you realise that it is not, or is no longer, correct. This obligation lasts for six months from the date of service of this notice, but an exception is explained in the next paragraph. If you need to correct information already given, you must do so within one month of becoming aware that the information is incorrect.

The obligation will cease if, after transferring your tenancy, you notify the landlord of the transfer and of the name and address of the person to whom your tenancy has been transferred.

If you fail to comply with the requirements of this notice, or the obligation mentioned above, you may face civil proceedings for breach of the statutory duty that arises under section 40 of the Landlord and Tenant Act 1954. In any such proceedings a court may order you to comply with that duty and may make an award of damages.

NOTES

The sections mentioned below are sections of the Landlord and Tenant Act 1954, as amended, (most recently by the **Regulatory Reform** (Business Tenancies) (England and Wales) Order 2003).

Purpose of this notice

Your landlord (or, if he or she is a tenant, possibly your landlord's landlord) has sent you this notice in order to obtain information about your occupation and that of any sub-tenants. This information may be relevant to the taking of steps to end or renew your business tenancy.

Time limit for replying

You must provide the relevant information within one month of the date of service of this notice (section 40(1), (2) and (5)).

Information required

You do not have to give your answers on this form; you may use a separate sheet for this purpose. The notice requires you to provide, in writing, information in the form of answers to questions (1) to (3) in the Table above and, if you answer 'yes' to question (3), also to provide information in the form of answers to questions (4) to (10) in that Table. Depending on your answer to question (2) and, if applicable in your case, questions (8) and (10), you must also provide the information referred to in paragraph 2(b), (d) and (e) of this notice. Question (2) refers to a person who owns an interest in reversion. You should answer 'yes' to this question if you know or believe that there is a person who receives, or is entitled to receive, rent in respect of any part of the premises (other than the landlord who served this notice).

When you answer questions about sub-tenants, please bear in mind that, for these purposes, a sub-tenant includes a person retaining possession of premises by virtue of the Rent (Agriculture) Act 1976 or the Rent Act 1977 after the coming to an end of a sub-tenancy, and 'sub-tenancy' includes a right so to retain possession (section 40(8)).

You should keep a copy of your answers and of any other information provided in response to questions (2), (8) or (10) above.

If, once you have given this information, you realise that it is not, or is no longer, correct, you must give the correct information within one month of becoming aware that the previous information is incorrect. Subject to the next paragraph, your duty to correct any information that you have already given continues for six months after you receive this notice (section 40(5)). You should give the correct information to the landlord who gave you this notice unless you receive notice of the transfer of his or her interest, and of the name and address of the person to whom that interest has been transferred. In that case, the correct information must be given to that person.

If you transfer your tenancy within the period of six months referred to above, your duty to correct information already given will cease if you notify the landlord of the transfer and of the name and address of the person to whom your tenancy has been transferred.

If you do not provide the information requested, or fail to correct information that you have provided earlier, after realising that it is not, or is no longer, correct, proceedings may be taken against you and you may have to pay damages (section 40B).

If you are in any doubt about the information that you should give, get immediate advice from a solicitor or a surveyor.

Validity of this notice

The landlord who has given you this notice may not be the landlord to whom you pay your rent (sections 44 and 67). This does not necessarily mean that the notice is invalid.

If you have any doubts about whether this notice is valid, get advice immediately

Form 5

TENANT'S REQUEST FOR INFORMATION FROM LANDLORD OR LANDLORD'S MORTGAGEE ABOUT LANDLORD'S INTEREST

Section 40(3) of the Landlord and Tenant Act 1954

To: (insert name and address of reversioner or reversioner's mortgagee in possession [see the first note below])

From: (insert name and address of tenant)

1. This notice relates to the following premises: (insert address or description of premises)

2. In accordance with section 40(3) of the Landlord and Tenant Act 1954 I require you—

    (a)   to state in writing whether you are the owner of the fee simple in respect of the premises or any part of them or the mortgagee in possession of such an owner,

    (b)   if you answer 'no' to (a), to state in writing, to the best of your knowledge and belief—

        (i)   the name and address of the person who is your or, as the case may be, your mortgagor's immediate landlord in respect of the premises or of the part in respect of which you are not, or your mortgagor is not, the owner in fee simple;

        (ii)   for what term your or your mortgagor's tenancy has effect and what is the earliest date (if any) at which that tenancy is terminable by notice to quit given by the landlord; and

        (iii)   whether a notice has been given under section 25 or 26(6) of the Landlord and Tenant Act 1954, or a request has been made under section 26 of that Act, in relation to the tenancy and, if so, details of the notice or request;

    (c)   to state in writing, to the best of your knowledge and belief, the name and address of any other person who owns an interest in reversion in any part of the premises;

    (d)   if you are a reversioner, to state in writing whether there is a mortgagee in possession of your interest in the premises; and

    (e)   if you answer 'yes' to (d), to state in writing, to the best of your knowledge and belief, the name and address of the mortgagee in possession.

3. You must give the information concerned within the period of one month beginning with the date of service of this notice.

4. Please send all correspondence about this notice to:

Name:

Address:

Signed: Date:

*[Tenant] *[on behalf of the tenant] (*delete whichever is inapplicable)

IMPORTANT NOTE FOR LANDLORD OR LANDLORD'S MORTGAGEE

This notice contains some words and phrases that you may not understand. The Notes below should help you, but it would be wise to seek professional advice, for example, from a solicitor or surveyor, before responding to this notice.

Once you have provided the information required by this notice, you must correct it if you realise that it is not, or is no longer, correct. This obligation lasts for six months from the date of service of this notice, but an exception is explained in the next paragraph. If you need to correct information already given, you must do so within one month of becoming aware that the information is incorrect.

The obligation will cease if, after transferring your interest, you notify the tenant of the transfer and of the name and address of the person to whom your interest has been transferred.

If you fail to comply with the requirements of this notice, or the obligation mentioned above, you may face civil proceedings for breach of the statutory duty that arises under section 40 of

the Landlord and Tenant Act 1954. In any such proceedings a court may order you to comply with that duty and may make an award of damages.

NOTES

The sections mentioned below are sections of the Landlord and Tenant Act 1954, as amended, (most recently by the Regulatory Reform (Business Tenancies) (England and Wales) Order 2003).

Terms used in this notice

The following terms, which are used in paragraph 2 of this notice, are defined in section 40(8):

> 'mortgagee in possession' includes a receiver appointed by the mortgagee or by the court who is in receipt of the rents and profits;

> 'reversioner' means any person having an interest in the premises, being an interest in reversion expectant (whether immediately or not) on the tenancy; and

> 'reversioner's mortgagee in possession' means any person being a mortgagee in possession in respect of such an interest.

Section 40(8) requires the reference in paragraph 2(b) of this notice to your mortgagor to be read in the light of the definition of 'mortgagee in possession'.

A mortgagee (mortgage lender) will be 'in possession' if the mortgagor (the person who owes money to the mortgage lender) has failed to comply with the terms of the mortgage. The mortgagee may then be entitled to receive rent that would normally have been paid to the mortgagor.

The term 'the owner of the fee simple' means the freehold owner.

The term 'reversioner' includes the freehold owner and any intermediate landlord as well as the immediate landlord of the tenant who served this notice.

Purpose of this notice and information required

This notice requires you to provide, in writing, the information requested in paragraph 2(a) and (c) of the notice and, if applicable in your case, in paragraph 2(b), (d) and (e). You do not need to use a special form for this purpose.

If, once you have given this information, you realise that it is not, or is no longer, correct, you must give the correct information within one month of becoming aware that the previous information is incorrect. Subject to the last paragraph in this section of these Notes, your duty to correct any information that you have already given continues for six months after you receive this notice (section 40(5)).

You should give the correct information to the tenant who gave you this notice unless you receive notice of the transfer of his or her interest, and of the name and address of the person to whom that interest has been transferred. In that case, the correct information must be given to that person.

If you do not provide the information requested, or fail to correct information that you have provided earlier, after realising that it is not, or is no longer, correct, proceedings may be taken against you and you may have to pay damages (section 40B).

If you are in any doubt as to the information that you should give, get advice immediately from a solicitor or a surveyor.

If you transfer your interest within the period of six months referred to above, your duty to correct information already given will cease if you notify the tenant of that transfer and of the name and address of the person to whom your interest has been transferred.

Time limit for replying

You must provide the relevant information within one month of the date of service of this notice (section 40(3), (4) and (5)).

Validity of this notice

The tenant who has given you this notice may not be the person from whom you receive rent (sections 44 and 67). This does not necessarily mean that the notice is invalid.

If you have any doubts about the validity of the notice, get advice immediately from a solicitor or a surveyor.

The Code for Leasing Business Premises in England and Wales 2007

Leasing Business Premises: Landlord Code

Introduction

This revised lease code is the result of pan-industry discussion between representatives of landlords, tenants and government. The objective is to create a document which is clear, concise and authoritative.

However, our aims are wider. We want the lease code to be used as a checklist for negotiations before the grant of a lease and lease renewals. Landlords should be transparent about any departures from the code in a particular case and the reasons for them.

We have provided model heads of terms and whilst we recognise the code will apply to leases in England and Wales, we believe its intent should apply to the whole of the UK.

Most importantly, we are launching the code with an objective to ensure that parties to a lease have easy access to information explaining the commitments they are making in clear English. We will encourage trade and professional bodies, lenders and government (at all levels) to ensure small businesses are made aware of the code and the advisory pages which accompany it.

Although the code applies to new leases, please also see the British Property Federation declaration, which applies to existing leases, in relation to applications for consent to sublet where there is an existing lease covenant requiring subleases to be at the higher of the passing rent and the market rent.

We hope the code will help the industry in its quest to promote efficiency and fairness in landlord and tenant relationships.

1 Lease Negotiations

Landlords must make offers in writing which clearly state: the rent; the length of the term and any break rights; whether or not tenants will have security of tenure; the rent review arrangements; rights to assign, sublet and share the premises; repairing obligations; and the VAT status of the premises.

Landlords must promote flexibility, stating whether alternative lease terms are available and must propose rents for different lease terms if requested by prospective tenants.

2 Rent Deposits and Guarantees

The lease terms should state clearly any rent deposit proposals, including the amount, for how long and the arrangements for paying or accruing interest at a proper rate. Tenants should be protected against the default or insolvency of the landlord.

State clearly the conditions for releasing rent deposits and guarantees.

3 Length of Term, Break Clauses and Renewal Rights

The length of term must be clear.

The only pre-conditions to tenants exercising any break clauses should be that they are up to date with the main rent, give up

occupation and leave behind no continuing subleases. Disputes about the state of the premises, or what has been left behind or removed, should be settled later (like with normal lease expiry).

The fallback position under the Landlord and Tenant Act 1954 is that business tenants have rights to renew their lease. It is accepted that there are a number of circumstances in which that is not appropriate. In such cases landlords should state at the start of negotiations that the protection of the 1954 Act is to be excluded and encourage tenants to seek early advice as to the implications.

4 Rent Review

Rent reviews should be clear and headline rent review clauses should not be used. Landlords should on request offer alternatives to their proposed option for rent review priced on a risk-adjusted basis.

For example, alternatives to upward only rent review might include up/down reviews to market rent with a minimum of the initial rent, or reference to another measure such as annual indexation.

Where landlords are unable to offer alternatives, they should give reasons.

Leases should allow both landlords and tenants to start the rent review process.

The Code for Leasing Business Premises
in England and Wales 2007
www.leasingbusinesspremises.co.uk

5 Assignment and Subletting

Leases should:

- allow tenants to assign the whole of the premises with the landlord's consent not to be unreasonably withheld or delayed; and

- not refer to any specific circumstances for refusal, although a lease would still be Code compliant if it requires that any group company taking an assignment, when assessed together with any proposed guarantor, must be of at least equivalent financial standing to the assignor (together with any guarantor of the assignor).

Authorised Guarantee Agreements should not be required as a condition of the assignment, unless at the date of the assignment the proposed assignee, when assessed together with any proposed guarantor:

- is of lower financial standing than the assignor (and its guarantor); or

- is resident or registered overseas.

For smaller tenants a rent deposit should be acceptable as an alternative.

If subletting is allowed, the sublease rent should be the market rent at the time of subletting.

Subleases to be excluded from the 1954 Act should not have to be on the same terms as the tenant's lease.

6 Service Charges

Landlords must, during negotiations, provide best estimates of service charges, insurance payments and any other outgoings that tenants will incur under their leases.

Landlords must disclose known irregular events that would have a significant impact on the amount of future service charges.

Landlords should be aware of the RICS 2006 Code of Practice on Service Charges in Commercial Property and seek to observe its guidance in drafting new leases and on renewals (even if granted before that Code is effective).

7 Repairs

Tenants' repairing obligations should be appropriate to the length of term and the condition of the premises.

Unless expressly stated in the heads of terms, tenants should only be obliged to give the premises back at the end of their lease in the same condition as they were in at its grant.

8 Alterations and Changes of Use

Landlords' control over alterations and changes of use should not be more restrictive than is necessary to protect the value, at the time of the application, of the premises and any adjoining or neighbouring premises of the landlord.

Internal non-structural alterations should be notified to landlords but should not need landlords' consent unless they could affect the services or systems in the building.

Landlords should not require tenants to remove permitted alterations and make good at the end of the lease, unless reasonable to do so. Landlords should notify tenants of their requirements at least six months before the termination date.

9 Insurance

Where landlords are insuring the landlord's property, the insurance policy terms should be fair and reasonable and represent value for money, and be placed with reputable insurers.

Landlords must always disclose any commission they are receiving and must provide full insurance details on request.

Rent suspension should apply if the premises are damaged by an insured risk or uninsured risk, other than where caused by a deliberate act of the tenant. If rent suspension is limited to the period for which loss of rent is insured, leases should allow landlords or tenants to terminate their leases if reinstatement is not completed within that period.

Landlords should provide appropriate terrorism cover if practicable to do so.

If the whole of the premises are damaged by an uninsured risk as to prevent occupation, tenants should be allowed to terminate their leases unless landlords agree to rebuild at their own cost.

10 Ongoing Management

Landlords should handle all defaults promptly and deal with tenants and any guarantors in an open and constructive way.

At least six months before the termination date, landlords should provide a schedule of dilapidations to enable tenants to carry out any works and should notify any dilapidations that occur after that date as soon as practicable.

When receiving applications for consents, landlords should where practicable give tenants an estimate of the costs involved.

Landlords should normally request any additional information they require from tenants within five working days of receiving the application. Landlords should consider at an early stage what other consents they will require (for example, from superior landlord or mortgagees) and then seek these. Landlords should make decisions on consents for alterations within 15 working days of receiving full information.

The Code for Leasing Business Premises
in England and Wales 2007
www.leasingbusinesspremises.co.uk

Leasing Business Premises: Occupier Guide

Introduction

A business lease is a legally binding contract between the legal owner (Landlord) and the occupier (Tenant). Failure by either party to comply with the terms of the agreement could result in court action.

The 2007 Code for Leasing Business Premises ('the Lease Code') provides a framework within which a prospective tenant can reasonably expect a landlord to operate. As a prospective tenant, you should not assume that a landlord complies with the Lease Code. The Lease Code does not provide all of the protection you need for your business in leasing premises.

Sometimes the Landlord is also the tenant of another owner. This may restrict the flexibility of terms the Landlord can offer. The Landlord should always state in advance if this is so and provide a copy of the current lease.

If it is proposed to buy an existing lease (assignment) from someone else, be aware that, though parts of this Occupier Guide may help in interpreting some of the terms of the lease, there may be many additional liabilities. Professional advice from a qualified surveyor and a lawyer should be sought.

In this document the following terms have been used:

Landlord   This is the owner of the property or the person owning an existing lease of the property

Tenant   This is the occupier of the property or the person paying rent to a landlord (this Occupier Guide assumes the tenant will be you)

Heads of Terms This is a summary of the agreement between the parties and is used to instruct lawyers to produce the formal lease. Both the lease and the Heads of Terms should comply with the recommendations of the Lease Code but the Heads of Terms will be superseded once the lease has been granted.

For more information on the Lease Code see Useful Links.

1   Lease negotiations

You should expect the Landlord to make very clear exactly what you are being asked to agree.

You should be able to understand the total extent and duration of the cost and liability you will be taking on if you sign a lease based on the terms being offered by the Landlord.

Tip 1

Make sure you understand every term and condition in the offer including the total cost until the lease ends and ask the Landlord or the Landlord's representative to confirm in writing that the offer meets the Lease Code.

You should know from the offer exactly what the property is.

Tip 2

Make sure the offer clearly shows the extent of the property, with the boundaries clearly marked on plan and the floor area noted, together with all means of access, any access or areas you must share with other occupiers, any limitation of hours of use, any restrictions in the type of use, any legal or planning limitations or obligations that come with the property.

You should also remember that, however good your relationship is or seems to be with the Landlord, the Landlord may sell to another party; the terms you agree and the lease you take on must reflect everything you rely on to conduct and safeguard your business.

The Code for Leasing Business Premises in England and Wales 2007
www.leasingbusinesspremises.co.uk

Tip 3

Make sure the offer sets out clearly who the Landlord is, together with any superior landlords, and assume that any Landlord will sell his interest to someone else and that you will have to deal with the new owner.

You should request alternative terms if you are not happy with the initial terms of the Landlord's offer, always bearing in mind that any variation (such as lease length, rent review terms – including frequency and basis – break options, etc) may change the level of rent or other terms.

Tip 4

Request written responses from the Landlord, where you expect to need to rely on them. Check that all the things which are important to you and your business have been accurately written down in the Heads of Terms and documented in the lease.

2   Financial matters, rent deposits and guarantees

The Landlord should provide full details of your expected costs involved in leasing the property. This should include all personal or company guarantees, security deposits or other bank guarantees.

Not all costs will be fixed at the time of agreeing the lease. You should expect the Landlord to explain how any costs are calculated so that you can understand the risks and make sure you can afford all of the costs of leasing the property.

Tip 5

It may be helpful to use a checklist (such as that set out below) so that you can ask the Landlord to be explicit about costs and obligations in the lease.

If the Landlord demands a deposit, you should make sure you understand the conditions under which it is held and the basis on which it will be returned to you. You should remember that this is YOUR money that the Landlord is holding as a protection against any failure on your part.

Tip 6

Keep thinking of the deposit as your money and demand that interest on it is accrued at a fair rate. Ask the Landlord to make sure it is held in an account that belongs to you (escrow or stakeholder account) in case the Landlord becomes insolvent. Throughout the term of the lease, make sure you obtain statements from the Landlord to confirm that the money is still in the account and that all interest earned has been paid to you or, if required by the lease, has been held on your behalf within the account. Check that your deposit will be transferred to the new Landlord if the Landlord sells the property to another owner.

Tip 7

Make sure you know when and how you can get your deposit back, such as when you no longer have an interest or have satisfied agreed conditions.

If you are asked to give a personal guarantee, you should avoid using your home as security. You should be able to understand both when and how the Landlord may call on your guarantee, and also what the guarantee would actually cover.

Tip 8

Think of any guarantee as if it WILL be called on the first day of the lease; what would be the personal consequences for you? Can you afford it?

Cost Item	Who pays?	How much? How often?	What is the occupier's cost each year?	If this cost is not fixed, what does it depend on?
Rent	e.g. Tenant			
VAT				
Rates				
Service charges				
Insurance				
Utilities				
Repairs/Dilapidations				
Fitting out/Alterations				
Total each year				
Total lease cost				

4

The Code for Leasing Business Premises
in England and Wales 2007
www.leasingbusinesspremises.co.uk

3   Rent review

Your lease may contain provisions allowing the Landlord to change the rent. The rules by which the rent can be changed should be clear and understandable. It should be arranged that the Landlord cannot simply impose a rental increase. The basis of rent review should be to the market rent unless clearly stated otherwise. If you agreed increases fixed to an index, the basis should be a published, independent, authoritative source.

If there is an open market rental value provision, it should specifically exclude (or disregard) any improvements you make, other than as part of an explicit obligation, or any value arising from your business. You should also make sure there are controls in the event of disagreement that will be referred to an independent expert or arbitrator to settle.

Tip 9

Check that you understand the basis on which the rent can be changed. Can the rent go down as well as up? You should see if the Landlord is prepared to allow upward or downward rent reviews and if not, you should consider asking for a break option exercisable only by the tenant.

Your lease should include a provision allowing you to serve a rent review notice on the Landlord. If the Landlord does not initiate the rent review, think very carefully before deciding not to serve notice on the Landlord as you may be responsible for paying interest on any increase in rent above the original rent from the appropriate rent review date until the review has been agreed.

Tip 10

Make sure that the interest rate on the difference is no higher than bank base rate. Try to introduce a provision whereby the Landlord forfeits interest on the difference if he/she does not initiate the rent review process prior to the review date.

Tip 11

Avoid strict time limits in the rent review clause (other than referred to in Tip 10) – these could result in you losing the ability to negotiate.

4   Subletting and assignment

Subletting (creating a new lease of all or part of the property)

If your lease allows subletting, you should understand any limitations (in terms of the amount of space, the use and the rent you can charge and the nature of the subtenant you can sublet to).

It is usual for Landlords to insist that subleases are granted outside the protection of the Landlord and Tenant Act 1954 and on similar terms to your lease.

Tip 12

Try to make sure you are NOT required to sublet at the same or higher rent than you pay. You should not be limited other than by reference to the market rent at the time of the subletting.

Be careful that restrictive subletting provisions do not prevent you from, say, sharing your space with a supplier or service provider (for example, an outside cleaning company which you provide with its own cleaner's cupboard)

Tip 13

Ask your Landlord to reflect the flexibility you require in the sharing provisions of the lease. This probably means you must not create a tenancy for your supplier.

Landlord's written consent is likely to be required for subleases.

Tip 14

Make sure your Landlord, including any superior landlords, is required to give consent within a defined (and short) period of time and that he is not allowed to refuse without good reason.

Assignment (disposing of your existing legal interest in the whole premises)

It is common for Landlords to require you to guarantee the lease once you have assigned it to a third party. The form of guarantee (an Authorised Guarantee Agreement or AGA) usually makes you responsible, as a guarantor, for the lease obligations until your assignee (the person to whom you sold your lease) assigns the lease to another party.

Tip 15

Ask the Landlord to limit his requirement for an Authorised Guarantee Agreement to those cases where your proposed buyer (assignee) is financially weaker than you are at the date of assignment. Ask the Landlord to include provisions that will allow you to cancel the Guarantee if defined conditions are met and/or after an agreed period.

Tip 16

Try to agree alternative conditions to avoid you having to enter into an Authorised Guarantee Agreement (for example, by having the new tenant pay a rent deposit).

The Landlord should not impose any condition which requires you to be in compliance with the lease at the time of assignment.

Tip 17

Try to make sure the only precondition for assignment is obtaining the Landlord's consent in writing and that the Landlord may not unreasonably withhold or delay giving his consent.

The Code for Leasing Business Premises
in England and Wales 2007
www.leasingbusinesspremises.co.uk

5   Lease length, break clauses and renewals

The Landlord should make clear the length of the lease, whether there are any rights to break the lease and whether you will be entitled to an extension of the lease on expiry (see section 11 below).

Make sure that the length of the lease is appropriate for your business needs; ask the Landlord to offer you a break option exercisable only by the tenant (this will be you unless you have assigned your lease) to give you the opportunity to cancel the lease at a time that suits your business.

A right to break should allow you to walk away from the lease at a given time after informing the Landlord in writing. This should be conditional only upon having paid the rent due under the lease and giving up occupation of the property, leaving behind no continuing subleases. You may have other liabilities to fulfil, but these should not be used to invalidate the right to break.

Tip 18

Be careful that it is only the principal rent and not any other sums (such as service charges) that must be paid in cleared funds before the break date.

When your lease ends, whether by expiry or by exercise of a break option, you will be liable to the Landlord for any sums due and for any repairs you should have carried out during the lease (dilapidations).

Tip 19

When granting any subleases or in sharing possession with any suppliers or business partners, always make sure your agreement with them expires on a date before your right to break, AND that you have not given them any rights to stay in the property beyond the term of your agreement with them.

Be sure that you understand what notices you would be required to serve on the Landlord to end the lease, and how and when these should be served.

The Landlord and Tenant Act 1954 gives you the right to extend your tenancy when your lease runs out.

Unless both you and the Landlord have agreed (in the correct procedure) that the lease is to be excluded from the relevant sections of the Landlord and Tenant Act 1954, you will be entitled to renew your lease unless your Landlord can prove certain specific circumstances, which include redeveloping the property or occupying the space himself.

You should make sure you understand the options available to you when your lease expires. Take professional advice to make sure all notices are properly served and that your interests are protected.

Tip 20

Take professional advice at least six months before the end of the lease and on receipt of any notice from the Landlord under the Act.

6   Service charges

You should expect the Landlord to be explicit in his offer about any service charges, including how these costs are calculated, what they cover (and don't include) and the extent to which you will be obliged to pay towards any capital improvements and long-term repairs or replacements of structure, fabric or machinery and equipment.

Tip 21

Ask the Landlord whether he complies with the Service Charge Code 2006, and ask for a clear estimate in writing of the likely service charge costs for each year of the lease term (to include any known or planned capital costs).

Tip 22

As you are likely to be responsible for the repairs to a proportionate part or the whole of the building you should satisfy yourself that there are no major repairs required at the beginning of your lease or that are likely shortly afterwards.

Tip 23

Make sure the Landlord cannot charge you a greater proportion of cost when he has other space vacant in the estate or building.

7   Repairs

UNLESS you specifically agree at the time of taking the lease to carry out works or to reinstate the property to its original state, check that the lease does not require you to put the property into a better condition than when you take the lease.

Tip 24

It is worthwhile either getting a formal photographic schedule of condition carried out by a firm of surveyors or taking plenty of photographs on or before taking the lease to record the condition at the beginning of the lease.

Tip 25

If you take the photographs yourself, make sure you get the photographs dated and witnessed and keep a set with your lease documents. If you produce your own video schedule of condition, send the Landlord a copy by Recorded Delivery Post.

You should bear in mind if you buy an existing lease (take an assignment of someone else's lease), that the condition of the property when you take it may be poorer than it was at the beginning of the lease. You may be required to put the property back into its original condition so it is worth taking professional advice.

The Code for Leasing Business Premises
in England and Wales 2007
www.leasingbusinesspremises.co.uk

8 Alterations and changes of use

Your lease will limit the use of the property to a specified purpose (for example, B1 (Offices). The lease will usually put the responsibility on you to check that your proposed use complies with any planning consent.

Tip 26

Make sure the Landlord provides you with all relevant information and, if possible, confirms to you that your use complies with his planning consent.

The lease may be quite restrictive in terms of any signage and any alterations you are permitted to make. Before you enter into the lease, you should make sure you are permitted to carry out any works your business needs.

Tip 27

Check what you need to do to the property in order to trade. Make sure the Landlord agrees in writing any changes you intend to make at the beginning of the lease period. Check whether you will be required to remove your alterations at the end of the lease.

The Landlord should be required to give his consent within a reasonable time period (say 21 days) and should not be able to refuse your proposed alterations without good reason.

Tip 28

Make sure your lease allows you to make non-structural alterations except where the Landlord can demonstrate it would affect the operation of the building. You should remember that you should notify the Landlord of any non-structural alterations you do make.

You should be aware of statutory requirements (such as Construction (Design and Management) Regulations 2007 (CDM) that you must comply with when carrying out any works or alterations to the Property. The CDM regulations require you to keep full and detailed formal records and your Landlord will require you to maintain these records throughout the lease.

9 Insurance

You may be required to reimburse the Landlord for his insurance premiums, and the Landlord should tell you what commission payments (if any) he receives.

Tip 29

Ask for a copy of the Landlord's insurance policy and before signing the lease, check with alternative insurers that you are getting value for money for the given level of premium and that the insurance company is reputable. Ask him to confirm to you that he has no intention of changing the scope (and, therefore, the cost and nature) of the insurance cover.

The lease should provide for the Landlord's policy to be used to repair or rebuild the property unless the insurance is invalidated by anything you do, in which case you may be liable for the reinstatement.

Tip 30

Remember to inform the Landlord and his insurer if you intend to change the way you use the property; let them know if you are storing any hazardous chemicals in the context of your business or if you propose to leave the property vacant and unattended at any time. Ask the Landlord to ensure inclusion of such activities in the insurance policy and to consult you over any changes in the insurance policy terms.

Tip 31

Check whether your alterations or improvements would be covered under the Landlord's policy.

10 Tenant's defaults and applications for consent

Tenant default

The lease forms a legal contract between you and your Landlord. Any breach of contract may have serious consequences and you should take care to understand your obligations and steps the Landlord may take against you and, if applicable, your guarantors, including Court action.

The laws relating to Landlord and Tenant relationships are complex and you should seek professional advice so you are clear on your obligations and rights.

A fair lease is one which allows you enough opportunity to fix any problems (without loss to the Landlord) before any legal action is taken.

Tip 32

Check that the Landlord must let you know you are in breach and give you a reasonable opportunity to remedy the breach before taking legal action against you.

You may find that you have failed or forgotten to carry out some obligations under your lease. It is usually best if you are able to carry out these obligations yourself. It may be better sometimes to approach the Landlord and negotiate a reasonable payment to have the Landlord carry out the obligations after your lease has expired.

Tip 33

Try to stay on good terms with the Landlord. This should help make any situation easier to handle and should allow you to run your business without unnecessary outside interruptions.

The remedy for a breach of your agreement may range from the Landlord sending in bailiffs, who may seize goods to the value of the breach, to the Landlord taking back the property from you ('Forfeiture'). You should note that this would not take away your liability to pay arrears of rent.

The Code for Leasing Business Premises
in England and Wales 2007
www.leasingbusinesspremises.co.uk

Tip 34

Make sure the 'Forfeiture' provisions in the lease are clear; they should allow you enough time to pay, and should allow you to restructure your business without necessarily making your lease vulnerable to forfeiture.

The Landlord may try to forfeit your lease by locking you out of the Property or by obtaining a court order. In either case you can apply to the Court to give you time to put matters right or to pay what you owe. Seek urgent professional advice in that situation.

New legislation often brings new obligations for owners and occupiers of property. Leases often require tenants to comply with statute at their own cost. You should ensure your obligations under the lease are proportionate to the length and terms of your lease and you should take professional advice and make your own estimate of any expected costs. You should research possible new Regulations that could affect your occupation and your business.

This provision should not be taken lightly and you should ensure that the Property is in compliance with existing regulations (for example, with Disability Discrimination Acts, Town and Country Planning Acts, Health & Safety Acts or Environmental Protection Acts) when you take the lease.

Tip 35

Ask the Landlord to confirm to you in writing that the Property complies with all regulations (some of which are "Statutory Instruments") before entering into the lease.

Tip 36

Stay aware of potential new legislation and Regulations that will affect occupiers of business premises (many trade bodies and professional firms send out newsletters which can help to identify significant changes). Identify the costs and take professional advice to ensure you comply where you are obliged to by your lease.

Applications for consent

You will need to make applications to the Landlord during the lease, for example, if you intend to carry out alterations (see Section 8) or if you propose to sublease or assign your lease (see Section 4). The lease should specify that the Landlord may not unreasonably withhold or delay his consent.

The Landlord's duty to respond only applies from when he has received from you adequate information about the proposed alterations or about the proposed assignee or subtenant and full details of the proposed transaction.

Tip 37

Check what information will be required before making an application and make sure you are able to give the Landlord full details. Ask the Landlord in advance what other consents he may have to get and ask for assurances that this will not add any further delay to the approval process.

Useful Links

The Code for Leasing Business Premises in England and Wales 2007
www.leasingbusinesspremises.co.uk

Bills before Parliament
www.publications.parliament.uk/pa/pabills.htm

Building Regulations
www.communities.gov.uk/index.asp?id=1130474

Health and Safety Executive
www.hse.gov.uk

Service Charge Code
www.servicechargecode.co.uk

Town Planning (Link Site)
www.ukplanning.com/ukp/index.htm

Uniform Business Rates
www.voa.gov.uk

Organisations Endorsing the Code

Association of British Insurers
www.abi.org.uk/

British Council for Offices
www.bco.org.uk

British Property Federation
www.bpf.org.uk

British Retail Consortium
www.brc.org.uk

Communities and Local Government
www.communities.gov.uk

Confederation of British Industry
www.cbi.org.uk

CoreNet Global
www.corenetglobal.org.uk

The Forum of Private Business
www.fpb.org.uk

Federation of Small Businesses
www.fsb.org.uk

Investment Property Forum
www.ipf.org.uk/

The Law Society of England and Wales
www.lawsociety.org.uk

The Royal Institution of Chartered Surveyors
www.rics.org

Welsh Assembly Government
www.wales.gov.uk/index.htm

Leasing Business Premises: Model Heads of Terms

Note: These Model Heads of Terms follow a similar format to the Code for Leasing Business Premises: Landlord Code.

1.0	**Initial information**	Lease to be Code compliant: Yes / No.
1.1	**Property address**	Detailed description (and Land Registry compliant plan if available) and measured area if relevant, e.g. for rent, service charge and rent reviews.
1.2	**Landlord**	[ ] (Registered no. [ ]) Registered office: Correspondence address: Contact name: E-mail: Telephone: (Fax:) Mobile:
1.3	**Tenant**	[ ] (Registered no. [ ]) Registered office: Correspondence address: Contact name: E-mail: Telephone: (Fax:) Mobile:
1.4	**Rent**	£ per annum exclusive of VAT. Payment dates monthly/quarterly. Is the property VAT elected?
1.5	**Rent free period (and other Incentives)**	
1.6	**Type of lease**	Head lease or sub lease.
1.7	**Landlord's initial works (including timing)**	Long stop date by which works must be done. Is the specification agreed/if not who is providing it?
1.8	**Tenant's initial works (including timing)**	
2.0	**Guarantor/rent deposits**	(a) Identity of guarantor (if any). (b) Rent deposit amount (if any).
3.0	**Lease length, breaks, extensions and rights**	
3.1	**Lease length and start date**	
3.2	**Break clauses or renewal rights**	(a) Notice periods for exercising? To be at least [ ]. (b) Any break clause payments?
3.3	**1954 Act protection**	Does the lease have 1954 Act protection?

| 3.4 | Rights | eg. Satellite dish, air conditioning platforms, remote storage areas, signage, etc. Any rights of access, servicing, wayleaves or other matters inc. fire escape. For car parking – state number and attach plan if relevant. |

| 4.0 | Rent reviews | (a) Type (market rent, fixed increases, link to an index?).
 (b) How often do reviews occur?
 (c) For market rent, are there any unusual disregards or assumptions. Arbitrator/Expert. |

5.0 Assignment and subletting
See check box >

	Prohibited	If not prohibited is CNUW	Permitted without consent
Assignment of whole	Yes/No	Yes/No	Yes/No
Sub-Lease whole	Yes/No	Yes/No	Yes/No
Sub-Lease part	Yes/No	Yes/No	Yes/No
Sub-sub-lease	Yes/No	Yes/No	Yes/No
Concession	Yes/No	Yes/No	Yes/No
Group sharing	Yes/No	Yes/No	Yes/No

For sub lettings consider: Maximum number of occupiers, limitations
Code requires sublettings to be at market rent.
CNUW = Consent not to be unreasonably withheld.

| 6.0 | Services and service charge | Provide estimate or actual budgets and confirm proportion. Any special provisions, eg. exclusions special services, e.g. enhanced security? Any unusual provisions, e.g. sinking fund?

 Note: Owners and Occupiers should be aware of the RICS 2006 Code of Practice on Service Charges in Commercial Property and seek to observe its guidance in drafting new leases and on renewals. |

| 7.0 | Repairing obligations | |

| 7.1 | FRI and schedule of condition | (a) is it full repairing; if so
 (b) is it the Landlord who repairs and recovers the cost, or the Tenant who repairs at its own cost?;
 (c) is there to be a schedule of condition? |

| 7.2 | Collateral warranties | Who is giving them? |

| 8.0 | Alterations and use | |

8.1 Alterations
See check box >

	Prohibited	If not prohibited is CNUW	Permitted without consent
External	Yes/No	Yes/No	Yes/No
External structural	Yes/No	Yes/No	Yes/No
Internal structural	Yes/No	Yes/No	Yes/No
Internal non structural	Yes/No	Yes/No	Yes/No

Note: Is an agreed form of licence to be attached to lease?

| 8.2 | Permitted use | Specify use and any ability to change use. |

| 9.0 | Insurance | (a) Landlord insures and recovers the premium from the Tenant.
 (b) Will terrorism be an insured risk?
 (c) Mutual break clause on:
 • Insured damage?
 • Uninsured damage? |

10

10.0	**Lease management**	
10.1	**Dilapidations**	e.g. Dilapidations to be scheduled and given to the Tenant six months before the termination date.
11.0	**Other issues**	
11.1	**Rates and utilities**	Confirm that the Tenant is responsible. Tenant must check actual amount with Local Authority and utility provider.
11.2	**Legal costs**	Each party to pay own including costs of approval for tenant's fit out.
11.3	**Conditions**	e.g. 1. Board approvals 2. Planning 3. Local authority consents. 4. References 5. Superior landlord's consent 6. Survey.
11.4	**General**	1. DDA 1995? 2. Asbestos register? 3. Environmental issues? 4. Health & safety file and other Issues? 5. Energy efficiency certificate?
11.5	**Landlord's solicitors**	[ ] Company address: Contact name: E-mail: Telephone: (Fax:) Mobile:
11.6	**Tenant's solicitors**	[ ] Company address: Contact name: E-mail: Telephone: (Fax:) Mobile:
11.7	**Timing and other matters**	e.g. Exclusivity period, target for exchange?
11.8	**No contract**	These Heads of Terms are subject to contract.
11.9	**Landlord's agent(s)**	[ ] (Registered no. [ ]) Registered office: Correspondence address: Contact name: E-mail: Telephone: (Fax:) Mobile:
11.10	**Tenant's agent(s)**	[ ] (Registered no. [ ]) Registered office: Correspondence address: Contact name: E-mail: Telephone: (Fax:) Mobile:

11

Lease of floor(s) of an office block with guarantee and prescribed clauses

DATED

LEASE

relating to

[DESCRIPTION OF THE PROPERTY]

between

[PARTY 1]

and

[PARTY 2]

and

[PARTY 3]

Contents

1. Interpretation
2. Grant
3. Ancillary rights
4. Rights excepted and reserved
5. Third Party Rights
6. The Annual Rent
7. Review of the Annual Rent
8. Services and Service Charge
9. Insurance
10. Rates and taxes
11. Utilities
12. Common items
13. VAT
14. Default interest and interest
15. Costs
16. [Compensation on vacating
17. No deduction, counterclaim or set-off

18. Registration of this lease
19. Prohibition of dealings
20. Assignments
21. Underlettings
22. Sharing occupation
23. Charging
24. Registration and notification of dealings and occupation
25. Closure of the registered title of this lease
26. Repairs
27. Decoration
28. Alterations and signs
29. Returning the Property to the Landlord
30. Use
31. Management of the Building
32. Compliance with laws
33. [Energy performance certificates
34. Encroachments, obstructions and acquisition of rights
35. Breach of repair and maintenance obligations
36. [Indemnity
37. Landlord's covenant for quiet enjoyment
38. Guarantee and indemnity
39. Re-entry and forfeiture
40. Liability
41. Entire agreement and exclusion of representations
42. Notices, consents and approvals
43. Governing law and jurisdiction
44. Exclusion of LTA 1954 protection
45. [Tenant's break clause
46. Contracts (Rights of Third Parties) Act 1999
47. New tenancy under 1995 Act

Schedules

1. Guarantee and indemnity
2. Break Notice
3. Services, Service Costs and Excluded Costs

PRESCRIBED CLAUSES

LR1. Date of lease
[DATE]

LR2. Title number(s)

LR2.1 Landlord's title number(s)
[INSERT TITLE NUMBER(S) OR LEAVE BLANK IF NONE]

LR2.2 Other title numbers
[TITLE NUMBER(S)] OR [None]

LR3. Parties to this lease

Landlord
[COMPANY NAME]
[REGISTERED OFFICE ADDRESS]
[COMPANY REGISTERED NUMBER]

Tenant
[COMPANY NAME]
[REGISTERED OFFICE ADDRESS]
[COMPANY REGISTERED NUMBER]

Other parties
[[COMPANY] NAME]
[[REGISTERED OFFICE] ADDRESS]
[COMPANY REGISTERED NUMBER]

Guarantor

LR4. Property
In the case of a conflict between this clause and the remainder of this lease then, for the purposes of registration, this clause shall prevail.
See the definition of 'Property' in clause 1.1 of this lease.

LR5. Prescribed statements etc.

LR5.1 Statements prescribed under rules 179 (dispositions in favour of a charity), 180 (dispositions by a charity) or 196 (leases under the Leasehold Reform, Housing and Urban Development Act 1993) of the Land Registration Rules 2003.
None.

LR5.2 This lease is made under, or by reference to, provisions of:
None.

LR6. Term for which the Property is leased
The term as specified in this lease at clause 1.1 in the definition of 'Contractual Term'.

LR7. Premium
None.

LR8. Prohibitions or restrictions on disposing of this lease
This lease contains a provision that prohibits or restricts dispositions.

LR9. Rights of acquisition etc.

LR9.1 Tenant's contractual rights to renew this lease, to acquire the reversion or another lease of the Property, or to acquire an interest in other land
None.

LR9.2 Tenant's covenant to (or offer to) surrender this lease
None.

LR9.3 Landlord's contractual rights to acquire this lease
None.

LR10. Restrictive covenants given in this lease by the Landlord in respect of land other than the Property
None.

LR11. Easements

LR11.1 Easements granted by this lease for the benefit of the Property
The easements as specified in clause 3 of this lease.

LR11.2 Easements granted or reserved by this lease over the Property for the benefit of other property
The easements as specified in clause 4 of this lease.

LR12. Estate rentcharge burdening the Property
None.

LR13. Application for standard form of restriction
The Parties to this lease apply to enter the following standard form of restriction [against the title of the Property] [against title number]
None.

LR14. Declaration of trust where there is more than one person comprising the Tenant
[OMIT ALL INAPPLICABLE STATEMENTS]
[The Tenant is more than one person. They are to hold the Property on trust for themselves as joint tenants.]
[The Tenant is more than one person. They are to hold the Property on trust for themselves as tenants in common in equal shares.]
[The Tenant is more than one person. They are to hold the Property on trust [COMPLETE AS NECESSARY]]
THIS LEASE is dated [DATE]

PARTIES

(1) [COMPANY NAME], incorporated and registered in England and Wales with company number [NUMBER] whose registered office is at [REGISTERED OFFICE ADDRESS] (**Landlord**).

(2) [COMPANY NAME], incorporated and registered in England and Wales with company number [NUMBER] whose registered office is at [REGISTERED OFFICE ADDRESS] (**Tenant**).

[(3) [COMPANY NAME], incorporated and registered in England and Wales with company number [NUMBER] whose registered office is at [REGISTERED OFFICE ADDRESS] **OR** [NAME] of [ADDRESS] and [NAME] of [ADDRESS] (**Guarantor**).]

AGREED TERMS

1. INTERPRETATION

1.1   The definitions and rules of interpretation set out in this clause apply to this lease.

Act of Insolvency:

(a)   the taking of any step in connection with any voluntary arrangement or any other compromise or arrangement for the benefit of any creditors of the Tenant [or any guarantor]; or

(b)   the making of an application for an administration order or the making of an administration order in relation to the Tenant [or any guarantor]; or

(c)   the giving of any notice of intention to appoint an administrator, or the filing at court of the prescribed documents in connection with the appointment of an administrator, or the appointment of an administrator, in any case in relation to the Tenant [or any guarantor]; or

(d)   the appointment of a receiver or manager or an administrative receiver in relation to any property or income of the Tenant [or any guarantor]; or

(e)   the commencement of a voluntary winding-up in respect of the Tenant [or any guarantor], except a winding-up for the purpose of amalgamation or reconstruction of a solvent company in respect of which a statutory declaration of solvency has been filed with the Registrar of Companies; or

(f) the making of a petition for a winding-up order or a winding-up order in respect of the Tenant [or any guarantor]; or

(g) the striking-off of the Tenant [or any guarantor] from the Register of Companies or the making of an application for the Tenant [or any guarantor] to be struck-off; or

(h) the Tenant [or any guarantor] otherwise ceasing to exist (but excluding where the Tenant [or any guarantor] dies); or

(i) the presentation of a petition for a bankruptcy order or the making of a bankruptcy order against the Tenant [or any guarantor].

The paragraphs above shall apply in relation to a partnership or limited partnership (as defined in the Partnership Act 1890 and the Limited Partnerships Act 1907 respectively) subject to the modifications referred to in the Insolvent Partnerships Order 1994 (SI 1994/ 2421) (as amended), and a limited liability partnership (as defined in the Limited Liability Partnerships Act 2000) subject to the modifications referred to in the Limited Liability Partnerships Regulations 2001 (SI 2001/1090) (as amended).

Act of Insolvency includes any analogous proceedings or events that may be taken pursuant to the legislation of another jurisdiction in relation to a tenant [or guarantor] incorporated or domiciled in such relevant jurisdiction.

Annual Rent: rent at an initial rate of £[ ] per annum and then as revised pursuant to this lease [and any interim rent determined under the LTA 1954].

[**Break Date:** a date which is at least [NUMBER] [weeks][months] after service of the Break Notice.]

[**Break Notice:** written notice to terminate this lease [in the form set out in Schedule 2] specifying the Break Date.]

Building: [DESCRIPTION OF THE BUILDING] shown edged blue on Plan 2.

Certificate: a certificate prepared by the Landlord or the Manager setting out the Service Charge and the Service Costs for the preceeding Service Charge Year.

Certified Accounts: service charge accounts prepared [and audited] by the Landlord's [independent accountants] [or] [managing agents].

CDM Regulations: the Construction (Design and Management) Regulations 2007.

Common Parts: the Building other than the Property and the Lettable Units.

Contractual Term: a term from and including [DATE] to and including [DATE].

Default Interest Rate: [four] percentage points above the Interest Rate.

Deliberate Damage: damage caused deliberately [with the intention of causing damage] by the Tenant [or anyone at the Property or on the Common Parts with the express or implied authority of the Tenant [other than anyone deriving title under the Tenant]].

[**Energy Assessor:** an individual who is a member of an accreditation scheme approved by the Secretary of State in accordance with regulation 25 of the Energy Performance of Buildings (Certificates and Inspections) (England and Wales) Regulations 2007 or regulation 30 of the Building Regulations 2010 (SI 2010/2214).]

[**Energy Performance Certificate:** a certificate which complies with regulation 11(1) of the Energy Performance of Buildings (Certificates and Inspections) (England and Wales) Regulations 2007 or regulation 29 of the Building Regulations 2010.]

Excluded Costs: the costs set out in paragraph 3 of Schedule 3.

Insurance Rent: The aggregate in each year of:

(a)   a fair and reasonable proportion of:

    (i)   the cost of any premiums (including any IPT chargeable thereon) that the Landlord expends ([before][after] any discount or commission is allowed or paid to the Landlord); and

    (ii)   any fees and other expenses that the Landlord reasonably incurs,

    in effecting and maintaining insurance of the Building in accordance with this lease, including any professional fees for carrying out any insurance valuation of the Reinstatement [Cost][Value];

(b)   a fair and reasonable proportion of the cost of any premiums (including any IPT chargeable thereon) that the Landlord expends ([before][after] any discount or commission is allowed or paid to the Landlord) in effecting public liability insurance in relation to the Common Parts;

(c)   the cost of any additional premiums (including any IPT chargeable thereon) and loadings that may be demanded by the Landlord's insurer as a result of any act or default of the Tenant, any person deriving title under the Tenant or any person at the Property with the express or implied authority of any of them;

(d)   the cost of any premiums (including any IPT chargeable thereon) that the Landlord expends ([before][after] any discount or commission is allowed or paid to the Landlord) in effecting insurance against loss of the Annual Rent from the Property for [three] years; and

(e)   any VAT payable on any sum in (a) to (d) inclusive.

Insured Risks: fire, lightning, explosion, impact, earthquake, storm, tempest, flood, bursting or overflowing of water tanks or pipes, damage to underground water, oil or gas pipes or electricity wires or cables, subsidence, ground slip, heave, riot, civil commotion, strikes, labour or political disturbances, malicious damage, aircraft and aerial devices and articles dropped accidentally from them, and such other risk against which the Landlord may reasonably insure from time to time, and **Insured Risk** means any one of the Insured Risks.

Interest Rate: interest at the base lending rate from time to time of [NAME OF BANK], or if that base lending rate stops being used or published then at a comparable commercial rate reasonably determined by the Landlord.

IPT: Insurance Premium Tax chargeable under the Finance Act 1994 or any similar replacement or additional tax.

Landlord's Neighbouring Property: each and every part of the adjoining and neighbouring property in which the Landlord has an interest known as [DESCRIPTION/ADDRESS OF THE LANDLORD'S NEIGHBOURING PROPERTY] [registered at HM Land Registry with title number[s] [INSERT TITLE NUMBER[S] IF REGISTERED]] [shown edged green on the attached plan marked [INSERT PLAN REFERENCE].

LTA 1927: Landlord and Tenant Act 1927.

LTA 1954: Landlord and Tenant Act 1954.

LTCA 1995: Landlord and Tenant (Covenants) Act 1995.

Lettable Unit: a floor [or part of a floor] of the Building other than the Property, that is capable of being let and occupied.

Management Fee: the total of the reasonable costs, fees and disbursements of the Manager which are properly incurred by the Landlord relating to the carrying out and provision of the Management Service.

Management Service: any service provided by, or any function of, the Manager in relation to the provision of the Services and the administration of the Service Charge.

Manager: any managing agent, team, individual or in-house person or persons employed by the Landlord, or by managing agents themselves, or otherwise retained by the Landlord to act on the Landlord's behalf, to budget for, forecast, procure, manage, account for, provide and otherwise administer any of the Building, the Services or the Service Charge.

NIC: National Insurance Contributions or any similar, replacement or additional contributions.

Permitted Use: offices within Use Class B1 of the Town and Country Planning (Use Classes) Order 1987 as at the date this lease is granted.

Permitted Hours: [LIMITS OF NORMAL WEEKDAY HOURS] Mondays to Fridays and [LIMITS OF NORMAL SATURDAY HOURS] on Saturdays other than days which are bank holidays or public holidays in [England][Wales].

Plan 1: the plan attached to this lease marked 'Plan 1'.

Plan 2: the plan attached to this lease marked 'Plan 2'.

Property: the [part of the][ ] [and [ ]] floor[s] of the Building (the floor plan[s] of which [is][are] shown edged red on Plan 1) [in respect of each of those floors] bounded by and including:

(a)   [the [floorboards] [floor screed] [OTHER FLOORING BOUNDARY]];

(b)   [the [DESCRIPTION OF CEILING BOUNDARY];]

(c)   [the interior [plasterwork and] finishes of exterior walls and columns;]

(d)   the [plasterwork and] finishes of the interior [structural][load-bearing] walls and columns that adjoin [another Lettable Unit or] the Common Parts;]

(e)   [the doors and windows within the interior, [structural] [load-bearing] walls and columns that adjoin [another Lettable Unit or] the Common Parts and their frames and fittings;]

(f)   [one half of the thickness of the interior, [non-structural] [non-load-bearing] walls [and columns] that adjoin [another Lettable Unit or] the Common Parts;] [and]

(g)   [the doors and windows within the interior, [non-structural][non-load-bearing] walls [and columns] that adjoin the Common Parts and their frames and fittings;]

but excluding:

(h)   [the windows in the exterior walls and their frames and fittings;]

(i)   [the whole of the interior [structural] [load-bearing] walls and columns within that part of the Building [other than their plasterwork and] finishes and other than the doors and windows and their frames and fittings within such walls;] and

(j)   [all Service Media within that part of the Building which do not exclusively serve that part of the Building].

[**Recommendation Report:** the recommendation report required by regulation 10 of the Energy Performance of Buildings (Certificates and Inspections) (England and Wales) Regulations 2007, including a report issued by an Energy Assessor for the purposes of regulation 29(5) of the Building Regulations 2010 or regulation 20(1) of the Building (Approved Inspectors etc.) Regulations 2010 (SI 2010/2215).]

Reinstatement [Cost][Value]: the full [cost of reinstatement][reinstatement value] of the Building as reasonably determined by the Landlord from time to time, taking into account inflation of building costs and including any costs of demolition, site clearance, site protection, shoring up and any other work to the Building that may be required by law and any VAT on any such costs.

[**Rent Commencement Date:** [SPECIFY DATE].]

Rent Payment Dates: [25 March, 24 June, 29 September and 25 December] **OR** [SPECIFY ALTERNATIVE RENT PAYMENT DATES].

Reservations: all of the rights excepted, reserved and granted to the Landlord by this lease.

Review Date: [SPECIFY EACH REVIEW DATE].

Rights: The rights granted by the Landlord to the Tenant in clause 3.1.

Service Charge: a fair and reasonable proportion of the Service Costs, calculated by a recognised method on a consistent basis across the Building and the occupiers of the Building, having regard to the physical size, nature of use and benefits to and use by each occupier.

Service Charge Account: any account set up and maintained by the Landlord into which the [estimated] Service Charge paid by the occupiers of the Building is paid.

Service Charge Code: the RICS Code of Practice known as 'Service Charges in Commercial Property' which came into effect on 1 April 2007.

Service Charge Year: the annual accounting period relating to the Services and the Service Costs beginning on [SPECIFY DATE] in [YEAR] and each subsequent year during the term.

Service Costs: the costs listed in *paragraph* 2 of Schedule 3.

Service Media: [lifts and lift machinery and equipment and] all media for the supply or removal of heat, electricity, gas, water, sewage, [air-conditioning,] energy, telecommunications, data and all other services and utilities and all structures, machinery and equipment ancillary to those media.

Service Provider: any body, individual, contractor or sub-contractor which is responsible for providing any of the Services, excluding utility providers.

Services: the services listed in paragraph 1 of Schedule 3.

Third Party Rights: all rights, covenants and restrictions affecting the Building including the matters referred to at the date of this lease in [the property register] [and [entry][entries] [STATE RELEVANT ENTRY NUMBER(S)] of the charges register] of title number [] **OR** [DESCRIPTION OF RELEVANT MATTERS AFFECTING AN UNREGISTERED REVERSION].

VAT: value added tax chargeable under the Value Added Tax Act 1994 or any similar replacement or additional tax.

1.2   A reference to this **lease**, except a reference to the date of this lease or to the grant of this lease, is a reference to this deed and any deed, licence, consent, approval or other instrument supplemental to it.

1.3   The Schedules form part of this agreement and shall have effect as if set out in full in the body of this agreement. Any reference to this agreement includes the Schedules.

1.4   Except where a contrary intention appears, a reference to a clause or Schedule is a reference to a clause of, or Schedule to, this lease and a reference in a Schedule to a paragraph is to a paragraph of that Schedule.

1.5   Clause, Schedule and paragraph headings shall not affect the interpretation of this lease.

1.6   A reference to the **Landlord** includes a reference to the person entitled to the immediate reversion to this lease. A reference to the **Tenant** includes a reference to its successors in title and assigns. A reference to a **guarantor** [is a reference to any guarantor] [includes a reference to the Guarantor and to any other guarantor] of the tenant covenants of this lease including a guarantor who has entered into an authorised guarantee agreement.

1.7   A **person** includes a natural person, corporate or unincorporated body (whether or not having separate legal personality).

1.8   Unless the context otherwise requires, a reference to one gender shall include a reference to the other genders.

1.9   The expressions **landlord covenant** and **tenant covenant** each has the meaning given to it by the LTCA 1995.

1.10   Any obligation in this lease on the Tenant not to do something includes an obligation not to agree to or suffer that thing to be done and an obligation to use best endeavours to prevent that thing being done by another person.

1.11   References to the **consent** of the Landlord are to the consent of the Landlord given in accordance with clause 42.5 and references to the **approval** of the Landlord are to the approval of the Landlord given in accordance with clause 42.6.

1.12   Unless the context otherwise requires, references to the **Building**, the **Common Parts**, a **Lettable Unit** and the **Property** are to the whole and any part of them or it.

1.13   The expression **neighbouring property** does not include the Building.

1.14   A reference to the **term** is to the Contractual Term [and any agreed or statutory continuation of this lease].

1.15   A reference to the **end of the term** is to the end of the term however it ends.

1.16   Any phrase introduced by the terms **including, include, in particular** or any similar expression shall be construed as illustrative and shall not limit the sense of the words preceding those terms.

1.17   A reference to **writing** or **written** includes faxes but does not include e-mail.

1.18   Unless the context otherwise requires, words in the singular shall include the plural and in the plural include the singular.

1.19   A **working day** is a day other than a Saturday, Sunday or public holiday in [England][Wales].

1.20   A reference to a statute, statutory provision or subordinate legislation is a reference to it as it is in force [from time to time **OR** as at the date of this lease], taking account of any amendment or re-enactment [and includes any statute, statutory provision or subordinate legislation which it amends or re-enacts].

1.21   A reference to a statute or statutory provision shall include any subordinate legislation made [from time to time **OR** as at the date of this lease] under that statute or statutory provision.

2.   GRANT

2.1   [At the request of the Guarantor, the] [The] Landlord lets [with full title guarantee][with limited title guarantee] the Property to the Tenant for the Contractual Term.

2.2   The grant is made together with the Rights, excepting and reserving to the Landlord the Reservations, and subject to the Third Party Rights.

2.3   The grant is made with the Tenant paying the following as rent to the Landlord:

(a)   the Annual Rent and all VAT in respect of it;

(b)   the Service Charge and all VAT in respect of it;

(c)   the Insurance Rent; [and]

(d)   all interest payable under this lease[; and

(e)   all other sums due under this lease].

3. ANCILLARY RIGHTS

3.1 The Landlord grants the Tenant the following rights:

(a) the right to support and protection from the Common Parts to the extent that the Common Parts provide support and protection to the Property to the date of this lease;

(b) [the right to use external areas of the Common Parts shown hatched [ ] on Plan 2 for the purposes of vehicular and pedestrian access to and egress from the interior of the Building [and to and from the parts of the Common Parts referred to in clause 3.1(c) to clause 3.1(f);]

(c) [the right to park [ ] private cars or motorbikes belonging to the Tenant, its employees and visitors within the area edged [ ] on Plan 2;]

(d) [the right to use the area edged [] on Plan 2 for keeping bicycles belonging to the Tenant, its employees and visitors;]

(e) [the right to use the area edged [ ] on Plan 2 for loading and unloading goods and materials;]

(f) [the right to use [ ] bins in the area edged [ ] on Plan 2;]

(g) the right to use the hallways, corridors, stairways, [lifts] and landings of the Common Parts [shown hatched [ ] on Plan 2] for the purposes of access to and egress from the Property [and the lavatories and washrooms referred to in clause 3.1(h)];

(h) [the right to use the lavatories [and washrooms] on the [ ] [and [ ]] floor[s] of the Building;]

(i) the right to use and to connect into any Service Media at the Building that belong to the Landlord and serve (but do not form part of) the Property which are in existence at the date of this lease or are installed or constructed during the period of [INSERT AGREED PERIOD] years from the commencement of the Contractual Term;]

(j) [the right to attach any item to the Common Parts adjoining the Property so far as is reasonably necessary to carry out any works to the Property required or permitted by this lease;]

(k) [the right to display the name and logo of the Tenant (and any authorised undertenant) on a [sign or noticeboard] provided by the Landlord [in the entrance hall of] the Building [and on the Common Parts at the entrance to the Property, in each case] in a form and manner [reasonably] approved by the Landlord; [and]

(l) the right to enter the Common Parts or any other Lettable Unit so far as is reasonably necessary to carry out any works to the Property required or permitted by this lease[; and]

(m) [ANY OTHER SPECIFIC RIGHTS THAT NEED TO BE GRANTED].

3.2 The Rights are granted in common with the Landlord and any other person authorised by the Landlord.

3.3 The Rights are granted subject to the Third Party Rights insofar as the Third Party Rights affect the Common Parts and the Tenant shall not do anything that may interfere with any Third Party Right.

3.4 The Tenant shall exercise the Rights (other than the Right mentioned in clause 3.1(a)) only in connection with its use of the Property for the Permitted Use and only during the Permitted Hours and in accordance with any regulations made by the Landlord as mentioned in clause 3.1(a).

3.5 The Tenant shall comply with all laws relating to its use of the Common Parts pursuant to the Rights.

3.6   In relation to the Rights mentioned in clause 3.1(b) to clause 3.1(h), the Landlord may, at its discretion, change the route of any means of access to or egress from the interior of the Building and may change the area over which any of those Rights are exercised.

3.7   In relation to the Rights mentioned in clause 3.1(c) and clause 3.1(f) the Landlord may from time to time designate the spaces or bins (as the case may be) in respect of which the Tenant may exercise that Right.

3.8   In relation to the Rights mentioned in clause 3.1(i), the Landlord may, at its discretion, re-route or replace any such Service Media and that Right shall then apply in relation to the Service Media as re-routed or replaced.

3.9   [In relation to the Right mentioned in clause 3.1(j), where the Tenant requires the consent of the Landlord to carry out the works to the Property, the Tenant may only exercise that Right when that consent has been granted and in accordance with the terms of that consent.]

3.10   In exercising the Right mentioned in clause 3.1(l), the Tenant shall:

(a)   except in case of emergency, give reasonable notice to the Landlord and any occupiers of the relevant Lettable Unit(s) of its intention to exercise that Right;

(b)   where reasonably required by the Landlord or the occupier of the relevant Lettable Unit(s), exercise that Right only if accompanied by a representative of the Landlord and/or the tenant and/or the occupier of the relevant Lettable Unit(s);

(c)   cause as little damage as possible to the Common Parts and the other Lettable Units and to any property belonging to or used by the Landlord or the tenants or occupiers of the other Lettable Units;

(d)   cause as little inconvenience as possible to the Landlord and the tenants and occupiers of the other Lettable Units as is reasonably practicable; and

(e)   promptly make good (to the satisfaction of the Landlord) any damage caused to the Common Parts (or to any property belonging to or used by the Landlord) by reason of the Tenant exercising that Right.

3.11   Except as mentioned in this clause 3, neither the grant of this lease nor anything in it confers any right over the Common Parts or any Lettable Unit or any neighbouring property nor is to be taken to show that the Tenant may have any right over the Common Parts or any Lettable Unit or any neighbouring property, and section 62 of the Law of Property Act 1925 does not apply to this lease.

4.   RIGHTS EXCEPTED AND RESERVED

4.1   The following rights are excepted and reserved from this lease to the Landlord for the benefit of the Building and the Landlord's Neighbouring Property [and to the extent possible for the benefit of any neighbouring or adjoining property in which the Landlord acquires an interest during the term]:

(a)   rights of light, air, support and protection to the extent those rights are capable of being enjoyed at any time during the term;

(b)   the right to use and to connect into Service Media at, but not forming part of, the Property which are in existence at the date of this lease or which are installed or constructed during the period of [INSERT AGREED PERIOD] years from the commencement of the Contractual Term; the right to install and construct Service Media at the Property to serve any part of the Building (whether or not such Service Media also serve the Property); and the right to re-route any Service Media mentioned in this clause;

(c)   at any time during the term, the full and free right to develop the Landlord's Neighbouring Property [and any neighbouring or adjoining property in which the Landlord acquires an interest during the term] as the Landlord may think fit;

(d)   the right to erect scaffolding at the Property or the Building and attach it to any part of the Property or the Building in connection with any of the Reservations;

(e)   the right to attach any structure, fixture or fitting to the boundary of the Property in connection with any of the Reservations;

(f)   the right to re-route any means of access to or egress from the Property or the Building and to change the areas over which the Rights mentioned in clause 3.1(a) to clause 3.1(e) are exercised; [and]

(g)   the right to re-route and replace any Service Media over which the Rights mentioned in clause 3.1(i) are exercised; [and]

(h)   [ANY OTHER SPECIFIC RIGHTS THAT NEED TO BE RESERVED].]

notwithstanding that the exercise of any of the Reservations or the works carried out pursuant to them result in a reduction in the flow of light or air to the Property or the Common Parts or loss of amenity for the Property or the Common Parts [provided that they do not materially adversely affect the use and enjoyment of the Property for the Permitted Use].

4.2   The Landlord reserves the right to enter the Property:

(a)   to repair, maintain, install, construct, re-route or replace any Service Media or structure relating to any of the Reservations;

(b)   to carry out any works to any other Lettable Unit; and

(c)   for any other purpose mentioned in or connected with:

(i)   this lease;

(ii)   the Reservations; and

(iii)   the Landlord's interest in the Property, the Building or the Landlord's Neighbouring Property.

4.3   The Reservations may be exercised by the Landlord and by anyone else who is or becomes entitled to exercise them, and by anyone authorised by the Landlord.

4.4   The Tenant shall allow all those entitled to exercise any right to enter the Property, to do so with their workers, contractors, agents and professional advisors, and to enter the Property at any reasonable time (whether or not during usual business hours) and, except in the case of an emergency, after having given reasonable notice (which need not be in writing) to the Tenant.

4.5   No party exercising any of the Reservations, nor its workers, contractors, agents and professional advisors, shall be liable to the Tenant or to any undertenant or other occupier of or person at the Property for any loss, damage, injury, nuisance or inconvenience arising by reason of its exercising any of the Reservations except for:

(a)   physical damage to the Property; or

(b)   any loss, damage, injury, nuisance or inconvenience in relation to which the law prevents the Landlord from excluding liability.

5.   THIRD PARTY RIGHTS

5.1   The Tenant shall comply with all obligations on the Landlord relating to the Third Party Rights insofar as those obligations relate to the Property and shall not do anything (even if otherwise permitted by this lease) that may interfere with any Third Party Right.

5.2   The Tenant shall allow the Landlord and any other person authorised by the terms of the Third Party Right to enter the Property in accordance with its terms.

6.   THE ANNUAL RENT

6.1   The Tenant shall pay the Annual Rent and any VAT in respect of it by four equal instalments in advance on or before the Rent Payment Dates. The payments shall be made by banker's standing order or by any other method that the Landlord requires at any time by giving notice to the Tenant.

6.2   The first instalment of the Annual Rent and any VAT in respect of it shall be made on [the date of this lease and shall be the proportion, calculated on a daily basis, in respect of the period from the date of this lease until the day before the next Rent Payment Date] **OR** [the Rent Commencement Date and shall be the proportion, calculated on a daily basis, in respect of the period from the Rent Commencement Date until the day before the next Rent Payment Date].

7.   REVIEW OF THE ANNUAL RENT

7.1   In this clause the **President** is the President for the time being of the Royal Institution of Chartered Surveyors or a person acting on his behalf, and the **Surveyor** is the independent valuer appointed pursuant to clause 7.7.

7.2   [The amount of Annual Rent shall be reviewed on each Review Date to the open market rent agreed or determined pursuant to this clause.]

OR

[The amount of Annual Rent shall be reviewed on each Review Date to equal:

(a)   [the Annual Rent payable immediately before the relevant Review Date (or which would then be payable but for any abatement or suspension of the Annual Rent or restriction on the right to collect it)] **OR** [£[] per annum]; or, if greater;

(b)   the open market rent agreed or determined pursuant to this clause.]

7.3   The open market rent may be agreed between the Landlord and the Tenant at any time before it is determined by the Surveyor.

7.4   If the open market rent is determined by the Surveyor, it shall be the amount that the Surveyor determines is the best annual rent (exclusive of any VAT) at which the Property could reasonably be expected to be let:

(a)   in the open market;

(b)   at the relevant Review Date;

(c)   on the assumptions listed in clause 7.5; and

(d)   disregarding the matters listed in clause 7.6.

7.5   The assumptions are:

(a)   the Property is available to let in the open market:

(i)   by a willing lessor to a willing lessee (which may be the Tenant);

(ii)   as a whole;

(iii) with vacant possession;

(iv) without a fine or a premium;

(v)   for a term equal to the unexpired residue of the Contractual Term at the relevant Review Date or a term of [SPECIFY MINIMUM LENGTH OF HYPOTHETICAL TERM] years commencing on the relevant Review Date, if longer; and

(vi) otherwise on the terms of this lease other than as to the amount of the Annual Rent but including the provisions for review of the Annual Rent [, and other than the provision in this lease for a rent-free period];

(b)   the willing lessee has had the benefit of any rent-free or other concession or contribution which would be offered in the open market at the relevant Review Date in relation to fitting out works at the Property;

(c)   the Property may lawfully be used, and is in a physical state to enable it to be lawfully used, by the willing lessee (or any potential undertenant or assignee of the willing lessee) for any purpose permitted by this lease;

(d)   the Landlord and the Tenant have fully complied with their obligations in this lease;

(e)   if the Property or any other part of the Building or any Service Media serving the Property, has been destroyed or damaged, it has been fully restored;

(f)   no work has been carried out on the Property or any other part of the Building that has diminished the rental value of the Property [other than work carried out in compliance with clause [INSERT DETAILS OF CLAUSE CONTAINING TENANT'S OBLIGATION TO COMPLY WITH STATUTORY OBLIGATIONS]];

(g)   any fixtures, fittings, machinery or equipment supplied to the Property by the Landlord that have been removed by or at the request of the Tenant, or any undertenant or their respective predecessors in title (otherwise than to comply with any law) remain at the Property; and

(h)   the willing lessee and its potential assignees and undertenants shall not be disadvantaged by any actual or potential election to waive exemption from VAT in relation to the Property.

7.6   The matters to be disregarded are:

(a)   any effect on rent of the fact that the Tenant or any authorised undertenant has been in occupation of the Property;

(b)   any goodwill attached to the Property by reason of any business carried out there by the Tenant or by any authorised undertenant or by any of their predecessors in business;

(c)   any effect on rent attributable to any physical improvement to the Property carried out [before or] [after the date of this lease,] by or at the expense of the Tenant or any authorised undertenant with all necessary consents, approvals and authorisations and not pursuant to an obligation to the Landlord (other than an obligation to comply with any law);

(d)   any effect on rent of any obligation on the Tenant [to fit out the Property or] [to reinstate the Property to the condition or design it was in before any alterations or improvements were carried out]; [and]

(e)   any statutory restriction on rents or the right to recover them[.][; and]

(f)   [any effect on rent attributable to the asset rating in any Energy Performance Certificate in respect of the Property.]

7.7   The Surveyor shall be an independent valuer who is a Member or Fellow of the Royal Institution of Chartered Surveyors. The Landlord and the Tenant may, by agreement, appoint the Surveyor at any time before either of them applies to the President for the Surveyor to be appointed. Any application to the President may not be made earlier than three months before the relevant Review Date.

7.8   The Surveyor shall act as an expert and not as an arbitrator. The Surveyor shall determine the open market rent [and shall have power to determine any issue involving the interpretation of any provision of this lease, his jurisdiction to determine the matters and issues referred to him or his terms of reference]. The Surveyor's decision shall be given in writing[, and the Surveyor shall provide reasons for any determination]. The Surveyor's written decision on the matters referred to him shall be final and binding in the absence of manifest error or fraud.

7.9   The Surveyor shall give the Landlord and the Tenant an opportunity to make written representations to the Surveyor and to make written counter-representations commenting on the representations of the other party to the Surveyor. The parties will provide (or procure that others provide) the Surveyor with such assistance and documents as the Surveyor reasonably requires for the purpose of reaching a decision.

7.10 If the Surveyor dies, or becomes unwilling or incapable of acting, or unreasonably delays in making any determination, then either the Landlord or the Tenant may apply to the President to discharge the Surveyor and clause shall then apply in relation to the appointment of a replacement.

7.11 The fees and expenses of the Surveyor and the cost of the Surveyor's appointment and any counsel's fees, or other fees, [reasonably] incurred by the Surveyor shall be payable by the Landlord and the Tenant in the proportions that the Surveyor directs (or if the Surveyor makes no direction, then equally). [If the Tenant does not pay its part of the Surveyor's fees and expenses within ten working days after demand by the Surveyor, the Landlord may pay that part and the amount it pays shall be a debt of the Tenant due and payable on demand to the Landlord. The Landlord and the Tenant shall otherwise each bear their own costs in connection with the rent review **OR** If either the Landlord or the Tenant does not pay its part of the Surveyor's fees and expenses within ten working days after demand by the Surveyor then:

(a) the other party may pay instead; and

(b) the amount so paid shall be a debt of the party that should have paid due and payable on demand to the party that actually made the payment.

The Landlord and the Tenant shall otherwise each bear their own costs in connection with the rent review].

7.12 If the revised Annual Rent has not been agreed by the Landlord and the Tenant or determined by the Surveyor on or before the relevant Review Date, the Annual Rent payable from that Review Date shall continue at the rate payable immediately before that Review Date. [On the date] [No later than five working days after] the revised Annual Rent is agreed or the Surveyor's determination is notified to the Landlord and the Tenant, the Tenant shall pay:

(a) the shortfall (if any) between the amount that it has paid for the period from the Review Date until the Rent Payment Date following the date of agreement or notification of the revised Annual Rent and the amount that would have been payable had the revised Annual Rent been agreed or determined on or before that Review Date; and

(b) interest at the Interest Rate on that shortfall calculated on a daily basis by reference to the Rent Payment Dates on which parts of the shortfall would have been payable if the revised Annual Rent had been agreed or determined on or before that Review Date and the date payment is received by the Landlord.

7.13 Time shall not be of the essence for the purposes of this clause.

7.14 If at any time there is a guarantor, the guarantor shall not have any right to participate in the review of the Annual Rent.

7.15 As soon as practicable after the amount of the revised Annual Rent has been agreed or determined, a memorandum recording the amount shall be signed by or on behalf of the Landlord and the Tenant and endorsed on or attached to this lease and its counterpart. The Landlord and the Tenant shall each bear their own costs in connection with the memorandum.

8. SERVICES AND SERVICE CHARGE

8.1 Subject to clause 8.5 the Landlord shall provide the Services.

8.2 The Landlord shall administer the Services and the Service Charge in good faith and, except where there are sound reasons for implementing alternative procedures that can be justified and explained, the Landlord shall have regard to the provisions and recommendations of the Service Charge Code.

8.3 The Landlord shall:

(a)   ensure that the Services are provided in a commercial and professional manner and that the quality and cost of the Services are appropriate for the Building and are regularly reviewed;

(b)   require that Service Providers comply with written performance standards and regularly review, monitor and measure the performance of Service Providers against those written performance standards;

(c)   regularly review the cost of each of the Services against the market cost of similar services and, where appropriate, require contractors and suppliers to submit competitive tenders for the supply of any of the Services;

(d)   require that each Service Provider regularly reviews the methods, procedures, value and efficiency of the Services that it provides and, where possible, that it demonstrates that it is reviewing the Services where so required, that the Services are being provided to an appropriate standard and that value for money is being achieved;

(e)   provide sufficient, capable and appropriately qualified staff of the right type who are capable of administering and providing the Services efficiently and cost-effectively;

(f)   establish and maintain a written management policy which shall identify the aims of the Landlord and/or the Manager and any other members of any management team, the method of procurement, administration and management of the Services and shall [make this management policy available for inspection by the Tenant] [provide a copy of the management policy to the Tenant as soon as possible upon request];

(g)   establish and operate sound management procedures to ensure that the respective obligations of the Landlord and the Tenant which are set out in this clause are complied with and the Landlord shall record these procedures in the management policy referred to in clause 8.3(f);

(h)   ensure that the Management Fee:

(i)   is transparent so that the basis on which it is charged and the way in which it is calculated is clear;

(ii)   relates only to, and is reasonable for, the Management Service;

(iii)   has due regard to the duty of the Manager to observe the principles of the Service Charge Code;

(iv)   is charged to the Tenant in accordance with the relevant provisions of the Service Charge Code;

(v)   is not linked to a percentage of expenditure on the Services; and

(vi)   shall be fixed for a reasonable period of time (subject to indexing);

(i)   at reasonable intervals review the cost and quality of the Management Service and compare it against the market cost and quality of similar services. Unless the Landlord and the majority of the occupiers in the Building are satisfied with the results of such review, the Management Service shall be put out to tender in the open market and the tenderer providing the best value for money shall be appointed as the Manager;

(j)   require the Manager and the Service Providers to, respectively, operate the Management Service and provide the Services, in accordance with all procedures which are established by the Landlord, pursuant to this clause, in order to maintain the quality of the Services to the standard required by the Service Charge Code;

(k)   establish standard procedures for the Building in order to maintain the quality of the Services and shall require that the Manager ensures that the Service Providers comply with those procedures;

(l)   deal promptly and efficiently with any reasonable enquiry made by the Tenant which relates to the Service Charge or any of the Services;

   (m)   invite (and, where appropriate act upon) comment from the Tenant on the performance of the Service Providers, the standard of the Management Service and delivery of the Services;

   (n)   ensure that (where appropriate) regular meetings are held between the Landlord, the Tenant, the other occupiers in the Building and the Manager;

   (o)   ensure that any interest earned on the Service Charge Account (in each case, after bank charges, tax and all other appropriate deductions have been accounted for) is credited to the Service Charge Account;

   (p)   allocate the whole of the Service Cost relating to any of the Services which benefits only one occupier, to that specific occupier; and

   (q)   as soon as practicable but not later than four months after a disposal of the reversion immediately expectant on the determination of this lease, provide the purchaser with full details of the Service Costs, accruals, prepayments, and all other relevant information for the last [ ] Service Charge Years or any other Service Charge Year for which any part of the procedure set out in clause 8.8 remains outstanding and up to the date of sale.

8.4   The Landlord shall provide to the Tenant:

   (a)   details of any proposed works or Services which may substantially increase the Service Charge due for the relevant Service Charge Year and shall notify the Tenant promptly (and in any event within the relevant Service Charge Year) of any likely significant variation in the actual Service Costs of which the Landlord becomes aware;

   (b)   at the Tenant's request, a summary of the process of any tender which is undertaken in accordance with clause 8.3 and the results of any tender which applies to any proposed substantial works that would fall within the Service Costs together with full information on the programme of works, costs and the process for keeping the Tenant informed;

   (c)   information contained in any report or other item where the cost of obtaining this information is a Service Cost;

   (d)   a schedule showing the apportionment of the Service Costs for each Lettable Unit, together with a commentary on how the apportionments have been calculated;

   (e)   full details of any plans for the Building where such are likely to affect the Service Costs; and

   (f)   the Manager's (and where appropriate other Service Providers') contact details and details of each of their respective roles and responsibilities.

8.5   The Landlord shall not be required to:

   (a)   carry out any works where the need for those works has arisen by reason of any damage or destruction by a risk against which the Landlord is not obliged to insure;

   (b)   provide any of the Services outside the Permitted Hours; or

   (c)   replace or renew any part of the Building or any item or system within the Building which has not become beyond economic repair.

8.6   [The Landlord shall not be liable for any interruption in, or disruption to, the provision of any of the Services for any reason that is outside the reasonable control of the Landlord.]

8.7   The Landlord shall not charge any of the Excluded Costs as part of the Service Charge.

8.8   The procedure and obligations of the parties relating to operation of the Service Charge are as follows:

   (a)   at least one month before the start of each Service Charge Year, the Landlord shall prepare and send to the Tenant an estimate of the Service Costs for that Service Charge Year (in such form to enable the Tenant to compare it with the last issued Certified

Accounts) together with an explanatory commentary where appropriate and a statement of the estimated Service Charge for that Service Charge Year;

(b)   the Tenant shall pay the estimated Service Charge for each Service Charge Year in four equal instalments on each of the Rent Payment Dates;

(c)   in relation to the Service Charge Year current at the date of this lease:

(i)   the Tenant's obligations to pay the estimated Service Charge and the actual Service Charge shall be limited to an apportioned part of those amounts, such apportioned part to be calculated on a daily basis for the period from the date of this lease to the end of the Service Charge Year; and

(ii)   the estimated Service Charge for which the Tenant is liable shall be paid in equal instalments on [the date of this lease and] the [remaining] Rent Payment Days during the Period from the date of this lease until the end of the Service Charge Year;

(d)   as soon as reasonably practicable and no later than four months after the end of each Service Charge Year, the Landlord shall prepare and send to the Tenant a Certificate together with Certified Accounts and the Certificate shall:

(i)   be in a form which is reasonably consistent from year to year;

(ii)   provide an appropriately detailed and comprehensive summary of Service Costs;

(iii)   provide full details of and reasons for any material variations against the estimated Service Charge;

(iv)   be accompanied by a separate report providing any other relevant information which is required by the Service Charge Code; and

(v)   specify the name and role of the person who has given the Certificate;

(e)   if any cost is omitted from the calculation of the Service Charge in any Service Charge Year, the Landlord shall be entitled to include it in the estimate of the Service Charge and the Certificate in any following Service Charge Year;

(f)   subject to clause 8.8(e) and except in the case of manifest error, the Certificate shall be conclusive as to all matters of fact to which it refers, subject to the Tenant's right to reasonably challenge the expenditure by [referring the matter for Alternative Dispute Resolution (ADR)], and in the event of any such referral to ADR, each party shall bear its own costs;

(g)   the Landlord shall allow the Tenant a reasonable period in which to raise enquiries in respect of the Certified Accounts, shall respond promptly and efficiently to any reasonable enquiries of the Tenant and shall [make] [provide copies of] all relevant paperwork and copies of any supporting documentation [available for inspection by the Tenant] [to the Tenant upon request and upon payment by the Tenant of a reasonable fee];

(h)   at the Tenant's request the Landlord shall agree to an independent audit of the Service Costs which shall be undertaken at the Tenant's cost; and

(i)   if in respect of any Service Charge Year, the Landlord's estimate of the Service Charge is less than the Service Charge, the Tenant shall pay the difference immediately upon the expiry of the period specified in clause 8.8(g) (unless the Tenant shall challenge the Service Charge pursuant to clause 8.8(f) in which case the Tenant shall pay the difference immediately upon the final determination of that challenge). If in respect of any Service Charge Year, the Landlord's estimate of the Service Charge is more than the Service Charge, the Landlord shall promptly repay to the Tenant the difference.

8.9   In addition to the Tenant's obligations contained in clause 8.8 the Tenant shall:

(a)   co-operate fully with the Landlord and the Manager in order that the Landlord and the Manager may administer the Service Charge in accordance with the provisions of this clause;

(b)   promptly advise the Landlord and the Manager of any changes within the Tenant's organisation that may affect the operation of the Service Charge;

(c)   promptly make a written record upon being advised by the Landlord or the Manager of any changes to the operation of the Service Charge;

(d)   respond promptly and efficiently to any reasonable enquiry of the Landlord or the Manager; and

(e)   be proactive in assisting the Landlord and the Manager with operating and using the Services on a value for money and quality standard basis and follow all procedures reasonably required by the Landlord or the Manager in order to maintain and promote the quality and economic effectiveness of the Services. Such procedures include, but are not be limited to, separating waste to facilitate appropriate and cost effective recycling.

8.10   Where the Landlord is required to comply with any obligation contained in this clause such obligation shall, where relevant, include, in the alternative, an obligation on the Landlord to ensure that the Manager complies with that obligation.

9.   INSURANCE

9.1   The Landlord shall effect and maintain insurance of the Building (but excluding [any plate glass and] any Tenant's and trade fixtures in the Property) in accordance with this clause:

(a)   unless the insurance is vitiated by any act or omission of either:

(i)   the Tenant, any person deriving title under the Tenant or any person at the Property with the express or implied authority of any of them; or

(ii)   any tenant of the Landlord of any part of the Building other than the Property, any person deriving title under them or any person in the Building with the express or implied authority of any of them; and

(b)   subject to:

(i)   any exclusions, limitations, conditions or excesses that may be imposed by the Landlord's insurer; and

(ii)   insurance being available on reasonable terms in the London Insurance market.

9.2   Insurance of the Building shall be with reputable insurers, on fair and reasonable terms that represent value for money, for an amount not less than the [Reinstatement Cost][Reinstatement Value] against loss or damage caused by any of the Insured Risks, and shall include additional cover, if practicable, against damage arising from an act of terrorism.

9.3   In relation to any insurance effected by the Landlord under this clause, the Landlord shall:

(a)   at the request of the Tenant supply the Tenant with:

(i)   full details of the insurance policy;

(ii)   evidence of payment of the current year's premiums; and

(iii) details of any commission paid to the Landlord by the Landlord's insurer;

(b)   procure that the Tenant is informed of any change in the scope, level or terms of cover [as soon as reasonably practicable after][within five working days after] the Landlord or its agents have become aware of the change;

(c)   use all reasonable endeavours to procure that the Landlord's insurer waives its rights of subrogation against the Tenant and any lawful sub-tenants or occupiers of the Property and that the insurance policy contains a non-invalidation provision in favour of the Landlord in respect of any act or default of the Tenant; and

(d)   procure that the interest of the Tenant is noted on the policy of insurance either specifically or by way of a general noting of tenants' interests under the conditions of the insurance policy.

9.4   The Tenant shall pay each of the following to the Landlord on demand:

    (a)   the Insurance Rent; and

    (b)   a reasonable proportion of any amount that is deducted or disallowed by the Landlord's insurer pursuant to any excess provision in the insurance policy.

9.5   The Tenant shall:

    (a)   comply at all times with any requirements or recommendations of the Landlord's insurer that relate to the Property or the use by the Tenant of the Common Parts, where written details of those requirements or recommendations have first been given to the Tenant;

    (b)   give the Landlord notice immediately that any matter occurs in relation to the Tenant or the Property that any insurer or underwriter may treat as material in deciding whether or on what terms, to insure or continue insuring the Building; and

    (c)   give the Landlord notice immediately that any damage or loss occurs that relates to the Property.

9.6   If the Tenant makes any alteration or addition to the Property, the Tenant shall arrange at its own cost, for a current, independent, VAT inclusive valuation of the [Reinstatement Cost][Reinstatement Value] of the Property, taking into account the alteration or addition, such valuation to be prepared in writing and given to the Landlord within [four weeks] of the alteration or addition being completed.

9.7   In relation to any insurance arranged by the Landlord under this clause, the Tenant shall not do or omit to do anything and shall not permit or suffer anything to be done that may:

    (a)   vitiate the insurance contract; or

    (b)   cause any money claimed under the insurance to be withheld; or

    (c)   cause any premium paid for the insurance to be increased or cause any additional premium to be payable[, unless previously agreed in writing with the Landlord].

9.8   Other than [plate glass and] Tenant's and trade fixtures, the Tenant shall not insure the Property against any of the Insured Risks in such a manner as would permit the Landlord's insurer to cancel the Landlord's insurance or to reduce the amount of any money payable to the Landlord in respect of any insurance claim.

9.9   Notwithstanding the obligation on the Tenant in clause 9.8, if the Tenant [or any person deriving title under or through the Tenant] shall at any time be entitled to the benefit of any insurance of the Property, the Tenant shall immediately cause any money paid to the Tenant under that insurance to be applied in making good the loss or damage in respect of which it was paid.

9.10   If the Building or any part of it is damaged or destroyed by an Insured Risk, the Landlord shall:

    (a)   make a claim under the insurance policy effected in accordance with this clause;

    (b)   notify the Tenant immediately if the Landlord's insurer indicates that the [Reinstatement Cost][Reinstatement Value] will not be recoverable in full under the insurance policy; and

    (c)   subject to clause 9.11, use any insurance money received (other than for loss of rent) and any money received from the Tenant under clause 9.4(b) to repair the damage in respect of which the money was received or (as the case may be) to rebuild the Building.

9.11   The Landlord shall not be obliged under clause 9.10 to repair or reinstate the Building or any part of it:

    (a)   unless and until the Landlord has obtained any necessary planning and other consents for the repairs and reinstatement work; or

(b) so as to provide premises or facilities identical in size, quality and layout to those previously at the Building so long as the premises and facilities provided are reasonably equivalent; or

(c) after a notice has been served pursuant to clause 9.13 or clause 9.14.

9.12 If the Building is damaged or destroyed (other than by Deliberate Damage [that causes either the insurance policy to be vitiated or any money claimed under the insurance to be withheld]) so that the Property is wholly or partly unfit for occupation and use, or the Common Parts are damaged or destroyed so as to make the Property inaccessible or unusable, then payment of the Annual Rent or a fair proportion of it according to the nature and extent of the damage, shall be suspended until the earlier of the following:

(a) the date the Tenant can occupy and use the Property in the manner contemplated by this lease prior to the date of the damage or destruction; and

(b) the end of [three] years from the date of damage or destruction.

9.13 Subject to clause 9.15, the Landlord may give the Tenant notice terminating the lease with immediate effect if:

(a) the Property is damaged or destroyed or the Common Parts are damaged or destroyed so as to make the Property inaccessible or unusable; and

(b) the Landlord reasonably decides that it is either impracticable or impossible to reinstate the Property and the Common Parts within [three] years from the date of the damage or destruction.

9.14 The Tenant may give the Landlord notice terminating this lease with immediate effect (subject to clause 9.15) in either of the following situations:

(a) where the Property is:

(i) damaged or destroyed in whole [or in part] [other than by Deliberate Damage] so that it is unfit for occupation or use, or the Common Parts are damaged or destroyed so as to make the Property inaccessible or unusable; and

(ii) is not accessible and/or not fit for occupation and use by the end of [three] years from the date of damage or destruction; or

(b) where:

(i) the Property is damaged or destroyed in whole [or in part] [other than by Deliberate Damage and] other than by an Insured Risk[or is not covered by the Landlord's insurance by reason of a limitation in the insurance policy] so that it is unfit for occupation or use, or the Common Parts are damaged or destroyed so as to make the Property inaccessible or unusable; and

(ii) the loss or damage was caused other than by an Insured Risk [or is not covered by the Landlord's insurance by reason of a limitation in the insurance policy] and the Landlord has not given notice to the Tenant within [six months] of the date of damage or destruction that the Landlord will reinstate the Property at the Landlord's own cost.

9.15 Any notice to terminate this lease by either the Landlord or the Tenant under this clause shall be without prejudice to the rights of either party for breach of any of the covenants in the lease.

9.16 If this lease is terminated by either the Landlord or the Tenant under this clause, then any proceeds of the insurance effected by the Landlord shall belong to the Landlord.

10. RATES AND TAXES

10.1 The Tenant shall pay all present and future rates, taxes and other impositions payable in respect of the Property, its use and any works carried out there, other than:

(a)   any taxes payable by the Landlord in connection with any dealing with or disposition of the reversion to this lease; or

(b)   any taxes, other than VAT and insurance premium tax, payable by the Landlord by reason of the receipt of any of the rents due under this lease.

10.2   If any such rates, taxes or other impositions are payable in respect of the Property together with other land (including any other part of the Building) the Tenant shall pay a fair proportion of the total.

10.3   The Tenant shall not make any proposal to alter the rateable value of the Property or that value as it appears on any draft rating list, without the approval of the Landlord.

10.4   If, after the end of the term, the Landlord loses rating relief (or any similar relief or exemption) because it has been allowed to the Tenant, then the Tenant shall pay the Landlord an amount equal to the relief or exemption that the Landlord has lost.

11.   UTILITIES

11.1   The Tenant shall pay all costs in connection with the supply [and removal] of [electricity, gas, water, sewage,] telecommunications [and] data [and other services and utilities] to [or from] the Property.]

11.2   The Tenant shall comply with all laws and with any recommendations of the relevant suppliers relating to [the use of those services and utilities] [the supply and removal of electricity, gas, water, sewage, telecommunications, data and other services and utilities to or from the Property].

12.   COMMON ITEMS

12.1   The Tenant shall pay the Landlord on demand a fair proportion of all costs payable by the Landlord for the maintenance, repair, lighting, cleaning and renewal of all Service Media, structures and other items not on the Building but used or capable of being used by the Building in common with other land.

12.2   The Tenant shall comply with all reasonable regulations the Landlord may make from time to time in connection with the use of any of those Service Media, structures or other items.

13.   VAT

13.1   All sums payable by the Tenant are exclusive of any VAT that may be chargeable. The Tenant shall pay VAT in respect of all taxable supplies made to it in connection with this lease on the due date for making any payment or, if earlier, the date on which that supply is made for VAT purposes.

13.2   Every obligation on the Tenant, under or in connection with this lease, to pay the Landlord or any other person any sum by way of a refund or indemnity, shall include an obligation to pay an amount equal to any VAT incurred on that sum by the Landlord or other person, except to the extent that the Landlord or other person obtains credit for such VAT under the Value Added Tax Act 1994.

14.   DEFAULT INTEREST AND INTEREST

14.1   If any Annual Rent or any other money payable under this lease has not been paid by the date it is due, whether it has been formally demanded or not, the Tenant shall pay the Landlord interest at the Default Interest Rate (both before and after any judgment) on that amount for the period from the due date to and including the date of payment.

14.2   If the Landlord does not demand or accept any Annual Rent or other money due or tendered under this lease because the Landlord reasonably believes that the Tenant is in breach of any of the tenant covenants of this lease, then the Tenant shall, when that amount is accepted by the Landlord, also pay interest at the Interest Rate on that amount for the period from the date the amount (or each part of it) became due until the date it is accepted by the Landlord.

15. COSTS

15.1 The Tenant shall pay the costs and expenses of the Landlord including any solicitors' or other professionals' costs and expenses (incurred both during and after the end of the term) in connection with or in contemplation of any of the following:

(a) the enforcement of the tenant covenants of this lease;

(b) serving any notice in connection with this lease under section 146 or 147 of the Law of Property Act 1925 or taking any proceedings under either of those sections, notwithstanding that forfeiture is avoided otherwise than by relief granted by the court;

(c) serving any notice in connection with this lease under section 17 of the LTCA 1995;

(d) the preparation and service of a schedule of dilapidations in connection with this lease; or

(e) any consent or approval applied for under this lease, whether or not it is granted [(unless the consent or approval is unreasonably withheld by the Landlord in circumstances where the Landlord is not unreasonably to withhold it)].

15.2 Where the Tenant is obliged to pay or indemnify the Landlord against any solicitors' or other professionals' costs and expenses (whether under this or any other clause of this lease) that obligation extends to those costs and expenses assessed on a full indemnity basis.

16. [COMPENSATION ON VACATING

Any right of the Tenant or anyone deriving title under the Tenant to claim compensation from the Landlord on leaving the Property under the LTA 1954 is excluded, except to the extent that the legislation prevents that right being excluded.]

17. NO DEDUCTION, COUNTERCLAIM OR SET-OFF

The Annual Rent and all other money due under this lease are to be paid by the Tenant or any guarantor (as the case may be) without deduction, counterclaim or set-off.

18. REGISTRATION OF THIS LEASE

Promptly following the grant of this lease, the Tenant shall apply to register this lease at HM Land Registry. The Tenant shall ensure that any requisitions raised by HM Land Registry in connection with that application are dealt with promptly and properly. Within one month after completion of the registration, the Tenant shall send the Landlord official copies of its title.

19. PROHIBITION OF DEALINGS

Except as expressly permitted by this lease, the Tenant shall not assign, underlet, charge, part with or share possession or share occupation of this lease or the Property or hold the lease on trust for any person (except pending registration of a dealing permitted by this lease at HM Land Registry or by reason only of joint legal ownership).

20. ASSIGNMENTS

20.1 The Tenant shall not assign the whole of this lease without the consent of the Landlord, such consent not to be unreasonably withheld.

20.2 The Tenant shall not assign part only of this lease.

20.3 For the purposes of section 19(1A) of the LTA 1927, where at the date of assignment, either:

(a) [the assignee is an individual resident overseas or is a company not incorporated in the United Kingdom; or]

(b)   in the reasonable opinion of the Landlord, the proposed assignee, when assessed together with any proposed guarantor, is of a lower financial standing than the tenant and its guarantor (if any),

the Landlord and the Tenant agree that the Landlord may impose the condition in clause 20.4 upon assignment.

20.4   A condition that the assignor enters into an authorised guarantee agreement which:

(a)   is in respect of all the tenant covenants of this lease;

(b)   is in respect of the period beginning with the date the assignee becomes bound by those covenants and ending on the date when the assignee is released from those covenants by virtue of section 5 of the LTCA 1995;

(c)   imposes principal debtor liability on the assignor (and any former tenant);

(d)   requires (in the event of a disclaimer of liability of this lease) the assignor (or former tenant as the case may be) to enter into a new tenancy for a term equal to the unexpired residue of the Contractual Term; and

(e)   is otherwise in a form reasonably required by the Landlord.

20.5   The Landlord and the Tenant agree that [if reasonable] the Landlord may give its consent to any assignment subject to a condition that a person of standing acceptable to the Landlord enters into a guarantee and indemnity of the tenant covenants of this lease in the form set out in Schedule 1 (but with such amendments and additions as the Landlord may reasonably require).

20.6   For the purposes of section 19(1A) of the LTA 1927, if the Tenant wishes to assign this lease to any company that, at the date of assignment is a member of the same group (within the meaning of section 42 of the LTA 1954), the Landlord and the Tenant agree that the Landlord shall not be unreasonable in refusing its consent if in the reasonable opinion of the Landlord, the proposed assignee, when assessed together with any proposed guarantor, is of a lower financial standing than the tenant and its guarantor (if any).

20.7   Nothing in this clause shall prevent the Landlord from giving consent subject to any other reasonable condition, nor from refusing consent to an assignment in any other circumstance where it is reasonable to do so.

21. UNDERLETTINGS

21.1   The Tenant shall not underlet the whole of the Property except in accordance with this clause nor without the consent of the Landlord, such consent not to be unreasonably withheld.

21.2   The Tenant shall not underlet part only of the Property.

21.3   The Tenant shall not underlet the Property:

(a)   together with any property or any right over property that is not included within this lease; nor

(b)   at a fine or premium or reverse premium; nor

(c)   allowing any rent free period to the undertenant that exceeds the period as is then usual in the open market in respect of such a letting.

21.4   The Tenant shall not underlet the Property unless, before the underlease is granted, the Tenant has given the Landlord:

(a)   a certified copy of the notice served on the undertenant, as required by section 38A(3)(a) of the LTA 1954, applying to the tenancy to be created by the underlease; and

(b)   a certified copy of the declaration or statutory declaration made by the undertenant in accordance with the requirements of section 38A(3)(b) of the LTA 1954.

21.5   Any underletting by the Tenant shall be by deed and shall include:

(a)   an agreement between the Tenant and the undertenant that the provisions of sections 24 to 28 of the LTA 1954 are excluded from applying to the tenancy created by the underlease;

(b)   the reservation of a rent which is not less than the open market rental value of the Property at the date the Property is underlet and which is payable at the same times as the Annual Rent under this lease [(but this shall not prevent an underlease providing for a rent-free period of a length permitted by clause 21.3(c)];

(c)   provisions for the review of rent at the same dates and on the same basis as the review of rent in this lease, unless the term of the underlease does not extend beyond the next Review Date;

(d)   a covenant by the undertenant, enforceable by and expressed to be enforceable by the Landlord (as superior landlord at the date of grant) and its successors in title in their own right, to observe and perform the tenant covenants in the underlease and any document that is supplemental or collateral to it; and

(e)   provisions requiring the consent of the Landlord to be obtained in respect of any matter for which the consent of the Landlord is required under this lease,

and shall otherwise not conflict with the terms of this lease and shall be in a form approved by the Landlord [such approval to be given, or refused with reasons, in writing within [ ] days of receipt by the Landlord of the final draft of the underlease and] such approval not to be unreasonably withheld.

21.6   In relation to any underlease granted by the Tenant, the Tenant shall:

(a)   not vary the terms of the underlease nor accept a surrender of the underlease without the consent of the Landlord, such consent not to be unreasonably withheld;

(b)   enforce the tenant covenants in the underlease and not waive any of them; and

(c)   ensure that in relation to any rent review the revised rent is not agreed without the approval of the Landlord, such approval not to be unreasonably withheld.

22. SHARING OCCUPATION

The Tenant may share occupation of the Property with any company that is a member of the same group (within the meaning of section 42 of the LTA 1954) as the Tenant for as long as that company remains within that group and provided that no relationship of landlord and tenant is established by that arrangement.

23. CHARGING

23.1   The Tenant shall not charge the whole of this lease without the consent of the Landlord, such consent not to be unreasonably withheld.

23.2   The Tenant shall not charge part only of this lease.

24. REGISTRATION AND NOTIFICATION OF DEALINGS AND OCCUPATION

24.1   In this clause a **Transaction** is:

(a)   any dealing with this lease or the devolution or transmission of, or parting with possession of any interest in it; or

(b)   the creation of any underlease or other interest out of this lease, or out of any interest, underlease derived from it, and any dealing, devolution or transmission of, or parting with possession of any such interest or underlease; or

(c)   the making of any other arrangement for the occupation of the Property.

24.2   In respect of every Transaction that is registrable at HM Land Registry, the Tenant shall promptly following completion of the Transaction apply to register it (or procure that the relevant person so applies). The Tenant shall (or shall procure that) any requisitions raised by

HM Land Registry in connection with an application to register a Transaction are dealt with promptly and properly. Within [one month] of completion of the registration, the Tenant shall send the Landlord official copies of its title (and where applicable of the undertenant's title).

24.3   No later than one month after a Transaction the Tenant shall:

(a)   give the Landlord's solicitors notice of the Transaction; [and]

(b)   deliver two certified copies of any document effecting the Transaction to the Landlord's solicitors[; and

(c)   pay the Landlord's solicitors a registration fee of £30 (plus VAT)].

(d)   [deliver to the Landlord's solicitors a copy of any Energy Performance Certificate and Recommendation Report issued as a result of the Transaction.]

24.4   If the Landlord so requests, the Tenant shall promptly supply the Landlord with full details of the occupiers of the Property and the terms upon which they occupy it.

25.   CLOSURE OF THE REGISTERED TITLE OF THIS LEASE

[Within one month] [Immediately] after the end of the term (and notwithstanding that the term has ended), the Tenant shall make an application to close the registered title of this lease and shall ensure that any requisitions raised by HM Land Registry in connection with that application are dealt with promptly and properly; the Tenant shall keep the Landlord informed of the progress and completion of its application.

26.   REPAIRS

26.1   The Tenant shall keep the Property clean and tidy and in good repair [and condition] [except that the Tenant shall not be required to put the Property into any better state of repair or condition than it was in at the date of this lease as evidenced by the schedule of condition initialled by the parties to this lease and annexed to this lease].

26.2   The Tenant shall not be liable to repair the Property to the extent that any disrepair has been caused by an Insured Risk, unless and to the extent that:

(a)   the Landlord's insurance has been vitiated or any insurance proceeds withheld in consequence of any act or omission of the Tenant, any person deriving title under the Tenant or any person at the Property or on the Common Parts with the actual or implied authority of the Tenant or any person deriving title under the Tenant; or

(b)   the insurance cover in relation to that disrepair is excluded, limited or unavailable.

27.   DECORATION

27.1   The Tenant shall decorate the Property as often as is reasonably necessary and also in the last three months before the end of the term.

27.2   All decoration shall be carried out in a good and proper manner using good quality materials that are appropriate to the Property and the Permitted Use and shall include all appropriate preparatory work.

27.3   All decoration carried out in the last three months of the term shall also be carried out to the satisfaction of the Landlord and using materials, designs and colours approved by the Landlord.

27.4   [The Tenant shall replace the floor coverings at the Property within the three months before the end of the term with new ones of good quality and appropriate to the Property and the Permitted Use.]

28. ALTERATIONS AND SIGNS

28.1 The Tenant shall not make any alteration to the Property without the consent of the Landlord, such consent not to be unreasonably withheld, other than as mentioned in clause 28.2.

28.2 Subject to clause 28.3, the Tenant may make non-structural alterations without the consent of the Landlord provided that the Tenant shall:

(a) make good any damage to the Property and to any part of the Common Parts; and

(b) immediately after completion of such alterations give to the Landlord copies of the plans and specifications for the alterations.

28.3 The Tenant shall not install nor alter the route of any Service Media at the Property, nor do anything that may affect the Service Media, without the consent of the Landlord, such consent not to be unreasonably withheld.

28.4 The Tenant shall not attach any sign, fascia, placard, board, poster or advertisement to the Property so as to be seen from the outside of the Building.

28.5 Where the consent of the Landlord is required under this clause, the Landlord shall determine the Tenant's application for consent within [15] working days of receiving all the information that the Landlord [reasonably] considers necessary to allow the Landlord to determine the application.

28.6 [The Tenant shall not carry out any alteration to the Property which would[, or may reasonably be expected to,] have an adverse effect on the asset rating in any Energy Performance Certificate commissioned in respect of the Property.]

29. RETURNING THE PROPERTY TO THE LANDLORD

29.1 At the end of the term the Tenant shall return the Property to the Landlord in the repair and condition required by this lease.

29.2 If the Landlord reasonably so requires and gives the Tenant notice no later than six months before the end of the term, the Tenant shall remove items it has fixed to the Property, remove any alterations it has made to the Property and make good any damage caused to the Property by that removal.

29.3 At the end of the term, the Tenant shall remove from the Property all chattels belonging to or used by it.

29.4 The Tenant irrevocably appoints the Landlord to be the Tenant's agent to store or dispose of any chattels or items it has fixed to the Property and which have been left by the Tenant on the Property for more than ten working days after the end of the term. The Landlord shall not be liable to the Tenant by reason of that storage or disposal. The Tenant shall indemnify the Landlord in respect of any claim made by a third party in relation to that storage or disposal.

29.5 If the Tenant does not comply with its obligations in this clause, then, without prejudice to any other right or remedy of the Landlord, the Tenant shall pay the Landlord an amount equal to the Annual Rent at the rate reserved immediately before the end of the term for the period that it would reasonably take to put the Property into the condition it would have been in had the Tenant performed its obligations under this clause. The amount shall be a debt due on demand from the Tenant to the Landlord.

30. USE

30.1 The Tenant shall not use the Property for any purpose other than the Permitted Use.

30.2 [The Tenant shall not use the Property outside the Permitted Hours [without the approval of the Landlord].]

30.3 [If the Landlord gives its approval to the Tenant using the Property outside the Permitted Hours, the Tenant shall observe all [reasonable and proper] regulations that the Landlord makes relating to that use and shall pay the Landlord all costs incurred by the Landlord in connection with that use, including the whole of the cost of any Services provided by the Landlord attributable to the use by the Tenant of the Property outside the Permitted Hours.]

30.4 The Tenant shall not use the Property for any illegal purpose nor for any purpose or in a manner that would cause loss, damage, injury, nuisance or inconvenience to the Landlord, the other tenants or occupiers of the Lettable Units or any owner or occupier of neighbouring property.

30.5 The Tenant shall not overload any structural part of the Building nor any Service Media at or serving the Property.

31.   MANAGEMENT OF THE BUILDING

31.1 The Tenant shall observe all [reasonable and proper] regulations made by the Landlord from time to time in accordance with the principles of good estate management and notified to the Tenant relating to:

(a)   the use of the Common Parts;

(b)   the management of the Building; and

(c)   the use of any Service Media, structures or other items outside the Building which are used or capable of being used by the Building in common with other land.

31.2 Nothing in this lease shall impose or be deemed to impose any restriction on the use of any other Lettable Unit or any neighbouring property.

32.   COMPLIANCE WITH LAWS

32.1 The Tenant shall comply with all laws relating to:

(a)   the Property and the occupation and use of the Property by the Tenant;

(b)   the use of all Service Media and machinery and equipment at or serving the Property;

(c)   any works carried out at the Property; and

(d)   all materials kept at or disposed from the Property.

32.2 Without prejudice to any obligation on the Tenant to obtain any consent or approval under this lease, the Tenant shall carry out all works that are required under any law to be carried out at the Property whether by the owner or the occupier.

32.3 Within five working days after receipt of any notice or other communication affecting the Property or the Building (and whether or not served pursuant to any law) the Tenant shall:

(a)   send a copy of the relevant document to the Landlord; and

(b)   in so far as it relates to the Property, take all steps necessary to comply with the notice or other communication and take any other action in connection with it as the Landlord may require.

32.4 The Tenant shall not apply for any planning permission for the Property.

32.5 The Tenant shall comply with its obligations under the CDM Regulations including all requirements in relation to the provision and maintenance of a health and safety file.

32.6 The Tenant shall supply all information to the Landlord that the Landlord reasonably requires from time to time to comply with the Landlord's obligations under the CDM Regulations.

32.7 As soon as the Tenant becomes aware of any defect in the Property, it shall give the Landlord notice of it. The Tenant shall indemnify the Landlord against any liability under the Defective Premises Act 1972 in relation to the Property by reason of any failure of the Tenant to comply with any of the tenant covenants in this lease.

32.8   The Tenant shall keep the Property equipped with all fire prevention, detection and fighting machinery and equipment and fire alarms which are required under all relevant laws or required by the insurers of the Property or reasonably recommended by them or reasonably required by the Landlord and shall keep that machinery, equipment and alarms properly maintained and available for inspection.

33.   [ENERGY PERFORMANCE CERTIFICATES

33.1   [The Tenant shall:

(n)   cooperate with the Landlord so far as is reasonably necessary to allow the Landlord to obtain an Energy Performance Certificate and Recommendation Report for the Property or the Building [including providing the Landlord with copies of any plans or other information held by the Tenant that would assist in obtaining an Energy Performance Certificate]; and

(o)   allow such access to any Energy Assessor appointed by the Landlord as is reasonably necessary to inspect the Property for the purposes of preparing an Energy Performance Certificate and/or Recommendation Report for the Property or the Building.]

33.2   [The Tenant shall not commission an Energy Performance Certificate for the Property [without the Landlord's consent [such consent not to be unreasonably withheld]].]

33.3   [At the written request of the Tenant, the Landlord shall provide the Tenant with a copy of any Energy Performance Certificate relating to the Property held by the Landlord, provided that the Tenant shall pay [the sum of [AMOUNT] **OR** the reasonable cost of providing the copy **OR** [OTHER]] to the Landlord.]]

34.   ENCROACHMENTS, OBSTRUCTIONS AND ACQUISITION OF RIGHTS

34.1   The Tenant shall not grant any right or licence over the Property to any person nor permit any person to make any encroachment over the Property.

34.2   The Tenant shall not obstruct the flow of light or air to the Property.

34.3   The Tenant shall not make any acknowledgement that the flow of light or air to the Property or any other part of the Building or that the means of access to the Building is enjoyed with the consent of any third party.

34.4   The Tenant shall immediately notify the Landlord if any person takes or threatens to take any action to obstruct the flow of light or air to the Property.

35.   BREACH OF REPAIR AND MAINTENANCE OBLIGATIONS

35.1   The Landlord may enter the Property to inspect its condition and state of repair and may give the Tenant notice of any breach of any of the tenant covenants in this lease relating to the condition or repair of the Property.

35.2   If the Tenant has not begun any works needed to remedy that breach within two months following that notice (or if works are required as a matter of emergency, then immediately) or if the Tenant is not carrying out the works with all due speed, then the Landlord may enter the Property and carry out the works needed.

35.3   The costs incurred by the Landlord in carrying out any works pursuant to this clause (and any professional fees and any VAT in respect of those costs) shall be a debt due from the Tenant to the Landlord and payable on demand.

35.4   Any action taken by the Landlord pursuant to this clause shall be without prejudice to the Landlord's other rights.

35.5   Not less than six months before the end of the term, the Landlord shall serve a schedule of dilapidations on the Tenant and shall notify the Tenant of any other dilapidations that occur after the schedule of dilapidations has been served as soon as possible.

36.   [INDEMNITY

The Tenant shall keep the Landlord indemnified against all expenses, costs, claims, damage and loss (including any diminution in the value of the Landlord's interest in the Building and loss of amenity of the Building) arising from any breach of any tenant covenants in this lease, or any act or omission of the Tenant, any undertenant or their respective workers, contractors or agents or any other person on the Property or the Common Parts with the actual or implied authority of any of them.]

37.   LANDLORD'S COVENANT FOR QUIET ENJOYMENT

The Landlord covenants with the Tenant, that, so long as the Tenant pays the rents reserved by and complies with its obligations in this lease, the Tenant shall have quiet enjoyment of the Property without any lawful interruption by the Landlord or any person claiming under the Landlord.

38.   GUARANTEE AND INDEMNITY

38.1   [The provisions of Schedule 1 apply.]

38.2   [If an Act of Insolvency occurs in relation to a guarantor, or if any guarantor (being an individual) dies or becomes incapable of managing his affairs the Tenant shall, if the Landlord requests, procure that a person of standing acceptable to the Landlord, within [ ] days of that request, enters into a replacement or additional guarantee and indemnity of the tenant covenants of this lease in the same form as that entered into by the former guarantor.]

38.3   [Clause 38.2 shall not apply in the case of a person who is guarantor by reason of having entered into an authorised guarantee agreement.]

38.4   For so long as any guarantor remains liable to the Landlord, the Tenant shall, if the Landlord requests, procure that the guarantor joins in any consent or approval required under this lease and consents to any variation of the tenant covenants of this lease.

39.   RE-ENTRY AND FORFEITURE

39.1   The Landlord may re-enter the Property (or any part of the Property in the name of the whole) at any time after any of the following occurs:

(a)   any rent is unpaid 21 days after becoming payable whether it has been formally demanded or not; or

(b)   any breach of any condition of, or tenant covenant, in this lease; or

(c)   an Act of Insolvency.

39.2   If the Landlord re-enters the Property (or any part of the Property in the name of the whole) pursuant to this clause, this lease shall immediately end, but without prejudice to any right or remedy of the Landlord in respect of any breach of covenant by the Tenant [or any guarantor].

40.   LIABILITY

40.1   At any time when the Landlord, the Tenant or a guarantor is more than one person, then in each case those persons shall be jointly and severally liable for their respective obligations arising under this lease. The Landlord may take action against, or release or compromise the liability of, any one of those persons or grant time or other indulgence to any one of them without affecting the liability of any other of them.

40.2   The obligations of the Tenant and any guarantor arising by virtue of this lease are owed to the Landlord and the obligations of the Landlord are owed to the Tenant.

40.3 The Landlord shall not be liable to the Tenant for any failure of the Landlord to perform any landlord covenant in this lease [unless and until the Tenant has given the Landlord notice of the failure and the Landlord has not remedied the failure within a reasonable time of service of that notice **OR** unless the Landlord knows it has failed to perform the covenant, or reasonably should know this, and has not remedied that failure within a reasonable time].

41. ENTIRE AGREEMENT AND EXCLUSION OF REPRESENTATIONS

41.1 This lease constitutes the whole agreement between the parties relating to the transaction contemplated by the grant of this lease and supersedes all previous agreements between the parties relating to the transaction.

41.2 [The Tenant acknowledges that in entering into this lease it has not relied on] [The Tenant and the Guarantor acknowledge that in entering into this lease neither has relied on], and shall have no right or remedy in respect of, any statement or representation made by or on behalf of the Landlord.

41.3 Nothing in this lease constitutes or shall constitute a representation or warranty that the Property or the Common Parts may lawfully be used for any purpose allowed by this lease.

41.4 Nothing in this clause shall limit or exclude any liability for fraud.

42. NOTICES, CONSENTS AND APPROVALS

42.1 Except where this lease specifically states that a notice need not be in writing, or where notice is given in an emergency, any notice given pursuant to this lease shall:

(a) be in writing in the English language; and

(b) be:
  (i) delivered personally; or
  (ii) delivered by commercial courier; or
  (iii) sent by fax; or
  (iv) sent by pre-paid first-class post or recorded delivery; or
  (v) (if the notice is to be served by post outside the country from which it is sent) sent by airmail requiring signature on delivery.

42.2 A notice is deemed to have been received:

(a) if delivered personally, at the time of delivery; or

(b) if delivered by commercial courier, at the time of signature of the courier's receipt; or

(c) if sent by fax, at the time of transmission; or

(d) if sent by pre-paid first-class post or recorded delivery, 48 hours from the date of posting; or

(e) if sent by airmail, five days from the date of posting;

(f) if deemed receipt under the previous paragraphs of this clause is not within business hours (meaning 9.00 am to 5.30 pm on a working day in the place of receipt), when business next starts in the place of receipt.

42.3 To prove service, it is sufficient to prove that the notice:

(a) if sent by fax, was transmitted by fax to the fax number of the party; or

(b) if sent by post, that the envelope containing the notice was properly addressed and posted.

42.4 Section 196 of the Law of Property Act 1925 shall otherwise apply to notices given under this lease.

42.5 Where the consent of the Landlord is required under this lease, a consent shall only be valid if it is given by deed, unless:

(a)   it is given in writing and signed by a person duly authorised on behalf or the Landlord; and

(b)   it expressly states that the Landlord waives the requirement for a deed in that particular case.

If a waiver is given, it shall not affect the requirement for a deed for any other consent.

42.6   Where the approval of the Landlord is required under this lease, an approval shall only be valid if it is in writing and signed by or on behalf of the Landlord, unless:

(a)   the approval is being given in a case of emergency; or

(b)   this lease expressly states that the approval need not be in writing.

42.7   If the Landlord gives a consent or approval under this lease, the giving of that consent or approval shall not imply that any consent or approval required from a third party has been obtained, nor shall it obviate the need to obtain any consent or approval from a third party.

43.   GOVERNING LAW AND JURISDICTION

43.1   This lease and any dispute or claim arising out of or in connection with it or its subject matter or formation (including non-contractual disputes or claims) shall be governed by and construed in accordance with the law of England and Wales.

43.2   The parties irrevocably agree that the courts of England and Wales shall have [exclusive **OR** non-exclusive] jurisdiction to settle any dispute or claim that arises out of or in connection with this lease or its subject matter or formation (including non-contractual disputes or claims).

44.   EXCLUSION OF LTA 1954 PROTECTION

44.1   The parties confirm that:

(a)   the Landlord served a notice on the Tenant, as required by section 38A(3)(a) of the LTA 1954 , applying to the tenancy created by this lease, [not less than 14 days] before [this lease] [DETAILS OF AGREEMENT FOR LEASE] was entered into [a certified copy of which notice is annexed to this lease];

(b)   [the Tenant] [[NAME OF DECLARANT] who was duly authorised by the Tenant to do so] made a [statutory] declaration dated [DATE] in accordance with the requirements of section 38A(3)(b) of the LTA 1954 [a certified copy of which [statutory] declaration is annexed to this lease]; and

(c)   [there is no agreement for lease to which this lease gives effect.]

44.2   The parties agree that the provisions of sections 24 to 28 of the 1954 Act are excluded in relation to the tenancy created by this lease.

44.3   The parties confirm that:

(a)   the Landlord served a notice on the Guarantor, as required by section 38A(3)(a) of the LTA 1954, applying to the tenancy to be entered into by the Guarantor pursuant to paragraph 4 of the Schedule, [not less than 14 days] before [this lease] [DETAILS OF AGREEMENT FOR LEASE] was entered into (a certified copy of which notice is annexed to this lease); and

(b)   [the Guarantor] [[NAME OF DECLARANT], who was duly authorised by the Guarantor to do so], made a [statutory] declaration dated [DATE] in accordance with the requirements of section 38A(3)(b) of the LTA 1954 (a certified copy of which [statutory] declaration is annexed to this lease).

45. [TENANT'S BREAK CLAUSE

45.1 The Tenant may terminate this lease by serving a Break Notice [at any time on or after [EARLIEST DATE]] on the Landlord.

45.2 A Break Notice served by the Tenant shall be of no effect if, at the Break Date:

(a) the Tenant has not paid [in cleared funds] any part of the Annual Rent, or any VAT in respect of it, which was due to have been paid; or

(b) the Tenant remains in occupation of any part of the Property; or

(c) there are any continuing subleases of the Property.

45.3 Subject to clause 45.2, following service of a Break Notice this lease shall terminate on the Break Date.

45.4 Termination of this lease on the Break Date shall not affect any other right or remedy that either party may have in relation to any earlier breach of this lease.

45.5 If this lease terminates in accordance with clause 45.3 then, [within 14 days after] [on] the Break Date, the Landlord shall refund to the Tenant the proportion of the Annual Rent, and any VAT paid in respect of it, for the period from and excluding the Break Date up to and excluding the next Rent Payment Date, calculated on a daily basis.]

46. CONTRACTS (RIGHTS OF THIRD PARTIES) ACT 1999

A person who is not a party to this lease shall not have any rights under or in connection with it by virtue of the Contracts (Rights of Third Parties) Act 1999 [but this does not affect any right or remedy of a third party which exists, or is available, apart from that Act].

47. NEW TENANCY UNDER LTCA 1995

This lease creates a new tenancy for the purposes of the LTCA 1995.

This document has been executed as a deed and is delivered and takes effect on the date stated at the beginning of it.

SCHEDULE 1
GUARANTEE AND INDEMNITY

1. GUARANTEE AND INDEMNITY

1.1 The Guarantor guarantees to the Landlord that the Tenant shall:

(a) pay the rents reserved by this lease and observe and perform the tenant covenants of this lease and that if the Tenant fails to pay any of those rents or to observe or perform any of those tenant covenants, the Guarantor shall pay or observe and perform them; and

(b) observe and perform any obligations the Tenant enters into in an authorised guarantee agreement made in respect of this lease (the **Authorised Guarantee Agreement**) and that if the Tenant fails to do so, the Guarantor shall observe and perform those obligations.

1.2 The Guarantor covenants with the Landlord as a separate and independent primary obligation to indemnify the Landlord against any failure by the Tenant:

(a) to pay any of the rents reserved by this lease or any failure to observe or perform any of the tenant covenants of this lease; and

(b) to observe or perform any of the obligations the Tenant enters into in the Authorised Guarantee Agreement.

2. GUARANTOR'S LIABILITY

2.1   The liability of the Guarantor under paragraph 1.1(a) and paragraph 1.2(a) shall continue until the end of the term, or until the Tenant is released from the tenant covenants of this lease by virtue of the LTCA 1995, if earlier.

2.2   The liability of the Guarantor shall not be affected by:

(a)   any time or indulgence granted by the Landlord to the Tenant; or

(b)   any delay or forbearance by the Landlord in enforcing the payment of any of the rents or the observance or performance of any of the tenant covenants of this lease (or the Tenant's obligations under the Authorised Guarantee Agreement) or in making any demand in respect of any of them; or

(c)   any refusal by the Landlord to accept any rent or other payment due under this lease where the Landlord believes that the acceptance of such rent or payment may prejudice its ability to re-enter the Property; or

(d)   the Landlord exercising any right or remedy against the Tenant for any failure to pay the rents reserved by this lease or to observe or perform the tenant covenants of this lease (or the Tenant's obligations under the Authorised Guarantee Agreement); or

(e)   the Landlord taking any action or refraining from taking any action in connection with any other security held by the Landlord in respect of the Tenant's liability to pay the rents reserved by this lease or observe and perform the tenant covenants of the lease (or the Tenant's obligations under the Authorised Guarantee Agreement) including the release of any such security; or

(f)   [a release or compromise of the liability of any one of the persons who is the Guarantor, or the grant of any time or concession to any one of them; or]

(g)   any legal limitation or disability on the Tenant or any invalidity or irregularity of any of the tenant covenants of the lease (or the Tenant's obligations under the Authorised Guarantee Agreement) or any unenforceability of any of them against the Tenant; or

(h)   the Tenant being dissolved, or being struck off the register of companies or otherwise ceasing to exist, or, if the Tenant is an individual, by the Tenant dying or becoming incapable of managing its affairs; or

(i)   without prejudice to paragraph 4, the disclaimer of the Tenant's liability under this lease or the forfeiture of this lease; or

(j)   the surrender of part of the Property, except that the Guarantor shall not be under any liability in relation to the surrendered part in respect of any period after the surrender; or

(k)   by any other act or omission except an express [written] release [by deed] of the Guarantor by the Landlord

2.3   [The liability of each of the persons making up the Guarantor is joint and several.]

2.4   Any sum payable by the Guarantor shall be paid without any deduction, set-off or counter-claim against the Landlord or the Tenant.

3. VARIATIONS AND SUPPLEMENTAL DOCUMENTS

3.1   The Guarantor shall, at the request of the Landlord, join in and give its consent to the terms of any consent, approval, variation or other document that may be entered into by the Tenant in connection with this lease (or the Authorised Guarantee Agreement).

3.2   The Guarantor shall not be released by any variation of the rents reserved by, or the tenant covenants in, this Lease (or the Tenant's obligations under the Authorised Guarantee Agreement) whether or not:

(a)   the variation is material or prejudicial to the Guarantor; or

(b)   the variation is made in any document; or

(c)   the Guarantor has consented, in writing or otherwise, to the variation.

3.3   The liability of the Guarantor shall apply to the rents reserved by and the tenant covenants in this lease (and the Tenant's obligations under the Authorised Guarantee Agreement) as varied except to the extent that the liability of the Guarantor is affected by section 18 of the LTCA 1995.

4.   GUARANTOR TO TAKE A NEW LEASE OR MAKE PAYMENT

4.1   If this lease is forfeited or the liability of the Tenant under this lease is disclaimed and the Landlord gives the Guarantor notice not later than [six] months after the forfeiture or the Landlord having received notice of the disclaimer, the Guarantor shall enter into a new lease of the Property on the terms set out in paragraph 4.2.

4.2   The rights and obligations under the new lease shall take effect from the date of the forfeiture or disclaimer and the new lease shall:

(a)   be granted subject to the right of any person to have this lease vested in them by the court and to the terms on which any such order may be made and subject to the rights of any third party existing at the date of the grant;

(b)   be for a term that expires at the same date as the end of the Contractual Term of this lease had there been no forfeiture or disclaimer;

(c)   reserve as an initial annual rent an amount equal to the Annual Rent payable under this lease at the date of the forfeiture or disclaimer or which would be payable but for any abatement or suspension of the Annual Rent or restriction on the right to collect it and which is subject to review on the same terms and dates provided by this lease (subject to paragraph 5); [and]

(d)   be excluded from sections 24 to 28 of the LTA 1954; and

(e)   otherwise be on the same terms as this lease (as varied if there has been any variation).

4.3   The Guarantor shall pay the Landlord's solicitors' costs and disbursements (on a full indemnity basis) and any VAT in respect of them in relation to the new lease and shall execute and deliver to the Landlord a counterpart of the new lease within one month after service of the Landlord's notice.

4.4   The grant of a new lease and its acceptance by the Guarantor shall be without prejudice to any other rights which the Landlord may have against the Guarantor or against any other person or in respect of any other security that the Landlord may have in connection with this lease.

4.5   The Landlord may, instead of giving the Guarantor notice pursuant to paragraph 4.1 but in the same circumstances and within the same time limit, require the Guarantor to pay an amount equal to [six] months Annual Rent and the Guarantor shall pay that amount on demand.

5.   RENT AT THE DATE OF FORFEITURE OR DISCLAIMER

5.1   If at the date of the forfeiture or disclaimer there is a rent review pending under this lease, then the initial annual rent to be reserved by the new lease shall be subject to review on the date on which the term of the new lease commences on the same terms as those that apply to a review of the Annual Rent under this lease, such review date to be included in the new lease.

5.2   If paragraph 5.1 applies, then the review for which it provides shall be in addition to any rent reviews that are required under paragraph 4.2(c).

6.   PAYMENTS IN GROSS AND RESTRICTIONS ON THE GUARANTOR

6.1   Any payment or dividend that the Landlord receives from the Tenant (or its estate) or any other person in connection with any insolvency proceedings or arrangement involving the Tenant shall be taken and applied as a payment in gross and shall not prejudice the right of the

Landlord to recover from the Guarantor to the full extent of the obligations that are the subject of this guarantee and indemnity.

6.2   The Guarantor shall not claim in competition with the Landlord in any insolvency proceedings or arrangement of the Tenant in respect of any payment made by the Guarantor pursuant to this guarantee and indemnity. If it otherwise receives any money in such proceedings or arrangement, it shall hold that money on trust for the Landlord to the extent of its liability to the Landlord.

6.3   The Guarantor shall not, without the consent of the Landlord, exercise any right or remedy that it may have (whether against the Tenant or any other person) in respect of any amount paid or other obligation performed by the Guarantor under this guarantee and indemnity unless and until all the obligations of the Guarantor under this guarantee and indemnity have been fully performed.

7.   OTHER SECURITIES

7.1   The Guarantor warrants that it has not taken and covenants that it shall not take any security from or over the assets of the Tenant in respect of any liability of the Tenant to the Guarantor. If it does take or hold any such security it shall hold it for the benefit of the Landlord.

7.2   This guarantee and indemnity is in addition to any other security that the Landlord may at any time hold from the Guarantor or the Tenant or any other person in respect of the liability of the Tenant to pay the rents reserved by this lease and to observe and perform the tenant covenants of this lease. It shall not merge in or be affected by any other security.

7.3   The Guarantor shall not be entitled to claim or participate in any other security held by the Landlord in respect of the liability of the Tenant to pay the rents reserved by this lease or to observe and perform the tenant covenants of this lease.

SCHEDULE 2
BREAK NOTICE

[INSERT FORM OF BREAK NOTICE]

SCHEDULE 3
SERVICES, SERVICE COSTS AND EXCLUDED COSTS

1.   SERVICES

The **Services** are:

(a)   cleaning, maintaining, decorating and repairing the Common Parts, including the structural parts, the outsides of the windows and all Service Media forming part of the Common Parts, and remedying any inherent defect;

(b)   providing heating to the internal areas of the Common Parts [and the Lettable Units] during such periods of the year as the Landlord reasonably considers appropriate, and cleaning, maintaining, repairing and replacing the heating machinery and equipment;

(c)   lighting the Common Parts and cleaning, maintaining, repairing and replacing lighting machinery and equipment on the Common Parts;

(d)   supplying hot and cold water, soap, paper, towels and other supplies for any lavatories, washrooms, kitchens and utility areas on the Common Parts, and cleaning, maintaining, repairing and replacing the furniture, fittings and equipment in those areas;

(e)   keeping the lifts on the Common Parts in reasonable working order and cleaning, maintaining, repairing and replacing the lifts and lift machinery and equipment;

(f)   cleaning, maintaining, repairing and replacing refuse bins on the Common Parts;

(g) cleaning, maintaining, repairing and replacing signage for the Common Parts;

(h) cleaning, maintaining, repairing, operating and replacing security machinery and equipment (including closed circuit television) on the Common Parts;

(i) cleaning, maintaining, repairing, operating and replacing fire prevention, detection and fighting machinery and equipment and fire alarms on the Common Parts;

(j) cleaning, maintaining, repairing and replacing a signboard showing the names and logos of the tenants and other occupiers [in the entrance hall of the Building];

(k) maintaining the landscaped and grassed areas of the Common Parts;

(l) cleaning, maintaining, repairing and replacing the floor coverings on the internal areas of the Common Parts;

(m) cleaning, maintaining, repairing and replacing the furniture and fittings on the Common Parts;

(n) [providing air conditioning for the internal areas of the [Common Parts] [Building] and cleaning, maintaining, repairing and replacing air conditioning equipment serving the [Common Parts][Building];

(o) [providing [security] [reception] [cleaning and maintenance] staff for the Building;]

(p) [ANY OTHER SPECIFIC SERVICES REQUIRED]; and

(q) any other service or amenity that the Landlord may in its reasonable discretion (acting in accordance with the principles of good estate management) provide for the benefit of the tenants and occupiers of the Building.

2. SERVICE COSTS

The **Service Costs** (excepting the Excluded Costs) are the total of:

(a) all of the reasonable and properly incurred costs of:

    (i) providing the Services;

    (ii) the supply and removal of electricity, gas, water, sewage and other utilities to and from the [Common Parts][Building];

    (iii) complying with the recommendations and requirements of the insurers of the Building (insofar as those recommendations and requirements relate to the Common Parts);

    (iv) complying with all laws relating to the Common Parts, their use and any works carried out to them, relating to the use of all Service Media, machinery and equipment at or serving the Common Parts and relating to any materials kept at or disposed of from the Common Parts;

    (v) complying with the Third Party Rights insofar as they relate to the Common Parts;

    (vi) taking any steps (including proceedings) that the Landlord considers necessary to prevent or remove any encroachment over the Common Parts or to prevent the acquisition of any right over the Common Parts (or Building as a whole) or to remove any obstruction to the flow of light or air to the Common Parts (or the Building as a whole); and

    (vii) borrowing to fund major expenditure on any Service which is infrequent or of an unusual nature[.] [; and]

    (viii) [producing, and providing copies of, any Energy Performance Certificate and/or Recommendation Report commissioned by the Landlord in respect of the Building [provided that the cost of producing any Energy Performance Certificate and/or Recommendation Report shall not be included in the Service Costs more than once every three years].]

(b) the Management Fee and all of the reasonable and properly incurred costs, fees and disbursements of:

(i)   the accountants employed by the Landlord to prepare, audit and certify the service charge accounts; and

(ii)   a procurement specialist who is employed or retained to achieve greater value for money and cost effectiveness in relation to the Service Costs.

(c)   all costs incurred in relation to [security][reception][cleaning and maintenance] staff for the Building as follows:

(i)   salaries (and all appropriate benefits);

(ii)   employers' costs (including NIC and tax, costs of compliance with statutory requirements, pension, welfare, training and insurance contributions);

(iii) uniforms; and

(iv)   all equipment and supplies needed for the proper performance of their duties.

(d)   all rates, taxes and impositions payable in respect of the Common Parts, their use and any works carried out on them (other than any taxes payable by the Landlord in connection with any dealing with or disposition of its reversionary interest in the Building);

(e)   the reasonable and proper cost of complying with any of the Landlord's obligations contained in clause 8;

(f)   any VAT payable in respect of any of the items mentioned above except to the extent that the Landlord obtains credit for such VAT under the Value Added Tax Act 1994.

3. EXCLUDED COSTS

The **Excluded Costs** are any costs which relate to or arise from:

(a)   matters between the Landlord and an occupier in the Building, including, but not limited to, costs relating to or arising from:

(i)   enforcement of covenants to pay rent and other monies payable under the occupier's lease;

(ii)   the letting of any Lettable Unit;

(iii) any consents required under the relevant lease, including but not limited to consents to assign, sublet, alterations and extended opening hours; and

(iv)   rent reviews;

(b)   failure or negligence of the Landlord or Manager;

(c)   any Lettable Unit which is unlet;

(d)   any shortfall in the costs of providing any of the Services to a Lettable Unit for which the Landlord has agreed a special concession (not being a properly constituted weighting formula);

(e)   the maintenance or operation of:

(i)   any premises within the Building used by the Landlord for its own purposes (except where such use is wholly or partly in connection with the management of the Building itself, in which case the whole or a reasonable part, as the case may be, of such costs shall be a Service Cost);

(ii)   any cost centre within the Building that generates income for the Landlord (except where such income is credited to the Service Charge Account, in which case the whole of such costs shall be a Service Cost);

(iii) the initial provision of any items that are reasonably to be considered part of the original design and construction of the fabric, plan or equipment of the Building together with the initial setting up that is reasonably to be considered part of the original development of the Building;

(iv)   any future development of the Building;

(v)   the replacement of any item of the fabric, plant, equipment or materials necessary for the operation of the Building, except where it is beyond economic repair at the time of such replacement or except where the expenditure is necessary for the purposes of good estate management and following the analysis of reasonable options and alternatives (in which case the Landlord shall upon request provide to the Tenant evidence justifying such cost);

(vi)   the improvement of any item (where the cost exceeds the costs of normal maintenance, repair or replacement) except where the expenditure can be justified for the purposes of good estate management and following the analysis of reasonable options and alternatives (in which case the Landlord shall upon request provide to the Tenant evidence justifying such cost); and

(vii)   any service provided by reason of damage to or destruction of the Common Parts by a risk against which the Landlord is obliged to insure.

Executed as a deed by [NAME OF LANDLORD]
acting by [NAME OF FIRST DIRECTOR], a director
and [NAME OF SECOND DIRECTOR OR
SECRETARY], [a director **OR** its secretary]

....
[SIGNATURE OF FIRST DIRECTOR]
Director

....
[SIGNATURE OF SECOND
DIRECTOR OR SECRETARY]
[Director **OR** Secretary]

OR

Executed as a deed by [NAME OF LANDLORD]
acting by [NAME OF DIRECTOR], a director, in the
presence of:

....
[SIGNATURE OF DIRECTOR]
Director

....
[SIGNATURE OF WITNESS]
[NAME, ADDRESS [AND OCCUPATION] OF
WITNESS]

Executed as a deed by [NAME OF TENANT] acting by
[NAME OF FIRST DIRECTOR], a director and
[NAME OF SECOND DIRECTOR OR SECRETARY],
[a director **OR** its secretary]

....
[SIGNATURE OF FIRST DIRECTOR]
Director

....
[SIGNATURE OF SECOND
DIRECTOR OR SECRETARY]
[Director **OR** Secretary]

OR

Executed as a deed by [NAME OF TENANT] acting by
[NAME OF DIRECTOR], a director, in the presence
of:

....
[SIGNATURE OF DIRECTOR]
Director

....
[SIGNATURE OF WITNESS]
[NAME, ADDRESS [AND OCCUPATION] OF
WITNESS]

Executed as a deed by [NAME OF GUARANTOR]   ....
acting by [NAME OF FIRST DIRECTOR] and [NAME   Director
OF SECOND DIRECTOR/SECRETARY]

....

Director/Secretary

OR

Signed as a deed by [NAME OF GUARANTOR]   ....

[SIGNATURE OF GUARANTOR]

in the presence of [NAME OF WITNESS]   ....

[SIGNATURE OF WITNESS]

....

[NAME OF WITNESS]

....

....

[ADDRESS OF WITNESS]

Signed as a deed by [NAME OF GUARANTOR]   ....

[SIGNATURE OF GUARANTOR]

in the presence of [NAME OF WITNESS]   ....

[SIGNATURE OF WITNESS]

....

[NAME OF WITNESS]

....

....

[ADDRESS OF WITNESS]

Specimen Authorised Guarantee Agreement

THIS DEED IS DATED . . . .

Parties

- [FULL COMPANY NAME] incorporated and registered in England and Wales with company number [NUMBER] whose registered office is at [REGISTERED OFFICE ADDRESS](Landlord).

- [FULL COMPANY NAME] incorporated and registered in England and Wales with company number [NUMBER] whose registered office is at [REGISTERED OFFICE ADDRESS](Tenant).

Background

1   This agreement is supplemental and collateral to the Lease and to the Licence to Assign.

2   The Landlord is entitled to the immediate reversion to the Lease.

3   The residue of the term granted by the Lease is vested in the Tenant.

4   The Tenant intends to assign the Lease and has agreed to enter into an authorised guarantee agreement with the Landlord.

1. Agreed terms

1.1   The definitions and rules of interpretation set out in this clause apply to this agreement.

Assignee: the person or persons defined as assignee in the Licence to Assign.

Lease: a lease of [ADDRESS/DESCRIPTION OF THE PROPERTY] dated [DATE] and made between [PARTIES], and all documents supplemental or collateral to that lease.

Licence to Assign: a licence to assign the Lease dated [DATE] and made between [PARTIES].

Property: [ADDRESS/DESCRIPTION OF THE PROPERTY] as [more particularly described in and] demised by the Lease.

[1954 Act: Landlord and Tenant Act 1954.]

1.2   References to the Landlord include a reference to the person entitled for the time being to the immediate reversion to the Lease.

1.3   The expression Tenant Covenants has the meaning given to it by the Landlord and Tenant (Covenants) Act 1995.

1.4   References to the Completion of the Assignment are to the date on which the deed of assignment to the Assignee is dated and not to the registration of that deed at Land Registry.

1.5   Unless otherwise specified a reference to a particular law is a reference to it as it is in force for the time being taking account of any amendment, extension, application or re-enactment and includes any subordinate laws for the time being in force made under it.

1.6   A Person includes a corporate or unincorporated body.

1.7   Except where a contrary intention appears, a reference to a clause or schedule is a reference to a clause of, or schedule to this agreement, and a reference in a schedule to a paragraph is to a paragraph of that schedule.

1.8   Clause, schedule and paragraph headings are not to affect the interpretation of this agreement.

2.   Consideration and effect

2.1   The obligations on the Tenant in this agreement are owed to the Landlord and are made in consideration of the Landlord's consent granted in the Licence to Assign.

2.2   The provisions of this agreement shall take effect on the date the Assignee becomes bound by the Tenant Covenants of the Lease, and are to continue until the end of the term of the Lease (however it may end) and during any agreed or statutory continuation of it, or until the Assignee is released from the tenant covenants of the Lease by virtue of the Landlord and Tenant (Covenants) Act 1995, whichever is earlier.

2.3   If the Tenant is more than one person, then each of those persons shall be jointly and individually liable for their respective obligations arising by virtue of this agreement or the assignment. The Landlord may release or compromise the liability of any one of those persons or grant any time or concession to any one of them without affecting the liability of any other of them.

3.   Guarantee and indemnity

3.1   The Tenant guarantees to the Landlord that the Assignee will pay the rents reserved by the Lease and observe and perform the Tenant Covenants of the Lease and that if the Assignee fails to pay any of those rents or to observe or perform any of those Tenant Covenants, the Tenant will pay or observe and perform them.

3.2   The Tenant covenants with the Landlord as a separate and independent primary obligation to indemnify the Landlord against any failure to pay any of the rents reserved by the Lease or any failure to observe or perform any of the Tenant Covenants of the Lease.

4.   Tenant's liability

4.1   The liability of the Tenant shall not be affected by:

4.1.1   Any time or indulgence granted by the Landlord to the Assignee (or to any person to whom the Assignee has assigned the Lease pursuant to an assignment that is an excluded assignment under section 11 of the Landlord and Tenant (Covenants) Act 1995); or

4.1.2   Any delay or forbearance by the Landlord in enforcing the payment of any of the rents or the observance or performance of any of the tenant covenants of the Lease or in making any demand in respect of any of them; or

4.1.3   Any refusal by the Landlord to accept any rent or other payment due under the Lease where the Landlord believes that the acceptance of such rent or payment may prejudice its ability to re-enter the Property; or

4.1.4   The Landlord exercising any right or remedy against the Assignee for any failure to pay the rents reserved by the Lease or to observe or perform the tenant covenants of the Lease; or

4.1.5   The Landlord taking any action or refraining from taking any action in connection with any other security held by the Landlord in respect of the Assignee's liability to pay the rents reserved by the Lease and observe and perform the tenant covenants of the Lease (including the release of any such security); or

4.1.6   A release or compromise of the liability of any one of the persons who is the Tenant, or the grant of any time or concession to any one of them; or

4.1.7   Any legal limitation or disability on the Assignee or any invalidity or irregularity of any of the tenant covenants of the Lease or any unenforceability of any of them against the Assignee; or

4.1.8   The Assignee being dissolved or being struck off the register of companies or otherwise ceasing to exist; or

4.1.9   Without prejudice to clause 6, the disclaimer of the liability of the Assignee under the Lease; or

4.1.10   The surrender of part of the Property, except that the Tenant shall not be under any liability in relation to the surrendered part in respect of any period after the surrender; or

4.1.11   Any other act or omission except an express release of the Tenant made by the Landlord under seal.

4.2   Any sum payable by the Tenant under this agreement is to be paid without any deduction, set-off or counter-claim against the Landlord or the Assignee.

5.   Variations and supplemental documents

5.1   The Tenant shall, at the request of the Landlord, join in and give its consent to the terms of any licence, consent, variation or other document that may be entered into by the Assignee in connection with the Lease.

5.2   The Tenant is not be released from liability under this agreement by any variation of the rents reserved by, or the Tenant Covenants in, the Lease, whether or not:

5.2.1   The variation is material or prejudicial to the Tenant; or

5.2.2   The Tenant has consented to the variation.

5.3   The liability of the Tenant under this agreement shall apply to the rents reserved by and the Tenant Covenants of the Lease as varied except to the extent that the liability of the Tenant is affected by section 18 of the Landlord and Tenant (Covenants) Act 1995.

6.   Tenant to take a new lease

6.1   If the liability of the Assignee under the Lease is disclaimed and the Landlord gives the Tenant written notice within six months after the Landlord receives notice of that disclaimer, the Tenant shall enter into a new lease of the Property on the terms set out in clause 6.2.

6.2   The rights and obligations under the new lease are to take effect from the date of the disclaimer and the new lease shall:

6.2.1   Be granted subject to the right of any person to have the Lease vested in them by the court and to the terms on which any such order may be made and subject to the rights of any third party existing at the date of the grant;

6.2.2   Be for a term that expires at the same date as the end of the contractual term granted by the Lease had there been no disclaimer;

6.2.3   Reserve as an initial annual rent an amount equal to the rent which is payable under the Lease on the date of the disclaimer (subject to clause 7) and which is subject to review on the same terms and dates provided by the Lease; [and]

6.2.4   [Be excluded from sections 24 to 28 of the 1954 Act; and]

6.2.5   Otherwise be on the same terms as the Lease (as varied if there has been any variation other than a variation in respect of which and to the extent that the Tenant is not liable by virtue of section 18 of the Landlord and Tenant (Covenants) Act 1995).

6.3   [The parties confirm that:

6.3.1   the Landlord served a notice on the Tenant, as required by section 38A(3)(a) of the 1954 Act, applying to the tenancy to be entered into by the Tenant pursuant to clause 6.1 [not less than 14 days] before the authorised guarantee agreement was entered into (a certified copy of which notice is annexed to this agreement); and

6.3.2   [the Tenant] [[NAME OF DECLARANT], who was duly authorised by the Tenant to do so], made a [statutory] declaration dated [DATE] in accordance with the requirements of section

38A(3)(b) of the 1954 Act (a certified copy of which [statutory] declaration is annexed to this agreement).]

6.4 The Tenant shall pay the Landlord's solicitor's costs and disbursements (on a full indemnity basis) and any VAT on them in relation to the new lease and shall execute and deliver to the Landlord a counterpart of the new lease within one month after service of the Landlord's notice.

6.5 The grant of a new lease and its acceptance by the Tenant shall be without prejudice to any other rights which the Landlord may have against the Tenant or against any other person or in respect of any other security that the Landlord may have in connection with the Lease.

7. Rent at the date of disclaimer

7.1 If at the date of the disclaimer there is a rent review pending under the Lease, then:

7.1.1 the relevant review date in the Lease shall also be a rent review date in the new lease;

7.1.2 the rent to be first reserved by the new lease shall be the open market rent of the Property at the relevant review date as agreed or determined in accordance with the new lease;

7.1.3 until the rent is agreed or determined the rent under the new lease shall be payable at the rate that was payable under the Lease immediately before the disclaimer; and

7.1.4 the provisions in the new lease relating to the payment of any shortfall and interest following agreement or determination of a rent review shall apply in relation to any shortfall between the rent payable and the rent first reserved, in respect of the period after the date of the disclaimer.

7.2 If at the date of the disclaimer there is any abatement or suspension of the rent reserved by the Lease, then, for the purposes for this agreement, that rent shall be deemed to be the amount which would be payable under the Lease but for the abatement or suspension, but without prejudice to the provisions relating to abatement or suspension to be contained in the new lease.

8. Payments in gross and restrictions on the Tenant

8.1 Any payment or dividend that the Landlord receives from the Assignee (or its estate) or any other person in connection with any insolvency proceedings or arrangement involving the Assignee shall be taken and applied as a payment in gross and shall not prejudice the right of the Landlord to recover from the Tenant to the full extent of the obligations that are the subject of the guarantee and indemnity in this agreement.

8.2 The Tenant shall not claim in competition with the Landlord in any insolvency proceedings or arrangement of the Assignee in respect of any payment made by the Tenant pursuant to the guarantee and indemnity in this agreement. If it otherwise receives any money in such proceedings or arrangement, it shall hold that money on trust for the Landlord to the extent of its liability to the Landlord.

8.3 The Tenant shall not, without the consent of the Landlord, exercise any right or remedy that it may have (whether against the Assignee or any other person) in respect of any amount paid or other obligation performed by the Tenant under the guarantee and indemnity in this agreement unless and until all the obligations of the Tenant under the guarantee and indemnity in this agreement have been fully performed.

9. Other securities

9.1 The Tenant warrants that it has not taken and covenants that it will not take any security from or over the assets of the Assignee in respect of any liability of the Assignee to the Tenant. If it does take or hold any such security it shall hold it for the benefit of the Landlord.

9.2 This agreement is in addition to any other security that the Landlord may at any time hold from the Tenant or the Assignee or any other person in respect of the liability of the Assignee to pay the rents reserved by the Lease and to observe and perform the tenant covenants of the Lease. It shall not merge in or be affected by any other security.

9.3 The Tenant shall not be entitled to claim or participate in any other security held by the Landlord in respect of the liability of the Assignee to pay the rents reserved by the Lease or to observe and perform the tenant covenants of the Lease.

10. Costs

On completion of this agreement the Tenant is to pay the reasonable costs and disbursements of the Landlord's solicitors and its managing agents in connection with this agreement. This obligation extends to costs and disbursements assessed on a full indemnity basis and to any value added tax in respect of those costs and disbursements except to the extent that the Landlord is able to recover that value added tax.

11. Indemnity

The Tenant will indemnify the Landlord against all costs and claims arising from any breach of the terms of this agreement.

12. Notices

Any notice given pursuant to this agreement shall be in writing and shall be delivered by hand or sent by pre-paid first class post or recorded delivery or by any other means permitted by the Lease. A correctly addressed notice sent by pre-paid first class post shall be deemed to have been delivered at the time at which it would have been delivered in the normal course of the post.

13. Contracts (Rights of Third Parties) Act 1999

No term of this agreement shall be enforceable under the Contracts (Rights of Third Parties) Act 1999 by any third party.

Extracts from the Landlord and Tenant Act 1954, Part II

SECURITY OF TENURE FOR BUSINESS, PROFESSIONAL AND OTHER TENANTS

TENANCIES TO WHICH PART II APPLIES

23. Tenancies to which Part II applies

(1)   Subject to the provisions of this Act, this Part of this Act applies to any tenancy where the property comprised in the tenancy is or includes premises which are occupied by the tenant and are so occupied for the purposes of a business carried on by him or for those and other purposes.

(1A)   Occupation or the carrying on of a business—

(a)   by a company in which the tenant has a controlling interest; or

(b)   where the tenant is a company, by a person with a controlling interest in the company,

shall be treated for the purposes of this section as equivalent to occupation or, as the case may be, the carrying on of a business by the tenant.

(1B)   Accordingly references (however expressed) in this Part of this Act to the business of, or to use, occupation or enjoyment by, the tenant shall be construed as including references to the business of, or to use, occupation or enjoyment by, a company falling within subsection (1A)(a) above or a person falling within subsection (1A)(b) above.

(2)   In this Part of this Act the expression 'business' includes a trade, profession or employment and includes any activity carried on by a body of persons, whether corporate or unincorporate.

(3)   In the following provisions of this Part of this Act the expression 'the holding', in relation to a tenancy to which this Part of this Act applies, means the property comprised in the tenancy, there being excluded any part thereof which is occupied neither by the tenant nor by a person employed by the tenant and so employed for the purposes of a business by reason of which the tenancy is one to which this Part of this Act applies.

(4)   Where the tenant is carrying on a business, in all or any part of the property comprised in a tenancy, in breach of a prohibition (however expressed) of use for business purposes which subsists under the terms of the tenancy and extends to the whole of that property, this Part of this Act shall not apply to the tenancy unless the immediate landlord or his predecessor in title has consented to the breach or the immediate landlord has acquiesced therein.

In this subsection the reference to a prohibition of use for business purposes does not include a prohibition of use for the purposes of a specified business, or of use for purposes of any but a specified business, but save as aforesaid includes a prohibition of use for the purposes of some one or more only of the classes of business specified in the definition of that expression in subsection (2) of this section.

Continuation and Renewal of Tenancies

24. Continuation of tenancies to which Part II applies and grant of new tenancies

(1)   A tenancy to which this Part of this Act applies shall not come to an end unless terminated in accordance with the provisions of this Part of this Act; and, subject to the

following provisions of this Act either the tenant or the landlord under such a tenancy may apply to the court for an order for the grant of a new tenancy—

(a)   if the landlord has given notice under section 25 of this Act to terminate the tenancy, or

(b)   if the tenant has made a request for a new tenancy in accordance with section twenty-six of this Act.

(2)   The last foregoing subsection shall not prevent the coming to an end of a tenancy by notice to quit given by the tenant, by surrender or forfeiture, or by the forfeiture of a superior tenancy unless—

(a)   in the case of a notice to quit, the notice was given before the tenant had been in occupation in right of the tenancy for one month; . . .

(b)   . . . .

(2A)   Neither the tenant nor the landlord may make an application under subsection (1) above if the other has made such an application and the application has been served.

(2B)   Neither the tenant nor the landlord may make such an application if the landlord has made an application under section 29(2) of this Act and the application has been served.

(2C)   The landlord may not withdraw an application under subsection (1) above unless the tenant consents to its withdrawal.

(3)   Notwithstanding anything in subsection (1) of this section,—

(a)   where a tenancy to which this Part of this Act applies ceases to be such a tenancy, it shall not come to an end by reason only of the cesser, but if it was granted for a term of years certain and has been continued by subsection (1) of this section then (without prejudice to the termination thereof in accordance with any terms of the tenancy) it may be terminated by not less than three nor more than six months' notice in writing given by the landlord to the tenant;

(b)   where, at a time when a tenancy is not one to which this Part of this Act applies, the landlord gives notice to quit, the operation of the notice shall not be affected by reason that the tenancy becomes one to which this Part of this Act applies after the giving of the notice.

24A.   Applications for determination of interim rent while tenancy continues

(1)   Subject to subsection (2) below, if—

(a)   the landlord of a tenancy to which this Part of this Act applies has given notice under section 25 of this Act to terminate the tenancy; or

(b)   the tenant of such a tenancy has made a request for a new tenancy in accordance with section 26 of this Act,

either of them may make an application to the court to determine a rent (an 'interim rent') which the tenant is to pay while the tenancy ('the relevant tenancy') continues by virtue of section 24 of this Act and the court may order payment of an interim rent in accordance with section 24C or 24D of this Act.

(2)   Neither the tenant nor the landlord may make an application under subsection (1) above if the other has made such an application and has not withdrawn it.

(3)   No application shall be entertained under subsection (1) above if it is made more than six months after the termination of the relevant tenancy.

24B.   Date from which interim rent is payable

(1)   The interim rent determined on an application under section 24A(1) of this Act shall be payable from the appropriate date.

(2)   If an application under section 24A(1) of this Act is made in a case where the landlord has given a notice under section 25 of this Act, the appropriate date is the earliest date of termination that could have been specified in the landlord's notice.

(3)   If an application under section 24A(1) of this Act is made in a case where the tenant has made a request for a new tenancy under section 26 of this Act, the appropriate date is the earliest date that could have been specified in the tenant's request as the date from which the new tenancy is to begin.

24C. Amount of interim rent where new tenancy of whole premises granted and landlord not opposed

(1)   This section applies where—

(a)   the landlord gave a notice under section 25 of this Act at a time when the tenant was in occupation of the whole of the property comprised in the relevant tenancy for purposes such as are mentioned in section 23(1) of this Act and stated in the notice that he was not opposed to the grant of a new tenancy; or

(b)   the tenant made a request for a new tenancy under section 26 of this Act at a time when he was in occupation of the whole of that property for such purposes and the landlord did not give notice under subsection (6) of that section,

and the landlord grants a new tenancy of the whole of the property comprised in the relevant tenancy to the tenant (whether as a result of an order for the grant of a new tenancy or otherwise).

(2)   Subject to the following provisions of this section, the rent payable under and at the commencement of the new tenancy shall also be the interim rent.

(3)   Subsection (2) above does not apply where—

(a)   the landlord or the tenant shows to the satisfaction of the court that the interim rent under that subsection differs substantially from the relevant rent; or

(b)   the landlord or the tenant shows to the satisfaction of the court that the terms of the new tenancy differ from the terms of the relevant tenancy to such an extent that the interim rent under that subsection is substantially different from the rent which (in default of such agreement) the court would have determined under section 34 of this Act to be payable under a tenancy which commenced on the same day as the new tenancy and whose other terms were the same as the relevant tenancy.

(4)   In this section 'the relevant rent' means the rent which (in default of agreement between the landlord and the tenant) the court would have determined under section 34 of this Act to be payable under the new tenancy if the new tenancy had commenced on the appropriate date (within the meaning of section 24B of this Act).

(5)   The interim rent in a case where subsection (2) above does not apply by virtue only of subsection (3)(a) above is the relevant rent.

(6)   The interim rent in a case where subsection (2) above does not apply by virtue only of subsection (3)(b) above, or by virtue of subsection (3)(a) and (b) above, is the rent which it is reasonable for the tenant to pay while the relevant tenancy continues by virtue of section 24 of this Act.

(7)   In determining the interim rent under subsection (6) above the court shall have regard—

(a)   to the rent payable under the terms of the relevant tenancy; and

(b)   to the rent payable under any sub-tenancy of part of the property comprised in the relevant tenancy,

but otherwise subsections (1) and (2) of section 34 of this Act shall apply to the determination as they would apply to the determination of a rent under that section if a new tenancy of the whole of the property comprised in the relevant tenancy were granted to the tenant by order of the court and the duration of that new tenancy were the same as the duration of the new tenancy which is actually granted to the tenant.

(8)   In this section and section 24D of this Act 'the relevant tenancy' has the same meaning as in section 24A of this Act.

24D.   Amount of interim rent in any other case

(1)   The interim rent in a case where section 24C of this Act does not apply is the rent which it is reasonable for the tenant to pay while the relevant tenancy continues by virtue of section 24 of this Act.

(2)   In determining the interim rent under subsection (1) above the court shall have regard—

(a)   to the rent payable under the terms of the relevant tenancy; and

(b)   to the rent payable under any sub-tenancy of part of the property comprised in the relevant tenancy,

but otherwise subsections (1) and (2) of section 34 of this Act shall apply to the determination as they would apply to the determination of a rent under that section if a new tenancy from year to year of the whole of the property comprised in the relevant tenancy were granted to the tenant by order of the court.

(3)   If the court—

(a)   has made an order for the grant of a new tenancy and has ordered payment of interim rent in accordance with section 24C of this Act, but

(b)   either—

(i)   it subsequently revokes under section 36(2) of this Act the order for the grant of a new tenancy; or

(ii)   the landlord and tenant agree not to act on the order,

the court on the application of the landlord or the tenant shall determine a new interim rent in accordance with subsections (1) and (2) above without a further application under section 24A(1) of this Act.

25.   Termination of tenancy by the landlord

(1)   The landlord may terminate a tenancy to which this Part of this Act applies by a notice given to the tenant in the prescribed form specifying the date at which the tenancy is to come to an end (hereinafter referred to as 'the date of termination'):

Provided that this subsection has effect subject to the provisions of section 29B(4) of this Act and the provisions of Part IV of this Act as to the interim continuation of tenancies pending the disposal of applications to the court.

(2)   Subject to the provisions of the next following subsection, a notice under this section shall not have effect unless it is given not more than twelve nor less than six months before the date of termination specified therein.

(3)   In the case of a tenancy which apart from this Act could have been brought to an end by notice to quit given by the landlord—

(a)   the date of termination specified in a notice under this section shall not be earlier than the earliest date on which apart from this Part of this Act the tenancy could have been brought to an end by notice to quit given by the landlord on the date of the giving of the notice under this section; and

(b)   where apart from this Part of this Act more than six months' notice to quit would have been required to bring the tenancy to an end, the last foregoing subsection shall have effect with the substitution for twelve months of a period six months longer than the length of notice to quit which would have been required as aforesaid.

(4)   In the case of any other tenancy, a notice under this section shall not specify a date of termination earlier than the date on which apart from this Part of this Act the tenancy would have come to an end by effluxion of time.

(5)   . . .

(6)   A notice under this section shall not have effect unless it states whether the landlord is opposed to the grant of a new tenancy to the tenant.

(7)   A notice under this section which states that the landlord is opposed to the grant of a new tenancy to the tenant shall not have effect unless it also specifies one or more of the grounds specified in section 30(1) of this Act as the ground or grounds for his opposition.

(8)   A notice under this section which states that the landlord is not opposed to the grant of a new tenancy to the tenant shall not have effect unless it sets out the landlord's proposals as to—

(a)   the property to be comprised in the new tenancy (being either the whole or part of the property comprised in the current tenancy);

(b)   the rent to be payable under the new tenancy; and

(c)   the other terms of the new tenancy.

26.   Tenant's request for a new tenancy

(1)   A tenant's request for a new tenancy may be made where the current tenancy is a tenancy granted for a term of years certain exceeding one year, whether or not continued by section twenty-four of this Act, or granted for a term of years certain and thereafter from year to year.

(2)   A tenant's request for a new tenancy shall be for a tenancy beginning with such date, not more than twelve nor less than six months after the making of the request, as may be specified therein:

Provided that the said date shall not be earlier than the date on which apart from this Act the current tenancy would come to an end by effluxion of time or could be brought to an end by notice to quit given by the tenant.

(3)   A tenant's request for a new tenancy shall not have effect unless it is made by notice in the prescribed form given to the landlord and sets out the tenant's proposals as to the property to be comprised in the new tenancy (being either the whole or part of the property comprised in the current tenancy), as to the rent to be payable under the new tenancy and as to the other terms of the new tenancy.

(4)   A tenant's request for a new tenancy shall not be made if the landlord has already given notice under the last foregoing section to terminate the current tenancy, or if the tenant has already given notice to quit or notice under the next following section; and no such notice shall be given by the landlord or the tenant after the making by the tenant of a request for a new tenancy.

(5)   Where the tenant makes a request for a new tenancy in accordance with the foregoing provisions of this section, the current tenancy shall, subject to the provisions of sections 29B(4) and 36(2) of this Act and the provisions of Part IV of this Act as to the interim continuation of tenancies, terminate immediately before the date specified in the request for the beginning of the new tenancy.

(6)   Within two months of the making of a tenant's request for a new tenancy the landlord may give notice to the tenant that he will oppose an application to the court for the grant of a new tenancy, and any such notice shall state on which of the grounds mentioned in section thirty of this Act the landlord will oppose the application.

27. **Termination by tenant of tenancy for fixed term**

(1)   Where the tenant under a tenancy to which this Part of this Act applies, being a tenancy granted for a term of years certain, gives to the immediate landlord, not later than three months before the date on which apart from this Act the tenancy would come to an end by effluxion of time, a notice in writing that the tenant does not desire the tenancy to be continued, section twenty-four of this Act shall not have effect in relation to the tenancy unless the notice is given before the tenant has been in occupation in right of the tenancy for one month.

(1A) Section 24 of this Act shall not have effect in relation to a tenancy for a term of years certain where the tenant is not in occupation of the property comprised in the tenancy at the time when, apart from this Act, the tenancy would come to an end by effluxion of time.

(2)   A tenancy granted for a term of years certain which is continuing by virtue of section twenty-four of this Act shall not come to an end by reason only of the tenant ceasing to occupy the property comprised in the tenancy but may be brought to an end on any day by not less than three months' notice in writing given by the tenant to the immediate landlord, whether the notice is given after the date on which apart from this Act the tenancy would have come to an end or before that date, but not before the tenant has been in occupation in right of the tenancy for one month.

(3)   Where a tenancy is terminated under subsection (2) above, any rent payable in respect of a period which begins before, and ends after, the tenancy is terminated shall be apportioned, and any rent paid by the tenant in excess of the amount apportioned to the period before termination shall be recoverable by him.

28. **Renewal of tenancies by agreement**

Where the landlord and tenant agree for the grant to the tenant of a future tenancy of the holding, or of the holding with other land, on terms and from a date specified in the agreement, the current tenancy shall continue until that date but no longer, and shall not be a tenancy to which this Part of this Act applies.

29. **Order by court for grant of new tenancy or termination of current tenancy**

(1)   Subject to the provisions of this Act, on an application under section 24(1) of this Act, the court shall make an order for the grant of a new tenancy and accordingly for the termination of the current tenancy immediately before the commencement of the new tenancy.

(2)   Subject to the following provisions of this Act, a landlord may apply to the court for an order for the termination of a tenancy to which this Part of this Act applies without the grant of a new tenancy—

(a)   if he has given notice under section 25 of this Act that he is opposed to the grant of a new tenancy to the tenant; or

(b)   if the tenant has made a request for a new tenancy in accordance with section 26 of this Act and the landlord has given notice under subsection (6) of that section.

(3)   The landlord may not make an application under subsection (2) above if either the tenant or the landlord has made an application under section 24(1) of this Act.

(4)   Subject to the provisions of this Act, where the landlord makes an application under subsection (2) above—

(a)   if he establishes, to the satisfaction of the court, any of the grounds on which he is entitled to make the application in accordance with section 30 of this Act, the court shall make an order for the termination of the current tenancy in accordance with section 64 of this Act without the grant of a new tenancy; and

    (b)   if not, it shall make an order for the grant of a new tenancy and accordingly for the termination of the current tenancy immediately before the commencement of the new tenancy.

(5)   The court shall dismiss an application by the landlord under section 24(1) of this Act if the tenant informs the court that he does not want a new tenancy.

(6)   The landlord may not withdraw an application under subsection (2) above unless the tenant consents to its withdrawal.

29A. Time limits for applications to court

(1)   Subject to section 29B of this Act, the court shall not entertain an application—

    (a)   by the tenant or the landlord under section 24(1) of this Act; or

    (b)   by the landlord under section 29(2) of this Act,

if it is made after the end of the statutory period.

(2)   In this section and section 29B of this Act 'the statutory period' means a period ending—

    (a)   where the landlord gave a notice under section 25 of this Act, on the date specified in his notice; and

    (b)   where the tenant made a request for a new tenancy under section 26 of this Act, immediately before the date specified in his request.

(3)   Where the tenant has made a request for a new tenancy under section 26 of this Act, the court shall not entertain an application under section 24(1) of this Act which is made before the end of the period of two months beginning with the date of the making of the request, unless the application is made after the landlord has given a notice under section 26(6) of this Act.

29B. Agreements extending time limits

(1)   After the landlord has given a notice under section 25 of this Act, or the tenant has made a request under section 26 of this Act, but before the end of the statutory period, the landlord and tenant may agree that an application such as is mentioned in section 29A(1) of this Act, may be made before the end of a period specified in the agreement which will expire after the end of the statutory period.

(2)   The landlord and tenant may from time to time by agreement further extend the period for making such an application, but any such agreement must be made before the end of the period specified in the current agreement.

(3)   Where an agreement is made under this section, the court may entertain an application such as is mentioned in section 29A(1) of this Act if it is made before the end of the period specified in the agreement.

(4)   Where an agreement is made under this section, or two or more agreements are made under this section, the landlord's notice under section 25 of this Act or tenant's request under section 26 of this Act shall be treated as terminating the tenancy at the end of the period specified in the agreement or, as the case may be, at the end of the period specified in the last of those agreements.

30. Opposition by landlord to application for a new tenancy

(1)   The grounds on which a landlord may oppose an application under section 24(1) of this Act, or make an application under section 29(2) of this Act, are such of the following grounds as may be stated in the landlord's notice under section twenty-five of this Act or, as the case may be, under subsection (6) of section twenty-six thereof, that is to say:—

    (a)   where under the current tenancy the tenant has any obligations as respects the repair and maintenance of the holding, that the tenant ought not to be granted a new tenancy in view of the state of repair of the holding, being a state resulting from the tenant's failure to comply with the said obligations;

(b)   that the tenant ought not to be granted a new tenancy in view of his persistent delay in paying rent which has become due;

(c)   that the tenant ought not to be granted a new tenancy in view of other substantial breaches by him of his obligations under the current tenancy, or for any other reason connected with the tenant's use or management of the holding;

(d)   that the landlord has offered and is willing to provide or secure the provision of alternative accommodation for the tenant, that the terms on which the alternative accommodation is available are reasonable having regard to the terms of the current tenancy and to all other relevant circumstances, and that the accommodation and the time at which it will be available are suitable for the tenant's requirements (including the requirement to preserve goodwill) having regard to the nature and class of his business and to the situation and extent of, and facilities afforded by, the holding;

(e)   where the current tenancy was created by the sub-letting of part only of the property comprised in a superior tenancy and the landlord is the owner of an interest in reversion expectant on the termination of that superior tenancy, that the aggregate of the rents reasonably obtainable on separate lettings of the holding and the remainder of that property would be substantially less than the rent reasonably obtainable on a letting of that property as a whole, that on the termination of the current tenancy the landlord requires possession of the holding for the purpose of letting or otherwise disposing of the said property as a whole, and that in view thereof the tenant ought not to be granted a new tenancy;

(f)   that on the termination of the current tenancy the landlord intends to demolish or reconstruct the premises comprised in the holding or a substantial part of those premises or to carry out substantial work of construction on the holding or part thereof and that he could not reasonably do so without obtaining possession of the holding;

(g)   subject as hereinafter provided, that on the termination of the current tenancy the landlord intends to occupy the holding for the purposes, or partly for the purposes, of a business to be carried on by him therein, or as his residence.

(1A)   Where the landlord has a controlling interest in a company, the reference in subsection (1)(g) above to the landlord shall be construed as a reference to the landlord or that company.

(1B)   Subject to subsection (2A) below, where the landlord is a company and a person has a controlling interest in the company, the reference in subsection (1)(g) above to the landlord shall be construed as a reference to the landlord or that person.

(2)   The landlord shall not be entitled to oppose an application under section 24(1) of this Act, or make an application under section 29(2) of this Act, on the ground specified in paragraph (g) of the last foregoing subsection if the interest of the landlord, or an interest which has merged in that interest and but for the merger would be the interest of the landlord, was purchased or created after the beginning of the period of five years which ends with the termination of the current tenancy, and at all times since the purchase or creation thereof the holding has been comprised in a tenancy or successive tenancies of the description specified in subsection (1) of section twenty-three of this Act.

(2A)   Subsection (1B) above shall not apply if the controlling interest was acquired after the beginning of the period of five years which ends with the termination of the current tenancy, and at all times since the acquisition of the controlling interest the holding has been comprised in a tenancy or successive tenancies of the description specified in section 23(1) of this Act.

(3) ...

31. Dismissal of application for new tenancy where landlord successfully opposes

(1) If the landlord opposes an application under subsection (1) of section twenty-four of this Act on grounds on which he is entitled to oppose it in accordance with the last foregoing section and establishes any of those grounds to the satisfaction of the court, the court shall not make an order for the grant of a new tenancy.

(2) Where the landlord opposes an application under section 24(1) of this Act, or makes an application under section 29(2) of this Act, on one or more of the grounds specified in section 30(1)(d) to (f) of this Act but establishes none of those grounds, and none of the other grounds specified in section 30(1) of this Act, to the satisfaction of the court, then if the court would have been satisfied on any of the grounds specified in section 30(1)(d) to (f) of this Act if the date of termination specified in the landlord's notice or, as the case may be, the date specified in the tenant's request for a new tenancy as the date from which the new tenancy is to begin, had been such later date as the court may determine, being a date not more than one year later than the date so specified,—

    (a) the court shall make a declaration to that effect, stating of which of the said grounds the court would have been satisfied as aforesaid and specifying the date determined by the court as aforesaid, but shall not make an order for the grant of a new tenancy;

    (b) if, within fourteen days after the making of the declaration, the tenant so requires the court shall make an order substituting the said date for the date specified in the said landlord's notice or tenant's request, and thereupon that notice or request shall have effect accordingly.

31A. Grant of new tenancy in some cases where section 30(1)(f) applies

(1) Where the landlord opposes an application under section 24(1) of this Act on the ground specified in paragraph (f) of section 30(1) of this Act, or makes an application under section 29(2) of this Act on that ground, the court shall not hold that the landlord could not reasonably carry out the demolition, reconstruction or work of construction intended without obtaining possession of the holding if—

    (a) the tenant agrees to the inclusion in the terms of the new tenancy of terms giving the landlord access and other facilities for carrying out the work intended and, given that access and those facilities, the landlord could reasonably carry out the work without obtaining possession of the holding and without interfering to a substantial extent or for a substantial time with the use of the holding for the purposes of the business carried on by the tenant; or

    (b) the tenant is willing to accept a tenancy of an economically separable part of the holding and either paragraph (a) of this section is satisfied with respect to that part or possession of the remainder of the holding would be reasonably sufficient to enable the landlord to carry out the intended work.

(2) For the purposes of subsection (1)(b) of this section a part of a holding shall be deemed to be an economically separable part if, and only if, the aggregate of the rents which, after the completion of the intended work, would be reasonably obtainable on separate lettings of that part and the remainder of the premises affected by or resulting from the work would not be substantially less than the rent which would then be reasonably obtainable on a letting of those premises as a whole.

32. Property to be comprised in new tenancy

(1) Subject to the following provisions of this section, an order under section twenty-nine of this Act for the grant of a new tenancy shall be an order for the grant of a new tenancy of the holding; and in the absence of agreement between the landlord and the tenant as

to the property which constitutes the holding the court shall in the order designate that property by reference to the circumstances existing at the date of the order.

(1A) Where the court, by virtue of paragraph (b) of section 31A(1) of this Act, makes an order under section 29 of this Act for the grant of a new tenancy in a case where the tenant is willing to accept a tenancy of part of the holding, the order shall be an order for the grant of a new tenancy of that part only.

(2) The foregoing provisions of this section shall not apply in a case where the property comprised in the current tenancy includes other property besides the holding and the landlord requires any new tenancy ordered to be granted under section twenty-nine of this Act to be a tenancy of the whole of the property comprised in the current tenancy; but in any such case—

(a) any order under the said section twenty-nine for the grant of a new tenancy shall be an order for the grant of a new tenancy of the whole of the property comprised in the current tenancy, and

(b) references in the following provisions of this Part of this Act to the holding shall be construed as references to the whole of that property.

(3) Where the current tenancy includes rights enjoyed by the tenant in connection with the holding, those rights shall be included in a tenancy ordered to be granted under section twenty-nine of this Act except as otherwise agreed between the landlord and the tenant or, in default of such agreement, determined by the court.

33. Duration of new tenancy

Where on an application under this Part of this Act the court makes an order for the grant of a new tenancy, the new tenancy shall be such tenancy as may be agreed between the landlord and the tenant, or, in default of such an agreement, shall be such a tenancy as may be determined by the court to be reasonable in all the circumstances, being, if it is a tenancy for a term of years certain, a tenancy for a term not exceeding fifteen years, and shall begin on the coming to an end of the current tenancy.

34. Rent under new tenancy

(1) The rent payable under a tenancy granted by order of the court under this Part of this Act shall be such as may be agreed between the landlord and the tenant or as, in default of such agreement, may be determined by the court to be that at which, having regard to the terms of the tenancy (other than those relating to rent), the holding might reasonably be expected to be let in the open market by a willing lessor, there being disregarded—

(a) any effect on rent of the fact that the tenant has or his predecessors in title have been in occupation of the holding,

(b) any goodwill attached to the holding by reason of the carrying on thereat of the business of the tenant (whether by him or by a predecessor of his in that business),

(c) any effect on rent of an improvement to which this paragraph applies,

(d) in the case of a holding comprising licensed premises, any addition to its value attributable to the licence, if it appears to the court that having regard to the terms of the current tenancy and any other relevant circumstances the benefit of the licence belongs to the tenant.

(2) Paragraph (c) of the foregoing subsection applies to any improvement carried out by a person who at the time it was carried out was the tenant, but only if it was carried out otherwise than in pursuance of an obligation to his immediate landlord, and either it was carried out during the current tenancy or the following conditions are satisfied, that is to say,—

(a) that it was completed not more than twenty-one years before the application to the court was made; and

(b) that the holding or any part of it affected by the improvement has at all times since the completion of the improvement been comprised in tenancies of the description specified in section 23(1) of this Act; and

(c) that at the termination of each of those tenancies the tenant did not quit.

(2A) If this Part of this Act applies by virtue of section 23(1A) of this Act, the reference in subsection (1)(d) above to the tenant shall be construed as including—

(a) a company in which the tenant has a controlling interest, or

(b) where the tenant is a company, a person with a controlling interest in the company.

(3) Where the rent is determined by the court the court may, if it thinks fit, further determine that the terms of the tenancy shall include such provision for varying the rent as may be specified in the determination.

(4) It is hereby declared that the matters which are to be taken into account by the court in determining the rent include any effect on rent of the operation of the provisions of the Landlord & Tenant (Covenants) Act 1995.

35. Other terms of new tenancy

(1) The terms of a tenancy granted by order of the court under this Part of this Act (other than terms as to the duration thereof and as to the rent payable thereunder), including, where different persons own interests which fulfil the conditions specified in section 44(1) of this Act in different parts of it, terms as to the apportionment of the rent, shall be such as may be agreed between the landlord and the tenant or as, in default of such agreement, may be determined by the court; and in determining those terms the court shall have regard to the terms of the current tenancy and to all relevant circumstances.

(2) In subsection (1) of this section the reference to all relevant circumstances includes (without prejudice to the generality of that reference) a reference to the operation of the provisions of the Landlord and Tenant (Covenants) Act 1995.

36. Carrying out of order for new tenancy

(1) Where under this Part of this Act the court makes an order for the grant of a new tenancy, then, unless the order is revoked under the next following subsection or the landlord and the tenant agree not to act upon the order, the landlord shall be bound to execute or make in favour of the tenant, and the tenant shall be bound to accept, a lease or agreement for a tenancy of the holding embodying the terms agreed between the landlord and the tenant or determined by the court in accordance with the foregoing provisions of this Part of this Act; and where the landlord executes or makes such a lease or agreement the tenant shall be bound, if so required by the landlord, to execute a counterpart or duplicate thereof.

(2) If the tenant, within fourteen days after the making of an order under this Part of this Act for the grant of a new tenancy, applies to the court for the revocation of the order the court shall revoke the order; and where the order is so revoked, then, if it is so agreed between the landlord and the tenant or determined by the court, the current tenancy shall continue, beyond the date at which it would have come to an end apart from this subsection, for such period as may be so agreed or determined to be necessary to afford to the landlord a reasonable opportunity for reletting or otherwise disposing of the premises which would have been comprised in the new tenancy; and while the current tenancy continues by virtue of this subsection it shall not be a tenancy to which this Part of this Act applies.

(3) Where an order is revoked under the last foregoing subsection any provision thereof as to payment of costs shall not cease to have effect by reason only of the revocation; but

the court may, if it thinks fit, revoke or vary any such provision or, where no costs have been awarded in the proceedings for the revoked order, award such costs.

(4) A lease executed or agreement made under this section, in a case where the interest of the lessor is subject to a mortgage, shall be deemed to be one authorised by section ninety-nine of the Law of Property Act 1925 (which confers certain powers of leasing on mortgagors in possession), and subsection (13) of that section (which allows those powers to be restricted or excluded by agreement) shall not have effect in relation to such a lease or agreement.

37. Compensation where order for new tenancy precluded on certain grounds

(1) Subject to the provisions of this Act, in a case specified in subsection (1A), (1B) or (1C) below (a 'compensation case') the tenant shall be entitled on quitting the holding to recover from the landlord by way of compensation an amount determined in accordance with this section.

(1A) The first compensation case is where on the making of an application by the tenant under section 24(1) of this Act the court is precluded (whether by subsection (1) or subsection (2) of section 31 of this Act) from making an order for the grant of a new tenancy by reason of any of the grounds specified in paragraphs (e), (f) and (g) of section 30(1) of this Act (the 'compensation grounds') and not of any grounds specified in any other paragraph of section 30(1).

(1B) The second compensation case is where on the making of an application under section 29(2) of this Act the court is precluded (whether by section 29(4)(a) or section 31(2) of this Act) from making an order for the grant of a new tenancy by reason of any of the compensation grounds and not of any other grounds specified in section 30(1) of this Act.

(1C) The third compensation case is where—

(a) the landlord's notice under section 25 of this Act or, as the case may be, under section 26(6) of this Act, states his opposition to the grant of a new tenancy on any of the compensation grounds and not on any other grounds specified in section 30(1) of this Act; and

(b) either—

(i) no application is made by the tenant under section 24(1) of this Act or by the landlord under section 29(2) of this Act; or

(ii) such an application is made but is subsequently withdrawn.

(2) Subject to the following provisions of this section, compensation under this section shall be as follows, that is to say,—

(a) where the conditions specified in the next following subsection are satisfied in relation to the whole of the holding it shall be the product of the appropriate multiplier and twice the rateable value of the holding,

(b) in any other case it shall be the product of the appropriate multiplier and the rateable value of the holding.

(3) The said conditions are—

(a) that, during the whole of the fourteen years immediately preceding the termination of the current tenancy, premises being or comprised in the holding have been occupied for the purposes of a business carried on by the occupier or for those and other purposes;

(b) that, if during those fourteen years there was a change in the occupier of the premises, the person who was the occupier immediately after the change was the successor to the business carried on by the person who was the occupier immediately before the change.

...

(8)   In subsection (2) of this section 'the appropriate multiplier' means such multiplier as the Secretary of State may by order made by statutory instrument prescribe and different multipliers may be so prescribed in relation to different cases.

37A. Compensation for possession obtained by misrepresentation

(1)   Where the court—

(a)   makes an order for the termination of the current tenancy but does not make an order for the grant of a new tenancy, or

(b)   refuses an order for the grant of a new tenancy,

and it subsequently made to appear to the court that the order was obtained, or the court was induced to refuse the grant, by misrepresentation or the concealment of material facts, the court may order the landlord to pay to the tenant such sum as appears sufficient as compensation for damage or loss sustained by the tenant as the result of the order or refusal.

(2)   Where—

(a)   the tenant has quit the holding—

(i)   after making but withdrawing an application under section 24(1) of this Act; or

(ii)   without making such an application; and

(b)   it is made to appear to the court that he did so by reason of misrepresentation or the concealment of material facts,

the court may order the landlord to pay to the tenant such sum as appears sufficient as compensation for damage or loss sustained by the tenant as the result of quitting the holding.

38. Restriction on agreements excluding provisions of Part II

(1)   Any agreement relating to a tenancy to which this Part of this Act applies (whether contained in the instrument creating the tenancy or not) shall be void (except as provided by section 38A of this Act) in so far as it purports to preclude the tenant from making an application or request under this Part of this Act or provides for the termination or the surrender of the tenancy in the event of his making such an application or request or for the imposition of any penalty or disability on the tenant in that event.

(2)   Where—

(a)   during the whole of the five years immediately preceding the date on which the tenant under a tenancy to which this Part of this Act applies is to quit the holding, premises being or comprised in the holding have been occupied for the purposes of a business carried on by the occupier or for those and other purposes, and

(b)   if during those five years there was a change in the occupier of the premises, the person who was the occupier immediately after the change was the successor to the business carried on by the person who was the occupier immediately before the change,

any agreement (whether contained in the instrument creating the tenancy or not and whether made before or after the termination of that tenancy) which purports to exclude or reduce compensation under section 37 of this Act shall to that extent be void, so however that this subsection shall not affect any agreement as to the amount of any such compensation which is made after the right to compensation has accrued.

(3)   In a case not falling within the last foregoing subsection the right to compensation conferred by section 37 of this Act may be excluded or modified by agreement.

38A.   Agreements to exclude provisions of Part 2

(1)   The persons who will be the landlord and the tenant in relation to a tenancy to be granted for a term of years certain which will be a tenancy to which this Part of this Act applies may agree that the provisions of sections 24 to 28 of this Act shall be excluded in relation to that tenancy.

(2)   The persons who are the landlord and the tenant in relation to a tenancy to which this Part of this Act applies may agree that the tenancy shall be surrendered on such date or in such circumstances as may be specified in the agreement and on such terms (if any) as may be so specified.

(3)   An agreement under subsection (1) above shall be void unless—

(a)   the landlord has served on the tenant a notice in the form, or substantially in the form, set out in Schedule 1 to the Regulatory Reform (Business Tenancies) (England and Wales) Order 2003 ('the 2003 Order'); and

(b)   the requirements specified in Schedule 2 to that Order are met.

(4)   An agreement under subsection (2) above shall be void unless—

(a)   the landlord has served on the tenant a notice in the form, or substantially in the form, set out in Schedule 3 to the 2003 Order; and

(b)   the requirements specified in Schedule 4 to that Order are met.

40.   Duties of tenants and landlords of business premises to give information to each other

(1)   Where a person who is an owner of an interest in reversion expectant (whether immediately or not) on a tenancy of any business premises has served on the tenant a notice in the prescribed form requiring him to do so, it shall be the duty of the tenant to give the appropriate person in writing the information specified in subsection (2) below.

(2)   That information is—

(a)   whether the tenant occupies the premises or any part of them wholly or partly for the purposes of a business carried on by him;

(b)   whether his tenancy has effect subject to any sub-tenancy on which his tenancy is immediately expectant and, if so—

(i)   what premises are comprised in the sub-tenancy;

(ii)   for what term it has effect (or, if it is terminable by notice, by what notice it can be terminated);

(iii)   what is the rent payable under it;

(iv)   who is the sub-tenant;

(v)   (to the best of his knowledge and belief) whether the sub-tenant is in occupation of the premises or of part of the premises comprised in the sub-tenancy and, if not, what is the sub-tenant's address;

(vi)   whether an agreement is in force excluding in relation to the sub-tenancy the provisions of sections 24 to 28 of this Act; and

(vii)   whether a notice has been given under section 25 or 26(6) of this Act, or a request has been made under section 26 of this Act, in relation to the sub-tenancy and, if so, details of the notice or request; and

(c)   (to the best of his knowledge and belief) the name and address of any other person who owns an interest in reversion in any part of the premises.

(3)   Where the tenant of any business premises who is a tenant under such a tenancy as is mentioned in section 26(1) of this Act has served on a reversioner or a reversioner's mortgagee in possession a notice in the prescribed form requiring him to do so, it shall

be the duty of the person on whom the notice is served to give the appropriate person in writing the information specified in subsection (4) below.

(4) That information is—

(a) whether he is the owner of the fee simple in respect of the premises or any part of them or the mortgagee in possession of such an owner,

(b) if he is not, then (to the best of his knowledge and belief)—

(i) the name and address of the person who is his or, as the case may be, his mortgagor's immediate landlord in respect of those premises or of the part in respect of which he or his mortgagor is not the owner in fee simple;

(ii) for what term his or his mortgagor's tenancy has effect and what is the earliest date (if any) at which that tenancy is terminable by notice to quit given by the landlord; and

(iii) whether a notice has been given under section 25 or 26(6) of this Act, or a request has been made under section 26 of this Act, in relation to the tenancy and, if so, details of the notice or request;

(c) (to the best of his knowledge and belief) the name and address of any other person who owns an interest in reversion in any part of the premises; and

(d) if he is a reversioner, whether there is a mortgagee in possession of his interest in the premises and, if so, (to the best of his knowledge and belief) what is the name and address of the mortgagee.

(5) A duty imposed on a person by this section is a duty—

(a) to give the information concerned within the period of one month beginning with the date of service of the notice; and

(b) if within the period of six months beginning with the date of service of the notice that person becomes aware that any information which has been given in pursuance of the notice is not, or is no longer, correct, to give the appropriate person correct information within the period of one month beginning with the date on which he becomes aware.

(6) This section shall not apply to a notice served by or on the tenant more than two years before the date on which apart from this Act his tenancy would come to an end by effluxion of time or could be brought to an end by notice to quit given by the landlord.

(7) Except as provided by section 40A of this Act, the appropriate person for the purposes of this section and section 40A(1) of this Act is the person who served the notice under subsection (1) or (3) above.

(8) In this section—

'business premises' means premises used wholly or partly for the purposes of a business;

'mortgagee in possession' includes a receiver appointed by the mortgagee or by the court who is in receipt of the rents and profits, and 'his mortgagor' shall be construed accordingly;

'reversioner' means any person having an interest in the premises, being an interest in reversion expectant (whether immediately or not) on the tenancy;

'reversioner's mortgagee in possession' means any person being a mortgagee in possession in respect of such an interest; and

'sub-tenant' includes a person retaining possession of any premises by virtue of the Rent (Agriculture) Act 1976 or the Rent Act 1977 after the coming to an end of a sub-tenancy, and 'sub-tenancy' includes a right so to retain possession.

40B. Proceedings for breach of duties to give information

A claim that a person has broken any duty imposed by section 40 of this Act may be made the subject of civil proceedings for breach of statutory duty; and in any such proceedings a court may order that person to comply with that duty and may make an award of damages.

42. Groups of companies

(1) For the purposes of this section two bodies corporate shall be taken to be members of a group if and only if one is a subsidiary of the other or both are subsidiaries of a third body corporate or the same person has a controlling interest in both.

(2) Where a tenancy is held by a member of a group, occupation by another member of the group, and the carrying on of a business by another member of the group, shall be treated for the purposes of section twenty-three of this Act as equivalent to occupation or the carrying on of a business by the member of the group holding the tenancy; and in relation to a tenancy to which this Part of this Act applies by virtue of the foregoing provisions of this subsection—

(a) references (however expressed) in this Part of this Act and in the Ninth Schedule to this Act to the business of or to use occupation or enjoyment by the tenant shall be construed as including references to the business of or to use occupation or enjoyment by the said other member;

(b) the reference in paragraph (d) of subsection (1) of section thirty-four of this Act to the tenant shall be construed as including the said other member; and

(c) an assignment of the tenancy from one member of the group to another shall not be treated as a change in the person of the tenant.

(3) Where the landlord's interest is held by a member of a group—

(a) the reference in paragraph (g) of subsection (1) of section 30 of this Act to intended occupation by the landlord for the purposes of a business to be carried on by him shall be construed as including intended occupation by any member of the group for the purposes of a business to be carried on by that member; and

(b) the reference in subsection (2) of that section to the purchase or creation of any interest shall be construed as a reference to a purchase from or creation by a person other than a member of the group.

43. Tenancies excluded from Part II

(1) This Part of this Act does not apply—

(a) to a tenancy of an agricultural holding which is a tenancy in relation to which the Agricultural Holdings Act 1986 applies or a tenancy which would be a tenancy of an agricultural holding in relation to which that Act applied if subsection (3) of section 2 of that Act did not have effect or, in a case where approval was given under subsection (1) of that section, if that approval had not been given;

(aa) to a farm business tenancy;

(b) to a tenancy created by a mining lease;

(2) This Part of this Act does not apply to a tenancy granted by reason that the tenant was the holder of an office, appointment or employment from the grantor thereof and continuing only so long as the tenant holds the office, appointment or employment, or terminable by the grantor on the tenant's ceasing to hold it, or coming to an end at a time fixed by reference to the time at which the tenant ceases to hold it:

Provided that this subsection shall not have effect in relation to a tenancy granted after the commencement of this Act unless the tenancy was granted by an instrument in writing which expressed the purpose for which the tenancy was granted.

(3) This Part of this Act does not apply to a tenancy granted for a term certain not exceeding six months unless—

(a)   the tenancy contains provision for renewing the term or for extending it beyond six months from its beginning; or

(b)   the tenant has been in occupation for a period which, together with any period during which any predecessor in the carrying on of the business carried on by the tenant was in occupation, exceeds twelve months.

44.   Meaning of 'the landlord' in Part II, and provisions as to mesne landlords, etc

(1)   Subject to subsections (1A) and (2) below, in this Part of this Act the expression 'the landlord', in relation to a tenancy (in this section referred to as 'the relevant tenancy'), means the person (whether or not he is the immediate landlord) who is the owner of that interest in the property comprised in the relevant tenancy which for the time being fulfils the following conditions, that is to say—

(a)   that it is an interest in reversion expectant (whether immediately or not) on the termination of the relevant tenancy, and

(b)   that it is either the fee simple or a tenancy which will not come to an end within fourteen months by effluxion of time and, if it is such a tenancy, that no notice has been given by virtue of which it will come to an end within fourteen months or any further time by which it may be continued under section 36(2) or section 64 of this Act,

and is not itself in reversion expectant (whether immediately or not) on an interest which fulfils those conditions.

(1A)   The reference in subsection (1) above to a person who is the owner of an interest such as is mentioned in that subsection is to be construed, where different persons own such interests in different parts of the property, as a reference to all those persons collectively.

(2)   References in this Part of this Act to a notice to quit given by the landlord are references to a notice to quit given by the immediate landlord.

(3)   The provisions of the Sixth Schedule to this Act shall have effect for the application of this Part of this Act to cases where the immediate landlord of the tenant is not the owner of the fee simple in respect of the holding.

Index

adjudication 133
administration 317
  administrator
    appointment 321
    powers and duties 322
  covenants 334
  moratorium 322
  rent 333
advertising 234
agreement for lease
  completion date 151
  damage before completion 152
  deducing title 152
  defects in work or materials and 152
  example 149–53
  force majeure clause 151
  form of lease 152
  incorporation of conditions of sale 152
  incumbrances 152
  landlord's obligations 150
  liability for delay 151
  merging with lease 152–3
  penalties for delay 151
  practical completion 150–1
  premises 152
  responsibility for damage 152
  supervision 150
  when used 149
airspace 175
alienation 211–21
  notice of 220
  restrictions on 213–17
    consent 217–20, 269–70
    covenants 213–14
  see also **assignment of leases; subleases**
alterations
  alterations clause 232–4
  Code for Leasing Business Premises 2007 224, 236
  covenants against
    absolute covenants 232–3
    compensation for improvements 236
    fully qualified covenants 233
    landlord's concerns 231–2
    need for 231–2
    other lease clauses 234–5
    qualified covenants 233
    tenant's concerns 231
  landlord's consent 233–4
  lease controls 232–5
  nature of premises 231
  restrictions outside lease 235
  term 231–2
  type 232
  withholding consent 233–4
  see also **improvements**
alternative accommodation
  offer of 304

appeals
  certificates of lawful use or development 71
  contaminated land 92–3, 94
  enforcement notices 80–2
    costs 81
    documentation 81
    effect 81
    fees 81
    forum 81
    further appeals 82
    grounds 80
    procedure 81
    time limits 81
    who may appeal 81
    written representations 81
  planning obligations 61
  planning permission 51–5
    appeal form 54–5
    challenging appeal decision 55
    costs 55
    hearing 55
    initial procedure 52–3
    inquiry 54–5
    statement of case 54
    types 53–5
    who may appeal 51–2
    written representations 53
  refusal of certificate of lawful use or development 71
arbitration 133
architects 116–17
asbestos 84, 106–7
  Control of Asbestos Regulations 2006 107
  duty holder 107
  duty to assess if present 107
  enforcement 107
  landlord and tenant issues 107–8
  non-domestic premises 107
assignment of leases 211
  assignee's guarantor 172–3
  consent
    applications for 269–71
    consent not to be unreasonably withheld 218–20, 269–71
    delays in obtaining 220
    reasonable response time 270
    refusal 220
    restrictions on charging for consent 220
    superior landlord's consent 271
  covenants against 213–14
    remedies for breach 283
  covenants and 166–7, 269–70
  detailed provisions 214–17
  excluded 168
  guarantee agreements 168, 216
  indemnity and 166, 167, 168
  licence to assign 271–2
  privity of estate and 166–7

assignment of leases – *continued*
  virtual assignments 221
  see also **authorised guarantee agreement**
assignment of rights
  construction projects 130
authorised guarantee agreement 272, 284
  content 272
  LTA 1954 considerations 272
  specimen 423–7

bankruptcy 317, 320–1
  covenants 334
  effect 320–1
  forfeiture and 256
  guarantee for lease and 171
  non-payment of rent and 280
  rent 332
  restrictions 321
  trustee in bankruptcy 321
    powers 321
boundaries
  lease of part 259
breach of condition notice 73–4
breach of covenant
  default notice 279
  landlord's breach 284–6
  landlord's remedies 279–84
  obligation not to derogate from grant 286
  other covenants 283–4, 303–4
    forfeiture 253–5
  quiet enjoyment 285–6
  remedies for landlord 279–84
  repairing covenant 281–3, 285
  tenant's breach 279–84
  tenant's remedies 284–6
break clauses 162, 180–1, 288
building
  definition of 159
building contractors 115–16
building operations 31
  see also **construction projects**

call options 21
Carbon Reduction Commitment Energy Efficiency Scheme (CRC Scheme) 102
case law
  change of use 32–3
certificates of completion 150
certificates of lawful use or development
  appeals 71
  effect 71
  existing development 70
  issue 71
  offences 71
  onus of proof 71
  proposed development 71
change of use
  case law 32–3
  Code for Leasing Business Premises 2007 224, 236
  non-statutory guidance 33
  statutory clarifications 33
charges
  fixed 13, 213

charges – *continued*
  floating 13, 213
  priority 13
  restrictions 213
clawback *see* **overage**
climate change 84, 102
  Carbon Reduction Commitment Energy Efficiency Scheme 103
  Climate Change Act 2008 103
  enforcement 103
  European Union Emissions Trading Scheme 102–3
  Greenhouse Gas Permits 103
  Kyoto Protocol 102
Code for Leasing Business Premises 2007 155–6
  alterations 224, 236
  assignment of lease 272
  change of use 224, 236
  forfeiture 257
  guarantee agreements 217
  insurance 241, 243, 245
  rent 276
  service charges 267
  text 371–81
collateral warranties 128–30
commercial developments
  value added tax 135, 136–7
commercial property
  meaning 3
  purchasers 4–5
commercial rent arrears recovery 280
common parts 159
commons registration search 112
Community Infrastructure Levy 57–8, 61
  area subject to charge 62
  charging authorities 61
  charitable exemption 64
  charitable reliefs 64
  date rate payable 63
  enforcement 65–6
  exceptional circumstances relief 64–5
  exemptions 64
  figure payable 63
  fundamentals 61
  interest 65
  liability 62
  management of liability 65
  payee 62
  payment 63–4
  penalties for non-payment 66
  planning obligations and 66–7
  procedure 65
  rate payable 61
  reliefs 64–5
  social housing relief 64
  surcharges and interest 65
company voluntary arrangements 316, 318–19
  approval 318
  covenants 333
  moratorium 319
  rent 332
compensation
  exclusion 162
  for failure to obtain new tenancy 307–8

compensation – *continued*
for improvements 236
penalties for delay 151
stop notices 79
completion certificate 150
completion notice 46
conditional agreements 18–21
condition 19–20
time for performance 20–1
types 19
consent
alterations 233–4
assignment of leases
applications for 269–71
consent not to be unreasonably withheld 218–20, 269–71
reasonable response time 270
refusal 220
restrictions on charging for consent 220
superior landlord's consent 271
virtual assignments 221
delay in obtaining 220
disclaimer 335
subleases 274
consent not to be unreasonably withheld 218–20
refusal 220
restrictions on charging for consent 220
construction, design and management coordinator 117
construction management 124–5
construction projects 115–33
adjudication 133
agreement for lease and
completion date 151
damage before completion 152
deducing title 152
defects in work or materials 152
example 149–53
force majeure clause 151
form of lease 152
incorporation of conditions of sale 152
incumbrances 152
landlord's obligations 150
liability for delay 151
merging with lease 152–3
penalties for delay 151
practical completion 150–1
premises 152
responsibility for damage 152
supervision 150
when used 149
arbitration 133
construction management 124–5
contract types 118–25
design and build contract 120–2
dispute resolution 132–3
duties owed to third parties 125–8
legislation 126
liability for economic loss 127–8
liability for physical damage 127
tort liability 126–8
legislation 133
management contracting 122–3
pricing 125

construction projects – *continued*
protection for other parties
assignment of rights 130
collateral warranties 128–30
declaration of trust of rights 130
defect liability periods 132
forced enforcement of remedies 132
latent defects insurance 130–1
limiting repair covenants 131–2
reconstruction as ground for opposition to new tenancy 304–6
traditional procurement 118–19
who is involved
architect 116–17
building contractor 115–16
construction, design and management coordinator 117
costs consultant 117
employer 115
engineers 117
project manager 117
quantity surveyor 117
contaminated land 84, 87–95
appeals 92–3, 94
apportionment of liability 91–2
appropriate persons 88, 91–2
asbestos *see* **asbestos**
case law 92–3
contaminant linkage 89
DEFRA guidance 88
enforcement 93–4
exclusion tests 90–1
landlord and tenant issues 94–5
liability 92
local authority duties 88
planning and 94
regime 88
review 95
remediation notice 90, 93
appeals 92–3, 94
responsibility 90
risks 87
sanctions 93–4
searches and enquiries 112
significant harm 87, 88–9
special sites 90
contracts
conditional agreements 18–21
condition 19–20
time for performance 20–1
types 19
construction projects 115–16, 118–25
duties owed to third parties 125–8
estate contracts *see* **agreement for lease**
fixed price lump-sum 125
guaranteed maximum price 125
insolvency 318
joint ventures 6
measurement contracts 125
option agreements 21–3
put and call options 21
terms 22–3
uses 21–2
overage *see* **overage**

contracts – *continued*
  privity 163, 165–6, 167, 169
  for sale 17–18
  searches and enquiries 111
    enquiries of seller 112
    investigation of title 113–14
    local 111
  types 18–23
costs
  appeal against enforcement notices 81
  appeals 55
  value added tax on 140
county planning authorities 28
courts
  application under LTA 1954 300–1
    renewal lease 308–10
covenants 161, 163
  administration 333–4
  against alterations
    absolute covenants 232–3
    compensation for improvements 236
    fully qualified covenants 233
    landlord's concerns 231–2
    need for 231–2
    other lease clauses 234–5
    qualified covenants 233
    tenant's concerns 231
  against assignment 166–7, 213–14, 269–70
    remedies for breach 283
  against dealings 213–14
  against subletting 213–14
  bankruptcy 334
  direct 167
  liability of parties on covenants in lease 146–7
  limiting repair covenants 131–2
  liquidation 334
  named tenants 225–6
  negative 226
  positive 226
  quiet enjoyment 237–8
    remedies for breach 285–6
  receivership 333
  remedies for breach
    landlord's breach 284–6
    landlord's remedies 279–84
    non-payment of rent 280–1
    obligation not to derogate from grant 286
    other covenants 283–4, 303–4
    repairing covenant 281–3
    tenant's remedies 284–6
  repairing
    covenant to yield up in repair 209
    decoration 209–10, 234
    definition of subject matter 204
    enforcement 209
    insured risks 245–6
    landlords 210
    remedies for breach 281–3, 285
    tenants 204
    tenant's concerns and amendments 208–9
  subleases 277
  successors and 164–5
  to pay rent 183

covenants – *continued*
  user
    ancillary clauses 227–8
    competition legislation and 228–9
    extent of landlord's control 226–7
    need for 223–4
    permitted use 224–6
    remedies for breach 283
  voluntary arrangements 333
  which touch and concern 167
criminal offences
  certificates of lawful use or development 71
  Japanese knotweed 108
  non-compliance with enforcement notice 77
  obstruction of right of entry 72
  sentencing guidelines for environmental offences 108–9
  stop notices 79

damage
  construction projects 127
  insurance and 245–7
  termination of lease 248–9
damages
  breach of covenants 281–2, 283, 285
    quiet enjoyment 285–6
dealings with part 212–13
death
  guarantee for lease and 171
debt finance
  due diligence 11
  loan agreements 11–12
  security
    further advances 14
    need for 12–13
    perfection 13–14
  term sheet 10–11
declaration of trust of rights
  construction projects 130
decoration
  covenant to repair and 209–10, 234
  forfeiture 256
  lease of part 261–2
  subleases 277
default notice 279
defects
  agreement for lease and 152
  inherent defects 205
  latent defects insurance 130–1
  liability periods in construction projects 132
  see also **repairs**
defences
  non-compliance with enforcement notice 77–8
demolition 31–2
  grounds for opposition to new tenancy 304–6
Department for Communities and Local Government
  administrative powers 28
  circulars 28
  guidance 28
  legislative powers 28
  quasi-judicial powers 28
derogation
  obligation not to derogate from grant 286
design and build contract 120–2

developers
  planning obligations 67–8
  as purchasers 5
development
  certificates of lawful use or development 71
  change of use 32–5
  demolition 31–2
  operations not constituting development 31
  permitted
    GPD Order 35–40
    resumption of previous use 35
  use classes 33–5, 225
development plans
  definition 30–1
  importance 29–30
  new system 29–30
  regional planning 29–30
disclaimer
  consent 335
  effect 335–6
  meaning 334
  persons able to disclaim 334
  property disclaimed 334–5
  timing 335
Display Energy Certificates 105
dispute resolution 132–3
  adjudication 133
  arbitration 133
  legislation 133
distress remedy 184, 280
district planning authorities 28
doctrine of waste *see* **waste**
drafting of leases
  commencement 158
  covenants 161
  definitions section 158–9
  exceptions and reservations 160
  execution 162
  forfeiture clause 251
  habendum 160
  interpretation clauses 159–60
  Land Registry prescribed clause leases
    157
  lease of part 259–67
  letting 160–1
  operative words 160
  parcels clause 160
  prescribed clauses 157
  principles 156–7
  provisos 161–2
  reddendum 160
  schedules 162
  structure 158–62
  subleases 275–8
  testimonium clause 162
  value added tax 139
drainage
  searches and enquiries 112

easements
  lease of part 259–60
economic loss
  construction projects 127–8

employees
  lease of part 262
employers
  construction projects 115
Energy Act 2011 106
energy performance 84, 103–6
  air conditioning assessments 105
  enforcement 105
Energy Performance Certificates 102, 104
enforcement
  asbestos regulations 107
  contaminated land 93–4
  energy performance 105
  environmental regulation and permitting 101–2
  EU ETS 103
  forced enforcement of remedies 132
  notice *see* **enforcement notice**
  nuisance 97
  planning control 69–82
    definitions 69–70
    time limits 70
  planning law
    appeals 80–2
    breach of condition notice 73–4
    injunctions 80
    planning contravention notice 72–3
    right of entry 72
    stop notice 78–80
    time limits 75
  planning obligations 59
  Regulatory Enforcement and Sanctions Act 2008 106
  sentencing guidelines for environmental issues 108–9
enforcement notice 74–8
  appeals 80–2
  challenging 74–5
  contents 75–6
  defences 77–8
  effect 77
  invalidity 76–7
  issue 74
  non-compliance 77–8
  nullity 76
  offences 77
  service 76
  time limits 75
  validity 76–7
  variation 77
  withdrawal 77
engineering operations 31
engineers in construction projects 117
entry
  for repairs 209
  right of 72
    subleases 277
Environment Agency
  contaminated land 95
Environmental Damage Regulations 2009 98–9
Environmental Impact Assessment 48
environmental regulation and permitting 84, 99–102
  enforcement 101–2
  hazardous substances 101
  offences 100–1
  permit requirement 99–101

environmental regulation and permitting – *continued*
  waste 100–1
  water 100
environmental risk management 83
  desktop study 85
  enquiries of consultants 85–6
  enquiries of seller 85
  indemnities 86
  insurance 87
  warranties 86
environmental statement 48
Environmental Tribunal 109
equity funding 10
estate contracts *see* **agreement for lease**
European Union Emissions Trading Scheme (EU ETS)
  102–3
expiry of leases 287

finance
  debt finance
    due diligence 11
    loan agreements 11–12
    security 12–14
    term sheet 10–11
  equity funding 10
  forward funding 9–10
  methods 9–10
  sale and leaseback 4, 10
  share capital 9
fixtures 175–6
  removal 176
  repair 176
flooding
  insurance 244
  risks 108
  searches 112–13
***force majeure* clauses 151**
forfeiture 251–7
  breach of other covenants 253–5, 284
  breach of repairing covenant 255–6, 283
  clause 251
  Code for Leasing Business Premises 2007 257
  decoration 256
  express reservation of right 251–2
  insolvency and 256, 331–2
  non-payment of rent 252–3, 281
  particular premises 257
  s 146 notice 253
  subtenants/mortgagees and 257
  waiver of right 252
forward funding 9–10
frustration 184, 248

gender
  in deeds 160
goodwill
  rent review and 197–8
Green Deal 102, 106
green leases 84, 102, 105–6
Greenhouse Gas Permits 103
guarantees
  assignment of leases and 168, 216
  guarantors of leases 168–73

guarantees – *continued*
  assignee's guarantor 172–3
  bankruptcy or liquidation of tenant 171
  death of tenant 171
  discharge or release 170–1
  drafting points 172
  extent of guarantee 169–70
  giving time 171
  release of co-guarantor 171
  variations 170–1

habendum 160
hazardous substances 101
hearings
  appeals 55
heating
  lease of part 262
highways
  searches and enquiries 112

improvements
  compensation for 236
  rent review and 198
  repairing covenants and 206–7
indemnity
  assignment of leases and 166, 167, 168
  environmental issues 86
individual voluntary arrangements 316, 318–19
  approval 318
  covenants 333
  moratorium 319
  rent 332
injunctions 80, 284
inquiry
  planning appeals 54–5
insolvency
  administration 317, 321
    administrator appointment and powers 322
    covenants 333–4
    moratorium 322
    rent 333
  bankruptcy *see* **bankruptcy**
  compulsory liquidation 317
  contracts 318
  covenants 333–4
  disclaimer 334–7
  forfeiture and 256, 331–2
  guarantee for lease and 171
  identification of contract type 318
  importance 315
  insolvency official 317
  liquidation
    compulsory 317, 322–3
    covenants 334
    moratorium 323
    powers and duties of liquidator 323
    rent 333
    voluntary 317, 322
  non-payment of rent and 280
  preferences 323–5
  receivership 317, 319–20
    breach of repairing covenant 285
    covenants 333

insolvency – *continued*
    rent 332
    reducing perceived risk 315–16
    regimes 316–17
    rent 332–3
    setting aside transactions 323–5
    tenant, landlord's remedies 325–32
    transactions at an undervalue 323–5
    vesting orders 336–7
    voluntary arrangements 318–19
        approval 318
        company 316, 318–19
        covenants 333
        individual 316, 318–19
        moratorium 319
        rent 332
    voluntary liquidation 317
    see also **liquidation (winding up)**
insurance
    additional provisions 250
    breach of covenant to insure 283
    by landlord 242
    by tenant 250
    Code for Leasing Business Premises 2007 241,
        243, 245
    compliance with terms 245
    damage to premises 245–7
    environmental 87
    excess payable 245
    flood 244
    latent defects insurance 130–1
    lease of part 266
    loss of rent 244
    losses covered 243–4
    payment 244–5
    reinstatement 245–7
        impossible 249
    retention of monies 249
    risks covered 158, 243–4
    subleases 277
    sum insured 244
    terrorism 243–4
    uninsured risks 249–50
    what insured 242
    in whose name 242–3
interest 158
    rent and 184–5
interim rent 183, 301–2
interpretation clauses 159–60
investors
    as purchasers 4–5

Japanese knotweed
    impact 108
    liability 108
joint and several liability 159
joint ventures 5–6
    contractual 6
    partnerships 6–7
    special purpose vehicles 7–8

Kyoto Protocol 102

Land Registry
    prescribed clause leases 157
landlord
    breach of covenant by 284–6
    drafting points 171–2
    party to lease 163–5
    remedies for breach 279–84
latent defects insurance 130–1
leases
    agreements for *see* **agreement for lease**
    assignment *see* **assignment of leases**
    covenants 161
        assignment of lease and 166–7
        liability of parties on covenants in lease 146–7
        limiting repair covenants 131–2
        successors and 164–5
    distinguished from licences 145–6
    drafting
        commencement 158
        definitions section 158–9
        execution 162
        interpretation clauses 159–60
        lease of part 259–67
        letting 160–1
        principles 156–7
        provisos 161–2
        schedules 162
        structure 158–62
        subleases 275–8
        value added tax 139
    office blocks 383–422
    options to renew 181
    parcels clauses 160, 175–7
    of part
        boundaries 259
        demised premises 259
        easements 259–60
        insurance 266
        repairs 260
        service charges 261–6
        sinking and reserve funds 266
    parties
        guarantors 168–73
        landlord 163–5
        successors 164–5
        tenants 165–8
    rent *see* **rent**
    security of tenure *see* **security of tenure**
    stamp duty land tax and 141
    term 158, 179–81
        renewal lease 309
        subleases 275–6
    termination *see* **termination of leases**
    value added tax and 139, 159
licences
    distinguished from leases 145–6
    licence to assign 271–2
liquidation (winding up) 171, 280
    compulsory 317, 322–3
    covenants 334
    moratorium 323
    powers and duties of liquidator 323

liquidation (winding up) – *continued*
  rent 333
  types 317, 322–3
  voluntary 317, 322
  see also **insolvency**
local authorities 28–9, 29–30
  contaminated land 88
  development plans *see* **development plans**
  enforcement and *see* **enforcement**
  planning obligations *see* **planning obligations**
  planning permission *see* **planning permission**
local development frameworks 30
local development orders 40
local plans 30
local searches and enquiries 111
London 29
  development plans 30

major infrastructure projects
  planning permission 46
management contracting 122–3
managing agents
  lease of part 262
merger
  agreement for lease 152–3
  termination of leases 289
mining operations 31
misrepresentation 161
mortgages
  forfeiture and 257
  legal mortgage 13
  restrictions 213

National Planning Policy Framework (NPPF) 28, 29–31
  sustainable development 29
National Planning Practice Guidance 28
  enforcement of planning control 75
  guidance on planning conditions 44
neighbourhood development orders 40
neighbourhood development plans 30–1
neighbourhood forums 31
notice
  of assignment/subleases 220
  enforcement *see* **enforcement notice**
  s 146 notice 253
  service *see* **service of notices**
  stop *see* **stop notice**
  to quit 287–8
  under LTA
    counter-notices 300
    prescribed forms 357–70
    s 25 notices 297–8
nuisance 84
  enforcement 97
  environmental permitting and 96
  planning permission and 96
  private 95–6
  public 96–7
  rule in *Rylands v Fletcher* 97–8
  standing 96
  statutory 97
  trespass 98

occupation
  occupation by landlord as ground for opposition to new tenancy 306–7
  purchase by occupiers 4
offences *see* **criminal offences**
office blocks
  lease of floor(s) 383–422
operations
  definition 31
  not constituting development 31
option agreements 21–3
  pre-emption agreements 23
  put and call options 21
  terms 22–3
  uses 21–2
options to renew 181
overage 23–5
  bond 25
  clawback and 23–4
  drafting considerations 24–5
  freehold right of re-entry 25
  guarantee 25
  meaning 23
  mortgage or charge 25
  negative 24
  payment
    amount 25
    security for 25
  positive 24
  positive covenant 25
  ransom strips 25
  restrictive covenant 25
  securing payment 25
  seller's lien 25
  trigger event 24–5

parcels clauses 160, 175–7
  airspace 175
  fixtures 175–6
  rights granted and reserved 176–7
  underground 175
part, lease of
  boundaries 259
  demised premises 259
  easements 259–60
  insurance 266
  repairs 260
  service charges 261–6
  sinking and reserve funds 266
parties to leases
  guarantors 168–73
    assignee's guarantor 172–3
    bankruptcy or liquidation of tenant 171
    death of tenant 171
    discharge or release 170–1
    drafting points 172
    extent of guarantee 169–70
    giving time 171
    release of co-guarantor 171
    variations 170–1
  landlord 163–5
    drafting points 171–2
    successors 164–5

parties to leases – *continued*
  tenants 165–8
parting with possession 212
permitted development
  checklist 39–40
  GPD Order 35–40
  resumption of previous use 35
permitted use 224–6
planning contravention notice 72–3
planning law 27
  enforcement 69–82
    appeals 80–2
    breach of condition notice 73–4
    definitions 69–70
    enforcement notice 74–8, 80–2
    injunctions 80
    planning contravention notice 72–3
    right of entry 72
    stop notice 78–80
    time limits 70, 75
  sources, legislation 28
planning obligations 57–68
  developer 67–8
  enforceability 59
  formalities 59
  Government policy 59
  LPA 67
    enforcement by 59
  meaning 58
  modification and discharge
    appeals 61
    applications 60
    determination of applications 60
    powers 60
  reform 57–8
  unilateral undertakings 60
  when used 58–9
planning permission
  abandonment 44
  Agricultural Holdings Certificate 49
  amendments 50
    s 96A 51
  appeals 51–5
    challenging appeal decision 55
    costs 55
    form 54–5
    hearing 55
    initial procedure 52–3
    inquiry 54–5
    statement of case 54
    types 53–5
    who may appeal 51–2
    written representations 53
  application for
    action by planning authority 49
    certificates with 49
    covenants against 234, 235
    decision 49–50
    fee 49
    full or outline 40–1
    notification 49
    preliminary steps 46–7
    procedure 47–50

planning permission – *continued*
  submission 48–9
  article 12 certificate 49
  basis for decision 41–2
  completion notice 46
  conditional 42–4
    Central Government guidance 44
    judicial restrictions on power 43–4
    Section 73 and Section 73A applications 50–1
  contaminated land 94
  deemed refusal 50
  discrimination 42
  duration 44–5
  effect 44–6
  environmental considerations 42
  environmental statement 48
  full 40
  implementation 45–6
  major infrastructure projects 46
  modification 45
  nuisance and 96
  outline 40–1
  planning register entry 49
  power to decline to determine 49
  pre-application decision 46–7
  procedure after decision 50
  refusal, deemed 50
  renewal 46
  reserved matters 41
  revocation 45
  searches and enquiries 111
  time limit for decision 50
  when required 31
pollution *see* **contaminated land**
pre-emption agreements
  options 23
preferences 323–5
premises
  definition 158
privity of contract 163, 165–6, 167, 169
privity of estate 166–7
project manager 117
put options 21

quantity surveyors 117
quiet enjoyment
  breach of covenant 238
  covenant for 237–8
  remedies for breach 285–6

rack rent lease 4
receivership 317, 319–20
  breach of repairing covenant 285
  covenants 333
  rent 332
reddendum 160
Regional Development Agencies 30
registered property 14
Regulatory Enforcement and Sanctions Act 2008 106
remedies
  breach of covenant
    landlord's breach 284–6
    landlord's remedies 279–84

remedies – *continued*
    obligation not to derogate from grant 286
    other covenants 253–5, 283–4, 303–4
    quiet enjoyment 285–6
    repairing covenant 281–3, 285
    tenant's breach 279–84
    tenant's remedies 284–6
  distress 184, 280
  forced enforcement 132
  injunctions 80, 284
  non-payment of rent 184, 252–3, 280–1
  right to overriding lease 284
  self-help 282, 285
  specific performance 283, 284, 285
  see also **damages; forfeiture**
renewal lease 308–10
  duration 309
  premises 309
  rent 309–10
renewal of leases
  options to renew 181
rent 159
  amount 184
  Code for Leasing Business Premises 2007 276
  covenant to pay 183
  delay in payment 303
  insolvency and 280, 332–3
  interest charged 184–5
  interim 183, 301–2
  non-payment 184, 280–1
    commercial rent arrears recovery 280
    forfeiture for 252–3, 281
  other payments reserved as 184
  premiums and 193
    reverse premiums 192–3
  reddendum 160
  renewal lease 309–10
  rent-free periods 139–40, 183
  review *see* **rent review**
  subleases 276
  suspension 161, 184, 247–8
  time for payment 184
  value added tax 185
rent review
  assumptions 191–7
    duration of lease 193
    fitting out 195
    landlord's obligations 196
    premiums 193
    rent-free periods 192, 194–5
    restoration of damage 196
    reverse premium 192–3
    sub-tenancies 191–2
    tenant's obligations 196
    terms of lease 194
    use of premises 193
    vacant possession 191–2
    VAT 197
    whole or part 191
    willing parties 191
    work diminishing value 196–7
  dates 189–90
  disregards 197–9

rent review – *continued*
    goodwill 197–8
    improvements 198
    occupation 197
    statutory restrictions 198–9
  fixed increases 187
  index-linked 187
  late 200
  mechanics 199–200
  need for 187
  open market revaluations 188–9
    comparables 190
    defining 190
    instructions to valuer 190
    upwards only 188–9
    upwards/downwards 189
  penultimate day 189–90
  recording 200
  regularity 189
  time of essence 199
  turnover 188
  types of review clauses 187–9
  valuer
    appointment 199
    capacity 199–200
    costs 200
    instructions 190
repairs
  access for 209
  agreement for lease and 152
  covenants
    definition of subject matter 204
    enforcement 209
    insured risks 245–6
    landlord's 210
    limiting repair covenants 131–2
    remedies for breach 255–6, 281–3, 285
    tenant's 204
  decoration 209–10, 234
  extent of liability 204–8
    reducing 208–9
  failure to repair 303
  fixtures 176
  inherent defects 205
  lease of part 260
  meaning 204–5
  multi-occupied building 203
  scope 205–7
  standard of 207–8
  subleases 277
  whole building 203
  yielding up in repair 209
reserve funds
  lease of part 266
reserved matters
  planning permission 41
reserved rights 176–7
residential property
  value added tax on development 135, 136
resumption of previous use 35
reverse premiums
  value added tax and 139–40
RICS Code of Practice for Service Charges 266–7

Rylands v Fletcher, rule in 97–8

s 25 notices 297–8, 311
s 26 requests 298–9
sale and leaseback 4, 10
searches and enquiries
    commons registration search 112
    contaminated land 112
    drainage 112
    enquiries of seller 112
    flood searches 112–13
    flooding 112–13
    highways 112
    investigation of title 113–14
    local 111
    survey and inspection 113
security of tenure
    business tenants 146, 162, 291–311
        application of LTA 1954 291–3
        competent landlord 293–4
        continuation tenancies 296
        contracting out 294–6
        definitions 293–4
        exclusions 293
        holding 294
        order for new lease 310
        protection 291
        renewal lease 308–10
    interim rent 183, 301–2
    termination of leases under LTA 1954 296–300
        application to courts 300–1
        compensation for failure to obtain new tenancy 307–8
        counter-notices 300
        grounds of opposition to new tenancy 303–7
        LTA 1954 text 429–45
        prescribed forms of notice 357–70
        s 25 notices 297–8, 311
        s 26 requests 298–9
        service of notices and requests 300
self-help remedies 282, 285
seller
    searches and enquiries 112
sentencing guidelines
    environmental issues 108–9
service charges 184
    definition 159
    landlord's covenant to perform services 263–4
    payment
        advance payments 264–5
        certification of amounts due 265–6
        final payments and adjustments 265
    RICS Code of Practice 266–7
    services to be provided 261
    tenant's contribution 264
service of notices 161
    default notice 279
    enforcement notice 76
    stop notice 78–9
    under LTA 1954 300
services
    definition 159
share capital 9
sharing possession 212

signs 234
simplified planning zones 40
sinking funds
    lease of part 266
special development orders 40
specific performance 283, 284, 285
stamp duty land tax 141, 181
stop notice 78–80
    compensation 79
    contents 78
    offences 79
    service 78–9
    temporary 79–80
    withdrawal 79
structure plans 30
subcontractors
    construction projects 115
subleases 211–12
    alienation 277
    break clauses and 181
    consent 274
        consent not to be unreasonably withheld 218–20
        delays in obtaining 220
        refusal 220
        restrictions on charging for consent 220
    covenants 277
    covenants against 213–14
    dealings with part 212–13
    decoration 277
    disclaimer effect 336
    drafting points 275–8
    forfeiture and 257
    grounds for opposition to new tenancy 304
    head landlord liability 275
    headlease and 277
    insurance 277
    liability of subtenants 275
    licences to sub-let 274
    nature of 273
    non-payment of rent 281
    reasons for subletting 273–4
    rent 276
    repair 277
    restrictions 274
    rights of access 277
    sub-tenant's concerns 278
    term 275–6
succession
    landlords 164–5
surrender of leases 140, 288–9
surveys 113
sweeper clauses 263

taxation
    stamp duty land tax 141
    transfers of going concerns 140
    value added tax
        commercial developments 135, 136–7
        on costs 140
        drafting points 138–9
        option to charge 137–9
        rent and 185, 197
        rent-free periods and 139–40

taxation – *continued*
    residential developments 135, 136
    reverse premiums and 139–40
    surrenders and 140
term of lease 158, 179–81
    renewal lease 309
    rent review and 193
    SDLT impact 181
    subleases 275–6
termination of leases
    damage to property 248–9
        landlord 249
        tenant 248–9
    expiry 287
    forfeiture *see* **forfeiture**
    merger 289
    notice to quit 287–8
    operation of break clause 288
    restriction on *see* **security of tenure**
    surrender 140, 288–9
    under LTA 1954 296–300
        application to courts 300–1
        compensation for failure to obtain new tenancy 307–8
        counter-notices 300
        grounds of opposition to new tenancy 303–7
        prescribed forms of notice 357–70
        s 25 notices 297–8, 311
        s 26 requests 298–9
        service of notices and requests 300
terrorism
    insurance 243–4
time for performance
    conditional agreements 20–1
    liability for delay 151
    penalties for delay 151
time limits
    agreement to extend 301
    appeal against enforcement notices 81
    defect liability periods 132
    enforcement of planning law 70, 75
title
    agreement for lease and 152
    investigation 113–14
tort liability
    construction projects 126–8
transactions at an undervalue 323–5
transfers of going concerns
    value added tax and 140
trespass 98
trust of rights
    construction projects 130

underground 175
unilateral undertakings 60
uninsured risks 249–50
unitary councils 29
unregistered property 14
use
    certificates of lawful use or development 71
    change of use 32–5
    covenants *see* **user covenants**
    permitted 161
    resumption of previous use 35
    use classes 33–5, 225
user covenants
    ancillary clauses 227–8
    competition legislation and 228–9
    extent of landlord's control
        absolute covenants 226
        fully qualified covenants 227
        qualified covenants 226–7
    need for 223–4
        landlord's concerns 223–4
        tenant's concerns 224
    permitted use 224–6
    planning 223
    remedies for breach 283

value added tax
    commercial developments 135, 136–7
    on costs 140
    drafting points 138–9
    leases and 139, 159
    option to charge
        how election made 137
        should election be made 138
        who or what is affected 137–8
    rent and 185, 197
    rent-free periods and 139–40
    residential developments 135, 136
    reverse premiums and 139–40
    surrenders and 140
    transfers of going concerns 140
vesting orders 336–7

Wales 29
    regional planning 30
warranties
    collateral 128–30
    environmental issues 86
waste 100–1, 234
water 100
winding up *see* **liquidation (winding up)**